USAGE AND ABUSAGE

Eric Partridge

USAGE AND ABUSAGE
A GUIDE TO GOOD ENGLISH

ABUSUS NON TOLLIT USUM

NEW EDITION
edited by Janet Whitcut

W. W. NORTON & COMPANY
New York   London

Foreword to the Present Edition

Eric Partridge's lively and erudite books on the English language were, and are, all classics in their field. As such they have stood up remarkably well to the passage of time and have been much reprinted, at first with emendations by Partridge himself. Modern readers can still enjoy his wit and elegance and the forthrightness of his judgements. But language changes with time, and if *Usage and Abusage*, whose first edition appeared as early as 1942, is to continue to be a practical guide to its subject today, some updating is now necessary for several reasons.

First, because some of the battles Partridge fought with such vigour have been irrevocably lost so that they are no longer worth discussing, the usages he condemned being now generally accepted. Some of his once reasonable guesses about the future of the language have turned out to be simply wrong.

Second, because new problems (such as the use of 'hopefully') and new topics (such as 'sexism') have arisen, which really cannot be omitted from any book claiming to discuss the English of the 1990s.

And third, because Partridge's intended audience has changed. Fewer educated English readers have studied Latin, much less Greek, than a generation ago. On the other hand, there have been considerable advances in the study of English grammar in the last half century.

I have tried to approach reverently the task of modernizing this delightful book. I have retained as much as possible of Partridge's original text, including his own (perhaps sometimes rather outdated) examples, and his references to sources such as Jesperson and Onions – who were supreme in their day – since both examples and references form the basis for his arguments. I have sometimes added a more modern scholarly reference. Most of the longer essays remain substantially as he wrote them. The section on 'vogue words', however, is all mine and not his, since the 'vogue' changes more quickly than any-thing else. Wherever the first person pronoun 'I' appears in the text it means 'Partridge, though with Whitcut's agreement', never merely 'Whitcut alone'.

I hope the result is not too uneasy a blend of the old and the new.

Janet Whitcut

Abbreviations used in this book

abbr., abbreviation
adj., adjective
adv., adverb
c. (circa), about
cf. *(confer)*, compare
ch., chapter
COD, The Concise Oxford Dictionary
conj., conjunction
DNB, Dictionary of National Biography
e.g. *(exempli gratia)*, for instance
EP, Eric Partridge
esp., especially
etc. *(et cetera)*, and the rest
fig., figuratively
gen., general(ly)
ibid. (ibidem), in the same place
i.e. *(id est)*, that is
JIJ, Journal of the Institute of Journalists
lit., literally
n., noun
NB *(nota bene)*, note well
OE, Old English
OED, The Oxford English Dictionary
op. cit. (opus citatum), the work cited
opp., opposed; opposite
orig., original(ly)
p., page (pp., pages)
pl., plural
ppl., participial or participle
q.v. (quod vide), which see

RC, Roman Catholic
SE, Standard English
SOED, The Shorter Oxford English Dictionary
SPE Tract, Society for Pure English Tract
TLS, The Times Literary Supplement
v., verb
vbl., verbal
v.i., verb intransitive
viz. (*videlicet*), namely
v.t., verb transitive
WB, Wilson Benington
Webster's, Webster's Third New International Dictionary

USAGE AND ABUSAGE

A

a, an. The indefinite article is often introduced, though quite superfluously, in such sentences as: 'No more signal a defeat was ever inflicted' (quoted by Fowler). In 'He's the party as had a done it', its use is merely illiterate and may be due to the difficulty of pronouncing the two d's. It may represent *have* in 'I would 'a done it' and in *had'ave* (*q.v.*). It occurs also in illiterate speech such as Cockney 'I arst you wot you was a-doin' of' (D. Sayers), and American Southern Mountain 'He's a-singin' a love song' (ballad). Cf. 'Father's gone a-hunting.' It can hardly be condemned when used for lyrical euphony in 'all ablowing and agrowing'.

a-, an- for 'not' or 'without' should correctly be prefixed only to Greek stems, e.g. *anarchic.* 'Amoral' (says Fowler) 'being literary is inexcusable.' Nevertheless, both *amoral* and *asexual* are generally accepted today.

a or *an.* See **an.**

A in titles. See TITLES OF BOOKS AND PERIODICALS.

a + noun + or two takes a plural verb. The formula merely obeys the general rule governing an example such as 'Either the head or the legs *are* injured'; thus: 'Another good yarn or two [i.e. two good yarns] *are* to be found in *The Moon Endureth.*' Regarded in another way, *a good yarn or two* is synonymous with and tantamount to *several good yarns*, which obviously takes a verb in the plural.

Note that *a + noun + or so* must not be used as synonymous with *a + noun + or two. A pint or so = a pint or thereabouts = a pint (approximately)*. It would take a singu-

lar verb. If, however, you permit yourself to murder a woman or so, you must write *a woman or so are nothing to me*: jocular, maybe; bad writing, certainly!

abdomen. See **belly.**

aberration is not a synonym of *absentmindedness*, as John G. Brandon makes it in *The Mail-Van Mystery.* 'Once, in a moment of temporary aberration, Mr Dorgan drew a huge, hook-bladed knife from a hidden sheath, felt its razor-like edge carefully with a black and calloused thumb, then returned it with every sign of satisfaction.'

ability and **capacity.** *Ability* is a power to do something, or skill in doing it, whether the something be physical or intellectual. 'Here, promotion is by ability, not by birth'; 'He has outstanding ability as a surgeon – a writer – a pugilist …'. *Capacity*, apart from its physical sense ('power to receive or to contain': capacity of 1,000 gallons), means either 'power to absorb or learn knowledge as opposed to power-in-doing' or 'innate or native power as opposed to acquired power'. 'My capacity for mathematics is negligible.'

abjure, 'to renounce on oath', is very easily confused with *adjure*, 'to request earnestly, esp. under oath' (*COD*).

-able and **-ible.** See **-ible and -able.**

ablution is now intolerably pedantic for 'the act of washing one's hands and face'; *perform one's ablutions* is but a sorry jest; though the word is now institutionalized for a place where soldiers or sailors wash. *Ablution* should otherwise be reserved for its religious senses:

1. (General) 'The washing of the body as a religious rite.'

2. (Anglican; RC) 'The washing of the chalice and paten after the celebration.'

3. (RC) 'The washing of the priest's hands before assuming the sacred vestments, and during the celebration.'

4. (RC) 'The wine and water used to rinse the chalice, and wash the fingers of the celebrant after communion.'

(Definitions: *OED*)

abnormal; subnormal; supra-normal.
Any departure from the *normal* (or usual or
standard) is *abnormal*. To distinguish further: Any such departure that is *below* the
normal is *subnormal*; *above* the normal,
supra-normal.

about should be avoided in such phrases
as these: 'It is about 9 or 10 o'clock'; 'The
boy is about 9 or 10 years old'; 'It happened about the 9th or 10th of October
1939.' Correct thus: 'It is 9 or 10 o'clock'
or 'It is about 9.30'; 'The boy is 9 or 10
years old' or 'The boy must be somewhere
near 10 years old'; 'It happened on either
the 9th or the 10th of October' or, less
precisely, 'It happened about the 9th of
October.' These examples might have
been listed at **WOOLLINESS**.

above, misused for *more than*. 'Above a
yard' and 'above three months, a year, etc.'
are loose for 'more than a yard, three
months, a year, etc.'.

above and **below.** They may usefully
refer to what has been mentioned earlier,
or to what is to be mentioned later, in a
piece of official or technical writing. *Above*
functions here as an adjective, adverb, or
noun. 'The above facts', 'The statement
above'. *Below* in this sense can be only an
adverb. 'The information below'. The
device is somewhat stilted in ordinary
writing, where it may be more appropriate to say 'The preceding remarks', 'The
following information'. It is, of course,
absurd to use *above* and *below* in writing
intended to be read aloud.

above and **over; below** and **beneath** and
under (prepositions). *Above* is 'vertically
up from; on the top of, upon', as in 'Hell
opens, and the heavens in vengeance crack
above his head'; *over* is now more usual in
this sense. – 'Higher up a slope, nearer the
summit of a mountain or the source of a
river (also, of time, "earlier than")', as in
'Behind and above it the vale head rises
into grandeur.' – 'Literally higher than;
rising beyond (the level of reach of)', as in
'The citadel of Corinth towering high
above all the land'; hence of sounds, as in

'His voice was audible above the din.' –
Fig., 'superior to', as in 'He is above mere
mundane considerations.' – 'Higher in
rank or position than; (set) in authority
over', as in 'The conscience looks to a law
above it.' – 'In excess of, beyond; more
than', as in 'But above all things, my
brethren, swear not.' – 'Surpassing in
quality, amount, number; more than', as
in 'Above a sixth part of the nation is
crowded into provincial towns.' –
'Besides', occurring in *over and above*, as in
'Over and above his salary, he receives
commission' (*OED*).

Over is 'higher up than', either of position or of motion within the space above,
as in 'Flitting about like a petrel over those
stormy isles'; hence (after *hang, lean, jut,
project*, etc.) in relation to something
beneath, as in 'The upper storey projects
over the street.' Also, fig., as in 'His speech
was over the heads of his audience.' The
spatial sense 'above' passes into other
notions: the literal notion is (*a*) combined
with that of purpose or occupation, as in
[to sit] *over the fire*, [to talk] *over a bowl, a
glass*; (*b*) sunk in that of having something
under treatment, observation, or consideration, as in *to watch* or *talk over*, and in
make merry over. – In sense 'on' or 'upon':
'On the upper or outer surface of', sometimes implying the notion of 'covering the
surface of'; as in 'Over one arm is the lusty
courser's rein', 'Sitting with his hat low
down over his eyes', 'She had a net over
her hair.' 'Upon', with verbs of motion, as
in 'He threw a dressing-gown over the
recumbent man' and 'Let us draw a veil
over this dismal spectacle.' 'Upon', or
'down upon', as an influence, as in 'A great
change came over him at this point of his
life.' 'Everywhere on' or 'here and there
upon' as in 'Cottages scattered over the
moor' and 'Over (or, all over) his face
there spread a seraphic smile'; cf. the sense
'to and fro upon; all about; throughout',
with reference to motion, as in 'The
hunter crew wide straggling o'er the
plain', 'We may range over Europe, from
shore to shore', 'They travel all over the
country', and the sense 'through every part

of', occasionally with a connotation of examination or consideration, as in 'He went over my proofs for me.' – In sense 'above in amount, number, degree, authority, preference', as in 'This court has no jurisdiction over unnaturalized foreigners', 'It cost him over £50', 'A distance of over 500 yards', 'The preference given to him over English captains', 'He has no command over himself.' – The general sense of 'across', whether 'indicating motion that passes over (something) on the way to the other side; or sometimes expressing only the latter part of this, as in *falling* or *jumping over a precipice*' – e.g. 'The sun is peering over the roofs', 'She turned and spoke to him over her shoulder', 'The room looking over Nightingale Lane'; or indicating 'from side to side of' (a surface, a space), 'across; to the other side of' (a sea, a river), 'from end to end of; along', as in 'He fled over the plains', 'A free pass over this company's lines of railways', 'He passed over the Channel'; or (of position) 'on the other side of; across', as in 'The king over the water', 'Our neighbours over the way'. – Of time: 'during; all through', as in 'Extending over a century'; or 'repayment over a series of years'; or 'till the end of; for a period that includes', as in 'If we only live over today', 'If you stay over Wednesday' (*OED*).

The chief difference is that *over* implies 'vertically higher than', while *above* need not. Both words can express superiority of rank, but while any general is *above* a major, only one general is *over* any particular major.

In general, *over* is opposed to *under*, *above* to *below* (or *beneath*).

Below, beneath; under. Beneath covers a narrower field than *below*, it has the following senses: (*a*) 'Directly down from, overhung or surmounted by; under', as in 'To sleep beneath the same roof', 'To walk beneath the moon', 'The boat lay beneath a tall cliff'; (*b*) 'immediately under, in contact with the under side of; covered by', as in 'The dust beneath your feet', 'To sit with one's hand beneath one's head', 'No wise man kicks the ladder from

beneath him'; (*c*) 'farther from (the surface); concealed by; inside of or behind' (now usually *under*), as in 'His musical art lay beneath the surface', 'A woollen vest which sometimes had beneath it another fitting close to the skin'; (*d*) 'under, as overborne or overwhelmed by some pressure', fig. 'subject to; under the action, influence, control of', as in 'Bending beneath a heavy weight', 'Brisk goes the work beneath each busy hand', now generally *under*; (*e*) 'lower than, in rank, dignity, excellence, etc.' (now usually *below*), as in 'Beings above and beneath us probably have no opinions at all'; (*f*) 'unbefitting the dignity of, undeserving of, lowering to', as in 'Beneath the attention of serious critics', 'It's beneath his notice', hence 'lower than (a standard of quality or quantity)', as in 'Copies always fall beneath their original', *below* being preferable. *OED* thus summarizes the status and usefulness of *beneath*: 'In ordinary spoken English, *under* and *below* now cover the whole field (*below* tending naturally to overlap the territory of *under*), leaving *beneath* more or less as a literary and slightly archaic equivalent of both (in some senses), but especially of *under*. The only senses in which *beneath* is preferred' are (*f*) as in 'Beneath contempt', and the fig. use of (*d*) as in 'To fall beneath the assaults of temptation'.

What then of *below*? Primarily it = (*a*) 'at a less elevation than, i.e. lower than', as in 'Below the level of the ocean', 'He hit his opponent below the knee', *below stairs*, fig. in 'It is possible to be below flattery as well as above it'; hence (*b*) 'lower on a slope than, farther down a valley or a stream than', also 'nearer the (actual or considered) bottom of a room than', as in 'Below the village, the valley opens into a broad flat meadow', *below-bridge*, *below the gangway* (in the House of Commons); (*c*) 'deeper than' (lit. and fig.), as in 'Water was found about three feet below the surface', 'Language has to be studied both below the surface and superficially'; (*d*) 'Directly beneath; under the canopy or covering of; underneath', in which sense *under* (or *beneath*) is preferable, 'Books lay on tables and below tables'; (*e*) of position in a graduated scale, e.g. that of a barometer, hence 'lower in amount, weight, degree, value, price, than', as in 'a rainfall below the average', also 'lower in quality or excellence than, i.e. inferior to in either of these respects', as in 'Well I know how far my performance is below excellence', 'One places Marlowe below Shakespeare', also fig. ('lower in rank, station, dignity than') as in 'A man far below them in station', 'Unless he is sunk below a beast'; (*f*) 'Unbefitting, unworthy of, lowering to' (better *beneath*), as in 'Too far below contempt to be worth castigating' (*OED*).

To give, here, every sense of *under* would be to fall into inappropriate excess. Its senses fall into four main groups: (I) 'senses denoting position beneath or below something, so as to have it above or overhead, or to be covered by it', as in 'Under a broiling sun, they toiled manfully', 'Under the waves', *under ground* (dead; *above ground*, alive), 'Under a friend's roof one feels safe', 'He put his head under the tap', 'Under the veil was a lovely face', 'Under the American flag', *under water* (flooded), 'A letter addressed under cover to a third party', 'Under the rock where the fowls build they row their boat', 'Chance led him under an apple-tree', (II) 'senses denoting subordination or subjection', as in 'Under the major was a captain', 'He thanked me that had, under God, given him and so many miserable creatures their lives', 'An office under government', 'The great communistic uprising under Wat Tyler in 1381', 'He would have lost his head under Caligula', 'Under the direction of amateurish clerks', 'He is under medical treatment', *under the plough* (arable), *under steam*, 'Sent under a strong guard to the Tower', *under an obligation*, 'The glass vessels intended to retain gases under pressure', 'Under the ban of Rome', 'He is under the impression that ...'; (III) 'senses implying that one thing is covered by, or included in, another', as in 'The several types under which our Ladye was represented in England', 'Extreme vanity

sometimes hides under the garb of ultra modesty', *under the name of* (by the name of), 'Many matters that would come under this head are trivial', 'The word is explained under *house*' (i.e. at *house*, not in a separate entry of its own), 'Under the auspices of a great name', 'All things here are under a perpetual vicissitude and alteration', *under my hand and seal, under the provisions of the Act*; (IV) 'senses which imply falling below a certain standard or level', as in 'It is under his majesty', 'It was too great an honour for any man under a duke', 'The weight proved to be under 114,000 ounces', *under age* or *under 18*, 'Wheat was under three shillings a bushel', 'Barbarous orders to sink every ship under 100 tons', (of spirit) *under proof, under one's breath* (in a whisper, in a very low voice) (*OED*).

The chief difference is that *under* implies 'vertically lower than', while *below* need not. When they refer to rank, *below* corresponds to *above*, and *under* to *over*. 'She has three secretaries under her.'

abrogate. See **arrogate**.

absence gives rise to the cliché 'conspicuous by his (or her) absence'. Avoid it. And do not write 'in the absence of' where *without* would do instead.

absolute. See COMPARATIVES, FALSE.

ABSTRACT NOUNS. The use of too many of these makes the language heavy and turgid. One may often improve the flow of a passage by the simple device of replacing an abstract noun, usually with its attendant adjective, by a single adjective, adverb, verb, or more concrete noun. 'Far-reaching consequences' is neater than 'consequences of a far-reaching nature'; 'He will be employed as a consultant' (or 'for consultation') than 'He will be employed on a consultancy basis'; 'weather' than 'weather conditions', and 'She drinks too much' than 'She has an alcohol problem.' Some abstract nouns that seem to be particular candidates for such rephrasing are *aspect, case, character, degree, factor, instance, manner, position, situation*. See **VERBOSITY**.

abysmal; abyssal. Both = 'of the abyss', but whereas the former is figurative, as in 'abysmal ignorance' and 'abysmal despair', the latter is literal, with the specific sense, 'belonging to that belt of the ocean which is more than 300 fathoms down', as in 'abyssal zone', 'abyssal animals', 'abyssal mud'. Colloquially, *abysmal* also means 'very bad', as in 'The standard of writing was abysmal.'

academic. See VOGUE WORDS.

accelerate and **exhilarate** are more often confused, especially in the noun forms (*acceleration*; *exhilaration*), than one might expect. To *accelerate* is to quicken, speed up, hasten, increase, advance, dispatch and expedite. To *exhilarate* is to enliven, cheer, elate, arouse to mirth, and raise to high spirits. 'An exhilarating conversation accelerates the mental faculties.'

acceptable. See VOGUE WORDS.

acceptance; acceptation. The former is used in all senses denoting or connoting the act of accepting and the state (or condition) of being received, as in 'the acceptance of a gift or an offer'; *acceptation* is, in general usage, reserved for 'the current sense of a word, the prevailing sense of a word', as in 'The acceptation of *imply* differs from that of *infer*.'

access; accession. The former chiefly means the opportunity to reach or obtain something, as in 'access to confidential files'. It is used as a verb in data-processing, meaning 'gain access to'. *Accession* means entering upon an office, as in 'her accession to the throne'. As a verb, it means 'record the addition of (an item) to a library or museum'.

accessary and **accessory.** In British English, a minor participant in a crime has traditionally been an *accessary*; the corresponding adjective is also *accessary*. In American usage, *accessory* is usual as both noun and adjective, and this spelling is becoming common in Britain.

In the sense 'an adjunct, an accompa- niment', *accessory* is now general; as the corresponding adjective ('subordinate', 'accompanying', 'non-essential', 'adventi- tious') *accessory* is correct.

accidently for *accidentally*: a solecism occasionally met with both in spelling and in pronunciation.

accompanist, not *accompanyist*, is now the usual term for 'an accompanying musician'.

according to. See CONJUNCTIONS, DISGUISED.

accountable should be confined to per- sons. 'This wretched nib is accountable for my scrawl' is catachrestic.

accredit(ed). See **credit.**

accuse. See **charge.**

acquaint with (the facts) is feeble and pretentious for *tell* (the facts).

acquiescence to. See PREPOSITIONS WRONGLY USED.

acquirement; acquisition. The former denotes the power or faculty of acquiring; the latter, the thing acquired. 'His acquire- ments in music are greater than his acquisition of riches.'

act as a verb should correctly be followed by an adverb in Standard British English, not by an adjective. Persons *act* 'stupidly', not 'stupid'.

act on, misused for *react on*. 'The fear of losing his job acted on him in the perfor- mance of his duties and finally caused him to lose his precious job.' *Action* as a verb means 'take action on' in managerial jargon, but the longer phrase is better English.

activate; actuate. The first means 'make active, or reactive, or radioactive', and is best confined to physics and chemistry or at any rate to machines. It should not replace *actuate* in the sense 'motivate to action', as in 'She was actuated by malice.'

actual and **actually** are usually unnecessary, in precisely the same way as *real* and *really* are, for the most part, excessive; *actual* is especially uncalled-for in collocation with *fact*, as in 'He is said to have died on a Monday; the actual fact is that he died on a Tuesday.' See **really.**

adapt and **adopt** are often confused. To *adapt* a thing is to change it for one's own purpose; to *adopt* it is to accept it unchanged and then use it. Moreover, *adopt* must be distinguished from *assume*: one adopts a child, a religion, but one assumes a pose, an attitude – a debt, a task, a duty.

adapted for *suitable* is infelicitous. 'Ordinary language is not adapted to describe processes within the atom' (Stuart Chase, *The Tyranny of Words*).

add. See **annex.**

addict. See **subject to.**

addicted (to) is a pejorative. Do not, for instance, say, 'Addicted to benevolent action' – unless you are being facetious. And do not use the infinitive construction, as in 'She was addicted to lie.'

address should not be synonymized with *speech*, but reserved for 'a formal speech', 'a set discourse', a speech to celebrate an important occasion; thus, 'The Queen's inaugural speech' is inferior to '... inaugural address'. An *address* in church is less systematic and less formal than a *sermon*.

adduce is applied only to arguments, speeches, statements, or to persons, animals, objects as illustrations or samples, the sense being 'to bring forward (verbally) for consideration; to cite; to allege', but especially the first of these nuances. 'In proof of this they adduced many arguments' (historian Robertson, 1765). – 'He adduced Tilden as the supreme example of the value of physical fitness in lawn tennis.' – 'She adduced some absurd reasons for her very odd preference.'

adequate enough is incorrect for 'sufficient' or 'suitable', and tautological for 'adequate'. The idea of 'enough' is contained within that of 'adequate'.

adequate standard of living. Enough money. [Gobbledygook.]

adherence; adhesion. In general, the former is figurative ('He was noted for his adherence to the principles of free thought'); the latter, literal ('The adhesion of this stamp to that envelope is in itself sufficiently remarkable'). See also **PREPOSITIONS WRONGLY USED.**

adjacent; contiguous. The latter = 'touching', as in 'France and Spain are contiguous', 'France is contiguous to Belgium'; loosely, 'neighbouring; near but not touching' – a sense to be avoided. But *adjacent* has, in correct usage, both of these senses.

ADJECTIVE FOR ADVERB. Even a tolerably educated person may, in a slovenly moment, fall into such an error as this: 'The home team pressed *stronger* [for *more strongly*] towards the close of the game' (cited by Harold Herd in *Watch Your English*). Some adverbs, however, may occur with or without the suffix '-ly'; e.g. *slow(ly)*, *quick(ly)*, *cheap(ly)*. The *-ly* forms are more polite, the root forms are more vigorous. Sometimes there is a difference in meaning: 'The ball went as *high* as the steeple'; 'I value it *highly*.'

Use an adjective when the verb refers to the subject of the sentence, in which case it could be replaced by the verb *to be*; as in 'The market closed steady' (It closed and it *was* steady) or 'The cat looked hungry' (It seemed *to be* hungry). Use an adverb when the verb refers to the activity, as in 'The market rose steadily' or 'The cat looked hungrily at the fish.'

ADJECTIVES, POSITION OF. Make sure that the adjective immediately precedes the noun it qualifies: look out for group-words like *children's language*, *women's college*, *men's shoes*. Harold Herd points out the absurdity of *stylish gentle-*

men's suits for *gentlemen's stylish suits*. Is *an excellent women's college* as clear as *an excellent college for women?*

ADJECTIVES, UNCOMPARA-BLE. See COMPARATIVES, FALSE.

adjure. See **abjure.**

admission. See **admittance.**

admit, admit of; permit of; allow of. *Admit of* is a rather literary variation of one of the senses of *admit*, viz. 'to allow of the presence, or the coexistence, of; to be capable of; be compatible with', as in 'Sublimity admits not of mediocrity' and 'It hardly admits of the possibility of error.'

Permit of is rather rare, and rather literary, for *permit* in the sense, 'to give opportunity to; to allow', as in 'The facts permit of only one interpretation', and is thus synonymous with *admit of* and *allow of* (OED).

admittance and **admission.** The former is physical ('No admittance here', as a sign or a notice); the latter, figurative and applied especially to 'reception or initiation into rights and privileges', as in 'His admission to the Athenaeum Club was duly noted' and 'The admission of immigrants into the United States of America has been much restricted of late years'; the latter example leads us to the fact that 'when physical entrance and access to privileges are combined, *admission* is the preferred form, as "admission to a concert, a play, a game"' (Weseen); cf. 'The charge for admission was one shilling.'

adopt. See **adapt.**

advance; advancement. The two nouns are not interchangeable. *Advance* means 'progress, going forward', as in 'an advance in computer technology'. *Advancement* means 'promotion, bringing forward', as in 'work towards the advancement of socialism'.

advantage and **vantage.** The latter is 'the position or a condition that is above another, either literally or figuratively', as in 'He viewed the struggle from the *van-*

tage (or, the vantage point) of a safe job' and 'He viewed the valley from the *vantage* (point) of the hill': *advantage* is here admissible. But 'He has an *advantage* over me, for he knows something about the subject.'

advent and **arrival.** The former connotes importance, deep significance, fate, the operation of natural law: 'The advent of summer had been preceded by the return to summer time'; 'The advent of death is of supreme importance to at least one person.' But 'His arrival at Marseilles took place on the first of June': *arrival* is neutral and it connotes comparative unimportance.

adventure; venture. 'In present use *venture* applies chiefly to business undertakings, especially such as involve chance, hazard, and speculation. *Adventure* applies chiefly to bold and daring experiences in the meeting of danger. Both words are used as verbs, but *venture* more commonly. It means to risk, hazard, take a chance, speculate, expose, and dare' (Weseen).

ADVERB, POSITION OF THE. See ORDER OF WORDS, Section B.

adverse to; averse to (or from). Respectively 'opposed to' and 'strongly disinclined to' or 'having a (strong) distaste for'. *Averse* is used chiefly of persons, but *adverse* is not properly so used: 'He was averse to violence'; 'Conditions adverse to swimming'. *Averse from*, though etymologically correct, is decidedly pedantic.

advert; avert. Lit., these respectively mean 'to turn to (something)' and 'to turn (something) away' or 'to prevent': 'He adverted to the plan that had been suggested'; 'He said that, at all costs, the danger had to be averted.'

advice is the noun, **advise** the verb.

advise for *tell* or *mention* is a piece of commercialese that has invaded the august halls of bureaucracy. 'As advised in our letter of the …'.

advisedly; intentionally. *Advisedly* = 'done judiciously, without haste, and after careful planning or consideration', whereas *intentionally* is much weaker, for it merely = 'done not by accident but *purposely*'. As Professor Weseen has shrewdly remarked, 'Many intentional acts are not carried out advisedly.'

aeroplane. See **airplane.**

aesthetic; beautiful. Correctly, *aesthetic* refers to the appreciation of beauty or to concern with beauty, so that a concrete building may be faced with stone for *aesthetic* reasons. This may make it *beautiful*, but one should not speak of the building as *aesthetic*.

affect and **effect** as verbs are frequently confused. *Effect* is 'to bring about', 'to accomplish'; *affect* is 'to produce an effect on'; 'to attack, move, touch' (*SOED*). An example occurs in *The Sessions Papers of the Old Bailey*, January 1737: 'Mr Bell, Surgeon, deposed, that upon his examining the Body of the Deceased, he found several Bruises and Wounds upon it, but not of consequence enough to effect her life.' Possibly the surgeon had, when he commenced his deposition, intended to say 'effect her death'. Even the nouns are occasionally confused, though only *effect* is in common usage.

AFFECTATION. Affectation is a putting-on of literary airs and graces: artificiality of style, of phrasing, of words. It may go so far that it becomes 'hollow or false display' (*OED*). 'The essence of affectation', said Carlyle, 'is that it be assumed.'

Some critics synonymize it with PRE-CIOUSNESS, but the two terms are not co-extensive. Preciousness might perhaps be considered as a special kind of affectation; that this, however, is too sweeping a statement may be perceived from the fact that whereas a good writer may fall into preciousness, he or she will not fall into affectation.

'The man who writes good English', we are told by Harold Herd in his valuable book, *Watch Your English*, 'avoids frills and verbal tricks. Gone are the virtues of polysyllabic words and lumbering sen-

tences. To load a composition with inflated phrases and far-fetched words is now a gross literary vice.

'If you would write plainly, beware of affected words and phrases. Do not write *eventuate* when you mean *happen*, *conversed* for *talked*, *demise* for *death*, *a member of the sterner sex* for *man*, *organ of vision* for *eye*, *voiced the opinion* for *said*. These are a few examples of tinsel expressions that try to usurp the place of simple words.'

Herd then picks on the device known as 'elegant variation'. 'If', he says, 'the mayor has been mentioned, he makes further appearances as "the civic chief"', "the leader of our official life", "our official head", "the town's chief representative" – and so on. Variation of this kind should be employed only when it is absolutely necessary' – in my opinion, it is never necessary. 'In most cases it is better to use a pronoun' – and when you can't, say 'the mayor' and have done with it.

affinity. An *affinity* may exist *between* persons or things, or *with* another thing or person. The use, here, of *to* or *for* is now common in scientific writing, where the word means the tendency of one substance to combine with another, but this construction should not be encouraged to proliferate.

affirm. See **assert.**

affirmative, reply in the. See **answer was …**

afflict. See **inflict.**

affluent. Prefer the simpler word *rich*.

AFRICAN ENGLISH. See STAN-DARD ENGLISH, Section IV.

Africander (or *Afrikander*) is not to be synonymized with *African* (n. and adj.). An *African* is a person, whereas an *Africander* is a kind of South African cow or sheep. A white South African of Dutch descent is an *Afrikaner*.

after. The senses 'on the analogy of' and 'according to' are Standard English, but they must be used with care, for they often lead to ambiguity, as in 'The word (*exist*), after *be*, has come to possess many nuances' and 'This statement is after Darwin.'

agenda, though a Latin plural, is now always treated as a singular noun, with the plural *agendas*. A single part of it is 'an item in the agenda', rather than 'an agendum'.

aggravate, aggravation. Already, in 1896, John Davidson, in *Baptist Lake*, remarked that the use of *aggravate* was beyond cure. It is incorrectly used in the sense *to annoy* (a person); properly it means *to intensify*, usually for the worse. On the misuse of this word see especially *The King's English*, by H. W. and F. G. Fowler. Stylists avoid *aggravate* in the sense 'to annoy, to exasperate, to provoke'; but humdrum writers and hurried journalists may, if they wish, take heart of disgrace from the fact that *aggravate* has been used in these nuances since early in the 17th century – for instance, it is enshrined in Cotgrave's famous French–English dictionary, 1611. *Aggravation* is likewise avoided by stylists, but pedants must cease from stigmatizing the word as bad English; it can no longer be classified as anything worse than an infelicity.

aggregate, 'to amount to a total of' (say $10 or £2), is a colloquialism perhaps less frowned-on in the USA than in Britain.

aggressive. See VOGUE WORDS.

agnostic and **atheist.** Whereas the latter denies the existence of God, the former merely says that His existence cannot be proved; a liberal agnostic admits that His existence cannot be disproved. (With *agnostic*, cf. **sceptic**.)

ago should not be combined with *since*. Write either 'It is many years since he died' or 'It was many years ago that he died', but not 'It is many years ago since he died.' See also **since**.

agrarian for *agricultural* 'is still rather bookish'; in the main, it is confined to the *Agrarian Reforms* of Ancient Rome and the *agrarian policies* of political parties. As a

noun, *agricultur(al)ist* is loose for 'a farmer', but it is justifiable when used as the opposite of *pastoralist* (a farmer of live stock); an *agrarian* is 'one who recommends an equitable division of land'.

agree. One *agrees with* a person or an opinion, *agrees on* a plan, *agrees to* a demand or proposal, or *agrees to do* something. But in British (though not in American) use, it is now common to use *agree*, and especially *agreed*, with no following preposition to mean 'reach agreement about', as in 'We agreed a procedure', or 'They issued an agreed statement.'

AGREEMENT, FALSE. False Agreement* affects two groups of grammar; constitutes two pitfalls of writing.

A. NUMBER. Particularly verb with subject, as in 'He and I am going to Town'; but also in such phenomena as 'those kind of books'. Contrast 'that breed of horses', which, theoretically correct, is unidiomatic; as, idiomatically, we say, 'that kind of book' (*not* 'that kind of books'), so, idiomatically, we say 'that breed of horse'. See **kind of, all.** Note that the verb *to be* agrees with its subject, not with its complement: thus, not 'A man *are* thousands of different persons' but 'A man *is* thousands of different persons' is correct. Charles Robert Fanshawe, *Memoires of Lady F.*, 1829, has 'All which' – we should say 'all that' – 'is required in compositions of that nature *are*, that the writer should record what he saw and heard': for *are* substitute *is*: Fanshawe seems to have been led astray by *compositions*. In 'The vividness of these delightful images *were* intensified by the desperateness of my own affairs' (C. H. B. Kitchen, *Birthday Party*), the subject is *vividness*, not *images*. In 'The rapidity of Lord Roberts's movements are deserving of the highest praise' (*The Daily Express*, 14 May 1900: cited by J. C. Nesfield in *Errors in English Composition*), the journalist has lost sight of the fact that

*For the beginner, there is a useful introduction in Harold Herd, *Watch Your English*, at pp. 12 (foot)–15 (top).

it was the *rapidity* which deserved praise. See '**one**, use of plural in v. after', for a very common type of false agreement between subject and verb: here I give two further examples: 'Sorel's *Reflections on Violence* is one of the few works upon Socialism that can be, or *deserves* to be, read by the non-professional student' (A. R. Orage, *c.* 1937); 'Mr Yeats has written one of the simplest accounts of poetical composition that *has* ever appeared' (Michael Roberts, in *The Spectator*, 19 Nov. 1937). *What* sometimes causes confusion, as in the following sentence from one of Agatha Christie's novels, 'I don't really see what my personal relationships *has* to do with the matter in hand, M. Poirot.' (See also **POSSESSIVE PRONOUN, agreement**.)

B. POSITION. Theoretically, this kind of false agreement could be taken to include all wrong positions, whether of words in a phrase, or of words or phrases in a clause, or, indeed, of words, phrases, clauses in a sentence. And, practically, it is most convenient to treat first of (I) relative clauses (subordinate clauses beginning with *who, which, that, when, where*, and such rarities as *wherever, whereof, wherefore, whenever*) that have slipped their moorings, got out of position, departed from apposition, departed therefore from positional agreement; and then consider (II) phrases and words (e.g. adjectives) that are out of position – that are, in other terms, in false agreement; and, finally, (III) several examples of pronominal falsity in agreement.

NB The position of adverbs, however, is discussed in **ORDER OF WORDS**, Section B, and confused or misrelated participles will be found at **CONFUSED PARTICIPLES**.

I. *Relative clauses out of position.* Relevant to this section is the use or misuse of the relative pronouns, *who* and *that, which* and *that*: see '**which and that; who and that**'. The importance of the correct use of the relatives may be gauged by such a sentence as, 'It is the question of the house that Jack built which is important in architecture.'

The danger of separating the relative from its antecedent should be obvious: that it isn't obvious may be guessed from the following examples (selected from an astounding abundance of infelicities):

'I had in the County of Northampton deposited my Heart in a Virgin's Breast, who failed in Credit and Sincerity' (*The Life of Benjamin Stratford*, 1766): the writer's sense of position was as defective stylistically as it was cardially. A rearrangement is necessary; thus, 'I had ... deposited my heart in the breast of a virgin, who failed ...'.

'He stripped off the drunkard's covering (who never stirred)' (Richard Hughes, 'Poor Man's Inn' in *A Moment of Time*). Correct to: 'He stripped off the covering of the drunkard, who never stirred' (i.e. did not stir).

In 'There is room for a persistent, systematic, detailed inquiry into how words work that will take the place of the discredited subject which goes by the name of Rhetoric' (I. A. Richards, *The Philosophy of Rhetoric*), the very acute and intelligent author has the excuse that if he attaches to 'words' its relative clause 'that will take the place of ... Rhetoric', he thrusts 'work' to the end of the sentence; true, but why not recast the sentence thus, 'There is room for a persistent ... inquiry into the workability (or activities or operations or potentialities) of words that will take the place of ... Rhetoric'? One is not always obliged to knock down a brick wall; often it is easier – and occasionally it is much more effective – to go through the gate or to walk to the end of the wall or to scale the wall.

'The modes of causal recurrence on which meaning depends are peculiar through that delegated efficacy I have been talking about' (*ibid.*). The uninstructed reader would probably suppose that *which* referred to 'causal recurrence'; it refers to 'the modes'. The ambiguity would not have arisen if the anticipatory *those* had been used; 'Those modes of causal recurrence on which meaning depends are ...' is unambiguous.

'The operational approach makes knowledge about the world outside no longer absolute, but relative. The operation is performed relative to' – i.e. in relation to – 'some standard, say the gauge or the meter stick. Concepts emerge from these operations which are definite and verifiable' (Stuart Chase, *The Tyranny of Words*). Does 'which' refer to 'operations', or to 'concepts'? If to 'operations', should there not be a comma after 'operations'? But does not 'which' refer to 'concepts'? Perhaps rewrite thus: 'Such concepts emerge from these operations as are definite and verifiable.'

'The latest major engagement [struggle between science and theology] was over Darwin, which lingered on to the Scopes trial in Tennessee' (*ibid.*): no ambiguity here; merely slovenliness.

'C. E. M. Joad wrote a book to drive home the message of Radhakrishnan, in which he states flatly that his hero has attained to truth about the universe which is "from its nature incommunicable"' (*ibid.*): 'such truth about the universe as is "from its nature incommunicable"'?

'Many factors affect judicial decisions, of which the rules of law constitute but one' (*ibid.*): 'of which' refers to 'many factors', not – as one might think – to 'judicial decisions'.

'The girl, furious, goes to Mr Frost's club to complain *who*, at first, thinks her visit is one of the practical jokes of his inventive friend. (And the heavens forbid that I should mar that choice sentence with any bracket of mine!) But eventually he agrees to carry out his forgetful wife's undertaking' (James Agate, in *The Tatler*, 15 Dec. 1937). The omission of the comma after 'complain' increases the clumsiness of the sentence. And what did Agate mean by bracket? See **bracket.**

II. *In the agreement of words other than antecedent and relative*, we find that the implication of incorrect or foolish order is as strong as in the foregoing examples. Witness the following:

'What is the ultimate nature of matter? The question we know by now is mean-

ingless' (Stuart Chase, *The Tyranny of Words*). Here the false agreement is flagrant. The writer means, 'By now, we know that this question is meaningless.'

'He arranges a meeting of his suspects to find out whether anyone reacts in any way peculiar to the sight of the body' (C. McCabe, *The Face on the Cutting-Room Floor*). Obviously the author does not intend us to understand a 'way peculiar to the sight of the body'; he does mean, 'react to the sight of the body'. Therefore he should have written '... reacts in any peculiar way to the sight of the body'.

'They sat at ease in the boat, which lay moored in a tiny creek of the island, canopied by an overhanging willow' (Gerald Bullet, in his powerful and poignant novel, *The Snare of the Fowler*). What was canopied? The island (as grammatically it should be)? The creek (as is possible though improbable)? Or the persons? Apparently the persons, for the spread of a willow's branches is not very large. Therefore the sentence should read, 'Canopied by an overhanging willow, they sat at ease in the boat, which lay moored in a tiny creek of the island.' (This sentence might have been included in the entry **CONFUSED PARTICIPLES.**)

'But, unlike North, it was not necessary for him to surrender his own judgment to that of George III' (J. R. Green, *A Short History of the English People*, 1874: cited by Nesfield in *Errors in English Composition*). Read, 'But it was not necessary for him, as it was necessary for North, to surrender his own judgment to that of George III.'

'"You'll like the Ole Man. ... Treats you as if you were a human being – not a machine." – Ten minutes later Meredith endorsed this opinion for himself. Alert, efficient, quiet both in manner and speech, he found the head of the borough police not only ready to condone his presence on the scene but to thank him for his co-operation' (John Bude, *The Cheltenham Square Murder*). 'Alert, efficient, quiet both in manner and speech' does not, as it should, refer to Meredith but to the head of the borough police ('the Ole Man').

'When they were gone, still carrying me, she sat down on a great smooth stone that was beside the well' (Wilfranc Hubbard, 'The Road to Eleusis' in his *Tanagra Figures*). Who was carrying 'me' – 'they' or 'she'? Presumably 'they'. The sentence should be rewritten in some such manner as this: 'When, still carrying me, they were gone [better: they went], she sat down on a great smooth stone.'

III. *Pronominal agreement, or lack of agreement*, has, in part, been exemplified in the section on relative pronouns. Here are several examples where other pronouns are involved:

'Left without a father at the age of $3\frac{1}{2}$, her mother was her only guide.' It was not her mother who had, at the age of $3\frac{1}{2}$, been left without a father; it was the little girl. Recast thus: 'To the girl left without a father at the age of $3\frac{1}{2}$, the mother was the only guide.' Cf. this: 'An only son, his mother had died when he was a child' (W. H. Lane Crauford, *Murder to Music*): his mother was not an only son, *he* was: therefore read, 'He was an only son, and his mother had died when he was a child' or, less happily, 'He was an only son, whose mother had died when he was a child.'

'A sensation would be something that just was *so*, on its own, a datum; as such we have none' (I. A. Richards, *The Philosophy of Rhetoric*): ? '...; we have no sensations – no data – as such'.

'It is well known that once a man or woman has become a town councillor, they are never quite the same again' (a letter in *Time and Tide*). By the advocates of expedience, 'they' may be defended on the ground that it avoids the clumsiness of 'he or she'; but why not 'It is well known that once persons have become town councillors, they are never quite the same again'? '"Neither Emilienne nor I really understands pictures"' (Naomi Royde-Smith, *The Younger Venus*). 'I', being the nearer, governs; therefore, 'understand'.

agricultural; agricultur(al)ist. See **agrarian.**

ain't for *isn't* or *are not* is an error so illiterate that I blush to record it. As for *ain't* for *hasn't* or *haven't* ...! More is to be said for *ain't = am not*, but it is now – and long has been – adjudged to be illiterate in Britain, although some educated Americans use it in speech, particularly in the question form *ain't I?* For this, the British have preferred the illogical but well-established *aren't I?*

airplane is the usual American, *aeroplane* the usual English form. But *air-* is standard in most words connected with aviation, as with *aircraft, airlift, airmail, airport.*

akin with for *akin to*. A not uncommon error. Eric Partridge fell into it in his *Eighteenth Century English Romantic Poetry*, 1924. *Akin* is a contraction of *of kin*, that form being occasionally found in literary English. (See also COMPARATIVES, FALSE.)

alarum is archaic for *alarm* (n.).

albumen; albumin. Respectively, 'the white of an egg' and 'a member of a class of proteins rich in sulphur and nitrogenous substance'; the former is a general scientific term, the latter a chemical technicality.

alcoholic. See **drunk.**

alias is sometimes – though less now than formerly – misused for a disguise, a concealment. 'He dressed up as a costermonger; *that* was his alias.'

alibi is sometimes used for an *excuse* or *pretext* of almost any kind, whereas, properly, it is only 'the plea that when an alleged act took place one was elsewhere' (*COD*). '"I was too ill to write." "That's no alibi for failing to let me know – somebody could have phoned that information."'

alien (adj.) is followed by *to*, not *from*, as in 'ideas quite alien to ours'.

alike, misplaced. 'For the moment it appeared quite convenient to regard myself as an executioner about to terminate a life alike forfeit to the laws of God and man', for a 'life forfeit to the laws of

God and man alike' (Eden Phillpotts, *Physician, Heal Thyself*).

alike ... or for *alike ... and*. '... He was taking, in colonial parlance, *a dry smoke* – that is, it was alike destitute of fire or tobacco' (Parker Gilmore, *Days and Nights in the Desert*).

all, colloquially used with the genitive (e.g. *all their sakes* instead of (*for*) *the sake*(*s*) *of all of them*). See GENITIVE, VAGARIES OF THE, the last paragraph but one.

all alone is tautological for *alone*, but can be excused when 'all' is a genuine intensive.

all-powerful, like **omnipotent**, is uncomparable. See COMPARATIVES, FALSE. The same restriction holds for the other *all*-compounds – e.g. *all-seeing*.

all right. See **alright**.

all that is normal in speech with adjectives and adverbs after negatives, as in 'He isn't as old as all that', or 'I wasn't driving all that fast.' The construction does not belong in formal writing.

all the lot. See **lot** and **whole, the.**

allege commonly means 'to declare or assert on insufficient grounds' and it must not be made synonymous with *affirm, assert, declare*.

allegiance and **alliance,** often confused. The former is the loyalty (theoretical and practical) that one owes to a person (e.g. one's king, one's overlord), whereas the latter is a pact between two nations or states.

ALLEGORY. 'When a comparison is protracted and sustained through numerous details, it is named an Allegory.

'Allegories on the grand scale are exemplified by Spenser's *Faery Queen*, Bunyan's *Pilgrim's Progress*, and Swift's *Tale of a Tub* and *Gulliver*. In these a whole series of adventures is sustained with a double meaning.

'... The short Allegory is frequent in literature. In *The Spectator*, we have the Vision of Mirza, No. 159; Luxury and Avarice, 55; Truth, Falsehood, and Fiction, 460' (Alexander Bain).

A short allegory with moral content is a *parable*, as with the stories Jesus tells in the Gospels. A *fable* also conveys a message, but by means of impossible (fabulous) events; particularly involving animal characters, as with Aesop's *Fables*.

alleluia is the Greek form of the word, and is the prevailing spelling today. *Hallelujah* derives directly from Hebrew, and is the form Handel used for the 'Hallelujah Chorus'.

allergic. To *be allergic to* is being grossly misused – and in its incorrect senses, fatuously overused – for 'to dislike (intensely)', 'to be opposed to', 'to be antipathetic to', as in 'He is allergic to music, you to noise', 'I am allergic to propaganda.' Originally and usefully it is a medical word (the noun being *allergy*); its correct and – may I add? – its sensible use appears in this statement made, in 1926, by a medical man: 'Allergic hypersusceptibility is a special type of idiosyncrasy in which the patient reacts to special substances' (cited by *OED*). *Allergy* is 'altered physiological reactivity': so don't go using it for 'dislike', 'intense dislike', 'antipathy', 'enmity or hostility', for it means nothing of the sort. A VOGUE WORD.

ALLITERATION. 'Apt alliteration's artful aid' (Charles Churchill, *The Prophecy of Famine*, 1763).

In his *English Composition and Rhetoric*, enlarged edition, Part II, 1888, Alexander Bain has the following short section, which may serve as an introduction.

'The term *Alliteration* is employed to signify the commencing of successive words with the same letter or syllable [as in *u-, ewe, yew, you*]. Unless' – read *except* – 'when carried out on a set purpose, it offends the ear: as *long live Lewis, come conqueror, convenient contrivance*.' Several other examples (likewise from Bain): 'That is *also altered*'; 'He i*mitated it at* once'; 'To per*manently imp*air the *p*ower of the *P*eers'.

Alliteration is employed either stylistically (that is, to obtain emphasis, effectiveness, pointedness, humour, euphony) or as a mnemonic device. It is frequent in advertisements: *beautiful Bournemouth, Guinness is good for you, pink pills for pale people, the sunny South.*

The poets have made a happy use of it: for instance, Keats's 'the winnowing wind'; Swinburne's 'welling water's winsome word' and

> Even the weariest river
> Winds somewhere safe to sea,

but then, of all poets writing in the English language, Swinburne is the most frequent, versatile, and felicitous alliterator.

But alliteration can be, and has been, employed no less felicitously by the prose writers. The two great masters, in the present century, are G. K. Chesterton and Frank Binder.

Chesterton is the more impressive and at the same time the more pointed and epigrammatic manipulator of alliteration; Binder the more rhythmical and euphonious, the more sophisticated and yet the more profound: but, in their different ways, they 'know their job'.

Of Chesterton's works I choose one of the less famous, *The Paradoxes of Mr Pond*, 1936. It opens thus: 'The curious and sometimes creepy effect which Mr Pond produced upon me, despite his commonplace courtesy and dapper decorum, was possibly connected with some memories of childhood; and the vague verbal association of his name.' And here are a few other examples: 'At this moment could be seen, striding across the sun-chequered lawn, the large and swaggering figure of Captain Gahagan'; 'The Asa-Smith school of drama, in which every sentence stops as soon as it starts'; 'Paradox has been defended on the ground that so many fashionable fallacies still stand firmly on their feet, because they have no heads to stand on. But it must be admitted that writers, like other mendicants and mountebanks, frequently do try to attract attention': (concerning Shakespeare's clowns and

fools) 'The Fool is like a fantastic dancing flame lighting up the features and furniture of the dark house of death'; 'Nobody who looked at the baldish, rather corrugated brow that bulged between the streaks of black hair, and the anxious, though angry eyes, could doubt that he was in fanatical good faith'; 'the trail of official fussing that crossed the track of the tragedy'.

Frank Binder has, I believe, published only two books: *A Journey in England*, 1931, and *Dialectic; or, the Tactics of Thinking*, 1932. From the former: 'It may be ..., a craving for echoes that never come, but I still lose myself in the solemn and insinuating stillness of the North German Plain, in its long, quiet, contemplative stretches of wistful woodland, its calm and grey religious skies.' (Of Ely) 'I had stepped into a lofty sepulchre of stone, a mausoleum of mediaeval memory, one of the stately desolations of Isaiah which served as proof of the failing frailty of humanity, and as a wrecking rebuke to perspiring ambition and pride. ... All was empty, dark, and still. Not a breath, not a footfall! Nothing to move the emotion, nothing to dispel the deadening dread of death, but all shrouded in shadow, grey as a forgotten grave, built up and barricaded above like a tomb, and all below, in the sombre seclusion of the aisles, the hard flags of unremembered burials, tablets to long-since nameless names, mural memorials to the well-noted unknowns of past time. Never have my thoughts been so reduced to the downtrodden dust of human destiny and of human despair as in the nave and in the aisles of Ely Church ... I am a poor pagan, but as I beheld the work of our own Alan of Walsingham I was prepared to believe in inspiration, to believe in a benevolent breathing from the beyond, and in courteous communications from some superior spirit who takes our favoured ones by the hand, and who leads them with a studied certainty of step to the sure summits of art.'

And from *Dialectic*: 'The debates of today are not, as the wrangles of the Middle

Ages, the battles of brain against brain, but a duet of defiances hurled from behind the fortifications, a banging of the big drum and a deciding of the issue in favour of the bigger din.

'The opinions of most people rarely spring from a principle by which their knowledge is selected and their thoughts arranged, but may be referred to little forts of fact and to blockhouses of bias where the defender lies entrenched for life, deeply enough as a rule to assure himself of safety and safely enough to bring any besieger to despair. A prejudice is early acquired, and as we are doubly attentive to those who agree with us and deaf to all we do not wish to hear, not a day goes without our piling Ossas of absolute assent on Pelions of dubious belief.

'The peddlers of practicability ... the criers-up of so-called common sense.

'The perennial personality of God.

'... The seers and astrologers of long ago who, looking at nature as we look at a printed page, saw in fact phenomena, events, and beings, symbols of celestial significance and emblems of immanent meaning, types of figures in the splendid speech of all things where, from the quaint contingency of eclipses and calamities, comets and the comings of greater kings, planetary aspects and the collapse of kingdoms, the mystical mind might come to read the alliteration of life, the assonance of the soul, the far-off arpeggios in the concords of God.

'Life in this embracing sense is not a fact but a faculty of nature, not a thing unique, discrete, and segregated with a poor and temporary place in our provincial bosoms, but a power both absolute and universal, a lasting possibility to which each atom has some trend and latent inclination. Each has a bias or bent to the spirit, a final predisposition, and allowing this, how shall we speak of men as being apart or as moving in a mystic remove from the world which holds us at one with itself? But not only are we so held, and not only the fabric of earth and sky is seen to fall into the bigger form and ... personality of being, but all

our aery estate of thoughts and dreams, of virtue and vice, of blessings and blasphemies, of purity and filth, of beauty and abomination, has, whether good or bad, its palpable part in the plan of things. For the world is an irrespective place, full, plenteous, and cosmopolitan, so free from prohibitions that he who seeks will find, who hopes will be sustained, who despairs will be left to despondency; a place so infinite in the forms of fact and fancy that men appear as everything and nothing, as the elect of heaven, as items of nature, or as poor parochial pawns in the one imperial purpose of God.'

allow. See **admit; admit of.**

allowing for. See CONJUNCTIONS, DISGUISED.

allude, vaguer than *refer*, is applied to a mention either incidental (or casual) or indirect, whereas *refer* is specific and direct. 'She often alludes to her early life'; 'He refers to Clemenceau on page 89.'

allure (v) is 'to attract' (a person), favourably or neutrally; **lure** is 'to attract' (a person) to his disadvantage. 'Allured by the prospect of fame, he was lured into indiscretion by the purveyors of publicity.'

allusion; reference. One makes an *allusion* to something not actually named. To make a *reference* to something is to name it. The distinction corresponds to that between *allude* (*q.v.*) and *refer*.

almost for *virtual*, esp. in *almost certainly* for *virtual certainty* or *near certainty*. *Almost*, I believe, should not be used to qualify a *noun*, abstract or concrete; correct uses are, 'he was almost certain', 'he almost succeeded'. Nesfield quotes from *The Review of Reviews*, April 1900 – 'The almost impossibility of frontal attacks, &c', which he corrects to 'the practical impossibility'. (But see **practical.**)

almost never is feeble – so feeble as to be incorrect – for *hardly ever* or *very seldom*. 'He almost never visits me any more' = 'He rarely visits me (nowadays).'

alone (adj.) is sometimes misused for the adv. *only*, as in 'It [the seizure of Kiaochau] was undertaken not alone without the knowledge of the Chancellor, but directly against his will', quoted by Nesfield from Wolf von Schiebrand, 'Germany as a World-Power' (*The Daily Telegraph*, April 1903), and in 'The roads, in these days of wireless and wireless-carrying cars, were not the proposition in a get-away that they had been in the era which depended alone upon telephonic communication' (John G. Brandon, *The Mail-Van Mystery*); in the latter quotation, 'alone' could be changed to 'only' or retained and placed after 'communication'. The use of *alone* in this sense is, however, permissible where it functions as an adv. after a noun or pronoun, as in 'You alone can help me.' See also **lonely.**

along of for (1) *owing to* and (2) *with* is used only by the uneducated.

along with, in the sense of *beside* or *in company with*, is inadmissible.

already is an adverb; **all ready,** an adjective. 'Are they already all ready?' illustrates the usage.

already sometimes requires a progressive tense (*am doing, was doing, has been doing*, etc.) instead of a simple one (*do, did, shall do*, etc.). One cannot draw up a rule; here, as so often in the finer points of idiom, literary tact or grammatical intuition or, indeed, both are required. 'If the legacy gave him a motive [in the past: complete], it's too late now to remove that motive. It operated, or it did operate [,] already' (Vernon Loder, *The Button in the Plate*). Here I should, for 'operated ... already', substitute, according to the precise time point required (only the author could tell us that), either 'was operating already' or, less probably (I feel), 'had been operating already'. Yet the above quotation does assign *already* to an implied past time. This use is more defensible than that of *already* with a past tense to mean 'before now', which requires a perfect tense (*have done, has done*). Do not write 'He already left.'

alright is an incorrect spelling of *all right*. There is a great temptation to spell it thus, to distinguish 'They are all right' (= all of them are right) from 'They are alright' (= they are safe, or satisfactory) just as *already* is distinguished from *all ready, almost* from *all most*, or *altogether* from *all together*; but the spelling *alright* is nevertheless unacceptable in serious writing.

also is often misused for *and*, as in 'He speaks Swedish and Danish, also French'; 'He speaks Swedish and Danish, also he can read French.' Avoid this practice.

altercation and **fight.** The former is verbal; the latter, physical. An *altercation* is a wrangle, a quarrelsome dispute, a heated controversy: 'Their altercation developed into a fight.'

alternate and **alternative.** The first means 'every other'. *Alternate* days are Monday, Wednesday, Friday ... The related adverb is *alternately*, meaning 'by turns'. 'He walked and ran alternately.' *Alternate* cannot replace *alternative*, which means 'available instead of another', as in 'We took an alternative route.' The adv. of *alternative* is *alternatively*, 'offering a choice'. 'You could fly, or alternatively go by sea.'

Alternative has been overused in official jargon, in such contexts as 'alternative accommodation', 'make alternative arrangements', 'find alternative employment', where it is often better replaced by *other* or *new*. But there is no really satisfactory synonym for the more recent sense 'nontraditional, offering a substitute for the conventional thing', as in 'alternative medicine', 'alternative cinema', 'alternative technology'. In this sense, it is a VOGUE WORD.

alternative and **choice.** There has been a long-standing objection to the use of *alternative* where more than two choices are involved, but this view is now discredited as pedantic. Today, it is good English to write 'What are the various alternatives?' or 'We must consider all the alternatives.' The near-synonyms *choice* and *option* do not always cover so neatly the idea of 'other things we can do'. It is redundant, however, to speak of 'no other alternative', since *alternative* itself contains the idea of 'other'.

although is more dignified, more literary than *though*, except in *as though* and *even though*, and (colloquially) at the end of a clause ('We enjoyed it, though'), where *although* could not be substituted for *though*. See also **though**.

although ... yet. To use both in a short sentence ('Although he returned only yesterday, yet he left again today') is unnecessary, but to imply that *although ... yet* is always redundant is wrong, as can be seen from almost any long sentence. In long sentences, as also in short, *(al)though* posits a handicap, an obstacle, or an advantage, and *yet* emphasizes the result – the victory or the defeat. Of the two, *yet* is, in any sentence, the more safely omitted, for the omission of *(al)though* leaves the sense unresolved for too long, as in 'He came only yesterday, yet he departed this morning.'

altogether and **all together** are often confused: the former = 'entirely, on the whole'; the latter implies collocation or coincidence or unanimity of individuals. The misuse can lead to strange ambiguities; 'The house party came altogether' (Anthony Wynne, *The Holbein Mystery*) should read: '... came all together'.

alumnus has the plural *alumni*. A former pupil of any school or college or, whether graduate or not, of any university. Properly, a male pupil or student; but the pl. *alumni* is used generically of both sexes, unless it is scientifically opposed to *alumnae* (sing. *alumna*, a girl pupil or student); the feminine is rarely used in Great Britain. [In American usage, *alumnus* is a graduate or former student of a university or a college: less commonly of a school, *former student* or *old student* being there more usual except in phrases like *alumni association*. The feminine *alumna, alumnae* is a cause of confusion at our colleges for women, especially because the 'English' pronunci-

ations of *alumni* and *alumnae* are similar to the 'Roman' pronunciations of *alumnae* and *alumni*.]

always, improperly employed. 'I have been a militant Communist and a constitutional Socialist and a Pacifist, and always there have been moments when I see all people ... as frightened children' (article 'Under Thirty' in *The Spectator*, 17 Dec. 1937). Existence only in 'moments' is contradictory of 'always'.

a.m. = in the morning, **p.m.** = in the afternoon and up to midnight. Avoid such phrases as '11 a.m. in the morning', and '11 p.m. at night'.

amatory and **amorous.** In current usage, *amorous* means 'moved by sexual love', as in 'amorous glances', 'amorous girls'. The more literary *amatory* means merely 'connected with sexual love', as in 'amatory poetry', 'his amatory affairs'.

amazement is 'overwhelming wonder, whether due to mere surprise or to admiration'; in the sense 'mental stupefaction', it is obsolete. It must not be confused with the *surprise* (or the *wonder*) itself.

amazing means 'astounding' – capable of amazing a person. It should not be debased to mean *unusual* or *good* (or even *very good*) or *bad* (or even *very bad*). Many journalists and many popular novelists and almost innumerable careless speakers have combined to make it a verbal counter – a 'rubber-stamp word', as Frank Whitaker has called it along with *ban, bid* (as noun), *chief* (as noun), *coup, drama, dream* (as adjective), *gang, gem, girl-wife, haul, pact, rail* (noun), *revelation, riddle, rush, trek, thrill* (both noun, especially, and verb), *wonder* (as adjective). Whitaker's witty and trenchant address, delivered on 13 Dec. 1938 to the Institute of Journalists, was reproduced in the Institute's *Journal*, January 1939. See also OFFICIALESE.

ambience. See VOGUE WORDS.

AMBIGUITY. 'I have often been apprehensive, that the manner in which I express myself, may lead you into some mistakes of my meaning, the signification of words, in the language of men, being so unsettled, that it is scarce possible to convey a determinate sense …; for where different, or perhaps contrary meanings are signified by the same word, how easy it is for a mind, prone to error, to take the wrong one?' (C. Johnston, *Chrysal*, 1768).

Ambiguity springs from woolly and muddled thinking; from a hasty fitting of words to the thought; from ignorance of the right uses of words; from the wrong order of words; from defective punctuation; and from a multiplicity of minor causes.

That ambiguity which springs from vague and muddled thinking – general ambiguity rather than particular ambiguities – is treated at **WOOLLINESS**, which is ambiguity on a large scale and is especially to be found in political speeches, in the words of publicists, and in the writings of such numerous vulgarizers as have failed to understand the views and thoughts of those whom they seek to vulgarize.

Obscurity is treated at **OBSCURITY**, where clarity is also dealt with. Ambiguity arising from defective punctuation is briefly treated at **PUNCTUATION**. Ambiguity arising from misuses of single terms is touched on in the ensuing paragraphs based on Jevons; but see also **CATACHRESIS**.

The relation of ambiguity to logic is so close that a chapter on ambiguity is to be found in every reputable treatise on logic. Instead of utilizing such works as Wm Ernest Johnson's *Logic*, 3 vols., 1921 (the Cambridge school of thought) and H. W. B. Joseph's *An Introduction to Logic*, 2nd edition, 1916 (the Oxford school of thought), which are excellent for dons and dons-to-be but a trifle difficult for the ordinary man and woman, I shall draw – and draw copiously – on a mid-Victorian logician (and economist), Wm Stanley Jevons, whose *Elementary Lessons in Logic* was recast as *The Elements of Logic*, 1883, by an American professor well known in the 1870s and 1880s – David J. Hill. What

follows is in parts an adoption, in parts an adaptation of the revised work.

Of Logic, the most general practical part is that which treats of the ambiguity of terms – of the uncertainty and the variety of meaning possessed by words. Nothing can be of more importance to the attainment of correct habits of thinking and reasoning than a thorough acquaintance with the imperfections of language. Comparatively few terms have one single clear meaning and one meaning only; and whenever two or more meanings are confused, we inevitably commit a logical fallacy, darken counsel, render hazardous the way of communication. If, for instance, a person should argue that 'Punishment is an evil', and that, according to the principles of morality, 'No evil is to be allowed even with the purpose of doing good', we might not immediately see how to avoid the conclusion that 'No punishments should be allowed', because punishments cause evil. A little reflection will show that the word *evil* is here used in two totally different senses: in the first case it means 'physical evil', 'pain'; in the second, 'moral evil'. Because moral evil is never to be committed, it does not follow that physical evils are never to be inflicted. – The more one studies the subtle variations in the meaning of common words, the more one will be convinced of the dangerous nature of the tools one has to use in all communications and arguments; the more careful should one therefore be in one's use of words, and the more critical one will be of propagandist writings.

In Logic, terms are said to be *univocal* when they can suggest no more than one definite meaning; to be *equivocal* (or *ambiguous*) when they have two or more different meanings. The word *cathedral* is probably univocal or of one logical meaning only. *Church*, on the other hand, sometimes means the building in which religious worship is performed; sometimes the body of persons who belong to one sect and assemble in churches; and *the church* means the body of the clergy as distinguished from the laity. *Equivocal* itself is ambiguous: its meaning in logic, as in philology, has been defined above; but in common life, *equivocal* is applied to the statements or the terms of one who uses words consciously and deceitfully in a manner designed to produce a confusion of the true and apparent meanings; in the moral sphere, it means 'questionable', 'of suspect or dubious character or reputation'.

Equivocal words fall into three classes, according as they are equivocal: in sound only; in spelling only; in both sound and spelling. Words equivocal in sound only or in spelling only give rise to trivial mistakes. When we hear them, we may confuse *right, rite, wright, write; rain, reign; might* and *mite*; but the context usually precludes misapprehension. Compare, too, *air* and *heir*, *hair* and *hare*. Words equivocal in spelling but not in pronunciation are a *tear*-(drop) and a *tear*, or rent, in cloth; *lead*, the metal, and the *lead* given by a person. We might add here such combinations as *French teacher*, which is stressed differently according to whether the person teaches, or is, French.

Much more important are the words equivocal in both spelling and pronunciation. These in their turn may be divided into three groups according as they arise: (i) from the *accidental confusion* of different words; (ii) from that *transference of meaning which is caused by an association of ideas*; and (iii) from the *logical transference of meaning to analogous objects*.

(i) *Accidental Confusion.* In this class we have those odd and interesting, though comparatively unimportant, cases in which ambiguity has arisen from the confusion of entirely different words (whether from different languages or from different roots of the same language) that have in the course of – and from the rough usage by – time come to have the same sound and the same spelling. Thus *mean* signifies either 'medium', 'mediocre', from the Medieval French *moien* (Modern French *moyen*), and 'base', 'vulgar', from Old English *gemæne*, 'belonging to the many'. The verb *mean* can hardly be confused with either of the adjectives *mean*, and it has, moreover, a distinct root.

(ii) *Transference of Meaning by Association of Ideas.* By far the largest proportion of equivocal words have become so by a transference of the meaning from the thing originally denoted by the word to some other thing so habitually connected with it as to be closely associated in thought. We have already seen the equivocality of *church*. In Parliamentary language, *the House* means either the chamber in which the members meet or the body of members that happen to be assembled in it at any time. Consider *foot*: the *foot* of a man; a *foot* measure; the *foot* (or base) of a mountain; those soldiers who fight on *foot*. Take *post*: that which is *posited* or *posted* firmly in the ground; a military *post*, the *post* of danger; *posts*, or horse-stages; the *post(s)*, or conveyance of news. *Man* is a male person, but it is also man or woman (*man* = mankind).

(iii) *Transference of Meaning by Analogy or by Real Resemblance.* A good example is afforded by *sweet*: a sweet taste, a sweet face, a sweet tune, a sweet poem. For *brilliant*, we have the original sense 'sparkling' or 'glittering'; a person who 'shines' is brilliant, perhaps because he or she has a brilliant or sparkling wit. It must, however, be admitted that in this group, there is little chance of confusion.

Related to Logic is Rhetoric; and in this connection we may recall I. A. Richards's dictum (*The Philosophy of Rhetoric*, 1936), that '[Whereas] the old Rhetoric treated ambiguity as a fault in language, the new Rhetoric sees it as an inevitable consequence of the powers of language and as the indispensable means of most of our most important utterances – especially in Poetry and Religion.'

Ambiguity, however, is found not merely in single words but also and especially in phrases, clauses, and sentences (whether single or compound; simple or complex). On ambiguity in general, the *locus classicus* is William Empson's *Seven Types of Ambiguity*, 1930; whence the following paragraph (direct borrowings being within quotation marks).

'There are three possible scales of dimensions [that] seem of reliable importance, along which ambiguities may be spread out; the degree of logical or grammatical disorder, the degree to which the apprehension of the ambiguity must be conscious, and the degree of psychological complexity concerned. Of these, the first seems to be the one about which there is least danger of talking nonsense, the one it is most important to be clear about ... My seven types, so far as they are not merely a convenient framework, are intended as stages of advancing logical disorder.' For us, there is, however, an obstacle in Empson's seven types: some of them constitute, not actual errors but mere potentialities of error or ambiguity; they are theoretic rather than practical. From this book, therefore, I select a few passages illustrative of such ambiguities as the ordinary reader – or, for that matter, the ordinary writer – is likely to encounter.

There is, for instance, that type of equivoque in which ambiguity – in word or syntax, or in both word and syntax – 'occurs when two or more meanings all add to the single meaning of the author'. In

> Cupid is winged and doth range;
> Her country so my love doth
>   change.
> But change she earth, or change
>   she sky,
> Yet I will love her till I die

'*change* may mean "move to another" or "alter the one you have got", and earth may be the lady's private world, or the poet's, or that of mankind at large'; the third verse shows that in the second verse the subject of *doth change* is *my love*, not *her country*, – a fact that in the second verse is still a doubt; also, does *yet* = the second member of an *although ... yet* antithesis, or does it = *still* (in time)? A moment's thought shows that *yet* is the concomitant of *although* understood after *But*. 'All meanings to be extracted from these

[terms] are the immediate meanings insisted upon by the words, and yet the whole charm of the poem is its extravagant, its unreasonable simplicity.'

'However, as a rule, complexity of meaning is produced by complexity of thought, even where ... there is only one main meaning as a resultant.' In

> If th' Assassination
> Could trammel up the Consequence,
>   and catch
> With his surcease, success ...

'*Consequence* means causal result. ... *Trammel* was a technical term used about netting birds, hobbling horses ... *Surcease* means completion, stopping proceedings in the middle of a lawsuit or the overruling of a judgment. ... *His* may apply to Duncan, *assassination* or *consequence*. *Success* means fortunate result, result whether fortunate or not, and succession to the throne. ... The meanings cannot be remembered all at once.'

'It is clear that ambiguity ... of grammar, though common enough in poetry, cannot be brought to this pitch without chaos. ... Sometimes the [ambiguity resides in] a relative clause, with "that" omitted, which is able to appear for a moment as an independent sentence on its own, before it is fitted into the grammar', as in *Their images* [which] *I lov'd* in

> Their images I lov'd, I view in thee,
> And thou (all they) hast all the all of
>   thee.

'There is some suggestion that the first clause may be wholly independent, and that *I view in thee* means "I look for them in you"; but on the whole the device merely puts "which I loved" into special prominence.'

After subjecting Shakespeare's 16th Sonnet, 'But wherefore do not you a mightier way', to a searching analysis of the equivocal words, the slightly ambiguous grammar, and the danger of inserting more punctuation-marks with a view to simplification, Empson draws this conclusion: 'Ambiguities of this sort may profitably be divided into those which, once understood, remain an intelligible unit in the mind; those in which the pleasure belongs to the act of working out and understanding, which must at each reading, though with less labour, be repeated; and those in which the ambiguity works best if it is never discovered.'

Another type of ambiguity 'occurs when two ideas, which are connected only by being both relevant in the context, can be given in one word simultaneously. This is often done by reference to derivation; thus Delilah is

> That specious monster, my
> accomplished snare.

Specious, "beautiful and deceitful"; *monster*, "something unnatural and something striking shown as a sign of disaster"; *accomplished*, "skilled in the arts of blandishment and successful in undoing her husband". The point here is the sharpness of distinction between the two meanings [of each of these three words], of which the reader is forced to be aware; they are two pieces of information, two parts of the narrative; if ingenuity had not used an accident, they would [each of them] have required two words.' Note, however, that Classical readers feel no ambiguity, for they perceive the pairs of meanings, and that modern non-Classical readers feel none, for they become aware of only *one* sense in each pair. Yet (Empson adds) 'it must seem trivial to use one word with an effort when there is time enough to say two more simply; even if time is short it seems only twice as useful, in a sort of numerical way'.

Another type of ambiguity 'occurs when two or more meanings of a statement do not agree among themselves but combine to make clear a more complicated state of mind in the author. ... One is [primarily] conscious of the most important aspect of a thing, not the most complicated; the subsidiary complexities, once they have been understood, merely leave an impression in the mind that they were

to such-and-such an effect and they are within reach if you wish to examine them.' This being a matter rather of psychological ambiguity and of a cumulative atmosphere and meaning arising from that psychological complexity than of verbal ambiguity, I shall refrain from examples and merely refer the inquirer to the subtle Fourth Chapter of Empson's book.

Germane to our article, however, is the type in which ambiguity 'occurs when the author is discovering his idea in the act of writing, or [is] not holding it all in his mind at once, so that, for instance, there is a simile which applies to nothing exactly, but lies half-way between two things when the author is moving from one to the other. Shakespeare continually does it:

> Our natures do pursue
> Like rats that ravin down their
> proper bane
> A thirsty evil, and when we drink
> we die.

Evidently the first idea was that lust itself was the poison; but the word *proper*, introduced as meaning "suitable for rats", but also as having an irrelevant suggestion of "right and natural", and more exact memory of those ... poisons which are designed to prevent rats from dying in the wainscot, produced the grander and less usual image, in which the eating of the poison corresponds to the Fall of Man, and it is [the] drinking [of] water, a healthful and natural human function, which it is intolerable to avoid, and which brings death. By reflection, then, *proper bane* becomes ambiguous, since it is now water as well as poison.'

Another interesting type 'occurs when a statement says nothing, by tautology, by contradiction, or by irrelevant statements, if any; so that the reader is forced to invent statements of his own and they are liable to conflict with one another'. This type is perceived the most clearly when a joke is implied, for the reader is meant to be conscious of the joke – the intelligent reader, of the means also. Take Max Beerbohm's remark that 'Zuleika [Dobson] was not strictly beautiful.'

Empson tackles it thus: ' "Do not suppose that she was anything so commonplace as [merely beautiful]; do not suppose that you can easily imagine what she was like, or that she was, probably, the rather out-of-the-way type that you particularly admire"; in this way (or rather, in the gambit of which this is a parody) jealousy is placated, imagination is set free, and nothing has been said (what is this strict [i.e. particular] type of beauty, anyway?) which can be used against the author afterwards.'

In 'Let me not love thee, if I love thee not' (Herbert) there is 'an ambiguity by tautology'.

Empson's seventh type, 'the most ambiguous that can be conceived, occurs when the two meanings of the word, the two values of the ambiguity [or equivocality], are the two opposite meanings defined by the context, so that the total effect is to show a fundamental division in the writer's mind. … A contradiction of this kind may be meaningless, but can never be a blank; it has at least stated the subject which is under discussion …; it is at once an indecision and a structure. … It seems likely … that words uniting two opposites are seldom or never actually formed in a language to express the conflict between them; such words come to exist for more sensible reasons, and may then be used to express conflict … People much more often need to mention the noticeable than the usual, so that a word which defines a scale comes to be narrowed down more and more to its two ends; the English "temper" is an example of this. Another reason is that, of relational opposites one cannot be known without the other; to know what a ruled person is you must know whether the ruler is a general or an archbishop. Thus a word which names both parts of a relation may be more precise than a word which only names half of it. … In so far, in short, as you know that two things are opposites, you know a relation which connects them. … [This]

type of ambiguity involves both the anthropological idea of opposite and the psychological idea of context, so that it must be approached warily.' Empson is wary, in that he begins 'by listing some very moderate and sensible examples'. Of the numerous excellent examples, this seems to me to be one of the best: 'Macbeth, faced suddenly with the Thaneship of Cawdor and the foreknowledge of the witches, is drowned for a moment in the fearful anticipation of crime and in intolerable doubts as to the nature of foreknowledge. Then throwing the problem away for a moment (he must speak to the messengers, he need not decide anything till he has seen his wife) –

> Come what come may,
> Time, and the hour, runs through
> the roughest day.'

Two interpretations lie open to us. 'Either, if he wants it to happen: "Opportunity for crime, or the accomplished fact* of crime, the crisis of action or decision, will arrive whatever happens; however much, swamped in the horrors of the imagination one feels as if one could never make up one's mind. I need not, therefore, worry about this at the moment"; or, if he does not want it to happen: "This condition of horror has only lasted a few minutes; the clock has gone on ticking all this time; I have not yet killed him; there is nothing, therefore, for me to worry about yet." These opposites may be paired with predestination and free will: "The hour will come, whatever I do, when I am fated to kill him [less ambiguously, "Whatever I do, that hour will come in which I am fated to kill him"], so I may as well keep quiet; and yet if I keep quiet and feel detached and philosophical, all these horrors will have passed over me and nothing can [? rather "will"] have happened." And in any case (remembering the martial sug-

---

*Obviously Empson would have avoided *fact* if he had remembered that, in Latin, *factum* = 'a fact' and 'a crime' and that, in legal terminology *fact* = 'a crime' (as in 'to confess the fact').

gestion of *roughest day*), "Whatever I do, even if and when I kill him, the sensible [= tangible and visible] world will go on, it [the murder] will not really be as fearful as I am now thinking it, it is just an ordinary killing like the ones in the battle."'

In the course of summing up, Empson says that 'Of the increasing vagueness, compactness, and lack of logical distinctions in English, the most obvious example is the newspaper headline. I remember a very fine one that went

ITALIAN ASSASSIN BOMB PLOT DISASTER.'

He notes that the assassin was not an Italian and that therefore *Italian* must qualify the rest of the headline; that the dominant noun is *disaster*, hints that the adjective qualifying *disaster* is *bomb-plot*, that *assassin* should be *assassin's* and that *Italian* should be *in Italy*; and concludes that 'the main rhythm conveys: "This is a particularly exciting sort of disaster, the assassin-bomb-plot type they have in Italy."' I suggest that the following rearrangement explains the headline:

ITALIAN DISASTER ASSASSIN'S BOMB-PLOT,

which = 'There has been in Italy a disaster caused by a bomb in an assassin's plot.' Empson's comment is delightful: 'Evidently this is a very effective piece of writing ... It conveys [its point] with a compactness which gives the mind several notions at one glance of the eye, with a unity like that of metaphor, with a force like that of its own favourite *bombs*': and he gently refrains from pointing out that it has one slight drawback, in that its meaning – even after an exasperating amount of cogitation by the reader – is far from clear.

It was this example and an ensuing pronouncement of Empson's which caused Frank Whitaker, in an address delivered to practising journalists on 13 Dec. 1938, and reproduced in the *JIJ*, January 1939, to speak as follows:

'Headlines are a good starting point, not only because they offer the greatest temptation to the debaser owing to the stress under which they are often written, but also because they have created an important problem of another kind. They remind us every day, particularly in our more popular newspapers, that the grammatical sentence is no longer the only way of expressing a thought in modern English. We are, indeed, rapidly evolving a distinct headline language which bears little relation to everyday speech. That cannot be a good thing, because it means that we are approaching a stage, if we have not already reached it, at which a word will mean one thing when it is written and another when it is spoken.

ANTI-POSSESSIVE CRAZE

'In this headline language logical distinctions in the meaning of words are being ruthlessly flattened out. It is a counterfeit language within a language, in which nouns are habitually made to do the work of adjectives, commas the work of heaven knows what, and from which the possessive case has almost disappeared. "Beware of the possessive", I read in one Fleet Street style sheet which in many respects is admirable – "beware of the possessive; it shows up a headline".

'What does that mean? I can quite understand the desire for action in headlines – the preference for lively, vigorous words – and there are no doubt many contexts in which the possessive case can be avoided without creating ambiguity. But this anti-possessive craze should be carefully watched. For example, I read in the *Star* last week the headline, "Question on Earl de la Warr speech", from which it was impossible to tell whether the speech was by Earl de la Warr or about Earl de la Warr. The distinction might be important, and it should be jealously preserved. Ambiguity is the enemy we have to watch, and our new headline language is full of it.'

After the felicities of Empson and Whitaker, it is a sad decline to pass to some particular examples collected by myself; but they may serve as warnings. They fall roughly into five unequal and fortuitous groups of horrible examples: Misrelated Construction; Wrong Pronoun; *when* and *where*; Wrong Order; and Miscellaneous.

A good instance of misrelated construction occurs in Froude's *Henry the Eighth*: 'The Reformation ... in the sixteenth century would have been left to fight its independent way unsupported by the moral corruption of the church from which it received the most powerful impetus': the *impetus* comes from corruption, not from *church*: if *that* had been written for *the*, there would have been no ambiguity. A very different example of this is double-pointedness (where only one point was intended) in a mid-Victorian's commencement of an article: 'We are all born idiots.'

Pronouns have to be handled with care; their misuse engenders some queer ambiguities, as in:

'He put his feet upon the stove as *it* was cold' (examination question). Was the stove cold? – This example illustrates the potential ambiguity of the impersonal (or *it*) verbs – *it rains, it is raining*, etc.

'Such preparation may occupy six or seven stages. First of all *it* may be necessary to bleach the object, though it is by no means universal' (Nigel Morland, *The Conquest of Crime*). The first *it* at first sight appears to refer to *preparation*; reflection shows that *it* is part of the verbal phrase *it may be necessary*. The second *it* should refer to *object*, but it obviously doesn't: this *it* = 'this practice'.

'He succeeded in dominating large meetings of operatives and in them causing them to think' (EP, *A Critical Medley*, 1926). The first *them* is condonable, although *at them* would have been preferable; but the second *them* is unforgivable, and should be *those men*.

'Although it [an estate] was not then specially laid out for shooting, a century and a half has, in fact, made it a very attractive *one*' (*Country Life*). *One* refers to *shooting*, but in a sense not yet mentioned: 'a tract of country over which one has the exclusive right to shoot'.

'Overtopping all was the knoll planted with cedars *that* always served as assembly point; as watch-tower before sunrise shot golden darts into the mists that flounced on the hills; as platform for a parting chant or chorus at night' (an article in *The Times*, 1938). Not the cedars but the knoll constituted the assembly point; change either to 'the cedar-planted knoll that always served' or to 'that knoll which, planted with cedars, always served' or 'the knoll that, planted with cedars, always served'. Nor is the repetition of *as* without a shade of ambiguity.

'Jack and Florence met George and Lily at *his* place. I had told *them* to arrange something, but *they* thought if *he* asked one of *them* to lunch *she* wouldn't come – *they* never quite hit it, perhaps *they* told you': a monstrous mass of ambiguity, cited by C. C. Boyd in his useful book, *Grammar for Great and Small*.

When and *where* look innocent enough, but they are very far from being so innocent as they look. 'When did you arrange to meet him on Saturday night?' is a question that, when I read it, I took to mean 'On what date did you arrange that you should meet him on the Saturday night?'; I was mildly annoyed when I saw that the reply was 'Somewhere about 7 o'clock, I think.' During the First World War, the constantly recurring 'Where were you wounded?' obviously admitted of two answers – locality (e.g. 'On the Somme'); part of the body ('In the arm'). Experienced men soon learnt to reply, 'In the arm; on the Somme.'

Often the ambiguity springs from a careless arrangement of words. 'Smart men's suiting' and 'Stylish gentlemen's suits' are likely to be misunderstood.

'The flames ... destroyed almost the last vestiges of past eras ... vestiges which the ruthlessness of Henry VIII failed entirely to erase' (J. A. Froude): the context shows that 'failed to erase entirely' or 'failed to entirely erase', not 'entirely failed to erase', is intended. See also **SPLIT INFINITIVE, THE.**

'Europe desires to see weakened the

non-warlike influence of China over Russia, which has increased enormously of late' (*The Daily Telegraph*, October 1900 – cited by Nesfield). Preferably: 'Europe desires the weakening of China's non-warlike influence over Russia, for that influence has enormously increased of late.'

'*Paradise Lost* is the name of Milton's great epic poem on the loss of Paradise divided into twelve separate parts' is cited by Nesfield, who proposed: '*Paradise Lost*, divided into twelve separate parts, is the name of Milton's great epic poem', which is a poor improvement. Read: '*Paradise Lost* is the name of Milton's great epic poem on the loss of Paradise; the poem is divided into twelve separate parts.'

'I shall begin by listing some very moderate and sensible examples' (Wm Empson, *Seven Types of Ambiguity*). This author, as modest as he is subtle, does not mean that his examples are 'very moderate and very sensible': he would have avoided this ambiguity of intention if he had written 'some sensible and very moderate [i.e. unexaggerated or simple] examples'.

'I was speaking to Miss Worsley of Holly Tye' (Adrian Bell, *By Road*). He was not speaking to a Miss Worsley that lived at Holly Tye, but of Holly Tye to Miss Worsley.

And here is a miscellaneous lot, of which the first five are drawn from Charles Boyd's *Grammar for Grown-Ups*:

'I am not going out because it is warm'; a comma after 'out' would remove the ambiguity.

'I do not write for that reason'; does the costive fellow mean that he doesn't write at all? Or that, although he writes, it is not for *that* reason (e.g. praise)?

'Miss B will probably never give another performance as the result of a motor smash': this example might have been included in the preceding group, for ambiguity disappears if we change the order, thus: 'As the result of a motor smash, Miss B will probably never give another performance.'

'I shall hope to see you next week' should be 'I hope to see you next week', for the meaning is not 'Next week, I shall be hoping to see you.'

'Complaints are made of the system of forwarding permits for the removal of cattle to Ireland by post' (quoted by *Punch* from an Irish newspaper).

'Jewels of unimpeachable genuineness gleamed upon white arms and necks of a value enough [i.e. sufficient] to make up a king's ransom' (John G. Brandon, *The Dragnet*).

'One remarks it as a defect only when judging the plan of the book apart from the contents – a practice that leads one into illogical statements concerning things that are illogical only in appearance' (FP, *Eighteenth Century English Romantic Poetry*, 1924): for *a practice* read *the practice of thus judging books*.

' "You won't catch the flu germs walking in the open air", states a health enthusiast' (*Punch*). Ambiguity would have been removed if the statement had been written in the form, 'You won't catch flu germs while you are walking' – or 'Walking in the open air, you won't catch flu germs.'

'The railway will be long before it approaches paying' (cited by Nesfield).

'Removers of distinction' is the proud slogan of a firm of carriers. Many of us would refrain from so cynically philistine a boast.

'Sullen, grey dawn crept over an equally sullen and grey lake, and Search watched its coming. But some time, from exhaustion, she slept' (M. G. Eberhart, *The Hangman's Whip*). But does 'some time' mean 'for some time – for some considerable time' or 'at a certain time (*or* hour)' or 'by a certain hour'?

ambivalence, ambivalent. See VOGUE WORDS.

ameliorate, misused for *appease* or *mitigate*. ' "How about taking advantage of Mrs Burleigh's invitation [to lunch] and ameliorating the more animal wants?" ' (Ellery Queen, *The Spanish Cape Mystery*).

One may *ameliorate* conditions, but not hardships.

amend,   amendment;   emend, emendation. To *amend* is 'to better; to improve by changing' (something imperfect); politically, 'to make professed improvements in (a measure before Parliament)'. In present use, *emend* is 'to remove errors from the text of (a document, a book)'.

America or **the States** for **the United States of America.** The former is commonly used, but obviously it is illogical, for it ignores the existence of Canada, Mexico, and the many nations of Central and South America. The same objection applies to *American*. There is, however, no other convenient adjective for *USA*. The English language is not rich in proper adjectives. *The States* is not incorrect, but it is colloquial; in Australia, *the States* would, to a native-born Australian, refer rather to the various *States* of Australia than to the *States* of the USA.

AMERICANISMS. See BRITISH AND AMERICAN USAGE.

amiable and **amicable.** *Amiable*, 'agreeable and good-natured', is applied to persons and their disposition: 'He was an amiable fellow', 'His was a most amiable nature.' *Amicable*, 'friendly', 'peaceable and pleasant', refers to relationships, attitudes (towards other persons), arrangements, settlements, conferences – in short, to the manner or process of doing: 'Amiable people generally have amicable relationships'; in law, an *amicable* suit is a pre-arranged test case between friendly parties.

amid, amidst. See **among** and **amongst.**

amity and **enmity** must be carefully enunciated or a considerable misunderstanding may arise.

amok is now more usual than *amuck* in *run amok* or *amuck*, but both spellings are acceptable. The Malay word *amok* means 'rushing in a frenzy' (*COD*).

among and **amongst; amid, amidst; while, whilst.** The *st* forms are falling into disuse, partly because they are less easy to pronounce; partly because, when pronounced, they are less euphonious than their alternatives.

among and **between.** See **between and among.**

among other reasons; among other things. 'I am not ... going to take you far into technical depths, because, among other reasons, I do not know enough' (Stuart Chase, *The Tyranny of Words*). If Chase intended *along with other reasons*, why did he not say so? If *aside* (anglice *apart*) *from*, why not say so? If *in addition to*, then why not *in addition to*? *Among other things* is generally excused as an idiom: but even if it is an idiom, it is so blatantly self-contradictory and absurd that careful writers avoid it. To extend the absurdity and thus to propagate the contradiction is – well, careless, to say the least of it.

amongst is obsolescent for *among.*

among(st) is occasionally misused for the somewhat literary *amid(st)*, as in '... Reveille, the voice of Western order among the babble of the East' (Humfrey Jordan, *The Commander Shall...*). *Among* is used with separable objects and is usually followed by the plural, or by a collective noun such as *crowd* or *congregation*. *Amid(st)* is a better choice with other singular nouns, or for two events concurrent in time, as in 'He dived into the lake amid shouts of applause.'

amoral = non-moral, not connected with morality; *immoral* = wicked; corrupt, licentious. 'A physiological text-book is amoral, but immoral persons may use such a text for immoral purposes'; 'A person ignorant of morality may easily become immoral because of his amoral training'; 'The bright amoral virtue of courage' (Rachel Taylor: *OED*). See also **unmoral.**

amorous. See **amatory.**

amount applies to mass or bulk, not to number. 'A large amount of animals' is absurd; 'a large amount of books' becomes ludicrous when juxtaposed to 'a large amount of paper'.

ample for *enough* (absolutely) is a colloquialism to be avoided in all self-respecting writing. 'Have you enough?' – 'Yes, ample.' Probably short for the pretentious *an ample sufficiency*.

amuck. See **amok.**

an; a. Before vowels and silent *h*, *an*; before consonants (other than silent *h*) and before *u* sounded *yoo*, *a*. Thus '*an* airy room', '*a* bad boy', '*a* use not known before', '*a* horse', '*an* hour ago', '*an* honest fellow', '*a* unique signature', '*a* eulogy as unexpected as it was flattering', '*a* union of two countries'. The same rule applies to groups of letters and initials: *a* before B, C, D, G, J, K, P, Q, T, U, V, W, Y, Z; *an* before A, E, F, H, I, L, M, N, O, R, S, X. Thus, '*a* PhD', but '*an* MP'. Words beginning with *h* and an unstressed syllable formerly took *an*, but *a* is now usually preferred here. Thus, '*a* hotel', '*a* historian'.

analogous and **similar.** See **similar and analogous.**

analyst (one who analyses); **annalist** (a writer of annals). These should not cause confusion, except in such a statement as 'He's an analyst (annalist).'

ancient is opposed to *modern*; it refers to the remote past, especially to primitive languages and civilizations and to very early buildings, statues, writings, etc. Something *ancient* may or may not still exist. An *ancient* civilization might be that of China, or of Babylon. Something that is no longer used – discredited because no longer in the style or the fashion – is *antiquated*; but unless it is some hundreds of years old, it is not *ancient*. Words and phrases no longer used are *obsolete*; words used only in poetry or by very old people are *archaic, historical, obsolescent* – but the obsolescence of a word that has not long

been in use cannot properly be called archaism.

and. There has been a long-standing prejudice against beginning a sentence with *and*, but there seems to be no basis for it. The device can be very effective, though it should not be allowed to become a mannerism.

and is unnecessary and incorrect in such a sentence as the following, from the Introduction to *Tom Thumb's Diary and Proverb Book*, 1893, 'But of all dwarfs none has bulked as largely in the public imagination ... as "General Tom Thumb", and with whom all successors have had to stand invidious comparison.' Here 'and' should be omitted or 'and with him' substituted for 'and with whom'.

and all is often meaninglessly tacked on to the end of a statement in British English. The same is true of *and that*, as in 'They sell bacon and sausages and that.' Neither expression is appropriate in serious writing.

and etc. is a vulgarism for *and so forth, and so on, and other things, and the rest.*

and moreover may occasionally be justified as an emphasized *and* – or an emphatic *moreover*. Generally, however, it is a tautological form of *and*, as in 'And, moreover, when Big Tito had started a vicious fight, certainly for liberty if not for life ...' (John G. Brandon, *The Mail-Van Mystery*).

and nor is occasionally found; all it can mean is 'nor', and literally ('and not ... not') it is nonsense. 'But he did not move and nor did Julia' (Margery Sharp, *The Nutmeg Tree*).

and/or is occasionally useful in legal and official contexts, since 'soldiers *and/or* sailors' is so much more concise than 'soldiers or sailors or both'. It should not, however, be allowed to infect general writing.

and that. See **and all.**

and which is permissible only when there is a preceding *which* clause, as in 'The house, which was empty and which was likely to remain empty, stood on the hill.' 'The house, situated on the hill and which was empty, was destroyed by fire' is inadmissible.

and who, and whom are merely the personal counterparts of **and which**, *q.v.*

and whose. See **whose, and.**

and yet which is extremely clumsy for *which yet* or *and which yet*. In 'They were countryman's hands, which could break a rabbit's neck as scientifically as possible; and yet which could set a dog's leg … with as much kindness as any woman would show' (Robert Eton), change *and yet which could* to *which could, however, set.*

anent, 'about, concerning', is archaic and pretentious.

angle, 'point of view', is not objectionable, but to be used sparingly. See **standpoint.** The word should not properly be used to mean 'technique for accomplishing something', as in 'He has a new angle for reducing the overdraft.' A VOGUE WORD.

angry at; angry with. The former of things and events; the latter of persons. 'He was angry *at* this incident – and *with* the policeman for having been too slow to prevent it.'

annex. In British usage this is the spelling for the verb, the noun being *annexe* or *annex* (of a building) or *annexation* (acquisition – esp. political acquisition of territory). [In American usage *annex* serves as verb and noun.]

annunciation, 'announcement', is not to be confused with *enunciation*, 'manner of, or degree of distinctness in, pronouncing one's words'.

another must not be used for *one other*. 'There is only another stile to cross before we reach the wood'; 'Talking of stiles, there's only another to cross before we reach the wood.'

another … also is excessive for *another*, as in 'There was another idea also at the back of his mind' (John G. Brandon).

another to is misused when made synonymous with *different from*. 'He wore another cap to mine.' *Another than* is legitimate, as in 'another century than this'.

answer for, misused for *answer to*. In the following example, *answer for* is not wrong; it is merely feeble: 'It is possible to substitute yards or … kilometres to apply to oblongs anywhere … and get an answer for what you want to know' (Stuart Chase, *The Tyranny of Words*).

answer was, or **is, in the affirmative** or **negative, the** = *The answer is Yes* or *No*; better: *He replies*, or *replied, Yes* or *No*, or whatever else the person and tense may be.

antagonist; opponent. An *opponent* is one who is on the opposite side, or one who opposes an idea, a measure; it is neutral – one's opponents in games are merely the other competitors or the opposing team. *Antagonist* is stronger; it connotes personal opposition in combat – duel, battle, war.

antagonize. 'To *antagonize*' is much stronger than 'to *oppose*'. To *oppose* is simply 'to be on the opposite side to', hence 'to resist'; to *antagonize* is to cause a strongly inimical reaction in another person by active opposition or by unfriendly behaviour, as in 'She antagonizes him by her personal remarks.'

ante = 'before' (in place or in time); *anti* = 'against; in opposition to'. See any good dictionary for examples. One of the commonest errors is *antichamber* for *antechamber*. Cf. *antedate* and *antidote*. But, exceptionally, in *anticipate*, *ante* has been changed into *anti*.

anterior to is officialese for *before*.

anticipate and **expect.** The former is now commonly used both for the latter and for *await*, but its proper sense is 'to forestall' an action or a person, or 'to foresee' an event and take appropriate action.

OED registers, as blameless English, the senses, 'to take into consideration before the appropriate or due time' (e.g. 'to anticipate consequences and provide for the future') – 'to realize beforehand (a certain future event)', as in 'Some real lives ... actually anticipate the happiness of heaven' (C. Brontë) – 'to look forward to, look for (an uncertain event) as certain', as in 'Those, not in the secret, anticipated an acquittal.'

ANTI-POSSESSIVE CRAZE, THE. See AMBIGUITY.

antiquated; antique. The former = 'out of use by reason of age; obsolete'; 'so old as to be unworthy to survive', as in 'the antiquated delusion of a papal supremacy'; 'old-fashioned, whether as survival or as imitation', as in 'antiquated phraseology'; 'advanced in – or incapacitated by – age', as in 'His antiquated aunt was a sore trial to him' (*OED*).

Antique = 'of the "good old times"; antiquated; no longer extant', as in 'an antique courtesy'; 'of or after the manner of the ancients, esp. of Greece and Rome', as in Byron's

And thus they form a group that's
    quite antique,
Half naked, loving, natural and
    Greek;

and 'archaic', as in 'the antique mystery of the Sphinx' (*OED*). Its chief modern use, however, is with reference to things made valuable by age, as with 'antique furniture'. Cf. the entry at **ancient.**

antisocial (or hyphenated). This chiefly means 'harmful or hostile to society', but it can also mean 'withdrawn, unfriendly', thus overlapping with the meaning of *unsociable. Unsocial,* and the rarer word *asocial,* refer chiefly to exclusion from or rejection of society. Those who have to work 'unsocial hours' are thereby excluded from social life.

anxious is now often used as a synonym of *eager* ('He is anxious to go on this journey') or *desirous* ('She is rather anxious to paint').

Those who dislike this use regard it as permissible for *solicitous* or *earnestly desirous.*

anxious of. 'I am not hopeless of our future. But I am profoundly anxious of it' (Beverley Nichols, *News of England,* 1938): which made us profoundly anxious *for* (or *about*) – not *of* – Nichols's literary future.

any, in a blended genitive. See GENITIVE, VAGARIES OF THE, last paragraph.

any, misused for **any other.** Examples: 'That winter was colder than any he had experienced' for '... any other'; better change to 'That winter was the coldest he had experienced.' – 'It is a longer book than any he has yet written.'

any, misused for *at all.* 'It did not hurt him any.' A colloquialism, more common in the USA than elsewhere.

anybody's (or **anyone's**) **else.** See **else's.**

anyday; anyrate; anytime. Incorrect for *any day, any rate, any time.*

any one; anyone. *Anyone* is synonymous with *anybody; any one* occurs, e.g. in 'He can beat any one of you.' The pronunciation is: *'any' one; any one".*

anyone is incorrect for either *any one (of* ...) or *any* (pronoun); e.g. 'Mr Huitt ... did not ... summon anyone of the clients who were waiting to see him' (E. P. Oppenheim, *The Bank Manager*).

anyone, anybody or **everybody (everyone)** or **nobody (no one)** or **somebody (someone) ... they.** They all take a singular verb, but (illogically) they often take plural pronouns in speech. This avoids both the tendentious use of *he, him, his* for both sexes, and the awkward *he or she, him or her.* But the use of these plural pronouns and possessive adjectives is not yet acceptable in serious writing. Thus, in Ruskin's 'Anyone may be a companion of St George who sincerely does what they can to make themselves useful', *they* should be *he,* and *themselves* should be *himself* (Onions); in 'Somebody came into the restaurant, ordered their meal, ate it; and then hurriedly they departed with a friend of theirs', *their* should be *his*, *they* should be *he*, and *theirs* should be *his*. The problem can often be evaded by rephrasing. 'Nobody cares what they do on holiday' might become 'People do not care ... '.

anyplace; anyways; anywheres. The first is an informal American synonym for *anywhere*. The others are dialectal.

any thing is justifiable when there is an opposition (whether explicit or implicit) to *any person*. Thus, 'He'll believe anything', but 'He is a fool to believe that any thing will ensure happiness.'

anyway, not *any way*, is correct for 'in any case'.

apart from ('in addition to'; 'without counting or considering') is both British and American, *aside from* being chiefly American.

apiary (a place for bee-hives) and **aviary** (a place for captive birds) are occasionally confused.

apiece; a piece. The latter is a noun ('a portion'); the former is an adverb ('singly', 'each by itself'). 'Their pork pies cost six-pence apiece; a piece [i.e. the half of a pie] cost threepence.'

apology is too important to be used as a synonym of *excuse*. Nowadays an apology connotes recognition that one is in the wrong, whereas an *excuse* is a plea offered in extenuation or justification of a minor fault or neglect, or an explanation of such a fault or oversight. Further, *excuse* can be extended to the impersonal, as in 'The derailing of the train was the doctor's excuse for failing to attend his extremely important patient.' But do not, from that example, fall into the error of synonymizing *excuse* with *reason*.

appendix. The usual plural is *appendixes* for the anatomical organ, *appendices* for material at the end of a book.

appraise; apprise; apprize. To *appraise* something is to estimate its value. To

apprise is to notify (someone of something). To *apprize* is to *evaluate*, and is obsolescent except in Scottish Law.

appreciate is incorrectly used in 'Do you appreciate that something terrible may happen?' The established uses of *appreciate* are these: To form (or make) an estimate of the worth, price, quality, or quantity of (a person or thing); to estimate correctly or perceive the full force or significance of; to esteem adequately, esp. to esteem highly; to recognize the value or excellence of or in; (commercially) to raise the value of (opp. *depreciate*), or, intransitive verb, to rise in value; to be aware of or sensitive to (a delicate impression, a nice distinction). It is very common in officialese, esp. in the bloodless passive. 'It will be appreciated that your motives were exemplary' = Clearly you acted for the best.

apprehend. See **reprehend.**

apprehended that, it is = I suppose, or He supposes. Officialese.

apprehensive. See **timid.**

apprise; apprize. See **appraise.**

approaches, 'preliminary efforts to obtain or effect something', is depreciative in tendency, and, in my opinion, one does well to avoid it in favourable contexts.

approximately, misused for *almost* or *comparatively*. 'With ... everything open it would be cool, or approximately cool, in the tropics' (Humfrey Jordan, *The Commander Shall ...*).

apt (to do something) = fit, suitable, or inclined to do it. Not to be identified with *likely*, as it is in 'He is not apt to gain that distinguished honour' when all that is meant is that he is unlikely to gain it. But *be apt to* (*do*) is good English in the following nuances:
> (Of things) to be habitually likely, to be ready, to (do); (of persons) to be given, inclined, or prone to (do); to tend to (do).

See also **liable.**

Arab; Arabian; Arabic. *Arab*, as both noun and adjective, applies to the people; *Arabian* (in modern use) to the peninsula of Arabia; and *Arabic* to the language, literature, or script of the Arabs.

arbiter; arbitrator. The former is general; the latter specific for one who has been chosen or appointed to adjudge and settle a specific question.

archaic. See **ancient.**

ARCHAISMS. These are of two kinds: actual and potential. The potential ones will be found at CLICHÉ and at SIMILES, BATTERED. True archaisms – not, of course, all of them! – are listed here.

The modern word (or phrase) is given in the second column; and when the archaism is, in some special context, not an archaism but a technicality, e.g. *whereas* in Law and *morn* and *eve* in poetry, an indication is made parenthetically.

ARCHAISM	MODERN EQUIVALENT
abed	in bed
abide	to stay
aforetime	formerly, previously
Afric (adj.: poetic)	African
albeit	although
Albion	England
amid(st)	among
an one	a one
anent	about, or concerning (preposition)
annoy (n.: poetic)	annoyance
Araby	Arabia
Arcady (poetic)	Arcadia
aright (only slightly archaic)	correctly
astonied	astonished
aught	anything
aye, for ever and	for all time; for ever
bale	evil; woe
Barbary	Saracen countries along North African coast
behest; hest	an order
behove or US *behoove* (vv.); *behoof; it behoves me*	to be an obligation on; an obligation; I ought ...
benison	a blessing
betide	to happen to
betimes	early
betrothal; betrothed	engagement (to be married); engaged [*Betrothal* and *betrothed* are current in American newspaper-English.]
betwixt	between
bewray	to expose, reveal, indicate
blackamoor	black
bootless	useless
bounden	bound (except in *bounden duty*)
bridal	a wedding [*Bridal* is American journalese.]
burgess	a citizen
burthen	burden

ARCHAISM	MODERN EQUIVALENT
caitiff	a coward
Caledonia	Scotland
castor	a beaver
Cathay	China
chiefer; chiefest	more important; most important
Christmastide	Christmas-time
citizenry	a body of citizens; citizens collectively
clang (preterite and past participle of *cling*)	clung
clime (poetic)	climate
clomb	climbed
clyster	an enema; a suppository
coal oil	paraffin [*Coal oil* is still common in the USA, though it will probably give place to *kerosene*.]
coolth	coolness
cruse	an earthenware pot or jar
damosel (or *-zel*)	damsel (see ELEGANCIES), girl
date	limit, term, end
deceptious	deceptive
deem	to think or believe [*Deem* in this sense is in American usage a false elegance.]
delicate (n.)	a delicacy or dainty
delve (not obsolete but obsolescent)	to dig
demesne; demesnes	domain; estates
despiteful	spiteful
destrier or *destrer*	war-horse
dight (ppl. adj.: poetic)	clad, clothed
doughty	brave; formidable
doxy	mistress; sweetheart; whore
drear (poetic)	dreary
drouth (poetic)	dryness; drought [*Drouth* is current in parts of the USA.]
durst	dared
dwell	to live (at a place)
eke	also
eld (poetic)	old age
emprise	enterprise
engraven	engraved
ensample	an example, a sample
ere (poetic)	before
eremite	hermit
errant (adj.)	wandering
erst (poetic)	formerly; once upon a time
erstwhile (poetic)	former; formerly; some while ago
essay (v.)	to attempt
Ethiop	Ethiopian
eve (poetic)	evening
exceeding	exceedingly

ARCHAISM	MODERN EQUIVALENT
faërie or *faëry*	fairy
fain (poetic adj. and adv.)	glad, gladly; ready, readily
fair, the (poetic)	beautiful, lovely or merely pretty women
fare (v.)	to travel
fealty	fidelity, loyalty
foison	abundance
forgat (preterite)	forgot
forgot (past participle)	forgotten
forsooth!	truly!
fraught (poetic)	filled, laden
froward	haughty
Gaul	France
gentle	well-born
glad (v.); *glad oneself*	to make glad; to rejoice
goodly	good; attractive
gotten	(in Britain) got [in the USA often *gotten*]; see entry at **gotten**
grammatic	grammatical
habit; habits	clothing
haply (poetic)	by chance or accident
helpmeet	helpmate
hereof (legal)	of this
heretofore (legal)	before this; up to this time
hereunto (legal)	unto this
hest (poetic)	see *behest*
Hibernia	Ireland
hight (ppl. adj.)	called, named
hindermost	hindmost
howbeit	nevertheless
I wis	I know
illume	illuminate
Ind (poetic)	India
ken	knowledge
kin (only slightly archaic)	relatives; one's family
kine	cows
leal	loyal
leman (Romance)	sweetheart (either sex); lover or mistress
lief; I'd as lief	willing, glad; I'd gladly or willingly
liefer was to me, him, etc.	I (or he or ...) had rather (do ...)
liege	liege lord or liege man
mart	a market
maugre	despite (preposition)
meet	fitting, proper, seemly
meseems	it seems to me
methinks	I think
minion	a male favourite
monstrous	exceedingly
moon	a month

ARCHAISM	MODERN EQUIVALENT
morn (poetic)	morning
mummer	actor in dumb show
Muscovy	Russia
Musselman	a Muslim
natheless	nevertheless
nether; nethermost (poetic)	lower; lowest
nigh	near
oft; ofttimes (both poetic)	often
olden (times)	the past, the distant past
Orient (adj.: poetic)	Oriental
orison (poetic)	prayer
otherwhile(s)	at times; at another time
pard	leopard
parlous	perilous, dangerous [Dialectal in the USA.]
pecunious	wealthy
perchance (poetic; facetious); *peradventure* (facetious)	perhaps
plaint	a weeping; a complaint
plight	to pledge
price, of	precious; (of persons) excellent
proven (except in the legal *not proven*)	proved [*Proven* is now as common as *proved* in American usage, and preferred there before a noun.]
psyche	cheval-glass
quick (except in 'the quick and the dead')	living; alive
quoth; quotha	said; said he
rufous	red
saith	says
sate	sat
save (poetic)	except
scarce (adv.)	scarcely
seigneur	lord
selfsame	(very) same
sideling	oblique(ly); sidelong
silly	simple; innocent
silvern	of silver; silvery
simples	herbs, or medicines therefrom
sire	father
something (adv.)	somewhat
spake	(he) spoke
span	(he) spun
speed (v.)	to thrive
spilth	a spilling; something spilled
stoup (poetic; ecclesiastic)	a tankard; holy-water vessel
subtile	subtle
surcease	(a) ceasing; relief (from pain)
swoon (n. and v.: poetic)	faint

ARCHAISM	MODERN EQUIVALENT
talesman (legal)	juror
tarry	linger
Tartary	the land of the Tartars
teen (poetic)	grief
tend (poetic)	attend to
testimony (legal)	an open attestation; a confession
thenceforth	from that time on(wards)
thereafter (legal)	after that time
thereof (legal)	of that
theretofore (legal)	up to that time
thrall	a slave
tilth	tillage
troth (also v.)	truth; faith
troublous	troublesome, tiresome
trow	to believe
trusty (e.g. one's trusty sword)	trustworthy
tryst (poetic)	a meeting; esp. a lovers' meeting
twain	two
umbrage, take	to take offence
unhand (v.), as in *unhand me, villain!*	to take one's hands off (a person)
unwitting	unknowing; ignorant
vagrom (adj.)	vagrant, vagabond; hence, erratic
Van Diemen's Land	Tasmania
varlet	a groom, a menial; a rogue
verily	truly
vicinage (legal)	neighbourhood, vicinity
void	empty
wax (v.i.)	to grow or increase
weal	welfare; the general good
ween	to think
whereas (legal)	since or because
whereat	at which
wherefore (legal)	for which reason
whereof (legal)	of which
whereon	on (or upon) which; immediately after which
whilom	once upon a time; some time before
whomso; whoso	whomever; whoever
whosesoever	of whatever person's
wight	a human being; gen. a man
wit, in *to wit*	namely
withal (except as an elegancy)	in addition, as well; nevertheless; therewith
wondrous (adv.)	wonderfully
wont	custom, habit
wot	know
woundy	extremely; excessively
writ (past participle)	written
yare	ready, alert, nimble

ARCHAISM	MODERN EQUIVALENT
yclept	named; known by the name of
yon	yonder
yore, of	in ancient times; in the past
Yule; Yuletide	Christmas; Christmas-time
zany	a clown; a fool

archetypal, archetype. See VOGUE WORDS.

aren't. See **ain't.**

Argentina; Argentine. It is best to retain *Argentina* as the name (based on the Spanish *la República Argentina*) of the South American Republic, *Argentine* or *Argentinian* as that of a native of Argentina. The related adjective is *Argentine* or *Argentinian*. The tendency to speak of *the Argentine* instead of *Argentina* is to be resisted.

arise is now, in ordinary speech, used in preference to *rise* only in the transferred sense of a discussion (controversy, argument), a quarrel, a war arising. In formal writing, however, we may still *arise* from a sick bed or from a seat.

arising. See CONJUNCTIONS, DISGUISED.

arm for *sleeve* is sometimes condemned, but as this sense (a natural one, after all) is passed as blameless by *OED*, it certainly is good English.

around for *about* or *round* is somewhat of an Americanism in 'I'll visit you around Easter' and 'He wandered around the city.'

arrogate and **abrogate.** To *abrogate* a law is to repeal it; to *abrogate* a custom is to discontinue it; the sense, 'to do away with, put an end to' is obsolescent. To *arrogate to oneself* (the simple verb is falling rapidly into disuse) is to claim or assume that to which one is not entitled, or to claim or assume unreasonably or arrogantly, as in 'They arrogated to themselves the right of approving or rejecting all that was done' (Brougham) and 'She arrogated to herself a certain importance' (Wm Black) (*OED*).

artifice is usually derogatory.

artist; artiste. The latter has been introduced into English 'in consequence of the modern tendency to restrict *artist* to those engaged in the fine arts, and especially painting' (*OED*, 1888); an *artiste* being there defined as 'a public performer who appeals to the aesthetic faculties, as a professional singer, dancer, etc.'. A gifted cook or hairdresser may be referred to as an *artist*, and that word is coming to supersede *artiste* in all contexts.

artless; ignorant. The former is favourable (with a connotation of ingenuousness); the latter unfavourable.

as for *because* is heavily taxed – grossly overworked – by many writers, who are apparently enamoured of its brevity; often *as* is ambiguous ('He could not work as he was ill in bed'). It is difficult to lay down rules for the use and discrimination of *as*, *because, for, since*, their correct employment being a matter of idiom. *As* is colloquial both for *because* and for *for*, either of which is to be preferred to *as* in good writing and dignified speech. In *since* there may also be a connotation of time: as a causal conjunction it derives from the temporal *since* (= after).

as for *that* (conjunction) is a solecism. 'He did not say as he liked it'; 'Not as I've heard or know of'. Read: 'He did not say that he liked it'; 'Not that I know of' – or 'Not so far as I know'.

as, unnecessary in such a sentence as: 'He expressed himself as anxious to do everything in his power to help' (F. W. Crofts).

as, wrongly omitted, esp. after *such*. 'The only thing that spurred [annoyed] me was me being such a flat [as] to buy the home' ('Autobiography of a Thief' in *Macmillan's Magazine*, October 1879). And it is better to retain the *as* introducing a simile; thus 'as dry as a bone' is preferable to 'dry as a bone'.

as, equally. 'It was accompanied by a hissing inbreath from Ferradi which was equally as vicious' (John G. Brandon), for 'equally vicious' or 'as vicious'. *Equally as* also = 'as much as' (no less than) in, e.g. 'He feels it equally as you do.' Both of these uses are abuses.

as a rule ... always. 'As a rule he was always in the drawing-room before the first gong sounded.' This is no less excessive and unnecessary than *generally ... always*.

as and when is tautological either for *as* or for *when*.

as ... as. The second *as* should not be abandoned in such a sentence as 'The younger Pitt was as great and even greater than his father': read, 'The younger Pitt was as great as and even greater than his father', or 'The younger Pitt was as great as his father or even greater.'

as ... as and so ... as. The former is neutral, colourless; the latter, emphatic. 'As soon as they were ready, they departed'; 'So soon as you are ready, we shall depart.' Where *to* + an infinitive follows, the formula is *so ... as* (e.g. 'They were so clumsy as to be dangerous to their companions'), not because there is *to* + an infinitive but because there is considerable emphasis: here, there is – in addition to the idea of comparison – an unmistakable connotation of degree, so that *so ... as* + infinitive has a different psychological origin from that of *as ... as*. In negative assertions and questions implying a negative answer, *so ... as* and *as ... as* are now generally used interchangeably.

as follow is wrong for *as follows*. 'There were many articles in the room, as follow: a large table and a small one, a bookcase, six chairs, twelve maps, etc.' *As follows* is

short for *as it follows* and, because it is impersonal, it is of the same order as the italicized words in 'I shall act *as seems* best', 'So far *as* in me *lies*' (Onions).

as if and **as though** are often synonymous, but should they not be differentiated? To define the difference is not easy: to exemplify is easy enough. 'Could you drive a ball four hundred yards?' 'As if I could!' – 'Jack X is an exponent of personal publicity, you know.' 'Oh yes, as though he lived aloud!' Clearly, *as though* connotes comparison, whereas *as if* stresses possibility or potentiality – or their opposite, impossibility. Clearly, whereas *as though* emphasizes similarity or implies comparison, *as if* emphasizes or implies contingency or a condition. The basic meaning, however, is the same.

Logically or even semantically, *as if* makes sense, *as though* makes (virtual) nonsense. One can hardly postulate a rule. The most one can say is that unless the nuance or, of course, euphony demands *as though*, you will do well to use *as if*. Examine the following:

1. He reprimanded me severely. As if it were *my* fault!
2. He reprimanded me, as though it were my fault.
3. She sobbed bitterly, as though her heart would break (= like one whose heart was breaking).
4. He struck the ball as though he intended to shatter it.
5. He struck the ball, as if he intended, etc.
6. She walked away as though she were leaving the room.
7. She walked away, (just) as if she, etc.

Sometimes the two idioms – and both of them are clearly idioms – are interchangeable, as in (4)–(5) and in (6)–(7). One point emerges: *as though* is rarely preceded by a comma; *as if* is usually preceded by a comma. Moreover, in (1) *as though* would not have been preceded by a full stop.

as is (or **was** or **will be**) **the case with** is an intolerable tautology for *like*: 'As was the case with Bonner, Bartlett is a mighty hitter.' Sometimes it is misused for *as for* or *as with*: 'As will be the case with the future, the past has been falsified by historians'; 'As is the case with you, I fear the unknown less than I do the known.'

as many as is loose – indeed, it is incorrect – for *such persons as* or *those who* (or *all those who*) in 'As many as require the book should order it before the edition (strictly limited) is exhausted.'

as per, 'in accordance with', is such horrible commercialese that even merchant princes are less than riotously happy when their secretaries wish it on them.

as to for *of* or *on* or *for*. 'A brief indication as to the English [influence] ... affords a useful comment ... ' (EP, *The French Romantics' Knowledge of English Literature*, 1924), where *of* was the right word to use.

as to is sometimes introduced quite unnecessarily, as in: 'One can only guess as to how Mr Jaggers knew ...' (Cecil Freeman Gregg, *Tragedy at Wembley*). One would not insert *as to* before a 'why', so why insert it before a 'how'? A less reprehensible example is this, cited by Dr C. T. Onions in *An Advanced English Syntax*: 'They could not agree as to whom they should elect', concerning which Onions comments: ' "As to" may be omitted. It is not at all necessary, and is inserted in such cases probably in imitation of "They could not agree as to that." ' *As to* in such senses is well described by Whitten (*Good and Bad English*, 1938) as 'fog-English'. It is defensible when it synonymizes *in respect of* or *in the matter of*; it is defensible, too, though unnecessary, as a synonym of *about* or *concerning*.

as to whether is unnecessary for **whether.**

as too. In the following, from J. A. Froude, *English Seamen in the Sixteenth Century*, 'As often happens with irresolute men, when they have once been fixed to a decision they are as too hasty as before they were too slow', *as too* is a very awk-

ward construction, though perhaps not demonstrably ungrammatical; 'as much too hasty' or 'as over-hasty' would be better.

as well as is often ambiguous, as in 'The captain, as well as the sailors, suffered this bitter reverse', which may convey the fact that both the captain and his crew suffered it – or the different fact that the captain's power of endurance was equal to the crew's.

as what. See **what, as.**

as yet is often unnecessary for *yet*. 'His mind ... was not as yet completely ossified' (Francis Brett Young). It is better, though, to retain *as* at the beginning of a sentence, where *yet* alone might be taken to mean 'nevertheless'. 'As yet, his mind ...'.

ascend up is absurd for 'to *ascend*'.

ascent; assent. *Ascent* is 'going up', as in 'the ascent of Everest'. *Assent* is 'agreement'. 'He gave his assent to our request.'

ascribe and **attribute.** To *ascribe* something is to enter it in an account, to reckon or count it; to consider or allege as belonging *to*, to claim *for*. To *attribute* is to consider or regard (something) as belonging *to* ('To attribute to a word a sense it does not possess'); to declare or impute as a quality belonging or proper *to*, or inherent in ('A mystical character is apt to be attributed to the idea of moral obligation'); to reckon as a consequence of ('His shrivelled arm was attributed to witchcraft'); to consider as belonging *to*, declare to belong *to* an author ('A play attributed to Shakespeare'); to assign to its proper place or time ('This manuscript may be attributed to the 4th century, AD') (*OED*).

Asian; Asiatic. Use the former, as both noun and adjective, for the peoples and culture of Asia. *Asiatic* is today considered offensive.

aside from. See **apart from.**

aspect. See ABSTRACT NOUNS.

aspen, frequently applied as a name to the branching poplar tree, is properly only an adj. derived from the obsolete designation of that tree, 'asp', and means *quivering, tremulous*, like the leaf of the poplar.

assemble together (v.i. or v.t.) is excessive, and wrong, for *assemble*. For 'The people assembled together' read 'The people assembled'; for 'He assembled the people together', read 'He assembled the people.'

assent. See **ascent.**

assert is a strong word: do not debase it to equivalence with *say*.

assert, like *affirm* and *declare*, cannot be used with the infinitive unless a noun or a pronoun is put with that infinitive. 'I assert [or affirm or declare] you [or her or him or John or that fellow] to be a thief' is correct, though less idiomatic than 'I assert [etc.] that you [etc.] are [or is] a thief.' But one cannot say 'I affirm [etc.] to be a thief' instead of 'I declare [idiomatically *not* 'affirm', nor 'assert'] myself to be a thief.' (Note that the first person requires, not *me* or *us* but *myself* or, after 'we', *ourselves*.) In C. McCabe's *The Face on the Cutting-Room Floor*, we find this example of 'the infinitive in the air': 'The reader, knowing, just as McCabe does, that Robertson's telephone was engaged between 6.30 and 6.35 …, more than two hours after the time at which Robertson now asserts to have left the room, …'.

assignation; assignment. The former is a rendezvous, particularly to meet a lover secretly. The latter is a task 'assigned' to someone.

assist to (do something) is incorrect for *assist in* (doing). We *help* a person to do, we *assist* in the action. Nesfield gives an example from that fruitful source of error in his time, *The Daily Telegraph* (8 Aug. 1900). 'He is looked upon as a great authority on these questions, and will assist to examine scientifically a number of these questions.' The first meaning of *assist* is *to be present at*; to *help* or *give aid* is now more common, but the word *help* is usually better.

assume. See **adapt and adopt.**

assume and **presume.** *Presume* (v.i.), 'to be presumptuous', and *presume (up)on*, 'to take for granted', offer no difficulty: *assume* can never be substituted, here, for *presume*. As a transitive verb, *presume* has the following extant senses: 'to take upon oneself, to undertake without permission or adequate authority', as in 'To presume to sit in judgement on the actions of kings'; 'to take for granted', especially in Law, as in 'to presume the death of the man that disappeared eight years before' or 'to presume that he who disappeared so long ago is dead'. To *assume* is 'to take unto oneself; to adopt', as in 'to assume a partner', 'to take upon oneself, to put on', as in 'Habits are soon assumed' (obsolescent), 'The Netherland revolt had … assumed world-wide proportions' (Motley); 'to take to oneself formally' (insignia of office; symbol of a vocation) and to 'undertake' (an office, a duty), as in 'The community which he had assumed the spiritual charge of' (Mrs Oliphant), 'He assumed the monastic habit' (Freeman); 'to take as being one's own, to claim, to take for granted', as in 'That disposition … to assume … jurisdiction over other men's conduct'; 'to simulate or feign', as in 'scepticism, assumed or real'; 'to take for granted as the basis of an argument, a negotiation', as in 'William assumes the willingness of the assembly', 'To assume that we have the most accurate possible translation', 'The entire length of our farm is assumed to be about thirty-two miles.' In Logic, *assume* = 'to add the minor premiss to a syllogism' (*OED*).

It is over the sense 'taken for granted' that the two verbs overlap in meaning. On the whole, one *presumes* a fact from the available evidence. 'Dr Livingstone, I presume?' but to *assume* is to put forward a hypothesis as a basis for argument. 'Assuming he doesn't marry, where will he live?'

assuming. See CONJUNCTIONS, DIS-
GUISED.

assumption and **presumption** correspond exactly to *assume* and *presume* (*q.v.*).

assurance and **insurance.** In British use,
assurance is the technical word in respect of
certainties, particularly death, in contrast
with possibilities such as fire. But it is coming to be replaced by the more everyday
word *insurance*, so that *assurance* is falling
into disuse. [It is obsolescent in the USA.]

astonish, astonishment are stronger
than *surprise* (n. and v.); *astound* and
astoundment are even stronger. Note, however, that 'to *surprise*' originally = 'to take,
come upon, unprepared, off guard, at
unawares', senses that belong neither to
astonish nor to *astound*. Cf. **amazement**
and **amazing.**

astronomical. See VOGUE WORDS.

at about (six o'clock; half-way) is incorrect for *about* (six o'clock; half-way).

at all is misapplied by a writer of a letter
quoted by *The New Statesman and Nation*,
who wonders 'if it is at all possible for us
to be warned if there is likely to be a return
of the aurora borealis'. A thing is either
'possible' or not. See COMPARATIVES,
FALSE.

at and **in.** See **in and at.**

at length = *at last* but it also = 'fully' or
'in detail'.

at that. See **that, at.**

atheist. See **agnostic.**

**atmosphere, stratosphere, tropo-
sphere.** See **troposphere.**

attach together. Read *attach.*

attached hereto. Read *attached.*

attend. See **tend to.**

attire; attired: clothes; clothed. Genteelisms and, latterly, officialese.

attorney. See **lawyer.**

attorney general. The preferable plural
is *attorneys general*. See **-general.**

attribute (v.) is misused in the following:
'Mr Collier, remembering that this (1593)
was the very year *Venus and Adonis* was
published, attributes some great gift of the
Earl of Southampton to Shakespeare to
have immediately followed' (Thornbury,
Old and New London, 1880). The latter half
of the sentence is awkwardly constructed
and would be better expressed, '*assumes
that some great gift was made by the Earl to
Shakespeare immediately afterwards*'. See also
ascribe and attribute. Note, too, the different pronunciation of the noun and the
verb.

attributed is misplaced and misunderstood in this deplorable sentence set for
correction in a school examination paper.
'Though Shakespeare had a fair education,
it was not acquired knowledge that can be
attributed to his brilliance'; the second
clause should read, 'his brilliance cannot
be attributed to acquired knowledge'.

auger; augur. The former is a tool
for boring holes; the latter a soothsayer,
particularly in ancient Rome. *Augur* is
now chiefly used as a verb meaning
'portend'. 'This weather augurs well for
the harvest.'

aught, 'anything', is incorrectly used for
the cypher, *nought*, which represents
'nothing'. 'For aught I know, he may be
there' is correct, though slightly archaic;
'Put an *aught* (or *ought*) after 7 and you
have 70' is incorrect – indeed, illiterate.

aura. 'McCarthy ... lit his cigarette, holding the lighter so that it etched an aura
upon its owner's face' (John G. Brandon,
The Dragnet, 1936), exemplifies a not
infrequent misconception, for the *aura* of
a person or thing is an *emanation from* him
or it, *not shed* by something outside.

Aura is occasionally misused for figurative *air* (or *atmosphere*), as in 'In view of
Lord Northcliffe's famous maxim, "When
a dog bites a man, that's not news; but
when a man bites a dog, that is news", it

appears as if every happening of importance should be given an aura of drama' (examination essay script, June 1939).

aural, 'of the ear', hence 'of hearing'; *oral*, 'of the mouth', hence 'spoken'.

Aurora Borealis. 'All over England last night the Aurora Borealis gave a magnificent display of their beauty' (*The Evening News*, 26 Jan. 1938). – The writer, thinking perhaps unconsciously of the *northern lights*, and ignorant of Latin, supposed *Aurora Borealis* to be a plural formation.

AUSTRALIAN ENGLISH. See STANDARD ENGLISH, Section IV.

author. It is pompous for a writer to use *The author* for *I, me*. As a verb *author* is best avoided where *write* will serve. See also **man of letters**.

authoress. Authoresses generally prefer to be called *authors*. See SEXISM.

authoritive is wrong for *authoritative*. *Authoritarian* (n. and adj.) means '(one who is) favourable to the principle of authority as opposed to that of individual freedom' (OED).

autocracy and **autonomy** are occasionally confused. The meaning of *autocracy* is 'absolute government (by an individual or a paramount authority)'; of *autonomy*, 'the right of a state or institution to govern itself' (or the condition of a state possessing such right). According to OED there was formerly a use, 'now obsolete', of the former for the latter, but not vice versa.

autography for *autobiography* is dead – despite misguided efforts to keep it alive. The surviving senses are: the action of writing with one's own hand; an author's own handwriting; autographs collectively (a rare sense); and especially a lithographic process 'by which a writing or drawing is transferred from paper to stone' (OED).

automation. See **mechanization**.

automaton has learned plural *automata*; ordinary – i.e. English – plural *automatons*.

avail for *afford, provide*. 'Behind all variants and shades, there stands the absolute certainty that fingers are not the fonts of knowledge, and sucking them will avail no information.' *Avail* is here misused; a correct construction would be 'such action will not avail (or, be of value to) them'.

avenge and **revenge** (vv.); **vengeance** and **revenge** (nn.). The noun that corresponds to *avenge* is *vengeance*; that which pairs with *revenge* is – *revenge*. One *avenges* another or, less commonly, the wrong done to another, but one *revenges* oneself or the wrong done to oneself; *vengeance* is the exaction of justice (' "Vengeance is mine," saith the Lord') or, for oneself, what one considers justice (a 'getting even'), whereas *revenge* is satisfaction accorded to personal resentment ('He shall have his revenge the next time we meet'). The nouns are less often confused than the verbs, and it is particularly to be noted that, in idiomatic English, one does not say 'I shall avenge – or, revenge – the person that does the wrong.' In short, *revenge* (n. and v.) is the more subjective or personal, *avenge* and *vengeance* the more objective and impersonal. See also Fowler's *Modern English Usage*.

avenue, explore every. See **explore every avenue.** Other strange uses of the word *avenue* have been noticed by Sir Alan Herbert, who quotes J. H. Thomas's reported statement, '... I certainly did not shut the door to any avenue of peace.'

average = 'estimated by average' or 'equal to what would be the result of taking an average', hence 'of the prevalent (or, the usual) standard', as in 'A modern drawing of average merit' (Ruskin) (OED). It can also mean 'ordinary, typical' or sometimes 'mediocre'.

averse to (or from). See **adverse to.**

avert. See **advert.**

avocation and **vocation.** One's *vocation* is one's occupation, one's work or employment; an *avocation* is that which calls one away from one's vocation –

hence, a minor or subsidiary occupation, a by-work, hence even a hobby. 'But as, in many cases, the business which called away was one of equal or greater importance ..., the new meaning was improperly foisted upon the word: Ordinary employment, usual occupation ...' (*OED*).

avoiding for *excepting* or *except*. 'I have found Guinness ... the only thing – avoiding drugs – to give me ... natural sleep' (an advertisement). Though it implies deliberate exception, it is too much to expect *avoiding* to = 'except if, and as, I avoid'.

avoirdupois as a synonym for 'a person's weight' is permissible only as a jocular colloquialism.

await and **wait**. *Await* is used, (*a*) of persons, 'to wait for' (a coming event or person), as in 'King Brindi awaited them at the head of the Picts' (J. R. Green) and 'I shall await your answer with the greatest eagerness' (Seeley); and (*b*) of events, fate, honours, offices, duties, 'to be in store for', as in 'Honours and rewards which he little deserved awaited him' (Macaulay) and 'What fates await the Duke of Suffolk?' (Shakespeare). To *wait* is intransitive (with occasional transitive uses) and has a transitive form *wait for*: to *wait for* persons is to *await* them (*OED*). See also **wait**.

awake; awaken. The past tenses are *awoke* and *awakened*; the past participles *awoken* and *awakened*. 'I was awoken by that rather flashy young woman' (Agatha Christie). Moreover, the past tense of *wake* is *woke* or *waked*; the past participle is *woken* or *waked*. Of *waken*, both the past tense and the past participle are *wakened*.

award and **reward**. The latter is either a recompense or a recognition of merit; the former is usually 'a judicial sentence, esp. that of an arbitrator or umpire', hence 'that which is ... assigned, as payment, penalty, etc. by the terms of the judge's sentence or arbitrator's decision' (*OED*). So, too, for the verbs.

aware. See VOGUE WORDS.

awful now means 'inspiring awe' only in poetry. Its modern meaning is 'very bad', as in 'awful weather', or 'extreme', as in 'an awful lot of money'. Similarly, *awfully* now means 'very', as in 'awfully glad'. Neither *awful* nor *awfully* should be used in serious writing.

awhile for **a while** is catachrestic when *while* is a noun. 'I shall stay here for awhile' is incorrect for '... for a while'. Such a sentence as 'They followed it [an inlet] for awhile along the edge of the bank' (Hulbert Footner) brings one up with a jerk; *for a while* or, simply, *awhile* would have been correct.

AWKWARD PHRASING. The worst awkwardnesses are so idiosyncratic and so obvious that they require no comment; of the others, the majority will be found under such headings as False Agreement (*q.v.* at AGREEMENT, FALSE) and ORDER.

One cannot prescribe against awkward phrasing except in a general way: reread everything you write, and do it as externally as you can by putting yourself in the place of the reader; any awkwardness will then manifest itself to you, and it will, indeed, hit you in the eye. Awkwardness is, if you like, the opposite of elegance; I prefer to call it the opposite of economy of words on the one hand, and on the other, the opposite of clarity.

Here is an example from a writer in whom such awkwardness is a rarity: '[There] stood, a slight, white-clad figure, in the bright circle of light cast by one of the lamps which was still alight, of the car from which she had been flung' (Mrs Belloc Lowndes).

awoke; awoken. See **awake**.

ay and **aye**. In the sense 'ever', *ay* is to be preferred; in that of 'yes', *aye* is to be preferred, though *ay* is etymologically as correct as *aye*. *Ay(e)*, 'ever', is pronounced like the *ay* of *hay*; *ay(e)*, 'yes', is pronounced 'eye' (*OED*).

B

baby. See **infant**.

Bacchic, misused for *gastronomic*. 'Ellery engulfed the last mouthful, put aside his serviette, and sighed with Bacchic repletion' (Ellery Queen).

back again is superfluous for *back* ('He gave me the coat back again'); also for *returned* ('I see you're back again').

back log, now **backlog.** Arrears (Whitehall *ex* Washington *ex* American commerce).

back of and *in back of* for *behind* are colloquial American English. *In front of* is good British English. So is *at the back of*, as in 'At the back of all this lay the conviction ...' (Krapp).

backlash. See VOGUE WORDS.

bad for *ill*, as in 'She was taken bad in the street', is a low colloquialism – a solecism. *Bad* is an adjective and correct in 'She feels bad.'

bail, bale. The two spellings have become almost inextricably mixed. One *bails* out a prisoner, who is then 'on bail'. To jump from an aircraft by parachute is to *bale* (or *bail*) out. One *bails* (or *bales*) out water from a boat. A bundle of hay or wood is a *bale*, but the crosspieces of a wicket are *bails*.

balance for *remainder* is catachrestic. 'The considerable balance of this list will be found in *Modern Criminal Investigation* ... from which the above extract is taken' (Nigel Morland). Its use for *the rest* or *remainder* may be justifiable where two amounts of money are involved. But I remember hearing, fifty years ago, of an Irishwoman at Killarney offering bog-oak ornaments to American tourists and saying 'Sure, I'm the Belle of Killarney!' To which one of the Americans replied, 'Are

you the Belle? Then I wouldn't give much for the balance!' (WB).

baleful and **baneful.** *Baleful* is 'pernicious; destructive', also 'malignant'; as 'unhappy; distressed' it is an archaism. *Baneful* is 'life-destroying; poisonous', also 'pernicious, injurious'. The points to note are that *baneful* does not mean 'malignant' and that *baleful* does not mean 'poisonous' (*OED*).

ball game. See VOGUE WORDS.

balmy and **barmy.** *Balmy* is 'fragrant and soothing'. It is also an alternative spelling (and the preferred American one) of the colloquial *barmy*, meaning 'crazy'.

baluster and **banister.** Wescen is misleading on this point. The facts are these: A *baluster* is a short, circular-sectioned, double-curved pillar or column, slender above and larger, pear-shaped below, 'usually applied in a series called a *balustrade*'; hence, 'a slender upright post or pillar of any shape supporting a rail; in pl. a railing or balustrade'; hence, usually in plural, 'the upright posts or rails which support the handrail, and guard the side, of a staircase; often applied to the whole structure of uprights and handrail. Now more usually banister(s)' (*OED*).

balustrade. See the preceding.

banister(s). See **baluster**.

bank (n.). The left and right *banks* of a river depend on the direction of movement. See **shore**.

Barbados, rather than *Barbadoes*, is now more usual for the island in the West Indies. The river in Brazil is always *Barbados*.

barbarian (adj.) = 'non-Hellenic' or 'non-Roman' (with reference to Classical times); as a synonym of *barbarous* (uncivilized in a derogatory sense), it is best avoided, and *barbarous* used in its place; *barbarous* also = 'cruelly harsh' and (of speech) 'harsh-sounding'.

barbaric = 'uncivilized', 'illiterate', 'non-Latin', 'outlandish'; it is well to reserve it for 'in the characteristic style of barbarians, as opposed to that of civilized countries or ages' as in 'Barbaric pearl and gold' (Milton), 'Each maiden's short barbaric vest', 'Barbaric splendour of decoration' (Wm Black), and 'barbaric art'.

To all these adjectives, the corresponding agential noun is *barbarian* (OED).

barely (or hardly or scarcely) than is catachrestic for *barely* (etc.) ... *when*. 'Barely had her spirits fallen, leaving her to brood over the sea, than the pinch was repeated' (Louis Bromfield). See also the entry at **hardly ... than**.

barmy. See **balmy.**

barrage. A barrage (of gunfire) is a military term, defined by *COD* as 'gunfire so directed as to make a given line impassable': it is, therefore, synonymous with *curtain(-)fire*. The term falls within our scope on two counts.

1. It is often misused for *fusillade*.
2. It is often used metaphorically for a rapid successive attack, as in 'a barrage of questions'.

barring. See CONJUNCTIONS, DISGUISED.

barrister. See **lawyer.**

base or basis. In brief, *base* is literal for 'the lowest or supporting part', with various derivative technical senses, and *basis* is figurative, 'the main constituent, fundamental ingredient', 'foundation; groundwork', 'a principle, or a set of principles' as in 'Society rested on the basis of the family' (J. R. Green), and 'a basis of legislation' (OED). The plural of *base* is *bases*. The plural of *basis* is *bases*, though with a different pronunciation. See also ABSTRACT NOUNS. The adjectives *basal* and *basic* are both related to *base*; but *basal* is confined chiefly to technical contexts, as in 'basal metabolism', while *basic* chiefly means 'fundamental'.

basic, basically. See VOGUE WORDS and COMPARATIVES, FALSE.

bathos and **pathos** (adjectives **bathetic** and **pathetic).** The former is a 'ludicrous descent from the elevated to the commonplace' (in Rhetoric); the latter is that artistic, musical, or literary quality – hence that quality in life – which excites either pity or sadness.

BATTERED SIMILES. See SIMILES, BATTERED.

bay window; bow window. The latter is segmentally *curved*; the former, rectangular or polygonal, though some writers make the term include curved windows, *bay* thus becoming generic and *bow* specific.

be (or become) + a single active verb. Ambiguity or awkwardness often results, as in 'They were not uncreative in their work, had to tackle new problems all the time, and so they were interested and worked with zest' (J. B. Priestley).

be being + past participle.

'He will not *be being* wounded every day but perhaps only once – possibly not at all – in the fighting.'

Though inelegant, this construction is sometimes unavoidable. I first wondered about it when I heard myself saying, 'I should not be being disturbed all the time by rushed jobs if I had independent means.' If I can say 'I am being disturbed all the time', why not 'I shall (or should or may or might) be being disturbed'? Is there a difference between 'I should not be disturbed all the time' and 'I should not be being disturbed all the time'? There is. The latter – 'I should not be being disturbed all the time' – conveys the idea of a *continual* act or a recurring state of things.

beau ideal, as *COD* usefully points out, does not mean 'a beautiful ideal' but 'the ideal beauty', one's idea of the highest type of beauty.

became + past participle. This construction is often ambiguous and always awkward or, at the least, infelicitous, as in 'Alan Kent became roused from sleep by the rattle of distant thunder' (Henry Holt). That this construction is to be avoided will be the more readily perceived when we add another example: 'Her eyes became filled with tears.' Certain persons would suggest: 'Kent was roused from sleep by ... distant thunder' and 'Her eyes were filled with tears': but both those sentences are time-ambiguous. I think that, in all such instances, the simple *active* tense is the best: 'Her eyes filled with tears'; 'The rattle of distant thunder roused Alan Kent from sleep.'

because is sometimes misused for *that*, as in 'The value of the book to civilized Europeans is because it is an anthology of Chinese ideas and anecdotes'; cf. 'Because terms are muzzy ... does not mean that nothing can be accomplished on the economic front' (Stuart Chase). [See Fannye Cherry, 'The Reason Is Because' (*American Speech*, February 1933) for an arresting list of examples of this misuse.]

because and **for**. See **for and because** and **as for because**.

become to be for *become*. In 'He became to be known as a most reliable person' there is confusion between *became known* and *came to be known*.

befall has a chiefly pejorative connotation; *happen to* is neutral and, occasionally, favourable; *fall out for* is favourable ('It might so fall out for anyone').

before for *until*. 'Not *until* I have passed that examination, shall I be able to go out to parties' is correct; 'Not *before* I have ...' is catachrestic. Perhaps the reason is that *until* connotes inclusion in the following act or event, whereas *before* emphasizes not so much the ensuing act or event as the time or events preceding it.

beg leave (to say, etc.); **beg permission** (to differ, etc.). These forms are preferable

to 'I beg to say' and 'I beg to differ.' Especially nauseating is 'I beg to advise you', and 'I beg to remain Yours faithfully, —' is insufferable.

beg the question. This is to assume the truth of something that cannot be taken for granted. The phrase does not correctly mean either 'pose a question' or 'avoid giving a straight answer to it'.

begin. See **commence.**

begrudge and **grudge** are not quite synonymous. To *begrudge* is particularly to envy (a person) the possession of something; to *grudge* is to be resentfully unwilling to give, or do, something.

behalf of, in and **on.** *On behalf of* in British use means 'in the interests of' or 'as a representative of' (another), as in 'An application was made on behalf of the prosecutor for a remand' (Sir J. Mathers). The Americans use *in behalf of* in the same way. Neither phrase means 'on the part of', so that 'an objection raised on John's behalf' is not raised by John himself.

behind is the most serviceable of all the words for that portion of the anatomy on which one sits. See my *Slang Today and Yesterday*, at the section on Vulgarisms. So late as 1882, it was a low colloquialism.

beholding is obsolete for *beholden*, 'obliged (*to* a person)', 'under a personal obligation for services or favours'.

behove and **behoove.** The former spelling is British, the latter American. The verb is used only impersonally, as in 'it behoves us to resist'.

being to be. See **be being.**

belief of. See PREPOSITIONS WRONGLY USED.

believable. See **unbelievable.**

bellicose; belligerent. Respectively 'warlike' and 'occupied in waging war'.

belly is 'that part of the body which receives food', i.e. the stomach with its adjuncts; *stomach* is now more general than *belly* in this sense. The prevailing current sense of belly is 'that part of the human body which lies between the breast and the thighs, and contains the bowels', the medical term being *abdomen*, which, by the euphemistic and the mealy-mouthed, is used in preference to the good English word (a doublet, by the way, of *bellows*).

below and **beneath**. See **above and over**.

beneath for **under**. This misuse occurs especially in 'This (that, etc.) fell beneath my notice (or observation)'; *beneath* = 'lower than'.

benefaction, misused for *benefit*. 'Gypsies were such a nuisance, they would say, that whoever had killed this man had probably conferred some benefaction upon the community at large' (Bernard Newman).

beneficence is occasionally misused for *benevolence*, as *maleficence* is for *malevolence*; and vice versa. *Beneficence* and *maleficence* are the doing of good and evil respectively; *benevolence* and *malevolence* are the corresponding sentiments. An instance of *beneficence* misused for *benevolence* occurs in the following quotation from Vernon Loder's detective novel, *The Button in the Plate*: 'Floating on a serene plane of airy beneficence, he suddenly discovered that people were not looking up to him among the stars, but somewhere on the ground near their feet.'

benzene; benzine. The non-scientist needs to be very careful with these two words; he or she should consult a technical rather than an ordinary dictionary.

bereaved; bereft. Prefer the former for 'deprived by death', the latter for more general deprivation. 'A bereaved husband'; 'a man bereft of hope'. Do not use *bereft* to mean merely 'without (something never possessed)', as in 'a countryside bereft of streams'.

beside, as used by Coleridge in

> The moving moon went up the sky
> And nowhere did abide,
> Softly she was going up,
> And a star or two beside,

is incorrect if he meant *as well, in addition*; he chose to avoid sibilance and to get the rhyme he wanted. He is perhaps not to be censured, for, according to *COD*, *beside*, the preposition, was 'formerly also adverb' and equivalent to *besides*.

Harold Herd, in *Watch Your English*, rightly insists on the distinction, giving examples of correct use: 'I first saw him beside the main entrance', and 'Have you any money besides this?' also 'Besides, the season will not be over, etc.'

besides means 'in addition to', not *other than*. Clearly, then, it is misused in '"Otherwise the wound must have been on the right side of his face – unless it was made by something besides the handle of the gear-lever"' (Lee Thayer).

best two (or **three** or …) and **two** (or **three** or …) **best**. Usage has tended to justify *two best*, probably on the ground that if we can say 'The most popular writers are X and Y', we can also say 'The two most popular writers are X and Y' – as we do. Contrast *first two* (etc.) which is correct, and *two first*, which is incorrect.

bête noir is a very frequent error for *bête noire*. Even *bête noire* is to be used with caution, for it is a cliché. What is wrong with *bugbear* that it should be supplanted by a Gallicism?

betide, meaning *happen to* or *come to pass*, is sometimes misused to mean *betoken* or *bode*, as in 'His slipping as he crossed the threshold betided a misfortune.'

betray for *exhibit* or *disclose* is sometimes ambiguous. 'Only once … did I see J. W. H. T. Douglas betray his punishing powers [as a batsman].' In fact the younger Douglas was a fine bat so that, here, *betray* must = 'exhibit'; but the uninformed might be pardoned for thinking that, on this occasion, he failed to do justice to an ability and habit of smiting the ball.

better. Than what? – 'Better buy Capstan, they're blended better' – a tobacco advertisement.

better and **bettor,** as the noun-agent of *bet* (v.). *OED* admits the two forms. Despite one's first feeling of prejudice against it, the *-or* form has much to be said for it.

better for *longer*. See **better than.**

better than for *more than* is not Standard English but dialect. 'Better than a mile' is a frequent example. *Better* in the sense of *longer* (in time) – ' "When did he marry his mistress?" "About four weeks ago, or better" ' (*The Sessions Papers of the Old Bailey*, 1759) – is obsolete in Standard English.

between, misused. 'The Trades Union' as nickname of the 1st Dragoon Guards is derived, according to Frazer & Gibbons, 'from the K.D.G.'s being constantly employed in suppressing Trade Union disturbances in Lancashire and the Midlands between 1825–34'. It should be 'from 1825 to 1834' or 'between 1825 and 1834'. The same error occurs in 'I got between five or six toont [sovereigns]' ('Autobiography of a Thief' in *Macmillan's Magazine*, October 1879). Note too the error in 'In 1926 [Louis Bromfield] returned to France, and since then has lived between there and the USA.'

between and **among.** One divides money, goods, property *between* two persons, but *among* three or more. The distinction, however, is not so simple. When speaking either of group action, or of precise spatial relationship, one must use *between* however many participants are involved; as in 'The children raised £25 between them', or 'Switzerland lies between France, Germany, Austria, Liechtenstein and Italy.'

between each. See **each, between.**

between [noun] **to** [noun] is incorrect – and silly – for *between ... and ...* as in 'Between London to Manchester, there are several large cities'; 'Between 9 a.m. to 6 p.m., I saw a battle.'

between you and I. *Between*, being a preposition, takes the accusative case equally with all other prepositions (*after me, after him and me, for you and me*): therefore, *between you and me*. The common error of using *I* here may be due to a widespread distrust of *you and me* by those who have been correctly instructed not to use this combination as the subject, as in 'You and me will have to talk.'

betwixt is now archaic for *between*, except in poetry.

bevy, misused, 'A bevy of men's voices reached them from the hall' (G. Pleydell Bancroft, *The Ware Case*).

biannual means 'half-yearly'; **biennial** is 'two-yearly'. I myself, however, prefer *half-yearly* to *biannual*. It may sometimes also be safer to use *two-yearly* for *biennial*. Avoid the equally ambiguous *biyearly*.

biased or **biassed.** *OED* sanctifies usage: and permits either form.

bibliography must not now be used – as before *c.* 1925 it could be used – of a *list of authorities and sources, a list of books (and documents) read* (or *consulted*), a *list of books to read and study* (or a *reading list*); nor of a *catalogue raisonné*, which is a list of works, authorities, sources, with the addition of descriptive or critical details (e.g. 'Esp. valuable for the French influence on English drama'). A *bibliography* is properly, in general 'the' and in particular 'a', 'systematic description and history of books, their authorship, printing, publication, editions, etc.' (*OED*); that 'etc.' includes format, number of pages (e.g. viii + 288), typefount (or *font*), number and kind of illustrations. The list of books by or on an author, or on a subject, becomes a bibliography only when the preceding particulars are noted against each book-title.

bid – preterite *bid* (archaic: *bad, bade*) – past participle *bid* (archaic: *bidden*).

bid is a popular noun in newspaper headlines, not only in the sense of 'offer', as in 'Lloyds Scraps Bid for Midland', but in the special journalistic sense of 'attempt, effort', as in 'Swimmer's Bid for World Record'. The device may be justified here as a space-saver, but headline language should not be allowed to spread into the rest of the article, much less to infect general writing.

biennial. See **biannual.**

biggest share for the *majority* or *most* is incorrect, as in 'The biggest share of the students were in uniform.'

billion is, in older British use, a million million. The British are now coming to follow the practice of the USA and of international scientific and financial writing, where it means a thousand million. Be careful to avoid ambiguity.

bimonthly means either 'twice a month' or 'every two months'. Similarly, *biweekly* is either 'twice a week' or 'every fortnight'. It is therefore probably safer to spell it out as 'twice a month', 'fortnightly', etc. *Semi-monthly* and *semi-weekly* can only mean 'twice a month/week'.

birth date, or **date of birth; birthday.** Respectively 'date on which one was born' and 'anniversary of one's birth'.

bison. See **buffalo.**

biyearly. See **biannual.**

black (v.) is chiefly literal (e.g. to black one's shoes); **blacken** (v.t.) is figurative as in 'She blackened his character in the most unscrupulous manner.' But as an intransitive, *blacken* is used both lit. and fig. – as in 'I ... believe that rain will fall when the air blackens' (Johnson) and 'It may blacken into cynicism' (Morley) (*OED*). Note also the trade-union sense of *black*, which here means 'boycott'.

black (n. and adj.) is now the term preferred by black people themselves, as in 'a black doctor' or 'young blacks'. It should not be capitalized, and should not be used of people of Asian descent. If it is necessary to refer to both these groups together, the inoffensive term is *nonwhite*. Avoid *coloured* outside South Africa, where it is a technical term for those of mixed race. Avoid also *Negro* and *Negress* except in technical anthropological contexts, where they should be capitalized. See also **nigger.**

blame (something) **on** (a person) is colloquial – and unnecessary – for *blame* (a person) *for* (something); but the construction is now well entrenched.

blank cheque (or, in USA, **check**) is needlessly and wrongly stigmatized by Weseen.

blatant for *flagrant*. Anthony Eden, in a speech delivered in December 1936, said 'a blatant breach of good faith'. *Blatant* emphasizes the brazenness of the offence, and *flagrant* its gravity.

-ble. This is a defective series: we have *double* and *treble*, but there it stops. For the difference between *treble* and *triple*, see **treble and triple.**

blend into is incorrect for *blend with* and for the preferable *merge into* or *with*. 'Professional gardeners blend into their surroundings, and it is often possible to miss them completely in a walk around the garden.'

blend together is a foolish, redundant variation of *blend* (v.).

BLENDED GENITIVE. See GENITIVE, VAGARIES OF THE, last paragraph.

BLENDS. See PORTMANTEAU WORDS.

block ought not to be used for a political *bloc*, a political group formed for a special purpose. [*Webster's* approves *block* in the sense of *bloc* in American usage.]

bloody 'is entirely without improper significance in America' (the USA), as H. L.

Mencken remarked in *The American Language*. But Americans writing for a British public and American visitors to Britain should remember that, in Great Britain, this word, despite its growing popularity there and its consequent weakening, is still regarded as unsuitable for, and in, respectable circles and dignified writing. (For a full account, see 'The Word *Bloody*' in my *Here, There, and Everywhere*, 1950.)

blueprint. See VOGUE WORDS.

bluff, misused for *simulate*. 'To bluff intelligence is the easiest thing possible', a crass Philistine once remarked: to simulate stupidity (or even to be stupid) is much easier.

bogey; bogie; bogy. These three spellings are interchangeable for the three meanings, 'one stroke more than the number of strokes a good golfer may be assumed to need for a hole or a course' – 'an open railway freight-car' or 'a revolving undercarriage' – 'a bogle, a goblin'. Writers would do well to attach the first meaning to *bogey*, the second to *bogie*, the third to *bogy*, as Weseen recommends.

Bohemian is 'a native of Bohemia', hence 'a Gypsy'; **bohemian,** a transferred use, is 'a Gypsy of society', esp. 'a writer, artist, musician, actor that leads a vagabond or a free and irregular life (*OED*).

bona fide is occasionally misused for *bona fides*. In a manuscript I read on 9 March 1939, I came upon the curious information that 'Mussolini's *bona fide* has never been questioned.' *Bona fide* is a Latin ablative; it = 'with good faith'. In English *bona fide* is an adverb, and it = 'in good faith: sincerely; genuinely'; hence it is used as an adjective = 'acting, or done in good faith; sincere; genuine'. *Bona fides* is the Latin nominative, and in English it can be used both as nominative and as accusative. Properly it is a Law term = 'good faith; freedom from intent to deceive' (*OED*). *Bona fides* is singular, not plural as in '… As though Kingdom's *bona fides* were not accepted' (R. Philmore).

book for *magazine, periodical*, etc. A book is a complete volume, not a single issue of a serial publication.

book-learned and **bookish** are now uncomplimentary. The corresponding complimentaries are *erudite, learned, scholarly*. *Book-learned* and *bookish* connote 'ignorant of life, however much book-learning one may possess'.

born, borne. Correct uses are 'He was born on the first day of the New Year' and 'He was borne by his mother after three hours of labour.' Also, 'The body was borne (not *born*) into the house.'

born-again. See VOGUE WORDS.

borrow (money) **of** (a person) is correct but slightly obsolescent; *borrow from* is now the usual construction; *borrow off* is non-standard.

boss (n.) is colloquial, both for one's employer and in its political sense, 'a manager or dictator of a party organization in the USA'.

both for *alike*. *Both* refers to two persons, things, groups, classes, kinds, etc., not to three or more thereof. '… A shrewd common sense, which kept her safe … from all the larger follies, whilst still permitting her to give full run to minor eccentricities, both in speech, deed and dress' (R. B. Cunninghame Graham). Cf. *both alike*, redundant for *alike*, in 'Both of the suits are alike' and 'The sisters are both alike.'

both for *each*. 'There is a garage on both sides of the street' should be 'There is a garage on each side of the street' unless the author means that a garage is partly on one, partly on the other side of the street.

both, the. This is catachrestic for *the two*: 'The both bowlers were unsuccessful' and also for *both*. ' "Good for the both of you", grinned Punch' (Robert Eton, *The Journey*, 1938).

both + noun, misused for *the* + noun + *together*. 'Then *x* plus 650 is her share. Both shares equal $5,000' (read 'The shares together equal $5,000') (Stuart Chase, *The Tyranny of Words*).

both ... as well as incorrect for *both ... and*. 'There are few more gloomy places in the early morning than a restaurant. Both the personnel – such as are about – as well as the furniture are in *déshabillé*' (Anthony Weymouth, *Tempt Me Not*).

both of us – you – them are correct; *we both* and *us both, you both, they both* and *them both* are equally correct though perhaps less formal.

both our fathers, both your husbands, both their books correspond to *the fathers of both of us, the husbands of both of you, the books of both of them*. 'The need for a compact expression of this kind is often felt. We may sympathize with the little girl who, wishing to state that a certain pet was the common property of herself and her brother, said "It's both of our donkey"!' (Onions). But although one can say *both our fathers*, what happens when the reference is to the father of two children? *Both our father* is (at present, anyway) impossible. *Both your husbands* is clear enough, at first sight; but it may refer to a young film star's two husbands (the present one and the divorced one). *Both their books* may, to the unthinking, appear innocuous: but there may be two persons, who have one book apiece, and therefore the reference could as well be to the entire book-stock of these two book-lovers ('*Both* their books are at the bindery') as to the thousands of books owned by a pair of bibliophiles. The ambiguity is often best resolved by recasting the sentence in the singular, and writing 'The book of each of them...'.

both the last is catachrestic for *the last two*. 'He could not have received both her last letters and not answered them' (Sheila Kaye-Smith). *Both of her last two letters* and *her last two letters* are equally correct; the latter, the more idiomatic.

bottleneck should be reserved for industry and transport; even there it has been overworked. *Congestion* is usually more effective.

bounden. See ARCHAISMS.

bow window. See **bay window.**

bracket, singular, is not to be used for *brackets* (pl.), a pair of brackets. In British usage, ( ) are *brackets* or *round brackets*, [ ] are *square brackets*. The Americans call the former *parentheses* and the latter *brackets*. The word, phrase, or sentence within brackets is often said to be a *parenthesis*. To employ *bracket* for the *brace* used in coupling two lines of writing or printing, thus

$$\left\{ \begin{array}{l} \text{L. } vinculum \\ \text{Eng. } bond, \end{array} \right.$$

is a catachresis. And to use it for an income-tax group is officialese.

brand, a trademark, or the make of goods distinguished by such mark, can also be metaphorically applied when the intention is humorous; but it is highly inappropriate in the following: 'The Queen had her own brand of services in her own private chapel' (Samuel Putnam).

bran-new; brand-new; brank-new. The third is incorrect, except in Scottish; the second is the original and best form; the first is etymologically senseless, and unnecessary, but – on the score of usage – is uncensoriously admitted by *OED*.

bravado and **bravery.** The former is never synonymous with the latter. *Bravado* is defined by *OED* as 'boastful or threatening behaviour', an archaic nuance; 'ostentatious display of courage or boldness; bold or daring action intended to intimidate or to express defiance; often, an assumption of courage or hardihood to conceal felt timidity, or to carry one out of a doubtful or difficult position'.

breach and **breech** are synonymous in none of their senses.

breadth; broadness. *Breadth* is the physical noun. It is also used in the transferred senses, *breadth of mind* (never *width of mind*), an extensive display of a quality ('breadth and accuracy of vision', Morley), and, in art, a broad effect. *Broadness* was, from the 14th to early 18th centuries, employed for 'breadth' (physical – as a measure, etc.): long disused and to be avoided. But as the abstract noun corresponding to *broad*, 'coarse, indelicate', *broadness* is the correct term.

breakdown can mean a statistical division into categories, and to *break* something *down* may mean to classify it. Avoid these words where there is any danger of confusion with the literal senses, as in 'a complete breakdown of national trade'.

breakthrough. See **VOGUE WORDS.**

breath (*breth*) is the noun; **breathe** (*brethe*) is the verb.

brethren is archaic for *brothers* except 'in reference to spiritual, ecclesiastical, or professional relationship' (*OED*); for certain technical and highly specialized senses, consult *OED*.

BREVITY.

> Since brevity is the soul of wit …
> I will be brief. (Shakespeare)

> I labour to be brief and become
>   obscure. (Horace)

'On the principle of attaining ends at the smallest cost, it is a virtue of language to be brief. If a thought can be properly expressed in five words, there is a waste of strength in employing ten', as Bain remarks (*English Composition and Rhetoric*).

In one sense, brevity is the enemy of tautology (see **TAUTOLOGY**) and the opposite of verbosity (see **VERBOSITY**). But to avoid tautology and verbosity 'is not all; there are direct means of attaining Brevity by the help of various devices of style' (Bain).

I. *The Choice of Words.* 'The extension of our vocabulary by classical and other foreign words has greatly enhanced the power of brief yet adequate expression. Many of the words thus acquired have in themselves a great fulness of meaning, the consequence of their being employed in

the higher kinds of knowledge, and in the complicated operations of society. Such are – strategy, census, codification, autonomy, altruism, hedonism, correlation.' To which we may add such words as *adaptability*, *complex* (in the psychological sense), *flair*.

'Take', continues Bain, 'a few quotations to illustrate this point:
'Man is described by Pope as –

> The *glory*, *jest*, and *riddle* of the world;

the words summing up very happily the substance of a preceding paragraph, which expatiates on the greatness of man's powers, the frequent absurdity of his conduct, and the mysteries of his nature. Again.

> And he, who now to sense, now
>   nonsense leaning,
> Means not, *but blunders round*
>   *about a meaning.*

Thomson has the following, in reference to birds teaching their young to fly:

> The *surging* air receives
> Its plumy burden; and their
>   self-taught wings
> *Winnow the waving element.*

The expressions here used bring before us in a few words the fan-like stroke of the wings on the one hand and the corresponding motion of the air, like that of waves, on the other.

> But as along the river's edge
> They went, and brown birds in the
>   sedge
> *Twittered* their *sweet* and *formless*
>   tune. (William Morris)

Here, *twittered* describes the short tremulous notes characteristic of the songs of the birds; *sweet* conveys the mental impression of the listener; while *formless* gives in one word the idea that the song is not shaped after any fixed standard but is poured forth in endless variety.

"Governments are not *made*, but *grow*."

'"The progress of civilization has been from *status* to *contract*" (Maine). A large amount of meaning is at once conveyed by each of the two contrasted words.'

II. *Grammatical Forms and Syntactical Usages.*

(1) *Abstract nouns.* 'His *refusal* justified my *adherence* to my plan' = '*The fact that he refused* justified me *in adhering* (or, *when I adhered*) to my plan.' Still more condensed is 'The *mazy-running* soul of melody', 'The *astonished* mother finds a *vacant* nest.' So too the *adverb*, or the adverb and adjective, or the adverb and adjective and abstract noun, as in –

(2) *The attributive use of nouns*, i.e. *nouns used as adjectives* or as elements of compound nouns; e.g. 'a *bosom* friend', '*table* talk', 'an *earth* worm, 'a *birthday* present'.

(3) *Adjectives* are rather obviously short-cuts, as in –

Goodness and wit
In *seldom-meeting* harmony combined,

'The *mazy-running* soul of melody', 'The *astonished* mother finds a *vacant* nest.' So too the *adverb*, or the adverb and adjective, or the adverb and adjective and abstract noun, as in –

See nations *slowly wise* and *meanly just*
To *buried merit* raise the *tardy* bust.

(4) *Participial phrases for clauses.* '*Enraged and mortified*, he soon returned to his mansion' = 'Because he was enraged and mortified, he soon returned to his mansion.' 'The Romans, *having* now *set foot* in Sicily, determined to declare war against Carthage' = 'The Romans had now set foot in Sicily, and therefore they determined to declare war against Carthage.'

An excellent example –

Vanished every fear, and every
power
Roused into life and action, light
in air
The acquitted parents see their
soaring race,
And once rejoicing never know
them more.

(5) *Prefixes and suffixes; and compounds.* Consider '*re*turn', '*re*unite', '*re*fund'; '*absentee*ism' and '*admiss*ibility'; 'forcible-

feeble', 'semi-popish', 'little-minded'.

III. *Rhetorical Devices.* To go adequately into these, I should require inordinate space. But perhaps a hint may be conveyed by the following examples:

'He lives to build, not boast,
a generous race.'

'And read their history in a
nation's eyes.'

'Leave to the nightingale
her woods;
A privacy of glorious light is
thine.'

'A hand-to-mouth liar.'

'Murder will out.'

A great – perhaps the greatest – master of brevity is Shakespeare. Here are two examples:

My thought, whose murder yet
is but fantastical,
Shakes so my single state of man,
that function
Is smothered in surmise.

If th' assassination
Could trammel up the
consequence, and catch,
With his surcease, success; that
but this blow
Might be the be-all and the
end-all here,
But here, upon this bank and
shoal of time,
We'd jump the life to come.

Both of these passages come, of course, from *Macbeth*; the latter passage occurs in a speech that I once set to be paraphrased; the whole speech (I, vii) would repay study, for it is of the essence of forceful brevity. Pope is another master of brevity: neater than Shakespeare, but less connotation-suggestive. 'Of the following four lines on the origin of Society' (as Bain says), 'Mark Pattison observes that they are "expressed with a condensed energy which it would be difficult to improve upon"':

Heaven forming each on other to
    depend,
A master, or a servant, or a friend,
Bids each on other for assistance call
Till one man's weakness grow the
    strength of all.

BREVITY, leading to obscurity. See
OBSCURITY.

brief and **short.** *Brief* = 'of short duration,
quickly passing away or ending', hence (of
speeches, writings) 'concise or short'; it is
virtually obsolete in reference to extent in
space; though it is applied to clothes. *Short*,
on the other hand, refers to either time or
space; but when it refers to the latter, it
often has a connotation of curtailment or
incompleteness, or sudden cessation, as in
'a short nap', 'a short description'.

briefness is now rare for *brevity.*

bring is confused with *take* only by the
illiterate or the unthinking. See esp. the
introductory note (to I) in *OED*.

bring to a (satisfactory) conclusion is
verbose for *conclude* (*satisfactorily*).

Britain. See **Great Britain.**

British; English. The people of the
United Kingdom are *British*. Their
language, spoken all over the world, is
English, but only the people of England
are correctly called the *English*, the others
being Irish, Scottish, or Welsh. *Briton*
is properly used of the Ancient Britons,
but the word is otherwise best confined
to newspaper headlines. *Britisher* is an
Americanism. *Brit* is colloquial and slightly
offensive.

**BRITISH AND AMERICAN
USAGE.** The written English of the
educated is more or less intercomprehen-
sible throughout the English-speaking
world. (See STANDARD ENGLISH.)
However, the two most firmly established
national varieties are British English and
American English, the others tending to
follow one or other of these two. Many
differences between British and American
usage are discussed at individual entries in

this book. There are some differences in
spelling, a matter not dealt with systematically here, and a few in punctuation.
When we come to grammar, a few verbs
inflect differently, as with *dove* for *dived* and
gotten for *got*; the Americans use the subjunctive more widely than do the British,
even in such negative sentences as 'It is
better that he not ask'; and they are reluctant to use plural verbs and pronouns with
such words as *audience*, in situations where
the British might readily do so. (See COL-
LECTIVE NOUNS.)

   The differences between British and
American vocabulary are of a different
order of frequency and importance. Since
the two languages are in constant contact,
the boundaries are constantly shifting:
what is regarded in Britain today as
an Americanism (or, come to that, in
America as a Briticism) may be accepted
without comment within a decade. But
British readers should be aware of a few
vocabulary differences that may cause
actual misunderstanding. Examples are the
American *cot* (for camp-bed), *gas* (for
petrol), *first floor* (already coming into
British use for ground floor), *public school*
(for state school), and *fender, hood, muffler,*
and *trunk* (for the wing, bonnet, silencer,
and boot of a car).

   There follows a selection from the
numerous relevant publications:

H. L. Mencken, *The American Language*,
    ed. R. I. McDavid Jr, 1963, New
    York.
M. Nicholson, *A Dictionary of American-
    English Usage*, 1957, New York.
Wilson Follet, *Modern American Usage*,
    1961, Longmans.
Roy H. Copperud, *American Usage and
    Style*, 1980, New York.
Guy J. Forgue, *Les Mots Americains*, 1976,
    Presses Universitaires de France.
The most authoritative American
    dictionary is *Webster's Third New
    International Dictionary*, 1961,
    Springfield, Mass.

broad and **wide.** See **wide and broad.**

broadcast, to; he *broadcast* or *broadcasted*; the news was *broadcast*.

broadness. See **breadth.**

Bruxelles, Firenze, Gand, Gdansk, Genf, Livorno, Lyon, Marseille, München, Reims are coming to be widely used in British and American writing, rather than their 'English' forms *Brussels, Florence, Ghent, Danzig, Geneva, Leghorn, Lyons, Marseilles, Munich, Rheims*. This must be attributable either to increased foreign travel or to a becoming increase in linguistic modesty.

buffalo and **bison.** *Bison* originally was 'a species of Wild Ox ... formerly prevalent in Europe' but now the term is applied properly to the North American species, which, therefore, is improperly called *buffalo*. *Buffalo* is that species of ox which was 'originally a native of India' (*OED*). [Nevertheless, in the USA, the North American bison is generally known as the buffalo and under this name figures in the national stock of stories. 'The bison nickel' would be unintelligible to young America and a British boner to their elders.]

Buhl (as in *Buhl table*) should be *Boule*. *Buhl*, says *OED*, 'seems to be a modern Germanized spelling' and *Boule* is 'the more correct form of the word commonly spelt *Buhl*': but this is a far too lenient comment, for *Buhl* has no justification – not even that of a universal error, *Boule* being, among the educated, an equally common spelling. 'Boule (André Charles), célèbre ébéniste, né à Paris en 1642, mort en 1732. Il éléva l'ébénisterie à la hauteur d'un art, et acquit une grande réputation' (Larousse, *Grand dictionnaire universel du xixᵉ siècle*).

build a building is, at the lowest estimate, ugly in sound and redundant in sense.

bulk, the (never *a*). *Bulk* should be reserved for 'volume' or 'mass'. It is incorrect for *the majority*, as in 'The bulk of slow bowlers prefer the eight-ball over, but the bulk of fast bowlers prefer the six-ball over.'

BULLS. A *bull* is 'an expression containing a manifest contradiction in terms or involving a ludicrous inconsistency unperceived by the speaker' (*OED*). Often called *Irish bulls*: but *bull* was used in this sense long before it came to be associated with that people which has given us the best examples of felicitous incongruities.

See Maria and Richard Edgeworth's *Essay on Irish Bulls*, 1802, and Walter Jerrold's *Bulls, Blunders and Howlers*, 1928.

Here are two bulls, said to be of Irish perpetration:

the entrance out.

'If there was twelve cows lyin' down in a field and one of them was shtandin' up, that would be a bull.'

bumble-bee. See **humble-bee.**

bunch. 'Good usage does not sanction the indiscriminate use of *bunch* for any and every group, and certainly not for groups of people' (Weseen).

bungalow. In India, where the word originated, it means a spacious detached house. But in Britain a bungalow is a (lightly built) one-storeyed house; hence Arnold Bennett's 'two-storeyed bungalow' in *The City of Pleasure* is absurd.

burglarize (American) and *burgle* have been objected to as verbs for the committing of burglary, but they are convenient as being more specific than the vaguer verb *rob*.

burn down and **burn up** are excessive, unnecessary for *burn* – unless an intensive force is required. A house 'burnt *down*' connotes total destruction, a burning right to the ground; a letter 'burnt *up*' connotes total destruction, not a mere scorching.

burthen. See ARCHAISMS.

bus (not *'bus*) is now Standard English for *omnibus*. The plural is *buses* or *busses*.

BUSINESS ENGLISH. See OFFICIALESE, JOURNALESE, COMMERCIALESE.

busyness, the state of being busy, is, according to *OED*, a modern formation, made to distinguish it from *business*, which has come to have another meaning. It is a necessary word.

but (adv.) (= *only*) is tautological in such sentences as this: 'There was but very little room for him in the small over-crowded cottage' (Hugh Walpole).

Like the adverb *only*, the adverb *but* sometimes gets into a foolish or illogical position – as in 'A semantic analysis of economic theory would fill a book ... Here we have space but for a few examples' (read. 'space for but a few examples'), (Stuart Chase). Also it can be ambiguous when it is used for *only*, as in 'Yes, but a portion of my tribe is with me, yet I cannot say that anyone is missing' (Bernard Newman). And 'We splashed out on to the lane ... its mud was but less fathomless than the yard's' (Adrian Bell), is very awkward if not entirely incorrect.

but (conjunction) is wrongly used in the following, quoted by C. C. Boyd (*Grammar for Grown-Ups*) from a newspaper: 'A gale swept the roads, and his (Mr Cobham's) machine was unprotected. At midnight he attached a second anchor, but the machine weathered the gale undamaged.' This is what is called a *non sequitur*. *But* must be used instead of *and*; the sentence should read: '... his machine was unprotected, but weathered the gale ... because he had attached a second anchor.'

The conjunction *but* is also incorrect in the following: 'He will certainly say of Mallet that as a detective he was remarkable not so much for the questions he put but for those he avoided putting' (John Ferguson); *not so much ... as* is correct, but the sentence might also read: '...not for the questions he put, but for those...'.

J. B. Priestley, in *English Humour*, falls into the same error: 'He [Munden] was not so much a comic actor, consciously presenting an amusing part, but a real comedian ...': here *but* should be as.

but (preposition). The clearest exposition I have seen is the following, from Dr Onions's *An Advanced English Syntax*: 'But is a Preposition meaning "except", and, like other Prepositions, governs the Accusative [or Objective]:

"No one would have thought of it *but him*."

'If, however, a sentence like this is otherwise arranged, the Nominative is very commonly put instead of the Accusative:

"No one *but he* would have thought of it."

The Accusative, in fact, is felt to be inelegant. *But* thus becomes a Conjunction, and the sentence must be regarded as equivalent to "No one would have thought of it, *but* he thought of it."
'Compare:

"The boy stood on the burning
   deck,
Whence all *but he* had fled." '

but (adv.) does not equal *more than*. '"I won't go into the house yet. Just give it the once over. Won't take me but a few minutes"' (Lee Thayer, *Death in the Gorge*). The negative misled him. Equally bad is: 'It is not possible in a short article to mention but a few of the, etc.' (Edward C. Ash).

but, misused for *than*. 'The choice of war or peace is now in other hands but ours' (Arthur Bryant).

but in *help but* and *cannot help but* (do something) is awkward and to be deprecated. 'Millions of hearts could not help but thrill in response.' Why not 'could not help thrilling', or simply 'thrilled'? Here is an example from *Murder at the Polls* by Milton Propper: 'The detectives could not help but accept his statement about the brawlers' should read '... help accepting his statement', or 'could not but accept ...'.

but ... however, used where either *but* or *however* (or *notwithstanding*) is needed, is incorrect; e.g. 'After judgement [in court], she pleaded her belly, and a jury of matrons being impanelled, they found her not quick with child; but, however, she was afterwards reprieved.' Trial of Mary Roberts in July 1728, sentenced to death for stealing (The Rev. John Villette, *The Annals of Newgate*, 1776).

Gerard Manley Hopkins, in *The Bugler's First Communion*, wrote thus:

Recorded only, I have put my lips on pleas
Would brandle adamantine heaven with
    ride and jar, did Prayer go disregarded:
Forward-like, but however, and like
    favourable heaven heard these.

but that after *doubt*. See **doubt**.

but that used, unnecessarily, for *that ... not*. 'Brington was not yet so overgrown but that the unspoilt country was within easy reach of it' (Archibald Marshall).

but what, in, e.g. 'I don't know but what ...', is a clumsy alternative to *but that*.

but yet (cf. **but ... however**) is, at the least, infelicitous; *but* is strong, *yet* is mild, and *but yet* rings oddly. It is rather surprising to find it in so good a writer as R. B. Cunninghame Graham: 'Born when the echoes of the '45 were ringing (though faintly) through the land, he held the Stuarts in abhorrence, but yet hated the Hanoverians, whom he termed German Boors.'

by. I regret that *by* is being used more and more in place of the merely instrumental *with*. E.g. 'She moved him rather by her tears than by her appeal to his chivalry.'

by for *beside* can be dangerously (and indeed ridiculously) ambiguous. 'Two bottles which contained poison were found by the deceased' (*The Daily Chronicle*, 1899), quoted by Nesfield in his admirable chapter, 'Errors in Prepositions'.

by a long way is verbose for *far* or *much*, as in 'The starlings are by a long way the greediest.'

by the name of and **of the name of** are intolerably wordy for *named* (or *called*). And **go by the name of** is ambiguous in that it implies – usually or often – that the name is an assumed one.

C

cacao, coca, cocoa, coco(nut). Confusion is common among these. *Cacao* is a tropical American tree from the seed of which the beverages *cocoa* and chocolate are made; *coca* is a Bolivian shrub whose leaves are chewed as a stimulant and from which cocaine is derived; the *coco* is a tropical palm-tree bearing the *coconut*.

cache, for any hiding place whatsoever, is loose, and *cache* for 'to hide' anything anywhere is catachrestic. To *cache* is 'to put in a cache', 'to store (provisions) underground' (*OED*).

caddy; caddie. Tea is kept in a *caddy*. A *caddie* (alternative spelling, *caddy*) carries golf clubs.

calculate is an Americanism – and, even as an Americanism, it is colloquial – for 'to think, opine, suppose ...; to intend, purpose' (*OED*).

calendar; calender. The latter is 'a rolling machine used in glazing paper or in smoothing cloth' (Weseen).

caliber (American), **calibre** (English). Don't use it indiscriminately to = *order of merit, class, kind,* and *type.* 'A poem of high calibre' and 'an artist of low calibre' are not absolutely wrong: they are merely ludicrous.

calk. See **caulk.**

calligraphy is frequently misused; i.e. it is a catachresis for 'handwriting'. David

Frome, 1933, 'The calligraphy expert';
Ngaio Marsh, 1945, 'A pointed irritable
calligraphy'. Its correct sense is 'beautiful
handwriting'.

callous; callus. The former, as an
adjective, chiefly means 'emotionally
unfeeling'. As a noun it is an alternative
spelling of *callus*, 'a hardened patch of
skin'. Hardened skin can be called *callused*
or *calloused*.

calvary. See **cavalry.**

camel; dromedary. The dromedary is
the one-humped Arabian camel. The
Bactrian camel has two humps.

can and **may.** On 10 Sept. 1665, Pepys
joined a party at Greenwich, where Sir
John Minnes and Evelyn were the life of
the company and full of mirth. 'Among
other humours, Evelyn's repeating of
some verses made up of nothing but the
various acceptations of *may* and *can*, and
doing it so aptly upon occasion of something of the nature, and so fast, did make
us all die almost with laughing, and did so
stop the mouth of Sir J. Minnes in the
middle of all his mirth (and in a thing
agreeing with his own manner of genius),
that I never saw any man so outdone in all
my life; and Sir J. Minnes' mirth too to see
himself outdone, was the crown of all our
mirth.' Unfortunately, Pepys does not
quote the verses on *may* and *can*.

Briefly, *can* is used of ability (or capacity) to do something; *may* now chiefly of
possibility, as in 'It may snow tonight.' In
addition, both words express the idea of
permission, for which *can* is now more
usual than *may* except in very formal writing. 'Where appropriate, the court may
award higher damages.' *Can't* almost universally takes the place of the awkward
mayn't: *Can't I go now? We can't have lights
after twelve o'clock.*

CANADIAN ENGLISH. See STAN-
DARD ENGLISH, Section IV.

candelabra, plural **candelabras.** These
are the modern forms of *candelabrum*, plural
candelabra.

**candidacy; candidateship; candida-
ture.** The first = 'the position or status of
a candidate': *candidateship*, 'the position of
a candidate'; *candidature* is the most 'active'
of the three terms, for it = 'standing as a
candidate' (*OED*). [Only the first of these
words is commonly found in American
usage.]

cannot help but. See **but in** *help but.*

cannot seem to is misplacement of words
= 'seem not to be able to'. Kathleen
Norris, 'I must be nervous this afternoon.
I can't seem to settle down to anything.'
Change to '... I seem unable to settle
down ...'. [American usage accepts *cannot
seem to* as a useful colloquial idiom. *I seem
unable to settle down* is, in comparison, awkward though logical.]

canon (ecclesiastic and textual), **cañon** (a
chasm or ravine), **cannon** (warfare and
billiards), **canyon** (the Anglicized form of
cañon).

CANT. The everday sense of *cant* is 'an
affected or unreal use of religious or
pietistic phraseology; language implying
the pretended assumption of goodness
or piety', as in 'He had a horror of cant'
and 'The whole spiritual atmosphere was
saturated with cant' (*OED*).

But in philology, *cant* is the technical
term for the vocabulary peculiar to the
underworld (criminals; tramps and beggars; prostitutes and 'ponces'; and such
hangers on as 'fences'). It is to be hoped
that the use of this short, convenient term
will become more general.

Cant, in this sense, is often called
'thieves' (or underworld) slang'. It is true
that the underworld employs a great deal
of slang, whether general or Cockney or
provincial or vocational; nevertheless,
when – as often it does – the underworld
wishes to converse, or to communicate, in
a manner incomprehensible to more
respectable citizens (once lumped together,
by the British underworld, in the generic
term, *mugs*), it employs what cannot
accurately be designated as slang, for it is
a 'secret language': but even 'secret

language' is slightly misleading, for only the keywords, the significant words, are 'secret'. The words for departure, escape, flight; for dying and killing; for thief, cheat, swindler, confidence man, professional tough, receiver of stolen property, prostitute, pathic; for policeman, detective, prison warder; for arrest and imprisonment; for begging, and professional tramping; for the victims of criminals and beggars; for means of conveyance (ship, train, car, aeroplane); for money, whether money in general or money in particular denominations; for food and drink in general and for certain specific drinks and foods; for such buildings as banks and houses, hospitals, barns, and casual wards; for doors, windows, stairs; for certain household effects (linen, plate); for jewellery and gems; for telephones and other means of communication; for such animals as dogs and horses; for certain geographical and topographical features (e.g. roads); for the tools and devices used by criminals (a jemmy; dynamite); for such weapons as a cudgel, a life-preserver, a revolver, a machine-gun, mustard (or other offensive) gas; for such verbs as 'do' or 'make', 'unmake', 'destroy', 'hide', 'discover', 'place', 'forge', 'look', 'examine', 'handle', 'bungle'; for 'man', 'woman', 'child', 'father', 'mother', 'wife', 'husband'; for 'marriage'; for the sexual act and its preliminaries; for unnatural sexual acts; for physical functions; and so on, and so on.

With regard to the secrecy and vocationalism of cant, it must, however, be remembered that, as Henri Bauche has pointed out, 'Il faut reconnaître que l'argot des malfaiteurs, l'argot des prisons, entre pour une part importante dans la formation du langage populaire. La cause en est évidente: le crime naît plus souvent du besoin et de la misère des classes inférieures que parmi les gens qui ne manquent de rien.' In the staple as in the slangy portion of uneducated speech there is, therefore, a considerable number of terms that are found also in cant: 'It's the poor as 'elps the poor': from the poor around them,

criminals do not wish, do not even think, to hide their secret vocabulary: and often it is to the advantage of criminals that parts of their specialist vocabulary should be known by their non-criminal relatives and friends. (This holds equally for beggars and tramps.) Cant terms leak out from time to time, with the result that many of them are ultimately included in some dictionary or other; nor always only there. As Bauche has said, 'Les divers argots des prisons, des différentes catégories de malfaiteurs, de la prostitution ont … laissé des traces nombreuses dans le bas peuple, sans distinction de métier: de là ces termes spéciaux sont montés dans le peuple et parfois jusqu'aux classes cultivées.' Here are a few examples of such promotion or elevation in British English: – *Beak*, a magistrate; *bilk*, to cheat; *booze* (noun and verb), and *boozer* (drunkard and public-house); *cove* and *cull* (or *cully*); *doxy*; *duds* (clothes); *filch*; *hick* (a rustic); *jemmy*; *moll* (a woman); *nab* (to take, steal, arrest); *nob* (the head); *ponce* (a prostitute's bully); *prig* (to steal); *queer* and *rum* (odd, 'shady'); *ready* and *rhino*; *rig* (a swindle, to swindle); *scamp* (noun) and *scamper* (verb); *shicer*; *stow it!*; *tip* (to give); *tout* (noun and verb); (to) *work* (a district, a street); *yokel*. In American, *hobo*, *stool pigeon*, and *yegg* form excellent examples.

Strictly then, cant is neither slang nor a secret language, but both; in its essence, however, it is a secret language, more precisely a secret vocabulary (the freemasonry of the underworld). John Farmer's opinion is here of great importance, for one of the most authoritative pronouncements on the relation of cant to slang is that of the operative editor of the seven-volumed *Slang and Its Analogues*. In the Preface to *Musa Pedestris*, 1896, he wrote thus: 'As to the distinction to be drawn between Slang and Cant it is somewhat difficult to speak. Cant we know; its limits and place in the world of philology are well defined. In Slang, however, we have a veritable Proteus, ever shifting. … Few, save scholars and suchlike folk, even distinguish between the two. … Slang is universal, whilst Cant is restricted in usage. ... Slang boasts a quasi-respectability denied to Cant, though Cant is frequently more enduring, its use continuing without variation of meaning for many generations.'*

Many writers of 'thrillers' and, especially, 'deteccers' sprinkle their pages – chiefly their low-life dialogue – with cant words and phrases. Most of them, however, have but a slight knowledge of cant, and of the few words they know, some are obsolete; in one of the most popular crime-plays of recent years, a character was made to say *crack a crib*. Now, since 1900, to 'burgle a house (flat, etc.)' is not *crack a crib* but *screw a joint*. Among the most reliable cant-users are (to confine ourselves to the early 20th century) Josiah Flynt, Jack London, Edgar Wallace, Bart Kennedy, W. H. Davies, Edwin Pugh, Arthur Stringer, George Bronson-Howard, Jim Tully, Charles F. Coe, Fred D. Pasley, E. D. Sullivan, Jack Bilbo, George Dilnot, Netley Lucas, James Spenser, John G. Brandon, 'David Hume', Nigel Morland, James Curtis, Robert Westerby, Damon Runyon, Courtney R. Cooper, and Don Castle. The only trustworthy and comprehensive glossary of American cant is Godfrey Irwin's *American Tramp and Underworld Slang* (Oxford University Press, London; Sears, New York) – a most valuable work of reference. For British cant, many of its words and phrases are scattered about the pages of my *A Dictionary of Slang and Unconventional English* (revised and enlarged 3rd ed., 1948); my dictionary of cant, both British and American, planned on historical lines, appeared in 1950 [D. W. Maurer has published a number of relevant articles in *American Speech*.]

can't seem to. See **cannot seem to.**

canvas is a cloth material; **canvass** is 'to examine, discuss, solicit', as in 'to canvass votes'. As a noun, *canvass* = 'a solicitation

* The preceding paragraphs are taken (and modified) from my *Slang Today and Yesterday*, 3rd edition, revised, 1949.

of support [esp. at an election], custom, etc.' (Harold Herd: *OED*).

canyon. See at **canon.**

capable of (e.g. *locomotion*). Able to (e.g. walk).

capacious in the sense of *spacious* is now so little used that it rings almost oddly enough to be designated a misuse, though admittedly it isn't one. 'Chewing hay in Don Angel's capacious stable' (Bernard Newman). The word is more currently used of 'containers', as in 'her capacious handbag'.

capital; capitol. The correct spelling is always *capital*, except for the meeting-place of an American legislature.

CAPITALS IN TITLES. See **TITLES OF BOOKS.**

caption means the legend either above or underneath an illustration. The mistaken idea that it should mean only a heading stems from the impression that the word derives from the Latin *caput*, a head, whereas the true derivation is from *capere*, to capture.

carat; karat; caret. The first is either a unit of parity for gold (spelt *karat* in American English) or a unit of weight for gems. A *caret* is a mark ($\wedge$) indicating an insertion in a piece of writing.

carbolic acid; carbonic acid. The former is 'a substance more systematically called *Phenol* or *Phenyl alcohol*'; the latter, 'a name originally given to the gas now more systematically called *Carbon(ic) Dioxide* or *Carbonic anhydride*. ... This is still popularly called *carbonic acid gas*, but the name *Carbonic acid* is applied in Chemistry to the hydrate or compound CH_2O_3'; **carbonic oxide** is now *carbon monoxide* (*OED*).

carburetter, -or. *COD*, giving both, seems to prefer the latter, as does *Webster's*. *Webster's*, however, prefers – or seems to prefer – *carburetor* to *carburettor*. Britain knows not *carburetor, -er*.

careen. To careen a ship is to tilt it on one side for cleaning. In American usage the verb also means 'lurch rapidly along', influenced by *career.*

carefree; careless. The former = 'free from care or anxiety'. So does *careless,* which also = (of persons) 'inattentive, negligent thoughtless', hence 'inaccurate', and (of things) 'artless', 'unstudied', 'done, caused, or said heedlessly, thoughtlessly, negligently' (*OED*).

cargo and **shipment.** The former is a shipload or aircraft load, a lading, a freight; the latter has the same sense, but with the nuance 'a consignment of goods', and the active sense, 'an act of shipping (goods)'. On trains, *freight* or *load*; on lorries, in motor-cars, and in trucks (USA), generally *load.*

caring. See VOGUE WORDS.

carousal, carousel. *Carousal* (v.: *carouse*) is a carouse, a drinking bout, a drunken revelry; *carousel* (or *carrousel*) is a rotating delivery system at an airport, or a special kind of chivalric tournament, and it has no corresponding verb. Historians and historical novelists confuse these two terms. [In American usage, *carrousel* is a merry-go-round.]

carping has occasionally been misused for *carking,* the former meaning 'fault-finding', the latter 'oppressive'.

Carta, Magna. See **Magna Carta.**

case (of), in the, is frequently misused for *in this* (or *that*) *connection;* also it is often quite unnecessarily used, as in 'There was a greater scarcity of crabs than in the case of herrings', which we owe to Sir Alan Herbert (from a newspaper). Despite Sir Arthur Quiller-Couch's furious and witty onslaught, *case* is still used with nauseating frequency. See ABSTRACT NOUNS.

caseine is incorrect for *casein* (*kayseen*).

cast = *dramatis personae* – the list, hence the personnel, of actors and actresses performing a play, whereas **caste** is an exclusive class (of persons); the term having originally been, as in India it still is, used of hereditary classes; hence, *caste* is applied to a rigid system of class-distinctions within a community.

caster; castor. The former is one who casts, e.g. a (metal-)founder, or a machine for casting type; both spellings are used for a small wheel on furniture, for a sugar container, or for the sugar itself. A *castor* is an archaism for a beaver; the unctuous substance also named castoreum; and *castor* (*oil*).

casualty; causality. *Casualty,* 'a fatal or serious accident or event' (*OED*), is now used of any kind of victim, as in 'Small businesses were the first casualties of the recession.' *Causality* is 'the principle of causal relationship'. [*Webster's,* concerning *casualty,* has this: '… a soldier unavailable for service, because of death, wounds, … or any cause'. This usage, for anyone killed or injured, is established.]

CATACHRESIS. A catachresis is a word misused (e.g. *anachronism* for *anomaly, to subject* for *to subordinate*); catachresis, as a fault in writing, is 'an improper use of words' (*OED*); etymologically, 'contrary-to-usage-ness'. The adjective is *catachrestic.*

This book deals with the commonest catachreses of the English language: to write at length on the nature of catachresis is therefore unnecessary.

cataclasm and **cataclysm.** *Cataclasm,* lit. 'a breakage' (Gr. *kata,* 'down'), means 'a break or disruption', as in 'The cataclasms of the moral and social world' (Southey) and 'Any cataclasm, any violent disruption of what is the usual course of nature' (Bowen); hence, in Geology, 'a breaking down, or crushing into fragments, of rocks', with adjective *cataclastic.* A *cataclysm* is 'a great and general flood of water', esp. the Noachian deluge, 'the Flood'; hence used vaguely for a sudden convulsion or alteration of physical conditions'; fig., 'a political or social upheaval that sweeps away the old order of things', e.g. the French Revolution of 1789, the Russian Revolution of 1917 (*OED*).

catalyst. See VOGUE WORDS.

catastrophic is occasionally misused by violent journalistic writers, for *severe* or *drastic*; it affords an excellent example of 'sending a man on a boy's errand'. Nigel Morland, *The Conquest of Crime*, chapter on finger-prints: 'The permanence of the prints against damage from wounding or burning was demonstrated painfully but conclusively by Dr Locard and Dr Witkowski of Lyon, who subjected their fingers to the action of boiling water, hot oil and to the pressure of hot plates. It was proved that while these catastrophic measures did destroy the marks on the epidermis, or outer skin, the patterns impressed on the corium, or underlying true skin, were unaffected, and that as soon as the wounds or the burns were healed, the original pattern returned in all its detail.'

catch afire is unnecessary for *catch fire*.

catchup or **catsup.** See **ketchup.**

category for *class* or *division*, and *categorize* for 'to *class*' or 'to *classify*' belong to officialese and are to be avoided by all.

catholic, Catholic, Roman Catholic. See **Roman Catholic.**

caulk is to be preferred to *calk*.

causality. See **casualty**

cause and **reason.** A *cause* is that which produces an effect; that which gives rise to any action, phenomenon, or condition. '*Cause* and *effect* are correlative terms' (*OED*). A *reason* is that which is advanced in order to explain the effect or result, or to justify it; the reason may or may not correspond to the facts; the reason one gives oneself may not be the true motive. 'The reason of (or for) the seasons is physical' affords an obvious example of *reason* misused for *cause*. See also **source and cause.**

cause to be informed = to tell.

cavalcade; procession. To use the former for the latter is not incorrect, but it is unnecessary and loose. Properly, *caval-*cade is 'a procession on horseback, esp. on a festive or solemn occasion'; hence 'a company of riders on the march or in procession' (*OED*). The word is now often used of a procession of motor vehicles, particularly by those who dislike the comparative neologism *motorcade*. The use of *cavalcade* for *pageant*, or for *march of events* (or *history*), is to be deprecated.

cavalry and **calvary** are occasionally confused by the ignorant. The less ignorant, however, tend to lose sight of the fact that whereas *Calvary* is 'the place where Christ was crucified', *calvary* is 'a life-sized representation of the Crucifixion', properly 'on a raised ground in the open air' and in Roman Catholicism it is also 'a series of representations, in a church or [a] chapel, of the scenes of the Passion' (*OED*).

ceiling, the theoretical acme of an aircraft's flight, has become a bureaucratic counter or rubber-stamp word for 'limit' or 'maximum' or, as an adjective 'highest', 'furthest', 'utmost'; e.g. 'the price-ceiling of whisky' – 'the ceiling figure for demobilization' – 'a new ceiling in exports'. If the word is to be used at all, one should not in any case refer to 'increasing' or 'waiving' a *ceiling*, or say that it is beginning to 'bite'. (Cf. **priority**.)

celebrity, 'fame', 'famousness', 'notoriety', is correct; correct, too, is the derivative sense, 'a celebrated (or distinguished) person', 'a famous person' – but it is grossly overworked.

Celt and **celt.** *Celt*, usually pronounced 'kelt' rather than 'selt', means the race of early inhabitants of Britain and their descendants. The Scottish football team is pronounced 'seltic'. A *celt*, pronounced 'kelt', is a prehistoric stone or metal implement. [In American usage, *Celt* and *Celtic* may be pronounced with *k*- or *s*-. The implement is pronounced 'selt'.]

cement and **concrete** are not synonymous. The latter is 'a composition of stone chippings, sand, gravel, pebbles, etc., formed into a mass with cement; used for building under water for foundations, pavements, walls, etc.'. *Cement* is a substance – esp. a strong mortar – 'used to bind the stones or bricks of a building firmly together, to cover floors, etc.'; hence, almost any cohesive, as, e.g. for stopping (or [American] filling) teeth (*OED*).

censer (a vessel in which incense is or may be burnt) is not to be confused with *censor*.

censor (v.) and **censure** (v.). To *censor* is 'to act as censor to or of', 'to examine rigorously for moral or political fault, or for the untimely disclosure of official or military or other state secrets', applied esp. to news, letters, plays, films. To *censure* is 'to criticize harshly or unfavourably; to condemn; find fault with; blame'. The corresponding nouns are *censure* and, to *censor*, the agential *censor* and the abstract *censorship*. The adjective *censorial* belongs to *censor*, and *censorious* to *censure*.

centenary (n. and adj.) should be employed as a noun only, for the more usual adjective is *centennial*, used also by the Americans as a noun.

centre (American **center**) and **middle**. *Centre* is applied properly to a circle, a (literal) revolution, and centripetal attraction; in Geometry, it is the middle point of figures other than circles; it is the point of equilibrium; and in general use, it is 'the middle point or part, the middle or midst of anything', as in 'Full in the centre of the grove' (Addison). 'The puniness of man in the centre of a cruel and frowning universe'. But one would not say 'in the centre of the road'. *Middle* applies to time, whereas *centre* does not; and spatially, *middle* 'applies to mere linear extension … but *centre* does not. *Centre* …, more precise than *middle*. The *centre* of the floor is a definite point; the middle of the floor is the indefinite space around or near the centre.' The line constituting the *middle* of any geometrical figure or physical space must run through its *centre*; but whereas there is only one centre, there are many

middles – any point on the line stands in the middle – all according to the subject's position. In May 1938, a certain newspaper, with unconscious humour, related that 'Colonel Woodhouse sat in the centre of a long table and on either side of him were officials of the Board.' One feels rather uncomfortable about 'centre' for 'middle' in '[The ships] ran down towards the islands; a brief order from the Admiral corrected the course a trifle to allow for the leeway the clumsy ship was making and which was carrying her a trifle away from the exact centre of the passage' (C. S. Forester, *The Earthly Paradise*, 1940). In military phraseology, however, *centre* is 'the main body of troops occupying the space between the two wings'; cf. political use of centre (mostly: *OED*).

centre round for 'to gather, or to be arranged around a centre' is ungrammatical, though often used by respectable writers. To *centre on* is correct. So are *centre in*, *be centred in*, but these imply an exact position or precise point. Also one can say that a thing is 'centred at' such and such a place, when the thing's *centre* is situated or has been placed in that locality. But one cannot with grammatical propriety (nor, for that matter, with good sense) speak of *centre about* or *(a)round*, *be centred about* or *(a)round*.

century is not always synonymous with *hundred years*, as is seen in 'The connexion between the law and medicine, although it has reached its fullest development only during the past century, is by no means new' (Nigel Morland, *Conquest of Crime*, 1937). Here, obviously, 'past hundred years' would be better. 'During this century' would certainly mean 'since 1900'.

cerebellum and **cerebrum** are ignorantly confused. *Cerebrum* is, loosely, the whole brain, 'the chief organ of mind'; *cerebellum* is 'the mass of nervous matter forming the posterior part of the brain, and looked upon as the centre of the higher order of combined actions' (*OED*).

ceremonial (adj.); **ceremonious.** The former corresponds to the noun *ceremonial*, as in 'ceremonial dress'; it also = 'of the nature of a ceremony or rite; ritual, formal'; hence, 'relating to or involving the formalities of social intercourse'. *Ceremonious* is obsolete in the sense 'ritual, formal'; of sacrifices, shows, displays, it means 'full of ceremony; showy'; as a synonym of *ceremonial*, 'relating to the formalities of social intercourse', it is obsolescent; its prevailing current sense is (of persons) 'given to ceremony; punctilious'. *Ceremonial*, therefore, is now applied only to things; *ceremonious* to both persons and things (*OED*).

certain. *A certain* is sometimes employed uselessly, as in 'Upon the other hand, the Inspector's feeling for "The Wallflower" was, perhaps, more than anything a certain admiration for an adversary who combined keen brain with utter fearlessness' (John G. Brandon). See also COMPARATIVES, FALSE.

cession (yielding, surrender) and **cessation** (end, ending) are occasionally confused. Do not confuse *cession* with *session*.

Ceylon. See **Sinhalese.**

chairman is now unpopular with feminists, though the word has often been applied to women, as in the form of address 'Madam Chairman'. The alternatives are *chairperson* or simply *chair*, as in 'Address your remarks to the chair'; but whatever choice you make becomes inevitably a statement of your views on this sensitive subject. See SEXISM.

change from and **change to** are often confused. 'A pleasant change *from* something *to* something else' is correct; 'Comfort is a pleasant change *to* discomfort' is incorrect.

chaperon is correct, **chaperone** incorrect. The careless are misled by the pronunciation (-ōn). [*Webster's*: 'The form *chaperone* is often used for a woman chaperon.']

character is much wider than **reputation;** the former includes the latter term and may be used as a synonym for it, as in 'His character for sanctity' (Freeman) (*OED*).

character, of a (stated), is verbose for the simple adjective. 'These goods are of a dangerous character' = These goods are dangerous. See ABSTRACT NOUNS.

character of. See PREPOSITIONS WRONGLY USED.

characterized by, be. Verbose for *be* or *have* (or *possess*) or *show* (or *display*). Thus 'His verse is characterized by obscurity' = His verse is obscure; 'The idea is characterized by stupidity' = The idea lacks sense or is stupid.

charge. To *charge* a person *with* (a crime or even a fault) is to *accuse* him or her of it; *charge*, though synonymous with *accuse*, is more formal. Only the former can be used absolutely, as in 'It has been charged that Coleridge appropriated the ideas of Lessing' (*OED*).

charisma, charismatic. See VOGUE WORDS.

chart is obsolete in the general sense 'map'. In current use, it is short for *sea-chart*, or is a map for navigation by air; it is used in certain technical senses, as in *magnetic chart, temperature chart, barometric chart*; where there is not a map but a graph, *graph* is displacing *chart*; hence it may be used for 'a sheet bearing information of any kind arranged in a tabular form' (*OED*).

Charta, Magna. See **Magna Carta.**

cheap price; dear price. Use *low price* and *high price*. To buy goods at a low price is to *buy* them *cheap*; *buy cheaply* is to do business at a low cost of buying.

check is the American form of *cheque*.

cheery is more positively lively than *cheerful*, which might mean merely 'contented'.

cherub has the pl. *cherubim* when it means an angel, but *cherubs* for beautiful chubby children.

chief. See COMPARATIVES, FALSE; *chiefest* is a literary antique.

child. See **infant**.

childish; childlike. *Childlike* is 'like a child'; (of qualities, actions) 'characteristic of a child', as in 'To place a childlike trust in Providence' (Southey), 'childlike simplicity'; it is usually a favourable adjective, whereas *childish* is usually unfavourable with sense 'puerile', '*too* childlike', e.g.

> What cannot be avoided,
> 'Twere childish weakness to lament
> (Shakespeare),

'He's becoming childish', 'Don't be so childish!' (based on *OED*).

Chinese. See **Jap.**

chiropody; chiropractic. The former is 'the art of treating corns, warts, defective nails, etc., on feet or hands'; now, generally restricted to the feet. The practitioner is a *chiropodist*.

Chiropractic is 'manipulation of the spinal column as a method of curing disease'; the practitioner is a *chiropractor*.

In these words *chiro* is a combining-element = 'manual', 'of the hand'.

choice (n.). See **alternative** (adj.). Avoid *choice* as an adjective, for it is commercialese.

chord, for the string (or *cord*) of a musical instrument, allowed by *OED* (but 'now only poetic'), may create confusion by its use in this sense, as in Tennyson, *Locksley Hall*:

> Love took up the harp of Life, and
>   smote on all its chords with
>   might,
> Smote the chord of Self, which,
>   trembling, passed in music out of
>   sight.

If 'chords' in the first line are the harp-strings, what is 'chord' in the second? The *string* cannot 'pass … out of sight'. Yet if we are to understand 'chords' as harmonious combinations of notes (as in 'I struck one chord of music like the sound of a great Amen', 'The Lost Chord', famous song by Sullivan), it is obvious that one does not strike *on* them; nor even in this sense can the chord be said to 'pass out of sight': it is the 'Self' of which the chord is the expression that does so.

It is likely that the confusion in this case was caused by Tennyson's ignorance of music (WB).

chorography. See **topography**.

Christian name is inferior to *given name*, for what are non-Christians to make of *Christian*? **Forename** and **first name** are other possibilities.

Christmas is now generally used in Britain instead of *Christmastide* or *Christmastime* (24–26 December); 25 December is *Christmas Day*, but formerly it was simply *Christmas*. [In American usage, *Christmas Holidays*, *Christmas Season*, *Christmas Day* are current. *Christmas* alone may mean 25 December or the week or ten days of the 'holidays' or 'season'.]

The abbreviation *Xmas* should not be used in formal contexts, and the pronunciation *Exmas* is an abomination.

chronic. As applied to diseases, *chronic* = 'lingering', 'inveterate', and is the opposite of *acute*; derivatively, then it = 'continuous, constant'. The sense 'severe' or 'bad' is slangy. The variant *chronical* is obsolescent and unnecessary.

cicada and **cicala.** The former is the usual, the English form; *cicala* is the Italian form which is coming to be Anglicized. [The term *locust* is common in the USA for the cicada.]

cinema. See **motion pictures**.

Cingalese. See **Sinhalese**.

CIRCUMLOCUTION. See TAUTOLOGY.

circumlocution. See **locution**.

circumstances, in the and **under the.** Certain newspaper editors recommend the one and forbid the use of the other (*under the circumstances*). If one turns to *OED* one finds that both phrases are correct but that they have different functions: '*In the circumstances* is the phrase to use when mere situation is to be expressed; *under the circumstances* when one's action is affected by the circumstances' – and that is usually the sense to be conveyed.

cite and **quote.** One may *cite* or *quote* a passage, a book, an author; for book and author, if only the title or the name is mentioned, it is better to use *refer to* or *mention* or *adduce*. It would be a convenience if *quote* were restricted to 'repeating the actual words', and *cite* to 'referring to the words (i.e. to the passage), the book, or the author': but usage has, so far, refused to yield to the need for precision.

city and **town.** *City* is correctly applied only to a town that has been created a city by charter; the presence of a cathedral does not, as often supposed, make a city, nor has every city a cathedral. In general, a *city* is larger, more important than a town; but usage differs in different countries. Idiom decrees that 'we go to town, but we go to *the* city. We live in town or live in *the* city. We leave town but leave *the* city' (Weseen). In England, *Town* = London, and *the City* (short for *the City of London*) is 'that part of London which is situated within the ancient boundaries' and esp. 'the business part ... in the neighbourhood of the Exchange and Bank of England, the centre of financial and commercial activity' (*OED*, *q.v.* for admirable historical accounts of *city* and *town*).

claim is catachrestic when used for *assert*, *contend*, or *maintain*, constructed with *that* ..., as in 'He claims that this is true', He claims that he was absent', 'He claims that it would be better to ...'. *Claim to be* is not wrong, but it is to be used with care; 'This book claims to be superior to the other' would read less oddly in the form, 'The

author of this book contends that it is superior to the other' (*OED*).

clang – **clanged** – **clanged**; **cling** – **clung** – **clung**.

CLARITY. The opposite of OBSCURITY, *q.v.*

class, as in 'He's no class', is an invidious colloquialism. [The phrase *no class*, when it occurs in American usage, is a vulgarism or 'illiteracy'.]

classic for 'important – or, the most important – event' is overdone by writers in sports and games.

Classical and **classic.** The former refers to the Greek and Latin Classics; the latter to the accepted literary works in other languages; or to the qualities thereof. In addition, *classical* is used of what was outstanding in its day, but is now superseded, as with the 'chemical physics' of Newton which preceded relativity and quantum theory. In the visual arts, Classicism is contrasted with Romanticism; in music, with popular or folk music.

Classic may mean 'outstanding', as in 'a classic example of misplaced confidence', or 'typical', as in 'a classic case of pneumonia'. When used of clothes, it means 'timelessly simple and elegant'.

classified into classes. See TAUTOLOGY.

cleanly = 'habitually clean' and (of things) 'habitually kept clean'; *clean*, therefore, is not to be used in these senses, the only ones now possessed by *cleanly*. The same applies to *cleanliness* and *cleanness*.

cleanse should be reserved for moral, spiritual, religious, ceremonial (or ritual) cleaning. But since it conveys the idea of 'purity', the word is widely used of such products as scouring powders and skin creams.

cleave. (1) 'to hew asunder, to split': preterite, *cleaved* or *clove* or *cleft*; past ppl. *cleaved* or *cleft*; ppl. adj., *cleft* ('a cleft stick') and *cloven* ('the cloven hoof').

(2) 'To adhere *to*': preterite, *cleaved* or *clove*; past ppl., *cleaved*.

clench and **clinch.** *Clench* is 'to fix securely, make fast', but in reference to nails, *clinch* is more usual, as in 'The girder which was clinched into the plaintiff's party wall' and 'to clinch the nails'. One either *clenches* or *clinches* a matter, affair, argument, bargain, but one *clenches* one's fist, fingers, jaw, lips, or, fig., one's nerves. In the sense 'to grip, to grasp firmly, to hold firmly in one's grasp', *clench* is used, as in 'Men who clench with one hand what they have grasped with the other' (Coleridge). *Clinch* is a later variant of *clench* (*OED*).

CLERGYMAN'S DICTION IN THE CHURCH OF ENGLAND. The following passage, caustically true of many clerics, occurs in Ernest Raymond's *Mary Leith*, 1931 (Part I, ch. iii): '"All", when Mr Broadley was in high emotional state, showed a strange tendency to become "ull" – "Brethren, we shall ull now rise and sing a hymn"; the holy Apostles, on the crest of the wave of very strong feeling, changed most distinctly into "The holy Aparcels, O Lord"; and at times – at really stirring times – "Lord" enriched and strengthened itself into something very like "Lorder".' This passage is preceded by an equally pertinent one on cleric clichés. [It is often difficult for Americans to appreciate the British re-spelling to indicate peculiarities of pronunciation. In British Standard English, *r* is not pronounced after vowels; therefore 'Aparcels' = '*a* p ä s'ls' and 'Lorder' = 'l ô d *e*' (i.e. there is a perceptible vowel sound after the *d*, or at least there is perceptible plosion).]

clever, 'good-natured, amiable', is an American colloquialism; as 'well, fit in health', it is Australian slang, from English dialect.

clew and **clue.** As 'an indication, a "key" to a puzzle or a problem', *clew*, formerly common in general English, is now chiefly an American spelling. This sense derives from *clew*, 'a ball of thread' – esp. as used in the legend of the Cretan Labyrinth. The nautical term is *clew*.

CLICHÉ. 'As to clichés, I daresay we are all in agreement. Haste encourages them, but more often they spring from mental laziness. I have, however, heard their use in football reports defended on the ground that the public expects them, and would feel lost without them. I may be wrong but I don't believe it' (Frank Whitaker in an address to the Institute of Journalists, 13 Dec. 1938). (For the nature, kinds, origins of clichés – for a study and a glossary – see my *A Dictionary of Clichés*, 1940; 4th edition, revised, 1950.)

'It was wonderful ... And most wonderful of all are words, and how they make friends with one another, being oft associated, until not even obituary notices do them part' (O. Henry, *Whirligigs*, 1910).

'There is no bigger peril either to thinking or to education than the popular phrase' (Frank Binder, *Dialectic*, 1932).

A cliché is an outworn commonplace; a phrase (or virtual phrase) that has become so hackneyed that scrupulous speakers and writers shrink from it because they feel that its use is an insult to the intelligence of their auditor or audience, reader or public. 'A coin so battered by use as to be defaced' (George Baker). They range from fly-blown phrases (*explore every avenue*), through soubriquets that have lost all point and freshness (*the Iron Duke*), to quotations that have become debased currency (*cups that cheer but not inebriate*), metaphors that are now pointless, and formulas that have become mere counters (*far be it from me to* ...). See also SIMILES, BATTERED.

client and **customer.** As 'a dependant', *client* is obsolescent; it now = 'one who goes to a lawyer, one who has an advocate'; hence, 'one who employs the services of a professional man or woman'. In relation to tradesmen, the correct term is *customer.* and what's wrong with *customer*, anyway? (*OED*, *q.v.* for several highly specialized senses.) See also **patron.**

climactic and **climatic; climacteric(al).** *Climactic* = 'of or pertaining to or resembling a climax' (an ascending series or scale); *climatic* = 'of or pertaining to climate'. *Climacteric* is 'constituting or pertaining to a *climacter* or a critical period in human life', as in 'climacteric period', 'a climacteric year'; hence, 'constituting a crisis or an important epoch', as in 'This age is as climacteric as that in which he lived' (Southey) (*OED*).

climate, clime, and **weather.** *Clime* is archaic, and poetic for *climate*. *Climate* has two senses: 'a region considered in relation to its weather or to its atmospheric conditions' (obsolescent); 'a country's or region's weather and atmospheric conditions, esp. as these affect life – human, animal, vegetable'. *Climate* has been neatly defined as 'the sum and average of weather', *weather* as 'the atmospheric condition of a particular time and place'. Thus, 'In such a climate as that of Britain, there is no weather – only specimens of weather' (based on *OED*).

climate. See VOGUE WORDS.

climb by itself means 'ascend', so that *climb down* is as necessary as *climb through* or *climb in*. But *climb up* is tautological for *climb* if *climb* is transitive; if it is intransitive, *up* is obviously necessary when the verb is not used absolutely.

clime. See **climate**.

clinch. See **clench**.

cling. See **clang**.

clone. See VOGUE WORDS.

close and **conclude**. See **conclude and close**.

close and **shut**. *Close* is the more general verb, '*shut* being properly only a way of closing; hence the former is generally used when the notion is that of the resulting state, rather than the process', the process demanding rather *shut* than *close*. Although one either *closes* or *shuts* a door, an eyelid, the distinction just made holds good:

properly, therefore, one *shuts* the door and then it is *closed*; one *shuts* one's eyelids and then one's eyes are *closed*. To say that 'The British Museum Library is shut up in the first week of May every year' is loose and colloquial for *is closed* (*to the public*) (*OED*). But *shut* is the word for preventing access or escape, as in 'He shut the dog in the kitchen.'

close down (a shop, a business); 'His shop closed down.' *Close* (*closed*) is sufficient, except nautically (of hatches). The same applies to *close up*, except in certain technical contexts – military, architectural, geographical. In short, make sure that *down* or *up* is necessary before you use it.

close proximity is tautological for *proximity*. For *in close proximity to*, say *close to* or *near*, according to the context.

cloture is an American word for the closure of a debate. But the British *closure* is much to be preferred, even in the parliamentary sense.

clove, cloven. See **cleave**.

clue. See **clew**.

COCKNEY speech is not itself slang, although it has certain slang words of its own. It is an urban dialect; no less a dialect than that of Devonshire or Yorkshire. The best book on the entire subject is Julian Franklyn's *The Cockney* – history, character, sociology, speech.

cocoa-nut, coco(nut). See **cacao** ...

coed. In British use, a coeducational school. In America, a girl attending such an establishment.

cognizance of, to take, is officialese for *notice* or *heed*.

cognomen is incorrect when it is used for 'given (or Christian) name', for 'full name' or for 'nickname'. For 'surname' it is not incorrect, but it is an objectionable Latinism. Correctly and impeccably it means 'the last of the three names by which a Roman of good family was designated' (*Nuttall's Standard Dictionary*).

cold glass of water is incorrect for a glass of cold water.

collect together is tautological for *collect* (or *put together*), for *collect* means 'gather together'. To apply *collect* to a single object is loose – though pardonable when it is intended facetiously.

COLLECTIVE NOUNS; when singular and when plural. Such collective nouns as can be used either in the singular or in the plural (*family, clergy, committee, Parliament*) are singular when unity (a unit) is intended; plural, when the idea of plurality is predominant. Thus, 'As the clergy are or are not what they ought to be, so are the rest of the nation' (Jane Austen), where *clergy = members of the clergy*; 'Is the family at home?', i.e. the family as a whole, a unit, but 'The family are stricken with grief at father's death', where the various members (other than father) are affected; 'The committee of public safety is to deal with this matter', but 'The Committee of Public Safety quarrel as to who its next chairman should be'; 'Parliament rises (*or*, goes into recess) at the beginning of August', where MPs are viewed as one body, but 'Parliament differ over the question of war', where the differences of opinion are emphasized; set 'The club is to be closed down at the end of the year' over against 'The club all know that he is a disappointed man' (De Quincey); 'Our army was in a sad plight' but 'The military were called out'; 'The majority is thus resolved' but 'The majority are going home.'

Collective nouns include proper names; 'Pakistan (i.e. the team) are just going in to bat'; 'Volvo (i.e. the company) have raised their prices.'

It is important to preserve consistency here between singular and plural in the use of pronouns as well as verbs. 'The family is well and send their regards' is wrong. Note also the choice between 'a jury *which* is' and 'a jury *who* are'.

[American writers are more reluctant than the British to pluralize collective nouns.]

COLLOQUIALISMS. 'The colloquial' – 'Colloquialisms' – is the name applied to that large tract of English which lies between Standard English and slang; it is of a status higher than that of slang, and, at its highest, it is scarcely distinguishable from familiar English (informal Standard English). 'Every educated person has at least two ways of speaking his mother tongue. The first is that which he employs in his family, among his familiar friends, and on ordinary occasions. The second is that which he uses in discoursing on more complicated subjects, and in addressing persons with whom he is less intimately acquainted. … The difference between these two forms consists, in great measure, in a difference of vocabulary' (Greenough and Kittredge, *Words and Their Ways in English Speech*, 1902). Other and frequent features are a syntax so flexible as to become at times ungrammatical, a fondness for sentences with a single verb, the omission of *I* at the beginning of a sentence or a clause. A rapid leaping from one subject to another, and the use of words and phrases that, unintelligible or at best obscure in print, are made both clear and sometimes arresting by a tone or a gesture, a pause or an emphasis. 'The basis of familiar words must be the same in Standard as in colloquial English, but the vocabulary appropriate to the more formal occasion will include many terms which will be stilted or affected in ordinary talk. There is also considerable difference between familiar and dignified language in the manner of utterance' – in pronunciation and enunciation. 'In conversation, we habitually employ such contractions as *I'll, don't, won't, it's, we'd, he'd* … which we should never use in public speaking unless with set purpose, to give a marked colloquial tinge to what one has to say' (Greenough and Kittredge, *op. cit.*).

Colloquialisms, like familiar and spoken English in general (of which it is the more lowly and racy part), vary tremendously from class to class, set to set, group to group, family to family, individual to individual, and even, according to the individual's mood or aspiration, from one *alter ego* to another. 'His social experience, traditions, and general background, his ordinary tastes and pursuits, his intellectual and moral cultivation are all reflected in each man's conversation. ... But the individual speaker is also affected by the character of those to whom he speaks. ... There is naturally a large body of colloquial expressions which is common to all classes ... but each class and interest has its own special way of expressing itself. The average colloquial speech of any age is ... a compromise between a variety of [vocabularies]' (H. C. K. Wyld's *History of Modern Colloquial English*).

The colloquial is difficult to confine within practicable limits: and that difficulty is made none the easier by the fact that, as Henry Bradley once remarked, 'at no period ... has the colloquial vocabulary and idiom of the English language been completely preserved in the literature' or even in the dictionaries. 'The homely expressions of everyday intercourse ... have been but very imperfectly recorded in the writings of any age'; in the 20th century, however, they have been far more fully and trustworthily recorded than in any earlier period. In the United States of America, the border-line between colloquialism and slang, like that between slang and cant, is less clearly marked than in Britain: but the general principles of differentiation remain the same.

It is far more possible today than it was in the past to study the spoken language generally, owing to the existence of a vast body of recordings of spontaneous speech.

collusion should not be used of favourable or neutral association or co-operation, for it implies a secret understanding, a pre-concerted plan, for an illicit, illegal, or evil purpose. Do not, therefore, employ *collusion* as a synonym of *co-operation*. – Only the semi-literate confuse it with *collision*, 'a violent encounter of a moving body with another body, whether moving or stationary'.

colossal is an adjective that is overdone by undiscriminating writers (and speakers). Even so good a writer as Louis Bromfield falls into this error in *The Strange Case of Miss Annie Spragg*.

coloured. See **black.**

combat and **contest.** A *combat* is a fight, a struggle between enemies; a *contest* may be merely a competition, and is often between neutrals or friends.

combine (n.) is a specific kind of commercial combination and must not be used for any other sort.

combine (v.) for *coordinate* is careless, for the former does not comport the quite unmistakable and very particular senses of the latter: 'to place or class in the same order, rank, or division'; 'to place or arrange (things) in proper position relatively to one another and to the system of which they form parts'; 'to bring into proper combined order in accordance with a stated law, rule, or arrangement'; (v.i.), 'to act in combined order to ensure a specific result' (*OED*). *Combine together* is a manifest tautology, far too often used by the unreflecting.

come and **go.** Of their use, Alford writes: 'We say of a wrecked ship that she *went* to pieces; but of a broken jug that it *came* to pieces. Plants *come up*, *come* into flower, but *go* to seed ... The sun *goes* in behind a cloud and *comes* out from behind it. But we are not consistent in speaking of the sun. He is said to *go down* in the evening; but never to *come up* in the morning.' But what about Coleridge's

The sun came up upon the right,
Out of the sea came he?

Idiom is paramount, as we see in *come loose* (cf. the slang *come unstuck*) and *go to pieces* (of a person); (of events) *come about*, but *so it went* (happened).

come in contact (with) should be *come into contact (with)*.

comic; comical. In current usage, only *comic* = 'belonging, or proper, to comedy' (opposite to tragedy, in the dramatic sense) as in 'comic opera'; but *comical* is more usual in the nuances 'mirth-provoking, humorous, funny; laughable, ludicrous' and is used particularly of the unintentionally funny, as in 'a comical seriousness'. *Comical* alone has the colloquial sense, 'odd, strange; queer'; and *comic* that of 'comic actor', or *comedian* (*OED*). [In the USA, *the comics*, or *the funnies*, is displacing *the funny paper* as a name for the infantile stories told in consecutive cartoons, which appear as a separate section of the Sunday newspapers.] See **-ic and -ical.**

coming. See CONJUNCTIONS, DISGUISED.

commander-in-chiefs is incorrect for *commanders-in-chief.*

commence, in its ordinary meaning of *begin*, is a wholly unnecessary word and its use is to be discouraged. *Commence* is more formal, and it should be reserved as a continuation of Anglo-French use; in association with law, official procedure, ceremonial, church service, (grave) combat. See esp. *OED.* [*Commence* in circumstances where *begin* or *start* would be more suitable is not uncommon in American usage, especially in the South and West. Perhaps it was once a genteelism but it is idiomatic today.]

commencement, in the. At the beginning; at first.

comment to. See PREPOSITIONS WRONGLY USED.

COMMERCIALESE. See at OFFICIALESE.

committed. See VOGUE WORDS.

common, basically 'belonging equally to more than one', 'possessed or shared alike by both or all (the persons or things in question)', as in 'The common ruin of king and people' (Burke), 'two triangles with a common base'; hence, 'belonging to all mankind alike', as in 'The higher attributes of our common humanity' (Nettleship); arising from or closely connected with those two senses are these others – 'belonging to the community at large, or to a specific community; public', 'free to be used by all alike; public', 'of general application; general', as in 'common notions', and 'belonging to more than one as a result or sign of co-operation or agreement; joint, united', esp. *to make common cause with*: – all these are excellent English. Good English also are the following senses; but, as they are apt to cause ambiguity, they should be displaced by: 'ordinary'; 'frequent'; 'undistinguished'; 'of low degree'; 'mean, of little value'; (of persons or their qualities) 'unrefined, vulgar' (*OED*).

COMMONPLACES. See CLICHÉ.

communicate; communication. If all you mean is *write, tell*, a *note* or a *letter*, then say so.

company, 'guests collectively; one or more persons invited or entertained' (*OED*), is not a colloquialism, but familiar SE, as in 'We do not often have company.'

COMPANY terms or names (e.g. a *flock* of sheep, a *herd* of cattle). See SPORTS TECHNICALITIES.

comparative, like *relative* (and the same holds for their adverbs), is often used where comparison has been neither stated nor implied. See also COMPARATIVES, FALSE.

COMPARATIVE CLAUSES present few difficulties. There is often an ellipsis, as in 'You do not play cricket so (*or*, as) well as he', i.e. 'as he does'; 'It concerns you as much as me', i.e. 'as much as it does me'; 'He is shorter than I', i.e. 'than I am'. If the use of the subjective pronoun ('as he', 'than I') is felt to be too formal, and the objective pronoun ('as him', 'than me') too colloquial, the safe middle course is to spell it out as a full clause, which is always best if the objective pronoun would be ambiguous. 'She likes John more than me' might be taken to mean either 'than I do' or 'than she likes me'. But, as Dr Onions points out in *An Advanced English Syntax*, a relative pronoun after *than* is always in the accusative.

'And then there is Woolley, than whom I have never seen a more gracious batsman';

'Beelzebub ... than whom none higher sat' (Milton).

Note: 'He is as tall as me', 'She is as wise as him', and all other such *as* sentences are colloquial, not Standard English. [As C. C. Fries says, speakers of English have a feeling that when a verb does not follow a pronoun, the pronoun is probably in an objective relationship.]

COMPARATIVES, FALSE, and False Superlatives. There are certain adjectives which are uncomparable: which do not admit of *more* or *most* before them, *-er* or *-est* tacked on to them. They are absolute and, in this respect, unmodifiable. One can speak of *nearly* or *almost* or *not quite* 'infinite' or 'perfect' or 'simultaneous' or 'unique', but not of 'more infinite', 'more perfect', 'most simultaneous', 'most unique'.

Here is a short list of these uncomparable intransigents:

absolute
akin
all-powerful (see separate entry)
basic
certain (sure, convinced) (see separate entry)
chief
comparative
complete (see separate entry)
contemporary (see separate entry)
crystal-clear
devoid (see separate entry)
empty (see separate entry)
entire
equal
essential (see separate entry)
eternal
everlasting

excellent (see separate entry)
fatal (see separate entry)
final
fundamental
harmless
ideal (see separate entry)
immaculate
immortal
impossible (see separate entry)
incessant (see separate entry)
incomparable (see separate entry)
indestructible
inevitable (see separate entry)
inferior (see separate entry)
infinite (see separate entry)
innocuous (see separate entry)
invaluable (see separate entry)
invulnerable (see separate entry)

There are many such such adjectives in *in-*

main
major and *minor*
manifest
meaningless
mortal (see separate entry)
obvious
omnipotent (see separate entry)
omniscient
perfect (see separate entry)
possible (see **impossible**)
preliminary
primary
primordial
principal (see separate entry)
pure (see separate entry)
replete (see separate entry)
rife
sacrosanct (see separate entry)
simultaneous
sufficient (see separate entry)
superior
superlative
supreme
sure (convinced)

ultimate
unanimous
uncomparable (see separate entry)
unendurable
uninhabitable
unique (see separate entry)
universal
untouchable
    and other *un-* adjectives
utter, uttermost, utmost (*q.v.* at **utmost**)
vital
void
whole
worthless

Note, too, that the corresponding nouns are likewise uncomparable: it is folly to speak of 'the utmost absolute', 'absolute perfection', 'complete indestructibility', 'partial universality', and so forth. The same restriction applies to such nouns as *acme*. 'The acme of comfort' is permissible, but 'the utter acme of comfort' is not merely absurd but weak; 'the omnipotence of God' is dignified, but 'the omnipotence of the President' is demonstrably false.

So too of the adverbs corresponding to the adjectives listed above. 'Utterly exhausted' may be a fact, whereas 'too utterly done up' is a slangy misstatement. [Many of the best American grammarians are more tolerant than Mr Partridge of 'false comparatives and superlatives'. Some of these are illogical, some are not; almost all of them occur occasionally in the writings of the wise and judicious.]

compare and **contrast.** See **contrast and compare.**

compare for **liken.** *Compare* is commonly used in this sense, though comparison implies difference as well as similarity. When *compare* = *liken*, it is followed by *to*. Thus, in Shakespeare's 'Shall I compare thee to a summer's day?', meaning 'to state or observe a likeness', the substitution of *with* for *to* would change the sense to 'to set up a comparison'.

compare to; compare with. See the preceding entry.

For other senses and nuances, the rulings of *OED* are these: 'To mark or point out the similarities and differences of; to collocate or juxtapose, in order to note the differences and similarities': *with*, as in 'Property, compared with personal ability, stands for more in England than elsewhere': but *to* is not wrong, though it should be avoided: moreover, one can *compare* two or more things *together*. Intransitively, *compare* = 'to bear comparison, to vie or rival', always takes *with*, as in 'As athletes, men cannot ... compare with ... monkeys' (Jevons).

compendious may be applied to something that is *briefly* comprehensive, for its meaning is 'compact', 'concise', 'summary', 'succinct'; but *comprehensive* is regarded as catachrestic when careless writers, ignorant of the history of the word, use it in the sense 'containing much in small compass'. Properly employed, *comprehensive* = 'extensive', 'embracing many things', 'widely sympathetic'.

competence is a fairly high degree of ability (in performance), but it falls short of *talent*, far short of *genius*: the following, therefore, rings oddly: 'He showed ... extraordinary military competence' (John Gunther, *Inside Asia*, 1939). [*Competence*, to the American reader, is more suggestive of performance and may therefore be a stronger word than *talent* for Gunther's purpose.]

compilation is occasionally misused for *symposium* and for *collection* (of essays or articles). It is used properly of a (literary) work 'built up of materials from various sources' (*OED*) and not of original compositions.

complacence and **complaisance** are easily confused; the former is *self-satisfaction*, the latter *obligingness, politeness* (*COD*). The adjectives are *complacent and complaisant. Complaisance* and *complaisant* may suggest an excessive desire to avoid trouble.

complement, -ary. See **compliment, -ary.**

complement and **supplement.** See at **supplement.**

complete is uncomparable when it means 'having all its parts'. See COMPARATIVES, FALSE. When it means 'thorough', however, it is reasonable to speak of 'a more complete survey'. See also:

complete; entire; whole. The need to distinguish these terms was brought sharply to my notice when, in so competent a writer as Inez Irwin, I came upon this instance of *whole* misused for *entire*: 'The whole investigations of this murder-case rests [sic] on my shoulders'; as Wilson Benington remarked to me, *whole* is now 'a singular adjective'; it is used only with a singular noun, except in certain technical contexts.

complete: 'Having all its parts or members' ('The preface is complete in itself', Ruskin); (of a period) 'whole'; (of an action) 'concluded'; 'realized in its full extent' ('A complete historical cycle'), 'thorough'; 'without defect'; (of a person) 'fully equipped, endowed, or trained' ('a complete horseman').

entire: 'With no part excepted'; 'constituting a whole'; (of a quality, state of feeling, condition; fact, action); 'realized in its full extent, thorough' ('Entire sincerity is a virtue'), 'thoroughly of the character described' ('An entire believer in Christianity'); 'unbroken, unimpaired, intact, undiminished' ('Even after this ordeal his faith remained entire'); (in science) 'wholly of one piece, continuous throughout, undivided ('The calyx is entire'), of unbroken outline'; (in Law) 'unshared' (*entire tenancy*).

whole: (of man or animal) 'uninjured, unwounded'; (of inanimate objects) 'unbroken, intact, untainted'; 'having all its parts or elements' – cf. *complete* and *entire* – 'full, perfect'; 'all, all of', the prevailing current sense, used only attributively and preceding the noun ('The whole Anglican priesthood', Macaulay); with rhetorical emphasis ('Whole libraries are filled with records of this quest'); 'undivided' ('apples baked whole'); (in mathematics) 'integral,

not fractional'; 'unmixed, pure', as in *whole blood* and *whole holiday* (a full day's freedom from work) (*OED*).

complex; especially **inferiority complex.** See VOGUE WORDS.

compliment, -ary (flattering), is often confused with *complement, -ary* (in completion of).

COMPOSITION. To schoolchildren and freshmen, the word means an essay or a formal exercise in literary self-expression. A very common definition is – with slight variations – that of *OED*: 'The mode or style in which words and sentences are put together': but composition is, I think, best regarded as the mode of putting together not merely words in a sentence, and sentences in a paragraph, but also paragraphs in an essay or a chapter, and chapters in a book; it comprises, therefore, arrangement and ordonnance.

This work of mine, however, is not a manual of composition. But I should perhaps be shirking a duty – certainly I should be missing an opportunity – if I did not give a short list of at least some of the basically important or practically useful works.

A. Bain: *English Composition and Rhetoric*, 1887–8; old-fashioned, but, to the mature student, still useful and suggestive.

J. C. Nesfield: *Senior Course of English Composition*, 1903; like Leonard's book, it is less advanced than Canby's and Krapp's; but very sound.

J. C. Nesfield: *Errors in English Composition*, 1903.

H. W. & F. G. Fowler: *The King's English*, 1906 (but use latest edition).

*Joseph M. Thomas and others: *Composition for College Students*, 1922; an excellent formal presentation of the subject.

H. W. Fowler: *A Dictionary of Modern English Usage*, 1926; at the risk of appearing impertinent, I must emphasize the inestimable value and usefulness of this work.

*H. S. Canby: *Better Writing*, 1927.

*G. P. Krapp: *A Comprehensive Guide to Good English*, 1927.

*Sterling Leonard: *Juniors' Own Composition Book*, 1928.

*J. R. & V. P. Hulbert: *Effective English*, 1929.

EP: *English: A Course for Human Beings*, 1948 (4th edition, 1954).

G. H. Vallins, *Good English*, enlarged Library Edition, 1952, and *Better English*, ditto, 1955.

Sir Ernest Gowers: *The Complete Plain Words*, 1954 (but use latest edition).

Frederick T. Wood: *Current English Usage*, 1962 (but use latest edition).

S. Greenbaum and J. Whitcut, *Longman Guide to English Usage*, 1985.

John E. Kahn and others, *The Right Word at the Right Time*, 1985, and *How to Write and Speak Better*, 1991.

Note also the entries at **GRAMMAR** and **STYLE**.

But remember this: theory is very useful, both for the check and brake it applies and also for the suggestions it offers; nevertheless, the only way in which to learn to write is – to write. With the proviso that you cease from writing so soon as you become mentally stale or physically tired, write as much as you can on all sorts of subjects. Revise what you write; revise it carefully, but do not pace the floor in an agonized search for the right word, for in that stylistic agony, you may lose the inspiration and you probably will lose the thread of your discourse. There is no merit in costiveness: meagreness is a sour-grapers' preoccupation, the ideal of one-bookers. While you have the inspiration, the energy, the verve, the gusto: write! The letter is important; but let it wait on the spirit, and, above all, do not allow it to parch up the springs and wells of the spirit.

I do not mean that writers should think everything they write to be God-inspired and heaven-sent. It isn't. By all means let writers prepare themselves to write; let

* Indicates American works. And how good they are!

them study Fowler and Gowers and Kahn (they will benefit you enormously), but you must not be discouraged by their advice; from theory you must pass to practice. Having passed to practice, you should write, full steam ahead: revision should come after, not in the course of, composition. Any writer worth the name thinks out a theme beforehand in its broad outlines and in its order of development; you know, or should know, the goal towards which you are working, and how you will arrive there: but you do not stay 'the genial current of your soul' *while* you are writing.

Having written and having perhaps been severely criticized for your composition, your style, you should take advantage of the surcease from work to examine carefully your writing and to look again at Fowler and Hulbert and Wood. Where formerly you thought of them as talking pedantically or professionally in the air, as being merely impractical, you will, if you are modest, come to recognize that what they say is thoroughly sound and extremely useful.

comprehend. See **reprehend**.

comprehensive. See **compendious**.

comprehensive(ly), misused for *comprehensible* (*-bly*); **incomprehensive(ly)** for *incomprehensible* (*-bly*). 'All jabbering incomprehensively at the top of their powerful voices' (E. C. R. Lorac).

comprise and **constitute**. *Comprise*, 'to constitute, to compose', is rare and, I think, to be avoided, as in 'Ten dogs comprise the pack.' Whereas *constitute* = 'to form, to make up', as in 'Reading, writing, and arithmetic ... do not in themselves constitute an education' (Lubbock), *comprise* = 'to include', esp. in a treatise; 'to sum up' (e.g. 'to comprise much in a short speech'); 'to comprehend or include *under* or *in* a class or denomination'; (of a thing) 'to contain, as parts forming the whole; to consist of (certain specified parts)', as in 'The house comprises box-room, nine bed-rooms, bath-room, etc.'; and 'to embrace as its contents, matter, or subject', as in 'The word politics ... comprises, in itself, a difficult study' (Dickens) (*OED*).

compulsive and **compulsory.** *Compulsive* behaviour results from an inner compulsion, as in 'a compulsive liar'. *Compulsory* behaviour is enforced by someone else.

compute, computation. Mostly gobbledygook for to, an, *estimate*. But correct when used with reference to computers.

concensus. See **consensus.**

concerned about; concerned with. Respectively; anxious about; having an interest in or business with. Careless writers confuse them.

concerning. See CONJUNCTIONS, DIS-GUISED.

CONCESSIVE CLAUSES. Usually, the verb in concessive clauses is in the indicative; always, when the concessive verb implies a fact, as in '*Although you are poor*, you are happy' – or, where there is less emphasis on the concession, 'You are happy, *although you are poor*'; '*Though he talks so much*, he never says anything worth saying'; '*Young as he looked*, he was no fool'; '*Small though their army was*, the French fought bravely.'

In such concessive clauses as refer to future time and in such others as show an action in prospect or under consideration, it is possible, though old-fashioned, to employ the subjunctive mood (or its equivalent – *may* or *should* + infinitive); present-day writers often prefer the indicative, 'Though everyone *deserts* you, I shall (or, will) not' rather than 'Though everyone *desert* (or, *should desert*) you, I shall (or, will) not.'

In certain concessive clauses – '*Cost what it may* ...'. '*Be he* (or, *she*) *who he* (or, *she*) *may*, he (or, *she*) must see me' – the verb comes at the beginning: but, these clauses being in the nature of formulas, there is less danger of one's going wrong in them than of one's using them too much.

Here, as in comparative clauses, the concession may be elliptical: 'Though no player, he appreciated the finer points of lawn tennis' is merely 'Though he was no player ...'; cf. 'Though [they are] outnumbered, they are fighting to the death.' See especially C. T. Onions, *An Advanced English Syntax.*

conclude and **close** (a speech). To *close* it may connote merely to end it, esp. if one has nothing more to say; to *conclude it* (a more formal phrase) is to bring it to a predetermined or rhetorical end.

conclude, misused for *decide*, as in 'The matter must wait, and Stone concluded to go to bed' (Carolyn Wells). *To conclude*, to make a considered judgement, is followed by a clause: 'He concluded that resistance was futile.'

CONCORD, WRONG. See AGREE-MENT, FALSE.

concrete. See **cement.**

condemn and **contemn.** In ordinary usage, *condemn* is the right word except in literary (formal, lofty) Standard English and in the following, very precise senses of *contemn*: – I, (as applied to persons and personal feelings or characteristics) 'to despise, disdain, scorn, slight', as in 'I have done penance for contemning love' (Shakespeare), 'Not that your father's mildness I contemn' (Dryden), 'It lay in Deronda's nature usually to contemn the feeble' (George Eliot). – II, 'To treat (law, orders, pacts, customs; advice) with contemptuous disregard', as in 'Mr Cooper contemned my lord's order, and would not obey it' (Mrs Hutchinson, *c.* 1665), 'They ... contemned and violated the engagement of treaties' (James Mill) (*OED*).

condition, in a (stated), as in 'He was found in an intoxicated condition' = drunk. Verbosity: cf. the similar use of *character* and *nature*. See ABSTRACT NOUNS. It is inelegant, though common, to use *condition* for 'ailment, abnormality', as in 'suffering from a heart condition'.

CONDITIONAL CLAUSES have always caused trouble to the semi-educated and the demi-reflective; to the illiterate they give no trouble at all. Most well-educated or well-speaking persons have little difficulty.

The whole subject has been treated with the utmost clarity and an illuminating virtuosity of arrangement by Dr C. T. Onions in *An Advanced English Syntax*: on his much fuller exposition and from his far more numerous examples the following cursory presentation is based, the following instances drawn.

The vast majority of conditional sentences fall into one of two classes, these being determined by the form (and meaning) of the principal clause, thus:

Group I: Those sentences in which the principal clause speaks of what is, or was, or will certainly be (i.e. *not* of what would be or would have been), and in which the *if* clause states, or implies, no fact and no fulfilment. This is what grammarians call Open Condition, as in 'If you are right, I am wrong', which does not imply that you actually are right. It does not matter whether the tenses are present or past ('If you did that, you were wrong') or future ('If you do this, you will be wrong') – or mixed, as in 'If he did it, he is a fool', 'If you have forged a cheque, you will be ruined.' Nor does it matter what the mood of the principal clause: 'If I did that, forgive me!'; 'If I do that, may I die!'

Group II: Those sentences in which the principal clause speaks of what would be or would have been, and in which the *if* clause states, or implies, a negative. Grammarians call this: Rejected Condition, as in 'If wishes were horses, beggars would ride' (but wishes are not horses – 'much virtue in an *if*').

In this group, there is a special conditional form, as in 'If John were right, I should be wrong', to connote the remoteness of the supposition. See also **was or were.**

But most sentences in this group belong to two kinds:

(*a*) When the time referred to is the same in both clauses, we have:
Present. 'If he did this, he would sin' or 'If he were doing this, he would be sinning.'
Past. 'If he had done this (or 'Had he done this'), he would have sinned'; 'Had we done this, we should have let you know.'
Future. 'If he did this (or 'If he were to do this') he would sin.'

(*b*) When the time is not the same in both clauses, we get the sentence-types, 'If he had not done this, he would be happier now' (or 'If I had not done this, I should be ...') or 'I should (or 'He would') be happier now, if I (or, he) had not done this'; and 'If I were doing that now, I should not have been wounded' (or 'If he were doing that now, he would not ...') or 'I should not (or 'He would not') have been wounded, if I were (or 'If he were') doing that now.'

It is worth observing that in this group, the *if* clause has its action thrown back in time and has its grammatical mood readjusted (subjunctive for indicative).

There is also a not unimportant Group III: Here, there are conditional sentences in which, as in Group I, the principal clause does not state, nor imply, what would be or would have been, but in which the *if* clause not only indicates an action that is contemplated (under consideration) or planned but also connotes some degree of reserve on the part of – some reservation hinted by – the speaker. Here it is possible, though old-fashioned and formal, to employ the subjunctive mood. 'If this be true, we are all wrong' (but it is neither stated nor implied that the fact *is* known or even said to be true); 'Should this be true, we shall all be wrong' (but so far as our knowledge goes, we may be right).

In such sentences as '*Tell me a liar*, and I'll tell you a thief', '*Bid me discourse*, I will enchant thy ear' (Shakespeare), the italicized portions are virtual *if* clauses, i.e. they are disguised conditionals; but conditional clauses are generally introduced by *if* or *unless* (i.e. if not): of the former, many examples have already been given; an example of the latter is 'I shall do as you ask, unless you countermand your instructions.'

Other disguised conditionals are those in which *were I* is used instead of *if I were*, and *had I* instead of *if I had*, and *should it* for *if it should*: 'Should it be wet, you had better remain in London'; 'Had I gone, I should have regretted it'; 'Were it possible, he would gladly do it.'

Semi-disguised conditionals are of the following kinds: '*Provided* (*that*) he leaves immediately, I agree to the plan'; '*Supposing* (*that*) it does not turn out as you say, what compensation if any shall I get?', '*Supposing* it happened, what should you do?'; 'They were always prepared for the worst *in case* the worst should happen'; '*So long as* you hold fast to me, you'll be all right', where *so long as* is merely a rather colloquial synonym of *if only*.

Not disguised but elliptical are such conditional sentences as 'If inevitable, why complain?' = 'If it is (or, be) inevitable, why do you complain?'; 'If necessary, we'll take drastic steps to prevent it' = 'If it is (or, be) necessary ...'; 'Whether safe or unsafe, the bridge will have to be crossed' = 'Whether it is (or, be) safe or unsafe ...'.

The last examples illustrate the rule that alternative clauses of condition are ushered in by 'whether ... or'. This 'whether ... or' formula is simply a syntactical synonym of 'if ... or if': 'If the bridge is safe or if it is unsafe, it'll have to be crossed' is less convenient, and unidiomatic, for 'Whether the bridge is safe or unsafe ...'.

conducive of. See PREPOSITIONS WRONGLY USED. See also **conducive**.

conduct. See **decorum**.

conductive and **conducive**. *Conductive* is extant in only one sense, that (in Physics) of 'having the property of conducting heat, etc.; of or pertaining to conducting: esp. used of conductors of electricity'. An extension of this idea is 'conductive education', for those with motor disorders. *Conducive* (constructed with *to*, not with

of) = 'having the property of conducting or tending to (a specified end, purpose or result); fitted to promote or subserve', as in 'A treaty conducive to American interests'; also a noun, as in 'Walking is a great conducive to health.' The verb is *conduce to* (OED).

conduit is pronounced 'kŭnd'it' or 'kŏnd'it' (less fashionable); so is *Conduit* (*Street*). [In the USA, the usual pronunciations are 'kŏn'dit and 'kŏn'doo-it', the latter the pronunciation of the engineers and electricians who install *conduits*.]

confidant(e); confident. The latter is the adjective ('assured', 'trusting or trustful', 'bold'), the former the noun (feminine in *-e*) – 'a person either trusted or being habitually or professionally trusted with secrets'.

CONFUSED METAPHORS. See METAPHOR, Part II.

CONFUSED PARTICIPLES. See also FUSED PARTICIPLES. Here will be treated what are variously known as disconnected or dangling or misrelated participles, 'misrelated participles' being the commonest of the three designations. (Compare the misrelated gerund, *q.v.* at GERUND, last paragraph.)

On this matter, as on all that he treats in *An Advanced English Syntax*, Dr C. T. Onions is both explicit and helpful. 'Avoid the error of using a Participle which has no subject of reference in the sentence, or which, if referred to its grammatical subject, makes nonsense. This mistake is not uncommonly made when a writer intends to use the Absolute construction [as in "*This done*, we went home" and "The signal being given" – or "having been given" – "we set off"]. ... A sentence like the following is incorrect because the word to which the Participle refers grammatically is not that with which it is meant to be connected in sense: "*Born* in 1850, a part of his education was received at Eton." Correct thus: "*Born* in 1850, *he* received part of his education at Eton."'

Dr Onions cites the following additional examples:

Calling upon him last summer, he kindly offered to give me his copy. [Say: *When I called.*]

Being stolen, the Bank of England refused to honour the note. [Say: *It being stolen*; or better: *The note being stolen,* the Bank of England refused to honour it.]

Having left daughters only, the property was sold for the immense sum of £135,000 (Boswell, 1765). [Say: *He* or *she having left* ...]

Looking out for a theme, several crossed his mind. [Who was looking out? Not 'several'.]

Being a long-headed gentlewoman, I am apt to imagine she has some further designs than you have yet penetrated (*The Spectator,* 1711).

Compare the following error in Addison's 'Tory Fox-Hunter' essay, 'His heart misgave him that there were so many meeting-houses; but upon communicating his suspicions to me, I soon made him easy in that particular.'

Two examples not from Dr Onions's book: 'Completely surrounded by a deep wide moat, access to it was only possible by a brick bridge' (R. H. Mottram, *The Spanish Farm,* 1924); 'He knew he would fail unless he could discover a main theme to which everything he said to Merle would be related ... Lacking a main theme, she would be almost certain to guess that he was hiding something' (Claude Houghton, *Passport to Paradise,* 1944). 'Lacking' should refer to 'he', not to 'she' at all; the result is ambiguity and mental malaise.

As Dr Onions points out, this sort of error is easy to fall into when one has such ellipses as 'while fighting' (while they were fighting), 'though fighting' (though he was fighting), where a conjunction (e.g. *while, though*) is coupled with a participle: 'While fighting, a mist rendered the combatants indistinguishable'; 'Though fighting bravely, his defeat was imminent.'

The error, however, will be avoided by all those who bear in mind the simple rule

posited by that grammarian: 'The only case in which it is permissible to omit the subject in an Absolute Clause [or phrase], is when the unexpressed subject is indefinite (= one, people, French *on*).' Here are two of his examples:

Taking everything into consideration, our lot is not a happy one. [*Taking* = one taking, i.e. if one takes]. See also CONJUNCTIONS, DISGUISED.

These prayers are to be said *kneeling* [= the people kneeling].

CONFUSION. See AMBIGUITY.

confute. See **refute and deny.**

congenial, 'to one's taste or liking' (as in 'Controversies congenial to his temperament', 'a congenial task')'; 'suited to (the nature of a thing)', as in 'Transplanted to a congenial soil, the hitherto sickly plant thrived wonderfully'; 'kindred, sympathetic', as in 'We are congenial spirits', 'He had a character congenial with mine', 'Poetry and music are congenial.' It is not to be confused with *genial*, 'affable', 'cordial', 'kindly and easily accessible' (*OED*).

conjugal and **connubial.** The former = 'of, belonging to, appropriate to marriage, the married state, married persons', as in Milton's 'conjugal rights' and the Law's 'conjugal rights' (*Webster's*). *Connubial* is eruditely facetious in the sense 'pertaining to a husband or a wife', as in Barham's 'Provoking from connubial toes a hint'. Reserve it for the senses 'nuptial', 'matrimonial', as in 'connubial rites', 'the connubial state', 'connubial contracts' (Johnson) (*OED*).

CONJUNCTIONS, DISGUISED. The rules discussed at CONFUSED PARTICIPLES do not apply to certain -*ing* words which have in fact beome either conjunctions (introducing a clause) or prepositions (introducing a noun). There is surely no objection to *according to* ('according to Peter, it is unnecessary'); *allowing for* wastage; *assuming* you are right; *barring* accidents; *coming* down to details; *concerning* your problem; *considering* the

time; (not) *counting* the office staff; *depending* on the weather; *excluding/excepting*
John; *failing* that; *granted/granting* that it is
true; *including* the children; *knowing*
Edward; *owing to* the flood; *provided/pro-
viding* he pays; *regarding* your question; *seeing* that he is ill; strictly *speaking*; *supposing*
he came; *taking* everything into account;
talking of cricket; *touching* this matter.

Some such forms belong particularly to
bureaucratic jargon, as with '*arising* out of
this correspondence', '*referring* to your
letter', '*respecting* the damage', '*pending*
further discussion'. Scientific writers are
much addicted to the construction '*Using*
familiar techniques, the substance was then
analysed.'

In marginal cases, one should err on the
side of caution in using these forms:
replacing, perhaps, 'Looking into the
future' by 'When we look'; 'Judging by
the volume of traffic' by 'If we may judge';
'Following the lecture' by 'After the lecture'; and 'Putting it simply' by 'To put it
simply'. Cf. **due to.**

connection and **connexion.** See
-ection and -exion.

connotation, connote are sometimes
confused with *denotation, denote.* Make
quite sure that you know the difference in
meaning between these two pairs.

consensus (not *concensus*) is 'agreement in
opinion', esp. 'the collective unanimous
opinion of a number of persons'; therefore
consensus of opinion is, at the best, loose.
One can, however, speak of a *consensus of
MSS*, or a *consensus of evidence, testimony,
authority*: but with care.

consequent and **consequential.** The
former adjective = 'resulting', 'as a result',
'in the result', as in 'He made a seditious
speech in that stronghold of Toryism; the
consequent uproar was tremendous, the
subsequent proceedings, lively.' (*Subsequent* = 'after', 'following', 'ensuing'.) *Consequential* is obsolescent – and to be
avoided – as a synonym of *consequent*; in
Law, it = 'resulting indirectly', as in *consequential damages*; in general usage, it = 'self-

important', as in 'Pampered and consequential freedmen' (Farrar) and the colloquial 'He's a cocky and consequential little blighter' (*OED*).

consequent to. See PREPOSITIONS
WRONGLY USED.

consider for *to think, believe, hold the
opinion* is not strictly incorrect, but, in
these senses, it loses its proper meanings of
think over, ponder, meditate. Thus Eric
Partridge, *The French Romantics' Knowledge of English Literature*, 1924: 'He
[Chateaubriand] always bore a grudge
against Byron, whom he considered to
have plagiarised, etc.'

considerable is properly used of abstractions, as in 'considerable experience', or
'considerable numbers'. Do not use it
of concrete things. One may lose 'a considerable amount of blood' but not
'considerable blood'.

considering. See CONJUNCTIONS,
DISGUISED.

consist in and **consist of.** *Consist in* is, in
general, 'to have its being in'; specifically,
'to be comprised or contained in (actions,
conditions, qualities', or other things non-
material); 'to be constituted of', as in
'Moral government consists … in rewarding the righteous, and punishing the
wicked' (Butler, 1736), 'Not every one
can tell in what the beauty of a figure consists' (Jowett). *Consist of* is 'to be made up
– or, composed – of; to have as its constituent parts, or as its substance', as in
'Newton considered light to consist of
particles darted out from luminous bodies'
(Tyndall), 'An ordinary fence, consisting
of a ditch and a bank' (Edge) (*OED*).

consist of and **constitute.** 'A whole consists of parts; the parts constitute the
whole', as Weseen has concisely and
shrewdly noted. See also **comprise.**

consistently and **persistently.** The
former = 'uniformly'; 'without incongruity or absurdity', as in 'To act consistently, you must either admit Matter or

reject Spirit' (Berkeley); 'compatibly', as in 'consistently with my aims'.

Persistently = chiefly 'with continuously repeated action', as in 'My frequent applications have been persistently ignored' (*OED*). It carries the implication of infuriating perseverance.

Confusion between the adjectives is much less common.

constant, as applied to actions, processes, conditions = 'perpetual, incessant, continuous; continual, but with only such intermissions as do not break the continuity': 'The supply of water may be either intermittent or constant', 'In a state of constant flux', 'The constant ticking of a watch', 'Constant repetition of a phrase renders it nauseating' (*OED*).

constitute. See **comprise** and **consist of.**

constrain and **restrain.** To *constrain* is to compel or oblige (someone to do something); it may be used with a simple object, as in 'The love of Christ constraineth us'; as 'to enforce (an action)', which is an obsolescent sense; 'to confine forcibly, to imprison', now only literary. – To *restrain* is 'to hold back' (oneself or another), 'to impose a deterrent influence on', 'I restrained the madman from throwing himself in the river', 'Only fear restrained him' (based on *OED*).

constructive. See VOGUE WORDS.

consume is to *use up*, not to *use*. The basic sense of *consume* is 'to destroy'. As Weseen has put it, 'A fire consumes a house, but does not use it; a man uses air, but without consuming it [unless he is in a hermetically sealed chamber]; a man both uses and consumes food.'

contact (v.). If you feel that without this originally American synonym for 'to establish contact with' or, more idiomatically, 'get in(to) touch with' [a person], life would be too unutterably drear and bleak and 'grim', do at least say or write 'to contact a person', not *contact with*, as in John G. Brandon's 'I've questioned every CID man I've contacted with.' [Many Americans of the interbelligerent period felt that *contact* supplied a lively and energetic metaphor, as indeed it does, and the word was grossly overused. Extremes of fashion bring their own corrective, and *contact*, the great word of the era of sales promotion and consolidation, shows signs of retiring to its rightful place.]

contagious. See **infectious.**

contemn. See **condemn.**

contemporaneous and **contemporary.** Both = 'belonging to the same time or period; living, existing, or occurring at the same time', but the former is now applied mostly to things, the latter mostly to persons. There is, however, a further distinction that may – other things being equal – be held to overrule the preceding distinction: *contemporaneous* tends to refer to the past, *contemporary* to the present. Thus, 'Chatham and Johnson were contemporaneous, Thatcher and Major are contemporary'; as a noun, *contemporary* has to do duty for both of these adjectives. In other words *contemporary* and *contemporaneous* might profitably be made, not synonyms but distinctions: it would help the cause of clarity if *contemporary* were confined to the actual present, *contemporaneous* to past periods that are under consideration as present times in those past periods, as in 'The novels contemporaneous with Fielding are more leisurely than contemporary novels (are).' The chief modern sense of *contemporary*, however, is 'modern, current, present-day'. For *contemporary*, see also COMPARATIVES, FALSE.

contemptible, properly 'despicable', is, in educated use, obsolete as a synonym of *contemptuous*, 'full of contempt; disdainful, scornful'.

content (v.). One *contents* oneself *with*, not *by*, things or actions, as in 'He contented himself with imprisoning his opponents.'

contest. See **combat.**

contiguous. See **adjacent.**

continual and **continuous** must not be confused. The former is defined as 'constantly recurring', the latter as 'connected, unbroken: uninterrupted in time or sequence' (*COD*). Cf. **constant**.

continuance; continuation; continuity. *Continuance* is obsolete in the senses 'continuity' and 'continuation'; properly it is the noun both of *continue* (v.t.), i.e. 'prolonging' or 'maintaining', as in 'The continuance of the unending task of human improvement' (John Morley), and of *continue* (v.i.), esp. as 'the going on (of an action or process), the lasting or duration (of a condition or state)', as in 'The sole cause of the continuance of the quarrel' (Froude). *Continuity* is lit. and fig. 'connectedness, unbrokenness, uninterruptedness'; hence, also, 'a continuous whole'. *Continuation* is 'continued maintenance; resumption', also, 'that by which or in which anything is maintained or prolonged': 'A continuation of fine weather' combines these two ideas (*OED*).

Thus, one might speak of 'a continuation of last week's episode' of a serial. In film production, *continuity* is 'consistency, avoidance of discrepancy' between individual shots.

continue to say is ambiguous for *continue by saying*. 'Smith asserted that the world was always square, and he continued to say, "If not square, at least oblong".' He did not continue the latter statement; he went on to make it: it was the statement about squareness which he continued.

contrary and **opposite**. *Opposite* is stronger than *contrary*, and in Rhetoric, Dialectics, and Logic, there is a distinction. To adapt Fowler's admirable exposition (in *Modern English Usage*), we notice that *All humans are mortal* has as its contrary *Not all humans are mortal* (which is untrue); as its opposite, *No humans are mortal* (also untrue). The converse, by the way, is *All mortals are humans*. Likewise, *I hit him* has no opposite; but its contrary is *I did not hit him* and its converse is *He hit me*. See **converse**.

contrast and **compare**. To *compare* is to align the two (or more) sets of similarities and identities; to *contrast* is to align the two sets of differences and distinctions. In doing either, one is conscious of the other; whence that favourite type of examination question. 'Compare and contrast (e.g. Caesar and Napoleon).'

conversation. See **dialogue**.

converse, inverse, obverse, reverse. By far the most general of these terms is *reverse*, 'the opposite or contrary of something', as in 'His speech was the reverse of cheerful'; in coinage, *reverse* is the back of a coin, whereas *obverse* is the front (that side which bears the head or other principal design).

Except the last, these terms are technicalities of Logic and Dialectics: venturesome journalists and dare-all writers should employ them with care and discretion. The corresponding abstract nouns are *conversion, inversion, obversion*; the verbs are *convert, invert, obvert*.

In general a *converse* is 'a thing or action that is the exact opposite of another'; in Rhetoric it is 'a phrase or sentence derived from another by the turning about or transposition of two important antithetical members', thus the converse of 'the possession of courage without discretion' is 'the possession of discretion without courage'; in Logic, *converse* is 'the transposition of the subject and predicate of a proposition ... to form a new proposition by immediate inference', thus the converse of 'No A is B' is 'No B is A.' – For the relation of *converse* to *contrary* and *opposite*, see **contrary**.

Inverse: In general, it is 'an inverted state or condition; that which is in order or direction the direct opposite of something else': the inverse of ABC is CBA. In Logic, it is that form of immediate inference in which there is formed a new proposition whose subject is the negative of that of the original proposition.

Obverse: In general, it is 'the counterpart of any fact or truth'; in Logic, 'that form of immediate inference in which, by changing the quality, from one proposition another is inferred, having a contradictory predicate'.

These definitions come, either verbatim or slightly changed, from OED.

convince should not be used like *persuade*. One convinces a person *of* something, or convinces a person *that* something is true, but one cannot correctly convince a person *to do* something.

co-operation. See **collusion.**

coordinate. See **combine.**

coppice and **copse** are partly synonymous. Both can mean 'a small wood or thicket consisting of underwood and small trees grown for the purpose of periodical cutting'. To *coppice* young trees is to cut them back periodically to stimulate growth of young shoots. In addition, *copse* is generally used for any small wood (*COD*).

copyright (v.). The past tense and past participle are *copyrighted*.

cord. See **chord.**

co-respondent. See **correspondent.**

corn means the chief cereal crop of a region, so that in British English it is wheat, oats, or barley. In American English it means maize (*Indian corn*), which is what *cornflakes* are made from.

corporal and **corporeal** are no longer interchangeable. *Corporal* = 'of or belonging to the human body', as in 'A favourite topic of ancient raillery was corporal defects' (Gibbon); in legal language, 'personal', as in 'Corporal possession of a benefice'; *corporal punishment* is punishment inflicted on the body, esp. flogging. *Corporeal* is 'of the nature of the animal body as opposed to the spirit; physical, mortal', as in 'That which is corporeal dies at our death' and 'The corporeal frame of every human being'; hence, 'of the nature of matter as opposed to mind and spirit; material', as in 'The Devil is punished by a corporeal fire'; in Law, 'tangible; con-

sisting of material objects', esp. in *corporeal hereditament* (*OED*).

corps; corpse; corpus. A *corps* is an organized group of people as in 'the press corps'. A *corpse* is a dead (usually human) body. A *corpus* is a collection of language or writings, and this word has also a specialized sense in anatomy.

CORRECTNESS or **CORRECTITUDE.** See STANDARD ENGLISH, Section III.

correspond to and **with.** The question is often asked whether *to* or *with* is correct: both are correct, but their senses should be carefully distinguished. *Correspond to* = answer to in character or function, answer or agree in regard to position, amount, etc.; *correspond with* = communicate by interchange of letters (*OED*). *Correspond with* is now widely used, however, for *correspond to*, though not vice versa.

correspondent is one who corresponds (writes letters); a **co-respondent** (or *corespondent*) is the external offending party in a divorce case.

could for *can*. See PAST MODAL FOR PRESENT.

could, misused for *might*. 'If there's no more need to sew your shirt on' – the reference is to the taking of risk – 'you could just as well jump in [properly, 'into'] the lake' (a detective novel). Either word is correctly used for estimating probabilities, as in 'He might/could have cut himself'; but there is some danger of ambiguity here. 'The door might/could be locked' can mean either that it is perhaps locked or that locking it is possible, so write either 'Perhaps it is locked' or 'We could lock it.'

council and **counsel** are often misused one for the other, the former being 'an advisory or deliberative assembly or body of persons', the latter meaning 'advice and opinion given or offered' (*OED*); *counsel* is also the correct spelling for a counsellor-at-law, a barrister, an advocate. A counsellor gives advice; a councillor is a member of council.

counting. See CONJUNCTIONS, DISGUISED.

coup is correct English (and well established by the end of the 18th century) in the sense 'a successful move (that one makes); a "hit"', but journalists are overworking it.

couple, a. When it means two persons, as in 'the happy couple', it takes a plural verb. Today, *couple* often means 'a few, two or three', as in 'a couple of minutes', but only in informal use.

course. *Of course* is to be used sparingly. (I say this with much feeling, for I myself tend to use it far too often.)

courtesy. See **curtesy** ...

courts-martial is the correct plural of *court-martial*. [The plural *court-martials* has wide currency in the USA.]

coverage, extent, scope, hence protection, is horrible (orig. American).

crape. See **crêpe.**

crash (adj.). See VOGUE WORDS.

crawfish is American for *crayfish*, 'a freshwater crustacean'. Both words are used in Britain for the marine spiny lobster, often called *langouste* on menus.

credible; creditable; credulous. (Negatives: *incredible*; *discreditable*; *incredulous*.) *Credible* = believable; worthy of belief; susceptible of belief. *Creditable* = worthy of praise or credit; redounding to one's credit or reputation. *Credulous* = gullible; showing – or given to – excessive readiness or willingness to believe.

credit and **accredit.** In no sense are these two terms interchangeable. The latter = 'to invest with authority', 'to vouch for'.

creole (capitalized) is a descendant of European (chiefly Spanish and French) settlers in West Indies, Louisiana, Mauritius, etc.; or a half-breed of white and native races in those colonized countries. It also means 'the French patois spoken in Louisiana'. Not capitalized it means any language based on two or more languages and serving as somebody's mother tongue.

crêpe (or *crepe*) is a light wrinkled gauzelike fabric, or else a thin pancake. *Crape* is the same fabric as *crêpe*, but in the form of a black mourning material.

crescendo means 'a gradual increase in volume'. It does not mean 'a climax', so it is nonsense to speak of 'reaching (or rising to) a crescendo'

crevasse and **crevice.** A *crevice* is, in general, a cleft or rift, a small fissure, and in mining a crevice is 'a fissure in which a deposit of ore or metal is found', whereas a *crevasse* is a fissure, usually of great depth and sometimes very wide, in the ice of a glacier, and in the USA, 'a breach in the bank of a river, canal, etc.; esp. a breach in the *levée* (or artificial bank) of the lower Mississippi' (*OED*). Do not use *crevice* for *crevasse*, nor, except of extensive breaches, *crevasse* of ordinary chasms or deep cracks in the earth.

crime should not, except in jest, be debased to = 'an error, a minor fault or offence'. Cf. the misuse of **tragic.**

criterion has the plural *criteria*, not *criterions*. Do not use *criteria* as a singular; it should be 'these (not this) criteria'.

critical. Weseen is wrong in his assertion that '*Critical* is not in good use as a general substitute for *serious* or *dangerous*, as "The invalid is in a critical condition", "He is critically ill."' It certainly is not a general substitute for *dangerous*: obviously one wouldn't speak of 'critical animal'. But following from the medical sense, 'relating to the crisis or turning-point of a disease' (as in pneumonia), are the closely related nuances, 'of decisive importance in relation to the issue', as in 'Socrates taught that on great and critical occasions he was often directed by a mysterious voice' (J. B. Blackie), and 'involving suspense or grave fear as to the issue; attended with uncertainty or risk', as in 'Relations ... were ... in a critical state; in fact, the two countries were on the eve of a war' (Washington Irving) and 'His throat had been cut; his condition was critical.' *Critical* also = 'crucial' (*OED*).

crossways, crosswise. They are synonyms, except that *crossways* is only an adverb, while *crosswise* functions also as an adjective. Both mean 'in the form of a cross' ('A church built crosswise', Johnson) or 'so as to intersect' ('Four of these streets are built crosswise', Nugent, 1754); 'across, athwart, transversely' ('A frame of logs placed cross-wise', Jowett); hence fig. 'perversely, wrongly' ('He seeks pleasure cross-wise').

crowd for *group* is extremely colloquial.

crumby; crummy. Both = 'like, or of the nature of, the crumb of bread', but only the former = 'full of, or strewed with, crumbs' and only the latter is used in the slang senses (*OED*). [The two are pronounced alike, i.e. without *b*; and in American English *crumby* may carry the slang senses (*Webster's*).]

crystal-clear. See COMPARATIVES, FALSE.

crystallized. We are tempted to borrow from Sir Alan Herbert (*What a Word!*) the following: '"A Daily Mail reporter who made inquiries in London learned that among Church leaders there is no *crystallized viewpoint* towards spiritual healing." Note: The *crystallized viewpoint* is not to be confused with the Standard *Glacé* or Frosted Angle.' *Crystallized* is here used metaphorically: for the dangers of this practice see METAPHOR.

ct and **x** as variants (*connection, connexion*). See -ection and -exion.

CUMULATIVE NEGATION. See NEGATION, Section C, *a* from third paragraph to end; also sub-section *b*.

cunning, 'amusing' or 'attractive', is an Americanism.

curb and **kerb.** The latter is the usual spelling (in Britain but not in the USA) for the protective margin of a pavement (sidewalk, US).

currant, current. A *currant* is a dried grape, or a blackcurrant or redcurrant; a *current* flows. The adjective meaning 'present' is *current*, as in 'current affairs'.

curtesy, courtesy; curts(e)y. *Curts(e)y* is an obeisance; *curtesy*, an obsolete form of *courtesy* in all its senses. *Courtesy*, 'an obeisance', is obsolete. In current usage, *courtesy* is limited to 'graceful politeness or considerateness in intercourse with others'; 'a courteous disposition'; 'a courteous act or expression'; a form of legal tenure, and an American political custom. *Of* (or by) *courtesy* = 'by favour or indulgence; by gracious permission'. A *courtesy title* is 'one that, without legal validity, is accorded by courtesy or social custom'; cf. *courtesy rank*.

customer. See **client** and cf. **patron.**

cute for *acute* is a colloquialism; for 'amusing' or 'attractive', an American colloquialism. Cf. **cunning** and **clever.**

cyclone, tornado, typhoon, and **hurricane.** It is best to confine these terms to their meteorological senses. A *cyclone* is 'a general name for a low-area storm [with] high winds rotating about a centre of low atmospheric pressure'. *Tornado* is the name of a specific type of storm characterized by rapidly falling barometric pressure, a funnel-shaped cloud, vertical motion of the air, and a narrow path' (Weseen). A *typhoon* is (*a*) 'a violent storm or tempest occurring in India'; (*b*) the prevalent sense, 'a violent cyclonic storm or hurricane occurring in the China seas and adjacent regions, chiefly from July to October' (*OED*). *Hurricane* should be reserved for storms originating in the neighbourhood of the West Indies: a violent wind-storm, with a diameter of 500–1,000 miles, wherein the air moves at 80–130 m.p.h. round a central calm space that advances with the rest of the system in either a straight or a curved track. As a technical term in meteorology, a *hurricane* is a force 12 wind on the Beaufort scale.

Cymric, 'Welsh'. Both *c*'s are hard, i.e. pronounced as *k*.

D

'd and **'ld**. At present, *'d* is used both for *had* ('If I'd only known!') and for *would* ('If he'd only do it!'). Would it not be better to reserve *'d* for *had* and set *'ld* aside for *would*? The adoption of this recommendation (already observed by F. E. Brett Young, who had a sense of style) would at least serve to prevent an occasional ambiguity. According to certain authorities *should* has no shortened form. [American authorities regard *'d* as a colloquial contraction of *had*, *would*, and *should*.]

daily and **diurnal**. *Daily* is 'of or belonging to each day; occurring or done every day; issued or published every day (or every week-day)', as in 'A daily paper comes out call'd The Spectator' (Hearne) and 'The daily labour to gain their daily bread' (Brougham).

In current usage, *diurnal* is the opposite of *nocturnal*, and (of the motion of the heavenly bodies) it = 'performed in or occupying one day', as in 'the planet's diurnal rotation' (*OED*).

dam is incorrect for *damn* (n., v., and interjection); and *damn* ('It's damn cold') is colloquial for *damned* = *damnably*.

damaged is used of things (or, jocularly, of persons); *injured*, of persons and animal life. One should not, for instance, speak of one's teeth as being (or getting) *injured*.

dangerous. See **critical**.

DANGLING PARTICIPLES. See CONFUSED PARTICIPLES.

dare is used in two ways: as a full verb (*dares* to, *dared* to, didn't *dare* to) and as an auxiliary like *can* or *must*. The latter occurs correctly only in negatives ('I *daren't* go'), in questions, and in subordinate clauses ('whether I *dared* go'). The two patterns are not to be mixed. Write either 'whether she *dares* to go' or 'whether she *dare* go' but not 'whether she *dares* go'.

data is wrong when it is used for the correct singular, *datum*. 'For this data, much of it routine, it would be sensible to enlist the local authorities' (Milton Propper). But the word is now in constant use in the field of data processing, whose practitioners prefer to speak of 'an item of data' rather than using the rare singular *datum*.

date back to and **date back from**. Certain newspaper editors, on their style sheets, forbid the former and recommend the latter: actually, both usage and good sense tell us to prefer *date back to* to *date back from*. Style, prompted by economy of words, suggests that *date from* is preferable to either of the phrases under discussion.

daughters-in-law is the correct plural, so *sons-in-law*, *mothers-in-law*, *fathers-in-law*, etc.

deadly and **deathly**. Both = 'causing death, fatal, mortal', but *deathly* is obsolescent in this sense; as = 'of or pertaining to death', *deathly* is poetical; indeed, the only general extant sense of *deathly* is 'deathlike; as gloomy or still or silent or pale as death', as in 'Poor fellow, he looks deathly; can't last much longer, I fear', 'a deathly silence, stillness, pallor'.

Deadly is a more general word. In addition to the sense noted above, it = (of things) 'poisonous, venomous, pestilential, esp. if to a fatal degree'; in Theology, 'mortal' as opposite to 'venial', as in 'the seven deadly sins'; 'aiming at (or involving an aim) to kill or destroy; implacable; to the death', as in 'The contest …

becomes sharp and deadly' (Mark Pattison); and 'death-like' ('a deadly faintness'), though in this nuance *deathly* is more usual (*OED*).

deaf and dumb is the adjective; **deaf-mute** the noun.

deal, a, like **a good** (or **great**) **deal,** 'a large quantity or number', is a colloquialism, to be avoided in formal literary language.

deal in; deal with. Weseen neatly epitomizes the distinctions: 'In business we deal *in* commodities and *with* persons, as "They deal chiefly *in* iron products and deal *with* contractors in many cities." In discussion we deal *with* a subject, as "He dealt with all phases of the matter." '

dean and **doyen** are dignified words; therefore do not, as certain journalists do, speak of 'the dean (or doyen) of the caddies', 'the dean (or doyen) of polo-players', and so forth; as applied to a diplomatic corps, they are in place, though *doyen* is here the better term.

dear price. See **cheap price.**

deathless, immortal, undying. 'We have not only *immortal*, but also *undying* and *deathless*, expressing different shades of meaning, e.g. we would not speak of *immortal* admiration or affection' (Weekley, *Something about Words*). Cf. the following examples of correct use from *OED*: 'The faith that animals have immaterial and deathless souls' (Tyler, 1871). 'The deathless name of Godwine' (Freeman, 1876). 'Our deathlessness is in what we do, not in what we are' (G. Meredith, 1865). 'The word itself probably is not immortal' (Hume, 1752). 'The undying interest ever felt by kindly women in a question of love or marriage' (Mrs Alexander, 1885). For *deathless*, see also **deadly and deathly.**

deathlike. See **deadly.**

debar; disbar. The latter is used only in one sense, 'to expel from the bar'; *debar* ('to exclude, prevent, prohibit') is not so used.

debate (n.) is misused when it is made synonymous with *doubt, pondering, question,* or *cogitation.* 'He wasted no debates on what had happened, but concentrated on how it had happened, and attempted to guess how his own investigation might be involved' (Robert George Dean).

decease is the legal synonym of *to die,* which is preferable in every context other than the legal. The same applies to the noun.

decimate originally meant 'to take or destroy one in ten', but is now commonly used, and by good writers, for 'destroy a large proportion of'. 'Typhus fever decimated the school' (Charlotte Brontë, 1847). It should not be used for 'wipe out entirely'.

decisive(ly) for *decided(ly)*; the reverse is rare. A good example of this misuse is found in Philip MacDonald's excellent thriller, *The Nursemaid Who Disappeared*: 'It being clear that the play was going to be a success, the party given after the show by Brooks-Carew was a decisively alcoholic affair.'

declare. See **assert.**

decorum and **conduct.** The latter is neutral and it requires an adjective to determine it. *Decorum* is 'propriety of behaviour'; in plural it = 'proprieties', as in 'Hedged round by formalities and decorums' (Merivale) (*OED*).

decrease over; decrease under. 'A 15 per cent decrease over (or under) the takings of the last year': the former is absurd, the latter clumsy. Read 'A 15 per cent decrease in the takings as compared with those of last year'.

decry. See **descry.**

decumbent. See **recumbent.**

deduce; deduct. To *deduce* is to infer by reasoning; to *deduct* is to subtract.

deductive; inductive. As applied to the process of reasoning, *deductive* and *deduction* (related, of course, to *deduce*, not to

87

deduct) refer to the establishing of a particular instance from a general premiss. *Inductive* and *induction* refer to the establishing of a general rule from particular instances.

deem is a very formal word, needed only in legal contexts. Elsewhere, prefer *think*.

defective; deficient. *Defective* things are faulty in quality, *deficient* things are incomplete, or insufficient in quantity.

definite and **definitive.** The difference is neatly given by Harold Herd, in *Watch Your English*: *Definite* implies that a thing is *precise*; *definitive* means that it is *final* (beyond criticism or refutation).

definitely. See **really**.

deflection and **deflexion.** See **-ection and -exion.**

degree, in a (e.g. **disastrous**). Wordy for, e.g. *disastrously*. See **ABSTRACT NOUNS.**

deliver. See **VOGUE WORDS.**

deliverance need not be confused with *delivery*, the former now being used only for 'liberation or rescue', in several legal technicalities, 'a formal utterance or pronouncement', and 'a verdict' (obsolescent except in Law).

delusion, illusion. *Delusion* is 'believing – or causing another to believe – that the false is true'; 'a fixed false opinion', e.g. as a form of mental derangement. An *illusion* is 'a false conception or idea; a deceptive belief, statement, or appearance' (*OED*). Thus, the impression that the sun goes round the earth was formerly a *delusion*, but is now an *illusion*.

demand is not 'to *order*', but to ask authoritatively or peremptorily for (a thing); or that something be done, as in 'Assent was categorically demanded', 'He demanded to be allowed to enter' or 'that he should be allowed …'; and 'to ask formally or authoritatively to know or be told', as in 'He demanded the cause' and 'All the members demanded who it was' (*OED*).

demean is two equally current verbs, of which one is always and the other usually reflexive. The first requires an adverb, and means 'behave', as in 'He demeaned himself with courage.' The second means 'lower the dignity of', as in 'I would not demean myself to ask.' It is the lack of the reflexive that makes the following seem – well, infelicitous: 'Osaki had moved to a secluded position aft, where she sat rigidly aloof, as might some great lady who felt herself demeaned by contact … with her fellow beings' (John G. Brandon). *Demeanour* is 'bearing, (outward) behaviour'.

demi and **semi.** Both literally mean '(a) half'; the former, direct from French, the latter direct from Latin. In Heraldry, the term is *demi*; in armoury, *demi* = half-sized or smaller – so too in artillery, fortification, and military tactics; in weights and measures, music, geometry, *demi* = 'half'; in the names of fabrics and stuffs it = 'inferior'; with the class-nouns it often = 'of equivocal character', as in 'demi-pagan', 'demi-priest'; with nouns of action or condition, it = 'partial', as in 'demi-toilet'.

Semi follows the same tendencies: in technicalities, it = 'half' (or, less generally, 'on a reduced scale'); with class-nouns and nouns of action, it = 'partial'.

In correlative pairs, only *semi* is used; as in 'semi-chemical, semi-mechanical'. *Semi* is the only one freely available for making new words, such as 'semi-detached'; 'semi-darkness'.

demise is a legal term, to be employed only in specific contexts; as a synonym of *death*, it is infelicitous and unnecessary, and as a euphemism it is deplorable.

democrat and **Democrat.** The former is an advocate of or an adherent to democracy; a *Democrat* is a member of the Democratic party in American politics.

denominate and **name** and **nominate.** To *denominate* is 'to name, to call by name, to give a name or appellation to', as in 'From him [Guelpho] they … were denominated Guelphs' (Fuller, 1639),

'This is what the world ... denominates an itch for writing' (Cowper). It is, in current usage, constructed usually with a complement, i.e. as = 'to call' (witness the example from Cowper). In this, the only sense of *denominate*, *nominate* is a synonym – but obsolescent and, for the sake of clarity, to be avoided. *Nominate* is obsolescent also in the two senses, 'to specify by name' and 'to specify, appoint, fix' ('The woman has the privilege of nominating the day of her marriage'). The prevalent sense – indeed, the only general current sense – is, 'to appoint (a person) by name to discharge some duty or to hold some office', as in 'The House of Commons was crowded with members nominated by the Royal Council' (J. R. Green), with the derivative sense, 'to propose, or formally enter, (a person) as a candidate for election', as in 'Any one may challenge the person nominated and start another candidate' (Jowett) (*OED*).

denote. See **connotation.**

dent and **dint.** In the literary sense 'an indentation (in a material object)' *dent* is usual; in the figurative sense, 'an impairment, a shock or blow', almost 'a blemish', *dint* is usual, as in 'a dint in a character – a reputation'. But *dint* is the only choice for the phrase 'by dint of' = 'by means of'.

deny, misused for *contradict*. 'I said that there were 101; he denied me and said there were 102.' See also **refute and deny.**

deny and **refute.** See **refute and deny.**

depend is correctly followed by *on* or *upon*, as in 'It depends (on) what you mean', 'It all depends (upon) the weather.' Its use alone as a full sentence, 'It depends!' belongs only to speech.

dependant; dependent. As also for *pendant*, *pendent*, the -*ant* form is preferred for the noun, the -*ent* for the adjective. [In American English, the final syllable of the adjective is -*ent*, of the noun, -*ent* or -*ant* (*Webster's*).]

depending. See CONJUNCTIONS, DISGUISED.

deplete and **reduce.** The former is not synonymous with the latter, though almost so in the nuance 'to reduce the fulness of', as in 'to deplete a garrison'; even here, however, one speaks of a garrison's 'being depleted' as the result of, e.g. an attack, whereas 'to reduce a garrison' implies deliberation by its officers. In general usage, to *deplete* = 'to empty out, to exhaust', as in 'to deplete one's strength'.

deplore governs a thing or a quality, not a person. Thus the correct form of 'We may deplore him for his conceit' (set, for correction, in a Scottish Leaving Certificate examination) is either 'We may deplore his conceit' or 'We may condemn him for his conceit.'

deploy. See VOGUE WORDS.

depositary and **depository.** The former is 'a trustee' or, in Law, 'a bailee'; the latter is 'a receptacle; a storehouse or repository', but is also used (though not in Law) of a person to whom something (lit. or fig.) is entrusted (*OED*). [In American English the two spellings are interchangeable.]

depravation and **depravity.** In current usage *depravation* is '(the act or fact of) making depraved or corrupt', whereas *depravity* is '(the process or fact of) becoming, or esp. having become, depraved, bad, corrupt': 'depravation of instincts and morals'; 'an unspeakable depravity caused him to be shunned by all decent people' (*OED*).

deprecate for *depreciate* (and vice versa). *Depreciating*, -*ly*, are often misused for *deprecating*, -*ly*; *depreciation* is much less commonly misused for *deprecation*. (To) *depreciate* is the opposite of *appreciate* and is synonymous with *belittle*: to *deprecate* is to deplore, to express an earnest wish against or earnest disapproval of.

derisive; derisory. These two adjectives are often used interchangeably; but a useful distinction can be made between *derisive* = 'expressing derision, mocking' and *derisory* = 'deserving derision, laughable', and particularly 'absurdly small'.

describe for *indicate* or *designate* or *denote* is catachrestic, slovenly, feeble, as in 'This blueprint describes how the machine has been made'; 'The nickname "The Croucher" describes that famous cricketer, Jessop'; 'The term *accuracy* describes the result of accuracy.' As = 'to represent, picture, or portray', *describe* is obsolete, and should be avoided. As = 'to descry', it is a catachresis; so discriminating a writer as Gibbon fell into this error: 'The smallest blemish has not been described by ... jealous ... eyes' (*OED*). [The second sentence does not offend American usage, though *describes* might well be *characterizes*. *Designate* in this sense is not usual, although one would say, 'The insignia on his shoulder designate his rank.']

description. See ABSTRACT NOUNS.

description (or descriptive) about is incorrect for *description* (or *descriptive*) *of*. The former is exemplified in 'Instead of a long description about studies into human communication and the meaning of language, we fill the gap with a new symbol – *semantics*' (Stuart Chase). Perhaps by confusion with *a discourse about* (something).

descry, decry; discern. *Descry* is 'to catch sight of, esp. from a distance; to espy', as in 'To meet Albert, whom I descried coming towards us' (Queen Victoria, 1868) and 'At intervals we descried a maple.' Hence, 'to discover by observation; to detect; to perceive', and even – though this is a weakening of the sense – merely 'to see': 'To descry new lands, rivers or mountains in her spotty globe' (Milton); 'The bounds which separated that school from Romanism were very difficult to descry' (Brougham).

To *discern* is, in current usage, 'to recognize or perceive distinctly' ('to discern the truth' or 'to discern that the truth is ...)'; 'to distinguish (an object) with the

eyes', i.e. 'to descry', as in 'We could discern no trace of rupture [in the ice]' (Tyndall), 'Good sight is necessary for one to be able to discern minute objects' (*OED*).

Neither word should be confused with *decry*, which means 'disparage, belittle'.

desertion is dangerously ambiguous in the following: 'Pedro de Valdez was universally loved and honoured, and his desertion in the face of an enemy so inferior in numbers was regarded as scandalous poltroonery' (J. A. Froude, *English Seamen in the Sixteenth Century*). The context shows that Valdez did not desert his friends but was deserted by them.

deserving of serious consideration is officialese for *important*.

déshabille should, as a French word, be *déshabillé*, e.g. *en déshabillé* (in undress). The English form carries no accent and should be *dishabille* (less correctly *deshabille*); the English phrase is *in dishabille* – not those hybrids, *en dishabille* (or *deshabillé*) or *in déshabille* (or *déshabillé*).

desirable is 'worthy to be desired', 'to be wished for', whereas *desirous* is 'full of, or characterized by desire' and is always constructed with *of* ('desirous of doing something') or the infinitive ('desirous to learn all he could') or, obsolescently, *that* ('He was desirous that nothing should be said about it').

despatch. See **dispatch.**

despite, 'notwithstanding (an opponent, an obstacle)', is a shortening of *despite of*, itself a shortening of *in despite of*. The usual current form is *in spite of*; *spite of* is colloquial. *Despite of* is archaic, as also – except in lofty or poetical style – is *in despite of*.

despoil = 'plunder, pillage', and is not today a synonym of *spoil*, which now = 'damage, reduce in value'; although in biblical English it was possible to say that the Children of Israel '*spoiled* (= despoiled) the Egyptians'.

determinately and **determinedly** are occasionally confused. The latter = 'in a determined (i.e. resolute) manner', in which sense *determinately* is literary – but slightly obsolescent. As 'conclusively, finally', *determinately* is now rare; and as 'definitely, exactly, precisely' ('It was determinately discovered that ...') it seems to be going out of use.

detract and **distract** are sometimes confused. In current usage, *detract* is common only in *detract from*, as in 'Nothing detracts from one's virtue so much as too much boasting about it'; *distract* is 'to divert the attention of', hence 'to perplex, to agitate, perturb', as in 'Love distracts the student.' See also at **substract**.

develop (preferable, by the way, to *develope*) is often used catachrestically for 'to arise', as in 'The totalitarian states, which have developed since the Great War [1914–18], are opposed to the doctrines of democracy.' See also **envelop**.

device; devise. As a noun, *devise* occurs only in Law. In general usage, *device* is only a noun, *devise* only a verb ('to plan, arrange, contrive'); *device* is a means whereby one is assisted in achieving one's purpose. *Deviser* is general; *devisor*, legal.

devices should be used with caution as a synonym of *plans* or *activities*. 'Left to his own devices' is a stock phrase – a commonplace (or cliché); but escape from that cliché and you fall into the pitfall of the unidiomatic, as in 'It was some hours later that the two men met, ... because the Chief-Inspector [why the hyphen?] had been busy on his own devices' (E. R. Lorac, *Death of an Author*).

deviser; devisor. See **device.**

devoid of, to be. To lack. (Officialese.) See also COMPARATIVES, FALSE.

dexterous is usual, though **dextrous** is the sounder formation.

DIALECT. 'Dialect is essentially local; a dialect is [that] variety of a language which prevails in a district, with local peculiarities of vocabulary, pronunciation, and phrase' (H. W. Fowler); dialects, therefore, are languages *within* a language.

The peculiarities, especially if they are picturesque or forcible, are constantly being incorporated into general colloquial speech or into slang. At ordinary times, the incorporation is slow and inconsiderable, but on special occasions and during intense periods, as in a war (when countrymen mingle at close quarters with townsmen), numerous dialectal terms become part of the common stock and some few of them pass into formal speech and into the language of literature, whether prose or poetry. 'Burns's *croon* was ... a dialect term, but it almost immediately commended itself to the poets, and is now in good use' (Greenough and Kittredge, 1901). [Radio *crooners* in America have brought the word into disrepute.]

More fully than slang, much more fully and accurately than that hardly definable region of informal speech which we call 'colloquial and familiar', dialect has been charted and mapped. In 'Popular Speech' (see his *Words and Idioms*), Dr Logan Pearsall Smith has written: 'Of all the various forms of non-literary English, the local dialects* have been most carefully documented and studied; glossaries of all, and grammars of some of them, have been published, and the material in these has been put together, with that collected by the Dialect Society, in ... Dr [Joseph] Wright's immense *Dialect Dictionary*, which is ... a work for the lover of words of inexhaustible fascination, enabling him, as it does, to explore at ease the wild regions of English which lie around the streets and suburbs of our polite vernacular.'

Dialect has already contributed to Standard English and to colloquialisms, as we have seen: what we should like to see is a larger, more effectual contribution, for many effetenesses of Standard English would profitably be displaced by the pic-

---

*On dialect in general, there is an excellent account at pp. 1–16 of H. C. K. Wyld's *History of Modern Colloquial English*.

turesque and pithy words and phrases of much dialect. Those writers who deplore the outworn and senile-senseless character of many Standard English words and phrases and metaphors, would be better employed in rejuvenating the literary (and indeed the normal cultured) language by substituting dialectical freshness, force, pithiness, for Standard exhaustion, feebleness, long-windedness than in attempting to rejuvenate it with Gallicisms, Germanicisms, Grecisms, and Latinisms; and this holds for American Standard hardly less than for English Standard. There is, in English dialect, and in American dialects,[*] a 'wealth of expressive words …, seemingly crude because of their unfamiliarity …, which have not been admitted to standard literary use' (G. H. McKnight): a fact that has been borne in on me with particular vividness by the objectivity, the immediacy, the direct and simple force, and the correspondence of sound to sense that characterize the dialect in Eden Phillpotts's and Paul Horgan's novels.

It is to be hoped that dialect-speakers will not be shamed out of their words, phrases, and pronunciations by 'cultured' visitors, by near-visioned teachers, by BBC 'experts'. The influence of 'education' is already visible in the weakening of the local pronunciations of *Cirencester* (*Sissiter*), *Bodiam* (*Bodjum*), *Daventry* (*Danetree*), *Yealm* (*Yam*): it is time that the curb and snaffle of good sense should put a check to the nefarious teachings of the unimaginatively genteel. Country people are too modest. They must sturdily resist the insidious approaches of their 'betters'. They should boldly preserve the traditional pronunciations.

[Note: Students of language at the end of this century would modify Fowler's original definition, distinguishing *dialect*, which is a matter of vocabulary and grammar, from *accent*, which refers to pronun-

ciation. It is possible and indeed common to speak standard educated English with a regional accent.

Moreover, it is now usual to speak of 'social' as well as 'local' dialects, the former being based on age, sex, and socioeconomic status. Dialectal variety is now far more widely accepted than it was a generation ago.]

dialectal and **dialectical** are often confused; the former refers to *dialect*, the second to *dialectics* (the art of argument).

dialogue, duologue, monologue, conversation. In their speech senses, *dialogue* is a conversation (between two or more persons), a colloquy, a talk together; *duologue* is a conversation (esp. in a dramatic piece) between two persons; *monologue* is not a soliloquy (spoken by a person when alone), but a speech (or harangue) delivered by one person to others. *Conversation* is rather more dignified than *talk*, but it cannot be used, as *talk* is, for an informal address or short, familiar speech or discourse. [In American usage, *monologue* is often a synonym of *soliloquy*.] See also **VOGUE WORDS**.

dichotomy is division or differentiation into two, as for binary classification. It should not be used to mean simply 'discrepancy, conflict' as in 'the widening dichotomy between Left and Right'. A **VOGUE WORD**.

dicta, '(noteworthy) sayings', is the plural of L. *dictum* and therefore it must not be used as a singular as in ' "After all, speed is everything in our game!" With which dicta "Freddie the Fly" agreed. "Yes", he said, "it's all fast work" ' (John G. Brandon, *The Regent Street Raid*).

DICTIONARIES and what they can – and cannot – do: these are subjects that, especially in matters of usage, puzzle all those who are not lexicographers. Easily the best guide is J. R. Hulbert's *Dictionaries, British and American*, 1955.

didn't ought. See **ought, didn't …**

---

[*]Several sections of the *Dialect Atlas of the United States and Canada* have been published. It is noteworthy that the American dialects are not so distinct as the British.

differ from; differ with. To *differ from* is 'to be not the same as; to hold an opinion different from that of another person', as in 'Milk differs from water', 'I differ from you in that matter'; the second sense ('to be at variance') may also be construed with *with* ('I differed with him in that matter') (*OED*).

different is incorrectly followed by singular instead of plural in the following (from *Swift or the Egotist*, M. M. Rossi and J. M. Hone), 'Temple's basic mistake lay in failing to realize that the question had a completely different nature in France and in England', which should read 'had … different natures', or, more cumbrously, 'had a … different nature in France from that which it had in England'.

different should not be used for *several* or *various*, as in 'Different actors performed for the occasion'; nor unnecessarily, as in 'Three different statesmen came to dinner.'

different to; different than. See **than, different.**

differently than is incorrect for *otherwise than*, as in 'I felt about it differently than I had ever felt about it before' (Frank Tilsley, *I'd Hate to be Dead*).

DIFFUSENESS. See TAUTOLOGY.

digraph. See DIPHTHONGS.

dilemma, as 'a choice between more than two things or decisions' hence 'a predicament or "fix"', is loose English. Although this extended sense may be justifiable where there is a definite number of choices, and those all unattractive, *dilemma* should certainly not be used of a predicament entailing an open choice, as in 'the dilemma of how to pay for the car'.

dimension. See VOGUE WORDS.

dine is more formal – but also more economical – than *have dinner*.

dint. See **dent.**

DIPHTHONGS. A diphthong is 'a union of two vowels pronounced in one syllable' (as in *out, boil, boy*). The term is 'often applied to a combination of two vowel characters, more properly called a *digraph*. When the two characters represent a simple sound, as *ea, ou*, in *head* (hed), *soup* (soop), they have been termed an *improper diphthong*: properly speaking, these are *monophthongs* [single vowel sounds] written by *digraphs*. – In popular use, [diphthong is] applied to the ligatures æ, œ, of the Latin alphabet. As pronounced … in modern use, these are no longer diphthongs, but monophthongs; the OE ligatures œ and æ always represented monophthongs' (*OED*).

diplomatist is an ineptitude for *diplomat* (adj., *diplomatic*).

dipsomaniac. See **drunk.**

dipthong is incorrect for *diphthong*; **diptheria** for *diphtheria*. The spelling and the learned character of the words restrain but do not extirpate the tendency to dissimilate. In turn, the popular pronunciation creates a popular though erroneous spelling.

direction, misused for *quarter*. ' "It's our duty to act." "Oh, very well", said West wearily. "I'll mention the matter in the right direction and see what can be done about it" ' (John Bude).

directly for 'as soon as', i.e. for *immediately when*, is a British colloquialism, as in 'The book was suppressed directly it appeared.'

disassemble is to break up an assembly, or to take (esp. a machine) apart, to *strip* it; *dissemble* is to hide one's feelings or purpose.

disassociate. See **dissociate.**

disaster is a grave word: do not use it lightly. No more than *tragedy* is it to be made a synonym of a mere *misfortune*.

disbeliever is active, positive; *unbeliever* is neutral. 'He attacks *dis*believers, but has very little to say to mere *un*believers' (Whewell) (*OED*).

disc is the usual British spelling, *disk* the American. But the British use *disk* in connection with computers (*floppy disk*) and the Americans prefer *disc* for a gramophone record and for the cutting tool of a plough or harrow.

discern. See **descry.**

disclose (v.t.) is 'to reveal, declare'; *expose* is 'to unmask' or 'to place in a dangerous situation'.

discomfit; discomfort (v.). The latter is 'to make uncomfortable physically or uneasy mentally'; *discomfit* is both stronger and more general, for it = 'to thwart, to foil'; 'to throw into dejection, perplexity, confusion; to disconcert'. The noun is *discomfort*, but only in the senses, 'lack of physical comfort', 'uneasiness whether physical or mental', and 'a hardship'. The noun of *discomfit* is *discomfiture.*

discontinue is officialese for 'to *stop* or *cease* (*from*)'.

discourteous (n.: *discourtesy*) is 'rude', therefore stronger than *uncourteous* (n.: *uncourteousness*), 'wanting in courtesy'. Cf. the difference between **disbeliever** and **unbeliever.**

discover. Its prevailing current sense is 'to find out' (something already there). Cf. **disclose**, *q.v.*, and **uncover**, 'to remove the cover of'. And contrast **invent**, 'to originate or devise'.

discreditable. See **credible.**

discreet and **discrete.** The former is applied to sage or, at the least, prudent persons and circumspect behaviour; the latter is rare except among the philosophic-minded and those who possess a knowledge of logic, and it means 'individually distinct', 'belonging to or consisting of distinct or individual parts', 'discontinuous'. It is a learned term, to be used with cau-

tion. The negatives are formed with *in-*, and the related nouns are *discretion*, *discreetness* (from *discreet*) and *discreteness* (from *discrete*).

disenfranchise is inferior to *disfranchise*, but equally common.

DISGUISED CONJUNCTIONS. See CONJUNCTIONS, DISGUISED.

DISGUISED PREPOSITIONS. See CONJUNCTIONS, DISGUISED.

dishabille. See **déshabille.**

disillusionize. Now pedantic for to *disillusion'.*

disincentive (n.) is what you or I prefer to call a *deterrent.*

disinterested originally meant 'not interested; apathetic'. It then came to mean 'impartial; not studying one's own interest'. It now shows signs of reverting to its older sense, but should not be so used. If there is the least danger of ambiguity, the word might be replaced by *bored* or *impartial*, according to the sense.

disk. See **disc.**

dislike to is incorrect for *dislike of*. 'It may be just a dislike to getting mixed up in such things' (E. R. Punshon). [In American English, *dislike for* is probably more common than *dislike of*.]

disorient; disorientate. The first is the preferred American form, the second the British.

dispatch and **despatch** (n. and v.). '*Dispatch* is to be preferred, as at once historical, and in accordance with English analogy' (*OED*).

dispense with is erroneously used for *dispose of*. 'The moment he had dispensed with all the formalities ..., he was not long in starting', writes an able young novelist.

dispersal; dispersion. The former is chiefly the process of scattering, the latter is the resultant situation; 'the dispersal of a mob by troops'; 'the widespread dispersion of our family throughout the world'. *Dispersion* has also many technical senses in statistics, optics, and chemistry.

displace. See **replace.**

dispose and **depose** are ignorantly confused.

disposition. 'Of a quarrelsome disposition' = quarrelsome.

dissemble. See **disassemble.**

dissimulate and **simulate.** One *dissimulates* – pretends not to have or be – that which one has or is; one *simulates* – pretends to have or be – that which one has not or is not. 'He dissimulated his cowardice, envy, suspicion, etc.'; 'He simulated drunkenness, interest, disinterest, etc.'

dissociate is now preferred to *disassociate*, no matter what the context.

distinctive is often misused for *distinct* and *distinguished*. *Distinguished*, 'now almost always of persons', = 'remarkable, eminent, of high standing, famous'. *Distinctive* = 'characteristic; distinguishing'; it is very rare in the sense 'distinct'. *Distinct* = 'separate' ('Absolute as distinct from relative knowledge'); 'individual' (not identical); 'different in quality or kind' ('A distinct species of composition'); 'individually peculiar'; 'clear, plain, definite' (to the senses or to the mind); 'unmistakable, pronounced, positive, decided' ('A distinct change').

distract. See **detract.**

disturb. See **perturb.**

diurnal. See **daily.**

dived; dove. The preterite of *dive* is *dived* in British use. The alternative preterite *dove* is now acceptable in American English. But the past participle is *dived* everywhere.

divers and **diverse,** originally the same word and still frequently confused, now mean, (the former) *several* or *a certain number of*, (the latter) of *different natures or aspects*.

divorcee is generic English for French *divorcé* (a divorced man) and *divorcée* (a divorced woman). But the distinction in the French terms is not to be lightly dismissed in deference to the snortings of Gallophobes. To use *divorcée* of a man is, however, indefensible.

do. As a makeshift, the verb *do* is colloquial rather than literary, except where it is obviously the best word to use. But be sure to put it in the same tense as the verb is represents. Obvious? Maybe! Yet I have seen and heard instances of the wrong tense. The present tense can be represented only by *do*; the progressive present by *am, is, are doing*, not by *do*; the preterite (simple past), only by *did*; the progressive past (or imperfect) by *was* or *were doing*, not by *did*, as in C. McCabe, *The Face on the Cutting-Room Floor*, 'Another company was making almost the same triangle story as you did' – properly, 'as you *were* [*making*, or *doing*]'; the simple future, by *shall* (or *will*) *do*; the progressive future by *shall* (or *will*) *be doing*. The same applies to the perfect tenses (whether present, past, or future). And see VERB UNCOMPLETED.

dock is not to be synonymized with *pier* or *wharf* in British use, although it can mean those things to Americans.

domicile is in place as a legal term and as = 'the dwelling-place of an animal': otherwise, it is an affectation or, at best, an elegancy.

dominated with is incorrect in such a sentence as, 'They were enthusiasts dominated with one idea, but domination by one idea is often, if not usually, the equivalent of monomania' (*Church Times*, 1899), quoted by Nesfield, who points out that 'domination by' in the second clause is correct, since 'idea' is here the agent which dominates.

dominating, misused for *predominant*. The former = 'masterful'; the latter, 'principal' or 'outstanding'. Distinguish also *dominating* from *domineering* ('bullying', 'actively arrogant').

domino (cloak and mask; a piece in the game) has plural *dominoes*, with *dominos* as a chiefly American alternative.

don't is now a solecism for *doesn't, does not.*

double entendre for *double entente* is a curiosity. The French phrase is *d. entente*; the French language knowing not *d. entendre* – a figment of the English imagination.

DOUBLE GENITIVE. See **of her –** **of hers** and GENITIVE, VAGARIES OF THE.

DOUBLE NEGATIVE. See NEGA-TIVE, Section G.

DOUBLE SINGULAR. This device is at its most obvious in the hyphenated form, e.g. 'The you-and-I that forms the dominant chord in youthful love is not wholly selfish.' The less obvious, though more general, form is that which sets two disparate things (or actions) in a combination, as in 'The din and smell was overpowering.' Apparently a modification of the latter is 'The coming and going of passengers is variable'; but actually it is a mere typographical variant of the former, because one might equally well write 'the coming-and-going' (cf. the French *le va-et-vient*). Occasionally we find the double singular either misused or, at best, confused, as in 'The heat and the jam' – i.e. crowd – 'was so oppressive that Iris was actually glad to reach her own compartment' (Ethel Lina White).

doubt (if, that, whether, etc.). *Doubt*, verb, may be transitive or intransitive; no difficulty arises in its transitive use ('I doubt the man's honesty') , though J. R. Green, 1874, writes 'who never doubted of the final triumph of freedom and law', in which the 'of' is unnecessary. In its intransitive use, the sentence following 'doubt' begins with a conjunction, which in nearly every case should be *that* or *whether*, in spite of the employment by many writers of *if, but, but that*, and even (in the 16th century) of *at* and *lest*. In the two following examples *that* would be better than *but* and *but that*: Steele, 1711, 'I do not doubt

but England is at present as polite a nation as any in the world'; W. Selwyn, 1817, 'It was never doubted but that one partner might bind the rest.' It is, however, to be noted that in negative and interrogative sentences, doubt 'may take *but that* or (simply) *but*, with the same meaning as the ordinary *that*:

I do not doubt *but that you are surprised.*

Who doubted *but* [or *but that*] the catastrophe was over?',

as Dr Onions writes in *An Advanced English Syntax* (6th ed., 1932). But the following sentence in Crosbie Garstin's *The Owl's House*, 'Had not Carveth goods enough in this world but that he must have Tregors' as well', is an illicit extension of the *doubt but that* sentence-type: 'but that he must have' should be changed to 'without his having'. In the two following, *whether* would be more correct than *that* and *if·* Bayard Taylor, 1871, 'Schiller doubted that a poetic measure would be formed capable of holding Goethe's plan'; *The Law Times*, 1891, 'The master doubted if all remedies were not barred.' – Hawthorne, 1858, 'I doubt whether English cookery is not better', is correct. Some ambiguity arises when 'doubt' is used in the sense of *suspect* or *fear (that)*. Trollope's (1879) 'I doubt that Thackeray did not write the Latin epitaph', and Shelley's (1820) 'I doubt that they will not contain the latest news', would have been more clearly expressed, 'I doubt whether Thackeray wrote –' and 'I doubt whether they will contain –'. Pepys's (1655) 'Doubting that all will break in pieces in the kingdom' is an expression not of dubiety but of fear. (The above examples are from *OED*.) [American textbooks note that *doubt* (v.) is followed by *that* when there is little or no doubt, and by *whether* (formal usage) or *if* (informal usage) when there is uncertainty. In a sentence such as 'I doubt *whether* he will come or not', *if* would be loose and incorrect, because of the presence of *or not*.]

doubtless being both an adjective and an adverb, the adverb *doubtlessly* is unnecessary.

douse; dowse. To *douse* is to drench, or to extinguish ('douse the candles'). To *dowse* is to seek water or minerals with a divining rod.

dove. See **dived.**

dower and **dowry** should be kept distinct. *Dower* is that 'portion of a deceased husband's estate which the law allows to his widow for her life'; avoid it both in the legal sense of *dowry* ('that money or property which the wife brings her husband') and in the derivative sense of *dowry* ('gift or talent bestowed by nature or by fortune') (*OED*).

downstair. See **upstair.**

downward; downwards. The latter is adverb only. The former is chiefly an adjective, but often functions as an adverb in American English and in older British writing.

dowse. See **douse.**

doyen. See **dean.**

Dr, I believe, is preferable to *Dr.*; if you wish to be pedantic, you will write 'D'r': but who does so write it?

draft is in America preferred to *draught*, whether noun, verb, or adjective; in Great Britain, *draught* is preferred for a plan or sketch (hence *draughtsman*), although a preliminary version of a document is a *draft* (hence *draftsman*). The British use *draught* for a drink, a current of air, a ship's displacement, a draught horse, and the game of draughts (which the Americans call *checkers*).

drama. Do not use this powerful word in trivial contexts, as in 'Drama in the monkey's compound'.

dramatic for *drastic*. L. Seccombe, broadcasting on 19 Jan. 1937, 'Lynch will have to do something dramatic in the last round if he is to win the fight.' To lose it might have been equally 'dramatic'.

DRAMATIC IRONY. See IRONY, fifth paragraph.

drank is the past tense; **drunk** the past participle of *drink*.

drastic means 'vigorous', 'vigorously effective', 'violent', (of a medicine) 'acting strongly', or (of a person) 'acting severely'; it is incorrect to speak of 'a drastic result'.

dream, as an adjective, is journalese; e.g. 'his dream girl', 'my dream home'. (With acknowledgements to Frank Whitaker.)

drinker. See **toper.**

dromedary. See **camel.**

drunk (v.). See **drank.**

drunk (adj.); **drunken.** The former is predicative ('The man is drunk'); the latter, attributive ('The drunken man'). *Drunken*, however, is preferred in the nuance 'given to drink, habitually drunk', whereas 'drunk on a given occasion' is *intoxicated*. A person habitually drunk is a *drunkard*; one ungovernably given to drink is a *dipsomaniac* or *alcoholic* (the same form as the adjectives). See also **toper.**

due to rings false in such a sentence as this: 'Their masts, due to the sloping effect given by the after legs of the tripod, always looked from a distance to be falling in towards each other' ('Taffrail', *The Sub*, 1917, of a battleship). Preserve the distinction between *due to*, which means 'caused by', and *owing to*, which means 'because of'. Nouns are *due to* something, verbs happen *owing* to something. 'The delay was due to the snow'; 'We were late owing to the snow.'

duly noted rarely means more than *noted*.

duologue. See **dialogue.**

DUPLICATED POSSESSIVE. See POSSESSIVE, DUPLICATED.

dwarf has the plural *dwarfs*, although *dwarves* is permissible in fairy tales.

dyeing from to *dye*; **dying** from to *die*.

dynamic. See VOGUE WORDS.

E

-e- for *œ* or *æ* (*oe* or *ae*) is becoming fairly general, particularly in American spelling. In *eternal* and *coeval* (in Early Modern English, *œternal* and *cœval*), *e* is the rule; *medieval* is now the usual – the fully Anglicized – form of the formerly (even in the 19th century) general *mediaeval* (or, before the 19th century, *mediæval*). The *œ* form is now rare; still rarer is *æ*. In scientific and technical terms, however, *ae* is retained, as in *palaeontology*, although *archeology* is fast gaining ground at the expense of *archaeology*. When the English word comes from Greek (as *palaeontology* does) the *ae* represents Greek *ai* – though this is as true of *archaeology* as of *palaeontology*. But whether the origin is Greek *ai* or Latin *ae* (or *æ*), the pronunciation of the English *œ* or *æ* or *e* is always *ee*: hence the general trend towards the spelling in *e*. Some spellings, such as *esthetic* and *anemia*, are only American.

each as a plural. John Farmer, in Forewords to *Musa Pedestris*, says, in speaking of slang and cant: 'One thing, indeed, both have in common, each are derived from a correct normal use of language.' 'Both' *are* and *have* but 'each' *is* and *has*. Wilfrid Whitten, in *Good and Bad English*, p. 70, justifies the plural verb in the sentence, 'Brown, Jones and Robinson each have their plans', on the ground that the writer 'refers to B., J. and R. as being of one mind'. There, *each* is grammatically subordinate to a plural subject, so the verb is correctly plural.

each, between. 'The crack way of running over hurdles, in which just three strides are taken mechanically between each hurdle' is loose. *And the next*, following *hurdle*, is required.

each and **every** are constantly used with a plural pronoun in spite of the obvious inaccuracy; famous writers are guilty of this error, as in the following examples cited by Nesfield (*Errors in English Composition*). 'Each of them was busy in arranging their particular concerns' (Jane Austen). – 'Everyone must judge of their own feelings' (Byron). – 'Let each esteem other better than themselves' (Phil., ii, 3).

Usually *each* or *every* can be changed to *all* or *both* without injuring the sense.

each and every, as in 'I must thank each and every one of you', is redundant and verbose. Use either *each* or *every*.

each other. 'We know what each other are doing' is cited by Henry Bradley, as instance of wrong use as a nominative; it also illustrates the confusion of singular and plural so often caused by the word 'each'. 'We know each what the other is doing', is correct but stilted; 'Each of us knows what the other is doing' overcomes all difficulties.

each other and **one another.** 'Even the atmospheres of Italy and Spain are quite distinct from one another – or from each other; I leave this point for grammarians to decide; it leaves your humble preface-writer gravelled' (R. B. Cunninghame Graham).

There is a traditional rule that *each other* should apply to two persons, animals, or things, and *one another* to three or more, but it has never been consistently obeyed and seems to be of little practical utility.

each other's, misused for *each other*. ' "We're both biased … but perhaps your bias and mine will correct each other's" ' – i.e. 'will correct each other' or better, 'will cancel each other' (E. R. Lorac, *Death of an Author*).

each, them, and **they each; we each** and **us each; you each.** Here, the case of *each* is not quite parallel to that of *both* in *they* (or *them*) *both*, *we* (or *us*) *both*, and *you both*.

Each is often used by good writers after a subject pronoun, as in 'They each chose a different one', or 'You each knew your lessons', or 'We each ate too much.' But

them each, you each (accusative), and *us each*
are more doubtful – They should normally
be changed to *each of them, each of you, each
of us*, except where the pronoun functions
as the indirect object. There is no objection to 'She gave them each a biscuit.'

Heaven knows why the late Professor
George O. Curme should have permitted
himself the following laxity: 'In the case
of *each* we may say: "She kissed *them each*"
(or *each of them*)': and I gravely doubt the
Professor's saying it himself.

earlier on, popular with the BBC, is as
uneconomical as **later on.**

early date, at an. If it = 'soon', use *soon*;
otherwise it is too vague to be useful.

earth; globe; world. *OED* defines the
relevant senses thus: *Earth*, 'the world on
which we dwell' (land and sea), hence 'the
present abode of man' (often contrasted
with heaven or hell).

Globe, a synonym for *earth* (first sense):
also, 'One of the planetary or celestial
bodies', the earth being itself a planet.

World, 'the earth', also 'the universe or
a part of it'; *the world's end* (generic), 'the
farthest limit of the earth'. A *world* is also
'a planet or other heavenly body, esp. one
viewed as inhabited'.

earthly is opposed to 'heavenly'; **earthy**
is 'of earth or soil; like earth', and it is used
in *of the earth, earthy* for 'frail, human', and
particularly for 'gross, unrefined'.

easier or **more easy** (adj.); **more easily**
(adv.). Hence, *easier* is not an adverb,
although it is permissible in colloquial
speech.

easterly and **eastern.** In current use,
easterly is used mostly of winds, *eastern*
being the general adjective; *easterly*, however, is not incorrect in the sense 'situated
towards the east'. So also with *northerly,
southerly, westerly.*

eastern (or **E**) and **oriental** (or **O**). See
Oriental and Eastern.

eastward; eastwards. The latter is
adverb only; the former is chiefly an adjective, but often functions as an adverb in
American English and in older British
writing.

eatable; edible. Whether as noun or as
adjective, these two words are correct.
They are not quite synonymous. *Edible*
chiefly means 'suitable to be eaten, not
poisonous', whereas *eatable* and *drinkable*
tend to mean 'palatable'. Dr Harry C.
Schnur writes: 'An edible fungus, if badly
cooked, may be uneatable. Similarly coffee as made in England, is potable but not
always drinkable.'

echelon, which formerly meant a steplike
military formation, has become a somewhat pretentious fashionable synonym for
'grade, rank', as in 'The upper echelons of
the Civil Service'. A word to be used but
not overused.

echoism and **onomatopoeia; echoic**
and **onomatopoeic; echo-words** and
echoic words. *Onomatopoeia* is 'the
formation of names or words from sounds
associated with the object or action to be
named, or that seem naturally suggestive
of its qualities' (*COD*); Jespersen, the great
Danish philologist and grammarian,
proposed *echoism* for this formation.
Collectively, such words are now called
echo-words (or *echoic words*), a better term
than *onomatopoeia* or *onomatopoeic words*
(*onomatopoeia* means, literally, 'word-
making'). *Echoism* is preferable to *onomatopoeia*, but rings a trifle pedantically.
One says, 'That word is echoic', whereas
one may say either '*Cuckoo* is an echoic
word' or 'It is an echo-word.'

eclectic is occasionally misused, perhaps
more frequently misunderstood, in the
sense of *fastidious in choice of the best*, but has
the opposite meaning (*COD*), 'borrowing
freely from various sources, *not exclusive* in
opinion, taste, etc.'.

eco-. See **VOGUE WORDS.**

economic corresponds to Political
Economy, as in 'the economic factor', and
can mean 'reasonably profitable', as in
'charge an economic rent'; *economical* is

'thrifty' or, of a thing, 'inexpensive'. See also **-ic and -ical** and **stingy.**

ecstacy, a frequent misspelling of *ecstasy.*

-ection and **-exion.** In the nouns: *connection, connexion; deflection, -exion; inflection, -exion; reflection, -exion;* the spelling with *x* was common in older British use, but most British writers now favour *connection, reflection,* etc. [In American usage, *connexion, reflexion,* etc., are rare.]

-ed, termination of past participle. On the pronunciation of this we may quote *OED*: 'The pronunciation *-èd* regularly occurs in ordinary speech only in the endings *-ted, -ded;* but it is frequently required by the metre of verse, and is still often used in the public reading of the Bible and the Liturgy. A few words such as *blessèd, cursèd, [accursèd], belovèd,* which are familiar chiefly in religious use, have escaped the general tendency to contraction when used as adjectives; and the adjectival use of *learnèd* is distinguished by its pronunciation from its use as simple participle (*learn'd*).'

edible. See **eatable.**

edifice = 'a building, a structure', or, derivatively, 'a large and imposing building'. Do not, for the love of architecture, call a *house* an edifice.

edition; impression; reprint; state. A book in its first printing is inevitably an edition; but it may – as also may any later edition – have two or several *states.* For instance, if after a certain number of copies have been machined, a correction or a change is made, or even if a different paper is used, the copies containing the change or correction or different paper constitute a later (second, third …) *state,* the original being the *first state.* When an edition is reprinted without correction, the resulting copies form an *impression*: an edition may have one, two, or more impressions. The first uncorrected reprint of the first edition is the *second* impression of the book; the second uncorrected reprint thereof, is the *third* impression. But the several un-corrected impressions of the second or any later edition are numbered anew: *2nd edition, 1st impression; 2nd edition, 2nd impression*; and so on. The term *reprint* is sometimes used loosely for an impression; so too is *reprinting,* which properly applies to the process, not to the result. Nowadays, *reprint* is generally reserved for a new edition (or a new impression) brought out some or many years after the issue of the preceding edition or impression, especially if the type has to be reset or the photographic process employed.

editress. Avoid, unless there is an all-compelling reason for its being used. See **SEXISM.**

educational; educative; eductive. The first is the general adjective corresponding to *education.* The second can be used in much the same way, but its specific sense is 'that has the power of educating, i.e. potentially educational; conducive to education'. The third corresponds to *eduction* and it = 'having the function of eliciting or developing', as in 'An eductive method of education' (*OED*).

-ee is commonly attached to a verb to mean 'person who undergoes the action', as in 'employee', 'trainee'. More controversially, it is now also used to mean 'person who performs the action', as in 'returnee, escapee'. Such words should be used with caution; but they cannot always be replaced by the more conventional 'returner' or 'escaper', since they usefully carry the 'perfective' nuance that the person *has* returned or escaped, and is not merely engaged in doing so.

e'er and **ere** (both pronounced *air*), constantly met with in poetry, are sometimes misunderstood. The former is a contraction of *ever,* the latter is an old word meaning *before* (as in 'ere long').

effect, effective. See **affect.**

effect that, to the, rarely conveys more than the simple *that.*

effective; effectual. See **efficient.**

effectuate is unnecessary – and horrible – for 'to *effect*'.

effeminate is not 'womanly', but 'womanish', 'unmanly', applied to men, their character, tendencies, habits, actions.

efficiency, misused for *proficiency*; **efficient** for *proficient*. 'If an amateur, through specializing, reaches a certain state [? stage] of efficiency and becomes a professional player [of games], his motive for playing often changes with his status' (examination essay script).

efficient, effectual, effective, and **efficacious** are often confused. The *efficient* man (capable, *knowing his job*) is *effective* in action, and his action is *effectual* in achieving its purpose. An efficient doctor prescribes only such medicines as are *efficacious*.

effort for 'any kind of achievement', 'any result of activity', is trivial and it should be used only where the jocular is permissible. 'That drawing was a particularly good effort of the child's' is trivial; 'His greatest effort was to pull a cork out of a bottle' is – presumably – jocular.

-efy. See **-ify.**

ego and **id.** In French, these conjoint terms are translated *le moi et le cela* ('the *I* and the *that*').

Ego is Latin *ego*, 'I'; in psychology, the *ego* is 'the conscious thinking subject, as opposed to the *non-ego* or object'; *id* is Latin for 'it', and in psychoanalysis it represents 'the inherited instinctive impulses of the individual'. These two definitions, which are those of *OED*, serve to indicate why the two terms are so often contrasted in psychology, esp. in psychoanalysis.

egoism and **egotism.** The former is 'the habit of looking upon all questions chiefly in their relation to oneself', also, 'excessive exaltation of one's own opinion; self-opinionatedness': as in 'The egoism of man ... can ... read in the planets only prophecies of himself' (Robertson, 1852).

Egotism is 'too much *I* in conversation', 'the practice of talking about oneself or one's doings', as in 'the egotism of personal narrative'. Hence 'boastfulness' and 'selfishness', as in 'Without egotism, I can safely say ...'.

An egoistic man is not necessarily selfish, an egotistic one is (*OED*).

Eire. See **Great Britain.**

either, often incorrectly used for *any* or *any one*. 'Did you notice anything peculiar about the manner of either of these three?' (Henry Holt, *Murder at the Bookstall*). 'There have been three famous talkers in Great Britain, either of whom would illustrate what I say' (Holmes, *Poet at the Breakfast Table*, quoted by Nesfield).

either for *each*. Letter signed J. M. S., *The Observer*, 9 Jan. 1938: 'When I was a child at an elementary school I was taught that it was incorrect to say "There are trees on either side of the road", as "either" means on one side or the other, but not both. Yet I find nearly all novelists, a famous thriller writer, and the daily Press making this mistake.' Cf. 'They never spoke about it: Edward would not, and she could not; but either knew what was in the other's thoughts' (Guy Pocock, *Somebody Must*, 1931).

This usage is in fact well established and reputable, but should be avoided where there is danger of ambiguity. Buses that 'run on either side of the river' might be taken to run sometimes on one side and sometimes on the other.

either or **either of,** (*neither* or *neither of*) + n. with a pl. v.: these are incorrect; e.g. 'This was not to say that during those wearing days either of them were idle' (Freeman Wills Crofts). A similar error is made with *either ... or*; e.g. 'Religious rites by which either Thebes or Eleusis were afterwards distinguished', Thirlwall, 1833, quoted by *OED* – 'Both poets are on the verge of mystical vision; neither actually seem to express it' (Charles Williams, *Introduction to Poems of G. M. Hopkins*, 1930). Dean Alford, one of our best authorities (*The Queen's English*, 1870), himself commits this error, when he speaks of 'the requirements of parenthesis, neither of which are taken into account in the ordinary rule'. [When the whole thought has a plural character, such sentences 'have a natural if not a correct grammatical ring' (Krapp).]

either ... nor for **either ... or** is, one might say, the fantastic dream of a fanatical heresy-hunter: and yet it occurs, not rarely but – if one allows for the enormity of the error – fairly often. Philip MacDonald is not in the habit of doing this sort of thing, sometimes, however, the excitement of his stories carries him away (he has an excellent excuse), and he falls into an example of the pilloried error: 'Its small and neat exterior gives to the unsuspecting client who tries it for the first time no indication either of the excellence of Mons. Laplanche's food, wines and cooking, nor of the preposterous charges made by Monsieur Laplanche' (*The Rynox Mystery*).

either of their sakes. See GENITIVE, VAGARIES OF THE, penultimate paragraph.

either ... or, misused for *both ... and.* 'Until then, I must ask you to preserve an open mind in your opinions, either of me or of what happened last night' (Seamark, *The Man They Couldn't Arrest*).

either ... or, wrongly positioned. This is a frequent error. The only rule is that the division must be made with logical precision.

eke. Cowper, in *John Gilpin*, has 'and eke with all his might'. Some other child may be puzzled as I was by knowing the verb *to eke out* and being ignorant of the old adverb *eke*, meaning 'also'.

elapse and **lapse** (vv.). Time *elapses* or slips away, passes, expires; *lapse* is (of men) 'to err', (of things) 'to fail, fall into disuse, become invalid', as when a life-policy lapses because the insurance premiums have not been paid. [For all senses, the usual noun is *lapse*, *elapse* being obsolete or rare.]

elder and **older.** The former is used only in family relationships or in reference to two specified persons: 'the elder brother', 'the elder partner'; in the sense 'pertaining to an earlier period, or to ancient times' ('A writer in the elder, more formal style'), it is obsolescent. *Older* is 'of greater age', 'longer established', as in 'an older custom', 'He looks much older' (*OED*).

electric; electrical. The former is now much the commoner. *Electrical* = 'connected with, dealing with electricity', as in 'There are very few electrical books in that library'; also *an electrical machine* (*OED*). Fig., both are available. Both words refer to the use of electricity as a direct source of power, in contrast with *electronic*, which refers to systems whereby one electric current controls another by means of a transistor, or thermionic valve, involving the flow of electrons.

ELEGANCIES. Here is a short list of those words and phrases which the semi-literate and far too many of the literate believe to be more elegant than the terms they displace. Some are genteel; some euphemistic; some plain catachrestic. If in doubt, consult also ARCHAISMS and LITERARISMS.

ablutions, perform one's
abode (home)
adjust one's dress
al fresco
albeit (also an archaism)
anent
anno domini (age: old age)
anon
aroma
assemblage (collection; assortment)
assignation
at this juncture
attire (n. and v.)
au courant and *au fait*
bairn (except in Scotland)
bard
beauteous (except in poetry)
bereavement

beverage
boon (n.)
bosom
broidered
cachet (fig.)
can but (can only)
charger (any horse)
charlady
City Fathers
collation
connubial rites
consume (to eat)
converse (as exactly synonymous with talk, v.i.)
corpulent
couch, esp. if *virtuous* (for mere bed)
countenance (n.)
crave (to beg; to ask)
cull (v.)
Cupid
damsel (except in verse or jocularity)
deboshed
deem
demise
denizen
dentures
develop (v.i. = to happen)
devotions, at one's
distrait(e)
divers (several, sundry)
divulge
dolorous (permissible in poetry and lofty prose)
domicile (n., non-legally, non-scientifically)
éclat
edifice; esp. *sacred edifice*
effluvium (smell); *effluvia* (scents)
elegant sufficiency, an
emanate (incorrectly used)
emolument
employ of, in the
emporium (shop)
epistle (any letter)
ere (also an archaism)
espousal
evince
expectorate
fain (also an archaism)
festive board, the (also a cliché)
floral tribute(s)

fraught
function (n.: used trivially)
garb (n.), *garbed*
garments
genus homo
goodly
gratis
habiliments
haply
helpmeet
histrionic art
hither
honorarium
Hymen (marriage, wedding)
imbibe
impecunious
implement (v.)
indisposition
indite
individual
instanter
interred; interment
isle (except in place-names)
Jehu (a coachman)
Jupiter Pluvius
lapsus calami
lapsus linguae
Leo (a lion)
liaison
libation (any potation)
liquid refreshment
lonely couch
luminary (e.g. a legal luminary)
magnum opus
menial (a servant)
mentor
mine host
misalliance
missive (any letter or note)
modicum
monarch
(to) *moot*
my Lady Nicotine
myrmidons
natal day
neophyte
nigh
non compos mentis
nuptials; nuptial couch
obsequies
odour

of late (recently)
orb (sun, moon)
orient (or *O.*) *pearl*
ozone
panegyric (of any praise however trivial)
partake of (to eat)
paterfamilias
patronize (shop at; to go, visit)
perchance
perspire
peruse (to read)
petite
plight one's troth
post-prandial
posterior (back side) and *posteriors*
  (buttocks)
powder(-)room
prevaricate
purloin
raiment
realistic (course)
redolent
remuneration
repast
repose (n. and v. in the senses: rest; sleep)
reside at
retire (go to bed)
Sabbath, the (as used by Gentiles: merely
  Sunday)
sanctum (a study, a 'den')
satellite (a follower)
save (preposition; also an archaism)
soigné, soignée
soiled
soirée
sotto voce
spirituelle
spouse
steed
strand (shore)
sufficient
sumptuous repast
swain
swoon (n. and v.)
*tender one's apologies, condolences,
  congratulations,* etc.
Terpsichorean
terra firma
Thespian
thither
thrice (except in poetry or lofty prose)

tiro (or *tyro*)
to the full (e.g. appreciate to the full)
toilet (water-closet)
transpire (to happen)
truly (as in 'truly great')
tryst (also an archaism)
twain (also an archaism)
umbrage (offence)
verily
veritable
verve
very (*heart-strings, life,* etc.)
viands (food)
victuals
visage
weal (also an archaism)
welkin
well nigh
wend one's way
whither
withal
wont (custom, habit)
Yuletide (also an archaism)

elegant is not good English (nor yet good
American) as a synonym for 'excellent'
('an elegant party') or 'first-rate' ('an
elegant lawn-tennis player').

elegy; eulogy. The former is a poem of
lament for the dead. The latter is an oration in praise of someone, who may or
may not be dead.

elemental, elementary. The former =
'of, connected with, like one or more
of the four "elements" (earth, air, fire,
water)'; 'pertaining to the powers, forces,
agencies of the physical world', as in
'elemental gods or spirits', 'elemental
religion', or 'like those powers' ('elemental grandeur'); 'of the nature of an
ultimate constituent of physical substances' ('the elemental operations of
Nature – of thought – of passion');
hence, 'constituent', as in 'elemental
ingredients'.
  Elementary has a technical sense in
chemistry; in general usage, its prevailing
sense is 'rudimentary', as in 'an elementary
book' or one that deals (simply) with first
principles, 'elementary school' (one in

which primary instruction or lessons are given) (*OED*).

elements, misused. See OFFICIALESE.

elicit and **illicit** are often confused in careless speech.

eliminate and **isolate.** Confusion seems to have arisen from the fact that to *eliminate* is to *remove* (get rid of) something from something, *isolate* is to *separate* something from other things.

eloquent. See at **grandiloquent.**

else's. The following are correct although once they were colloquial:

> *anybody* (or *anyone*) *else's*
> *everybody* (or *everyone*) *else's*
> *nobody* (or *no one*) *else's*
> *somebody* (or *someone*) *else's*
> *who* (or *whoever* or *whosoever*) *else's*

What has happened is this: the *else* has, in essence, become incorporated with the pronoun (*anybody*, *someone*, *who*, etc.): although we do not write *anybodyelse*, *whoelse*, etc., yet we think of the combination as a unit. Therefore it is only *else* which takes the genitive form, *else's*. A possible exception is *whose else*, rarer than *who else's* but permissible.

emanate, misused. 'The crime has astonished me. It's not the kind of thing I could ever imagine emanating from that house' (Margery Allingham, *Dancers in Mourning*). The writer means 'happening in that house'. *Emanating* is *flowing from*, immaterially.

emend. See **amend.**

emerge and **issue.** To *emerge* is 'to come forth into view from an enclosed and obscure place', as in 'The stream emerges from the lake, the moon from the clouds'; 'to rise into notice' and esp. 'to issue (come forth) from suffering, subjection, danger, embarrassment, etc.', as in 'France emerged triumphant from the great Revolution'; (of a fact, a principle) 'to come out as the result of investigation, cogitation, discussion', as in 'At last

there emerged Einstein's Theory of Relativity.'

To *issue*: There is no difficulty about the transitive use. The intransitive verb is 'to go out or come out; come forth; flow out, sally out', as in 'A band of brigands issued from the stronghold', 'The river issued into the sea at a desolate point of the coast'; fig., it is used in much the same way as *emerge*, i.e. 'to go out, or come out, of a state or a condition', as in 'He issued scatheless from that peril', 'She will issue dazed from the coma'; legally, 'to be born or descended' (cf. '*bodily issue*') and, of revenue, income, etc., 'to accrue'; compare the more general sense, 'to take (its) origin; to spring; be derived', as in 'Can malevolence and misery issue from the bosom of infinite goodness?'; hence, 'to result', as in 'Excitement issuing from a stimulus'; hence, to *issue* (or end or result) *in*; 'to be published', as in 'Far too many books are issued nowadays' (*OED*).

emigrant and **immigrant.** The same person may be both, but not at the same time: leaving one's own for another country, one is an *emigrant*; arriving from another country, an *immigrant*.

eminent. See **immanent.**

employ is obsolescent for *employment*, even in *in the employ of.*

employée is incorrect for *employee* or, as a masculine, for (French) *employé*, which latter should be avoided. English *employee* is used for either gender. [The spelling *employe*, with no accent, is common in American usage.]

empty and **vacant.** Empty = 'containing nothing' (a jug without water, a room without furniture); 'carrying nothing' (*empty ship*, *empty hands*); of persons, 'frivolous'; of things, 'vain' (*empty pleasures*). But a *vacant* room or house is a room or house in which there are no people, i.e. 'unoccupied', as also in *a vacant post* (or *position*), *office*, *benefice*; as 'devoid of' (*vacant of generosity*), it is obsolescent; (of time) 'free, leisure(d)', as in 'a hobby for one's vacant hours'; 'idle' (*a vacant life*); 'meaningless, expressionless, inane' (*vacant stare* or *look* or *smile*) (*OED*). See also COMPARATIVES, FALSE.

enclose, enclosure are, by usage, preferred to *inclose, inclosure*.

enclosed herewith = *enclosed*. But prefer *with* or *inside*, where possible.

end by. See PREPOSITIONS WRONGLY USED.

endeavour to, it will be our = we shall try to.

ended is 'that *has* come to an end'; **ending** is 'that is ending' or, loosely, 'that is about to end'. In other words, *ended* refers to the past, *ending* to the present or the future. Actually, the future is often implied in the present, the present in the past; nevertheless this philosophical subtlety does not justify the use of *ended* for *ending*, as in 'We shall dismiss him in the year ended in four days' time.' But *ending* as, as a historic present, convey a past, as in 'We are sending a report for the quarter ending (on) March 31st, 19–.' We seen is too dogmatic on this point, for even in reference to an event (or a period) already passed, *ending* is usual.

endemic; epidemic. An *endemic* disease is habitually prevalent in an area. An *epidemic* spreads rapidly in a community at a given time, and then dies out.

endless is 'without actual or readily discernible end'; it does not, in sober prose, = *innumerable*, as it is made to do in 'endless platitudes', 'endless examples', but it is hyperbolical, not incorrect English.

endorse; indorse. See **indorse**.

endways and **endwise** are given by *OED* as interchangeable.

enervate is to weaken (a person or an animal) physically or mentally or morally; it does not mean to nerve or invigorate (a person).

enforce. One may *enforce* a regulation, or *enforce* behaviour *on* a person, but one cannot *enforce* a person *to do*, or *into doing* something. For that construction, use *force* or *coerce*.

engender for *cause* should be used with care (as an intransitive, *engender* is obsolete). Primarily (esp. of the male), it = 'to produce (a child)'; its transferred senses are 'to give rise to, produce (a state of things), a disease, force, quality, feeling, etc.' (*OED*). 'Hate engenders strife' and 'Heat engendered by friction' are correct, whereas 'Coal is engendered by buried forests' is incorrect.

ENGLISH, STANDARD. See STANDARD ENGLISH.

enigmae is an incorrect plural of *enigma* as though of Latin origin (*Notes and Queries*, 24 Apr. 1937). *Enigma* is Greek, but having become an English word, it takes the ordinary plural in -*s*.

enjoy; enjoyed. 'Fortunately the Wages Tribunal disallowed this claim, although it virtually invited the applicants to make an application for some further improvement in the terms enjoyed' – i.e. to be had – 'in the near future' (Stockholders' Union circular). To *enjoy* can indeed mean 'experience', as in the expression, 'he enjoys very poor health', and 'does not enjoy good health', where there is no question of 'enjoyment', but of *having* good or bad health, or even of *suffering* from some complaint.

enlarge and **enlargement.** C. C. Boyd (*Grammar for Grown-Ups*) quotes from a newspaper: 'For the enlargement of the activity of his department Mr N. Chamberlain, etc.', and points out that 'you do not *enlarge* activity: you *increase* it'.

enormity; enormousness. The former is correctly used only of extreme wickedness, a gross offence; the latter (which should not be replaced by *enormity*) only of great size.

enough, following an adjective, is equivalent to *sufficiently* preceding that adjective. Thus, *strange enough = sufficiently strange* except that the former emphasizes *strange*, whereas the latter throws the emphasis on the adverb. (One does not say *enough strange*: usage forbids it.) But if we separate *strange* from *enough* by inserting a noun, we create at best a strangeness, at worst an ambiguity, as in 'Nature, that moves in us by strange courses enough if need be, ...' (Michael Innes, *Lament for a Maker*), where usage demands 'Nature, that moves in us by courses strange enough ...'.

enough that, enough so that. Incorrect for *enough* to (+ infinitive).

enough and **sufficient.** See **sufficient.**

enquire, inquire; enquiry, inquiry. See also **query and inquiry.** In modern British use, *enquire* and *enquiry* are preferred for a simple request for information, *inquiry* for a formal investigation. The Americans prefer *inquire, inquiry* for both.

ensure is to make sure or make sure of (a thing, or that ...); **insure** is the more usual word in the field of *life-insurance* and similar contracts. See also **assurance.**

enthuse is to be avoided, though it has its apologists.

enthusiastic, misused for *excited.* 'The children are wildly enthusiastic as they push forward into the big tent (of the circus).'

entire. See COMPARATIVES, FALSE, also **complete, entire, whole.**

entirely. A witness in a notorious lawcase was reported as saying: 'I was put entirely in a rather awkward position.' – 'Entirely' and 'rather' are mutually contradictory – but a witness under crossexamination cannot always make a cool choice of his or her words.

entirely without being is very clumsy for *being without* or *being far from* or *although not at all,* as in 'Entirely without being distinguished, Meade had a brisk business-like way' (Carolyn Wells, *The Clue of the Eyelash*).

entomology; etymology. The former concerns insects; the latter the history of words.

entrance; entry. Both = 'the action of coming or going in', but *entrance* connotes the action, *entry* the result. *Entrance = right of entry* in 'Free entrance and safe egress' (Lytton). Both nouns are used of 'that (whether open or closed) by which one enters', as a door or gate or passage; but only *entrance* is used attributively (*entrance-hall*). In seamanship and book-keeping, only *entry* (*OED*). *Entry* can also mean *entrant* (in a competition or contest).

entrust. See **intrust.**

enumerable. See **innumerable.**

enunciation. See **annunciation.**

envelop and **envelope.** The former is the verb, the latter the noun.

envelope (n.). Pronounce *enn-*, I say, not *on-*; the latter being French. *On-* is the more absurd in that the French noun is *enveloppe.*

enviable, worthy of envy; **envious,** (of a person) feeling envy.

environmental. See VOGUE WORDS.

envisage is officialese for '*to face*' or 'to *plan*'.

epic is not to be used lightly of the merely exciting.

epidemic. See **endemic.**

epigraph and **epitaph.** The latter an inscription commemorating the dead, especially on a tomb; the former, on any building, but now rarely on a tomb. *Epigraph* is also a legend on a coin: a motto or key-quotation on a title-page or under a chapter number or heading.

epistle and **letter.** Do not use the former as an exact synonym of the latter: an *epistle* is a formal or didactic or literary or elegant letter.

equable. See **equitable.**

equal should not be used (as it is once used early in R. H. Mottram's *You Can't Have It Back*) for *equable* as applied to mind or temper. One says 'an *equable* or tranquil mind' and 'an *equable* or even or unruffled temper': to employ *equal* for *equable* is, at best, an archaism. See also COMPARATIVES, FALSE.

equally as. See **as, equally.**

equate. One *equates* one thing *with* another, or a compound subject joined by *and*.

equitable; equable. The former = 'fair and just', as in 'an equitable distribution of the assets'. *Equable* = 'moderate and steady', as in 'an equable climate'.

EQUIVOCAL WORDS. See AMBIGUITY.

ere. See **e'er.**

erratum, error, plural, *errata*, should be reserved for corrections in books. Do not, of course, use *errata* as a singular, or form the deviant plural *erratas*.

eruption is a bursting out, **irruption** a bursting in.

escalate. See VOGUE WORDS.

escapee. See **-ee.**

especial and **special.** As the opposite to *general*, *special* is preferred. But for 'preeminent, very distinguished', 'pertaining to one particular case' and also in the obsolescent phrase *in especial* (*for your especial benefit*), *especial* is used. The same applies to *especially* and *specially*. But in colloquial speech, *special(ly)* is displacing *especial(ly)*.

essential ('absolutely necessary') should not be debased to mean merely *necessary* or *needful*. See also COMPARATIVES, FALSE.

essential ... must. 'It is essential that pageant must play its part', for *should* play its part.

et cetera, etc., meaning 'and other things' (Latin plural neuter), is insulting

when applied to persons. Publishers sometimes put *etc.* at the end of an incomplete list of authors. In December 1937, there appeared a Christmas number with this inset on the front page:

Contributions by

HUGH WALPOLE

STEPHEN LEACOCK

LAURENCE HOUSMAN

etc.

8-Page Supplement

CURIOSITIES ROUND THE WORLD

The polite thing to use here would have been *et al.* (= and others).

In formal writing, *etc.* should be avoided: use either *et cetera* or, better, an English equivalent.

eternal. See COMPARATIVES, FALSE.

ethic and **ethical** (adjs.). Except occasionally in grammar (e.g. *ethic dative*), *ethical* is now the usual adjective corresponding to *ethics*. See **-ic and -ical.**

ethic and **ethics** (nn.) are occasionally confused by those who should know better, for *ethic* is a word unknown, or, at the least, unused by the great majority. OED defines *ethics* as 'the science of morals', but a person's (or institution's) particular system of moral science may be called his or her *ethic*; e.g. 'The drab discipline of his days was beginning to suggest that one may purchase too dearly the satisfaction of sticking to a private and unpopular ethic' (Richard Aldington, *Very Heaven*). The adjective *ethic*, now usually *ethical*, is defined as 'of or pertaining to morality or the science of ethics' (*OED*).

ethnic used to be merely the adjective associated with *ethnology*, the scientific study of peoples. It is now a VOGUE WORD (*q.v.*).

etymology. See **entomology.**

eulogy. See **elegy.**

euphemism, confused with *euphuism*. A *euphemism* is a prudish evasion (*to go to his eternal rest* = to die); a *euphuism* is a literary, stylistic excess (e.g. of antitheses) exemplified in and fathered by Lyly's *Euphues*, 1579, and *Euphues and His England*, 1580. (For a common misapprehension of the precise meaning of euphuism, see my *The World of Words*.)

EUPHEMISMS. *Euphemism* comes from a Greek word meaning 'to speak favourably', and Greek provides what is perhaps the most famous of all euphemisms: *Eumenides*, 'the Kindly Ones', for the Furies, the Avenging Gods.

In *The King's English*, the Fowlers define euphemism as the 'substitution of mild or vague expression for harsh or blunt one'. In *The Romance of Words*, Professor Ernest Weekley speaks of euphemism as 'that form of speech which avoids calling things by their names' and observes that it results from 'various human instincts which range from religious reverence down to common decency'. Often, I fear, it springs from nothing so decent as either reverence or decency: too often it is an indication of prudery or an exaggerated genteelism.

Perhaps I may here interpolate my belief that if there were no synonyms, there would be no euphemisms – and no obscenity. If it were made compulsory to use one word and one word only for 'to defecate', 'to urinate', 'to die', 'to kill', 'to copulate', and their nouns, as well as for certain bodily parts (especially the genitals), the squeamish would be reduced to using gestures and then, by force of public opinion and by a growing shamefacedness, to employing the sole terms. The same thing would apply to obscenities, which, after all, represent merely the polar counterparts of euphemisms.

But let us pass from speculation to fact. Three writers* have written pertinently

*On certain specific points and words, Allen Walker Read has contributed invaluable information and views.

and clearly and suggestively on the subject: Professor G. H. McKnight, Henri Bauche, and Professor Albert Carnoy.

McKnight, in *English Words and Their Background*, pointed out that, contrary to a rather general impression, 'one of the most distinctive features of sophisticated speech, as distinguished from unsophisticated speech in our time, is the absence of squeamishness and the ready courage to name things directly'. Since the War of 1914–18, indeed, it is only the semi-educated and the uneducated who have persisted in constant euphemism, and, since civilization began, it has always been the 'half-baked' who practise euphemism the most.

Bauche has contributed to the subject chiefly by pointing out that the distinction between the harsh or the gross word and the word not thought to be either harsh or gross is somewhat arbitrary in all languages; that the harshness or the grossness does not correspond exactly to the picture evoked by the word; that different peoples and different social classes vary considerably not only at different but at the same periods with regard to which things, which acts, and which words are to be treated as objectionable; and that, in one restricted but important group (physical intimacy and the sexual parts), the euphemisms are to some extent accountable by the fact that the anatomical terms would, with perhaps one exception (the male generative organ), be out of place and pompous, whereas the 'old Roman words' have become too gross to be used by the respectable – except among intimates.

In *La Science du mot* (a wholly admirable book), Carnoy has a very important chapter on euphemism and its opposites, dysphemism. Euphemism he neatly defines as discretion in speech. He shrewdly notes that euphemism is employed, not to hide the truth – the fact – the thing (silence were best for that), but merely to minimize the painful impression on the listener or the perhaps unpleasant results for the speaker; related to the latter purpose is the speaker's desire to make a favourable impression. Carnoy has classified the direct causes of euphemism and the particular reasons for its use. Here is that classification, which I have taken the liberty of slightly modifying.

1. *The desire to adapt oneself to the general sentiment suitable to, or the general atmosphere of, the time, the place, the company.* In an elevated form: anxiety to preserve a lofty or a beautiful style in poetry, oratory, etc., where unseemly trivial words or metaphors would jar on one. In addressing children, or in lowly or very friendly circles: avoidance of medical (or otherwise technical) or literary words by the employment of euphemistic terms; in addressing children, a euphemism is frequently due to a modesty that would be ludicrous or misplaced among adults, or to a wish to spare them painful knowledge.

2. *The desire to enhance the value of what one possesses or of what one wishes to give* (a form of hyperbole). As in *saloon* for a bar, *university* for a technical school, *engineer* for a mechanic, and *professor* for a teacher or simply an exponent.

3. *Respect for the person addressed (or referred to); or desire to impress or please or merely not offend the person addressed.* Titles; the stereotyped politenesses of the professions and of commerce; *senior citizen* for old-age pensioner, and *Down's syndrome* baby for mongol; *lady* for any woman, and especially *charlady* for charwoman.

4. *The need to diminish, to tone down a painful evocation or to soften tragic or painful news.* This, among civilized peoples and especially in refined circles, is the most frequent of all reasons. Death above all, but also madness (or idiocy), disease, ruin. *To pass away, be no more, leave this world, go to a better world, go west, pass over, expire, breathe one's last, fall asleep in the Lord, join the great majority,* and many other phrases, instead of the simple and infinitely dignified 'to die'; and this tendency has spread to undertakers and their functions: *mortician, funeral director, obsequies,* and other atrocities.

5. *Social and moral taboos.* There are actions and objects that are either blameworthy or very intimate: and therefore not

as a rule mentioned directly in good company. A mild example is drunkenness, which gives rise to many euphemisms: *tight, pissed, lit up.* The 'inferior' physical processes and functions afford a stronger and better example: for these, delicacy, reticence and politeness devise euphemisms as discreet as *retire* or *pay a visit* or (among women) *powder one's nose* or (among men) *wash one's hands.* All that relates to sex is heavily veiled: a pregnant woman is *in an interesting condition*; a person lacking in restraint is *fast*, whereas one that constantly exercises self-restraint is *slow* and *dumb*; a lover of either sex is a *friend*; the intimacy of marriage becomes *conjugal relations*; obscene (in the sense of rich in sexual detail) becomes *blue* or *hot* or even *frank*.

6. *Superstitious taboos and religious interdictions.* The word is God; speech has a mysterious power; the name evokes the thing.[*] These three points of view – these three facets of the one idea – explain many ancient and modern euphemisms; and the same emotion or attitude, at different stages, is represented by the philosophic concept of the *Logos* and the popular belief implicit in *speak of the devil.* The latter is seen in the old superstition that one must be particularly careful in speaking of God, the gods, important persons, the dead; with regard to the Deity and Jesus Christ, this belief survives in such mild oaths as *by gad!, by golly! drat it!, gee-whizz!* Superstition may, however, become pure reverence, and reverence of another kind is felt by those who are profoundly in love, for, to them, reverence dictates a euphemistic vocabulary of intimacy.

Frequently, euphemism causes successive synonyms to be suspect, displeasing, indelicate, immoral, even blasphemous. This we see in such words as *lover* and

---

[*]*Numen et nomen,* essence and name (or manifestation). In the scriptural 'the Word is God', the Latin is *verbum.* The taboo springs from the primitive notion: the name = the potence or reality of the god, person, or thing. (See my *Name This Child.* p. 2, n. 3.)

mistress, simple and *silly*, and French *fille.* As Weekley has said, 'a euphemism is doomed from its birth'; Carnoy has said much the same: 'La vertu adoucissante des termes euphémistiques n'est naturellement pas de très longue durée. Dès que les gens se sont pour de bon habitués à comprendre *B* quand on dit *A*, *A* exprime aussi clairement *B* que le symbole propre à ce dernier. Il faut donc recommencer et aller chercher un nouveau mot qui puisse voiler *B* sans l'obscurcir tout à fait. Dans l'entretemps, *A* s'est définitivement infecté du sens défavorable de *B* et s'est donc dégradé.' (Et ainsi de suite.) An excellent example is afforded by *mad*, which became *crazy*, which became *insane*, which became *lunatic*, which became *mentally deranged*, which became *deranged* and, a little later and in slang, *mental.*

Euphemism may be obtained by directing the thought in the desired direction, as in *honorarium* or *convey* (to plagiarize); by using an extremely vague phrase, as in *commit a nuisance*; by mentioning a significantly concomitant circumstance, as in *remove* (to murder); by being enigmatical or elusive, as in *pass away* (to die); by understatement, as in *have had a glass* (to be tipsy), or the negative litotes (*it's not too safe*); by irony; by employing another language (e.g. the Latin found in translations of *Daphnis and Chloe*); by reticence, as in *you know where to go* (to hell!); and by abbreviation, as in *w.c.* (itself euphemized to *w.*) and TB (more properly, Tb.: tuberculosis).

(This represents an adaptation and reduction of 'Euphemism and Euphemisms' in my *Here, There and Everywhere.*)

euphoria. See VOGUE WORDS.

euphuism. See **euphemism**.

Euro-. See VOGUE WORDS.

European requires *a* not *an*.

evacuate the wounded is a horrible variation of the dignified *remove the wounded.* Beginning as military officialese, it has become general, and is now proba-bly the main sense of the verb. I won't swear that I haven't used it myself.

even (like *actually*, *definitely*, and *really*) is often used where there is no need for it, with the result that, instead of the desired emphasis, there is weakness, as in 'That thoughtful, appraising look turned all the time upon himself, worried Granadi rather; even hard-bitten as he was, and plausible, specious liar that he knew himself to be at a moment's pinch' (John G. Brandon); 'hard-bitten though he was' would have served, with 'as' for 'that' as a further improvement.

This adverb requires to be watched for punctuation; often a comma will prevent its being apprehended as an adjective. It is important to place *even* as near as possible to the word or phrase it relates to.

eventuate. This bad, ugly, and wholly unnecessary word usually means no more than *to happen, to come to pass.* Sir Alan Herbert (*What a Word!*) gets good fun out of it and quotes a misuse supplied to him by a curate in the East End: 'If more people do not eventuate, the meeting will not be held.' *Eventuality* for 'event' or 'possibility' is no less deplorable.

ever is often used unnecessarily, as in 'It remains doubtful whether any evidence against McCabe could ever have been collected by any methods other than those which Smith used' (a detective novel). Where it is legitimately used after *when*, *where*, *who*, etc. to intensify a question, the result should be spelt as two words, not one. 'How ever did you know?' 'I wonder what ever she meant?'

ever, seldom or. See **seldom or ever**.

everlasting. See COMPARATIVES, FALSE.

every, misused, e.g.. by Gerald Balfour, speaking in February 1898, and quoted by Nesfield: 'We already possess four times as great a trade with China as every other nation put together' (*all other nations*). – Cf. '"We've got to have every possible information concerning him that we can get"'

(John G. Brandon), where *every* should be *all*, though *every piece of information* would also be correct.

every takes the singular. 'Every man must be at *their* desk' is incorrect. Cf. **each.**

every time for *always*. The former refers to separate occasions, *on each occasion*; the latter means *at all times*, or *all the time*.

everybody or **everyone** followed by *they*, etc. See **anyone ... they.**

everyone, misused for *every one*; e.g. 'Everyone of the things was in its right place.' *Everyone* is everybody, *every one* is every single person or thing.

everyone's (or **everybody's**) **else**. See **else's.**

everyplace is colloquial American English for *everywhere*, as in 'I looked everyplace for his book.'

evidence and **testimony.** If you are in doubt on this point, consult *Webster's New International* or *The Shorter Oxford Dictionary*. *Evidence* is 'an appearance from which inferences may be drawn; an indication'; hence, 'ground for belief', as in 'The weight of evidence appears strongly in favour of the claims of Cavendish' (T. H. Huxley); whence the legal senses, 'information given in a legal investigation, to establish the act or point in question', as in *to bear*, or *give*, or *give in evidence*; the *evidence* is 'the testimony which in any particular cause has been received by the court and entered on its records'; cf. *to turn King's* (or *Queen's*) or *State's evidence*.

In current usage, it is best to reserve *testimony* for its set scriptural senses; one may, however, still speak of 'the *testimony* of the physical senses', though 'the *evidence* ...' is now the general term (*OED*).

evidence (v.). *To be evidenced*, for *to be shown* (or *indicated*), is ugly – and overworked.

evince, originally meaning to *overcome*, *subdue*, but now obsolete in that sense, is used for *to show*, *exhibit*, *make manifest*, but

it is a bad word and unnecessary. Whitten (*Good and Bad English*) rightly says, 'it is still a favourite with callow journalists who like to write "he evinced a desire" instead of "showed, expressed", etc.'.

ex-. See **late and ex-.**

exactly similar. See **similar, exactly.**

EXAGGERATION. See **HYPERBOLE.**

exalt; exult. The first means 'elevate in rank' or 'praise highly'; the second means 'rejoice in triumph'.

examination paper for *script* is ambiguous, an 'exam paper' being strictly the paper of questions set for examination, not the candidate's written answers (his or her *script*). [In American English, *script* is not current in this sense. Commonly, 'examination questions' are passed to the students, who write their '(examination) papers' or 'books'.]

example. See **illustration.**

example where is incorrect for *example in which*, as in 'This is an example where great care must be exercised.'

exceeding. See **excessive.**

excellent. See COMPARATIVES, FALSE. It is true that there are degrees of excellence, but *excellent = excelling*. There is connoted a dichotomy comparable with that of *major* and *minor*: things that excel are *excellent*, things that do not excel are not excellent. 'Jones is an excellent chap, but Smith is more excellent still – and Robinson? Why! Robinson is the most excellent of these truly excellent fellows' rings oddly: such a sentence should be avoided. As for *the Queen's most excellent Majesty*, *most* here is absolute. See **most.** Whereas *a most excellent fellow* is defensible, *the most excellent fellow of them all* is – well, infelicitous.

except as a conjunction (= *unless*) is in the present century to be avoided: idiom has left it behind; it is now a barbarism. 'He said he saw nobody with her [*except she had* *somebody under the cloak]' (The Sessions Papers of the Old Bailey,* 1754), was all very well in the 18th century, but 'I won't go except you do' is indefensible nowadays, although 'except that it is so wet' is legitimate.

excepting. See CONJUNCTIONS, DISGUISED.

excepting and **except** as prepositions. In 20th-century usage, *excepting* is not an exact synonym of *except*: Mary Howitt's 'Nothing to be seen ... excepting some blocks of marble' (1863) would now be '... except ...'. It is obsolete in the sense 'unless'. Indeed, it is now virtually restricted to the phrases *not excepting, always excepting* and *without excepting* as in John Morley's 'Of all societies ... not even excepting the Roman Republic, England has been the most emphatically political' (*OED*).

exceptionable and **exceptional** are frequently confused. *Exceptionable* is that to which exception may be taken. *Exceptional* is that which is an exception.

excerpt and **extract** (nn.). *Excerpt* is a literary word, synonymous with *extract* in the sense 'a passage taken out of a manuscript or a printed book or periodical; a selection; a quotation'. As a synonym for *offprint, excerpt* is not in general use.

excess. See **in excess of.**

excessive means 'beyond arrangement, beyond reason,' as in 'excessive flattery', 'excessive expense'; *exceeding* means 'very great', as in 'We are grateful for your exceeding generosity.'

excluding. See CONJUNCTIONS, DISGUISED.

excuse me ...! *excuse my doing* (something). '*Excuse my (me) doing* is sometimes used in the positive sense "forgive me for doing", but not infrequently in the negative sense "forgive me for not doing". Examples of the latter ...: Hazlitt, She said she hoped I should excuse Sarah's coming up ...; Dickens, You must excuse my

telling you ...; Kingsley, Excuse my rising, gentlemen, but I am very weak ...; Philips, You must excuse my saying anything more on the subject at the present moment' (Jespersen, *Negation*). The former is the logical usage; it is also the sensible one, for the second (the negative) usage – unless the intonation or the context precludes doubt – is ambiguous, as the Hazlitt and Dickens examples show. 'She hoped I would excuse Sarah's not coming up' and 'You must excuse my not telling you' would have been unambiguous.

Idiomatically, the *excuse me doing* form is generally understood to be positive; but it is much rarer than the *excuse my doing* form, especially since *c.* 1920, when the fused-participle doctrine began to ravage the land.

executor, executer; executioner. Only the illiterate confuse *executioner* (headsman, hangman) with either of the other two words. An *executor* is a legal term for 'a person appointed by a testator to execute (or carry into effect) a will after the testator's decease'; but an *executer* is a general term for one who, not in Law, executes or carries out a plan, an arrangement, an order, a promise – it is, however, decidedly obsolescent (*OED*).

exert for *exercise* is a very common error – and a wholly useless synonym, productive also, at times, of ambiguity. 'This failure to identify exerted a depressing effect on the Chief of the Criminal Investigation Department which was not lessened by the garbled accounts published in the evening ·papers' (Anthony Wynne, *The Holbein Mystery*). Why not 'had'? (Moreover, it is a deplorable sentence in other ways.)

exhausting; exhaustive. *Exhaustive* (or very full; complete) instructions or information may, by the listeners, be found *exhausting.*

exhibit a tendency to = to tend to. See ABSTRACT NOUNS.

exhilarate. See at **accelerate.**

-exion. See **-ection and -exion.**

exist, 'to be', 'to have being', 'to possess reality', 'to live (on a low plane, or barely)', is a weak word when used for *subsist,* 'to support life', 'to find sustenance'; but not an error, for *subsist* can signify merely 'to remain in being', i.e. 'to exist', although this neutral sense is much less used now than formerly. Thus, in the following passage from a School Certificate candidate's précis of Macaulay's *Defence of Arcot* (1751), *subsist* would be an improvement on *exist*: 'The sepoys told Clive that they would give their share of rice to the Europeans; saying that they [the sepoys] could exist on the gruel drained from it.'

exotic. Don't overdo this word, and make sure that you are using it correctly.

expect. Some have argued that *expect* should be used only of future events, rather than as a synonym of *think* or *suppose.* It is safer, in formal contexts, to avoid using this word about the present or past, as in 'I expect they were hungry.' See also **anticipate.**

expertise, 'skill', should be used with caution, for it comes from French, where it means 'a survey', 'a valuation', 'an expert's assessment or report' (Chevalley). As a verb, to *expertise* (or *expertize*) is to give an expert opinion.

explain does not mean 'show', nor 'indicate', nor 'prove'. 'In this glossary I have reached only *E*. This explains my rate of progress.'

explicit. See **implicit.**

explore every avenue, one of the common clichés of politicians, is a feeble and even contradictory expression; to *explore* is to *search out* (where ways are difficult and unknown), but an *avenue* is a clear road made on purpose to lead directly to its object. One would 'explore' a by-path or a jungle, not an avenue. 'He' an MP – 'was tired of all the figures of speech about exploring every avenue, and leaving no stone unturned, and ploughing the

sands, and so on' (John Ferguson, *Death of Mr Dodsley*).

expose. See **disclose.**

exposé for *exposition* (formal explanation; orderly précis; etc.) is a Gallicism – and unnecessary. But it now chiefly means 'disclosure of something discreditable'.

expressed is occasionally confused with *express* (adj.). *Expressed* is not a true adjective at all.

extant. See **extent.**

extempore. See **impromptu.**

extemporize. See **temporize.**

extent is a noun; *extant* (surviving, still existing) is an adjective.

extenuate. One *extenuates* guilt, so that extenuating circumstances are those that mitigate the seriousness of a crime. This verb is not to be used with a human object – one does not extenuate a person.

extrapolate. See VOGUE WORDS.

EXTREME READINESS. See FACILITY.

exult. See **exalt.**

exultance, a favourite word with a certain writer of thrillers, has no authentic existence; *exultation* is correct.

F

-f, plural of nouns in. The reason for the plural in *-fs* is a desire to ensure regularity – to make all nouns in *f* have their plural in *fs*. Admirable; yet the *-ves* plural is much more euphonious, I think, and easier to pronounce. (*Hoof* – *hoofs, roof* – *roofs*; but *loaf* – *loaves*: these are the usual forms.)

fable. See ALLEGORY.

fabulous, 'fabled, mythical, of the nature of a fable, belonging to a fable', hence 'marvellous, splendid'. This word is being grossly overworked. Use it with care.

face up to for *face* or *look in the face*. A needless expression, the result of the tendency to add false props to words that can stand by themselves; though some may argue that while *face* means merely 'confront', *face up to* carries the extra meaning of 'confront unflinchingly'.

face-lift. See VOGUE WORDS.

facetiae is a booksellers' euphemism for 'pornography' or 'a book with a certain amount of sexual interest' and should be avoided by anyone who is not a bookseller, for this is an absurd distortion of the correct sense of *facetiae*: 'Refined witticisms conceived in a spirit of pleasantry' (*Nuttall's Standard Dictionary*). One does not much like to see a bookseller so bend to the exigencies of his precious trade as to fall into this ineptitude: 'FACETIAE, UNEXPURGATED EDITION. *The Confessions* of Jean-Jacques Rousseau …'

FACILITY, or Extreme Readiness. In speech, those who have 'the gift of the gab' usually elucidate their loosenesses by gesture and by emphasis or intonation. But in writing there is no equivalent to gestures unless it be emphasis (with its concomitant risk of over-emphasis); none to intonation.

'Easy writing is hard reading' is true of everything but the most elementary and unsubtle writing.

I do not mean that, in writing, one should lose the thread and the verve by pacing the floor in search of the right word, the inevitable phrase: but all writing should be very carefully revised: at the back of one's mind should be the constant admonition, 'This may be clear in *my* mind, but it may not be clear to the reader.'

facility is often misused for *faculty*. In the senses most likely to be confused, *facility* is the ability to do something with ease and

fluency, whereas *faculty* is the innate power to do something before the ability is tested. 'His faculty for learning languages was demonstrated when he quickly acquired considerable facility in Urdu.'

fact, misused for *factor* (*q.v.*) is frequent in crime-novels since *c.* 1922; e.g. A. Feilding, *Death of John Tait*, 'Altogether she was a strange fact of the case.' – Cf. the entry at **factor.**

factitious and **fictitious** are occasionally confused. The former = artificial, not natural; not spontaneous; made up for a particular occasion. The latter = not genuine; arbitrarily – not rationally – devised; (of a name) not real; (of a character) deceptively assumed, simulated; imaginary, unreal; belonging to or characteristic of fiction.

factor is often grossly misused to mean anything from *fact* to *feature* or from *causation* to *cause*; a 'factor' being correctly a contributory element in causation or the composition of anything. Sir Alan Herbert quotes R. Davies, as reported in Hansard, 'I am assured that the greatest income from any single factor in Switzerland is in connexion with the League of Nations.' Especially frequent is the misuse of *factor* for *occurrence*, as in 'Sunburn and sand in the food are usual factors of beach parties.' Frequent, too, is its misuse for *element* or *constituent*, as in 'If we did not have some other factor [than fat, starch, glycerine] in our make-up, we should all remain alike' (examination script). See ABSTRACT NOUNS.

faculty. See FACILITY.

faëry; fairy. *Faërie* or *faëry* (with or without the diaeresis) is fairyland; hence an adjective (always attributive, as in 'the faëry world'), 'of or belonging to fairyland', hence 'beautiful and unsubstantial', hence, 'visionary, unreal' but with a connotation of beauty. *Fairy* is a fay, a supernatural being that lives in fairyland; hence an adjective (always attributive), 'of or pertaining to fairies', hence 'fairy-like'; also it = 'enchanted, illusory'.

faker; fakir. The former (one who 'fakes', a swindler, an impostor) is incorrect for *fakir*, a Muslim (or sometimes Hindu) religious mendicant, naked ascetic, wonder-worker.

failing. See CONJUNCTIONS, DISGUISED.

fall (USA) is the British *autumn*; *fall* is the more Saxon, the more poetical word ('the fall of the leaf, the fall of the year').

FALSE AGREEMENT. See AGREEMENT, FALSE.

FALSE COMPARATIVES and **SUPERLATIVES.** See COMPARATIVES, FALSE.

FALSE ILLITERACIES – false because the pronunciations are standard; e.g. *iz* for *is*, *duz* for *does*, and in Britain *wot* for *what*.

FALSE TITLES. See JOURNALESE at OFFICIALESE I.

falseness; falsity. Both = 'contrariety to fact; want of truth'; both = 'duplicity, deceitfulness'; only *falseness* now = 'faithlessness, treachery', or an instance thereof; only *falsity* = 'error in general or a particular error, untrue proposition, statement, doctrine' (*OED*).

familiar to. Things are *familiar to* persons, and persons are *familiar with* things. One thing, idea, method, etc. cannot be *familiar to* another.

famous. See **notorious and famous**. Also see **celebrity**.

fantastic is overused as a blanket term of approval. Prefer *excellent*, *spectacular*, etc.

fantasy and **phantasy.** 'In modern use *fantasy* and *phantasy*, in spite of their identity in sound and in ultimate etymology, tend to be apprehended as separate words, the predominant sense of the former being "caprice, whim, fanciful invention", ... that of the latter is "imagination, visionary notion"' (*OED*).

Far East. See **Middle East** ...

farther, farthest; further, furthest. 'Thus far and no farther' is a quotation-become-formula; it is invariable. A rough distinction is this: *farther, farthest*, are applied to distance and nothing else; *further, furthest*, either to distance or to addition ('a *further* question').

fascination of – for – by – with. Something has a fascination for persons, i.e. it fascinates them. 'The fascination of Elaine by Lancelot' is clear; but 'the fascination of Elaine' without a modifying 'by Lancelot' might have meant 'Elaine's fascinating qualities, or power of fascinating'. One is fascinated *by a person*, but *with a thing* (or a happening).

fatal, 'deadly, mortal, resulting in death', should not be debased to mean *grave* or *serious*, as in the instance: 'He had a fatal motor accident last month, but has completely recovered now.' To debase it to synonymity with *unfortunate* is still worse. See also COMPARATIVES, FALSE.

fatherhood is the quality of being a father; not, as sometimes, of having a father.

father-in-law is occasionally used for *stepfather*; *OED* quotes examples of this from Goldsmith, Dickens, and George Eliot, but this use is both confusing and incorrect. See also **daughters-in-law.**

FAULTY PRECISION. 'If the burglar had chosen Vanderlyn's room, it would almost certainly be he [Vanderlyn] and not the English maid, who would be lying dead at Bella-colline' (Mrs Belloc Lowndes, *The House by the Sea*). The correct form would be, 'it would almost certainly be Vanderlyn, and not the English maid, who would be lying dead'.

favour, 'to regard with favour, to show favour to', even 'to have a liking or preference for' ('He favours Roman Catholicism'), should not be used as a synonym of *prefer*. A good example of its misuse is, 'He favours a dog to a cat.'

favourable reception with. See PREPOSITIONS WRONGLY USED.

fearful; fearsome. In current English, both of these terms = 'causing or inspiring fear'; *fearsome* is slightly obsolescent and rather literary. Only *fearful* = 'afraid'.

feasible does not mean 'likely, probable', but 'doable, practicable'.

feature for *achievement* is catachrestic. 'Until his retirement at 46, he retained his pace and accuracy in the field, a feature without parallel.'

feedback. See VOGUE WORDS.

feel (n.), 'feeling' is now more usual for a mental sensation, as a 'feel of excitement'.

female as 'a mere synonym for "woman" ' is 'now commonly avoided by good writers, except with contemptuous implication' (*OED*) or with a facetious one.

femineity and **femininity.** The former is an archaic word for 'womanliness', hence 'womanishness'; for 'the nature of the female sex', *femininity* is the usual noun formed from *feminine* (*COD*).

ferment; foment. Either verb can be used in the sense of stirring up disorder: one *ferments* or *foments* a riot. But owing to their respective literal meanings, to *ferment* disorder suggests making it bubble up, while to *foment* it may imply warming it; perhaps a more quietly subversive proceeding.

fervent, fervid. The first carries the favourable connotation of 'ardent', the second the somewhat unfavourable suggestion of 'feverish'. In addition, persons may be *fervent* ('her fervent admirer') but not *fervid*.

festal; festive. Both = 'of or pertaining to a feast or festivity', though the former is now more usual, as it also is in the senses (of a person) 'keeping holiday' and (of a place) 'given up to feasting or festivity'. Both = 'befitting a feast; hence, joyous, gay', but *festive* is now preferred in these

nuances. *Festive occasion* and *festive season* are now set phrases.

fetch and **bring.** Weseen excellently distinguishes them.. '*Fetch* implies that the [person] spoken to is some distance from the thing to be brought ... *bring* ... that he is already near it. "Please bring me that paper you have"; "Please fetch my book from the library". *Go* is redundant with *fetch*, as "Go and fetch the paper". *Fetch* means go to something, get it, and bring it here.' [For many Americans *fetch* is, unfortunately, a homely and obsolescent word.]

few and **a few.** (Cf. the entry at **good few, a; good many, a.**) The difference has been admirably determined by *OED*: 'Without prefixed word, *few* usually implies antithesis with "many", [whereas] in *a few, some few* the antithesis is with "none at all". Cf. "few, or perhaps none", "a few, or perhaps many".'

The few now generally = 'the minority' and is opposed to *the many*, i.e. 'the majority'.

fewer; less. See **less.**

fictional, fictitious, fictive. *Fictional* is 'of, pertaining to, or of the nature of fiction', as in 'fictional literature', 'It is a fictional work', 'His fictional friends give him more pleasure than he gets from his real ones.' Both *fictitious* and *fictive* = 'counterfeit, feigned, not genuine', but the latter is obsolescent; *fictitious* in the sense 'of, in, or like fiction (literature)' is now less common than *fictional*; both *fictitious* and (the now rare) *fictive* are applied to assumed names; both of these adjectives, though the latter now rarely, = 'existing in or created by the imagination'. But *fictive* is the correct term for 'imaginatively creative', as in 'Having a ... great fictive faculty' (J. M. Robertson); *fictitious* alone is correct in the legal sense, 'a fictitious son', i.e. an adopted one, and in the general sense, 'arbitrarily devised; not founded on rational grounds', as in 'a fictitious measure of values' (*OED*). See also **factitious.**

fiddle for violin is 'now only in familiar or contemptuous use' (*OED*). Unfortunately, the verb *fiddle* has gone the same way; we have to say, *play the violin*, and *violinist* rather than *fiddler*.

fiend is, in jocular usage, permissible for 'a person or agency causing mischief or annoyance', but in the sense 'addict' or 'devotee' – 'fresh-air fiend', 'coffee fiend' – it is slang (*OED*).

figure is not synonymous with *number*, but only with 'a number expressed in figures', i.e. in numerical symbols. A *number* is expressed in *figures*; figures represent a number or numbers.

FIGURES OF SPEECH. Those in common use today are probably HYPER-BOLE, METAPHOR, SIMILE, and UNDERSTATEMENT.

fill in; fill out. These two phrases are not interchangeable, as certain people seem to think. *Fill in* is to complete (an outline); to insert (into speech or writing) something that will occupy a vacancy, as in 'He left the date blank for me to fill in.' *Fill out* is to enlarge or extend to the desired size or limit; the Americans use it of a cheque or form, but *fill in* (or *fill out*) is the usual British phrase.

films. See **motion pictures.**

final (adj.). See COMPARATIVES, FALSE.

final (n.). See **finale.**

FINAL CLAUSES (clauses of purpose). Final or purposive clauses form one of the eight types of adverbial clause. They are introduced either by *that*, generally preceded by *in order* or *so* or – now only in literary language – *to the* (*end*) or by *lest* (equivalent to *that … not*). The rule for the right use of final clauses has nowhere been more clearly stated than in Dr C. T. Onions's *An Advanced English Syntax*.

'Final Clauses introduced by *that* take *may* with the Infinitive in present and future time, *might* in past time.'

'I eat that I *may* live' is the literary form of 'I eat in order that I may live' or the idiomatic 'I eat (in order) to live.'

'I shall eat well in order that I *may* keep fit.'

'They climbed higher that' – or *so that* – 'they *might* get a better view.'

'Conspirators are always secretive to the end that their secrets *may* not be divulged.'

'The conspirators were secretive to the end that their secret *might* not be divulged.'

Negative final clauses may be couched in the *that … not* mode; so far as the verbs are concerned, the sentences follow the *that* mode.

'I eat that I may not die' or '… in order that I may not die.'

'They climbed higher (in order) that they *might* not fall.' But even now in formal or literary language, as formerly in nearly all cultured or educated speech, *that … not* is less usual than *lest* in negative final clauses. *Lest* takes *should* (or, after the present or the future, *may*) with the infinitive.

> 'I eat lest I *should* (or *may*) die',
> 'I shall eat lest I should (or *may*) die',
> 'I ate lest I *should* die.'
> — (may being obsolescent)

A good example of the wrong verb after *lest* occurs in E. R. Lorac's *Death of an Author*. 'He hastened his steps a little, lest he were left in the lurch again', *were* being incorrect for *should be*.

'He forgets not his viaticum lest he *fail* to reach the happy shore.'

> To act that each tomorrow
> Find us farther than today,

where *tomorrow* is a noun.

'Relative Clauses with Final or Consecutive meaning sometimes take *shall* (*should*), equivalent to the Latin Subjunctive.'

> Build me straight a goodly vessel
> That *shall* laugh at all disaster.
>   (Longfellow)

'An act might be passed which *should* not entirely condemn the practice.' In this latter sentence, *did* would have been less formal than *should*. See SUBJUNCTIVE.

final upshot, like **final completion** and **final ending,** is a tautological absurdity.

finale and **final** (n.). The latter in athletics and (also as *finals*) in examinations; the former in music, in drama or variety, and fig. as 'the conclusion; the final catastrophe'.

finalize is perhaps a useful verb, in bureaucratic contexts, for 'put into final conclusive form', as in 'finalize the details'; but where possible prefer *complete, finish*, etc.

fine as an adverb ('He's doing fine') is colloquial.

Firenze for *Florence*. See **Bruxelles ...**

first for *at first* can lead only to ambiguity or to that momentary check which is more irritating though less dangerous. 'The murder might not be as commonplace in its occasion, nor its solution as simple as he had first been inclined to think' (Sidney Fowler, *Four Callers in Razor Street*).

first for *just* (*after*) may be ambiguous, as in 'When they were first married they took several trips': better, 'Just after they married, they ...'.

first, two; three first; four first, etc., are incorrect for *first two, first three*, etc. For 'the two first chapters in the book' read 'the first two chapters ...'. This is the English idiom; French has 'les deux premiers chapitres ...'.

first name. See **Christian name.**

firstly is traditionally said to be inferior to *first*, even when *secondly, thirdly* ... follow it. Yet a list that goes *first ... secondly ... lastly* ... may be judged to be inconsistent. One way out is to write *first ... second ... last* ..., at least where the words can be construed as adjectives. 'There are several implications of this rule: first ... second ...'

fist for '*un*clenched hand' is now permissible as a jocularity.

fit often takes *fit*, in American English, for the British past tense and past participle *fitted*, in the sense 'be the right size (for)' or 'be suitable (for)'.

flair. Don't overdo this noun (which properly = 'instinctive discernment', 'unusually keen perceptiveness') in such senses as 'inborn ability' ('He has a flair for cricket') and – much worse – 'liking' ('She has a flair for gimcracks') (*OED*). [For an informative discussion of the word, see Joseph E. Gillet, 'Flair', *American Speech*, vol. 12 (1937), pp. 247–57.]

flammable, despite appearances, is a synonym of *inflammable*, not an opposite, and is preferred today in technical contexts concerned with fire hazard. Things that will not burn are *non-flammable*.

flaunt for *flout* seems to be a strange error – and, some would say, a rare one. It may be strange, but it is not rare. I fell into it in the 1st edition of *Slang Today and Yesterday*: and saw it with horror. Reading *The Owl's House*, by Crosbie Garstin (who could write well), I came on this, 'He achieved strong local popularity, a priceless asset to a man who lives by flaunting the law.'

flautist is the British word for a flute-player, *flutist* the American.

flavour of the month. See VOGUE WORDS.

flee and **fly.** The former has become literary. Both words can mean 'leave abruptly', or 'run away from', but *fly* is not used like that in the preterite. 'He fled (not flew) the country.'

fleshly is now used only in the senses (1) 'carnal', (2) 'lascivious, sensual': in which senses *fleshy* is catachrestic.

flier; flyer. Both are correct, the latter (esp. for 'an aviator') being the more common.

floor and **stor(e)y.** Usage prefers *stor(e)y* in relation to height, *floor* in relation to part of building; thus, 'The apartment is on the tenth floor of a fifteen-storey building.' 'It's a ten-storey building, and only two floors are empty.'

flout. See **flaunt.**

flow – flowed – flowed; fly – flew – flown. These are the correct forms.

fluidly, misused for *fluently.* 'The tea-lounge was full. Guests continued to arrive; all were greeted fluidly by the manager.'

fly. See **flee,** also **flow.**

flyer. See **flier.**

-fold, as in *twofold, threefold, fourfold, fivefold,* etc., and in *manifold* (*q.v.,* separately), originally represents 'folded in 2, 3, 4, etc.,' or 'plaited of 2, 3, 4, etc. strands' ('a *threefold* cord'); hence it serves as an arithmetical multiplicative. The multiplicative sense, once very common, is now employed chiefly with reference to largish numbers ('He has repaid me tenfold') or large numbers ('That is a thousandfold worse'), where the force of *-fold* is adverbial. The adjectives express 'rather a plurality of things more or less different than mere quantitative multiplication: cf. "a double charm" with "a twofold charm"' (*OED*); the hyphenated form is now rare.

folks for *folk.* 'The old folks at home'. *Folk* is already plural, but the added *s* modifies its meaning from the group or collective sense to that of the individuals composing the group, as in the above quotation, and gives a sentimental flavour.

follow. See **succeed.**

follow behind is unnecessary for *follow.* 'I found certain men who had penetrated boldly into the heart of the subject ... I follow behind them here' (Stuart Chase, *The Tyranny of Words*). If the gap is to be emphasized, why not 'follow from afar'? So too for *follow after.*

following, misused for *after.* 'For "following" ... there is a quite satisfactory substitute, the simple preposition "after". What the luckless "after" has done to merit being quietly cold-shouldered out of the language I cannot conceive. ...

'"Following dinner, the band of the Guards played a selection of music in the blue drawing-room."

'One hopes that the band managed to overtake their dinner before the evening was out.

'"Following a chase half across Europe, a beautiful spy was captured at Bucarest." The lady was apparently following the chase that was following her. It sounds like a vicious circle' (G. V. Carey, *Mind the Stop*).

The word may be more acceptable where it means 'after and because of', but it is usually best avoided. See also CONJUNCTIONS, DISGUISED.

foment. See **ferment.**

footpath. See **pavement.**

for and **because.** The former is subjective ('Don't swear, for I dislike swearing'), the latter objective ('They did that, because events compelled them'); the former may represent the writer's own view, the latter the immediate and explicit cause. 'Hirst swerved somewhat more than any other bowler ... But he was not the first swerver, because' – read *for* – 'Rawlin and Walter Wright swerved occasionally before he was ever seen.'

for ever means 'for eternity', 'for one's lifetime'; **forever** means 'constantly or continually', as in 'He's forever singing that song.' The Americans use *forever* for both senses, a practice which will probably triumph in the end.

for what? See **what ... for?**

for your information is, 99 times out of 100, superfluous. Its use is justified only when one reassures a reader that no action is necessary.

forbear is now less usual than *forebear* for 'an ancestor'.

forbid ... from. See PREPOSITIONS WRONGLY USED.

forceful; forcible. A *forceful* (not *forcible*) person is vigorous or strong or powerful; 'acting with force, impetuous, violent' is *forceful*; a writer, a painter, an orator that produces a powerful effect is *forcible*; a cogent, impressive, or effective speech or style is either *forceful* or *forcible*; a weapon drawn with force or violence is a *forceful* weapon; something done by force, or involving the use of force or violence, is *forcible* (e.g. 'a *forcible* expulsion', '*forcible* means'), esp. in Law, as in *forcible detainer*, *forcible entry*, *forcible abduction*, *forcible dissolution* (of, e.g. Parliament) (*OED*).

forecast – preterite *forecast* or *forecasted* – past participle *forecast* or *forecasted*.

forego and **forgo** should be distinguished, I believe; the former meaning to *precede in time or place* (i.e. to go before), the latter meaning to *relinquish*, to *go without*. Yet the 'relinquish' sense is now often spelt *forego*.

forename. See **Christian name.**

Forensic Medicine, although found in the calendars and syllabuses of many universities, is less correct than *Medical Jurisprudence*; Nigel Morlands, *The Conquest of Crime*, 'Forensic Medicine – or, to use the correct title, Medical Jurisprudence ...'. Whichever term is used, *forensic* means 'used in connection with Law'.

forever. See **for ever.**

forgo. See **forego.**

former for *first*. 'Jeffrey, Alexander and Sutton met in the former's office to discuss the situation' (Freeman Wills Crofts, *The Loss of the Jane Vosper*). 'In Jeffrey's office' would be the best phrase, but if there is a wish to avoid repetition of the name, 'in the office of the first-named'.

Former and *latter* are used only when there are two persons or things. See also SUPERLATIVE DEGREE.

formerly and **formally** are often confused by some writers. (I had forgotten this fact until I consulted Harold Herd's *Watch Your English*.)

formula, plural of. Prefer *formulas* in general, but *formulae* in the chemical and mathematical senses.

fort; fortress. Only the latter is now used figuratively. As military terms, both = 'a fortified place', but the latter is specifically one that is capable of receiving a large force. In Canada and the USA, a fortified trading place is a *fort* (now only historical).

forte is, in Music, dissyllabic; elsewhere it may have only one syllable. A *forte* is a person's strong point – that in which he or she excels; in fencing, it is the strongest part of a swordblade.

fortress. See **fort.**

fortuitous means 'happening by chance', and should not be used, as it increasingly is, to mean 'fortunate'.

forward and **forwards.** *Forwards* is an adverb only; *forward*, both an adverb and an adjective. In Great Britain, the adverbs *forward* and *forwards* are used as in the following masterly verdict of *OED*: 'The ... distinction ... is that the latter expresses a definite direction viewed in contrast with other directions. In some contexts either form may be used without perceptible difference of meaning; the following are examples in which only one of them can be used: "The ratchet-wheel can move only *forwards*"; "the right side of the paper has the maker's name reading *forwards*"; "if you move at all it must be *forwards*"; "my companion has gone *forward*"; "to bring a matter *forward*"; "from this time *forward*".' [Of American usage, *Webster's* says: 'In general, *forward* tends to displace *forwards* in most or all contexts, although the latter is still often used to express the actual direction, as of a movement.' The military order is '(forward,) march'.]

fraction is infelicitous for *portion*; incorrect for *proportion*, 'A large fraction of what passes for human folly is failure of communication' (Stuart Chase, *The Tyranny of Words*).

Frankenstein is frequently misused for *Frankenstein's monster*, which became dangerous to its inventive creator. Mary Wollstonecraft (who was Shelley's second wife) published, in 1818, her tale of terror, *Frankenstein*, which owed its inspiration to current scientific research.

free, gratis, and for nothing is a cliché, excusable only as a jocularity: *free gratis* and *free for nothing* are ludicrous tautologies.

-free. See VOGUE WORDS.

free-thinker (freethinker) is, in thought, an independent, but this usage is obsolescent; a *free-thinker* refuses to allow authority to overrule his or her reason in religious matters – not to be confused with an *agnostic*, nor yet with an *atheist*.

freight. See **cargo.**

FRENCH TERMS MISSPELT. A delightful correspondent, whose name I have unforgivably lost, writes (June 1947) to say, 'I rather wish you could have found a place in which to dismiss three misspellings that appear wrongly in nine out of ten English texts:

Folies Bergères for *Folies Bergère*;

hors d'œuvres for *hors d'œuvre*, writers seeming to think that the former is a plural, but they are mistaken;

Mistinguette for *Mistinguett.*'

To that list add: *crime passionel* for *crime passionnel*. The most common mistake of all, *bête noir* for *bête noire*, is treated separately.

frequent is now, except in archaic or very literary writing, used only in the senses, 'happening at short intervals; often recurring; happening (or coming) in close succession; (of a pulse) faster than is normal', as in 'The crops suffered from frequent blights' and 'The snow was deep ... and our immersion in unseen holes very frequent' (Tyndall); and (of an agent), 'constant or habitual', as in 'He was a frequent guest at the villa, a frequent patient at the hospital.' I myself often speak of 'a frequent error'; this is a permissible sense, unfortunately obsolescent (*OED*).

friendlily is less frowned upon than it used to be, and when we become accustomed to the sound, we shall no longer find *friendlily* inferior to *in a friendly manner*, than which, obviously, it is much more economical. *Friendly* as an adverb ('He talked friendly to me') is an illiteracy.

-friendly. See VOGUE WORDS.

friends with. 'I am friends with Bill' is as correct as 'We are friends of theirs.' As Dr Onions has remarked (*An Advanced English Syntax*, §24, last paragraph), this 'interesting case ... is not so startling an anomaly as it seems; it is easy to see how (e.g.) "He and the Prime Minister are great friends", by assimilation to "He is very friendly with the Prime Minister", could give rise to "He is great friends with the Prime Minister."' On the analogy of *friends with* is *shipmates with*: 'Captain Bolton of the *Caligula*, who tells me he was shipmates with you in the old *Indefatigable*' (C. S. Forester, *A Ship of the Line*).

from every angle = in every way; wholly, entirely.

from hence is unnecessary; *hence* = from here, from this. The same applies to *from thence* and *from whence*.

froze, preterite; *frozen*, past participle. It is, therefore, an illiteracy to say 'I am nearly froze to death.'

-fs. See **-f.**

-ful, as in 'handful', cupful', now usually forms the plurals 'handfuls', 'cupfuls', etc. The alternative (cupsful) is old-fashioned.

function (v.) for *to act, to work*, should be used only of machinery or of an organ that works like a machine. As a noun it is pretentious when used of an *informal* social gathering or festive meeting.

fundamental. See COMPARATIVES, FALSE.

funds is permissible for one's pecuniary resources, money at one's disposal (see *OED*); but do not use it indiscriminately for *money* or *cash*.

funeral and **funereal.** Only the latter is used figuratively ('gloomy, dark, dismal, melancholy, mournful'), as in 'We marched at a funereal pace' (Leslie Stephen), 'funereal shades of night'. As 'of or pertaining to or appropriate to a funeral', *funereal* is now rare except in poetry and in archaeology (e.g. *funereal papyri*), precisely as *funeral* is archaic in figurative usage. *Funeral*, therefore, is the correct current term for 'of or pertaining to the ceremonial burial (or cremation) of the dead; used, observed, delivered, etc., at a burial' (*OED*), as in *funeral rites, funeral urn, funeral pall, funeral pile* or *pyre, funeral column.*

fungous is the adjective of *fungus*; the adjective *fungoid* is a botanical and a pathological technicality.

funny for *odd* or *strange* is a colloquialism. Also it tends to produce ambiguity: one is too often constrained to ask, '*Funny*, "strange", or *funny* "ha! ha!"?'

furnish particulars = to tell.

further, furthest. See **farther.**

further to that is a commercialized and verbose elaboration of *further* or *furthermore.*

fuschia, a very frequent error for *fuchsia.* (The plant is named after Leonard *Fuchs*, a 16th-century German botanist.)

FUSED PARTICIPLES. (For other problems with the participle, see CON-FUSED PARTICIPLES.)

'Fused Participle', says H. W. Fowler, at the beginning of his spirited article thereon in *A Dictionary of Modern English Usage*, 'is a name given to the construction exemplified in its simplest form by "I like

you pleading poverty", and in its higher development by "The collision was owing to *the signalling instructions* laid down by the international regulations for use by ships at anchor in a fog *not having been properly followed*"'; it was, by the way, Fowler who invented the name. An example midway between the two extremes is this, 'Y.Y.'s distillation of fun ... has done much to make up for *that paper having spoiled* other Christmas dinners besides his and the Professor's' (from a letter in *The New States-man and Nation*, early in 1938).

The fused participle has caused much heartburning. There are two main schools of thought: the Fowlerites, who consider it the abomination of abominations; the Onions men and the Jespersenites, who, on certain points, oppose the Fowlerites with a most English sturdiness.

Let us consider the pronouncements of the judicious Dr C. T. Onions in *An Advanced English Syntax*; the much-lamented and inadequately appreciated H. W. Fowler; the luminously sensible Professor Otto Jespersen. In that order.

'Notice', says Dr Onions, 'the following alternative constructions, the first involving the use of the Gerund, the second that of the Verb Adjective in -ing (Active Participle) [*being* or *having been*]:

What is the use of *his coming? – of him coming?*

He spoke of *its being* cold – *it being* cold.

We hear every day of *the Emperor's dying – the Emperor dying.*

Forts were erected to prevent *their land-ing – them landing.*' To which I should like to add:

What is the use of *his having come* – of *him having come?*

He spoke of *its having been cold – it having been cold,* &c., &c.

'Some people', continues Dr Onions, 'insist that the first of these constructions should always be used.' 'If', he remarks in a footnote, 'this rule were pressed, we should have to say: "His premature death prevented *anything's coming* of the scheme" – which can hardly be called English', i.e. it is unidiomatic. 'But the second is the older use, and, moreover, involves nothing illogical or inconsistent with other uses of the Participle, which may generally be paraphrased by "in the act of -ing". We find a good instance in Clarendon of the Gerund qualified by a possessive: "Sunday passed without *any man's taking* notice of *the keeper's being* absent." ' It is interesting to note that in the 18th century the apostrophized construction (possessive adjective + gerund) was common enough, e.g. in *The Sessions Papers of the Old Bailey*, one example (among many there) being, 'There was no indictment for the first fact [i.e. crime], which was the reason of *Hayes's being acquitted*' (4 April 1744).

H. W. Fowler considered the fused participle to be 'a usage ... rapidly corrupting modern style': but Dr Onions's positing of the historical facts has shown that the fused participle was formerly the general usage; the inference is that the apostrophized form (*his coming*) is a modern improvement, – for Dr Onions, Professor Jespersen, and other authorities fully admit that, in many instances, the apostrophized (or possessive adjective + gerund) form is an improvement, a very useful distinction, but do not enforce its application so widely, nor so rigidly, as does the tonic author of *Modern English Usage*.

Consider, too, the following examples from Professor Jespersen's 'On ING' in his masterly paper, *Some Disputed Points in English Grammar* (SPE Tract No. xxv, 1936), evoked in stern opposition to Fowler's article in *Modern English Usage* and based mainly on usage ('I have ... examples of this construction from nearly every prose writer of repute from the beginning of the eighteenth century till our own days') and partly on convenience:

'I cannot understand no *rain falling*', i.e. (the fact) that no rain falls or has fallen.

'Journeys end in *lovers meeting*' (Shakespeare).

'She had calculated on her *daughters remaining* at N' (Jane Austen).

Note: 'He had every day a chance of *this happening*' (Fielding), 'He wouldn't hear of *that being* possible' (Dickens), 'We are

mortified at the news of the *French taking* the town from the Portuguese' (Swift), 'I am not surprised at *young or old falling* in love with her' (Thackeray), 'No fear had they of *bad becoming* worse' (Wordsworth), 'Besides the fact of *those three being* there, the drawbridge is kept up' (A. Hope); here we have instances of words that cannot form a genitive; 'but are they therefore to be excluded from being used as the subject of an *ing*-combination?' as Jespersen pertinently asks. In fact, the genitive often sounds odd with non-personal nouns: 'She was annoyed to find *the pattern costing more than the wool.*'

Groups of nouns, long noun phrases, and non-personal pronouns do not readily form a genitive, and so the fused participle is preferred: 'The danger of *the chair and its occupant being* dashed against the rugged face of the precipice' (Scott) – not *the chair's and its occupant's* nor *the chair and its occupant's*; 'Laughing at *Sir John Walter and me falling* out' (Swift) – not *Sir John Walter's and my*, nor *Sir John Walter and my*; 'What is the good of *mother and me economizing?*' (Hardy); 'We were talking about getting away. *Me and you getting* away' (Kipling) and 'There is the less fear of *you and me finding* one' (Conan Doyle), '*I and you* or *All and you* or *my and your* getting away' being as unnatural as '*you and my* or *your and my* finding out'; *mine and yours* (for '*me and you* getting away') being even more absurd. 'How could public justice be pacified by *a female cousin of the deceased man engaging* to love, honour and obey the clerk?' (De Quincey); 'It consists in *the heart and soul of the man* never *having* been open to Truth' (Carlyle); 'Without *either of us knowing* that the other had taken up the subject' (Wordsworth); 'Nor the slightest chance of *any of them going* in rags' (Ruskin); 'On *the door being* opened, she perceived a couch' (Hardy).

The conclusion seems to be that the genitive is to be preferred for personal pronouns ('He spoke of its being cold'), particularly where the pronominal construction is the subject of the sentence: '*His going* away like that was a surprise.'

But this is not equivalent to saying that the *ing*-construction is not extremely clumsy at times. 'When it is clumsy, turn the sentence differently' is the safe and obvious practice to observe. It is, however, to be remarked that, even here, the fused participle is frequently less clumsy than is the possessive + gerund, as some of Jespersen's examples have shown.

The genitive construction is usually better with proper names: 'In the event of *Randall's not going*' (Iris Murdoch). But even there it should be avoided if it would lead to actual ambiguity. 'I don't like *Susan singing*' clearly = 'I don't want her to sing', while 'I don't like *Susan's singing*' might mean either that or 'I don't like the way she sings.' In such a case rephrase, perhaps with the infinitive: 'I don't like Susan to sing.'

And, whatever you do, avoid a mixture (unless there is an imperative reason for using the two different constructions). Sometimes a writer falls between two stools – between fusing and refusing, as in J. William Matthews's *Cockney Past and Present*, where we find 'For my own part, I have no great objection to *Cockney being described* as vulgar or even to *its being denied* officially the status of a dialect' (being officially denied' would have been preferable).

Note: The verb often appears to be followed by one extended object. In 'I saw him crossing the road' I saw both him and the fact of his crossing, a nuance that would be lost if *him* were to be changed to *his*.

future refers to something that has not yet happened; do not, therefore, use it for *subsequent* or *after*, as in 'We do not know her future manoeuvres when she made the decision.'

future, in the near, is insufferably verbose for *soon* or *shortly*. 'He will retire in the near future.' He will shortly retire (or, retire shortly).

G

Gaelic refers to the Celts or the Celtic languages, particularly those of Scotland, Ireland, and the Isle of Man. **Gallic** means 'Gaulish', or 'typically French'. Confusingly, the French call Wales 'le pays de Galles'.

gamble is to play games of chance for money, esp. for high stakes. It should not be applied to playing for trifling sums, for it is a pejorative term, whereas to *game* is neutral, literary, and slightly archaic: the same applies to the verbal nouns, *gambling* and *gaming* (*OED*). [Game (v.) seldom occurs in American English as a synonym of *gamble*. The expression less deprecatory is to *play* one game or another *for stakes*.]

game. 'Game in England – Hare, pheasant, partridge, grouse, and moor fowl. Game in Ireland – Same as [for] England, with the addition of deer, landrail, quail, black game, and bustard. Game in Scotland – Same as [for] England, with the addition of ptarmigan' (*Diary*, 1939 – issued by Messrs Hay & Son, Ltd of Norfold Street, Sheffield). [*Webster's*: 'The various animals (chiefly birds and mammals) which are considered worthy of pursuit by sportsmen. Among birds the order Galliformes, and the duck, plover, snipe, and rail families, contain the majority of those ordinarily considered game.']

Gand for *Ghent*. See **Bruxelles ...**

gang of workmen or of criminals is correct. But to apply *gang* to a set, a clique, a fortuitous assemblage of idle or harmless persons is to fall into slang.

gantlet is in Britain an obsolete form of *gauntlet*, whether independently or in the phrase, *run the gauntlet*. In the USA, the phrase is written *run the gantlet*, in order to distinguish *gantlet* from *gauntlet* (glove), for *ga(u)ntlet* of the phrase is a corruption of *gantlope*, a totally different word. See esp. *OED*.

gaol, gaoler; jail, jailer. The former pair is the earlier, but the latter is now the accepted one: *gaol, gaoler* are now literary and archaic. In 'literary and journalistic use both the G and J forms are now admitted as correct, but all recent dictionaries give the preference to the latter', said *OED* in 1900: this tendency is, by now, even more marked. [In the USA, *gaol, gaoler* are 'obsolete, except for occasional legal use' (*Webster's*).]

gargantuan, misused. 'The water was alive with traffic, Lilliputian tugs were performing gargantuan towing feats' (Robert Eton, *Not in Our Stars*). The author (Laurence Meynell) means either *gigantic* or, better, *Brobdingnagian*.

gasolene and **gasoline** (likewise pronounced *-ene*) are equally correct. *Gas* is a colloquial abbreviation, originally American, and is in Britain used mostly in *step on the gas*, 'to make haste'. [The original noun *gas* was the invention of Van Helmont and is one of the most successful of invented words.]

gay, as both adjective and noun, is the word that homosexuals prefer to use of themselves. This has now become such an important, though colloquial, sense of the word that it can scarcely be used without self-consciousness in its older senses.

Gdansk for *Danzig*. See **Bruxelles** ...

gem for *something greatly prized* (a 'treasure') is colloquial and therefore to be avoided in formal or dignified contexts; and it can easily be overdone in any kind of context. Frank Whitaker condemns it as a 'rubber-stamp' word.

gender refers to words: as a synonym for *sex* it is rapidly becoming a **VOGUE WORD** (*q.v.*).

-general forms a regular plural as part of a military title; *major-generals* are a particular kind of *general*. The correct plural

for non-military titles is *attorneys general, postmasters general,* etc.

generally for *usually* (as a general rule; in most instances) is not incorrect, but it may lead to ambiguity, as in 'It is generally wet and cold in S.W. New Zealand.'

generally always. The two adverbs used together are contradictory.

genetic, defined as 'pertaining to, or having reference to, origin' (*OED*), must not be confused with *generative*, 'productive, able to produce'.

Genf for *Geneva*. See **Bruxelles** ...

GENITIVE, GROUP. See GROUP GENITIVE.

GENITIVE*, VAGARIES OF THE. See also GROUP GENITIVE

‘ "And did they compare for size?" – "About right. But then, so were that other clerk's, Mason, and Dr Parsons', and half a dozen other people's" ',

(Josephine Bell,
Death on the Borough Council)

The basis from which we arrive at vagaries of the genitive (or possessive) case is the general rule that a singular *boy* takes apostrophe *s*: *boy's*; the plural *boys* takes apostrophe: *boys'*. The main exceptions are that those words with interior changes take apostrophe *s* in both the singular and the plural: *man's*, plural *men's*; *woman's*, plural *women's*; *child's*, *children's*; *cow's*, *kine's*; *pig's*, *swine's*: and that nouns that remain unchanged also take apostrophe *s* in both numbers: *one sheep's* (*wool*), *two sheep's* (*wool*).

Other exceptions are these: nouns ending in *-nce* take, in the singular, an apostrophe, as in *for patience' sake, for conscience' sake*, but in the plural they take *s'*, as in *for their consciences' sake*, in accordance with the general rule for the plural; *for goodness'*

---

*For an extremely good account of the genitive in general, see Geo. O. Curme, *Syntax*, 1931, pp. 70–88. The ensuing article is, in several parts, a précis of Curme's chapter.

sake is a formula – contrast *for mercy's sake*; nouns ending in *s*, followed immediately by a noun beginning with *s*, and nouns ending in *ses*, or *sess* or *sses* or *ssess*, or in *sis* or *siss* or *ssis* or *ssiss*, or in *-xes* (as in *Xerxes' army*), take in the singular an apostrophe, as in *Pears' Soap* (the three consecutive *s's* in 'Pears*'s* soap' being felt to be excessive) and in 'the *oasis'* verge', '*molasses'* attraction for children'.

In the past it was a very general, as it is now a not infrequent, practice to form the genitive singular of all nouns ending in *s* and especially those ending in *ss* (*hostess*) by adding an apostrophe to both the nominative singular (*a hostess' duties, your Highness' pleasure*) and of course in the plural ('The *three hostesses' houses* were in Park Lane'); but now it is usual to form the singular genitive by adding *'s* (*a hostess's duties, your Highness's pleasure*) – which seems to be a sensible idea, for if you can say *three hostesses' houses*, you can easily say *a hostess's duties*. There is, however, a strong tendency to retain *Jesus'* and *Demosthenes', Socrates',* and other such genitives of Greek proper names.

In these three paragraphs, there are no vagaries properly so called, at least in the rules enunciated, although it is true that certain idiosyncratic, law-unto-themselves writers fall into vagaries when, in defiance of rule and clarity, they depart from those rules. [American readers may wish to consult *Webster's* entry for '*possessive*', Perrin's discussion of *Jones,* and *A Manual of Style* (University of Chicago Press, 13th rev. ed., 1982), pp. 72, 95.] Nor perhaps do the following paragraphs contain vagaries, unless we classify several idioms as vagaries.

In the group genitive (*the King of England's power*), a group of words is made to conform to the rule that governs single words: an economical idiom and a very great convenience. See **GROUP GENITIVE.**

The same principle determines the genitive ending of two or even three nouns in apposition. Thus, *John Williamson, the aforementioned tenant* becomes in the genitive *John Williamson, the aforementioned tenant's house,* or, for legal clarity, *John Williamson's (the aforementioned tenant's) house*; *Albert, the Prince Consort* becomes *Albert, the Prince Consort's home*; *Arthur Wellesley, Duke of Wellington, the Field Marshal* becomes *Arthur Wellesley, Duke of Wellington, the Field Marshal's victory at Waterloo.* That these, or at least the shorter, genitival groups are equivalent to group genitives can be seen by the omission of the comma, as in *John Williamson the aforementioned tenant's house* – *Albert the Prince Consort's home* – but not in the third, for there *Arthur Wellesley Duke of Wellington* is possible, but *Duke of Wellington the Field Marshal* is impossible.

'If two names are connected by *and* and represent persons that are joined together in authorship, business, or a common activity, the second name alone assumes the genitive ending: "*Steevens and Malone's* Shakespeare", "in *William and Mary's* reign", but of course "*Steele's and Addison's* [work or] works" when we are speaking of the separate sets of two different authors' (Curme) and 'Elizabeth's and Victoria's reign [or, better, reigns]' when we are dealing with two separate reigns. In the same way, 'if two or more names connected by *and* represent persons that are joined together in possession, the second or [the] last name alone assumes the genitive ending: "*John and William's* uncle", "*John, William, and Mary's* uncle". "We paid a visit to *Messrs Pike and White's* works." "My *father and mother's* Bible". But we must give each genitive its genitive *-s* if there is not joint possession: "*My father's and my mother's* birthdays both fall in June, two days apart" ' (Curme).

Two pronouns (*you and I*) or three pronouns (*he, you, and I*) need careful handling: '*Your and my contract* (or *contracts*) has (or have) been signed'; '*His, your, and my contract* (or *contracts*) has (or have) been signed.' An alternative to *your and my contracts*, where the contracts are separate, is *your contract(s) and mine.*

Noun and pronoun (*John and you*) or pronoun and noun (*you and John*) follow the same rule: *John's and your contract(s)*, *your and John's contract(s)*.

There are to be noted several rules of a different order. 'First [the] use [of the genitive case] is now in ordinary prose almost restricted to personal beings [and animals], and even such phrases as "society's hard-drilled soldiery" (Meredith), where *society* is personified, are felt as poetical; still more so ... "thou knowst not gold's effect" (Shakespeare) or "setting out upon life's journey" (Stevenson). But in some set phrases the genitive is [well] established, e.g. "out of *harm's way*"; "he is at his *wits'* (or *wit's*) end"; so also in the stock quotation from *Hamlet*, "in my *mind's* eye", etc. Then to indicate measure, etc.: "at a *boat's* length from the ship", and especially time: "an *hour's* walk", "a good *night's* rest", "*yesterday's* post"; and this is even extended to such prepositional combinations as "*today's* adventures", "*tomorrow's* papers".

'Secondly, ... the subjective genitive ... is in great vigour, for instance in "the King's arrival", "the Duke's invitation", "the Duke's inviting him [gave him much pleasure]", "Mrs Poyser's repulse of the squire" (G. Eliot). Still there is, in quite recent times, a tendency towards expressing the subject by means of the preposition *by*, just as in the passive voice, for instance in "the accidental discovery by Miss Knag of some correspondence" (Dickens); "the appropriation by a settled community of lands on the other side of the ocean" (Seeley); "the massacre of Christians by Chinese". "Forster's Life of Dickens" is the same thing as "Dickens' Life, by Forster". The objective genitive' – where the genitival noun or pronoun is affected by the following noun instead of affecting that following noun (*his defeat* = *the defeat of him*, not *the defeat by him*), – 'was formerly much more common than now, the ambiguity of [this] genitive being probably the reason of its decline. Still, we find, for instance, "his expulsion from power by the Tories" (Thackeray)', where, however, 'by the Tories' dispels all ambiguity, ' "What was thy pity's recom-

pence?" (Byron). "England's wrongs" generally mean the wrongs done to England. ... In "my sceptre's awe" [Shakespeare, *Richard the Second*, I, i, 118] we have an objective, but in "thy free awe pays homage to us" (*Hamlet*, IV, iii, 63) a subjective genitive. But on the whole, such obscurity will occur less frequently in English than in other languages, where the genitive is more fully used' (Jespersen, *Growth and Structure of the English Language*). The same ambiguity attaches to *of* + noun, as in *the love of God*, which only the context can – but sometimes does not – make clear, for by itself it may = 'the love felt by God' or 'the love felt for God'. But practised writers and speakers, and indeed, all clear thinkers, avoid these pitfalls almost by instinct.

Stylistically, the *'s* and the *of* forms of the possessive are often varied or mingled. Thus Elizabeth Barrett Browning's 'all the hoofs of King Saul's father's asses' would probably, in good prose, become 'all the hoofs of the asses of King Saul's father' or, better, 'all the hoofs of the asses owned by King Saul's father'; and Pinero's 'He is my wife's first husband's only child's godfather' might be rendered a little less monotonous by a change to 'He is the godfather of the only child of my wife's first husband.'

There is an excellent guiding principle set forth by George O. Curme, who acutely remarks. 'The inflected genitive that stands before the governing noun usually has a weaker stress than its governing noun, while the genitive after the governing noun has a heavier stress: *Mr Smith's new house'*, but *the new house of Mr Smith''*; stress, obviously, is laid on the important word, and if there are two stresses, the heavier stress falls on the more significant of the two important words, thus: *Mr Smith's' new house'* and *the new house' of Mr Smith'*.

Note too the place of the genitive in 'The desire *of my heart* for peace', *of my heart* being less important than *for peace*; to stress the genitive, put it last, as in 'the desire for peace *of every man, woman, and child in that great nation*' (Curme).

Then there is the double genitive case, exemplified in such phrases as 'a friend of my *father's*', 'three friends of *mine*', 'that hat of *his*', and 'dress of *Jane's*'. For the pronominal type of this strange negative, see **of her – of hers**.

These pronominal examples are much less likely to lead to trouble than are the others: *that hat of his, that football of theirs, this pain of mine* are ambiguous; but what are we to say of *this beauty of my sister's* and *this famed beauty of my famous sisters'*? To the reader, they are clear; the listener, however, does not, in either example, know whether one or two or several sisters are concerned. Such double genitives as the two recorded in the last sentence but one are avoided by scrupulous writers, for the scrupulous remember the very sound rule that a piece of writing should be as clear to a listener as to a reader; especially do they avoid it with nouns in the plural, as in *in some retreat of his or his friends'* (John Burroughs, *Far and Near*), where the apostrophe after *friends* clarifies the thought of the author: listeners, unfortunately, do not hear an apostrophe. But nouns in the singular are often equally susceptible to misapprehension by a listener, as in ('It was no fault of *the doctor's*'). 'The *of*-genitive ['of the doctor'] is here, as often elsewhere [e.g. to distinguish between objective and subjective genitive], a clearer form, and is often preferred', remarks George O. Curme, who thereby implies a useful hint. The same authority has smilingly noticed that 'although the double genitive with nouns is in general subject to ambiguity, many [writers and speakers], desirous of its lively effect, take their chances with it, trusting to the [context or the] situation to help them out'. Make sure that the circumstances *do* make the reference clear.

'In the case of personal pronouns', Curme remarks, 'there has long been a tendency to differentiate … form and meaning, namely, to employ *his, her*, etc., in the possessive relation and *of him, of her*, etc., in the partitive relation, stressing the idea of an integral part …: "*His hair, his eyes*", etc., but "She was the daughter of a

lumberjack and woodcraft was bred into the very fibre *of her*" (*Saturday Evening Post*, 29 July 1916). "The man had something in the look *of him*" (Browning, *An Epistle*). "I don't do it for the honour *of it*". As this differentiation has not become thoroughly established, we still more commonly employ here the old undifferentiated forms *his, her*, etc., for either the possessive or the partitive relation: "*his* eyes" and "The man had something in his look". But we now always use the form *of* when the pronoun is modified by a relative clause: "Then first I heard the voice of *her* to whom … the Gods Rise up for reverence" (Tennyson, *Oenone*, 1.105)', it being loose English to write such a sentence as 'I put the money into *his* hand *who* needed it.'

In general, the 'very fibre *of her*', 'something in the look *of him*' form is poetic or, at the least, literary; Carlyle says, 'The chief quality of Burns is *the sincerity of him*'; Jack London, in *White Fang*, has 'They were moulding *the clay of him*.' These examples are cited by Curme, who then adds: 'In a number of expressions the partitive genitive of personal pronouns is also common in plain prose, usually, however, without the poetic [connotation] of the preceding examples, [but] merely stressing the idea of an integral part: "That will be the end *of it*, the last *of it*". In a vague way we feel life and death as parts of us, vital parts of our human experience: "I couldn't do it for *the life of me*". "That will be *the death of you*".'

Worth noting, though it presents few difficulties, is the genitive absolute: that genitive in which the governing noun is omitted and which applies especially to residences and to places of business, as in 'Buy a loaf at the baker's in the next street', 'I spent a pleasant hour at Smith's [house, flat, apartment, etc.], after an unpleasant half-hour at Robinson & Smith's [office or shop or factory]'; 'John has asked whether he might go for part of his holiday to his *uncle and aunt's*'; but if the uncle and the aunt occupy separate residences, the sentence must end: 'go … to his *uncle's and* (his) *aunt's*. Now, 'the governing noun is regularly omitted when the possessive genitive points forward or backward to a preceding or following governing noun, for the genitive here is now felt as a possessive pronoun, like *mine*, *hers*, etc. ... "John's auto is larger than *William's and mine*"' (Curme). Ezra Pound, in *Moeurs Contemporaines*, omits a necessary genitive absolute within a double genitive: 'At a friend of my wife's there is a photograph ...'; the sentence needs to be recast.

Finally we come to what Curme designates, by implication, as the Unclear Genitive and the Blended Genitive.

Unclear Genitives: 'The loss of distinctive genitive form ... in a number of pronouns and limited adjectives has weakened English expression.' Fielding wrote: '*Both their several talents* were excessive', whereas a Middle English author would have written *bothe their* (or *their bothe*) *talents*, where *bothe*, in either *bothe talents*, or *their bothe*, is a distinctive genitive form – *bothe* as distinctive from the nominative *both*. Fielding's *both their several talents* would, in correct Modern English, be *the several talents of both of them*, which is weak and wordy in comparison with the Middle English *bothe their* (or *their bothe*) *several talents*. 'This older usage', as Curme points out, 'is best preserved in the subjective genitive category in connexion with the gerund: "Your mother will feel *your both* going away"' (Mrs Gaskell, *Wives and Daughters*, Ch. xiv). "Isn't it dreadful to think of *their all* being wrong!"' (Sir Harry Johnston, *The Man Who Did the Right Thing*, Ch. ii). – It is also well preserved in the possessive category in such expressions as *both our lives* [are at stake], *both our minds* [are made up], but we now feel the old genitives as plural limiting adjectives. ... This old usage survives in popular speech: "She is *both their mothers*, i.e. "the mother of both of them". "It is *both their faults*" [i.e. the faults of both of them]. In the literary language it lingers on in *for both their sakes*, *for both our sakes* [for the sake(s) of both of them – of us]. Similarly when *of* is inserted after *all*, *both*, *none*, etc. to give expression

to the partitive idea: "I'm taking the trouble of writing this true history *for all your benefits*" (Hughes, *Tom Brown's School-Days*, I, vi), instead of the correct *for the benefit of all of you*. "A painful circumstance which is attributable to *none of our faults*" (Thackeray, *Pendennis*, II, Ch. xxxv), instead of the correct *the fault of none of us*.' This difficulty affects also *each* and *either* (and *neither*): 'for each of our sakes' should be 'for the sake of each [or, all] of us'; 'It was neither of our faults' should be 'It was the fault of neither of us.' Note, however, that *neither* of their faults, like *both of their faults*, *all of their faults*, etc., is correct in such sentences as 'Smith's fault was gluttony; Robinson's avarice. But *both of their faults* paled into respectability in comparison with Jones's, for that was a tendency to murder those who contradicted him' and '... But *neither of their faults* seems of much account when set beside Jones's ...'. This is a distinction that Curme failed to make – perhaps he thought it too obvious to be worthy of his nice discriminating mind.

Blended Genitives: These are more subtle: they constitute a nice test of the correctitude of even the best writers. 'In the partitive category', writes Curme, 'there is a tendency, once much more common than now, to blend the genitive with some other construction, resulting in illogical expression: "His versification is by far the most perfect *of any English poet*" (Saintsbury, *Nineteenth Century Literature*, 268), a blending of "His versification is far the most perfect *of all English poets*" and "His versification is more perfect than that of *any other English poet*"', but should not the first sentence read '... *of all English poets*'? Such 'omission of the word *other* after *any* ... is a form of blending still common. In comparisons where there is present the idea of a group or class, the superlative represents the group as complete, while the comparative represents the separation of one or more from all the others in the group. Hence we should say "[His versification] is [by far] the most perfect *of all English poets*"' – more logically, of all English poets' – 'or "is more perfect [by far] than that *of any other English poet*"' (Curme). Curme, however, should add that Saintsbury could also have written: 'He, of all English poets, has by far the most perfect versification' or 'Of all English poets', his is by far the most perfect versification', or even 'Of all English versifications [= systems of versification, and performance therein], his is by far the most perfect', or several other modifications. (For the further infelicity, *the most perfect*, see COMPARATIVES, FALSE.) In 1938, an English journalist perpetrated this objectionable sentence, 'On President Benes's shoulders now devolves the greatest burden of any man in Europe'; for this read, 'On President Benes's shoulders now devolves a burden greater than on those of any other man in Europe.'

genius, 'native intellectual power of an exalted type; instinctive and extraordinary capacity for imaginative creation, original thought, invention, or discovery. Often contrasted with *talent*' (*OED*), must not be debased to = *talent*, which should be confined to 'a special natural ability or aptitude; a natural capacity for success in some department of mental or physical activity' (*OED*), but without inspiration or ultimate power. Do not confuse *genius* with *genus*, class, category, kind.

gent, 'a gentleman', is an illiteracy except when it applies to such a man as might be expected to use the word.

genteel; gentle; Gentile. The last = 'non-Jewish'; the second is now confined to the senses 'mild, not savage, not cruel, not rough', the sense 'well-born' being archaic; *genteel*, in Standard English, is now pejorative or, at best, playful – the senses 'belonging to the gentry', 'appropriate to the gentry', 'having the habits characteristic of the gentry' being, except in sarcastic (or, occasionally, jocular) contexts, archaic.

GENTEELISMS. See ELEGANCIES.

gentleman. See **lady** and **Mister.**

GEOGRAPHICAL ARCHAISMS (*Albion, Cathay, Tartary*, etc.). See ARCHAISMS.

geography, chorography, topography. See **topography** ...

GERUND. An admirably clear treatment of the subject is to be found in Dr C. T. Onions's *An Advanced English Syntax* (6th ed., 1932). Here are various examples of correct current usage:
'The *digging* of the foundations was hard work';
'The train will be long in *coming*';
'Now cease *complaining* and start work.'
With constructions dependent:
'He spoke of there *being a danger*';
'Your *being friends* will ease the situation';
'There are more ways of *killing a cat* ... '.
With adverbial modifications:
'*Staring about aimlessly* will do no good';
'There is no *getting to the borders of space*.'
With adjectives:
'There's *no refuting* so cogent an argument';
'There was *some foolish staring, some more than foolish wondering*.'
Note that when the gerund governs – i.e. is followed by – an objective (an accusative), there are, in 20th-century English, two constructions:
'Much diffidence was felt about *demanding money*';
'*The demanding of money* was the cause of much diffidence.'
Demanding money is the more general usage when the gerund depends on a preposition. *The demanding money* is now obsolete: a good thing too, for it led to ambiguity: *the electing councillors* could either mean 'the election of councillors' (to the Town Council) or 'those Councillors who elect' (the Chairman of the council). Occasionally, even now, one sees *the mentioning this* for (*the*) *mention of this* or *the mentioning of this*.
The gerund governed (i.e. preceded) by *a* or *a-* (i.e. *on*), as in 'I went a-buying', is archaic – when, at least, it is not dialectal.

There is, however, a literal survival, with the preposition omitted:

'The church is *building*' (a-building, or in the course of building – or being built);

'The reformation must still be *doing*, never done.'

A purely syntactic, one might call it an academic, difficulty occurs in such sentences as these:

'What a long time you are *dressing*!';

'He was too much occupied *watching* the passers-by to notice what was being discussed';

'They continued *eating* until they could eat no more.'

Thus: 'What a long time you are *a-dressing*' or 'What a long time you, dressing, are';

'He was too much occupied, *a-watching* (or, in watching) ...' or 'Watching, he was too much occupied ...';

'They continued their eating ...' or 'Eating, they continued until they could eat no more.'

Finally, precisely as there are misrelated (or suspended) participles, so there are misrelated gerunds. 'The gerund', Dr Onions remarks, 'must be handled carefully with respect to its reference to the rest of the sentence. Do not write, e.g.: "After *fighting* the flames for several hours the ship was abandoned." Here, *fighting* refers grammatically to "the ship", which makes nonsense; say: "After they (the crew ...) had been fighting" or "After fighting the flames ... the crew abandoned the ship." Correct the following: "By pouring hard peas upon the hatches they became so slippery that the boarders could not stand." [Who poured?]'

GERUND AND PARTICIPLE CONFUSED. (See also preceding article, last paragraph proper.) An example from Cameron McCabe's *The Face on the Cutting-Room Floor* will show the error and affords material for the correction of the error. 'He describes ... how Smith rang him up at my place. But he does not realize how very odd it is that Smith should ring him there. ... McCabe *goes on telling*

us how he went back to the studio, how Smith took him up to Robertson's room, how Robertson ..., and how Smith suggested that ...'. Written as printed here, *goes on telling* connotes that McCabe had already begun to tell how he went back to the studio, etc., etc., but the context shows that not the gerund but the present participle is required, thus: 'McCabe *goes on, telling* how he went back ...' But a stylist would have written 'He describes ... ring him there. ... McCabe goes on to tell how (or, unambiguously, that) he went back ...'.

get. The verb *to get* should not be used much in formal writing, but replaced by *obtain, receive, become, buy*, etc. as appropriate. Sometimes, though, its use is unavoidable, as with 'get well' or 'get married'. See example under **have got.** See also **got.**

get the best of; get the better of. They both mean 'defeat, outwit' (*COD*)

gibberish. See **jabber.**

gibe; gybe; jibe. To *gibe* (or *jibe*) is to mock or jeer. The verb *gybe* (US spelling *jibe*) is used of the sudden swinging of a sail. A third verb *jibe* is a colloquial American word meaning 'be in accord', as in 'Her account doesn't jibe with theirs.'

gigantic, misused for *abundant, copious, heavy*. 'The waterfalls would have been a great nuisance if we had not been wet through, for the spray was so gigantic we couldn't have escaped a soaking' (Violet O. Cressy-Marcks, *Up the Amazon*).

gigantic, titanic. In their transferred senses, both of these words mean 'huge, colossal', but whereas the former is rarely, the latter is frequently employed with the sub-sense of 'extraordinarily powerful'. The stronger of the two words is *titanic*, but both of them are to be used in moderation.

gilded and **gilt** are both correct as preterites and past participles, though *gilded* is now much the commoner. But as adjectives, *gilt* is now confined to the literal sense, whereas *gilded* is not only figurative ('A gilded pollution', Dean Farrar), but also mediate as 'tinged with a golden colour' ('The gilded summit of that bright mountain') and literal; in the literal sense, *gilded* is more dignified than *gilt*. *Gilded*, moreover, appears in certain set phrases – *the Gilded Chamber* (the House of Lords), *gilded spurs* (of knighthood), and *gilded youth* (the French *jeunesse dorée*).

gipsy – gypsy; Gipsy – Gypsy. The word being a corrupted form of *Egyptian*, there is good ground for preserving the latter spelling, and it is indeed the preferred one in both British and American use. The capital G should be used when the people or language is meant (as *English*, *French*, etc.), but not when *gipsy*, *gypsy*, is adjectival.

give (particular) attention to = to heed (well), to attend (closely) to. See ABSTRACT NOUNS.

given name. See **Christian name.**

glamorous for *romantic* or (of a scene, a night, etc.) *lovely*, or (of a woman) *beautiful and attractive* or (of a way of life) *exciting* or *adventurous* or (of a love-affair or a flirtation) *sex-filled* or *amorous* belongs to the advertising of films – and should be treated as the dubious privilege of boss-driven copywriters.

glean, 'to gather in small quantities', 'to scrape together', is catachrestic when it is used as a mere synonym of *acquire* or *get* or *obtain* (as in 'He failed to glean the sense').

global. See VOGUE WORDS.

globe. See **earth.**

glycerine, glycerin. See **-ile and -ine.**

go and **come.** See **come and go.**

go by the name of. See **by the name of.**

gobbledygook is (originally) American for *officialese* or *official jargon*. (See my introduction to 'Vigilans', *Chamber of Horrors*.) A most expressive word.

golf course and **golf links.** Properly, the former is applied to an inland, the latter to a seaside set of greens and fairways. (With thanks to Frank Whitaker, lover of good English and exponent of good golf.)

good few, a; a good many. What is the difference? Cf. the entry at **few and a few.** *A good few* is 'a fair number', but it is a colloquialism. *A good many* is also a colloquialism; its sense is 'a very fair number'. Both phrases are vague but *a good many* represents a slightly larger number than *a good few*. ' "Were there any others there?" "There *were*!" "Quite a few?" "Oh, Lord, yes! A good many, in fact." '

The colloquial *quite a few* = 'a considerable number'.

good goods makes an ugly sound. Try *well-made, serviceable, excellent, superior,* etc.

good will; goodwill. In commerce, always *goodwill*, the privilege, granted by seller to buyer, of trading as his or her successor, esp. the ready-formed connection of clients or customers, considered as part of the saleability of a business and as additional to the plant, the stock-in-trade, the book-debts, etc. As the state of wishing well (to a person, a corporation, a cause, etc.), 'kindly or favourable regard', and as 'cheerful consent or acquiescence', 'readiness or zeal', it is written either *good will* (preferably) or *goodwill* (OED).

goose, plural *geese*, except for *goose*, 'a tailor's smoothing-iron', which has plural *gooses*.

gorilla. See **guer(r)illa.**

got and **have got.** The too frequent slovenly substitution of *got* for other verbs expressive of *possession, acquiring, attainment, arrival, achievement,* etc., was noted as early as 1789 by the author of *Aristarchus; or, The Principles of Composition. Contains a Methodical Arrangement of the Improprieties frequent in Writing and Conversation, with Select Rules for attaining to Purity and Elegance of Expression.* (This anonymous work is ascribed by the British Museum Library to the Rev. Philip Withers, but John Badcock ['Jon Bee'] says, in 1823, that it is Dr Thomas Birch.)

At pp. 141–4 of the second edition, 1789, the author writes:

'I GOT on Horseback within ten Minutes after I GOT your Letter. When I GOT to Canterbury, I GOT a Chaise for Town. But I GOT wet through before I GOT to Canterbury, and I HAVE GOT such a Cold as I shall not be able to GET rid of in a Hurry. I GOT to the Treasury about Noon, but first of all I GOT shaved and drest. I soon GOT into the Secret of GETTING a Memorial before the Board, but I could not GET an Answer then, however I GOT Intelligence from the Messenger that I should most likely GET one the next Morning. As soon as I GOT back to my Inn, I GOT my supper, and GOT to Bed, it was not long before I GOT to sleep. When I GOT up in the Morning, I GOT my Breakfast, and then GOT myself drest, that I might GET out in Time, to GET an Answer to my Memorial. As soon as I GOT it I GOT into the Chaise, and GOT to Canterbury by three: and about Tea Time, I GOT home. I have GOT Nothing particular for you, and so Adieu.'

'Every phrase in this Extract', says the author, 'is in popular and perpetual Use; and it is far from my Wish to deprive the Vulgar, and the wealthy illiterate of so convenient an Abridgement of Terms. On the Contrary, I recommend it to the pious care of Dr — to compose a History of the World, on this elegant Plan of Abbreviation. All the Events, from the Birth of Time to His Majesty's Journey to Cheltenham may be detailed without the Aid of a single Verb in the English Language, the omnipotent GET excepted.

'This Verb is of Saxon Origin; *Arrival* at the Place of Destination, the primitive Idea; hence *Acquisition*; and hence *possession*. With the latter Idea, the Illiterate use it in Construction with *Have* – *I have* HAVE; in other Words, *I have* GOT. E.g.

'*I have got* a Father ninety Years old.

'For obvious reasons, *I have got a Father* must be restricted to *I possess*; conse-

quently, it is absurd to prefix HAVE – *I have* POSSESS!!

'It may, therefore, be advanced as a general Rule – when *Possession* is implied, it is vulgar to use HAVE in construction with GOT.

'Permit me to add, our Ancestors have furnished us with innumerable Terms to express all the Ideas which the Vulgar affix to their FACTOTUM – GOT.

'Are you in Quest of any Thing? Do not exclaim with the Illiterate – I HAVE GOT it. But say – I have FOUND it or I HAVE it, HERE IT IS, etc.

'Again. "I *mounted* my Horse, or I *was on Horseback* within ten Minutes after I *received* your Letter: as soon as I *arrived* in Canterbury, I *engaged* (or *hired* or *stept into*) a Post Chaise for Town. I *was* wet through before I *reached* Canterbury, and I *have* (or *I have taken*) such a Cold as I shall not easily *remove* (or *cure*). I *arrived* at the Treasury about Noon, having previously *shaved* and drest. I soon *discovered* the Secret of *introducing* a Memorial to the Board; I could not, however, *obtain* an immediate Answer, but the Messenger told me, that I should probably *receive* one, next Morning. I *returned* to my Inn, *Supt*, *Went* to Bed, and *Slept* well. I *rose* early, and *drest* immediately after *Breakfast* that I might be in Time for the Answer to my Memorial. As soon as I *received* it, I *took* Post Chaise, *reached* Canterbury by three, and my home about Tea Time. I *have* nothing particular to add."

'It was not my Design to paraphrase the Extract in Terms of Elegance, I only wished to prove, that Men of common Education might express the usual Occurrences of Life, without the Aid of GET and GOT and I HAVE GOT, etc.' See also **have got.**

Note: The 1789 author is not quite right about the etymology of *get*. It comes from the Old Norse *geta* = 'obtain, beget, guess'; so that the idea of 'arrival' is not the 'primitive' one.

gotten is obsolete in Great Britain, except in the cliché, *ill-gotten gains*; but in the

USA, *gotten* (past participle) is common in the sense 'obtain', but not for 'possess'. 'I've gotten to go' means 'I've succeeded in going', not 'I must go.'

gourmand; gourmet. The former is greedy, the latter a connoisseur of food.

graduate is 'to admit (a candidate) to a university degree' or (of the candidate) 'to take a university degree'; *to be graduated* expresses a single nuance – that of 'to be admitted to a university degree'.

graffiti is a plural, whose much rarer singular is *graffito*. Do not use *graffiti* with singular verbs and pronouns.

GRAMMAR. (For the relation of grammar to logic, see the next article.)

This is no place for a general discussion of grammar, for in this book a knowledge of the essentials of accidence and the simplicities of syntax has been assumed.

For those who desire to examine 'the heart and soul' of grammar, there is one book that stands high above the rest: *The Philosophy of Grammar*, by Otto Jespersen. A simplified paraphrase (with comment) of the – to the general reader – most interesting part of Professor Jespersen's book will be found in my *The World of Words* (chapter entitled 'What Grammar Is – and Why').

Jespersen is the author of *A Modern English Grammar on Historical Principles*: a masterly work, though less consecutively written than the warmly to be recommended *A Grammar of the English Language* (vols 2 and 3, Parts of Speech, Accidence and Syntax, 1931–2), by George O. Curme.

Syntax has been treated with admirable clarity and orderliness by Dr C. T. Onions in *An Advanced English Syntax*.

Of short grammars, Jespersen's *Essentials of English Grammar* is perhaps the best; of medium-sized ones, J. C. Nesfield's *Manual of English Grammar and Composition* (in its latest edition) is still useful, but, owing to the modernization in terminology, E. A. Sonnenschein's *A New English Grammar*, 1916, is preferable. A suggestive

and entertaining book is C. C. Boyd's *Grammar for Grown-Ups*, 1927.

For a modern treatment, concise and adequate, of the grammar necessary to every educated person, I may, not immodestly, refer to my *English: A Course for Human Beings*, 1948 (4th edition, revised, 1954). In his *Good English* and *Better English*, especially in their Library Editions, G. H. Vallins has many excellent things to say.

A bird's-eye view of comparative grammar is offered by E. A. Sonnenschein's *The Soul of Grammar*. 'To the advanced student grammar is a fascinating subject, just because he knows that he is dealing with an organic writing.' But however far advanced he is, the student must beware of falling into the error of supposing that there is such a thing as a universal grammar, applicable to every language. Grammar is based on language – the particular language concerned – grammar has no existence apart from language; grammar is a set of rules codifying usage, not a code superimposed on language and predetermining usage; in short, grammar must modify itself if language changes, grammar being made for man, not man for grammar.

Nevertheless, where grammatical rules make for a clarity that would disappear with the disappearance of the rules, it is better to preserve and maintain the rules – until, at least, a simpler or more satisfactory rule is devised or (more probably) evolved. For instance, to ignore the useful distinctions between *shall* and *will*, *that* and *who* (or *which*), is, in my opinion, to set up ambiguity without any fully compensating gain. Also see **COMPOSITION**.

Note: Since Partridge compiled his list of recommendations, many more recent publications have emerged. Particularly valuable is *A Grammar of Contemporary English* by Quirk, Greenbaum, Leech and Svartvik (latest edition).

GRAMMAR (and language in general) **AND LOGIC*.**

'To write or speak, we must think; logic

---

*See also **NEGATION** Section *A*.

is the mechanism of formal reason, and grammar the mechanism of all writing and speaking; in so far as we think, we may – or may not – employ logic, for logical thinking is not the only kind of thinking, nor is it necessarily the most accurate. Logic may have been at the back of certain grammatical rules, but thought of some kind or other is at the back of all such rules' (*A Modern Scholiast*, 1938).

In *Logic and Grammar*, published as SPE Tract No. xvi, Otto Jespersen is, to use a modern slang term, 'devastatingly' on the side of good sense as opposed to both the determinists and the nihilists among grammarians. From this paper, which every lover and student of language should con, study, and remember, I take a few passages that not only illuminate the thorny path of theory but also establish a *modus vivendi* and a *modus operandi* – a sound ethic and a safe guide to the practice of speech and writing.

'In examining the relation between logic and grammar we are at once faced with two diametrically opposed views: one that grammar is nothing but applied logic, or, as John Stuart Mill has it, "*Grammar is the most elementary part of logic. The structure*" [? rather *the constructing*] "*of every sentence is a lesson in logic*"; the other that language has nothing to do with logic, but is essentially "alogical" [i.e. outside of logic, unconnected with logic]. The first view is found more frequently among philosophers or logicians than among philologists or linguists; it seems also to belong to a former period rather than to the present time. ... The second and opposite view must often be considered a kind of reaction against the pedantry of many grammarians of the old school, who wanted to coerce or entrammel language so as to bring it into accordance with a set of rigid rules, condemning everything that did not agree with the strictest classical' – rather, Classical – 'standard of correctness. To this the school of historical grammar opposed the right of life and urged the inevitableness of change in the linguistic domain, pointing out the infinite diversity

of human languages and thereby coming naturally to deny the possibility of one single strictly logical standard by which to measure correctness in every sentence and every language. These writers do not indeed maintain that language is *illogical*, because this expression implies that it is contrary to the laws of correct thinking, but they say that language has nothing to do with logic ...: linguistic laws, they say, are not logical, but merely psychological laws.'

'Which of these two opposed views', he asks, 'is the true one?' They cannot both be right, but they may both be wrong. Both of these views are one-sided, hence exaggerated, hence false. 'Many of the rules [of grammar] are so arbitrary that it is quite impossible to deduce them from the laws of universal logic; but, on the other hand, language as the vehicle of communication of thoughts cannot be exempt from obeying the most necessary laws of correct thinking. Grammar ... contains a practical, everyday logic; it embodies the common sense of untold generations as applied to those complex phenomena of human life which call for expression and communication: ... language has developed through an infinite number of momentary' and expedient 'solutions of such problems of communication as arise every instant of our daily life. Language has not come into existence as a well-thought-out system that would once for all preclude any possibility of misunderstanding; but the necessity for mutual comprehension has gradually eliminated all fruitful sources of permanent or continual misunderstanding. ... Language is never illogical where strict logic is required for the sake of comprehension, but neither is it pedantically logical where no ambiguity is to be feared in ordinary conversation: it steers adroitly between these two dangers.' In the conduct of his daily life, man proceeds by trial and error; he is quick to learn; he is shrewdly empirical. No less empirical in his language, he is quick to discard the useless and the grossly imperfect, the gravely obstructive.

Jespersen then becomes 'positively shattering'. Concerning that stock syllogism, *All men are mortal; John is a man; therefore, John is mortal*, he asks, 'Do we ever reason that way?' and drives home his point by taking another simple syllogism, *Both my brothers are teachers; John is my brother; therefore, John is a teacher.* Here, as in the other syllogism, it is 'evident to the simplest mind' that the major premisses connote or contain the conclusion; in other words, we could not know that *all* men are mortal unless we knew that *John* was mortal, and in my knowledge that both my brothers are teachers is implicit the (actually prior) knowledge that John is a teacher. In Höffding's *Logic* there occurs this syllogism, *Neptune is a planet; every planet moves in an ellipse; therefore, Neptune moves in an ellipse.* There isn't a deduction here, for unless we knew that *Neptune* moves in an ellipse, we could not have known that *all* planets so move. 'The syllogism about John's mortality', continues Jespersen, 'is merely an illegitimate trick to disguise the real character of the conclusion, which is this: we have seen in innumerable instances that men have died, therefore we conclude that there is an overpowering probability that this man John, who has so many traits in common with those that have already died, will also some day die. This of course is no syllogism, but then the part played by syllogisms in everyday life, and consequently in everyday language, is really negligible.'

FORM	FUNCTION	NOTION
-ed, as in *handed* *-t*, as in *fixed* *-d*, as in *showed* *-t* with inner change (*left*) unchanged, as in *put* inner change, as in *drank* different kernel or radical (*was*)	Preterite	Past time: 'He *knew* it long ago.' Unreality in present time: 'If we *knew*' and 'I wish we *knew*' (or 'If only we *knew*', of which the past is 'If only we *had known*'). Future time: 'It is time you *went* to bed.' Shifted present time: 'How did you know I was a Dane?' All times (universality): 'Men were deceivers ever.'

*But even in logicality, language is sometimes superior to logic itself. 'Sometimes the instinctive logic that underlies linguistic expression is subtler or suppler than the logic of the schools. Thus in some cases with negatives. "He spends £200 a year" and "He lives on £200 a year" are practically synonymous, but if we negative them everything is changed, for "He doesn't spend £200 a year" means that he spends less than £200 and "He doesn't live on £200 a year" means that he spends more.' In the former instance the numeral is negatived; in the latter, 'live on £200 a year ' is negatived. In language, the former negative yields 'less'; in the latter, 'more'. If we consider 'the way in which actual language uses two negatives together', we find that 'the result sometimes is a positive, sometimes a negative assertion'. See **NEGATION**.

In this relation of grammar and logic, there is a further aspect: Could our traditional system of grammar be more logically arranged? This is not the place for a detailed answer, which can be obtained in Jespersen's *The Philosophy of Grammar*, that great grammarian provides a short yet illuminating account on pp. 11–17 of his tract, *Logic and Grammar*. In brief, he urges us to consider all words (and word-groups) in their three aspects, form, syntactic function, and 'natural or logical meaning'; this third aspect he calls 'notional', the aspect

*Cf. **NEGATION**, third paragraph of Section A.

itself being *notion*. Syntax, he remarks, stands between form and notion, and Janus-like, it faces both ways. 'If we take such an example as the English preterite, we find, first, that it is expressed by different forms in different verbs, and, second, that it corresponds to different time-divisions and other rational categories.' He establishes the scheme shown above, in which the criterion of form is not spelling but pronunciation. This example serves to show, or at least to indicate, that 'the distinction between syntactic function and the notional meaning [or, briefly, notion] is extremely important, and may serve to settle disputed points in grammar'.

grammatical error is rejected by purists on the ground that, *qua* grammar, an error that is ungrammatical cannot be grammatical: but this is folly: *grammatical* means 'in grammar or of grammar or pertaining to or like or characteristic of grammar' and therefore *grammatical error*, as any sensible person assumes, signifies 'an error in (or of) grammar'.

gramophone is now an old-fashioned word, the modern electronic device being usually called a *record-player*. *Phonograph* is still current as a US synonym. A *music centre* combines radio, record-player [and/or compact disc player] and cassette tape recorder.

grand as a passe-partout of admiration is to be avoided, not merely because it is a colloquialism (the adverb *grand*, 'He's doing grand', is, by the way, an illiteracy) but also and especially because it is not a precise term but a lazy man's substitute for thought. See also GRANDIOSE.

grandiloquent, magniloquent and **eloquent**. *Eloquent* is a favourable term; the other two are pejorative. For *magniloquent*, see the separate entry. *Grandiloquent* is applied to a person, or to his or her speech or style, and it = 'characterized by swollen or pompous expression' (*OED*).

grandiose is more particular, more specific than *grand*. *Grandiose* = 'producing an effect or impression of grandeur or greatness; characterized by largeness of plan or nobility of design', as in 'The simple and grandiose taste of the Hellenic architects' (Leitch) and 'He recalls the past like "an Arab Ossian", monotonous and grandiose' (Dowden); also it = 'characterized by formal stateliness', a sense that is disparaging, as in 'Mr Urquiza entered first, with a strut more than usually grandiose', where the nuance is that of 'pompous' or 'aiming at grandeur' (*OED*).

granted, granting. See CONJUNCTIONS, DISGUISED.

grass roots. See VOGUE WORDS.

grateful and **gratified.** *Grateful* = 'feeling gratitude' and (only of things) 'pleasing to the mind or senses' (a literarism); but *gratified* = 'pleased – esp. pleased by compliance', 'satisfied, humoured, indulged', as in 'a gratified tone of voice', 'gratified acknowledgements', 'His vanity was gratified by the homage ... paid him' (Prescott) (*OED*).

gravamen. See **onus.**

gray is the usual US spelling, *grey* the British.

great is an infelicity for *much* in such a context as the following: 'During the last few years great publicity has been given to the Physical Fitness Campaign.'

Great Britain = England, Scotland, Wales; *the United Kingdom* adds Northern Ireland to these, but the official name is *The United Kingdom of Great Britain and Northern Ireland; the British Isles* is a purely geographical term, including the Irish Republic, the Isle of Man, and the Channel Islands.

greater part. See **major portion.**

greatly for *largely* or *mainly* is catachrestic. 'There is little doubt that hatred borne by one nation towards another is greatly due to a lack of understanding of their respective racial characteristics.'

Grecian and **Greek**. *Grecian* is gradually being superseded by *Greek* in almost every sense of both the adjective and the noun. The adjective is now rare 'except with reference to style of architecture and facial outline', and even *Grecian architecture* has become rarer than *Greek architecture*, except as an architectural technicality. As a noun, *Grecian* is extant in only three senses: (*a*) a person learned in the Greek language, a Greek scholar; (*b*) such a Jew of the Dispersion as spoke Greek, a Greek Jew; and (*c*) a boy in the highest form at Christ's Hospital, 'the Blue-coat School' (based on *OED*).

The Greeks is now obligatory. And the adjective *Greek* is preferred to *Grecian* in almost every context: e.g. *Greek art*; *Greek literature*; *Greek life*; *Greek history*; the *Greek character*; *Greek Earth*, as the title of Sydney Hopper's distinguished and delightful travel book, with aesthetic, literary, philosophical, and sociological commentary, published in 1939; *Greek cities*; *the Greek nation* and *people*; *the Greek army* and *navy*; etc., etc.

GREEK AND LATIN. To refrain from using Greek and Latin words when they are the best available, when indeed no others will perform the work that the Classical words will do, is childish. In science, philosophy, medicine, technology, they are inevitable.

But that Classicism may be overdone appears not only in **JOHNSONESE** (*q.v.*) but, as I see it, in such a sentence as this, 'Nor have I tried to plumb the subjects' minds for their fundamental credenda [? *beliefs*], philosophies and ideation' (G. J. Nathan, *The Intimate Notebooks of George Jean Nathan*).

On the immense number of current Latin words and phrases that an educated person must be familiar with, Sir Alan Herbert has eleven very useful pages (166–76), with notes on pronunciation, in *What a Word!*

green. See **VOGUE WORDS**.

green house is a house painted green; **greenhouse** (or, now obsolescent: **green-house**) is a glass-house for the rearing and preservation of plants, esp. of tender and delicate plants. The word probably appears most frequently today in the contexts *greenhouse effect* and *greenhouse gas*.

grey. See **gray**.

grisly; grizzly; grizzled. *Grisly* = 'causing horror or terror', hence 'causing uncanny or extremely unpleasant feeling', 'grim', 'ghastly'; *grizzly* and *grizzled* = 'grey', esp. 'grey-haired'. A *grizzly* is a large American or Russian bear.

ground(s). The word can be used in either the singular or the plural in the sense 'motive, reason', even when only one motive or reason is adduced. 'He retired on the ground(s) of ill-health.' Where *grounds* is used, it must take a plural verb. 'Our grounds for suspicion are as follows ...'

GROUP GENITIVE. The rule governing the use of the genitive (*boy's, boys'*; *woman's, women's*) is extended to any phrase that can be regarded as a unit and that is not of an inordinate length.

'The position of the genitive now', says Professor Jesperson in *Growth and Structure of the English Language*, 'is always immediately before the governing word, and this in [conjunction] with the regularity of the formation of the [genitive] case has been instrumental in bringing about the modern group-genitive, where the *s* is tacked on to the end of a word-group with no regard to the logic of the older grammar: *the King of England's power* (formerly "the kinges power of England"), *the bride and bridegroom's return*, *somebody else's hat*, etc.' Dr Onions adduces *A quarter of an hour's ride* and continues with the necessary caution: '[The group genitive] must not be extended beyond reasonable limits: such ludicrous phrasings as the following will be avoided: "*the father of the child's* remonstrances" (instead of "the remonstrances of the child's father"), "that's *the man I saw yesterday's son*", "that's *the passenger that missed the train's luggage*" ': with which it is interesting and instructive to compare Shakespeare's 'I do dine today at the father'*s* of a certain pupil of mine' (cited by Onions).

GROUP TERMS (*'flock* of sheep', '*herd* of cattle'). See SPORTS TECHNICALITIES.

grow smaller is condemned by many purists on the ground that it is impossible to *grow* smaller. A silly condemnation, for in idiomatic English *grow* has the derivative sense, 'to become'.

grudge. See **begrudge.**

guarantee is noun and verb; **guaranty** is noun only. The former noun is general, legal, and commercial; the latter, legal and commercial, is the more usual for 'the act of guaranteeing or giving a security' and 'something given or already existing as security'. Avoid – though it is correct – *guarantee* and – because it is obsolete – *guaranty* in the sense 'a guaranteeing party', i.e. a *guarantor*, the person to whom the guarantee (or guaranty) is given being the *guarantee*. Cf. **warrant, warranty.**

gubernatorial (mostly American) is permissible only when neither *governor's* nor *of the government* (or *the Government's*) will serve the purpose.

guer(r)illa (warfare) is correct, and a *guer(r)illa* is a member of a group engaged in irregular warfare; in current slang, a hired murderer employed by underworld gangs; a tough. There is sometimes confusion of *guer(r)illa* with *gorilla*, the much more usual underworld form.

guess is colloquial in the senses 'believe, think, suppose, expect'. In current Standard English its predominant senses are 'to estimate' (to guess a weight, a direction, a value, etc.) and 'to form an opinion or hypothesis respecting (some unknown state of facts), either at random or from indications admittedly uncertain; to con-

jecture', as in 'we may guess when its growth began' (Bayard Taylor), 'I ... little guessed the end' (Mrs Browning), and *as I guess, so I guess, one may guess*, etc.

guidelines. See VOGUE WORDS.

gybe. See **gibe.**

gypsy. See **gipsy.**

H

habitable, inhabit, inhabitable, uninhabitable. Respectively 'liveable-in', 'to live in', 'liveable-in', 'not liveable-in'. *Habitable* is nowadays applied mostly to houses or flats, *inhabitable* to countries. (In French, *habitable* is English 'inhabitable', but French *inhabitable* is English 'uninhabitable'.)

hacienda. See **ranch.**

had. See **would have.**

had is improperly used by Eric Partridge (*The French Romantics' Knowledge of English Literature*, 1924) in the following: 'At the former date, A. de Pontmartin's father had a prefect of police say to him, etc.'. The idiom is common where *have* means 'cause to'. A man introducing a friend may say: 'I'd like to have you shake hands with Mr So-and-So'; *OED* confirms this definition: 'To cause, procure, or oblige (a person to do something)', and extends it thus: 'To wish, will, require that something be done', and gives examples: 'I would have you make an essay to accomplish it'; 'I would not have it spoken about.' Now 'A. de Pontmartin's father' did not *will* or *cause* 'the prefect of police' to say something to him, but happened to be spoken to by that official.

had best; had better. See **would best** and **would better.**

had have ('If you had have come'). Redundant *have*; an error by no means confined to the illiterate. This construction, in which the *have* is intrusive and which has the still more illiterate variant *had of*, is not an error I should have signalized here, had it not been for the following sentence met with in a very good novelist, 'But then, thought Rome [an educated woman], should I have been any more understanding if I hadn't have happened to have been there that afternoon when Mark's name was mentioned?'

had rather. See **would rather.**

had used to be for *had been* or *used to be*, or for preterite + *formerly* (before or after the verb), seems an odd mistake; but it is not so infrequent as the paragons would have us think. 'To Basil Woolrich, sitting in the room at the top of Rynox House which had used to be that of F.X., came the clerk Harris' (Philip MacDonald, *The Rynox Mystery*).

hadn't ought. See **ought, didn't ...**

hail and **hale** (v.). The former is 'to salute with "hail!"'; to greet; to welcome'; hence, 'to call to (a ship, a person) from a distance in order to attract attention', but *hale* is 'to draw or pull', hence 'to drag or bring violently', as in 'He was haled to prison' (*OED*).

half. See **demi.**

half a dozen and **half-dozen** in British usage are the better ways of writing these phrases. *OED* gives them as equally English. Whereas one says *a half-dozen*, one does not say *a half a dozen*, and *the half-dozen* is more idiomatic than *the half a dozen*. [*Webster's* hyphenates the adj. *half-dozen* but not the noun phrase.]

half after (8 o'clock) is an American alternative to *half-past* (eight). An increasingly common British variant is *half eight*. The same applies to *a quarter after* (for *a quarter past*).

hallelujah. See **alleluja.**

hands-on. See VOGUE WORDS.

hangar; hanger. The former is used in only one sense, 'a shed for the shelter of aircraft'.

hanged is used of capital punishment only ('He was hanged – not *hung* – 'yesterday'; 'The executioner hanged the criminal'). *Hung*, preterite and past participle, is applied to things, as in 'The picture was hung too low', and 'I hung the picture as high as I could.'

happiness should not be debased to the sense, 'pleasure'.

hardly and **scarcely** are virtual negatives. 'Hardly a man was there' and 'Scarcely a run was scored in the first half hour' are correct, but 'I didn't hardly (or, scarcely) know him' is incorrect. 'Touring arrangements have been made. Why? Nobody hardly tours in that country now' is another example of an error that is an illiteracy – a solecism – a damning social lapse!

hardly none is solecistic for *hardly any*.

hardly ... than, like *scarcely ... than*, is a frequent misconstruction. 'Hardly was Edward dead than a struggle began for the possession of the reins of power', Ransome, *History of England* (Nesfield); substitute *when* for *than*. Cf. **barely ... than.**

hardly ... until is catachrestic for *hardly ... when*, as in 'I had hardly begun my work until I was called away.'

hari-kari is a common misspelling and mispronunciation of the Japanese *hara-kiri*, a method of suicide sometimes practised in Japan. The error is made by E. C. R. Lorac in *A Pall for a Painter*. 'He'd have committed hari-kari himself before he tipped her off her pedestal.'

harmless. See COMPARATIVES, FALSE. Cf. the synonymous **innocuous.**

haste; hasten. Keep the former as a noun, the latter as a verb (whether transitive or intransitive); as a verb, *haste* is obsolete, except as a literarism or as a poetic archaism.

hate is much stronger than *dislike*: do not, therefore, use these two terms synonymously.

haul is grossly overworked by journalists and by writers of crime novels. 'Meaning anything from herrings [properly, a *catch*] and diamonds [properly, a *theft* or a *booty*] to goals scored in a football match [properly, a *large number*]' (Frank Whitaker, in the *JIJ*, January 1939).

have. See **possess.**

have a right to is catachrestic when = *ought to*. Harold Herd happily cites the ludicrous 'He has a right to be hanged.' *Have a right to do* connotes privilege, not penalty.

have dinner. See **dine.**

have got is less formal than *have*. 'I can truthfully say that I have not got an enemy in the world' (Ethel L. White, *The Wheel Spins*). See **got.**

having reference to this, I think ... = About this, I think ...

he. See **they, their.**

healthful is archaic for *healthy* and should be reserved for 'promoting or conducive to bodily health' – hence, fig., '... to spiritual health' (*OED*).

Heaven (capital *H*) is 'God, Providence'; *heaven* (small *h*) is 'the habitation of God and his angels'; *the heavens* (small *h*) are 'that expanse in which the sun, moon, and stars are seen'. Other senses are obsolete, archaic, literary, or colloquial.

heavenward is the adjective and preferable adverb, *heavenwards* a later variant of the adverb.

Hebraic. See **Semitic.**

Hebrew. See at **Yiddish**; also see **Jew** and **Semitic.**

hectic (adj.) 'applied to that kind of fever which accompanies consumption' (*OED*),

is, because of the flush which it causes, now more often applied to any state of busy excitement as in 'Life has been so hectic lately.'

heighth, a misspelling of *highth*, a variant of (preferred) *height*.

heir. An *heir apparent* cannot be superseded by any subsequent birth; an *heir presumptive* may later be displaced by a baby with a superior claim.

help (it), with **can** or **could.** *Not*, though necessary to the sense, is often erroneously omitted, as in Newman, *Apologia* (quoted by Whateley), 'Your name shall occur again as little as I can help, in these pages', the sense being '– shall occur only when I cannot help (or prevent) it'. See also **NEGATION,** the final sentence.

help but, cannot. See **but.**

helpmate and **helpmeet.** Both of these words are applied especially to a wife or a husband; the latter is archaic.

hence is redundant in such a sentence as 'It won't be a long time hence, before we sail.' See also **from hence.**

henceforth and **thenceforth.** The former = 'from this time or point'; both have the connotation of *onwards*. Except in legal and formal contexts, they are obsolescent.

her, of, and **of hers.** See **of her – of hers.**

her's for *hers*, a frequent illiteracy. Cf. *it's* for *its*, *their's* for *theirs*, *your's* for *yours*, *our's* for *ours*.

hereabout; hereabouts. Both = 'in this neighbourhood'; usage appears to be adopting the latter to the exclusion of the former.

heretofore; hereunto; theretofore. See **ARCHAISMS.** Cf. **henceforth.**

herself. See **myself** and **oneself.**

hew – preterite, *hewed* – past participle, *hewn* or *hewed*: these are the correct forms of the verb.

hiccup, rather than *hiccough*, is the prevalent spelling of both noun and verb. Their pronunciation is identical.

hide – hid – hidden (or, now obsolescent, **hid**). See also at **cache**.

high is, in my opinion, misused in the sentence, 'Mexico City is 7,350 feet high' (Violet O. Cressy-Marcks, *Up the Amazon and over the Andes*). For *high* I should read *up*; in formal writing 'M. C. is at an altitude of 7,350 feet.' See also **tall**.

him, of and **of his**. See **of her – of hers**.

himself. See **myself** and **oneself**.

Hindi and **Hindustani**. *Hindi*, the chief vernacular of northern India, is an Indo-Aryan language; it is divided into two groups, the Eastern Hindi dialects and the Western Hindi dialects. The most important Western Hindi dialect is Hindustani, which, containing many words adopted from Arabic and Persian, is 'current as a lingua franca over nearly all India' (*Webster's*). A literary form of Hindustani is called Hindi and is an official language of India.

hindsight is a popular and useful word, for 'wisdom after the event'. It is contrasted with *foresight*.

hire and **lease** and **let** and **rent**. Of these four verbs, only *let* (or *let out*) is univocal ('to grant the temporary possession and use of [property] to another in consideration of payments of money', i.e. of rent). The other three have opposite senses: (1) to *let*; (2) 'to pay rent for, to take or occupy by payment of rent'. In Britain *rent*, however, is now used mostly in the second sense: it is the usual opposite of *let*. *Hire* is now little used of land or houses, and it is applied mostly in sense 2. *Lease* is a formal term; the one who lets is the *lessor*, the one who pays rent is the *lessee*. The Americans also use *hire* for 'employ (someone) for wages', and may *rent*, rather than *hire*, a dinner jacket for one night.

historic; historical. The latter = 'of the nature of history' (*historical novel*); the former = 'famous or important in history'. See **-ic** and **ical**.

histrionics are insincere over-dramatic behaviour, not to be confused with *hysterics*.

hoard. See **horde**.

hocus (v.) forms *hocussed, hocussing*, but *focus* (v.) forms *focused, focusing*: this is the ruling implied by *OED*.

hoi polloi means 'the masses, the riffraff'. Although it is strictly inaccurate to speak of '*the hoi polloi*' (since *hoi* is Greek for 'the') it would be quite unidiomatic to omit *the* here.

holily is obviously much more economical than *in a holy manner.* and, after all, it is not too difficult to pronounce.

holocaust is 'destruction by fire': do not synonymize it with *disaster*. With a capital *H* it means the mass murder of the Jews by the Nazis.

home is the residence of a family, a household; it should not be used (at any rate in Britain) as a synonym for *house*, as in 'Homes for Sale'.

home, be. To say that a person 'is home' for 'is at home' is, I think, both slovenly and ambiguous.

homicide. See **murder**.

homogeneous means 'of the same kind, uniform'. The technical word *homogenous* means 'similar owing to common descent'.

honeycombed has some odd uses: Sir Alan Herbert learns from one newspaper that 'Kalat City is another wilderness honeycombed with corpses' and from another that 'Stresa is honeycombed with detectives.'

honorarium (plural, *-iums*; pedantically, *-ia*) is not synonymous with *salary*. Originally (as still) it was an honorary reward; thence it came to be, and predominantly it is, a fee for services rendered, esp. services rendered by a professional person (barrister, architect, doctor). Sometimes it is a complimentary fee paid to one who is not entitled to either salary or fee, as e.g. to a non-professional club secretary.

honorary; hono(u)rable. The latter is applied to that which is worthy of honour; the former, apart from legal phrases, has, as its predominant current sense, these two allied senses: 'holding a title or position conferred as an honour either without emolument or without the usual duties or obligations on the one hand, the usual privileges on the other', as in *honorary colonel, honorary magistrate*, and 'rendered or conferred merely for the sake of honour', as in *honorary colonelcy*; the oldest sense, not yet archaic, is that of 'denoting – or bringing – honour; conferred (or rendered) in honour', as in 'The simple crown of olive, an honorary reward' (Grote, *The History of Greece*, vol. ii, 1847) (*OED*).

hopefully, besides meaning 'in a hopeful way', now often means 'it is hoped'. This new use seems no odder than the corresponding use of adverbs such as *naturally*: 'Hopefully/Naturally she'll come', but it has aroused the rage of many purists. Those who do use it should at least beware of ambiguity, since 'He will leave tomorrow hopefully' might be interpreted in either way.

horde; hoard. The former is a gang, swarm, or tribe; the latter a stock laid by for future use.

horrible, like *awful, dreadful, terrible*, is overdone. Don't. Above all, do not so shear it of its virtue that it becomes a mere equivalent of *disagreeable*.

hospitalize (n., **hospitalization**) is shocking officialese for *sent to hospital*.

host. *OED* does not record the word as a feminine; nor have I ever heard it so applied.

host for *large quantity*. 'Frank had arranged for a host of provisions to be laid up in the larder here' (Cecil Freeman Gregg,

Tragedy at Wembley). Host is properly a large number of individuals.

hot cup of cocoa, coffee, tea (etc.), is condemned by purists, who uphold *cup of hot cocoa* (etc.). The latter is more logical; but only at first sight.

housekeep for *keep house* has proved to be a convenient word. But *houseclean* to 'clean (the) house' has not proved much of a success.

how for *that* should be avoided except in indirect questions. Thus, 'He does not realize how very odd it is that Smith should ring him there' is correct and clear; but '[He] goes on telling me how he went back to the studio' is ambiguous for the intended meaning, which is 'that he went back to the studio', not 'in what manner' or 'in what conveyance he went back to the studio'. – 'I do not know how you contrive to make ends meet' is correct; but 'I told him how I had spent four years in France' is ambiguous, for it may mean either plain fact or coloured manner.

how for *what* is illiterate or, at the best, slovenly. ' "It will take my mind off the master, if you see how I mean" ' (John Bude, *The Cheltenham Square Murder*).

how, as, is vulgarly used for *that* or *whether*, e.g. 'He said as how he would be late tonight', 'I don't know as how I like that man,'

however can come at the beginning, in the middle, or at the end of a sentence, but is best positioned immediately after the item that is held up for contrast: 'In the morning, however, nothing was done' (in contrast to the preceding afternoon). It should be surrounded by commas unless it means 'no matter how', as in 'however hard I work …'. See also **ever.**

HOWLERS are such schoolboys' (and schoolgirls') errors of fact as arise from mis-apprehension or confusion of sense. They are catachrestic or, more often, the result of confusing a word with a word similar to it in form or pronunciation. 'The bystanders expressed deep sorrow at the passing of the beer', 'Histology is the dry bones of history', 'A conjunction is where railway lines cross.' Sometimes an epigram is unintentionally achieved, as in 'Elizabeth was known as the Virgin Queen. She was a great success as a queen.' [Cecil Hunt collects these things – and publishes them. Good Hunting!]

human, 'belonging to or characteristic of mankind'; **humane,** as 'kind' or (of knowledge) 'Classical'. As a noun, *human* is either a jocularity, or an affectation; it may, however, make its way as a convenience.

humankind. See **mankind.**

humble-bee and **bumble-bee** have caused a 'big-end, little-end' and a century-old discussion among the inexpert. The two forms are equally correct; the former is recorded by *OED* in 1450, the latter (by the same authority) not until some eighty years later; *bumble-bee* is now the main form.

humility; humiliation. The former is meekness, being humble. The latter is mortification, being humbled.

hurricane. See **cyclone.**

hyper- and **hypo-** (both from Greek). *Hyper* = *over, above,* and *hypo* = *under.* Thus all words beginning with *hyper-* convey the idea of excess (*hypercritical* = too critical; *hyperbole* = exaggerated statement); words with *hypo-* convey the opposite idea, so that *hyperthermia* is too high a bodily temperature, and *hypothermia* is too low.

HYPERBOLE, says Bain, 'is an effect gained by magnifying things beyond their natural bounds'; *OED* defines it as 'A figure of speech consisting in exaggerated or extravagant statement, used to express strong feeling or to produce a strong impression, and not intended to be understood literally.'

Here are two examples of literary, justifiable hyperbole:

> Not in the legions
> Of horrid hell can come a devil
>   more damn'd
> In evils, to top Macbeth;

>   I was all ear
> And took in strains that might create
>   a soul
> Under the ribs of death.

But hyperbole may be incongruous or ludicrous or painful; in this form, it has a second name – Exaggeration or Over-emphasis.

That the following examples are from one book by an American writer is accidental; one could easily find egregious examples from such British writers as Ossian and Hall Caine; and in any case the American was not an author.

'Crime, shielded beneath the garb of outward apparent virtue, stalks abroad unblushingly at noon-day, in the midst of society, or riots under cover of darkness, in its secretly guarded haunts of infamy. No community is free from its contamination' (opening words of the Preface to Geo. P. Burnham's *Memoirs of the United States Secret Service,* 1872).

'It is probably true that New York City is annually the scene of more crimes than are committed in any other five cities in the United States. Yet, in other places, colossal offences occur, and great criminals flourish, in spite of all effort to prevent or suppress the evil-doings of the wickedly inclined. The cloak of piety and the outward garments of "eminent respectability" hide a multitude of iniquities and very few instances of well dissembled charity and righteousness which parallel in depth the following veritable occurrence – are found even in the annals of the romance of crime' (*ibid.,* p. 144).

hypercritical (excessively, unduly, or finically critical) is occasionally confused with *hypocritical.*

HYPHENATION. In the life of compound words there are three stages: (1) two separate words (*cat bird*); (2) a hyphenated compound (*cat-bird*); (3) a single word (*catbird*).

Apart from that general process of language, there are, however, (*a*) many instances in which the hyphen is necessary; (*b*) others in which there is an important distinction between a hyphenated compound and two separate words; and (*c*) others in which the hyphen, by being misplaced, sets up an error or an ambiguity.

(*a*) *The hyphen that is necessary ... or, at least, advisable.*

'They were using it to mark straight lines for relaying some flagstones' (F. J. Whaley, *Trouble in College*). *Re-laying* is intended: cf. the difference between 'That umbrella needs to be *re-covered*' and 'He has *recovered* the umbrella that he lost two days ago.'

That the hyphen is especially useful in objective combinations – i.e. combinations in which the first noun is the virtual object of the action denoted or connoted by the second noun – may be indicated by 'General Curley ... known as "the Indian-fighter"' (Paul Horgan, *A Lamp on the Plains*), i.e. one who fights the Indians. General Curley is obviously not 'the Indian fighter', i.e. an Indian that is a fighter (subjective use).

In *Grammar for Grown-Ups*, C. C. Boyd quotes from a newspaper, in reference to a dog-show, the sentence, 'Every dog loving man should buy a ticket for this show', and remarks that 'without a hyphen between *dog* and *loving* it looks as if the editor has expected the dogs to buy the tickets'.

In *The Tyranny of Words*, Stuart Chase writes *antisurvival* for *anti-survival* (n.), *noneconomic* for *non-economic*, *nonresistance* for *non-resistance*, and *predepression* for *predepression*. Very little can be said in defence of this 'modernism', for *anti*, *non*, and *pre* are strong prefixes. [American readers will find that Mr Chase here follows good American usage; see *Webster's*, *anti-*, *non-*, *pre-*.]

'As for the little explored territory of [rhyming] slang, the fringe has been reached in ...' (EP at *beef* in his edition of Francis Grose, *A Classical Dictionary of the Vulgar Tongue*). For 'the little explored territory', read 'the little-explored territory'.

(*b*) *Hyphenated compound and two separate words.*

Compare 'The author's tense-sequence' (sequence of tenses) 'is defective in this passage', with 'A tense sequence of events' – a sequence of tense events – 'succeeded a dull sequence'.

Compare also *bull's-eye* (a sweetmeat) with *bull's eye* (the animal's eye), as in 'He hit the bull's eye with a bull's-eye.'

(*c*) *Hyphen misplaced.*

'I am an old cloathes-man' (Israel Israel in *The Sessions Papers of the Old Bailey*, 3rd session, 1773). The reporter should have written, ' an old-cloathes man', the reference being not to his age but to his profession.

'The Queen's Head ... where gin and water' – i.e. gin in water – 'is sold in three half-penny bowls, called Goes' (Francis Grose, at *Go Shop*, in *A Classical Dictionary of the Vulgar Tongue*). For 'three half-penny bowls' read 'three-halfpenny bowls'.

In *TLS* of 8 April 1938 appeared this very pertinent letter from Dr R. W. Chapman:

HYPHENS.

'Sir, All students of typographical practice must have noticed the awkwardness which results when a hyphen is used to connect compounds not themselves hyphenated. Thus "The Chipping Norton-Stony Stratford road" might be thought by a stranger to mean the road that leads from Chipping to Stratford by way of Norton Stony. The example which follows is extreme in my experience because the expression is tripartite. A writer in the American *Publishers' Weekly* (11 Feb. 1938) explains that Mr Stanley Morison believes that early printing types were influenced not only by manuscript but also by engraved or carved letters. "He would like to replace our present concept of a dual relationship calligrapher-typecutter with a new calligrapher-letter engraver-typecutting triangle." It needs an effort to realize that the three sides of this triangle are (1) calligrapher, (2) letter engraver, (3) typecutter.'

Here, admittedly, I have merely skimmed the surface of Hyphenation. In the Fowlers' *The King's English*, there is, at pp. 284–9, an excellent short account; in *Modern English Usage* there is an admirable long account. See also pp. 79–84 of G. V. Carey's *Mind the Stop*. [American readers may wish to consult *Webster's* at the entry *compound*, n.; also *The New Standard Dictionary*, 'Method of Compounding Words', pp. xxx–xxxi; and *The Style Manual of the Department of State* (Washington, DC, 1937); and the *Manual of the Government Printing Office* (Washington, DC).] *Webster's* is especially good; I have adapted and considerably developed *W.'s* treatment in *You Have a Point There*.

hysterics. See **histrionics.**

I

I easily becomes egotistical, but is preferable to 'your humble servant', 'the undersigned', 'your uncle', and all other such puerilities.

I is misused for *me* in such a sentence as 'He could only get tickets for you and I.' Boyd quotes 'a girl like I' from *Gentlemen Prefer Blondes.*

I (says). See **says.**

ib. or **ibid.**, short for *ibidem* ('in the same place'), is used chiefly in the sense, 'in the same chapter, passage; ... to avoid the repetition of a reference', thus: 'R. Whiston, *Cathedral Trusts*, pp. 2–4 ... *Ibid.*, pp. 10–12'. All forms of the word should be italicized; the same applies to the following three terms: *id.* is short for *idem*, 'the same word, name, title, author, etc., as mentioned before: used to avoid repeti-

tion'. – *l.c.* is the abbreviation of *locus citatus*, 'the passage quoted'; among printers, however, it = 'lower case' (small as opposed to capital letters). – *op. cit.* is short for *opus citatum*, the work (book, pamphlet, article) already mentioned as in 'Coleridge, *op. cit.*'.

-ible and **-able.** The former represents Latin -*ibilis*, as in *audible, flexible, legible, permissible, possible, terrible, visible*. It is often displaced by -*able* in such Latin words as have come through French, also in such words as are regarded as having been formed immediately on an English verb: *convertable* for the usual *convertible, dividable, readmittable, referable, washable.*

In phrases, only -*able* is permissible: *come-at-able, get-at-able.*

See *OED* (at -*able* and -*ible*), Jespersen's *Modern English Grammar*, Part I, and Quirk's *A Grammar of Contemporary English.*

-ic and **-ical.** It is impossible to predict which form will prevail. Sometimes both may coexist, as with *botanic, botanical; geologic, geological*; though -*ical* is often preferred for the adjective when the -*ic* form also serves as a noun, as with *cynic, fanatic, logic*. There is, however, often a nuance at stake, as in *comic, comical; ethic, ethical; economic, economical; historic, historical*. See esp. *OED.*

ice-water; iced water. The former is correct only in the sense 'water formed by melting a piece or block of ice'; *iced water* has been made cold with ice.

-ics as a noun ending takes a singular verb when it means a science, art, or field of study, as in 'Linguistics is a popular university subject.' It takes a plural verb when it means a manifestation of qualities or set of activities, as in 'The acoustics in this theatre are excellent', or 'Their tactics were inexcusable.'

id. See **ego.** See **ib.**

idea, misused for *principle* or *assumption*. 'Four kinds of explanations which people give to justify their beliefs: 1. *The impulsive*: Much used by primitive man in the idea that any explanation was better than none' (Stuart Chase, *The Tyranny of Words*).

idea of (or **notion of**) for *idea* (etc.) *that* is occasionally ambiguous, as in 'This ties in [= links up] with Korzybski's central idea of knowledge as structural [= that knowledge is structural]' (Stuart Chase).

ideal (adj.) does not admit of comparison. 'I think it is one of the most ideal spots in the whole of Scotland' (examination script). See COMPARATIVES, FALSE.

identification. See **identity.**

identify is sometimes misused for *compare*. A candidate in the Scottish Leaving Certificate examination, in dealing with Burke's metaphor of the French Revolution described as a chemical reaction, wrote, 'In this metaphor the speaker is identifying the unruly state of France with liquor on the surface of which a froth had formed.'

Identify (somebody) with is correctly used, though somewhat overused, for 'associate with', as in, 'He has been identified with church work for many years.' The same pattern is now often used intransitively for 'feel psychological sympathy with', as in 'She identifies with the heroine of the play.' In formal contexts it is better to write 'She identifies herself with ...'.

identity, 'a person's personality and individuality', must not be confused with *identification*, 'the establishment of a person's name and individuality'.

ideology was formerly used chiefly to mean 'visionary speculations', but the more modern sense is 'economic or political theory', as in 'Marxist ideology'. We need a word without religious connotations to cover these secular doctrines.

IDIOM AND IDIOMS. 'If there is one thing more than another that I have learnt in Fleet Street it is never to underrate the importance of usage. It is blind and often illogical, but when it makes its mind up nothing can withstand it; and whatever else may be said of it, it has done much to make our language the richest in the world' (Frank Whitaker, in the *JJJ*, 1939).

'Neither grammar nor rule governs the idiom of a people: and there will be a multitude of cases where *Sic volo, sic jubeo* is the only measure of the tyranny of usage' (Dean Alford, *The Queen's English*, 1863).

The best account of idioms is that in Dr Pearsall Smith's *English Idioms*, SPE Tract No. xii. The following remarks and quotations are based on and drawn from that delightful paper.

Generically, *idiom* is 'used ... to describe the form of speech peculiar to a people or nation'. Particularly, *idioms* are 'those forms of expression, of grammatical construction, or of phrasing, which are peculiar to a language, and approved by its usage, although the meanings they convey are often different from their grammatical or logical signification'.

'The idiosyncrasy of English, like that of other languages, is perhaps most strikingly exemplified in the use of prepositions. Prepositional usage in all languages contains ... much that is peculiar and arbitrary; the relations to be expressed by prepositions are often so vague and indefinite, that many times one might seem logically just as right as another, and it is only "that tyrannical, capricious, utterly incalculable thing, idiomatic usage", which has decreed that this preposition must be used in this case, and that in another' (Jespersen, *Progress in Language*). For instance, 'we tamper *with*, but we tinker *at*; we find fault *in* a person, but find fault *with* him; we act *on* the spur of the moment, but *at* a moment's notice; we are insensible *to*, but are unconscious *of*; we say *for* long, but *at* length. ... Americans speak of getting *on* or *off* a train, the British of getting *in* or *out of* it; "*up to* time" is the British idiom, "*on* time" the American. [Note: Current British idiom has more recently come to follow the American here.] The difference is one of usage; either is correct from the point of view of grammar.' Compare such terse prepositional phrases as *by fits, for ever, for good, in fact, in general.*

A large class of British idioms consists of phrases 'in which two words are habitually used together for the sake of emphasis', e.g. *hue and cry, fits and starts, free and easy, hard and fast; by and by, over and over, round and round; bag and baggage, safe and sound, spick and span; art and part, high and dry, fair and square; hither and thither, from top to toe, as bold as brass, as large as life, as thick as thieves.*

Perhaps the most interesting class of idioms is that in which metaphor renders the idiom more telling, more effective. Originally confined to that trade or profession, sport or game, which originated them, these idioms 'are found to be capable of a wider use; ... and little by little the most vivid and useful of these phrases make their way into the common vocabulary and come to be understood by all'. From sailors we get *take in a reef, turn adrift, cut the painter, on the rocks, when one's ship comes home* and a host of others; soldiers have passed on to us such phrases as *take alarm, pass muster, at close quarters, on the qui vive, to hang fire* and *lock, stock, and barrel*; from hunting (including dog-lore) come *to hunt down, to give tongue, to lead a dog's life, to have a hair of the dog that bit you,* and horses have given us *to saddle with, a run for one's money, out of hand, with a heavy hand,* etc., etc.; domesticity yields *to get on like a house on fire, next door to, on the shelf, a drop in the bucket, as stiff as a poker, to boil over, to butter up* and so forth.

Though slightly less true now than in 1923, the following verdict is to be taken to heart: 'Idiom is held in little esteem by men of science, by schoolmasters, and old-fashioned grammarians, but good writers love it, for it is, in Landor's phrase, "the life and spirit of language". It may be regarded as the sister of poetry, for like poetry it retranslates our concepts into living experiences, and breathes that atmosphere of animal sensation which sustains the poet in his flights' (Logan Pearsall Smith).

if, omission of. 'And yet, come to the rights of it, he'd no business there at all'

(Baumann); this colloquial abbreviation of *if you come* is slovenly; but the fixed phrases *come to that, come to think of it* could have been correctly used here.

if for *whether* is informal and often ambiguous, but the mixture of the two is wrong, ambiguous – and amusing. 'She was wondering if Rupert [her husband] would like an heir, and whether it was time that they moved from the doll's house in Bourdon Street into a house of more sensible proportions and if Makepeace would keep a supply of records from *Private Lives* and the best honey and produce them placidly on a tray whenever they were needed' (Barbara Worsley-Gough, *A Feather in Her Cap*). A particularly illuminating example is afforded by the second *if* in the following sentence from Margery Allingham's *The Fashion in Shrouds,* 'Rex was still speaking in an absent fashion, as if he were working round to a point and wondering if to make it.' In that good writer and erudite scholar Sir Maurice Bowra's *Sophoclean Tragedy,* we notice this lapse: '[Contemporaries] would catch his hints and suggestions, and know if he intended to surprise them with a paradox or to expose some familiar way of thought.'

if is often misused by competent but hasty writers, where the correct word is *and* or *but* (as though I had written 'by competent *if* hasty writers'); thus: 'Which picture ... is likely to be nearest the truth? – that neat, simplified one which our descendants will master from their text-book histories, or that more complicated affair with which we are so painfully, if confusedly, familiar.' *If,* in such a sentence, implies a contrast between qualities unexpectedly found together, whereas no such contrast is seen in 'painfully' and 'confusedly'.

if and when is usually tautological for *when* (or *if*), as in 'I'll pay when I see you', 'I'll shout if it's necessary.'

if need be is correct with Present ('He always does that, if need be') or Future ('He will always do that, if need be'); but with Past, the correct form is *if need were* ('He always did that, if need were'). Those who feel that whereas *if need be* is literary, *if need were* is both literary and archaic (actually it is not archaic), may, if they wish, use *if necessary*, which does away with the verb in the conditional, in all tenses.

if not, ambiguity of. An excellent example is quoted by Sir Alan Herbert (*What a Word!*): 'England's Captain ... played one of the greatest, if not the most attractive innings of his career ... (*The Observer*). A. P. H. invites us to think this over: 'Was the innings "the most attractive" (as well as "one of the greatest") or not? Honestly, I do not know.'

The same ambiguity is to be noticed in the following: 'The war had found me still at school; I had left at once, of course, and done my share – with decent competence if not with distinction ...', where '*though not with distinction*' would make the writer's lack of that quality definite: by '*if not* ...' he appears to mean that he is merely too modest to claim the 'distinction' to which he would like to think himself entitled.

-ify is incorrect for *-efy, -ifaction* incorrect for *-efaction*, in the following verbs and their corresponding abstract nouns:
liquefy, putrefy, rarefy, stupefy, torrefy, and in certain other scientific or technical terms.

ignoramus. See PLURALS, UN-ENGLISH.

ignorant. See **artless** and **illiterate**.

-ile and **-ine,** words ending in. The modern British pronunciation of such words as *fertile, docile, missile,* and *turbine* is with the *i* long. In American usage the *i* is more commonly short, or so reduced that, for instance, *fertile* rhymes with *turtle*. *Quinine* and *glycerine* take the sound 'een' in Britain, but *quinine* in America has the long *i*, and *glycerin* (US spelling) the short *i*.

ilk, of that. *Of that ilk* means 'of the same (estate)'; thus *Guthrie of that ilk* means

'Guthrie of Guthrie' (Ackermann). The word is now well established, particularly in a derogatory sense, for 'of that family, clan, class, or kind', but this usage is peculiarly irritating to the Scots.

ill and **sick,** as applied to persons. Both are used predicatively; the former, rarely otherwise: 'He is ill, or sick.' But 'He is a sick man' – not, in current British usage, 'He is an ill man.' As applied to other than living things, *sick* has a special reference to nausea, as 'a sick headache', or is used in such extended senses as 'sick leave' and 'a sick joke'. Cf. **sick and sickly.**

illegal; illegitimate; illicit; unlawful. They all mean 'contrary to the law', but *illegal* = 'prohibited by the law of the land'; *illegitimate* = 'lacking proper legal status'; *illicit* is used particularly of secret activities that in certain circumstances contravene the law, as in 'an illicit whisky still'; and *unlawful* refers particularly to what contravenes either natural justice or the law of God.

illegible. See **unreadable.**

illicit and **elicit.** See **illegal.** See also **elicit.**

ILLITERACIES, FALSE. See FALSE ILLITERACIES.

ILLITERACY. See SOLECISM.

illiterate and **ignorant.** The former = 'not knowing how to read or write', or merely 'badly educated'; the latter = 'markedly deficient in knowledge'. An illiterate person is not necessarily ignorant.

illusion. See **delusion.**

illustration and **example.** *Illustration,* in one of its derivative senses, does = *example* or *instance*; but it is more dignified than *example* and has a sub-tone connotation of 'image or picture', as in 'An illustration of the principle which runs throughout nature' (Tyndall), 'Charles James Fox afforded an excellent illustration of bohemianism-cum-integrity' (based on *OED*).

image. See VOGUE WORDS.

imaginary; imaginative. Respectively 'imagined', esp. in the sense 'unreal, non-existent'; and 'endowed with (a powerful or fruitful) imagination', 'pertaining to the imagination as a mental faculty', 'bearing evidence of high creative force' (e.g. *an imaginative poem*) (*OED*).

imbue, misused for *instil*. One is *imbued* or *inspired with*: one *instils* something *into* a person. Incorrect is 'The courage he imbued into his men'; equally incorrect is 'The address instilled every citizen with fresh confidence.'

immaculate. See COMPARATIVES, FALSE.

immanent, imminent, eminent. These and their corresponding nouns and adverbs are often interconfused; for their different meanings, see any good dictionary. But don't be too hasty in imputing error! Take 'Newt was aching with the immanence of what he had to tell Danny' (Paul Horgan, *A Lamp on the Plains*). One may at first think, 'Oh! he means *imminence*'; but reflection shows that *immanence* is, after all, intended.

immediately used in the sense of *as soon as* is well-established but informal English. '*Immediately* the police arrived the crowd began to disperse.' More formally, one might write 'When the police arrived the crowd dispersed immediately', or, of course, 'Immediately after the police arrived, the crowd began to disperse.'

immigrant and **emigrant.** See **emigrant.**

imminent. See **immanent.**

immoral. See **amoral.**

immortal. See **deathless.** Also see COMPARATIVES, FALSE.

immunity and **impunity.** Apart from its technical senses in Law, Ecclesiasticism, Medicine, *immunity* = 'exemption from any usual liability; freedom from anything evil or harmful', as in 'immunity from pain', 'immunity from snakes', 'immunity

from sin'. *Impunity* is less extensive in its meaning: it = 'exemption from penalty (e.g. a fine) or a punishment (e.g. imprisonment)', and, in a weakened sense, 'exemption from loss or injury, security': 'In England, one can't commit murder with impunity', 'Snake-venom may be swallowed with impunity' (*OED*).

impassable (**-ability**) and **impassible** (**-ibility**) are easily confused; the former = *that cannot be traversed*; the latter, *unfeeling, incapable of being hurt, impassive.*

impecunious is 'penniless, in want of money'; not 'unthrifty', as it is occasionally understood to be.

imperative and **imperious.** In 1794, Gouverneur Morris, American statesman and diplomat, wrote the useful words, 'Subject to the imperative, and too often the imperious, mandates of a committee'; 'An imperious ruler would naturally give imperative orders' (Weseen). The basic sense (apart from the grammatical one) of *imperative* is 'of or like or expressing a command', hence 'peremptory' ('He spoke in an imperative tone'); hence 'urgent' or 'obligatory', as in 'The condition of the sick and wounded made it imperative to ship them to Egypt', 'The work is imperative.' The predominant current sense of *imperious* is 'overbearing, domineering, dictatorial', as in 'A proud, imperious aristocrat, contemptuous ... of popular rights' (Froude) (*OED*).

implement. See VOGUE WORDS.

implicit and **explicit.** *Implicit* is 'implied though not expressly stated; naturally or necessarily involved in, or inferable from, something else', as in 'Proofs are either implicit and indirect, or explicit and direct'; hence 'virtually or potentially contained *in*', as in 'The blessing implicit in all heaven's chastenings' (C. Kingsley). *Explicit* is '(of utterances) distinctly expressing *all* that is meant' (*explicit promises*); hence, '(of persons) saying all that one means; outspoken' (*OED*).

imply for **infer.** See **infer.**

impossible. See COMPARATIVES, FALSE; and cf. **possible.**

A thing is either possible or impossible; therefore 'more possible' is catachrestic for 'more feasible' or 'more practicable'.

impracticable and **impractical.** The former = 'that cannot be effected or dealt with; unmanageable, unserviceable', as in 'an impracticable road', 'an impracticable plan'; the latter = 'unpractical', 'having perhaps the theory but certainly not the practice', as in 'He was a great poet but an impractical man' (but see also at **unpracticable**).

impressible and **impressive** are occasionally confused; so are the adverbs *impressibly* and *impressively. Impressible* = 'easily impressed'; *impressive* = 'likely or sure to impress others'. Misused in ' "Don't forget," said my uncle impressibly, "that you are unable to articulate" ' (Francis Beeding, *The Big Fish*).

impression. See **edition.**

impromptu; extempore. Both are adverbs = 'without preparation or premeditation'; only *impromptu* is a noun; both are adjectives, *impromptu* being 'improvised', as in 'an impromptu speech', hence 'makeshift', as in 'an impromptu raft'. An *extempore* speech may have been prepared, but not to the extent of being written down or memorized: it is not read, nor has the speaker any notes.

impudent, catachrestic for *impotent*, is recorded as early as 1612. Dekker, *O per se O*, represents the palliard (a beggar with artificial sores for the excitation of compassion) as employing this patter: 'Ah the urship' - i.e. worship – 'if God looke out with your mercifull eyne, one pittifull looke upon sore, lame, grieved and impudent [for impotent] people, sore troubled with the grievous disease ...'.

impunity. See **immunity.**

in and **at.** Concerning prepositional idioms, Dr Pearsall Smith in *English Idioms*, SPE Tract No. xii, has posed the distinc-

tion better than I've seen it put anywhere else: 'More interesting are the cases where the difference of usage is not really arbitrary, but may express a shade of meaning which we are ourselves perhaps unconscious of. A curious instance of this is the way we use the prepositions *in* and *at* with the names of places. We say someone is *in* London, *in* Rome, *in* Paris, but usually *at* Oxford, *at* Rouen. The general rule is that we use *in* for large cities and capitals, *at* for smaller places'; (in a footnote) 'Shakespeare used *at* London, ... when London was a smaller place than it is now.' He continues with the caution that 'we commonly use *in* rather than *at* even for a small place if we ourselves are there, probably because then it bulks more largely in our imagination'. (Today, we use *at* even for a large city when global distances are in question: 'We refuelled at London on our flight to Karachi.')

in- and **un-** in adjectives; **in** and **un** as prefixes. In general, *in* is the prefix that goes with words of Latin origin or with such words of French origin as spring from Latin; *un* is the prefix that goes with the words of Teutonic origin (i.e. from Old English, Scandinavian, German). Thus, *infelicitous*, but *unhappy*. Most words with *-ed* and *-ing* form their negative with *un-*: unexpected, unassuming. See also **non-.**

in for *into*. 'Plane dives in reservoir' (caption in *The Daily Mirror*, 24 Aug. 1937) – 'I went in the Perla [a café], and sat down at a table' (Ernest Hemingway, *To Have and Have Not*, 1937). Those examples were legitimate, but the next is ambiguous. 'Towards ten o'clock I slipped down in the street' (interview reported in *The Daily Sketch*, 24 Mar. 1938) conveys only that the speaker *slipped and fell*, until we read that his object in 'slipping down' was 'to buy a paper'. Cf. the opposite error (*into* for *in*).

in for *within* causes ambiguity; e.g. 'I can get up in five minutes.'

in as much as, in so much as, in so far as may be written *inasmuch as, insomuch as,* insofar as, but not in asmuch as, insomuch as, in sofar as. The usual modern forms are inasmuch as and insomuch as; but still often in so far as. In so far as = 'in such measure or degree as', 'to such extent that'; insomuch as (slightly obsolescent) is virtually co-extensive with inasmuch as, which = in so far as (as here defined), but also = 'in proportion as' or 'according as', hence, 'in that', 'considering that', 'since', 'because'. Nor can in so far (etc.) be made equivalent to in so far as (etc.): 'Winning this election meant nothing to me except in so far it was a fight' (Frank Tilsley, I'd Hate to be Dead).

in behalf of. See **behalf of.**

in comparison of. See PREPOSITIONS WRONGLY USED.

in connection with for about is officialese.

in despite of. See at **despite.**

in excess of is not to be used indiscriminately for more than, as in 'The fee was in excess of £5', 'He rode in excess of twenty miles.'

in isolation is not to be used for by itself or alone.

in my opinion. See **opinion.**

in rare cases = rarely. See ABSTRACT NOUNS.

in respect to and **in search for.** See PREPOSITIONS WRONGLY USED.

in spite of. See at **despite.**

in support for. See PREPOSITIONS WRONGLY USED.

in the circumstances. See **circumstances.**

in the event that = if.

in the nature of for about or approximately. From a bank manager's letter of November 1937: 'We are communicating with the Company to ascertain what rate of interest they charge and the amount they would be prepared to advance which

we imagine would be in the nature of £450 if required.' See ABSTRACT NOUNS.

inapt, 'inappropriate', hence 'unskilful, awkward', is preferable to unapt, which particularly means 'not apt, unlikely'. Inept is the word to use for inappropriate words, speech, tone, allusions, and for 'absurd, foolish' actions, consequences, as in inept interference; in Law, inept = 'of no effect; void'. The corresponding nouns are inaptitude, ineptitude.

inasmuch as. See **in as much as.**

inaugurate, 'to begin formally or ceremonially', is grandiose and excessive as a synonym for begin.

incapable connotes innate or permanent lack of ability: unable connotes inability 'in a specific situation or at a specific time': 'He is incapable of doing such a thing' and 'He is unable to do it.'

incessant, 'unceasing, ceaseless' (actions; persons), is not to be used as a synonym for everlasting. See also COMPARATIVES, FALSE.

incident (adj.) and **incidental.** Incident is 'likely or tending to befall or affect; hence, naturally appertaining or attached to', either with to ('The physical weaknesses incident to human nature', 'powers incident to government') or absolutely ('The Puerto Rico expedition, and the incident aggressive steps taken in the campaign'). Do not use it in the senses of incidental, which = 'casual, fortuitous', as in 'Even corruptness may produce some incidental good', and (of a charge or expense) 'incurred apart from the primary disbursement', as in 'The house rent, and the incidental charges of a family' (W. Tennant) and the new set phrase, incidental expenses. And do not use incidental in the sense attaching to incident (OED).

incidentally for by the way, deplored by former purists, has obtained a fourth-class degree into respectability, much as **aggravate** has done.

incidently for *incidentally* is commoner than one might think; I have seen it in the writing of a good American journalist.

inclined for *likely* (or *apt*), when it is applied to things, is an odd usage: a usage to be avoided. In reading an Oxford and Cambridge School Certificate script I felt myself pulled up with a jerk when I ran into this, 'They wrote the truth, which, though interesting, is inclined to shock us.'

inclosure. See **enclose, enclosure.**

including. See CONJUNCTIONS, DIS-GUISED.

incom'parable and **uncompa'rable.** See **uncomparable**; also COMPARA-TIVES, FALSE.

incomprehensive(ly) for *incomprehensible* (*-bly*). See **comprehensive(ly).**

inconsequent; inconsequential. They can both mean 'irrelevant, disconnected'. In addition, *inconsequential* = 'unimportant' (*COD*).

incorrect and *uncorrected* are the correct forms.

incredible, incredulous. See **credible.**

incubus. See **succubus.**

inculcate. One *inculcates* ideas or information *into* a person; one does not *inculcate* a person *with* ideas. Cf. **imbue.**

incumbent. See **recumbent.**

incumbent upon me to, it is = I am obliged to, I must. Beloved of officialese.

in-depth. See VOGUE WORDS.

indestructible. See COMPARATIVES, FALSE.

indexes. See **indices.**

Indian may, by a historical accident, be an ambiguous word even today. Make it clear, where necessary, whether you mean a person from India or a descendant of the indigenous peoples of America. *Indian*

restaurants often belong to Pakistanis and Bangladeshis.

INDIAN ENGLISH. See STANDARD ENGLISH, Section IV.

indicated, be, though much used in medical contexts, is not good general English for *advisable* or *that has been advised*, as in 'Prompt action is indicated.'

indices; indexes. The former is obligatory in Mathematics and Science; *indexes* is correct for 'an index of names, subjects, etc.'.

indict and **indite** are pronounced alike, but the former = 'to accuse', whereas the latter = 'to write'.

indifferent to (not *for* or *about*) means 'having no interest in'.

indigestible and **indigestion**, but **undigested**; these are the correct forms.

indignant was confused with *indigent* by the blind beggar whose card was inscribed, 'Pity the indignant blind.'

INDIRECT SPEECH. See REPORTED SPEECH.

indiscreet and **indiscrete.** For the distinction, see **discreet.**

indiscriminate. See **undiscriminating and indiscriminate.**

indite. See **indict.**

individual is not synonymous with *person*; it connotes a person as an entity – as distinct from a class.

individually is often used unnecessarily and tautologically.

indoor is the adjective, **indoors** the adverb.

indorse and **endorse.** The form *endorse* is now preferred in both British and American use for all senses, including 'express explicit approval of' and the British 'enter details of an offence on (a driving licence)'.

inductive. See **deductive.**

indulge, misused for *satisfy.* 'Amateur theatricals indulge my real bent.'

indulge in; engage in. The former may imply that the occupation is trivial or undignified.

industrial; industrious. Respectively 'connected with or characteristic of industry' and 'diligent'.

inelastic. See **unelastic.**

inept. See **inapt.**

inevitable has come to have what philologists term a pejorative connotation and what others call an unfavourable sense. It is, therefore, out of place in the following sentence: 'The most dramatic event was [Lord] Hawke's intrepidity in dropping Peel ... when it would certainly rob Yorkshire of almost inevitable championship': substitute *certain* for *inevitable.* (And delete *certainly*, for *almost certain* is certainly not *certain.*) See also COMPARATIVES, FALSE.

infant, child; baby (poetic and archaic: **babe**). In general use, an *infant* is a child in arms (*babe in arms* is the set phrase); in Law, a minor (a person under 18); in British education, a schoolchild under seven. A *child*, in general use, is under 14 or, more logically, below the age of puberty; in Law, (one of) the offspring; a *baby* is a child still at the breast or on the bottle. *Baby* is a less pretentious word than *infant.*

infectious and **contagious.** (*Infective*, by the way, is a medical term only.) A *contagious* disease is one that is spread by actual contact, either with the person or with some object that has been in contact with him or her; an *infectious* disease is spread by germs, in the air or in water.

infer for *imply. Infer* is 'to deduce; to derive, as a fact or [a] consequence' (*Nuttall's Standard Dictionary*); *imply* is 'to include in reality, to express indirectly: to mean: to signify' (*Chambers's*), also 'to hint'. 'I had a detailed report from Penfold Travers. ... Very terse indeed. ... He

inferred we were all blockheads in Bombay' (Graham Seton, *The K. Code Plan*) exemplifies the misuse.

inferior (or **superior**) **than** is a gross, yet alarmingly frequent error for *inferior* (or *superior*) *to.* Nesfield quotes *The Fortnightly Review*, September 1898: 'A man of far inferior abilities than Bismarck', which contains a further error; it would be better to write either 'a man far less able than Bismarck' or 'a man of abilities far inferior to Bismarck's'. See also COMPARATIVES, FALSE.

infinite is a dignified word; an uncomparable adjective; do not debase it to equality with '(very) great' or 'vast', as it is debased in 'His infinite worries caused him to become a victim of insomnia.' See also COMPARATIVES, FALSE.

infinitely small is loose, infelicitous English. **Infinitesimal** is the word required.

INFINITIVE, SPLIT. See SPLIT INFINITIVE, THE.

inflammable and **inflammatory.** The former is applied to that which (fig., that person who) is combustible (or can easily be set fire to); the latter, to that which causes the fire; especially if it is particularly likely to cause it; hence, to 'stimulating' (liquors). See also **flammable.**

inflection and **inflexion.** See **-ection and -exion.**

inflict. One *inflicts* something unpleasant *on* or *upon* a person, but one does not *inflict* a person *with* something. That is the proper use of *afflict.*

inform, for mere *tell*, is officialese and to be avoided by ordinary people.

informant; informer. Respectively, anyone who gives information on a stated (or implied) occasion, and one who lays information against another, especially if he or she makes a habit of so doing.

infrequent. See **unfrequent.**

ingenuous, 'innocent, artless', is sometimes confused with *ingenious*, 'clever at contrivance'.

inhabitable. See **habitable.**

inherent and **innate.** The latter (properly 'inborn', hence 'native' to a person, 'natural') is no longer used for the former. *Inherent* = 'existing in something as a permanent attribute; belonging to the intrinsic nature of that which is spoken of'; hence, 'intrinsic, indwelling'; hence, 'essential', hence, 'vested (*in*)', as in 'The supreme authority is inherent in the legislative assembly' (*OED*).

inhibit and **prohibit.** In Ecclesiastical Law, *inhibit* is to forbid or interdict; in general use, it is to restrain, check, prevent, stop, as in 'The reflex actions of the spinal cord may, by appropriate means, be inhibited'; in modern psychology, an *inhibition* is 'a (or the) restraining or checking of a thought or an action by the (unconscious) will'. *Prohibit*, in general use, is to forbid, as in 'The law prohibits larceny': cf. 'Fear can inhibit a man from action' (*OED*).

initiate, 'to begin, to introduce, to originate', is a dignified word. Do not use it as an easy synonym for *begin*. Its predominant sense is 'to admit (a person) with due rites to a society, etc.', hence, 'to instruct in the elements of a subject, a practice', as in 'to initiate into freemasonry', 'to initiate in(to) physical science'. As an intransitive verb, it is rare. Moreover, one *initiates* a person *into* something, but one does not *initiate* something *into* a person. Use *instil* for that.

injured. See **damaged.**

-in-law. See **daughters-in-law.**

innost; innermost. The latter = 'most – or furthest – within', as in 'The third and innermost barrier' (Scott) and 'innermost thoughts'; but both spatially and figuratively ('most intimate or secret'), *inmost* is preferable and more usual (*OED*).

innate. See **inherent and innate.**

innocuous. See COMPARATIVES, FALSE. Cf. **harmless.**

innumerable and **enumerable.** The former = uncountable, countless; the latter = countable.

input. See VOGUE WORDS.

inquire, inquiry. See **enquire;** also **query.**

insensible *of* = unaware of. *Insensible* (more usually *insensitive*) *to* = indifferent to.

insert in; insert into. The former emphasizes the general idea of the verb, the latter the inthrusting. *Insert in* = 'place in', whereas *insert into* rather = 'introduce into'. The former, in short, is static rather than dynamic; the latter is indubitably dynamic.

inside of. See **outside of.** *Inside of* is correctly, though colloquially, used for 'in less than (a period of time)'.

insignia is a plural; the rare singular is *insigne*.

insignificant does not mean 'small', but 'unimportant'. (The sense 'small in size' does exist, but it is obsolescent.)

insinuate, now a pejorative, should not be flattened to equivalence with *to suggest*.

insipid. See **vapid.**

insofar as; insomuch as. See **in as much as.**

inst. See **ult.**

instal is less usual than (to) *install*.

instance (n.). See **illustration.** As a verb, it is not rare in the sense, 'to cite as an instance or example', as in 'I may instance olive oil, which is mischievous to all plants' (Jowett).

instance where ('This is an instance where a doctor is powerless') is incorrect for *instance in which.* Cf. **example where.**

instances, in most, is verbose for *usually* or *mostly.* (Flayed by Sir Arthur Quiller-Couch.) See ABSTRACT NOUNS.

instanter (instantly) is properly a legal term; its use in other contexts is – except perhaps as a humorous term – to be discouraged. Some good people employ it as an elegancy.

instil. See **imbue** and **initiate**.

institute the necessary inquiries = to *ask*. (Attacked by Sir Alan Herbert.)

instructional and **instructive**. Both = 'educational' and 'conveying instruction or information', but the former stresses the teaching, the latter the information imparted. 'An instructional course' – i.e. a course of instruction – 'for young officers may be instructive' or informative, interestingly educative.

instrumentality of, by the = *by means of* or simply *by*. See ABSTRACT NOUNS.

insurance. See **assurance**.

insure. See **ensure**.

integrate. See VOGUE WORDS.

intellectual. See following entry.

intelligent (of persons), 'having the faculty of understanding', especially in a high degree, or (of things) 'displaying that faculty'; *intelligible*, (of either persons or things) 'easily understood; comprehensible'; *intellectual*, 'relating to the intellect', or (of persons) highly cultured, or (of things) requiring mental effort. One may be very *intelligent* without knowing much; the word is used of small children, animals and machines.

intensely for *very* must be used cautiously. One may say 'intensely hot (or cold)', even 'intensely unpleasant', but not 'intensely wealthy' (Agatha Christie, *Death on the Nile*).

intension is a learned term, to be used with great care. It is not synonymous with *intention*, 'a purpose'.

intentionally. See **advisedly**.

inter = 'between' or 'among', as in *intercede, intersection, intermarry; intra* = 'within', as in *intramural, intravenous*.

intercalate. See at **interject and interpolate**.

interesting. This passe-partout adjective is to be used very sparingly and, even when used, it must be only after soul-searching and intelligence-racking thought. If you mean 'puzzling', say so; if 'dramatic', say *dramatic*; if 'unusual', then *unusual*, if 'important', then *important*; if 'full of character or incident or implication(s)', then, for the sake of the right word, use the right words!

interface. See VOGUE WORDS.

interject and **interpolate**. The former is to interrupt a conversation; the latter is to insert something in a script or a publication – or indeed in a conversation, but without the abruptness or rudeness connoted by *interject*. To *intercalate* is to insert (a day) in a calendar or – a transferred use – to insert, in a series, something extraneous; generally in the passive.

internecine properly means 'mutually destructive', and should not be used, as it often is today, for 'quarrelling within a group, fratricidal', as in 'internecine squabbling within the Tory party'. Writers who attempt to use *internecine* correctly will often be understood in this new meaning.

interpretive. This is an acceptable variant of *interpretative*.

into for *in*. 'A far larger number [of compositions], cast (so to speak) into the same mould, have wearied the public' (E. Partridge, *The French Romantics' Knowledge of English Literature*, 1924); EP was wrong in speaking so. The error arises from the two meanings of 'cast' and from some ambiguity in his use of 'mould'. Another good example is 'He had understood at the beginning but failed to understand now as the threads ran away, on their own, into various directions' (a detective novel). And another is Fowler's example, 'Lord Rosebery took her into dinner' – which would have been very distressing for the lady.

into (*art*, etc.). This new sense of *into*, for 'keen on', is still colloquial.

intolerable, 'unbearable', hence, 'excessive'; **intolerant**, 'unwilling – or unable – to endure (something specified)', hence, 'disposed to persecute those who differ' (*OED*).

intoxicated. See **drunk** (**adj.**); **drunken.**

intra. See **inter.**

intrude. See **protrude.**

intrust; entrust. The former is a mere variant of the latter, in both British and American spelling.

invalid; invalidated; invalided. *Inval'id* = 'not valid'; and *in'valid* = '(a person) that is ill', whence the pun 'An invalid invalid'; *invalidated* = 'rendered not valid; null and void' (e.g. *invalidated evidence*); *invalided* = 'rendered – or accounted – an invalid, disabled by illness or injury', and as in 'invalided out of the Army'.

invaluable, like *priceless*, now means 'valuable to a high degree'; the senses 'without value', 'having no (high) price' are obsolete. The opposite of *invaluable* is *valueless*; that of *priceless*, is *worthless*. See also **COMPARATIVES, FALSE.**

invariably, for *always*, has long been overworked.

inveigh; inveigle. To *inveigh against* something is to protest vehemently; to *inveigle* (transitive) is to cajole.

invent. See **discover.**

inverse. See **converse.**

inversion. See **ORDER OF WORDS.**

investigation into, make (an) = to investigate. See **ABSTRACT NOUNS.**

invite for (an) *invitation* is incorrect and ill-bred and far too common.

involve the necessity of = *require*.

involved by. See **PREPOSITIONS WRONGLY USED.**

invulnerable, like *absolute* and *perfect* (see **COMPARATIVES, FALSE**), is a superlative, in that it implies a peak: one can say 'almost (or virtually) invulnerable', 'well nigh absolute', 'almost perfect', but, as one cannot say 'more absolute', or 'rather (or, more) perfect', so one cannot say 'rather invulnerable'. 'As long as he had Boss Warren's backing, he was fairly invulnerable' (Milton Propper, *Murder at the Polls*).

inward, inwards. The latter is adverb only ('with scales turned inwards', 'duties paid inwards'); the former is chiefly an adjective ('inward vitality', 'inward experience') but often functions as an adverb in American English and in older British writing.

ionosphere. See **troposphere.**

IRISH BULLS. See **BULLS.**

IRONY. 'Irony consists in stating the contrary of what is meant, there being something in the tone or the manner to show the speaker's real drift' (Alexander Bain, *English Composition and Rhetoric*, enlarged edition).

Bain gives many examples; several will suffice.

Job's address to his friends, 'No doubt but ye are the people, and wisdom shall die with you'; the Mark Antony oration ('honourable men') in *Julius Caesar*; Swift's *The Tale of a Tub*, *The Battle of the Books* and *Gulliver's Travels*, all three for sustained irony; *The Spectator*, No. 239 (the various kinds of argument); Bentham's constant references to English Law as a 'matchless institution'; in such commonplaces as 'so great a master', 'a superior person', 'how very kind!', '*too* charming!', 'It never entered his wise head.'

'The Socratic Irony', Bain remarks, 'consisted in an affectation of ignorance and a desire to be informed; but it was generally meant to be taken seriously by the hearer, at least at the beginning of a discussion.' It is a method of refutation.

Dramatic irony is that which consists in a situation – not in words; or rather, not in words alone, but in words plus situation; when the audience in a theatre or the reader of a book perceives a crux, a significance, a point, that the characters concerned do not perceive.

Irony must not be confused with sarcasm, which is direct: sarcasm means precisely what it says, but in a sharp, bitter, cutting, caustic, or acerb manner: it is the instrument of indignation, a weapon of offence, whereas irony is one of the vehicles of wit. In Locke's 'If ideas were innate, it would save much trouble to many worthy persons', *worthy* is ironical; the principal clause as a whole is sarcastic – as also is the complete sentence. Both are instruments of satire and vituperation.

IRREGULAR OR STRONG VERBS, as opposed to the *love-loved-loved* type. Many are cited in this book. For a comprehensive alphabetical list, see *English: A Course for Human Beings* (4th edition, 1954), Book I, pp. 75–9, and *A Grammar of Contemporary English* (latest edition).

irreligious. See **unreligious.**

irrespective of; irrespectively of. Usage tends to prefer the former, where, probably, *irrespective* has – or had originally – adverbial force. But where there is no *of*, *irrespectively* is obligatory.

irresponsive is being dispossessed by the longer established *unresponsive*.

irruption. See **eruption.**

is when is a stupid beginning for a definition, as in 'Quadratics is when the highest power of the unknown is a square.'

-ise and **-ize** (verb endings). See **-ize.**

ism, 'a theory', is disparaging; so is *ology*, 'an art, a science'. *Ism* comes direct from Greek. – See following entry.

-ism. Its basic use, a suffix forming a noun of action (*baptism; heroism*), does not concern us. Derivatively, it indicates the name of a system, whether of theory or of practice – e.g. religious, philosophical, social, etc., etc.; it may derive from the subject (or the object) or from the name of its founder: *Buddhism, Catholicism, Protestantism*. Allied are class-names, or descriptive terms for doctrines or principles: *atheism, bimetallism, scepticism*: whence such nonce-words and rarities as *rule-Britanniaism*. These two main groups lead naturally to that in which *-ism* denotes, not a system or a principle, but a peculiarity, e.g. of language or style. *Americanism, Anglicism, Scotticism; archaism, colloquialism, witticism; Browningism, Carlylism, Micawberism*. A new sense, now common, indicates a basis of prejudice: *racism, sexism*. See **VOGUE WORDS.**

The corresponding adjectives are formed in *-ist*. Ismatic (rarely *ismatical*) = 'pertaining to *isms*, to an *ism*, or to the suffix *-ism*'; *ismatize* = 'to name (something) an *ism*, or to furnish a radical (or root or stem) with the suffix *-ism* (*OED*).

isolate. See **eliminate.**

Israeli, Israelite. See **Jew.**

issue (n.) is misused in a dozen contradictory and confusing senses, especially by politicians and leader-writers. See Sir Alan Herbert for examples and comments.

issue (v.). See **emerge.**

issue with, 'to supply with', is condemned in America but standard in Britain.

it, misapplied. 'He put his feet up on the stove as it was very cold', meaning the weather, not the stove. – 'Londonderry Corporation decided to reconsider the decision to ban jazz on the Guildhall organ as it was injurious to the instrument' (provincial paper quoted by *The New Statesman and Nation*); grammatically, the 'decision' was 'injurious to the instrument'. See **OBSCURITY.**

it is me for *it is I* is today considered to be good colloquial English, acceptable in all but the most formal contexts. In fact, *It is I* (in isolation) would now sound insufferably pedantic, though it should correctly be preferred with a following clause, as in 'It was I who wrote that essay.'

ITALICS. Italics should, in good writing, be used with caution and in moderation; their most legitimate purpose is to indicate emphasis in dialogue, and, everywhere else (but there too), to indicate foreign words and phrases and titles.

The whole title should be italicized; not, e.g. 'Carlyle's great work, the *French Revolution*'.

(For a fuller treatment, see G. V. Carey, *Mind the Stop*, the Fowlers' *The King's English*, and esp. my *You Have a Point There*.)

item for *affair* or *matter* or *subject*, or *fact* or *incident*, is not merely slovenly but misleading; it is almost as bad as falling weakly back on *you know what I mean* when one is too lazy to try to remember the precise term or is gravelled by one's astounding ignorance.

item for (specific) *object* is of the same order as the preceding error, but is perhaps more objectionable, for some particular object should be named. It is certainly less justifiable than *gadget* or *thingummy*, the tools-for-all-occasions of the incurably slothful and the unashamedly woolly.

item is often misused in non-commercial writing; e.g. 'The bed ..., a table and a chair, were its only items of furniture' (Laurence Meynell, *The Door in the Wall*), where *pieces* would be better.

its is the genitive of *it*; **it's** = *it is* or *it has*. The number of persons that one might suppose to know better, who fall into the error of *it's* for *its* (= *of it*), is a source of constant surprise to any keen observer. Cf. **her's** for **hers**.

it's me. See **it is me**.

itself. See **myself**.

-ization, -isation. These noun endings, like the participle-adjective endings *-ized*, *ised*, correspond to: See following entry.

-ize and **-ise**, verb-endings. When there is a choice, as with *sympathize* (*sympathise*) or *dramatize* (*dramatise*), the spelling with *-z* is the only American form and is the one endorsed by the Oxford and Cambridge University Presses. A few verbs can take only *-z*, of which the commonest are *capsize*, *prize* (= value), *seize*, and *size*. Verbs that take only *-s* are: *advertise*, *advise*, *apprise*, *arise*, *chastise*, *circumcise*, *comprise*, *compromise*, *demise*, *despise*, *devise*, *disguise*, *enfranchise*, *excise*, *exercise*, *franchise*, *improvise*, *incise*, *merchandise*, *premise*, *promise*, *poise*, *praise*, *raise*, *revise*, *rise*, *supervise*, *surmise*, *surprise*, *televise*. The important thing is to be consistent throughout a piece of writing, remembering that to opt for *-z*, or *-s* for the verb entails the selection of *-ization* or *-isation* for the related noun, and *-izable* or *-isable* for the adjective.

J

jabber is an excellent term for 'incoherent, inarticulate, or unintelligible speech', a sense for which *gibberish* is also used. But as a synonym of 'chatter', 'prattle', 'voluble talk', *jabber* is somewhat discourteous.

jackeroo is a variant spelling of *jackaroo*. The word is a blend of *Jack* (from *Johnny Raw*, a 'new chum' or recent immigrant) and *kangaroo*. See especially Edward Morris, *Austral English*.

jail; jailer. See **gaol, gaoler**.

Jap (n. and adj.) is a colloquialism – not to be employed in the society of a Japanese, any more than *Chinee* or *Chinaman* is respectful to a Chinese. Use *Japanese* for the adjective, and for the singular and plural noun.

JARGON. 'The pure research chemist will say, "Chlorophyll makes food by photosynthesis." The practical engineer does not know what he – the scientist – is talking about. But if the statement is rephrased, "Green leaves build up food with the help of light", anyone can understand it. So, says [C. F.] Kettering, if we are going to surmount the boundaries between different kinds of technical men: "The first thing to do is to get them to speak the same language" ' (Stuart Chase, *The Tyranny of Words*).

In his masterly preface to *OED*, Sir James Murray sets the stage thus: 'The English Vocabulary contains a nucleus or central mass of many thousand words whose "Anglicity" is unquestioned; some of them only literary, some of them colloquial [i.e. "used in speech": not in my sense], the great majority at once literary and colloquial – they are the *Common Words* of the language. But they are linked on every side with words that are less and less entitled to this appellation, and which pertain ever more and more distinctly to the domain of local dialect, of the slang and [peculiar expressions] of "sets" and classes, of the popular technicalities of trades and processes, of the scientific terminology common to all civilized nations, of the actual languages of other lands and peoples. And there is absolutely no defining line in any direction: the circle of the English language has a well-defined centre but no discernible circumference. The centre is occupied by the "common" words, in which literary and colloquial [i.e. spoken] usage meet. "Scientific" and "foreign" words enter the common language mainly through literature; "slang" words ascend through colloquial usage; the "technical" terms of crafts and processes, and the "dialect" words, blend with the common language both in speech and in literature. Slang also touches on one side the technical terminology of trades and occupations, as in "nautical slang",

"Public School slang", "the slang of the Stock Exchange", and on another passes into true dialect. Dialects similarly pass into foreign languages. Scientific language passes on one side into purely foreign words, on another it blends with the technical vocabulary of art and manufactures.'

Jargon, originally (as in Chaucer) the warbling of birds, has been loosely employed for cant, slang, pidgin English, gibberish: it should be reserved for the technicalities of science, the professions, the Services, trades, crafts, sports and games, art and Art. A synonym is *shop* or *shop talk*. (See esp. my introduction to 'Vigilans', *Chamber of Horrors*.)

'Every social fact – and the language of a group is a social fact – is the result of two classes of cause: personal (or biological) causes, represented by the physiological and psychological characteristics of the individual; and external (or mesological) causes, represented by the great accumulation of the social pressures, economic and geographical and other factors, which so powerfully influence mankind', says Alfredo Niceforo (*Le Génie de l'argot*). He makes the further distinction that sometimes it is feeling or sentiment, sometimes one's profession or trade which determines the nature of one's speech, whether it be Standard, dialectal, or unconventional. The specialization that characterizes every vocation leads naturally to a specialized vocabulary, to the invention of either new words or new senses (i.e. the re-charging of old words). Such special words and phrases become slang only when they are used outside the vocational group and, even there, only if they change their meaning or are applied in other ways. Motoring, flying, and radio have already supplied us with a large number of slang terms and colloquial or even Standard English metaphors.

It is important for us to be clear as to the difference between jargon and slang, and to be able to place them accurately in the hierarchy of language. In *La Science du mot*, Professor Albert Carnoy remarks that '*Les langues spéciales* sont de deux types différents: 1. À la langue *soignée* (langue *noble*, langue *littéraire*) s'opposent le langage *familier* et la langue *triviale* (avec ses diverses nuances), qu'on emploie pour les usages ordinaires de la vie, les besoins journaliers, les sentiments élémentaires, etc.

2. À la langue *commune* (celle de tout le monde) s'opposent:

(*a*) le langage *intellectuel* (exprimant les notions philosophiques, morales, les conceptions que confère la culture) et les idiomes *techniques* ou *scientifiques* (en usage entre les gens du métier ou entre les initiés à une discipline).

(*b*) les langues développées plus ou moins *artificiellement* par des groupes sociaux particuliers: *argots* [slang and cant] *et jargons* [non-slangy technicalities].' Carnoy rightly adds that the distinctions between these diverse types of speech are a little confused by the borrowings made by familiar and colloquial language from the jargons and slangs and by the borrowings made by the various jargons (or technical 'languages') from slang.

Niceforo has the following significant passage on an aspect common to jargons and cant; an aspect common, moreover, to the various jargons and all vocational and social slangs:

'Les langages spéciaux, issus de la différente façon de sentir et de juger, et des différentes sortes de travail auxquelles chaque groupe est adonné, ne constituent pas l'argot [cant], qui est essentiellement un langage spécial né ou maintenu intentionnellement secret. Cependant, ils peuvent, spontanément, – nous dirions presque innocemment – remplir de façon plus ou moins complète l'une des fonctions de l'argot [cant]: la fonction de protection du groupe.

'Tout langage spécial ne peut-il constituer, en effet, une protection du groupe qui le parle? Lorsqu'un groupe qui sent d'une façon spéciale et qui accomplit les gestes spéciaux se forge spontanément un langage traduisant ces deux spécialités, il ne fait pas acte prémédité d'hostilité ou de cachotterie envers le monde qui l'environne; mais, vus du dehors, ces hommes

parlent une langue qui n'est pas de suite compréhensible dans toutes ses parties. Ils parlent, pour les non-initiés, une sorte de langue sacrée devenant par cela même un tissu de protection, formé spontanément autour du groupe social.

'Il est certain qu'un groupe parlant un langage spécial, s'apercevant que son dictionnaire constitue une barrière éclos dans l'atmosphère spécial où le groupe vit, pense et agit, devient une sorte de protection – tâche de tirer profit de ce fait; et on verra alors ces hommes complaire à leur langage. Mais il est également certain que ce dictionnaire n'en restera pas moins un dictionnaire de langage spécial' (i.e. a jargon).

A less specialist point of view is that expressed by Greenough and Kittredge: 'The arts, science, philosophy, and religion are not alone in the necessity which they feel for a special vocabulary [*these vocabularies being jargons*]. Any limited circle [not necessarily so very limited, either!] having common interests is sure to develop a kind of "class dialect", such as that of schoolboys, of university men, of travelling salesmen, of ... Civil Servants [these being either jargons or, as the case may be, slangs].' And these two authors display the same calm balance, the same exemplary 'stance' and that same sure 'seat in the saddle' which distinguishes the natural horseman, when they proceed to warn us of the cleavage between jargon and slang: 'A word or phrase which is slangy in general conversation stands in quite a different position when it is used in a limited circle, or under special circumstances. "Horsey" words are not slang when one is "talking horses", nor hunting terms in the hunting field, nor the [peculiar] phrases of politics on the hustings or on the stumps. They belong ... to the category of jargons or technical dialects, and are comparable to the special vocabularies of commerce, or medicine, or the law.'

There is a jargon that calls for special attention: the jargon of Society, as distinguished from its slang and catch-phrases. 'From the almost exclusive association of [the members of Society with one another] there arises a kind of special vocabulary … The society jargon is disseminated like the technical language of the philosopher or the man of science, by the same means and with even greater rapidity' (Greenough and Kittredge, 1901). We must, however, distinguish Society jargon from Society slang. And as the differences are, in the main, those between all jargon and all slang, we may dwell upon them for a moment. It is the procedure, the forms, the not so angelic 'hierarchy' of Society which make up almost the whole of its jargon, whereas the entire universe is the sport and plaything of the slang, properly so called, of Society. But, then, all jargon whatsoever consists of words and phrases concerning, or affected to the observance of, the letter of a profession, a trade, a social class, an art, a sport, whereas slang is concerned with the spirit of the universe, the world, life, and in that general, usually subconscious preoccupation, it also hovers, joyously or jauntily or jaundicedly over the objects and the practices of the slangster's own vocation, but with this difference: jargon treats with solemnity and respect the avocation it serves; slang, even where – as seldom – it retains respect towards it, treats that avocation with the detached amusement that, viewed from afar, every human activity seems to invite. In Society, as in all close corporations, all groups, and all sections of society, jargon tends to develop in proportion to the degree of its own exclusiveness, to its own place in the world's esteem, and to the difficulty experienced in learning it or perhaps rather to its learnedness (not that erudition affects Society! It does, however, affect science, the Law, the church, medicine, and so forth): but slang thrives only where this exclusiveness is tonic, not constrictive, and where, as among Cockneys and the Army, the users are very numerous. The more, for example in Society, jargon thrives – the more, that is, the latter prevails – the less does slang prosper. (Since the First World War, however, Society has become less

walled-in, less snobbish, less clannish, with the result that its speech is being increasingly fertilized with technical terms from the trades and professions, from manufactures and processes, and, more importantly, with colloquial and slangy terms from the world of commerce and manual work, from journalism, art, the theatre, and, in short, from life as it is lived, not life as it is permitted by a comfortable income, and not life in which attention need be paid only to one's social equals.)

Let us turn to art. Of artistic jargon, John Camden Hotten makes fun; yet, having selected such terms as *aesthetic, transcendental, the harmonies, keeping harmony, middle distance, aërial perspective, delicate handling, nervous chiaroscuro*, 'and the like', he confesses that 'it is easy to find fault with this system of doing work' – or writing about art – 'whilst it is not easy to discover another so easily understood by educated readers, and so satisfactory to artists themselves. … Properly used, these technicalities are allowable.'

In the familiar speech employed by those who participate in, by those who watch, and by those who write about a sport (e.g. hunting) or a game (e.g. football, whether Rugby or Association, whether Australian or American and, in Rugby, whether Union or League), one has to remember that what, to a complete outsider, seems mysterious and slangy may actually be mysterious but in no way slangy. Sport in general and every particular form of sport have their corpus of technical terms (their jargon). It is not always easy to say whether a term is jargon or slang; but a slang term is always a synonym of an accepted term, and that accepted term, if a technicality, is jargon. Sailors and soldiers have their jargon.

> Les mathurins ont une langue
> Où le verbe n'est point prison;
> L'image y foisonne à foison,
> Or vierge dans sa rude gangue.
> (Jean Richepin, *La Mer*)

The slang and the jargon of the sailor have exercised considerable influence upon familiar speech, whence they have sometimes passed into Standard English. 'Transporté dans un autre milieu, le professionnel', writes Albert Carnoy in *La Science du mot*, 'conserve ses habitudes de pensée. Les objets et les activités qu'il rencontre lui rappellent des aspects et des expériences de sa vie de travail. Il les assimile donc en fonction de celle-ci et comme à travers celle-ci qu'il "projette" sur l'autre. Rien de plus caractéristique à ce propos que le cas des hommes de mer qui trouvent de toutes parts des réminiscences de leur vie si spéciale.' Thus it is, he adds, that our everyday language has been affected by nautical terms: the *all aboard!* of bus, tram, and train conductors; *to land*, e.g. on one's feet; *to be on the stocks*, to be in preparation; *to catch (the turn of) the tide*, *to seize an opportunity*; *to drift around*, to idle about.

Much the same applies to soldiers' language, especially their jargon (by which the civilian often affects to be annoyed). 'L'armée, comme tout corps étroitement constitué, ayant sa vie propre … et arrachant l'homme à sa vie normale, a toujours eu un parler propre très développé; qui, naturellement, comme celui des marins, a servi à désigner bien des idées extra-militaires' (Carnoy).

Those are special aspects* of jargon; but the subject of jargon is so important, and so often misunderstood, that it would be well to pose, more firmly than we have yet done, the basis and establish the generality of jargon: to treat it in the large. In *Words and Their Ways in English Speech*, Greenough and Kittredge include an excellent chapter on jargon; it is entitled 'Technical or Class Dialects', which exemplifies *dialect* employed in a way that I strongly object to – but let it pass!

'Every profession or trade, every art and every science', they write, 'has its technical vocabulary, the function of which is partly to designate things or processes

which have no names in ordinary English, and partly to secure greater exactness in nomenclature. Such special dialects, or jargons, are necessary in technical discussion of any kind. Being universally understood by the devotees of the particular science or art, they have the precision of a mathematical formula. Besides, they save time, for it is much more economical to name a process than to describe it. Thousands of these technical terms are very properly included in every large dictionary, yet, as a whole, they are rather on the outskirts of the English language than actually within its borders.

'Different occupations, however, differ widely in the character of their special vocabularies. In trades and handicrafts, and [in] other vocations, like farming and fishery, that have occupied great numbers of men from remote times, the technical vocabulary is very old. It consists largely of native words, or of borrowed words that have worked themselves into the very fibre of our language. Hence, though highly technical in many particulars, these vocabularies are more familiar in sound, and more generally understood, than most other technicalities. The special [jargons] of Law, medicine, divinity, and philosophy have also, in their older strata, become pretty familiar to cultivated persons, and have contributed much to the popular vocabulary. Yet every vocation still possesses a large body of technical terms that remain essentially foreign, even to educated speech. And the proportion has been much increased [since about 1850], particularly in the various departments of natural and political science and in the mechanic arts. Here new terms are coined with the greatest freedom, and abandoned with indifference when they have served their turn.[*] Most of the new

---

*Taken, in a modified form, from my *Slang Today and Yesterday*.

*Note the corresponding process by which an entire set of words once so familiar to the educated as to be no longer jargon have fallen into so general a disuse that they are now, except by a few experts, regarded as 'deep' jargon: the nomenclature of Rhetoric.

coinages are confined to special discussions, and seldom get into general literature or conversation. Yet no profession is nowadays, as all professions once were, a closed guild. The lawyer, the physician, the man of science, the divine, associates freely with his fellow-creatures, and does not meet them in a merely professional way. Furthermore, what is called "popular science" makes everybody acquainted with modern views and recent discoveries. Any important discovery, [even if] made in a remote or provincial laboratory, is at once reported in the newspapers, and everybody is soon talking about it.'

They pass to a paramount point when they remark on the fact that 'the classifying habit of the natural sciences reacts on many scientific terms in a curious way. It is convenient for the naturalist to have the vernacular or "trivial" names of plants and animals coincide in their scope, so far as possible, with the orders and families and genera of his system. Hence we are bidden to limit the name *fly* to dipterous [two-winged] insects, *bug* to the hemiptera, *worm* to the order *vermes*, and are rebuked if we speak of a whale as a "big *fish*". This is all very well for the purposes of science, but we must not allow ourselves to be browbeaten. The whale was a "fish" when the "order *cetacea*" had never been heard of. ... The loose popular designations are quite as well established, and therefore as "correct", as the more limited terminology of science. Less "accurate" they may be, but language is not always bound to scientific accuracy. It has its inalienable right to vague terms when there is no question of system at stake.' – Which is all very refreshing and true.

Their summing-up is so sensible and practical and, from the viewpoint of usage, so sound, that it were a pity to refrain from quoting again from a book that had a very large sale in the first decade of this century and that deserves to go on selling. The position of technical dialects or jargons with respect to our language is this: so long as the terms in question are used in technical discussions only, they scarcely belong to the English vocabulary at all. If they wander out of their narrow circle and are occasionally heard in current speech, they become a part of our vocabulary, though they are still a very special or technical part of it. But the process may go much further: the objects or conceptions for which the [technical] terms stand may become very common, or the words may lose their strictly scientific sense and be applied vaguely or metaphorically. When this happens, the word has become fully naturalized, and its technical origin is pretty sure to be forgotten in the long run.

'The propriety of using technical terms in speaking or writing depends on a commonsense principle. A remark should be intelligible, not merely to the speaker, who is presumed to know what he wishes to say, but also to the person addressed. Otherwise, it can hardly be called language in any proper sense. To be very technical in conversation not only savours of pedantry but makes the speaker unintelligible; and the same is true of a book addressed "to a great variety of readers". Among specialists, however, one can hardly go too far in the employment of technicalities, provided the terms belong to the accepted vocabulary of the science or art in question. That form of pedantry which consists in changing well-established designations for others that seem to the writer more appropriate is extremely common, and, indeed, may be called one of the weaknesses of the scientific temperament.'

(Since EP wrote this article, many attempts have been made to restrict the use of jargon by 'insiders' addressing nonspecialists. See *The Complete Plain Words* by Sir Ernest Gowers, and the work of the Plain English Campaign in Britain and of the Committee on Public Doublespeak in America.)

Jew; Jewish. *Jews* are followers of Judaism, or their descendants. The *Israelites* were the ancient inhabitants of the land of Israel. *Israelis* are the citizens of modern Israel, not all of whom are Jewish. *Hebrew* is the ancient language, revived for use in modern Israel. The word *Hebrew* is used of the ancient Israelites, but not now of modern Jews, though an older use survives, for instance, in the title of the YMHA (Young Men's Hebrew Association).

The proper adjective is *Jewish*, not *Jew*, as in 'a Jewish scientist'.

A *Jewess* may prefer to be called a Jewish girl or woman.

There is no language called Jewish. But see **Semitic** and **Yiddish**.

jibe. See **gibe.**

jim-jams; jitters. The former is now obsolescent, the latter is still colloquial: neither, therefore, has yet qualified to appear in serious writing or in impassioned oratory.

JINGLES; UNINTENTIONAL RHYMES. In prose, avoid these unsought, infelicitous solicitors of sense; avoid them anywhere. 'In most *prose*, and more than we ordinarily *suppose*, the opening words have to wait for *those* that follow' (I. A. Richards, *The Philosophy of Rhetoric*) affords an excellent example of how *not* to write prose that is intended to be either effective or melodious.

This is the fault noticed by Alexander Bain when, in Part II of *English Composition and Rhetoric*, he says, 'Unpleasing are iterations within words or at the end of words: *indulgent parent, uniform formality, instead of a steady ...*, he is tempted to attempt.

'Even a short interval is not enough to allow the repetition of very marked sounds: as "I confess with humility, the sterility of my fancy, and the debility of my judgement." "What is of more importance, the principles, being propounded with reverence, had an influence on the subsequent jurisprudence." "The art of politics consists, or would consist if it existed ... "; "taking such directions as to awaken pleasant recollections".'

job for one's profession, trade, vocation is somewhat of a colloquialism; *job of work* is Standard English, dating from the 16th century. *Job description, job satisfaction* and *job evaluation* are popular management jargon. *Job* is an interesting word: look it up in *OED* (and its *Supplement*) the next time you get the chance.

JOHNSONESE. *Johnsonian* is defined by *OED* as 'a style in English abounding in words derived or made up from Latin, such as that of Dr Johnson'; but, in current usage, it is applied especially and indeed almost solely to 'stilted or pompous style, affecting polysyllabic classical words' (*Webster's*).

In *Squire's Companion to the British Pharmacopæia* I came upon the following definition of opium, 'the milky exudation of *papaver somniferum* obtained by incision from the unripe capsules, and inspissated by spontaneous evaporation', whereon I commented thus in *Literary Sessions*, 1932: 'If only the compiler had put *lacteal* for *milky*, and *immature* for *unripe*, Dr Johnson could not have bettered it. He would probably have been ungracious enough to translate the Latin as "soporific poppy"; *inspissated* (i.e. thickened) was a favourite word of his.'

Dr Jespersen, in *Growth and Structure of the English Language*, says, 'I can find no better example to illustrate the effect of extreme "Johnsonese" than the following:

'"The proverbial oracles of our parsimonious ancestors have informed us that the fatal waste of our fortune is by small expenses, by the profusion of sums too little singly to alarm our caution, and which we never suffer ourselves to consider together. Of the same kind is the prodigality of life; he that hopes to look back hereafter with satisfaction upon past years, must learn to know the present value of single minutes, and endeavour to let no particle of time fall useless to the ground." William Minto, in *A Manual of English Prose Literature*, translates that passage as follows: "Take care of the pennies," says the thrifty old proverb, "and the pounds will take care of themselves." In like manner we might say, "Take care of the minutes, and the years will take care of themselves." '

Jespersen continues, thus: 'In his Essay on Madame D'Arblay, Macaulay gives some delightful samples of this style as developed by that ardent admirer of Dr Johnson. Sheridan refused to permit his lovely wife to sing in public, and was warmly praised on this account by Johnson. "The last of men," says Madame D'Arblay, "was Doctor Johnson to have abetted squandering the delicacy of integrity by nullifying the labours of talent." To be starved to death is "to sink from inanition into nonentity". Sir Isaac Newton is "the developer of the skies in their embodied movements", and Mrs Thrale, when a party of clever people sat silent, is said to have been "provoked by the dulness of a taciturnity that, in the midst of such renowned interlocutors, produced as narcotic a torpor as, etc." … In the nineteenth century a most happy reaction set in in favour of "Saxon" words and natural expressions. … But still the malady lingers on, especially with the half-educated. I quote from a newspaper the following story. The young lady home from school was explaining. "Take an egg," she said, "and make a perforation in the base and a corresponding one in the apex. Then apply the lips to the aperture, and by forcibly inhaling the breath the shell is entirely discharged of its contents." An old lady who was listening exclaimed: "It beats all how folks do things nowadays. When I was a gal they made a hole in each end and sucked." '

In short, do not use a heavily Latinized style unless you wish to obtain an effect that can be obtained thus and only thus; an effect, maybe, of extreme formality or one of majestic impressiveness or again, one of sonorous euphony. *He died poor* is always preferable to *he expired in indigent circumstances*, but a *disastrous conflagration* might, in certain circumstances, be preferable to a *great fire* – especially if the results and not the extent are being referred to.

For further comments, see Jespersen, *op. cit.*

JOURNALESE. See OFFICIALESE and **amazing**.

journey. See **trip**.

judged as to whether it is (or **was** or **will be**) + adjective is a clumsy variation of *adjudged* + that adjective. Thus 'No word can be judged as to whether it is good or bad, correct or incorrect, beautiful or ugly, or anything else that matters to a writer, in isolation' (I. A. Richards, *The Philosophy of Rhetoric*) would be less wordy, more effective, if the author had written, 'No word can be adjudged good or bad …'. (Moreover, 'in isolation' is out of position.)

judgement and **judgment**. Both spellings are permissible. The former is a common British preference, the latter the more usual American form.

judging. See CONJUNCTIONS, DISGUISED.

judicial and **judicious** are frequently confused. The former = 'connected with, pertaining to, or proper to a court of law or a legal tribunal; belonging to or characteristic of a judge'; the sense 'showing sound judgement' fell into disuse so long ago as the 17th century. *Judicious* = 'having sound judgement; wise in thought or behaviour; prudent; showing sound judgement'; the sense 'belonging or proper to a court of law or to a judge' dropped out of use in the 17th century.

juncture, at this. Physically, 'at this point or junction'; hence, 'at this crisis'. Even the sense 'at this particular point of time' is not incorrect, but its usage has been so debased that *at this juncture* is now avoided by self-respecting writers, public speakers, and private persons of good sense and education.

junior is 'the younger', and it is appended to a full name (*James Smith, Junior*) 'to denote the younger of the two bearing the same name in a family, especially a son of the same name as his father'; also after the

K

simple surname (*Smith, Junior*) to denote the younger of two boys of the same surname at a rather traditional school. The elder of the two is *Senior*.

just is sometimes misused for *quite*. 'That forgetfulness had been well done, but not just well enough' (Freeman Wills Crofts, *Found Floating*). (Possibly an uncorrected printer's error for 'just not well enough'.)

just means either *precisely* or *only*: obviously, therefore, it is to be used with care. Moreover, it has, in time-contexts, the sense of 'at, but certainly not later than'; sometimes, in this sense, it is preceded by *only*, as in ' "Was it so late as 11 o'clock?" "Yes, but just" – *or* only just – "11." ' Hence, avoid *just* = 'precisely' except in time-contexts; and even there, *precisely* (or *exactly*) is preferable. In such time-contexts, British usage has traditionally preferred the perfect tense, as in 'He has just arrived.' Under American influence the British are now beginning to express this idea with the simple past ('He just arrived') but the practice is to be avoided.

just exactly. This combination of almost synonymous terms is justly – and exactly – described by Fowler as 'bad tautology'.

just the same does not equal *just as well*, as it is sometimes made to do. 'There is no need for grandeur in life to give happiness. The simple things provide it just the same.'

justify, 'to excuse, to exonerate', is occasionally confused with *rectify*, 'to correct', 'to redress': one can *justify an error*, but it is something different from *rectifying an error*. *Justify* means *rectify* only in the printer's sense 'to adjust (a line of type) to fill a space evenly'.

juvenile and **puerile.** Cf. the difference between **childlike** and **childish**. *Juvenile* is 'young', as in 'juvenile messengers', 'juvenile attendants'; hence 'belonging to, suited to, intended for youth', as in 'juvenile books'. *Puerile* is now confined to the sense 'childish'. Cf. **young and youthful.**

karat. See **carat.**

kerb. See **curb.**

ketchup, catchup, catsup. The earliest is *catchup* (late 17th century); the prevalent British 20th-century form is *ketchup*, but *catsup* is the common American form.

kind ... are for *kind ... is*. 'Kittens and good scientists tend to let new experience pour in until some kind of workable relationships with past experience are established.'

kind of (e.g. rare) for *rather* (rare) is a colloquialism.

kind of, all. Not a serious solecism; according to *OED*, 'still common colloquially, though considered grammatically incorrect'. (But *all manner of* is an established usage.) Similarly, *these* or *those kind of things*, pedantically judged incorrect, is a justifiable English idiom; Dean Alford (*The Queen's English*) is worth quoting on this point: '... it is evident that this tendency, to draw the less important word into similarity to the more important one, is suffered to prevail over strict grammatical exactness. We are speaking of "things" in the plural. Our pronoun "this" really has reference to "kind", not to "things"; but the fact of "things" being plural, gives a plural complexion to the whole, and we are tempted to put "this" into the plural. That this is the account to be given, appears still more plainly from the fact that not unfrequently we find a rival attraction prevails, and the clause takes a *singular* complexion from the other substantive, "kind". We often hear people say "this kind of thing", "that sort of thing". It must be confessed that the phrases "this kind of things", "that sort of things" have a very awkward sound; and we find that our best writers have the popular expression, *These kind, those sort*. Thus we have in Shakespeare, *King Lear*, "These kind of knaves I know"; *Twelfth Night*, "that crow so at these set kind of fools"; in Pope, "The next objection is, that these sort of authors are poor." ' In a gardening article in a daily paper, March 1938 we find 'The newer kind (of aubrietia) spread rapidly', which is certainly incorrect and should be 'The newer kinds', or 'Those of the newer kind'.

kind of a for *kind of* is excessive, for 'What kind of a house do you live in?' means no more than 'What kind of house ...?' But there may be a delicate distinction between 'What kind of lawyer is he?' (a solicitor, a barrister ...) and 'What kind of a lawyer is he?' (= is he competent?).

kindred to is wrongly used for *akin to* in the following: 'We need to know that other planets are inhabited by being fulfilled and moved by a fire and spirit kindred to our own – otherwise what a dreadful loneliness oppresses us!' (Don Marquis, *The Almost Perfect State*).

kingly, royal, regal. 'Who is able', asks Jespersen, 'to tell exactly how these adjectives differ in signification? And might not English like other languages (*royal* in French, *kongelig* in Danish, *königlich* in German) have been content with one word instead of three?' But only *kingly* can be used as the masculine counterpart to *queenly*. *Regal* is the least used of the three, and now is generally confined to the figurative or transferred senses, 'stately', 'splendid' as in 'She is a most regal woman', 'He wore his robes with a regal air.' *Royal* is the most general: 'of or pertaining to the sovereign; belonging to the royal prerogative', as in 'the Royal Family', 'royal power'; hence 'belonging to, or devoted to the service of the sovereign', as in 'the royal forest'; hence, 'befitting a sovereign; princely; munificent', as in 'royal splendour', 'royal hospitality', 'royal companions' – being in this nuance of 'splendid, magnificent', a synonym of *regal* (*Webster's*).

knee-jerk. See VOGUE WORDS.

kneeled and **knelt** are equally correct as the preterite and past participle of **kneel.** *Knelt* is the British preference, *kneeled* the American.

knit and **knitted.** Both of these forms are correct as the preterite and past participle of *knit.* Prefer *knitted* for things made of wool, *knit* for 'united', etc.

knowing. See CONJUNCTIONS, DISGUISED.

knowledge on. See PREPOSITIONS WRONGLY USED.

L

laded; laden; loaded. *Laded* is the preterite of *lade*, 'to put the cargo on board (a ship)'; but *laden* is the past participle. *Loaded* is the preterite and past participle of *load.*

lading. See **cargo.**

lady, which has a social – almost a Society – connotation, should not be used as a synonym for *woman*, any more than *gentleman* should be used as a synonym for *man.* Only those men who are not gentlemen speak of their women friends as *lady friends*, and only those women who are not ladies speak of themselves as *charladies* and their men friends as *gentlemen friends*. It is reasonable, though, to use both *lady* and *gentleman* in the presence of the persons concerned, as in 'Please show this lady where to sit.' Cf. the note at **Mister.**

laid; lain. See **lay and lie.**

lama, a Tibetan or Mongolian Buddhist priest, is sometimes confused with *llama*, a S. American animal between sheep and camel.

langouste. See **crawfish.**

LANGUAGE AND LOGIC. See GRAMMAR AND LOGIC.

lapse. See **elapse.**

large is not – whereas *great* is – the adjective that should go with *breadth* (or *width*), *depth*, *distance*, *height*, *length*.

large-scale is correctly used of maps, in opposition to *small-scale*; but as a synonym for *large* it is both long-winded and unnecessary. It smacks, too, of 'big business', where the phrase 'large-scale operations' is not unknown. In an examination script I came upon this: 'He is able to see a large-scale result of his labours.'

large-size ('a large-size apple') is incorrect for *large-sized*, which many (myself included) would say is excessive for *large*. Cf. the preceding entry.

last can mean 'most recent', but should be replaced by *latest* where there is danger of ambiguity, as in 'his last novel'. Cf. **latter** for *last.*

last for *end*. Incorrect, as in 'Towards the last of the chapter'.

last, two; three last; four last, etc. English idiom demands *last two, three, four*, etc. For 'the three last chapters of the book' read 'the last three chapters ...'; French idiom has 'les trois derniers chapitres du livre'.

last but one in such a phrase as 'in the last but one sentence' is top-heavy. Better 'in the last sentence but one'; or perhaps, 'in the penultimate sentence'; *last but one*, unchanged, should be used only in a predicate, as in 'In the sentence that comes last but one', 'It is the sentence last but one.'

lastly. See **firstly.**

last-mentioned. See **latter and last-mentioned.**

late and **ex-.** 'The late President' is dead; 'the ex-President' is alive, *ex-* meaning 'former' but excluding death.

lately. See **latterly and lately.**

later and **latter.** *Later* is the comparative of *late* (in time), superlative *latest*; *latter*, the second of two things mentioned, has also the special sense 'near the end' of a period of time, as in 'the latter part of the year'.

later on for *later* (adv.) is an uneconomical colloquialism: cf. **earlier on.**

LATIN ADJECTIVES, USELESS. See USELESS LATIN ADJECTIVES.

LATINISMS. See GREEK AND LATIN and JOHNSONESE.

latter, misused for *last*. John G. Brandon, *The Dragnet*, 'Over all, was an aura of life, and youth, and happiness. But ... there were others in that room whose countenances and general demeanour suggested anything but the latter emotion.' 'Latter' should be 'last' (of three). But *life* and *youth* are not *emotions*, and it is very doubtful whether *happiness* (except when *joy*) is one. See also SUPERLATIVE DEGREE.

latter and **last-mentioned** (or **named**) should be applied, respectively, to the second of two things, and to the last of three or more things: in 'Tennis and squash are good exercises but the last-mentioned is too strenuous', *last-mentioned* should be *latter*.

latterly and **lately.** Both refer to time; the former is rather literary in the sense 'of late' (*lately*), but is preferable to *lately* in the sense 'at the latter end' (of life or of some period); e.g. 'He died Sept. 23, 1766, at Hammersmith, though latterly he resided chiefly at Bath' (Horace Walpole) (*OED*).

launder (preterite *laundered*) is the verb corresponding to *laundry*; in good English the latter is not used as a verb. The sense of launder 'transfer (funds of dubious provenance)' is colloquial.

Lawd for *Lord* is a FALSE ILLITERACY.

lawyer; attorney; notary; solicitor, barrister. A *barrister* argues a case in the courts; a *solicitor* does not – he or she instructs barristers in their cases and clients before, during, and after cases, originally in equity only. An *attorney* performs the same work as a solicitor, but only in Common Law, and is properly a *public attorney* (as opposite to a *private attorney* or *attorney in fact*, one who has *power of attorney* to act for another in business and legal affairs) or *attorney-at-law*; in current English, *solicitors* include *attorneys*. A *notary* (in full; *notary public* or *public notary*) is 'a person publicly authorized to draw up or attest contracts or similar documents, to protest bills of exchange, etc., and discharge other duties of a formal character' (*OED*). *Lawyer* is generic; 'a member of the legal profession; one whose business it is to conduct suits in the courts, or to advise clients, in the widest sense embracing every branch of the profession, though in colloquial use often limited to attorneys and solicitors' (*ibid.*). [The American terms are *lawyer* and, occasionally in certain phrases, *attorney* (*-at-law*), nowadays without difference in meaning. *Barrister* and *solicitor* are not current. *Notary* (*public*) is as defined above.]

lay and **lie,** verbs active and passive, in the infinitive and present and past tenses, are continually misused and confused with each other, sometimes even in good literature; e.g. Byron, *Childe Harold*, iv. 7–9.

> And send'st him ... to his Gods,
>   where haply lies
> His petty hope in some near port or
>   bay,
> And dashest him again to earth: –
>   there let him lay.

in which 'lies' is correct, but 'lay' incorrect. Ernest Hemingway falls into this trap in *To Have and Have Not*, thus, 'Eddy went forward and laid down.' *Lie* – *lay* – *lain*; *lay* – *laid* –*laid*; these are the correct forms. (*Lie*, to tell a falsehood, takes *lied* both in the preterite and in the past participle.)

l.c. See **ib.**

'ld. See **'d and 'ld.**

leading question does not mean an unfair question but simply 'one that suggests the proper or expected answer', especially (in Law) 'a question which sug-

gests to a witness the answer which he is to make' (Wharton) (*OED*).

lean has preterite and past participle *leaned* (pron. *lēn'd*) or *leant* (pron. *lĕnt*); they are equally common in British use, but *leaned* is the American form. The British often pronounce *leaned* like *leant*.

leap has preterite and past participle *leaped* (pron. *lēp'd*) or *leapt* (pron. *lĕpt*). Both forms are equally common in both British and American use. The British often pronounce *leaped* like *leapt*.

learn has preterite and past participle *learned* and *learnt*. They are equally common in British use, but *learned* is the American form. The British often pronounce *learned* like *learnt*. – *Learn* for *teach* is a solecism. – The participial adjective *learned* is pronounced with two syllables.

lease (v.). See **hire.**

least for *lesser* (the smaller of two) is unfortunate; it destroys a valuable distinction.

leave, in *leave me be, leave go of me*, is a colloquial alternative to the more traditional *let*. But the idiom *leave me alone* is now well established in the sense of 'cease from bothering me' as well as for 'allow me to remain in solitude'.

legionary; legionnaire. A *legionary* is 'a soldier of a legion, whether ancient (especially Roman) or modern (especially French)'. As an adjective, *legionary* = 'of or belonging to or characteristic of a legion'. Note, however, that *Legionary* or *Legionnaire* is also – since 1918 – 'a member of the British or the American Legion'.

lengthways and **lengthwise.** Both are adverbs, with sense 'in the direction of length' ('A hollow tube split lengthways', Coleridge; 'downward lengthwise', Goldsmith); the latter seems to be gaining the ascendant. Only *lengthwise* is an adjective (*OED*).

less for *fewer, not so many* is incorrect in the example given by C. C. Boyd, *Grammar for Great and Small*, 'There were less people at the matc h than I expected.' – In the correct 'the number of people was less', *less* qualifies *number*, not *people*. Similarly, *less* is correct with numbers giving the size of a quantity, as in 'less than £50', 'less than six months'.

less and **lesser.** *Less*, adjective, is the comparative of *little*, with superlative *least*; it is also an adverb, the comparative of (the adverbial) *a little*. *Lesser* is adjective only – a double comparative (from *less*, with the comparative suffix *-er*). *Less* (adj.) is both attributive (as in 'in a less degree') and predicative ('And then the signs he would suppress ... grew less and less', Byron; 'It is less'); *lesser* is attributive only ('The lights of lesser craft dipped by', Howells). With reference to material dimension, *less* has given way to *smaller*, but it has been retained with reference to number or degree ('19 is less than 20') (*OED*).

lessee; lessor. See **hire.**

let takes the accusative, not the nominative; 'Let you and I go' is incorrect for 'Let you and me go.' – For *hire, let, rent,* see at **hire.**

level, at a high – esp. **the highest** – is being grossly overworked both by Whitehall and by Fleet Street.

lexicon, as a dictionary, is often restricted to one of Greek, Hebrew, Syriac, or Arabic. The word can now also mean 'the word-stock of a language, region, or speaker'.

lexigraphy is 'a system of writing in which each character represents a word'; **lexicography** is 'the art or practice of writing dictionaries' (Johnson) (*OED*)

liable (to do) for *likely* (to do), as in 'he is liable to make that mistake', is correct only if the 'mistake' is habitual, and is undesirable for 'him'. Otherwise, use *apt* for a general tendency, *likely* for a probability. It is always correct to use *liable* with an undesirable noun, as in 'he is liable (i.e. subject) to error'.

liaison, apart from its technical senses in cookery, phonetics, and military organization, has only one sense, 'an illicit intimacy (generally of some considerable duration) between a man and a woman'. To apply it to other associations, to combinations, to alliances, to coalitions, is to commit an error.

libation is properly a pouring out of liquid – especially wine – in honour of a god, hence the drink-offering itself. Its use for a liquid poured out to be drunk by mere mortals is either jocular or pretentious.

libel is printed (or written, broadcast, or in pictorial form), whereas *slander* is spoken; to prove *slander*, an independent witness is required.

licence (n.), **license** (v.). In *Six Years in the Prisons of England*, by 'A Merchant', 1869, the author gives a specimen of that form of licence which is familiarly called a ticket of leave and makes this comment: 'In the foregoing "ticket-of-leave" the word Licence is spelt with an *s*. In the Police Documents it is spelt with a *c*. So much for the education of Government Officials.' [According to *Webster's*, the preferred spelling of both noun and verb is *license*.]

lie. See **lay and lie.**

lifelong and **livelong.** The former is literal, 'lasting or continuing for a lifetime', as in 'The lifelong disability of deaf-mutism'; *livelong* is an intensive of *long*, as in 'Throughout the livelong day he had a presentiment of misfortune' and has come to have the connotation of 'long drawn out' or 'tedious'.

lifestyle. See **VOGUE WORDS.**

ligature. See **DIPHTHONGS.**

light, 'to dismount, to descend', is being displaced by *alight*. – The verb *light*, 'to give light; to set fire to', has preterite and past participle *lighted* or *lit*. As an attributive adjective, *lighted* is the more usual: *a lighted cigarette*.

lightening and **lightning.** The former = '(a) making lighter or less heavy'; *lightning* is the visible discharge of electricity in the sky.

like for *as* is not formally correct in, e.g. *to do like I do* (correctly *to do as I do*). It would appear to be going too far to call it an illiteracy; but it is at least 'a loose colloquialism ... avoided by careful speakers and writers' (Onions, *An Advanced English Syntax*).

like for *as if* is incorrect. 'Carted her out limp – looked like a chloroform-pad had been at work' (John G. Brandon, *The Dragnet*).

like for *as though.* 'She was lying on the floor like dead with ... wounds dark on her wrist and the blood squirting out' (a detective novel), where *like* should be *as though* (or *as though she were*) dead.

like for *likely* is incorrect, as in 'Is it like to happen soon?' But the phrase '(as) like as not' is established idiom.

like as if, e.g. 'it looks like as if it would rain' is illiterate, but Nesfield, who had the nose of a sleuth hound for these errors, found it in *The Daily Telegraph* in May 1900: 'The troop have set out with four days' supplies, so it looks like as if we were going no farther than Ladybrand.'

like that, 'in that way', is not absolutely wrong, but it is vague; and often it is slightly ambiguous. 'Does he care for you like that?' does not impress one as either vigorous or precise – or, for that matter, as elegant.

limited is now widely used, and overused, as a substitute for *small* or one of its synonyms. 'A man of limited (meagre) education and limited (inadequate) capital is likely to be limited to a limited (scant) income.' Properly it = 'restricted, narrow, closely circumscribed'.

linage, less happily spelt *lineage*, is the number of lines of printed (or written) matter, or payment according to the num-

ber of lines; *lineage* is ancestry or pedigree. The former has long *i* and only two syllables; the latter, short *i* and three syllables.

line, 'a profession or trade, an occupation, an activity', has been so overdone that one would be wise to avoid it – in good writing, at least. [In the USA, *line of goods*, trade jargon = the items dealt in.]

lineament 'a facial feature', is occasionally confused with *liniment*, 'an embrocation'.

linguistics is rather 'the science of language' and *philology* an older word used particularly for the historical and comparative study of languages, and of the language of earlier literature.

liquidate, liquidation. Sinister euphemisms for 'kill' and 'killing', as in 'the liquidation of the Kulaks'. Not, of course, to be confused with the literal *liquidize*.

listen at. See PREPOSITIONS WRONGLY USED.

lit; lighted. See **light.**

literal. See **literate.** – Do not confuse with *littoral*, 'adjacent to the shore'.

literally, when used, as it often is, as a mere intensive, is a slovenly colloquialism, its only correct use being to characterize *exactness to the letter.* 'William Hickie' once overheard the following in a woman's club: 'He literally turned the house upside down.'

LITERARISMS are either the journalese of the literary (these literarisms might almost be stigmatized as high-brow) or such unusual words as are used only by the literary or the learned.

And both kinds are to be distinguished from elegancies (*q.v.*); for elegancies are the 'literary or cultured English' of those who, as a rule, are neither literary nor cultured.

If in doubt consult ELEGANCIES and also ARCHAISMS.

acerb
acolyte (non-ecclesiastically)
adumbrate
alchemy (figuratively)
alembicated
amplitude (non-scientifically)
ancillary (subsidiary)
arcana
archetypal (cf. VOGUE WORDS)
aura
autochthonous
avid
avocation
balm
beatific
bedizened
bucolic
catharsis
certitude
cerulean
chieftain
chivalric
cognoscenti
confrère
continuum (used figuratively or non-technically)
converse (conversation)
couched (expressed)
crepuscular
crux
daedalian
darkling
deft and *deftly*
delectable and *delectation*
denigrate
derogate from
descant
desiderate
dichotomy
ebon (as in 'ebon night')
effete
emanate (correctly used)
empyrean
encomium
envoy (of a poem)
epicene
esurient
eternize
ethereal
ethos
etiolated

exacerbate; exacerbation
excerpt (v.)
exemplar
exordium
feral
firmament
flee
fleece (to cheat)
fount
froward (also an archaism)
fulvid and *fulvous*
gelid
gilded youth (also a cliché)
glabrous
grateful (of things: pleasing, acceptable)
gubernatorial
haste (v.)
heaven (sky)
helot
homo sapiens
hymeneal
imbrue (v.)
immarcescible
impedimenta
implement (to fulfil)
in very truth
ineluctable
inexpugnable
infinitude
intrinsic
inwardness
irrefragable
iteration and *iterate*
ivory tower
jocose
lassitude
laud (n. and v.)
lave (v.)
Lethe
liege-lord (non-feudally; non-facetiously)
literati
logorrhoea
longanimity
lustrum
magistral
mantle (figuratively)
meretricious
metempsychosis
mulct (of: to deprive of)
neophyte
nepenthe (or N.)

nimbus
no other, be able to do
obloquy
olden
opuscule
ordonnance
ordure
otherwhere
paramount
paramour
parergon
paucity
penumbra, penumbral
perdurable
peripatetic
peripheral
perspicacious; perspicacity
perspicuity
pestilence
plenteous
plentitude
plethora
polity
polymath
pother
prescience; prescient
proem
prolegomenon, prolegomena
provenance
pusillanimous
quietude
regimen
Renascence, the
respire
r(h)odomontade
scabrous
sempiternal(ly)
significant (important)
similitude
smite
something (somewhat or rather)
straightway
supererogatory
superimpose
supernal
surcease (n.)
suspire
susurrus
suzerainty
swart
tantamount

Tartarean (or-ian)
thrasonical
toper
transpire (used correctly)
turpitude
umbrageous
unobtrusive(ly)
untoward
vacant (of persons: idle)
vatic
vault (to leap)
verdant
verisimilitude
verities, the
viable
virtuoso (pl. virtuosi)
visitant
wain
warranty (but not as a legal term)
what time (while; when)
whence
whither
wilderness
wondrous (adj.) and wondrously
writ (written)
wroth

LITERARY ALLUSION. Is literary allusion a form of snobbery or is it not rather – in the scholarly and the unpretentiously cultured, the genuinely well-read – a legitimate source of pleasure and a kind of subtlety? William Empson, in *Seven Types of Ambiguity*, has pertinently asserted that 'It is tactful, when making an obscure reference, to arrange that the verse' – he is speaking of poetry – 'shall be intelligible when the reference is not understood'; the same applies to prose. Those very sound scholars and eminent philologists, J. B. Greenough and G. L. Kittredge (*Words and Their Ways in English Speech*), have, apropos of fashions in language, written thus: 'Another fashion is the knack of literary allusion. It is akin to the habit of quotation – itself a fashion ... that comes and goes; but it shows itself in a less formal and tangible way' – less formal because less tangible.

LITERARY STANDARD. See STANDARD ENGLISH, Section II.

literate means 'able to read and write'; the opposite of *illiterate*. For a confusion with *literal*, see the passage quoted at **malapropisms**.

literature for printed matter of any kind, e.g. for advertising matter, is a colloquialism – an extremely silly and unfortunate one, for it tends to degrade a good word and a fine thing.

littoral. See **literal.**

livelong. See **lifelong.**

Livorno for *Leghorn*. See **Bruxelles...**

-'ll. See **shall** and **will.**

llama for *lama*. See **lama.**

load. See **cargo.**

loaded. See **laded.**

loan as a verb for *lend* is good American, but it is not yet good British English; though it may be beginning to be countenanced in the sense 'a collection of miniatures loaned to the Victoria and Albert Museum'.

loath; loathe; loth. *Loth* is an alternative form of *loath*, 'disinclined', 'reluctant', as in 'I am loath (or loth) to believe it' or in the set phrase, *nothing loath* ('not at all unwillingly'). *Loathe* is a verb, 'to feel dislike or aversion for', e.g. for food: 'To dictate their terms to statesmen who loathe the necessity of submission' (Bryce); 'Your stomach soon must loathe all drink and meat' (J. Thompson) (*OED*).

locality and **location.** A *locality* is the situation or position of an object, or the place in which it is to be found; it is applied especially to geographical position or place; also a district, a place, regarded either as the site occupied by certain persons or things or as the scene of certain activities. 'A blind man ... feeling all round him with his cane, so as to find out his locality' (Hawthorne); 'This tremendous rainfall of the Khasi Hills, amounting in some localities ... to 559 inches of annual rainfall' (Haughton). *Location* is

local or definite position, as in 'location in space'; the two senses, 'a tract of land marked out or surveyed', e.g. a mining claim, and 'place of settlement or residence', were formerly American, as also was the cinematic *location* ('on location'), 'an exterior place where a scene is filmed' (adapted from *OED*).

locate, meaning *to place*, is misused for *to find*; as the maid said about some articles lost by the laundry, 'I expect they'll be able to locate them.' One can *locate* only something of fixed position, as in 'locate the enemy's camp'.

located. *To be located*, 'to reside'; 'to live (in a place)', is an Americanism, as in 'Are you located near here?'

loch. See **lough.**

locution and **circumlocution.** The predominant 20th-century sense of *locution* is 'a form of expression; a phrase; an expression', as in 'The introduction of new words and locutions' and 'The brisk and picturesque locutions of Cockneys'. A *circumlocution* is a roundabout, esp. if wordy, phrase or expression – e.g. *in respect of* and *with regard to* for *about* or *concerning* (*OED*).

LOGIC AND GRAMMAR. See GRAMMAR AND LOGIC.

logistics. See VOGUE WORDS.

lonely; alone. *Lonely* is solitary; *alone*, by oneself. One may be alone in a wood, yet by no means lonely; or one may be walking in a crowded street, yet be intolerably lonely.

look over. See **overlook.**

look well and **look good.** To *look good* is to appear good; to *look well* is to be well in health. Both can mean 'be attractive', so some trouble should be taken to avoid confusion there with the other senses of *well* and *good*.

looker-ons is incorrect for *lookers-on*.

looking. See CONJUNCTIONS, DISGUISED.

loose and **loosen**. The former is usual in the sense, 'to undo, to unbind, set free from material bonds', as in 'He loosed the dog'; hence 'to loose an arrow'. The latter is more general in the sense 'to relax or slacken', as in 'to loosen ligatures', 'loosen one's joints', 'loosen discipline'; hence 'to unfix or detach; to render less firm or cohesive', as in 'to loosen the stones in a wall', 'to loosen the soil'; cf. 'to loosen one's tongue' (*OED*).

loose for *lose* is a misspelling not infrequently met with; inexcusable, for the two words are pronounced differently.

lot. *A lot* for a large number or quantity; *the lot* for the whole number or quantity; are too common in our speech to be condemned as incorrect, but their use where any refinement or elevation of language is required is impossible, for they are not Standard English. *All the lot* is almost a vulgarism.

lough; loch. The former is in Ireland, the latter in Scotland. Both are pronounced the same, with the 'ch' sound which many people have to replace by 'k'.

louring. See **lowering**.

lovelily is good English and it means 'beautifully; in such a way as to stimulate love', as in 'How lovelily do the Graces cling to one another' and 'lovelily shines the moon'. Where it is cacophonous, use *in a lovely manner*.

low. See **lowly**.

low profile. See VOGUE WORDS.

lowering (n. and adj.) = 'depression' or 'depressing' ('Fever is very lowering') and 'frowning; gloom or gloomy' (*lowering looks, lowering sky*); *louring* is used only in the second sense. *OED* prefers the *lour* form for the 'frowning, gloomy' sense.

lowly should be avoided as the adverb of *lowly*, 'humble', for it is often ambiguous, as in 'The preacher spoke lowly': for 'in a low voice', use *low*; for 'in a lowly manner', use either *in a lowly manner* or *lowlily*.

There is an adverb *lowly*, and it occurs in both of these senses: but avoid it!

luncheon is a formal (e.g. a civic) *lunch*.

lure (v.). See **allure** (v.).

lustful; lusty. The former = 'pertaining to or full of sexual desire; libidinous', with adverb *lustfully*; the latter (with adverb *lustily*) = 'vigorous', as in 'He's a fine, lusty fellow', 'He dealt the bully a lusty blow.'

luxuriant for *luxurious*. The former, 'producing abundantly, growing profusely', is an adjective of active properties; the latter, 'given to luxury or self-indulgence, of or pertaining to, or characterized by luxury' (*OED*), is passive. Often confused in application, as are the adverbs *luxuriantly* and *luxuriously*. For misuse of *luxuriantly*, see the passage quoted at **malapropisms**; of *luxuriously*, note: 'All the plants in my garden are growing luxuriously.'

Lyon for *Lyons*. See **Bruxelles** ...

lyricist; lyrist. The latter is either 'a player on the lyre', or 'a lyric poet'; the former is 'a person who writes the words to a song'.

M

macintosh, not *mackintosh*, is the strictly correct name of the raincoat, for it was called after one Charles Macintosh; but the *ck* form has been so widely used that one feels pedantic in even mentioning the *c* form.

mad for *angry* is a colloquialism.

Madam is the correct English form of the French *Madame*; the plural is correctly as in French, *Mesdames*, but as that sounds pretentious today, prefer *Ladies*. When a *madam* is either a brothel-keeper or a conceited minx, the plural is always *madams*.

magisterial and **magistral**. In current, non-technical usage, *magistral* = 'masterly' as in 'a magistral arrangement of complex facts' and 'Magistral as Milton at his greatest, but subtle beyond his scope' (J. M. Robertson, 1889). An adoption from France.

The predominant sense of *magisterial* is 'of, belonging to, proper to a magistrate; holding the office of a magistrate', as in 'my magisterial neighbour', 'a magisterial inquiry', 'magisterial duties'. Two obsolescent nuances are: 'authoritative', as in 'a magisterial utterance', *magisterial* being here synonymous with the preferable *magistral*; and 'invested with authority', as in 'a magisterial superintendent'. But a useful sense is that of 'assuming authority, schoolteacher-like', hence 'dictatorial', as in 'He delivered his instructions in a magisterial voice' (based on *OED*).

Magna Carta; Magna Charta; The Great Charter; all three are correct.

magniloquent for *pompous* is an error due to misunderstanding, for by its Latin derivation *magniloquent* means 'talking big', a sense it retains in usage, although usage generally gives to it the meaning, 'lofty or ambitious in expression' (*OED*); and pomposity is not a form of speech though it may accompany magniloquence. See also at **grandiloquent**.

Mahomet. See **Muhammad**.

mail. See **post**.

main. See COMPARATIVES, FALSE.

maintain, misused for the intransitive *obtain* ('to exist; be practised, be habitual; be thus'), as in 'Does that puerile practice still maintain?' (Thorne Smith, *Topper Takes a Trip*). Perhaps cf. the French *se maintenir*.

maize. See **corn**.

major. See COMPARATIVES, FALSE. A thing or fact is either *major* or *minor* – and

that is all there is to it. This adjective is being overworked by Civil Servants.

major and **minor**. See VOGUE WORDS.

major portion and **greater part.** The latter would be preferable in such a sentence as 'He devotes the major portion of his time to gardening.'

majority, misused for *larger part* of a thing; e.g. 'The majority of the book is instructive.' *Majority* applies only to numbers; it = 'the greater number'.

majority of instances, in the; five words for one – either *usually* or *mostly*.

malapropisms. A malapropism – the adjective, by the way, is *malapropian* – is a 'ludicrous misuse of [a] word, especially in [a] mistake for one resembling it (e.g. *a nice derangement of epitaphs* for *arrangement of epithets*)', to quote *COD*. With this, compare the pleasing example perpetrated at the Old Bailey (the Central Criminal Court) in 1851, 'He struck me ... he called me all the *epitaphs* he could' (*Sessions Paper*, 21 June 1851). The term derives from Mrs Malaprop in Sheridan's *The Rivals*, produced in 1775; she was 'noted for her aptitude for misapplying long words, e.g. "as headstrong as an allegory on the banks of the Nile"' (Sir Paul Harvey, *The Oxford Companion to English Literature*). This kind of mistake, which is a sub-division of the *genus* catachresis (*q.v.*), has been felicitously used by many writers. In the General English Paper set in the Oxford and Cambridge School Certificate examination of July 1938, there occurred this question:

'Point out and correct any mistakes in word usage and idiom in the following passage:

'Mary entered the luxuriantly [*luxuriously*] furnished room and was welcomed by the baroness. She was indeed surprised by the warmth and pleasantry [*pleasantness*] of her reception considering all she had heard of her hostesses masterly [*hostess's masterful*] ways. It would not be difficult now, she thought, to explain her purport [*purpose*] in coming to the castle. Suddenly her eye was attracted by a small picture which hung [better, *was hanging*] between the tall French-windows, and the baroness interrupted [*intercepted*] her glance. "My dear, you are perspicuous [*perceptive*, or preferably, *observant*]; I see you have already noticed my Orozzi. It is indeed quite unique [see **unique**] and priceless, though some people find the colours crude and the drawing primary [*primitive*; better, *elementary*] and are worried [better, *perplexed*] because they find no allusion [*illusion*] of perspective in the background." "Ah yes," said Mary, "but these kind [*this* (or *that*) *kind*] of people always looks for a literate [*literal*] meaning in a work of art, and nothing else." "I see you are by no means ingenious [*ingenuous*; better, *ignorant*] in these matters," observed the baroness, and Mary smiled, well pleased with the complement [*compliment*].'

For an alphabetical list of malapropisms and similar confusions, see Book II of *English: A Course for Human Beings* (4th edition, 1954).

malapropos is the correct English way of writing the adopted French phrase, *mal à propos*. *Malapropos*, originally an adverb, has become also an adjective and even a noun.

Malay, used as the name of the country *Malaysia*, is a frequent error of ignorance. A *Malay* is a native of Malaysia or Indonesia.

male. See at **manlike.**

maleficence; malevolence. See **beneficence.**

Mall and **Pall Mall.** Uncertainty as to the pronunciation of these names is often shown and conclusive authority is wanting. In *the Mall* it may be *Mawl* or *Māl*, but *Mel* is considered incorrect, whereas in *Pall Mall* the pronunciation *Pĕl Mĕl*, usual in the 17th century when the game from which it is derived was fashionable, has been retained and is correct, as is also *Pāl Māl*, but not *Pawl Mawl*. A *mall*, meaning a shopping precinct, is a *mawl*.

man of letters; writer; author. What-

ever the nuances may have been in 1800 or 1850 or 1900, the differentiation now prevalent is this: The term *author* is applied particularly to a writer of *fiction*; *writer* to a writer of *fiction, history, biography, belles-lettres*; *man of letters* to such a (male) writer of any or all of these, plus poetry plus works of scholarship – but if his fiction is preponderant, he is usually relegated to the rank of *writers*, precisely as a *writer* that produces very little except fiction becomes an *author*. Note that a person that writes only – or mostly – poetry is generally called a *poet*, seldom a *writer*, never an *author*. A person that writes plays – or mostly plays – is generally called a *dramatist* (serious plays) or *playwright* (any kind, all kinds), not an *author* (despite the call 'Author! Author!').

Man of letters, however, is, even among those who merit that designation, avoided by the modest, for it has a slight taint of highbrowism and, if used by themselves, more than a tinge of pretentiousness; they prefer to be called *writers*. In any case, the term is applicable only to men – nobody is called a *woman of letters*. *Author* has also a generic sense, as in 'The Society of Authors', 'The Authors' Club', and in legal and official documents (e.g. income-tax returns) and in semi-official publications (e.g. *Who's Who*); in its restricted sense (a writer of fiction) *author* is a useful welder of *novelists* and *short-story writers* – a combination that calls for some such neologism as *fictioner* or *fictionist*. *Writer* is probably the most useful of these three terms; it is certainly the least invidious; underwriters and copy-writers may generally be trusted not to usurp the more general – and more complimentary – term.

manifest. See COMPARATIVES, FALSE.

manifold; multifarious; multiform; multiple. For *manifold*, see the remarks at **-fold**; but it does also = 'consisting of many of one kind combined; operating many of one kind of object', as in 'a *manifold* bell-pull'; further, it = 'numerous and varied', as in 'O Lord how *manifold* are thy works!'

Multifarious emphasizes 'the diversity, sometimes even the incongruity, of the elements involved', as in 'The *multifarious* complexities of human character' (Hare).

Multiform = 'having many forms, shapes, or appearances', as in 'A plastic and multiform unit' (Hare).

Multiple = 'containing (something) more than once, or containing more than one (of a thing); consisting of more than one', as in *multiple stores, a multiple vote, multiple solutions* (of a problem).

mankind should be followed by *it*, not by *he*, for it = the human race. 'By [the middle of the 15th century], through the application of science and invention, new possibilities were available to mankind which were likely to have an even larger effect on his future than those of agriculture and the techniques of early civilization' (J. D. Bernal, 'The Social Function of Science', in *The Modern Quarterly*, Jan. 1938). Probably the confusion is caused by taking *mankind* to be a synonym of *man*, as of course it is – but of *man* generically, not of *man*, the male human being. It is this misunderstanding that has caused many feminists to prefer *humankind* for our species.

manlike (or **man-like**); **manly**; **mannish**; **male**; **masculine**. *Manly* (falling into disuse in the sense 'mannish') is favourable, connoting the good qualities of a man; *mannish* is unfavourable if it is applied to a woman, and it means 'resembling a man' (in dress, manners, speech), but as a synonym of *manly* and *manlike*, it is obsolescent; of *manlike* the predominant sense is, 'characteristic of a man as opposite to a woman or a child', but when applied to an animal (esp. an ape), it = 'resembling a human being', – its other senses ('mannish' and 'manly') being obsolescent; *male* is 'of the masculine sex *qua* sex, as opposite to the feminine sex'; and *masculine*, the grammatical opposite of *feminine* (*gender*), is in general use in the senses 'peculiar to or assigned to males; consisting of males', as in *masculine attire, masculine primogeniture*, and 'virile; vigorous;

appropriate to (excellences of) the male sex', as in *masculine licence, masculine force, masculine style*, the sense 'mannish' being obsolescent (*OED*).

manner. See ABSTRACT NOUNS.

manslaughter. See **murder.**

mantel; mantle. The former is a shelf over a fireplace. The latter (among other meanings) is a cloak.

manuscript means 'written by hand' and *manuscripts* should be reserved for hand-written copies of, e.g. a book; that which is typed is a *typescript*. But *manuscript* is often used for *typescript* (whether noun or adjective): which seems a pity!

many is normally plural, but it takes a singular verb in *many a* ('many a student has wondered') and in *many's the* ('many's the time I've seen …').

marginal. See VOGUE WORDS.

marionette. See **puppet.**

Marseille for *Marseilles*. See at **Bruxelles** …

marshal for *martial* is an occasional error among the semi-literate. The former is noun and verb; the latter, adjective only ('war-like').

mart is slightly archaic, rather literary for *market*, but is in modern use for a trade centre or auction-room.

marten; martin. The former is a weasel-like carnivore, the latter a swallow.

martyr (to) for *victim (of)* or *one suffering (from)* is hyperbolical and to be used with care: *a martyr to epilepsy* is admissible, *a martyr to colds* is absurd.

marvel and **miracle** are overworked – and too often used hyperbolically.

masculine. See **manlike.**

masochism. See **sadism.**

massacre (n. and v.) refers to wholesale killing, mass-slaughter, not to the murder of one person. 'He swore the most dread-

ful oaths that he would "massacre her" '
(Thomas Reid, *Two Voyages*, 1822).

masseur, masculine; **masseuse,** feminine.
They may now be regarded as English
words; do not, therefore, print them in
italic.

massive. See VOGUE WORDS.

masterful; masterly. With a long interval between them, I wrote two accounts
of this pair. Here is the later:

In current usage, they are distinguished
thus: *Masterful* is 'imperious' or (of actions)
'high-handed, despotic', as in 'She was
proud and masterful' (Trollope), 'This
masterful disregard of logical thought';
'qualified to command; powerful and/or
vigorous in command or in rule', as in
'Henry VIII was a masterful King'; as a
synonym of *masterly*, it is obsolescent. *Masterly* is applied either to persons or their
actions or abilities, and it = 'resembling or
characteristic of a master or skilled workman; skilfully performed, done, exercised',
as in 'a masterly sportsman,' 'The thought
is masculine and the expression masterly'
(Leslie Stephen); 'a masterly stroke' (of
painter, tactician, batsman) (*OED*).

And here the earlier:
Masterful and *masterly* are often confused.
In the Oxford and Cambridge School
Certificate examination held in July 1938,
the English General Paper contained this
sentence for correction: 'She was indeed
surprised by the warmth ... of her reception, considering all she had heard of
her (hostess's) masterly ways.' And in the
same month I found in the Introduction
to Dr Selwyn Gurney Champion's
remarkable book, *Racial Proverbs*, this
reference to Bonser and Stephen's *Proverb
Literature* (1928), 'This unique and masterful compilation of the world's proverb
literature is indispensable to the paroemi-
ographer'. *Masterful* means 'self-willed',
'imperious', 'domineering';   *masterly*
signifies 'worthy of a master (at e.g. one's
art)', hence 'very skilful or expert'. – The
same remarks apply to *masterfulness* and
masterliness.

materialize, 'to become visible or perceptible; to become real, actual, actual fact;
against general opinion or serious obstacles
to succeed, make its way', is overdone, as
in 'There were doubts of his ability to
come at all, but he materialized', 'After
much discussion, a plan materialized',
'The house he longed to achieve did not
materialize.'

materially is not incorrect in the sense 'to
an important extent; substantially; considerably, greatly', as in 'Short cuts, by ...
which the road was materially shortened'
(Ralph Boldrewood), but there is,
especially among journalists, a tendency to
overdo it.

maximum and **minimum,** meaning the
absolute *most* and *least*, are often loosely
used.

may and **can.** See **can and may.**

may and **might.** Both *may have* and *might
have* are used of past possibilities; the
former properly means that the possibility
is still open, the latter that the possibility
no longer exists. Do not use *may have* for
might have, as in 'events which may never
have become known here if the coup had
succeeded' (BBC News). It is at least clear
there that the coup failed, but if the passage had ended after 'here' there would be
real doubt as to its outcome. See also **SUB-
JUNCTIVE,** and **PAST MODAL.**

may and **must.** See **NEGATION,** Section
A, last five paragraphs.

maybe is to be preferred to the original
may be as a colloquial synonym of 'perhaps'. ' "You'll say it's likely enough that
there was money and may be jewellery
sent over to him from France" ' (Ronald
Knox, *Double Cross Purposes*). It is permissible, though no longer usual, to write '...
money and (it may be) jewellery'.

me for *I.* See **it is me.**

mean time and **meantime.** *Meantime*
(adv.) is short for *in the meantime* (originally
in the mean time), 'during a specified interval'. In current usage, *mean time* is, by dis-

criminating writers, confined to the sense *mean solar time*, i.e. the time of day as shown by the *mean sun*, i.e. the time shown by an ordinary clock, correctly regulated.

meaningful. See VOGUE WORDS.

meaningless. See COMPARATIVES, FALSE.

means, 'an instrument, agency, method or course of action, by the employment of which some object is or may be attained, or which is concerned in bringing about some result' (*OED*), is plural in form, but it takes a singular verb after singular words such as *a* and *each*, and a plural verb after plural words such as *all* and *several*. The *means* is singular or plural according to meaning. 'The means of payment is for him to decide.' 'The means of payment are numerous.'

meantime. See **mean time.**

Mecca, being the birthplace of the Prophet, is a place of religious pilgrimage for Muhammadans, but to say (as the Southern Railway's *Holiday Hints*, 1938, says) that 'Ryde Pier is a Mecca for anglers' is to debase metaphor from the sublime to the piscatorial.

mechanism. See VOGUE WORDS.

mechanization is the substitution of machines for human (or animal) muscles; *automation* is the substitution of machines for human brains, in the controlling of other machines.

media. See **mediums.**

medium-size (adj.) is incorrect for *medium-sized*, and often *medium-sized* is unnecessary for *medium* or *average*.

mediums are spiritualistic, or (of persons) 'intermediaries' or 'mediators', or absolute as in 'The large hats are ugly, the mediums are tolerable, the small ones are pretty'; in all other senses, the plural is *media*, which in the sense 'means of mass communication' is now often treated as a singular noun – a practice to be eschewed. It

should be 'The media *are* (*not* is) responsible.'

memoranda is the plural of *memorandum*; and because the plural is more often used than the singular it is occasionally taken for and construed as a singular (cf. **strata**). The English plural, *memorandums*, is gaining ground: and there is no reason why you should not use it if you wish. The unforgivable sin is to form the plural in *-as*; *memorandas* is as absurd as *stratas*.

menace, 'a threat', should not be overdone. That Kenneth Farnes was a better bowler than writer appears from: 'McCabe is a good second-string to the Bradman menace' (*Lyons' Sport Sheet*, 8 May 1938).

mendacity and **mendicity.** The former is habitual lying or deceiving; the latter, the habit of begging, or the existence of the begging class (*mendicants*). See *Webster's* and *OED*.

mental to describe a mentally disordered person is a modern term – and no better than slang.

mentally maladjusted is psychiatric, thence official, jargon for *insane*.

mesdames. See **madam.**

Messrs should be confined to commerce; elsewhere *Messieurs*. The abbreviation *MM* is for *Messieurs*, the plural of *Monsieur*, but not (unfortunately) for *Messrs*, the plural of *Mr*.

metal is a substance; *mettle* is 'the stuff' of which a person is made, with reference to character.

METAPHOR

I. *General Considerations.*

Metaphor, as defined by *OED*, is that figure of speech in which 'a name or descriptive term is transferred to some object different from, but analogous to, that to which it is properly applicable'; derivatively, an instance of this, i.e. a metaphorical expression – a transference or transferred usage. The word comes from the Greek μεταφοά, 'a transference' (of the sense of one word to another), and its Latin synonym is *translatio*, lit. 'a carrying across'.

But, as the following précis of certain passages from 'Metaphor' and 'The Command of Metaphor' in Dr I. A. Richards's *The Philosophy of Rhetoric* – the two best chapters in a provocative and illuminating book – will (I hope) make clear, that is an insufficient definition.

Aristotle, in *The Poetics*, went so far as to declare that 'the greatest thing by far is to have a command of metaphor' and added that, 'to employ metaphors happily and effectively', it was necessary to have 'an eye for resemblances'. On this matter, Dr Richards says: 'We all live, and speak, only through our eye for resemblances. Without it we should perish early. Though some may have better eyes than others, the differences between them are in degree only and may be remedied, certainly in some measure, as other differences are, by the right kinds of teaching and study. ... As individuals we gain our command of metaphor just as we learn whatever else makes us distinctively human.'

Richards passes to that further assumption made by the 18th- and 19th-century writers on Rhetoric – 'that metaphor is something special and exceptional in the use of language, a deviation from its normal mode of working, instead of the omnipresent principle of all its free action.

'Throughout the history of Rhetoric', continues this able pleader for a revival and a re-assessment of Rhetoric, 'metaphor has been treated as a sort of happy extra trick with words, an opportunity to exploit the accidents of their versatility, something in place occasionally but requiring unusual skill and caution. In brief, a grace or ornament or *added* power of language, not its constitutive form.' He notes that Shelley developed his view that 'language is vitally metaphorical': and remarks, 'But that is an exceptional utterance and its implications have not yet been taken account of by rhetoricians.'

Richards proceeds to deal with a matter of primary importance: 'That metaphor is the omnipresent principle of language can be shown by mere observation. We cannot get through [even so much as] three sentences of ordinary fluid discourse without it. ... Even in the rigid language of the settled sciences we do not eliminate or prevent it without great difficulty. In the semi-technicalized subjects, in aesthetics, politics, sociology, ethics, psychology, theory of language and so on, our constant chief difficulty is to discover how we are using it [i.e. metaphor] and how our supposedly fixed words are shifting their senses. In philosophy, above all, we can take no step safely without an unrelaxing awareness of the metaphors we, and our audience, may be employing. ... And this is the more true, the more severe and abstract the philosophy is. As it grows more abstract we think increasingly by means of metaphors that we profess *not* to be relying on. The metaphors we are avoiding steer our thought as much as those we accept.

'In the simplest formulation, when we use a metaphor we have two thoughts of different things active together and supported by a single word, or phrase, whose meaning is a resultant of their interaction. ... There is an immense variety in [the] modes of interaction between co-present thoughts ... or, in terms of the context theorem, between different missing parts or aspects of the different contexts of a word's meaning. In practice, we distinguish with marvellous skill between these modes of interaction, though our skill varies. The Elizabethans, for example, were far more widely skilled in the use of metaphor – both in utterance and in interpretation – than we are. A fact which made Shakespeare possible. The 18th century narrowed its skill down, defensively, to certain modes only. The early 19th century revolted against this and specialized in other modes. The later 19th century and [the 20th] have been recovering from these two specializations.'

Dr Richards then 'gets down to brass tacks'. 'The traditional theory noticed only a few of the modes of metaphor; and limited its application of the term *metaphor* to a few of them only. And thereby it made metaphor seem to be a verbal matter, a shifting and displacement of words, whereas fundamentally it is a borrowing and [an] intercourse of *thoughts*, a transaction between contexts. *Thought* is metaphoric, and proceeds by comparison, and the metaphors of language derive therefrom.'

Having established a background and a principle, Richards asks us to consider certain simple analytic steps that render more facile the translation of our skill with metaphor into an explicit art. 'A first step is to introduce two technical terms to assist us in distinguishing from [each other] what Dr Johnson called the two ideas that any metaphor, at its simplest, gives us. Let me call them the tenor and the vehicle. ... At present we have only some clumsy descriptive phrases with which to separate [the two halves – or members – of a metaphor]. "The original idea" and "the borrowed one"; "what is really being said or thought of" and "what it is compared to"; "the underlying idea" and "the imagined nature"; "the principal subject" and "what it resembles"; or, still more confusing, simply "the meaning" and "the metaphor", or "the idea" and "its image".

'How confusing these must be', he continues, 'is easily seen. ... We need the word "metaphor" for the whole double unit.' The 18th-century rhetoricians assumed 'that figures [especially metaphors] are a mere embellishment or added beauty and that the plain meaning, the tenor' – the surface meaning, the general tenor of the discourse at any given point or stage of the discourse – 'is what alone really matters and is something that, "regardless of the figure", might be gathered by the patient reader'.

To this, 'a modern theory would object, first, that in many of the most important uses of metaphor, the co-presence of the vehicle and tenor results in a meaning (to be clearly distinguished from the tenor [a meaning richer, subtler, fuller than that

conveyed by the tenor alone]) which is not attainable without their interaction'. Modern opinion would object, secondly, 'that the vehicle is not normally a mere embellishment of a tenor which is otherwise unchanged by it, but that vehicle and tenor in cooperation give a meaning of more varied powers than can be ascribed to either [the tenor alone or the vehicle alone]. And a modern theory would go on to point out that with different metaphors the relative importance of the contributions of vehicle and tenor to this resultant meaning varies immensely. At one extreme the vehicle may become almost a mere decoration or colouring of the tenor, at the other extreme the tenor may become almost a mere excuse for the introduction of the vehicle, and so no longer be "the principal subject".

'How about [Lord Kames's] suggested rule that we should carefully avoid mounting metaphor upon metaphor? What would be the effect of taking it seriously? It would, if accepted and observed, make havoc of most writing and speech. It is disregarding the most sustaining metaphors of all speech. It would make, I think, Shakespeare the faultiest writer who ever held a pen; and it turns an obstinately blind eye upon one of the most obvious features of current practice in every minute of our speech.'

Arrived at 'the command of metaphor', Dr Richards remarks upon the contrast between our use of metaphors and our awareness of them. 'Our skill with metaphor, with thought, is one thing – prodigious and inexplicable; our reflective awareness of that skill is quite another thing – very incomplete, distorted, fallacious, over-simplifying. [The business of reflective awareness is] to protect our natural skill from the interferences of unnecessarily crude views about it; and, above all, to assist the imparting of that skill – that command of metaphor – from mind to mind!

'A very broad division can ... be made between metaphors which work through some direct resemblance between the two things, the tenor and vehicle, and those which work through some common attitude which we may ... take up towards them both. *That we like them both is ...* a common property that two things share, though we may, at the same time, be willing to admit that they are utterly different. ... This division, though it does not go very deep, may ... help us sometimes to avoid one of the worst snares – the assumption that if we cannot see how a metaphor works, it does not work.'

Let us take the simple word *leg*. 'We notice that even there the boundary between literal and metaphoric uses is not quite fixed or constant. To what do we apply it literally? A horse has legs literally, so has a spider, but how about a chimpanzee? Has it two legs or four? And how about a star-fish? Has it arms or legs or neither? And, when a man has a wooden leg, is it a metaphoric or a literal leg? The answer to this last is that it is both. It is literal in one set of respects, metaphoric in another. A word may be *simultaneously* both literal and metaphoric, just as it may simultaneously support many different metaphors, may serve to focus into one meaning many different meanings. This point is of some importance, since so much interpretation comes from supposing that if a word works one way it cannot simultaneously work in another way and have simultaneously another meaning.'

From that important point, Richards passes to another – 'the varying relations between tenor and vehicle. It is convenient to begin with the remark ... that a metaphor involves a comparison. What is a comparison? It may be several different things: it may be just a putting together of two things to let them work together; it may be a study of them both to see how they are like and how unlike [each other]; or it may be a process of calling attention to their likeness or a method of drawing attention to certain aspects of the one through the co-presence of the other. [Thus] we get different conceptions of

metaphor. If we mean calling attention to likenesses, we get a main 18th-century doctrine of metaphor. Dr Johnson ... praises Denham's lines on the Thames because "the particulars of resemblance are so perspicaciously collected" ...

> O could I flow like thee, and make
>   thy stream
> My great exemplar as it is my
>   theme!
> Though deep, yet clear; though
>   gentle, yet not dull;
> Strong without rage; without
>   o'erflowing, full.

'Here the flow of the poet's mind, we may say, is the tenor [or the subject of discourse, the primary matter under consideration], and the river the vehicle; and it is worth noting ... that in the last two lines there is a repeated alternation of the relative positions of tenor and vehicle and of the direction of the shift between them. "Though deep, yet clear": the words are literally descriptive of the vehicle, the river; derivatively or metaphorically descriptive of the mind. "Though gentle, yet not dull": "gentle" certainly is literally descriptive of the mind, the tenor, derivatively of the river, the other way about; but "dull", I suppose, goes from the river to the mind again'; *dull*, as applied to a river, means 'sluggish' – cf. Spenser's 'Thenceforth her waters waxed dull and slow.' ' "Strong without rage" goes, for me, unquestionably from mind to river, and "without overflowing, full" goes back again from river – does it not? – to mind. ... The more carefully and attentively we go over the senses and implications of *deep, clear, gentle, strong* and *full* as they apply to a stream and to a mind, the less shall we find the resemblances between vehicle and tenor counting [= significant] and the more the vehicle, the river, comes to seem an excuse for saying about the mind something which could not be said about the river. ... But the river is not a mere excuse, or a decoration only, a gilding of the moral pill. The vehicle is still controlling the mode in which the tenor forms.

'Comparison, as a stressing of likenesses, is not the whole mode of this metaphor though it commonly is in the 18th-century writing – where, too, the tenor is usually the [more] important partner in the metaphor. The opposed conception of comparison – as a mere putting together' (or juxtaposition) 'of two things to see what will happen – is a contemporary fashionable aberration, which takes an extreme case as the norm. ... This is André Breton, the leader of the French Super-Realists, stating the doctrine very plainly: "To compare two objects, as remote from [each other] in character as possible, or by any other method [to] put them together in [an abrupt] and striking fashion, this remains the highest task to which poetry can aspire" ... That as "the highest task to which poetry can aspire"! ... Like Mr Max Eastman, with his insistence (in *The Literary Mind*) that metaphor works by attempting "impracticable identifications", M. Breton sees no need to consider what should be put with what – provided they are sufficiently remote from [each other] – nor does he distinguish between the very different effects of such collocations. ... Mr Eastman shares this indifference as to the precise effect of the encounter of disparates.* For him the poet "communicates a kind of experience not elsewhere accessible", and, to do so, ... he "must arouse a reaction and yet impede it, creating a tension in our nervous system sufficient and rightly calculated to make us completely aware that we are living something" ... This ... heroism comes, I think, from a crude conception of the mode of action of metaphors, a conception which is an excessive reaction from the equative of metaphor to a mere comparison of likenesses.

'I conclude that these contemporary exploiters of the crude "clash them together – no matter what" view of the metaphor are beguiling themselves with

by-products of the process of interpretation and neglecting the more important cares of critical theory. But ... one point of importance emerges clearly from examining these exaggerations. We must not, with the 18th century, suppose that the interactions of tenor and vehicle are to be confined to their resemblances. There is disparity action too. When Hamlet uses the word *crawling* – "What should such fellows as I do crawling between earth and heaven?" – its force comes not only from whatever resemblances to vermin it brings in but at least equally from the differences that resist and control the influences of their resemblances. The implication there is that man should not so crawl. Thus, talk about the identification or fusion that a metaphor effects is nearly always misleading and pernicious. In general, there are very few metaphors in which disparities between tenor and vehicle are not as much operative as the similarities. Some similarity will commonly be the ostensive ground of the shift, but the peculiar modification of the tenor which the vehicle brings about is even more the work of their unlikenesses than of their likenesses.'

Richards then leads us gently to the crux. 'Words cannot, and should not attempt to "hand over sensations bodily"; they have very much more important work to do. So far from verbal language being a "compromise for a language of intuition" ..., language, well used, is a *completion* and does what the intuitions of sensation by themselves cannot do. Words are the meeting points at which regions of experience which can never combine in sensation or intuition, come together. They are the occasion and the means of that growth which is the mind's endless endeavour to order itself. That is why we have language. It is no mere signalling system. It is the instrument of all our distinctively human development, of everything in which we go beyond the other animals.

'Thus, to present language as working only through the sensations it reinstates, is to turn the whole process upside down. It overlooks what is important in Mallarmé's

Disparates are 'things so unlike that they cannot be compared with each other' (*OED*).

dictum that the poet does not write with thoughts (or with ideas or sensations or beliefs or desires or feelings, we may add) but with words. "Are not words", Coleridge asked, "parts and germinations of the plant? And what is the law of their growth? In something of this sort", he wrote, "I would endeavour to destroy the old antithesis of Words and Things: elevating, as it were, Words into Things and living things too." We must do so if we are to study metaphor properly ... It is the word which brings in the meaning which the image and its original perception lack.'

Richards then attacks 'the mistaking of what I have been calling the tenor-vehicle antithesis for that between the metaphor (the double unit including tenor and vehicle) and its meaning'. He attacks, too, 'those anxious, over-careful [and erroneous] attempts to *copy* perceptions and feelings *in words*, to "hand over sensations bodily", of which modern prose at its most distinguished too often consists. Words are not a medium in which to copy life. Their true work is to restore life itself to order.

'We are accustomed to distinguish between taking an utterance literally and taking it metaphorically, but, at the simplest, there are at least four possible modes of interpretation to be considered, not two. And the kinds of believing that will be appropriate will as a rule be different. We can abstract the tenor and believe that as a statement; or abstract the vehicle; or, taking tenor and vehicle together, contemplate for acceptance or rejection some statement about their relations; or we can accept or refuse the direction which together they would give to our living. We need not go to the Alexandrian schools of early Christian interpretation, or to the similar exegetical developments of other religions, to find instances to show how immense the consequences for belief of these choices may be. The varying possibilities of understanding of any metaphoric utterance will show them.'

That is but a poor and meagre presentation of Dr Richards's two perceptive and highly acute lectures on metaphor: if I succeed in sending readers to the source, I shall have achieved my purpose.

II. *Confused or Mixed Metaphors.*

In Alexander Bain's *English Composition and Rhetoric*, enlarged edition, Part I, at pp. 165–8, there is a sound, though perhaps unimaginative and rather too formal, section on mixed metaphor.

Bain introduces the section with the sibyllic words 'The brevity of the Metaphor renders it liable to the vice called Mixing Metaphors': is it the brevity or is it not rather the confused thinking of the perpetrator?

'This arises', Bain says, 'when metaphors from different sources are combined in the same subject: as "to *kindle a seed*". We may *sow a seed* or *kindle a flame*; but kindling a seed is incongruous and confusing to the mind.

'The following example from Addison is familiar –

> I *bridle* in my struggling muse with pain
> That longs to *launch* into a bolder strain.

Three different figures' – horse, ship, music – 'are conjoined in one action.

' "The very *hinge* and *centre* of an immense system": "hinge" is out of place': but is it? Here we have not a mixing but an adding or a collocation of metaphors, for 'centre' is as much a metaphor as a 'hinge'.

' "All my pretty *chickens* and their *dam*" is the mixing of two metaphors ...

' "Physiology and psychology thus become united, and the study of man passes from the uncertain *light* of mere opinion to the *region* of science."

' "The very recognition of these by the jurisprudence of a nation is a *mortal wound* to the very *keystone* upon which the whole vast arch of morality reposes." '

After citing other examples, of which several would, to the modern mind, seem not merely permissible but admirable, Bain goes on to say, 'There is no objection to different metaphors being successively applied to the same subject, provided they are kept distinct. Thus: "They admire the profundity of what is mystical and obscure, mistaking the *muddiness of water* for *depth* (1), and *magnifying* in their imaginations what is *viewed through a fog* (2)" (Whately).'

Nor do we now subscribe to the dictum that 'the mixture of the metaphorical and the plain or literal is also objectionable. Dryden, speaking of the aids he had in his translations, says, "I was sailing in a vast ocean without other help than the *pole-star* of the ancients, and *the rules of the French stage* among the moderns" ': *rules* itself is naught but a metaphor – originally.

Let me now adduce a few instances of a more glaring kind. Sir Boyle Roche (1743–1807), Irish politician, is reported to have said, in the version given in *Stevenson's Book of Quotations*:

'Mr Speaker, I smell a rat; I see him forming in the air and darkening the sky; but I'll nip him in the bud.'

But some 19th-century wit elaborated the original, and the form in which most of us know this delightful mixture is:

'Mr Speaker, I smell a rat. I see it floating in the air; and if it is not nipped in the bud, it will burst forth into a terrible conflagration that will deluge the world.'

'A house mortgaged up to the hilt.' Two from Sir Alan Herbert's *What a Word!*:

'... Ideas of individuality, freedom, tolerance, and eternal youth with which the aftermath of war was impregnated.'

'The Irish Free State had held out the olive branch but nothing concrete had come out of it' (Mr James Maxton, MP). Two examples of a different kind, from my own reading:

'They alone were concerned about the sharing of the bear's skin after the bear had been killed – perhaps because they are possessed by the illusion that they can win the election off their own bat' (leading article in *The Daily Telegraph*): not a mixing but a confusingly rapid change of metaphors.

'When Einstein broke ... open [the old concept of length], knowledge jumped forward' (Stuart Chase, *The Tyranny of Words*): 'jumped *out*' would have been preferable.

Finally, it is possible to associate a metaphor accidentally with a literal sense of one of its words. The result, though not a *mixed* metaphor, is certainly *confused*, and yields absurd results; as with 'a crash course for trainee pilots', or 'When they handed me the bill I agreed to foot it.'

meticulous is now often used to mean 'careful of detail in a praiseworthy manner'; properly, it implies excess of care and an overscrupulousness caused by timidity; but the modern favourable sense is appropriate everywhere except in the most formal writing.

mid, preposition, is – except in traditional and scientific phrases – rather literary (and poetic). Write *mid*, not *'mid*. As an attributive adjective, as in 'mid-July', the word is of course perfectly current.

middle. See **centre.**

Middle East, Far East, Near East. The Near East (Egypt, Israel, Syria, etc.) has unfortunately become the Middle East; apparently the Far East (Japan, China, Thailand, Malaysia) remains the Far East, and what used to be the Middle East is now simply the East (in so far as that term has not been pre-empted by the ex-Communist countries of Eastern Europe).

Middle West; Middle Western. See **Midwest.**

'midst is inferior to *midst* (whether noun, adverb or preposition); now rather literary than spoken English, it has, for the most part, been superseded by *among* or *in the midst of.*

Midwest, Midwestern; Middle West, Middle Western. As applied to the central United States. 'Usage', remarks Weseen, 'seems to favour *Midwest* and *Midwestern* as adjectives and ... *Middle West* as the noun. But *Midwest* [not *Midwestern*] is sometimes used as a noun and *Middle West* and [less often] *Middle West-*

em are often used as adjectives.' That, of course, is an American ruling; the longer form may be more common in British use.

might for *would*. See SUBJUNCTIVE (near end). – *Might* for *may*. See PAST MODAL ... – For the correct use of *may* and *might*, see **may** ... – For *might* and *could*, see **could**.

Milady and **Milord** as terms of address are British, not Continental, being indistinguishable in speech from *my lady*, *my lord*. As generics, they have the senses 'an English noblewoman', 'an English nobleman'.

mileage. See VOGUE WORDS.

militate. See **mitigate**.

millenary and **millinery.** The latter is noun only ('articles made and sold by milliners; the business of a milliner'); the former, both noun (a thousand years) and adjective ('consisting of, belonging to, characteristic of a thousand' – especially a thousand years, a millennium).

Milord. See **Milady**.

mind, 'to remind', is obsolescent; *mind*, 'to remember' (v.t.) is archaic.

miniature should, as an adjective, be used with care. It is not a synonym of *small* or *little* or *dainty*. For a misuse, see the quotation at **sound** (v.).

minimize, 'to reduce to the smallest possible size, amount, or degree', as in 'Clerical vestments are minimized', and 'to estimate at the smallest possible amount (or value of importance)', as in 'Jesus did not minimize sin': is not to be degraded to equivalence with to *decrease*, *diminish*, *lessen*, as in 'Why seek to minimize the danger?' (*OED*).

minimum (adj.) – cf. **maximum** – is being overworked, at the expense of *least*.

minor and **major.** See VOGUE WORDS. See also COMPARATIVES, FALSE.

miracle. See **marvel**.

mischievious is a too frequent mispronunciation of *mischievous*.

MISQUOTATIONS. ' "Similarity of style. ... Two or three times the fellow tried to disguise it ... ". "Oh, but there was more than that!" cried the other. ... "... Now, look at this. The Minister of Imperial Finance, in his efforts for advancement of self, would do well to remember that hackneyed line of Pope: 'A little learning is a dangerous thing.' Did you see that?" – Anthony opened his eyes. "I did. And thought how refreshing it was to see the quotation given right. They nearly all get it wrong, though you'd think anyone could see that Pope couldn't have been such a fool as to say a little knowledge was dangerous. Knowledge is always useful; learning isn't, until you've got plenty. But go on ..." – Masterson was searching feverishly. "... here we are! Listen ... 'when Greek joins Greek then comes the tug of war?' ... How many times d'you see that given right?" – "Never," said Anthony. "They all say 'meets'." – "There you are then. ... Style – similarity of style, I mean – isn't proof; but this orgy of correctitude *plus* that similarity is. ... There are plenty more instances ... There's one I remember well ... It said ...: '*facilis descensus Averno*'. What about that?" – Anthony sat up. " '*Averno*' is very rare", he said slowly. "But it's a better reading ..." ' (from Ch. xiii, sec. ii, of Philip MacDonald's first-class 'deteccer', *The Rasp*).

As this brief entry is not intended to cope with even the commonest of the many misquotations, I shall note only a few others; but these others are, at least, extremely common.

'That he who runs may read' should be '[Write the vision, and make it plain upon tables] that he may run that readeth it' (Habakkuk, ii, 2); the meaning was that 'he who reads the information may run away and act upon it' (Alfred Ackermann, *Popular Fallacies*).

'Fresh fields and pastures new' should be 'Fresh woods and pastures new' (Milton).

'A parting shot' was originally 'a Parthian shot', and originally 'All that glitters is not gold' was 'All that glisters …'.

'Water, water everywhere, and not a drop to drink' should be 'Water, water everywhere, nor any drop to drink' (Coleridge).

'Of the making of books there is no end' is properly (and originally) 'Of making many books there is no end', which occurs in the Bible. In

To die: to sleep;
No more; and, by a sleep to say
    we end
The heart-ache and the thousand
    natural shocks
That flesh is heir to, 'tis a
    consummation
Devoutly to be wish'd.
                        (Shakespeare)

shocks is frequently misquoted as *ills*.

Prunes and prisms is incorrect for *prunes and prism*; and *gild the lily* is incorrect for 'to gild refined gold, to paint the lily' (Shakespeare, *King John*, IV. ii.11).

'Cribbed, cabined and confined' is incorrect for Shakespeare's '[Now I am] cabin'd, crib'd, confin'd, bound in' (*Macbeth*, II, iv.24).

'Flat, stale and unprofitable' (or 'improfitable') is a misquotation of Shakespeare's 'How weary, stale, flat, and unprofitable, Seem to me all the uses of this world.'

MISRELATED GERUND. See **GERUND**, last paragraph.

MISRELATED PARTICIPLE. See **CONFUSED PARTICIPLES.**

misremember is correct in the sense 'to remember incorrectly or incompletely'; dialectal in the sense 'to forget'.

Miss and **Misses.** The former correct plural of *Miss Hume* is the *Misses Hume*; but *the Miss Humes* is permissible.

missis (or **missus**), **the,** is at best a colloquialism for '(one's) wife' and (also without *the*) 'the mistress' of the house.

mistaken, misunderstood. 'I was *mistaken*' = 'I was wrong, in error'; 'I was misunderstood' = 'Somebody (or some persons) failed to understand me.'

Mister, as a vocative (or term of address) without the surname, is avoided by the polite.

mitigate; militate. They are often confused. To *mitigate* something is to make it less severe. To *militate* (v.i.) against something is to have a significant effect against it.

MIXED METAPHORS. See **METAPHOR**, Part II.

MM. See **Messrs.**

mob is a dangerous or at least a potentially disorderly crowd.; it is colloquial to use it of *any* crowd, or of companies of animals. *The mob* is the populace, the masses.

model is a pattern or a representation in scale or proportion; do not use it where *copy*, *reproduction*, or esp., *replica* is the precise word. See, above all, *OED*, and also **VOGUE WORDS.**

MODIFIED STANDARD. See **STANDARD ENGLISH,** Section II.

Mohammed, Mohammedan See **Muhammad.**

moiré for *moire*. The fabric is *moire*; and *moiré* is an adjective, or as a noun it is the watered or cloudy appearance characteristic of moire.

momentary; momentous. *Momentary* is (of things) 'transitory'; (of persons or animal life) 'short-lived' – an obsolescent sense. But *momentous* is 'important' of events, and 'weighty' of statements or decisions.

monies and *moneys* are alternative plurals for *money*, but the latter is preferable.

monologue. See **dialogue.**

Mons., whether written or spoken, is regarded by Frenchmen as a gratuitous insult. Say or write *Monsieur*; write *M.*

monstrous, even when it means *enormous*, has a connotation either of abnormality or of ugliness. Subjectively, it means 'horrible, atrocious' or 'outrageously wrong; contemptibly absurd'. As an adverb ('exceedingly'), it is archaic. See esp. *OED*.

MOOD IN SYNTAX; right use of mood. See esp. SUBJUNCTIVE and TENSE-SEQUENCE but also CONCESSIVE CLAUSES and CONDITIONAL CLAUSES and FINAL CLAUSES.

moonlight (adj.) is used in *moonlight night*, and wherever it means 'done by moonlight', as in *moonlight flit* and *moonlight dancing*. For the visual effect, use *moonlit*, as in 'the moonlit landscape'.

moral and **morale.** In regard to the power of usage, Frank Whitaker, in the *JIJ*, January 1939, selects an excellent example. 'Take', says he, 'the word "moral", meaning "of good morals". We had used it for centuries in that sense when somebody discovered that the French used it [as a noun] to mean "the spirit of the troops". "Ah", said this person, "a useful word. We must bag that." So we took it, added an "e" to distinguish it both in spelling and [in] pronunciation from "moral", and made it our own. It didn't matter a pin to Mr Usage that the French have the two words, and use them in precisely the reverse sense. But although this happened years ago, it still matters to *The Times*. ... It still spells it without an "e" to remind us that we mustn't play tricks with other people's words. It might as well talk to the moon. The distinction is useful, and because it is useful it has established itself.'

Fowler upholds *morale* (pronounced *morahl*) and – for what that is worth – so do I.

moratorium is a dignified word, not to be used of trivial delays or postponements.

more for *other* is to be avoided, for often it leads to ambiguity, as in 'Most people have heard of Shaftesbury, Southwood, Smith and Chadwick, but there were many more ardent reformers who are now forgotten' (an examination essay script).

more -er (e.g. *more brighter*). Now a solecism, though in Middle and Early Modern English it was common and permissible.

more often. See **oftener.**

more perfect, like *more inferior, more superior, more unique, more universal*, is an absurdity. See COMPARATIVES, FALSE; and TAUTOLOGY.

Mormons is the popular name of the members of the *Church of Jesus Christ of Latter-day Saints*; cf. **Quaker**, the popular name of the members of the Society of Friends. In official and formal contexts, the longer names should, in mere respect and decency, be used.

moron is properly 'one of the highest class of feeble-minded; an adult having an intelligence comparable to that of a normal average child between eight and twelve years of age'; hence, as a colloquialism, 'a stupid person; a fool' (*OED*).

Morpheus, in the arms of, is commonly used to mean 'asleep', whereas Morpheus was god of dreams (maker of changing shapes); the god of sleep was Hypnos. Not only, therefore, is the phrase an intolerably overworked cliché: it is also an inaccurate one.

mortal, whether 'human' ('mere mortal man') or 'death-causing', is an uncomparable adjective. See the list at COMPARATIVES, FALSE. As meaning 'wearisome', it is a colloquialism.

mortar. See **cement.**

Moslem. See **Muslim.**

most is pleonastic before superlative of adjectives and adverbs. Shakespeare's 'This was the most unkindest cut of all', effective in its emphasis, affords no excuse.

most should not be used of comparison between two; 'Of those two men, Jack

is the most intelligent' should be '...
more ...'.

most and **mostly**. See **mostly**.

most and **very**. 'All those stories were
most interesting' is ambiguous. *Most* can
properly (though rather formally) mean
'very', as well as meaning 'more than all the
others'. 'A most interesting story' would
clearly be 'very' interesting, but without
the indefinite article one is in trouble.

most all for *almost all* is an American colloquialism.

most part is incorrect for *greater* (or *greatest) part* or *main part* except in the phrase
for the most part (whence springs the error).
'It was rough going, and more than once
Philip blessed the broad pair of bucolic
shoulders which were doing the most part
of the work' (Laurence Meynell, *The Door
in the Wall*). There are several alternatives,
all to be preferred: 'doing most of the
work', ' – the biggest share of the work',
' – the larger part of the work'.

mostly is 'in the main: for the most part',
as in 'A man whose mind has been mostly
fallow ground will not easily take to the
mental plough and hoe' (H. Black). Do
not misuse it for *most*, as it is misused in
'The people mostly in need of assistance
do not ask for it' (*OED*).

mother-in-laws is incorrect for *mothers-
in-law*. See **daughters-in-law**.

motif is not a synonym of *motive*. It has
four specific uses:
  i. In painting, sculpture, architecture,
decoration, etc., it is a constituent feature
of a composition or a distinct part of a
design, hence a particular type of subject,
hence the principal feature or the predominant idea of a work; as in 'The *motif*
is simple', 'That painter's favourite *motif* is
cherubs.'
  ii. Hence, in a novel, a biography, etc.,
a type of incident, a dominant idea, the
predominant idea or theme.
  iii. In dress-making, an ornament (e.g.
of lace or braid) sewn on to a dress.

  iv. In Psychology. But here it is obsolescent.
  v. In Music, be careful! (*Leitmotiv* or *subject* or *figure* is safer.)
  Originally an adoption from French, it
should now be written in roman characters. *Motiv*, a German term, has not been
Anglicized, except in *leitmotiv* (a technical
word) (based on *OED*).

motion pictures is a formal word for
films, though one might work either 'in
films' or 'in the motion picture industry'.
In Britain one goes to the *cinema* or to the
pictures to see a picture or a film, in
America to a *theater* or (colloquially) to the
movies or a *movie-house* to see a *movie*.

motivate, motivation belong to psychiatry and educational psychology: why
not leave them there? See VOGUE WORDS.

motorcade. See **cavalcade**.

moustache. See **whiskers**.

movies. See **motion pictures**.

mowed and **mown** as part participles.
Usage prefers 'He has mowed the grass',
'The grass was mowed yesterday', but
'Mown grass smells sweet', 'A mown field
looks bare.' As a true participle, *mown* is
archaic.

Mr. – Write *Mr* in Britain, *Mr.* in
America.

Mrs, not *Mrs.*, is the form preferred in
Britain, but *Mrs.* in America.

Ms, like *Mr* and *Mrs*, takes a full stop in
American usage. It is pronounced 'miz'. It
usefully indicates a woman's sex while
concealing her (perhaps unknown) mari-
tal status. Unhappily, its use also makes a
positive statement of feminism, which
may or may not be welcome to the
woman concerned. One should therefore
try to ascertain the woman's preference
and use *Ms* with caution, particularly in
correspondence with older women who
grew up before this locution was heard of.

MS for manuscript has plural *MSS*. No full
stop.

much and **many.** Do not use the former where the latter is idiomatic as in 'As much as twenty members have resigned'; *many* is the word for separables, for units, for entities. Weseen cites the absurd *much clothes* for *many clothes* – or *much clothing*.

much and **muchly.** Avoid the archaic *muchly* unless you are sure that as a jocularity it is inoffensive.

much and **very.** With ordinary (i.e. nonparticipial) adjectives and with adverbs, use *very*: not 'much unkind' but 'very unkind'; not 'much soon' but 'very soon'. With participial adjectives, *much* is correct, as in 'much admired' or 'much exaggerated', except with those which have come to be regarded as ordinary adjectives: 'very tired'; 'very pleased'; 'very worried'; *much obliged* is a set phrase. Note, however, that one says 'much too soon', 'much sooner', 'much worse', 'much better', 'much the more praiseworthy', 'much the largest'.

much less (or **still less**) is sometimes illogically used through lack of clear thinking, by writers usually competent; e.g. 'The task of keeping the fire under, much less of putting it out, was beyond the resources of the fire-engines' (G. B. Besant, *London Bridge*). Obviously, if 'the task of keeping the fire under' was difficult, that of extinguishing it was *much more so*.

much the same is a common but clumsy way of saying 'about the same'. Very weak in literary use, as e.g. in Alfred Austin's poem on the illness of Edward VII:

Across the wire the electric message came,
He is no better, he is much the same.

Muhammad is now the preferred spelling for the name of the founder of Islam. Its adherents are *Muslims*, rather than Muhammadans.

multifarious; multiform; multiple. See **manifold.**

multiplicity of, a, is nauseatingly verbose for *many* or *very many*.

München for *Munich*. See **Bruxelles ...**

murder; manslaughter; homicide. These three terms are often confused. Under British Law *murder* is planned, intentional killing; *manslaughter* is unplanned, though possibly intentional killing; *homicide* is the generic term for all killing of one person by another. More precisely:

Murder is 'the unlawful killing of a human being with malice aforethought; often more implicitly *wilful murder*'. In the USA there are two kinds of murder: *murder in the second degree*, where there are mitigating circumstances; *murder in the first degree*, where there are no such circumstances.

Manslaughter (in Scotland: *culpable homicide*) is 'committed when one person causes the death of another either intentionally in the heat of passion under certain kinds of provocation, or unintentionally by culpable negligence or as a consequence of some unlawful act' (*OED*).

Homicide, which includes both *murder* and *manslaughter*, occurs chiefly in: *culpable homicide*, which is *manslaughter*; *excusable homicide*, which is killing in self-defence or by accident or misadventure; *justifiable homicide*, which is a killing in the performance of certain legal duties (e.g. the hangman's), by unavoidable necessity, or to prevent the commission of an atrocious crime (*Webster's*).

[In the USA the *Homicide Squad* is that section of the detective force which deals with homicide.]

music centre. See **gramophone.**

musical is noun or adjective; **musicale** is noun. *Musicale* has taken on in America; not in Britain, where *musical evening, musical party, musical reunion*, etc., are preferred. But a musical film or comedy is a *musical* in both Britain and America.

Muslim, rather than *Moslem*, is now the preferred spelling for a follower of Islam. See **Muhammad.**

must and **may.** See NEGATION, Section *A*, last five paragraphs.

mustache. See **whiskers.**

mutual = 'reciprocal', as in 'mutual fear', 'mutual friendship' – this being the safest sense in which to use it; 'respective' as in 'the difference in their mutual years' – correct but obsolescent, so avoid it!; and 'pertaining to both parties; common; in common', since *c.* 1900 regarded as incorrect when applied to things, actions, sentiments, as in 'our mutual front door', (of a collaboration) 'their mutual work', 'your mutual opinion' – certainly a usage to be avoided; and in the same general sense, but applied to 'a personal designation expressive of a relation' – an application now regarded as incorrect except in *mutual friend(s)* and *mutual acquaintance(s)*, where the strictly correct *common* is ambiguous (still, one can always say *friends* – or *acquaintances* – *in common*), such collocations as *mutual father, mutual brother* now sounding very odd (*OED*).

myself, yourself, herself, himself, itself, ourselves, yourselves, themselves. There is a tendency to employ these pronouns where the simple *I* (or *me*), *you, she* (or *her*), *he* (or *him*), *it, we* (or *us*), *you, they* (or *them*) are sufficient. The *self* forms are either reflexives, as in 'I hurt *myself*', or emphatic additions, as in 'He *himself* did not know' (avoid the ambiguity of 'He did not know *himself*'). Here are three misuses:

'You and myself will arrange this
    between us.'
'Herself and himself will soon be getting
    married.'
'He sent the inquiry to yourself.'

See also **oneself.**

mystic, as an adjective, is more rhetorical and more formal than *mystical*, where the two forms are synonymous: cf. 'the mystical relation of man and God' and 'the mystic union of the soul with Christ'.

N

naif, naïf; naive, naïve. *Naif* is inexcusable; in English, *naïf* is unnecessary, being the masculine of Fr. *naïf, naïve,* 'artless'. *OED* implies its recommendation of *naïve* or *naive* written in roman and pronounced as a dissyllabic.

name (v.). See **denominate.**

name of, of (or **by**) **the.** See **by the name of.**

name ... who (or **that**). It is permissible to say, 'The editor telephoned to a big name from whom he wanted an article', although the present writer does not recommend such looseness. But the following use of *name* passes the bounds of decency: 'Picking up his telephone, he called for a certain number ... Getting it, he asked for a certain name, who, in less than a minute, was upon the phone to him' (John G. Brandon).

nary, 'not a; not one; no; neither', is a colloquialism or dialectalism.

nasty. Weseen is wrong in condemning this word as a colloquialism in the senses 'unpleasant, disagreeable' (as in 'a nasty day'), 'mean' ('a nasty trick'), and 'ill-natured, ill-tempered' ('to turn nasty'): they are faultless Standard English: admittedly not literary, they are familiar Standard. [*Webster's* and Krapp agree with Weseen. This use of *nasty* is much more common in Britain than in the USA.]

nationalize; naturalize. The former is to bring under state ownership; the latter to admit (an immigrant) to citizenship, to introduce (a plant or animal) into a region, or to adopt (a foreign word or custom). An older use of *nationalize* for *naturalize* is confusing, and best avoided.

native(s). There is something not only inexact but offensive in the general use of this word for the dark-skinned inhabitants of Africa, India, etc., as though it applied exclusively to them and implied an inferiority of race. The inhabitants born in England or any other country are the 'natives' of that country.

naturalize. See **nationalize.**

nature, like *condition* and *character* and *description*, is used in wordy phrases: and it should be avoided in e.g. 'The road was of such a nature that the man fractured his spinal cord', which apparently means 'The road was so bad that the man broke his neck.' See ABSTRACT NOUNS.

naught. See **nought and naught.**

naval (adj.); **navel** (n.); but a *navel* orange.

near and **near to.** *Near* and *near to* can be used of literal position, as in 'We lived quite near them', or, less usually, '... near to them'; *near to* is more general than *near* in transferred or derivative senses – sometimes, indeed, *near* would be wrong in such instances. As Dr C. T. Onions remarks in *An Advanced English Syntax*, 'Notice that the different senses of *near* take different constructions, e.g. "The Prince of Wales stood *near* (or *near to*) [i.e. close *to*] *the* throne" and "The German Emperor [was] *near to the throne* of Great Britain" (i.e. in respect of succession). In the second sentence "near the throne" would be undesirable, as being ambiguous and suggesting the wrong meaning'; a neat exemplification of the difference.

Near East, the, no longer exists. See **Middle East.**

nearly is an adverb, not a preposition. It is wrongly used in 'She came nearly falling' (for '... near to falling' or colloquially '... near falling').

neath is on the one hand dialectal, on the other poetic, for *beneath*.

necessaries and **necessities.** The former = 'essentials; requisites', as in 'A father provides his children with necessaries' and 'Food, sleep, and shelter are necessaries of life.' In this sense, *necessities* is obsolete –

or, at the least, obsolescent. The predominant current sense of *necessities* is 'pressing needs or wants; a situation of difficulty or of hardship', as in 'The necessities of every newly colonized country' and 'We must aim at a habit of gratitude, which has no relation to present necessities' (J. B. Mozley).

The adjective *necessitous* = 'living or placed in poverty' or 'characterized by poverty' (*OED*).

necessity is a misuse when made to synonymize (an) *essential*. 'Without the necessities of a good internal government, liberty is not likely to last long' (examination script, March 1938), meaning 'the needful elements' or 'essentials'.

need. See **want and need.**

NEGATION.

'And we none of us never said nowt'
(Yorkshire song, broadcast on
9 Dec. 1937)

The subject of negation may be divided into three sections: *A, THE MEANING OF NEGATION; B, NEGATION IN SYNTAX; NEGATIVE CONJUNCTIONS (OR CONNECTIVES);* and *C,* esp. the *DOUBLE NEGATIVE.*

A. THE MEANING OF NEGATION

'A linguistic negative', writes Professor Otto Jespersen in *Negation*[*], Copenhagen, 1917, 'generally changes a term into what logicians call the contradictory term (A and not-A) comprising everything in existence and is thus very different from a negative in the mathematical sense, where – 4 means a point as much below 0 as 4 (or + 4) is above 0.' There are, however, 'instances in which a negative changes a term into the "contrary term", as when *he begins not to sing* (for *he begins not-to-sing*) comes to mean "he ceases singing".'

---

[*]Perhaps the most acute and subtle, yet gloriously practical and serviceable, of all Jespersen's works; it is only his *The Philosophy of Grammar* which makes me write 'perhaps'.

'If we say, according to the general rule, that "not four" means "different from four", this should be taken with a general qualification, for in practice it generally means, not whatever is above or below 4 ..., but only what is below 4, thus less than 4, something between 4 and 0, just as "not everything" means something between everything and nothing (and as "not good" means "inferior", but does not comprise "excellent").' So, too, in 'He does not write three books in a decade', 'The mountain is not 10,000 feet high', 'He does not go to Paris once in three years', 'His income is not £300 a year.' When 'not + a numeral is exceptionally to be taken as "more than", the numeral has to be strongly stressed [in conversation], and [in writing] generally to be followed by a more exact indication', as in 'The mountain is not 10,000 feet high, but 11,000', 'His income is not £300 a year, but £400', 'Not once, but two or three times' (Defoe), and 'Not one invention, but fifty – from a corkscrew to a machine-gun' (W. J. Locke), 'He would bend to kiss her, not once, not once only' (E. F. Benson). 'But *not once or twice* always means "several times",' as in Tennyson, 'Not once or twice in our rough island-story The path of duty was the way to glory.'

*The import of 'a negative quantitative indication' often depends 'on what is expected, or [on] what is the direction of thought' – the trend of the conversation, the general sense of the subject-matter. Whereas 'the two sentences "he spends £200 a year" and "he lives on £200 a year" are practically synonymous, everything is changed if we add *not*: "he doesn't spend £200 a year" means [that he spends less than that sum]; "he doesn't live on £200 a year" means [that he spends more than £200 a year]; because in the former case we expect an indication of a maxi-

mum, and in the latter of a minimum. – Or, perhaps the explanation is rather this, that in the former sentence it does not matter whether we negative the nexus[†] or the numeral (he does-not-spend £200 he spends not-£200), but in the latter it changes the whole meaning, for "he does-not-live on £200" states' – ? rather 'connotes' – 'the impossibility of living on so little, and "he lives on not-£200 a year" (which is rendered more idiomatic if we add an adverb: "on not quite £200 a year") states the possibility of living on less than £200.

'... Compare also: *He is not content with £200 a year* and *he is content with not £200 a year.*

'Where a numeral is not used as a point in an ascending scale, its negative is really contradictory; "the train doesn't start at seven" says nothing about the actual time of starting, which may be either before or after seven. But "he won't be here at seven" implies "we can't expect him till after seven", because an arrival before 7 o'clock would naturally imply his being here also at that hour.'

Compare the point raised by Jespersen in the following: 'Not above 30 means either 30 or less than 30. But *less than* 30 may in English be negatived in two ways: *not less than* 30 means either 30 or more than 30, and *no less than* 30 means exactly 30, implying surprise or wonder at the high number.'

'He has not less than ten children' – I am not certain of the number, but it is at least ten. 'He has no less than ten children' – he has ten, and isn't that a large

---

*Cf. **GRAMMAR AND LOGIC**, par. 5 of the article proper.

†*Nexus*: 'The negative notion may belong logically either to one definite idea' – Special Negation – 'or to the combination of two ideas' – Nexal Negation, the notional combination being the Nexus. In 'never', 'unhappy', 'impossible', 'disorder' 'non-belligerent' – as also in 'not happy' and 'no longer' – we have special negation; in 'He does *not* come' the combination of two positive ideas, *he* and *coming*, and in 'He doesn't come today', the combination of *he* and *coming today*, are negatived, both sentences affording examples of negatived nexus.

family? Cf. 'He has not more than ten books' and 'He has no more than ten books.'

And here is an interesting case: *a little* is positive, *little* a virtual negative (cf. *absent* as contrasted with *present*). Jespersen equates these two terms with *a few* and *few* and arranges them thus:

1. *much*: much money	*many*: many people	*very*: very careless
2. *a little*: a little money	*a few*: a few people	*a little*: (He's) a little careless
3. *little*: little money	*few*: few people	*little*: little [idiomatically: slightly] careless.

If we negative these, we find that (1) becomes (3): *not much (money)* becomes *little (money)*; *not many (people)* becomes *few (people)*; *not very (careless)* becomes *little*, idiomatically *slightly (careless)*. But by negativing (2) we arrive at something that is either almost synonymous with (1) or standing between (1) and (2): *not a little (money)* becomes, or almost becomes, *much (money)*; *not a few (people)* roughly = *many (people)*; *not a little (careless)* is approximately equivalent to *very (careless)*.

Now, if we lengthen the series given above (*much – a little – little*) in both directions, we get on the one hand *all (everything)*, on the other hand *nothing*. These are contrary terms, even in a higher degree than *good* and *bad* are, as both are absolute. Whatever comes in between them (thus all the three quantities mentioned above) is comprised in the term *something*, and we may now arrange these terms in this way, denoting by *A* and *C* the two absolutes, and by *B* the intermediate:

A	B	C
all [noun], *everything*	*something*	*nothing*
and correspondingly:		
all [plural] ⎫	*some*	⎧ *none*
everybody (everyone) ⎭	*somebody (someone)*	⎩ *nobody (no one)*
all girls	*some girls (a girl)*	*no girls (no girl)*
all the money	*some money*	*no money*
So too with the adverbs:		
always	*sometimes*	*never*
everywhere	*somewhere*	*nowhere*

If we negative the *A* terms we get *B* terms; or, if you prefer it, *A* negatived = *B*; thus:

not all, not everybody	= *something*
not all, not everybody	= *some*
not all girls	= *some girls*
not all the money	= *some (of the) money*
not always	= *sometimes*
not everywhere	= *somewhere*

In other words, when we negative an *A* term, word-group or phrase, we negative the *absolute* element in that *A* term or phrase. 'Thus always when the negative precedes the absolute word [etc.] of the *A*-class', as in 'We are not cotton-spinners all,

But some love England and her honour yet' (Tennyson); 'I do not regard every politician as a self-seeker'; 'Not all Hugh's letters were concerned with these technicalities' (H. G. Wells).

That is a sensible as well as a logical positioning of the adverb *not*, but in *all*-sentences, *all* is frequently placed first for emphasis, and the negative is attracted to the verb in accordance with the prevailing tendency seen in 'He does not come today but tomorrow', which is so much more general than the more logical 'He comes not today but tomorrow.' 'All that glisters is not gold' is more usual than 'Not all that glisters is of gold', despite the fact that the latter is clear, the former ambiguous – but idiomatic. (Not that the latter is *unid-iomatic*.) In 'Thank Heaven, all scholars are not like this' (Richardson) the context removes all ambiguity, precisely as, in conversation, emphasis would make the statement clear. In 'For each man kills the thing he loves, Yet each man does not die' (Wilde) the first *each* = *every*, but *each man does not die* does not mean that every man dies (for a given reason). 'All men aren't fools' should, logically, mean 'All men are sensible'; idiomatically it means, 'Some men aren't fools' or 'Not all men are fools.'

'On the other hand', continues Jespersen, 'when a word of the *A*-class (*all*, etc.) is placed in a sentence with a special negative (or [a virtual or] an implied negative), the result is the same as if we had the corresponding *C*-word and a positive word; ... the assertion is absolute':

All this is unnecessary	= none of this is necessary*
Everybody was unkind	= nobody was kind
He was always unkind	= he was never kind
Everybody fails	= nobody succeeds
He forgets everything	= he remembers nothing.

If we examine what happens when a word of the *C*-class is negatived, we get the *not for nothing* = 'not in vain' or even 'to good purpose', as in Shakespeare's 'It was not for nothing that my nose fell a bleeding on Black Monday last' and in Professor Sir Walter Raleigh's 'He was not the eldest son of his father for nothing.' The result falls into class *B*: 'He was his son for something.' The same applies to 'It's not good for a man to have no gods.'

'Inversely if we begin with the word belonging to class *C* and place the negative adverb after it', we get an *A* result, as in Latin *nihil non videt* = *omnia videt*. Such sentences do not exist in English – not in workaday English, anyway; but precisely 'the same result is obtained when one of these words is followed by a word with a

*Jespersen's *nothing is necessary* is misleading, so I have taken the liberty of changing it.

negative prefix or [as in *fail*] with implied negative meaning':

Nothing is unnecessary	= everything is necessary
Nobody was unkind	= everybody was kind
He was never unkind	= he was always kind
Nobody fails	= everybody succeeds
He forgets nothing	= he remembers everything.

(It may be remarked that the second and third equations imply a gracious opinion of humanity.)

'When the negative is a separate word, the result is the same: but ... such sentences are generally avoided because they are not always clear or readily understood'; thus Thackeray's 'Not a clerk in that house did not tremble before her' is an obscure and verbose way of saying 'Every clerk (or all the clerks) in that house trembled before her.' 'There is, however, no difficulty if the two negatives are placed in separate clauses, as in "There was no one present that did not weep" (= everybody wept).'

Moreover, if we negative a *B* term (*something*, *somebody*), we get a *C* term: 'I met somebody' becomes 'I met nobody'; more generally, however, we use the *not* form: 'I did not meet anybody.' 'Obviously, obviously!' murmurs some intelligent person. Quite! Yet we find the intelligent Mr Cameron McCabe writing 'Maria looked back with a dead expression on her face – pale, indifferent, non-committal. She was not trying to hide something [properly, 'She was not trying to hide anything']: nothing she might have tried to hide was left in her.'

In the preceding paragraphs we have been dealing with the tripartite (threefold) arrangement of *A: all – B: some – C: none*. There is another tripartition that concerns both logicians and students of grammar in particular and of language in general:

> *A:* necessity
> *B:* possibility
> *C:* impossibility.

'If closely inspected, these categories', as is remarked by Professor Jespersen, who is nobody's dupe, 'are found to be nothing else but special instances of our three categories above, for necessity really means' – and fundamentally connotes – 'that *all* possibilities are comprised.' *Not necessary* = *possible*, or perhaps rather *not necessary* involves *possible*; *not impossible* = *possible*; *it is impossible not to admit* (that Shakespeare was a good writer) certainly implies that it is *necessary* to admit it.

The verbal correspondences, equivalences, counterparts, expressions of these three categories (*A:* necessity – *B:* possibility – *C:* impossibility) are:

A: must (or *need*)

B: can (or, *may*)

C: cannot (or, *be unable to*).

Their inter-relationship is evident in such instances as these:

He *must* run	= he *cannot* but run (or, cannot help running)
No one *can* deny	= everyone *must* admit
Nobody *need* be present	= everybody *may* be absent
He *cannot* succeed	= he *must* fail
He *cannot* forget	= he *must* remember.

If to these three categories (necessity, possibility, impossibility) we add an element of desire (or will) as it affects another person, we get the instructive tripartition:

A: command

B: permission

C: prohibition.

'But these three categories are not neatly separated in actual language, at any rate not in the forms of the verb, for the imperative is usually the only form available for *A* [command] and *B* [permission]. Thus *take that!* may have [either] of two distinct meanings, (*A*) a command: "You must take that", (*B*) a permission: "You may take that", with some intermediate shades of meaning (request, entreaty, prayer). Now a prohibition (*C*) means at the same time (1) a positive command to not (take that), and (2) the negative of a permission: "You are not allowed to (take that)"; hence the possibility of using a negative as a prohibitive:

> *Don't take that!*
> *Don't you stir!'*

This possibility helps us to understand certain peculiarities in the use of *must* and *may*. In *you must* (positive command) *not take* (negative) *that*, 'we have the usual tendency to attract the negation to the auxiliary ..., and thus we get: *you mustn't take that*, which ... has become the ordinary prohibitive auxiliary'. But in *you may not* (negative) *take* (positive) *that*, properly the negative of a permission, 'we have the competition with the usual combination of (positive) *may* + negative infinitive, as in "He may not be rich, but he is a gentleman"; this makes people shrink from *may not* in a prohibition, the more so as *may* is felt to be weaker and more polite than ... *must*. The result is that to the positive "we may walk on the grass" corresponds a negative "we mustn't walk on the grass" ... The old *may not* in prohibitions ... is now comparatively rare, except in questions implying a positive answer (*mayn't I* = "I suppose I may") and in close connexion with a positive *may*, thus especially in answers', as in ' "Perhaps I may kiss your hand?" – "No, you may not." ' – ' "May I tell you?" "No, you may not." '

'Positive *may* and negative *must not* are frequently found together:

'Ruskin ..., Your labour only may be sold; your soul must not.

'Stevenson ..., Prose may be rhythmical ..., but it must not be metrical.

'Shaw ..., You may call me Dolly if you like; but you mustn't call me child. ...

'*May* is thus used even in tag questions after *must not*: [Jane] Austen ..., "I must not tell, may I, Elinor?"

'Dickens ..., "You mustn't marry more than one person at a time, may you?" "Certainly not." "But if you marry a person, and the person dies, why then you may marry another person, mayn't you?" "You *may*, if you choose."

'On the other hand, *must* begins to be used in tag questions, though it is not possible to ask *Must I?* instead of *May I?* Thus: George Eliot ..., "I must not go any further, must I?" '

But this tendency is to be strongly resisted: any further break-down in the differentiation of *may* and *must* can result only in the blunting of the instrument and the slurring of the effect.

Two further points concerning *may* here present themselves: and Jespersen, as always, is lucid and helpful. *May* + a negative infinitive denotes possibility (*you may not know* = 'it is possible that you do not know'); usually, the *not* is attracted to the verb, in accordance with the general tendency of *not* to slip from its logical to what seems to be its idiomatic position. Shaw, 'Newcomers whom they may not think quite good enough for them'; A. Hope, 'I may not be an earl, but I have a perfect right to be useful'; W. J. Locke, 'What may be permissible to a scrubby little artist in Paris mayn't be permitted to one who ought to know better.' Then there is the semantic change caused by a negative. To the positive *may*, (past) *might*, there 'corresponds a negative *cannot, could not* (or *may not, might not*)'; Kingsley, 'His dialectic, though it *might* silence her, *could not* convince her'; George A. Birmingham, 'He *might* be a Turk. – No, he couldn't'; 'This cannot do harm and *may* do good.'

Section *B* falls into two parts: – *i. NEGATION IN SYNTAX; ii. NEGATIVE CONJUNCTIONS (OR CONNECTIVES).*

B.i. NEGATION IN SYNTAX

Obviously, much of the practice, as opposed to the theory, of negation has been dealt with or touched on in the preceding section; and much of it is being deferred to *B.ii.* (Negative Connectives). Nevertheless, a few general remarks may usefully be made at this point. The following short account is taken from George O. Curme's *Syntax*, 1931.

In general, the negative is a sentence adverb and, like the other sentence adverbs, it is, as a rule, stressed weakly and

placed between subject and predicate, as in 'I never do such things.' If there is an auxiliary in the sentence, the negative *not* (or *n't*), as is the way of sentence adverbs, 'stands before the stressed verbal form: "He has*n't* come yet." "He does*n't* do such things." "He *can't* do such things." The perfect infinitive without *to* is usually considered as a unit, so that the negative stands before the unaccented tense auxiliary of the infinitive: "He can *scarcely have arrived* by this time" [*scarcely* being a virtual negative] ... "He had spoken late, but he need *not have spoken* at all."

'In abridged infinitival or participial clauses the subject is usually understood, so that the negative stands before the verbal form: "He promises *not to do it again*", or now sometimes with split infinitive ..., since there is a tendency here to place the sentence adverb immediately before the stressed verb, as in the full clause: ... "There can be nothing between you and me, dear mother, that we can *not talk* about." ... In the compound form of the infinitive the negative usually stands before *to*, or now sometimes in accordance with the new drift, after the auxiliary, as in the full clause: "He claims *not* (or *never*) *to have seen her before*", or sometimes *to have not* (or *never*) *seen her before*, as in "He claims *that* he has not (or *never*) seen her before." '

In 'abridged participial clauses', as Curme designates them, *not* stands before the participle, whether simple ('*Not knowing the subject*, I failed in the examination'), or compound ('*Not having met him*, I failed to recognize him from his photographs in the newspapers'). *Never* is more amenable: '*Having never met him*, I ...' or, more emphatically but less usually, '*Never having met him*, I ...', as in the fuller sentences: '*As I had never met him*, I ...', or, less generally, '*As I never had met him*, I ...'.

When a statement as a whole is stressed the negative (like other sentence adverbs) is stressed: 'I *never* did it'; 'I have *not* done it.' When the *not* merges with the auxiliary, the auxiliary receives the stress, as in 'I *didn't* do it', 'I just *can't* do it!'

Usually the negative constitutes a sentence adverb and stands before the verbal form, but sometimes the negative is felt as 'a distinguishing adverb, i.e. as belonging to some particular word, phrase, or clause which is prominent in the sentence as a whole, and is then placed immediately before this word, phrase, or clause: *"He did it, not I." "He hit me, not him." '*

In 'I hope *not*' as an answer to 'You will shortly be dismissed' or as a comment on 'He thinks that soon he will die', and 'I thought *not*' as a comment on 'He didn't get what he expected', *not* 'represents all that is left of a subordinate clause, such as "that is *not* so". It does not strictly qualify "hope", "thought"' (Onions). Logically the construction is 'I hope that ... *not*', 'I thought that ... *not*', 'I feared that ... *not*', not 'I do not hope that', 'I did not think that', 'I did not fear that'. Here, as in so many English constructions, Latin influence (*non spero* ..., *non arbitrabor*, etc., etc.) has perhaps been at work.

B.ii. NEGATIVE CONJUNCTIONS (OR CONNECTIVES)

In his book *Negation*, Jespersen sets forth seven types of negative connection of sentences.

(1) '*Nor* seeks, *nor* finds he mortal blisses', where *nor* ... *nor* represents a shortening of 13th- to 15th-century *nother* ... *nother* (neither ... nor): archaic and/or poetical.

(2) 'I could *neither* run with speed, *nor* climb trees' (Swift); '*Neither* he nor his sister has come'; 'He neither loves nor hates her'; 'Neither are we ready, nor are you willing': the usual formula; the norm.

Where there are more than two alternatives, it is not uncommon to omit the connective with the middle terms (or one of them): thus Shakespeare, *Measure for Measure*, 'Thou hast neither heat, affection, limb, nor beauty.' *Julius Caesar*, 'I have neither writ nor words, nor worth, Action nor utterance, nor the power of speech.'

The conjunction may even be omitted poetically before all except the first alternative: Shakespeare, *Lear*, 'Nor rain, wind, thunder, fire are my daughters.'

(3) The *neither* ... *or* type, which is wrong in 'Having *neither* weapons *or* clothes' or 'He neither knew that fellow or wished to know him', is, in short, usually wrong; but it is correct in '*Neither* she nor your brother *or* sister suspected a word of the matter' (Jane Austen), for the principal dissociation (*neither* ... *nor*) is that between 'she' on the one hand, 'either your brother or your sister' on the other hand, and 'brother or sister' is felt as one idea, as indeed it is, being the second of the two parties concerned in the statement. Another good example of the correct use of *neither* ... *nor* ... *or* is afforded by the sentence, 'He wants neither [*a*] to solve any questions nor [*b*] to set them or [*b*¹] to evoke them in his readers' minds' (Cameron McCabe).

Compare the following sentences, where the negative word, be it adverb (*never, not*) or pronoun (*nobody*), covers everything: 'Faustus vows *never* to look to heaven, *Never* to name God, *or* to pray to him' (Marlowe); Jane Austen, 'She knew not what to think, *or* how to account for it' where, of course, 'knew not' = 'was ignorant'; 'He lived alone, and *never* saw her, *or* inquired after her' (Dickens); 'Nobody was singing or shouting' (H. G. Wells).

(4) 'They threatened that the cage *nor* irons should serve their turn' (Bunyan); 'She *nor* her daughters were ...' (J. Austen); 'My father, *nor* his father before him, ever saw it otherwise' – these are correct examples of a now archaic type, wrongly used in 'She struggled against this for an instant or two (maid *nor anybody* assisting)', perpetrated by Carlyle. The *nor* casts backward as well as forward.

(5) 'Never attaching herself much to us, *neither* us to her' (Ruskin); 'The royal Dane does not haunt his own mother – *neither* does Arthur, King John; *neither* Norfolk, King Richard II; *nor* Tybalt, Romeo' (Ruskin); 'Nothing makes us think ... *Nor*, I believe, are the facts ever so presented ... *Nor*, lastly, do we receive the impression ...' (Bradley); 'She said nothing, neither did I' (W. J. Locke). But

neither constitutes a slight variation: 'He did not for a moment underestimate the danger; but *neither* did he exaggerate its importance' (J. MacCarthy).

(6) 'I know nothing, *nor* you *neither*' is the double-negative form, now incorrect, of 'I know nothing: *nor* you *either*' (or, more neatly, 'I know nothing; nor do you').

(7) Analogous is 'Blush not ... *and* do not laugh *neither*' (Scott); 'I had no companions to quarrel with, neither' (Ruskin). This type is now frowned on: rightly, for it is misleading, clumsy, tautological.

An instructive example of the necessity for clear thinking in the use of negative connectives is afforded by this quotation from *A Ship of the Line*, by that excellent novelist, C. S. Forester: 'Close overside he saw a woman ... blubbering unashamed. ... It was *no more* than an even chance that she would *never* see her man again', where *never* should be *ever*, the author having been misled by *no*.

Summing up, we may say that *neither* calls for *nor*, as *either* calls for *or*; if *neither* appears in the second half, it is preceded not by *neither* but by *no* + noun and *not* (or *never*) + verb; *nor* unpreceded by *neither* properly = *and not*, but now improperly = *and no* (for examples, see **no ... nor**).

C. THE DOUBLE NEGATIVE

The most comprehensive, subtle, and informative treatment of the double negative – abstractly, a repeated (or even reiterated) negation – is that given by Professor Jespersen in *Negation*, 1917: but as it is designed rather for the professional grammarian and as it presupposes a considerable knowledge of comparative linguistics, I shall do no more than recommend it to the curious. The following account falls into two parts: (a) the double negative in its relation to logic and to good sense; (b) the double and the pleonastic negative in practice.

(a) *Logic and the Double Negative*

In his *Logic and Grammar*, SPE Tract No. xvi, 1924, Jespersen puts the case thus:

Both philosophers, especially logicians, and old-fashioned grammarians (back-to-

the-wallers; last-ditchers, die-hards) insist, with an absoluteness proper enough to cloudland metaphysics but improper to an empiric world, 'that two negatives make an affirmative, and that therefore those languages are illogical which use a double negative as a strengthened negative'. These intransigents generally refer to the mathematical law that $--1 = +1$ (i.e. 1); but a linguistic* negative is not equivalent to a mathematical negative. In actual as distinct from vacuum'd language, a combination of two negatives leads sometimes to a positive, sometimes to a negative.

'The first rule', says Jespersen, '... is that when two negatives are special negatives' – a negative applying to one idea only is a special negative, whereas a nexal negative applies to two ideas [section *A*, third par., footnote] – 'the meaning is always positive; ... [as in] "not uncommon", "not infrequent", "not without fear", etc. But it is important to observe that the double negative always modifies the idea, for "not uncommon" does not mean exactly the same thing as "common"; it is weaker; "this is not unknown to me" means "I am to some extent aware of it", etc. The psychological reason for this is that the *détour* through the two mutually destructive negatives weakens the mental energy of the listener and implies on the part of the speaker a certain hesitation which is absent from the blunt, outspoken *common* or *known*. "Not uncommon", therefore, cannot be classed exactly with the mathematical – (−1); the result is similar, though not identical.'

Now for the second rule: two nexal negatives may produce a negative result, as e.g. in the French *on ne le voit nulle part*, literally 'one not him sees no place' (one does not see him nowhere), but idiomatically 'one sees him nowhere' (or, in familiar English, 'you don't see him about at all').

'But wherever this cumulative negation is found, the negative elements are

---

*Cf. GRAMMAR AND LOGIC, par. 5.

attached not to the same word, but to different words, even though these belong to the same sentence, and under these circumstances ... we may say that though logically one negative suffices, two or three in the same sentence cannot be termed illogical; they are simply a redundancy, which may be superfluous from a stylistic point of view, just as any repetition [is] in a positive sentence (*every and any, always and on all occasions*), but is otherwise unobjectionable. There is no logical objection to combinations like these: "I shall never consent, not under any circumstances, not on any conditions, neither at home nor abroad"; it is true that here pauses, which in writing are marked by commas, separate the negatives, as if they belonged to so many different sentences [whereas] in "he never said nothing" and in similar phrases ..., the negatives belong to one and the same sentence. But it is [difficult*] to draw the [line] between what constitutes one and what constitutes two sentences. We see this in such resumptions as "he never sleeps, neither by night nor by day" and "he cannot sleep, not even after taking an opiate" [– two sentences in which the substitution of dashes for the commas would perhaps make the point clearer]; in such cases, with "neither – nor"† and "not even", all languages freely admit double negatives, though even here precisians object to them.'

The psychological reason for the use of a double negative in the majority of such sentences has been neatly posited by Jespersen, thus: 'Double negation in one and the same sentence generally arises under the influence of a strong feeling: the speaker wants to make absolutely sure that

the negative sense will be fully apprehended; therefore he attaches it not only to the verb, but also to any other part of the sentence that can be easily made negative. ... [Further,] it may be said that it requires greater mental energy to content oneself with one negative, which has to be remembered during the whole length of the utterance both by the speaker and [by] the hearer, than to repeat the negative idea whenever an occasion offers itself.

'... We have also what may be called paratactic negation, a negative being placed in a clause dependent on a verb of negative import like "deny", "forbid", "hinder", "doubt", as if either the corresponding positive verb had been used, or the clause had been an independent sentence; cf. "What hinders ... that you do not return to those habits?" (Lamb) ... Here, too, we have redundancy and overemphasis rather than irrationality or want of logic.

'Redundancy in the negatives should be judged in the same way as redundancies found in other departments of grammar. ... Languages differ greatly in their demands on explicitness ...; that, however, is a question of the economy of speech, but hardly one of logic.'

(b) *The Double and the Pleonastic Negative in Practice*

Practice, obviously, has been indicated and even stressed in the preceding subsection (from the fourth paragraph to the end); all that is necessary, now, is to state that 'I don't know nothing' is psychologically defensible but contrary to the present idiom of the educated, whereas, 'He can't sleep, not even after taking an opiate' is both psychologically justifiable and idiomatically justified; and to remark that 'What hinders ... that you do not return to those habits?' is perhaps based on the Latin *quominus* and *quin* and on that French *ne* which does not demand a succeeding *pas.*

But Dr George O. Curme's verdict on Double Negation and Pleonastic Expression with Negatives is so concise and pithy that to reproduce it here will probably be

---

*Jespersen wrote 'impossible': to me, 'impossible' seems rather too strong.

†A good example is this: 'He hated Jensen with the sound hatred of a jealous lover. He never hid either sentiment, neither his hate nor his jealousy' (C. McCabe), for the insertion of 'he hid' before 'neither his hate nor his jealousy' renders the sentence both logical and idiomatic.

a meritorious action. 'In older literary English, as in current popular speech, two or three negatives were felt as stronger than a single negative, on the same principle that we drive in two or three nails instead of one, feeling that they hold better than one: "I *can't* see *no* wit in her" (Lamb in a letter to Coleridge in 1797). "I *don't* know *nothing* about it" (current popular speech). Under Latin influence' – e.g. *non nihil vidi*, I did see something – 'we have come to feel that two negatives make an affirmative statement, although we still in an answer say *no, no,* to strengthen our negative reply. Even in the literary language, however, there is a survival of older usage after verbs like *doubt, wonder,* which are affirmative in form but negative in meaning. We sometimes still use the negative *but* after these words when preceded by a negative, not feeling that the two negatives make the statement affirmative without the help of *but*, so that *but* is really pleonastic: "I do not doubt *but that* (now usually simple *that*) you are surprised." "I wouldn't doubt *but* Hannah's upstairs all the while, splitting her sides" (St John Ervine, *John Ferguson*, Act II) ... Not feeling that *but* (= *only*) is a negative, we sometimes put a *not* before it, so that here *not* is pleonastic: "It will *not* take but a few minutes to dispose of it" (Mr Blanton, of Texas, in the House, 12 Aug. 1919). On the other hand, not feeling that *help* is negative with the force of *avoid*, we often say, "I won't do any more *than I can* (instead of the correct *can't*) help", after the analogy of *than I have to* or *than I must.*'

negative, the answer is or **was in the.** See **answer was ...**

neglect is *negligence* exemplified. When they are approximate equivalents ('Guilty of negligence', 'guilty of neglect'), *neglect* is the stronger word.

negligence should be used for *indifference* only in the senses 'careless indifference concerning one's appearance' and 'unaffected style'; not for *callousness*, as in

'Feigned negligence and real anxiety as it were cancelling each other out in his voice and rendering it quite toneless' (Nicholas Blake, *There's Trouble Brewing*).

negligent; negligible. Respectively 'careless' and 'not worth care (or attention)'. Cf. the entry at **intelligent.**

Negro. See **black.**

neighbourhood of, in the. 'The story ... on the making of which Hollywood is said to have lavished in the neighbourhood of £300,000' (*Sphere*). Here the expression is a bad and wholly unnecessary substitute for 'about' or 'nearly'.

neither followed by a plural verb: See **either.** But an excellent example of *neither ... are* for *neither ... is* is furnished by the following:

DESPATCH FROM THE BRITISH MINISTER AT PEKING TO THE CHINESE FOREIGN OFFICE
As printed in White Paper *China*, No. 2 (1898)
Sir C. MacDonald to the Tsung-li Yamen
Peking, February 9, 1898

MM. Les Ministres.
    Your Highnesses and your Excellencies have more than once intimated to me that the Chinese Government were aware of the great importance that has always been attached by Great Britain to the retention in Chinese possession of the Yang-tze region, now entirely hers, as providing security for the free course and development of trade.
    [Strictly speaking, this is not grammar. 'China' has not been mentioned, only 'Chinese possession' and the 'Chinese Government', neither of which are in the feminine gender. 'Hers' can only refer, according to the ordinary rules of grammar, to Great Britain.
    However, I suppose we must not be pedantic, but must leave Sir C. Mac-Donald and the Yamen to use bad grammar if they prefer.]

I shall be glad to be in a position to communicate to Her Majesty's Government a definite assurance that China will never alienate any territory in the provinces adjoining the Yang-tze to any other Power, whether under lease, mortgage, or any other designation. Such an assurance is in full harmony with the observations made to me by your Highnesses and your Excellencies.

I avail, etc.

(Signed) CLAUD M. MACDONALD

ELUCIDATORY NOTE.

Paragraphs 2 and 3 are marginal notes by Curzon, then Under-Secretary for Foreign Affairs, and form no part of the actual despatch which is composed of paragraphs 1 and 4. By some mishap in the printing the marginal note (which should have been suppressed) got incorporated in the text with the above result.

It is amusing to note that the careful grammarian has himself made a slip in 'neither of which *are*'.

(With thanks to Valentine Williams, *The World of Action*, 1938, and to the late Professor A. W. Stewart.)

neither should be restricted to two things, persons, actions, sets, groups, companies, etc. For three or more, *not any* or *none* is required. In 'Jack, Jill, and Jim were present; neither had much to say', substitute *none* (*of them*) for *neither*.

neither ... nor. See NEGATION, Section B.ii.

But the *number* of the verb has caused much trouble. The simplest general rule is that (*a*) if both of the subjects are in the singular, the verb is singular ('Neither Bill nor Jack is at fault'), and (*b*) if either of the subjects is in the plural, so is the verb ('Neither the men nor the woman are at fault' – 'Neither he nor they are at fault'). Obviously if both of the subjects are in the plural, so is the verb.

Pronouns in different persons increase the difficulty; that is, when both subjects are in the singular, for the case of either or both of the subjects in the plural has already been established. The rule that the nearer subject governs the verb in both person and number applies here as elsewhere. Thus:

> 'Neither he nor I *am* at fault'
> 'Neither he nor you *are* at fault'
> 'Neither you nor I *am* at fault'
> 'Neither you nor he *is* at fault'
> 'Neither I nor he *is* at fault'
> 'Neither I nor you *are* at fault'.

Neither ... nor has beguiled so brilliant a mind as that of Michael Innes when, merely and momentarily aberrant, he writes, 'Neither Pluckrose nor Prisk nor many of their colleagues has list [i.e. desire] or talent for this' (*The Weight of the Evidence*). It is, however, possible that 'many' is a printer's error for 'any'; if 'any' had been intended, 'has' was correct.

neither ... nor, misplaced. 'Bertrand Russell has characterized pure mathematics as "that science in which we neither know what we are talking about, nor whether what we say is true"' (Stuart Chase, *The Tyranny of Words*). Read '... we know neither what we are talking about nor whether what we say is true'.

neither ... nor ... nor. See no ... nor.

neither of their (sakes). See GENITIVE, VAGARIES OF THE: penultimate paragraph.

neither ... or should, (except in *neither ... nor ... or.* see NEGATION, *B.ii.* (3)) invariably be *neither ... nor*. A writer of detective thrillers perpetrated this in 1932, 'Looking neither to the right or the left'.

NEOLOGISMS. 'A novel word or phrase which has not yet secured unquestioned admission to the standard [language] is called a *neologism*, which is simply a "new form of speech". There is no test but time. If a neologism seems to most speakers to supply a lack in the language, or to be peculiarly fit for the expression of some special idea, it is sure to maintain itself against the protests of the literary and scholastic guild. On the other hand, nothing can force a new term into any language against the inclination of a large majority of those who speak it. The field of language is strewn with the dry bones of adventurous words which once started out with the paternal blessing to make their fortune, but which have met with an untimely end, and serve only, when collected, to fill the shelves of a lexicographical museum' (the Fowler brothers).

Concerning the origin of neologisms, the Fowlers, in *The King's English*, have written thus judiciously: 'The motive may be laziness, avoidance of the obvious, love of precision, or desire for a brevity or poignancy that the language as at present constituted does not seem to him to admit of. The first two are bad motives, the third a good, and the last a mixed one. But in all cases it may be said that a writer should not indulge in nonce-words unless he is quite sure he is a good writer.' (A *nonce-word* is a word 'coined for one occasion', in the definition of *COD*.)

To neologisms adopted direct from foreign languages there is little objection, provided always that the new words fill a gap.

neophyte: 'a beginner, a novice, a tyro': is not to be overdone!

nett for *net*, as in *nett profit*, *nett result*, is without justification.

neurasthenic and **neurotic.** There is a scientific distinction between *neurasthenia*, a non-technical word for 'a nervous weakness', and *neurosis*, 'a nervous disease' (*OED*), from which the adjectives are derived. Such terms should be left to the doctors who understand them; it is offensive to a person to be called 'neurotic' if he or she is only 'neurasthenic'.

never, as a mere equivalent of *not*, is a colloquialism and should, in serious writing, be used only after careful consideration. 'He never knew it was so chilly' for 'He did not know it was so chilly' is natural in dialogue, but incongruous in formal writing; cf. 'He spoke never a word' for 'He spoke *not* a word' (emphatic) or 'He did not speak a word' (neutral). In familiar speech 'He spoke never a word' is stronger than 'He did not speak a word'; in writing it is no stronger than 'He spoke not a word.' Students will find this matter treated suggestively in Jespersen's monograph, *Negation*, pp. 17–18.

never expected is incorrect – or, at best, loose – for *expected never*, as in 'I never expected to see her there.'

never so is no longer good English for *ever so*, as in 'Beer is beer, be it never so weak.'

nevertheless. The combination, *but nevertheless*, is tautological for *nevertheless*.

new and **novel.** The former refers to time ('It is new to me') or to state or condition ('His suit was new'); the latter to kind ('It's a novel way or method'). *New* is opposed to *old*, *novel* to *common* or *well-known*.

New York City. The official name is *The City of New York*, rare except in official papers or formal statements. *New York City* (abbr. *NYC*) is common in both speech and writing, as is simple *New York* except where it leads to confusion between the city and the state. *New York, NY* is a variant in writing and is sometimes preferred to *New York City*. Mail is addressed to *New York, NY* or *New York City*. Pretentious and formal communications such as wedding invitations may bear *New York, New York.*

news. Anxiety to be correct causes people sometimes to put the verb in the plural, but the singular is now the current choice, as in 'No news is good news.'

nice is a verbal counter, a passe-partout, a word-of-all-pleasant-work; permissible – though an indication of laziness – in conversation, it is to be avoided in serious writing.

nicely for *satisfactorily* or *well*, or *very well* is not, as Weseen states, a colloquialism; it is, however, far too common and should, as a general rule, be avoided. [According to *Webster's*, *nicely* (adj.) meaning *well*, *in good health*, is colloquial; *nicely* (adv.) is standard for *precisely*, *scrupulously*, *satisfactorily*.]

NICKNAMES are permissible among friends, and, for the great or the famous or the notorious, among all men (and women): but in writing, unless they are so apposite and effective that other considerations become negligible or inoperative, they are to be avoided. Gossip writers affect them, for nicknames in a gossip column give the impression that the writer knows intimately the person nicknamed or is at least in the enviable position of knowing the name if not the person; and readers, in the glow induced by intimacy at second hand, forgive the writer the gross tactlessness or the childish impertinence of this excessive familiarity. Especially offensive is the nicknaming of royalty: it is comparable with journalists' references to film and lawn-tennis stars by their pet names as in 'Betty plays magnificently in Wimbledon doubles' and 'Where is Greta?' [There is an increasing tendency in American businesses – particularly in the media – to call nearly everyone by his or her first name or by a nickname. It may produce a friendly atmosphere but it does not keep John from firing Charlie.]

nigger is very offensive when applied to the dark-skinned African races and their descendants in America and the West Indies, though black Americans sometimes use it inoffensively of one another. Its application to the native peoples of India is also ignorant and offensive. It is best to avoid even such phrases as *nigger brown* and *nigger in the woodpile*. See **black.**

nigh (adv.) for *near* is archaic in prose; current usage reserves it for poetry. Do not employ it as an adjective. *Well nigh* for *almost* or *very nearly* is a cliché.

no. See at **none.**

no, as in 'I didn't want no tellin'' (Baumann). An example of the double negative, common in illiterate speech.

no + superlative + noun ('no slightest sign') = '*no* + that noun, *not even the slightest*'. Idiomatically, 'There was no slightest sign' = 'There was no sign at all, not even the slightest', and not, as one might think, 'There was no very slight sign, but there was a big sign.'

no admission is occasionally used ambiguously for *no admission-charge*, to which *admission* (*is*) *free* is preferable.

no ... nor for *no ... and no* and *no ... or*. This *no ... nor* is permitted by *OED* in its use as an equivalent of *no ... and no*, as in 'We had no revolutions to fear, nor fatigues to endure' (Goldsmith, 1766). This equivalence, however, is obsolescent. The man in the street tends now to say 'We had no revolutions to fear and no fatigues to endure', and the modern stylist would write, 'We had no revolutions to fear; [or] no fatigues to endure.' 'She took no interest nor part in outdoor sports' seems nowadays old-fashioned. Sometimes *or* would be preferred to *and no* as the modern equivalent of this *nor*, as in 'He had in him ... no tincture of Scottish, Irish, Welsh, French, German, Italian, American nor Jewish [blood]' (Arnold Bennett, *Imperial Palace*), where a modern stylist would write 'He had ... no tincture of Scottish, Irish, Welsh ... American, or Jewish [blood]', with a comma after *American* to ensure dissociation. In the following sentence from Hugh Walpole's *John Cornelius* – 'They say that no novel in the first person can ever be true because no one can recall conversations as they actually occurred nor remember the physical details of past scenes' – I should have preferred '... no one can [either] recall conversations ... or remember the physical details', which is neater than 'no one can recall conversations ... and no one can remember the physical details'. Here, as in all nuanced writing, discrimination is required; not the bull-at-a-gate courage of desperation!

no object. See **object, no.**

no one; noone. The latter is incorrect.

no one (or **nobody**) ... **they.** See **anyone ... they.**

no one's (or **nobody's**) **else.** See **else's.**

no place is illiterate for *nowhere*, as in 'The jewel was no place to be found.'

no question. See **question.**

no such. Freeman Wills Crofts, *The Cask*, 'You can't have seen a letter from me, because no such exists', should be *no such letter* (or *thing*), for *such* ought not to be used as a pronoun except in the time-honoured formulas, 'such is life', 'such was the decision'.

no thing. See **nothing and no thing.**

noble for *charming, very kind, unselfish* is slang. Originally it was schoolgirls' slang.

nobody's else. See **else's.**

noisome means 'disgusting', and particularly 'evil-smelling'. It is not to be confused with *noisy*.

nom de plume is to be avoided: there is no such term in the best French (*nom de guerre* being usual). The correct English is *pen-name* or (literary) *pseudonym*, of which the former is a translation of the pseudo-French *nom de plume*; but in post-war French, *nom de plume* is very often employed; the popularity of *pen-name* + that of *nom de plume*, as used in England, has engendered a genuinely French *nom de plume* which is a writer's *nom de guerre*.

nomenclature means not, as in ' "Delpha" may be a popular nomenclature with the mystic sorority' (S. S. Van Dine, *The Gracie Allen Murder Case*), but 'a system of names' – as in 'The Linnaean nomenclature' – or 'the terminology used in a science or in technics'.

nominal is incorrectly used by Nigel Morland (*The Conquest of Crime*) in 'The figures are nominal'; he means *approximate*. 'Nominal' 'existing in name only, in distinction to real or actual' (*OED*). *Nominal*, in *at a nominal charge* or *cost, for a*

nominal fee, is not 'low' but 'so low' as not fairly to be considered a charge, a cost, a fee. In short, *nominal* is not synonymous with *low*.

nominate. See **denominate.**

NOMINATIVE ABSOLUTE. There's nothing mysterious about this! But example is better than precept: 'She failing to keep the appointment, he went off and got drunk.'

non- is shamelessly and usually quite needlessly overworked by Civil Servants. Why, e.g., *non-restricted* when *free* is available?

non-; in-; un-. They all negate adjectives; but while *non-* expresses simple negation, the others often imply a more forceful opposite or failure. Thus *non-scientific* work is not connected with science, but *unscientific* work is slovenly as regards scientific principles.

none. (i) When *none* = *not one*, use the singular, as in 'None of the newspapers has appeared this week.'

(ii) When *none* = *no one, no person, nobody*, the singular is correct; but, as indeed for (i) also, the plural is not regarded as a solecism; in both (i) and (ii), the plural is merely an infelicity, a defect that will not hinder the good-enoughists.

(iii) When *none* = *no persons*, the verb is plural, as in 'None have been so greedy of employments ... as they who have least deserved their stations' (Dryden). The corresponding singular pronoun is *no one* (based on *OED*).

Mr R. B. Hamilton of Nottingham has (17 Aug. 1947) written to me so pertinently that, with his very kind permission, I quote him word for word.

'It is bad form nowadays to mention the Ten Commandments; so I will, with apologies, take you no further than the first, as it appears in the Prayer Book: "Thou shalt have none other gods but me." The turn of phrase is archaic; but if you had pondered it, you might have cleared up, instead of thickening, the fog of pretentious misunderstanding which surrounds the use of "none".

'May I submit for your consideration the following sentences:

Q. Is there any sugar?
A. 1. No, there isn't any sugar. (colloquial)
2. No, there isn't any. (colloquial and elliptical)
3. No, there is no sugar. (formal)
4. No, there is none. (formal and elliptical)
Q. Are there any plums?
A. 5. No, there aren't any plums. (colloquial)
6. No, there aren't any. (colloquial and elliptical)
7. No, there are no plums. (formal)
8. No, there are none. (formal and elliptical)

'You will, I hope, agree that this arrangement has more than symmetry to recommend it. In the first place, all four replies in each case are exactly synonymous; secondly, they are all logical; and, thirdly, they are all idiomatic – they all slip off the tongue of careful and careless speakers alike; you hear them all every day of your life.

'Are they all equally grammatical? It seems that they should be; for they are logical and idiomatic, and what is grammar but a mixture of logic and idiom? There is no dispute as to Nos. 1 to 7; but when you come to No. 8, you will find that there is a superstition that, in formal contexts, it should be re-written with the verb in the singular. The awkwardness of this is apparent; for it seems to require the question to be either "Is there any plums?", which is bad grammar, or "Is there any plum?", which is not English at all. This awkwardness, however, recommends it to pompous or timid writers who, like fakirs, hope to gain merit by discomfort.

'The superstition was I think invented by some 18th-century sciolist, who, misled by appearances and regardless of history and logic, decided that "none" was a contraction of "no one" and decreed that it should be followed by a singular verb.

In point of fact, the truth is the opposite; for "no" itself is nothing but a shortened form of "none", standing in the same relation to it as "my" does to "mine"; so that "none other gods" is archaic only in retaining the longer form, before an initial vowel, in attributive use, and the phrase answers to the modern "no other gods" precisely as the Biblical "mine eyes" answers to the modern "my eyes". The phrase "no one" is therefore really a tautology (= not one one); and if Sentence No. 8 is wrong, No. 7 must be equally so.

'It is quite true that "none" contains the Anglo-Saxon *ān* (one), as also for that matter does "any". But Anglo-Saxon grammar is not English grammar; and both words have been indifferently singular and plural for six centuries.

'If you will now look back to the sentences, you will see that the facts are as follows: (1) "No" is merely the attributive form of "none"; (2) "None" and "no" do *not* (except by accident) mean "not one" or "no one" or "no persons"; they mean "not any", neither more nor less (it is impossible to construct any sentence which you cannot make into a question by substituting "any" for "none" and inverting the order of the words); and (3) "No", "none" and "any" are all singular or plural, according to the sense.

'Let me then urge you to throw in your lot with the "good-enoughists" (what is good enough for the Prayer Book should be good enough for you) and admit these simple facts. It is no disgrace to yield when etymology, logic, and idiom are all against you. To say (as you suggest we should) "None of the newspapers has appeared" is no better than to say "No newspapers has appeared." Indeed, it is worse; for vulgarity may be forgiven, but pretentiousness carries its own heavy punishment.'

After that, I retract.

none, misused with genitive. See GENITIVE, VAGARIES OF THE, penultimate paragraph.

none such is very awkwardly, if not absolutely incorrectly used in 'When he asked for the name, he was told that none such was in the register' (Nigel Morland). Cf. **no such.**

noone. See **no one.**

nor (in **neither ... nor**). See **neither ... or.** See also **or and nor.**

nor for *or* and for *and no.* See **no ... nor for** *no ... and no.*

nor for *than,* as in Thackeray, 1840. 'You're no better nor a common tramper' (*OED*), is still found in low colloquial speech, but is a mark of illiteracy.

nor ... neither. In general, see NEGA-TION, B (Negation in Syntax).

Occasionally, *nor ... neither* is misused for *nor ... either,* as in 'You've had a Boy Scout's training and they never have. Nor I neither' (Inez Irwin, *The Poison Cross Mystery*). One negatives not both members of *or ... either* (that would produce a double negative) but the first only in this formula, which is quite different from '*neither* (you) *nor* I'; *nor I either* is merely an elaboration of *nor I.*

nor none is occasionally misused for *nor any.* ' "They have no Libel Law in France." "Nor none in Brazil", says Miles' (Beatrice Kean Seymour, *The Happier Eden*); this Miles was a novelist.

normal, the. See the following entry.

normalcy, normalism, normality and **normalness.** The fourth is incorrect; the second, which is rare, has no special, no technical senses; the first is more American than British, but it is catching on in Great Britain; *normality* is the usual British form, although *the normal* is fast displacing it in the sense 'a normal variety of anything; an individual or specimen possessing normal characteristics or faculties' (*OED*). *Normally* has become far too common for both *usually* and *always.*

north is inferior to *northward(s)* as an adverb.

northerly and **northern.** See **easterly.**

northward; northwards. The latter is adverb only. The former is chiefly an adjective, but often functions as an adverb in American English and in older British writing.

nostalgia, nostalgic. *Nostalgia* formerly meant only 'acute homesickness', but its sense has been expanded to include any wistful yearning for the past, a usage now well established. The range of *nostalgic* is now even wider. It is overused to mean no more than 'touchingly reminiscent'.

In 1943 (and the remark still holds good), John P. Marquand, in what is, at least sociologically, his best novel, *So Little Time,* wrote, 'A perfectly good word has been worked to death in the last few years — the adjective "nostalgic". It has been applied to ladies' dresses, perfume, porch furniture, and even to saddle horses.'

not a one and **not one.** The former is incorrect: for 'Not a one of them did that' read 'Not one of them did that.'

not anything like. See **nothing like.**

not hardly is incorrect for *hardly.* So too **not scarcely.**

not ... nor, in the following sentence (J. B. Priestley, *English Humour,* 1929), is not only correct in itself, but leads Mr Priestley into a contradiction of his own meaning: 'He asks what it is that governs the Englishman. After replying that it is certainly not intelligence, nor seldom passion, and hardly self-interest, he goes on, etc.' The meaning is 'seldom passion' or 'not often passion'. It is unsafe for the ordinary person to use *nor* — except after *neither* (*q.v.*).

not ... nor ... nor is permissible when it is used instead of *neither ... nor ... nor.* Gladstone, 1870, writes 'Not a vessel, nor a gun, nor a man, were on the ground to prevent their landing', which woolly though it is, is preferable to 'Neither a vessel, nor a gun, nor a man ...'.

not only ... but (also), misplaced. 'This necessitated, not only the resignations of Essex and Manchester, against whom it was chiefly aimed, but also such valuable men as Lord Warwick, who as Lord High Admiral had successfully held the seas for Parliament during those anxious years': should read: 'This necessitated the resignations not only of Essex and Manchester, against whom it was chiefly aimed, but also of such valuable men as Lord Warwick, who ...' Quoted by G. V. Carey, *Mind the Stop*; he adds: 'If you prefer to put "not only" after the first "of", you will not need a second "of" before "such",' [*Not only ... but (also)* is overworked by writers of too little rhetoric. In short sentences a simple *and* is more emphatic.]

not scarcely. See **not hardly.**

notable and **noted.** The former stresses worth or worthiness; the latter, celebrity. The former is potential; the latter, actual. A notable man may not be noted; a noted man may not be notable – his fame may be notoriety, his title to fame may be factitious, adventitious, or meretricious. Cf. the entry at **noticeable.**

notary; notary public. See **lawyer.** The plural of *notary public* is *notaries public.*

note and **notice** (vv.). *Note*, as merely 'to take notice of', is fortunately passing out of use. Usage now prefers *note* to = 'to *notice closely*'.

noted that ... , it will be = *Please note that ...* (Officialese.)

nothing and **no thing.** In the latter, the stress is on *thing*, as in 'No thing perturbs him; many persons do.' 'Nothing perturbs him' connotes absence of, or freedom from perturbation. Whereas *nothing* is inclusive and general, *no thing* is exclusive and particular.

nothing but. In *nothing but* + a noun, it is *nothing* which determines the number of the verb; in other words, the verb after *nothing but* ... should be in the singular.

'Nothing but dreary dykes occur to break the monotony of the landscape' should be 'Nothing but dreary dykes occurs ...' (Onions, *An Advanced English Syntax*).

nothing like, as in 'nothing like so fast', is a colloquialism for *not nearly.*

notice. See **note and notice.**

noticeable and **notable.** The former chiefly = no more than 'perceptible', not – as *notable* does – 'striking'. Thus, 'a *notable* improvement' must be larger than 'a merely *noticeable* one'. See also **notable and noted.**

notorious and **famous.** Both mean 'very well known (to the general public)'; but the former is unfavourable, the latter favourable; thus, 'a famous writer' but 'a notorious criminal'. *Notorious*, in short, is 'famous in a bad way – for crime or excessive vice'. The cliché *it is notorious that* properly means no more than 'it is common knowledge that ...', but current usage invests it with pejorative connotation. Note, however, that a person may in his lifetime be so notorious that after his death he becomes famous: e.g. Charley Peace the murderer.

nought and **naught.** For the cypher or zero, *nought* is the British spelling and *naught* the American; for 'nothing' use *naught* – that is, if you use it at all, for it is archaic except in poetry.

NOUN ADJECTIVES. In the *JIJ*, January 1939, Frank Whitaker, having attacked the anti-possessive (or -genitive) craze (*q.v.* at **AMBIGUITY**), continues thus, under the caption, 'Dangerous Noun-Adjectives':

'The noun adjective mania is even more dangerous, in the sense that it is driving a wedge between written and spoken English. I read in a recent issue of *The Daily Sketch*, picked up haphazard, these headlines: "Minister's Milk Bill Climb-down" (we must be grateful for the possessive there: "Minister Milk Bill" would have been a little difficult); "Navy bid to save stranded Britons" (no possessive there, you will notice), and "Brothers' big boxing bid". Now I know what is meant by the first two of those headlines – the third puzzles me – but heaven forbid that one man should ever go up to another in the street and say "Have you heard the latest about the Minister's Milk Bill Climb-down, or of the Navy bid to save stranded Britons?"

'I read in another paper, "Crime chief to retire", and I think I know what that means. But I am wrong. The man who is about to retire is not a gangster but a Scotland Yard superintendent. And what are we to make of the headline noted by William Empson in his book, *Seven Types of Ambiguity*, which reads "Italian assassin bomb plot disaster"? We must be grateful again that the sub-editor did not follow the current fashion and write, "Italy assassin bomb plot disaster". But what did he mean? Was the assassin Italian? He was not. It was the disaster that was Italian. And what is an "assassin bomb plot"? I give it up.' See also JOURNALESE, at OFFICIALESE 1.

novel. See **new.**

noway; noways; nowise. All are correct: the third is the best; the second is the least used nowadays.

noxious. See **obnoxious.**

n't for *not* is colloquial and familiar; it should, in serious writing, be used with caution – or not at all.

number (v.), for *possess.* 'My *locum tenens* consented to perform the office of best man for me, since I numbered no personal friend to meet the occasion' (Eden Phillpotts, *Physician Heal Thyself*). Rather too pregnant for *number among one's acquaintances.*

number; whether it takes a singular or a plural verb. 'If a group of words, especially a partitive group, conveys the idea of plurality, a number of individuals, the verb is in the plural, even though the governing noun is singular, [but] the verb is singular if the group conveys the idea of oneness: "The greatest *part* of these years *was* spent

in philosophic retirement", but "The greatest *part* of the Moguls and Tartars *were* as illiterate as their sovereigns." In "*a large number* of the garrison *were* prostrate with sickness" and "There *are a large number* of things that I desire to say" *number* is now felt not as a collective noun but as a component of a compound numeral, [and] the indefinite ... *a large number* [as having] plural force, so that the verb is in the plural. ... *Number* as a singular noun is still found occasionally where a writer follows the outward form rather than the inner meaning: "Chicago has as many more [models] and besides these there *is* probably *an equal number* of occasional sitters, transients" (Beecher Edwards, "Faces that Haunt You", in *Liberty*, 22 May 1926).' Such is the pronouncement of that great American grammarian, George O. Currie, in *Syntax*.

It is observable that *number* is singular when it is used in a sentence commenting on the size of the number, as in 'The number of tourists has declined.' See also **figure.**

O

O and **Oh**. Is there a shade of human feeling which cannot be conveyed in speech by this simple vowel-sound? Yet we have no signs but these to represent to the eye their infinite variety of meanings, which prayer and imprecation, surprise, disgust, horror and delight, dubiety, incredulity, and a dozen phrases of interrogation can hardly summarize. ' "Here I am", said he; "Oh", said she': and how shall we indicate whether she was glad to see him? In the dialogue of a play, a stage direction might be required for the guidance of a (perhaps) stupid actress. To come to modern practice: *O* and *Oh* were at one time used indifferently, but now the use of *O* is almost confined to poetry. *O* without punctuation is an invocation (vocative case) to some person or object named in the words that follow it, as in Milton:

> O thou that with surpassing glory
> crowned,
> Look'st from thy sole dominion,
> etc.,

or in the humbler verse, 'O lovely night! O! [or Oh!] lovely night!', which is two exclamations, the second explaining the cause of the first. But *Oh, (a) lovely night, isn't it?* is not exclamatory; *Oh* in such cases implies a momentary pause for thought before speaking. Often it seems to call attention to a change of subject, a new idea: *Oh, have you heard, etc.?* Real hesitancy would be conveyed by *Oh –*. The mark of exclamation (*Oh!*) will always indicate some degree of feeling, surprise, pleasure, or the reverse. In James Thomson's tragedy, *Sophonisba* (1730), there is a line much quoted as an instance of unconscious bathos, i.e. strong feeling made ridiculous by affected and inadequate expression:

> *Oh! Sophonisba! Sophonisba! Oh!*

It is spoken by a young lover in a frenzy of delight and is perfectly natural in the circumstances. Each word is a separate exclamation capable of any change of intonation; spoken by a good actor as the author intended, it would be free from bathos and not open to ridicule.

Oh is capitalized only at the beginning of a sentence, and followed by any appropriate punctuation (or by none), whereas *O* is always capitalized and not usually followed by a stop.

Dean Alford (*The Queen's English*), complaining of the compositors' habit of inserting unnecessary and often misleading stops, says: 'If one has written the words *O sir* as they ought to be written, and are written in Genesis xliii, 20, viz., with the plain capital "O" and no stop, and then a comma after "sir", our friend the compositor is sure to write "Oh" with a shriek

(!) and to put another shriek after "sir".' (Wilson Benington, who, mentioned elsewhere as WB, contributed several short articles while the American edition was being prepared.)

object, no. E.g. 'distance no object', and especially, 'price no object': catachrestic when 'no obstacle' or 'not an objection' is meant. The correct sense, 'not a thing aimed at or considered important' has been vitiated by confusion with *no objection*. Its flagrant absurdity is seen in the undertaker's advertisement: 'Distance no object.'

objective. See VOGUE WORDS.

obligate (adj.), defined by *OED* as 'that is of necessity such', is applied with scientific meaning by biologists, but is better avoided by all others. As verb it is sometimes used for *oblige*, but means rather *to bind* (a person) *under an obligation*. An ugly and unnecessary word.

obliged. Correct uses:
   (1) 'I am obliged by circumstances to do it.'
   (2) 'I am much obliged to you for your kindness.'
   (3) 'I shall be obliged if you stop making that noise.'
   (4) 'I am' – or 'He or she is' – 'your obliged servant', an old-fashioned letter-ending.
.   Of Nos. 2 and 3, *OED* remarks, 'Now said only in reference to small services.' Except in dialogue, avoid the colloquialism exemplified in 'He obliged with a song.'

oblivion for *ignorance*. 'The necessity of keeping the common people in oblivion of the shortcomings of their material welfare'.

oblivious for *unconscious (of)*. *OED* quotes Buckle, *History of Civilization*, 1862, 'He was so little given to observation as to be frequently oblivious of what was passing around him.' The word formerly meant only 'forgetful', but the distinction is inevitably blurred, since an observer seldom knows whether the *oblivious* person has forgotten whatever it is, or never knew it. Moreover, one says *oblivious of.* Cf. 'She continued brightly, oblivious to Martha's expression' (Jennings Rice, *The Somers Inheritance*) – an error more common in the USA than in Great Britain.

oblivious to. See PREPOSITIONS WRONGLY USED.

obnoxious, 'aggressively disagreeable', must not be confused with *noxious*, which means 'injurious' e.g. of nuclear waste.

obscene. See VOGUE WORDS.

OBSCURITY.* 'It may be better to be clear than clever, it is still better to be clear and correct', as we are told by a correspondent in the *JIJ*, 1938.

'Without distinction of speech there is never much distinction of idea', remarks Frank Binder in *Dialectic*. And without distinction of idea there cannot be distinction of speech – or style. 'Real and offensive obscurity comes merely of inadequate thought embodied in inadequate language', declared Swinburne in 1870. On the other hand, as a certain grammarian has said, 'In contemplating the way in which our sentences will be understood, we are allowed to remember, that we do not write for idiots.'

To begin with, three examples of that obscurity which arises from the desire to be brief ('I labour to be brief and become obscure', as Horace once remarked).

'The foreign elements ... played a large part in the formation of the Romantic drama and constituted a large proportion of its maturity in the forties' (Eric Partridge, *The French Romantics' Knowledge of English Literature*, 1924).

'I began to get excited over my new photographic outfit. It was natural, since it was new' (Violet O. Cressy-Marcks, *Up the Amazon and over the Andes*).

'The bright naves of the wheels caught and played with the sun in their slow turn-

ing; and ... at every fourth revolution, one of them creaked with a sort of musical complaint at a world which was perfect but for a drop of oil' (Robert Eton, *The Journey*). One is abruptly pulled up: *but for the lack of a drop of oil* would be better: *but for* (= except for) makes the phrase almost too pithy.

And then a number of miscellaneous examples; for all their miscellaneity, they do, I think, serve to show the dangers of obscurity.

'There are, of course, many uses of *colorful* which have no such [damning-with-faint-praise] implications – where, for example, that a thing should be full of colour is all we can ask where no ironical reserves and no disparagement can be intended' (I. A. Richards, *The Philosophy of Rhetoric*).

'It is the rest of the poem that makes the connexion easy and obvious, which witnesses to a general truth' (*ibid.*). That should be *which*. But to what does *which* (*which witnesses*) refer? To *rest* or to *poem* or to the sentence, 'It is the rest of the poem that makes the connexion easy and obvious'? Presumably to the sentence.

'There is no warrant for the placing on these inevitably rather light heads and hearts, on any company of you, assaulted, in our vast vague order, by many pressing wonderments, the *whole* of the burden of a care for tone' (Henry James, *The Question of Our Speech*, 1905). Cited by I. A. Richards (*op. cit.*) without comment. I pass it on – without comment.

'This common professional attitude [courage and self-abnegation] to sea-going both sides of the pay-desk has one odd result' (Richard Hughes, *In Hazard*). The author might perhaps have written, 'This ... attitude – common to sea-going, on both sides of the pay-desk – has one odd result.'

'No, there was nothing left for him [David] in business ... he was surfeited with success. David, too, though, had ideas. Vague, true, but ideas' (Frank Tilsley, *Devil Take the Hindmost*). *Though* (= however) causes part of the trouble; *true* is

---

*The beginner will find pithy matter in Harold Herd, *Watch Your English*, pp. 42–3.

so short for 'it is true' that ambiguity has arisen. What the author intended was, 'No ... David, however, had ideas. *Vague ideas*, it is true; yet ideas.'

'He watched David talk, not too closely to make him self-conscious' (*ibid*). The sentence would have been clear had it been written, '... not too closely, lest he should make him self-conscious' or 'not so closely as to make ...'.

'I suppose that a few days before the place must have given some impression of a dwelling. Now ... there hung about it the atmosphere of an ancient monument. The tenancy of Ronald Guthrie had been a thread holding it to the present; that thread broken, *it* had slipped into the past as inevitably as a ripe apricot falls to the ground' (Michael Innes, *Lament for a Maker*). To what does the italicized *it* (italicized by me) refer? To 'the place' in the first sentence – rather too far away.

'Dales went first next day to the Registrar of Births and Marriages' (Vernon Loder, *The Button in the Plate*). Dales was not the first to go there; probably not the first on even that day. The author meant, 'Next day, Dales went, first to the Registrar (and then elsewhere)'. Not content with that piece of obscurity, the author continues, 'He found him a young man.'

'It was not Carol Berman alone to whom the jury's verdict came as a bewildering shock. Inspector Cambridge felt almost as dazed as she' (Sidney Fowler, *Four Callers in Razor Street*). Obviously the passage should begin thus: 'It was not to Carol Berman alone that the jury's verdict came as a bewildering shock.'

'Power Age communities ... rely increasingly on printed matter, radio, communication at a distance. *This* has operated to enlarge the field for words, absolutely and relatively, and has created a paradise for fakirs. A community of semantic illiterates, of persons unable to perceive the meaning of what they read and hear, is one of *perilous equilibrium*' (Stuart Chase, *The Tyranny of Words*). The italics are mine.

In conclusion, some of the main causes of obscurity are unclear reference, over-condensation and errors in word order. For yet further causes, see **AMBIGUITY; JARGON; NOUN ADJECTIVES; OFFICIALESE; ORDER OF WORDS; WOOLLINESS.**

observance and **observation**. The latter is no longer used for the former. *Observance* = the action or practice of keeping or paying attention to (a law, custom, ceremony, etc.)' also 'an act performed in accordance with prescribed usage; a practice customarily observed'. Thus 'the sternest observance of discipline'; 'religious ceremonies and observances' (*OED*).

observe is incorrect when used for 'to *preserve*' or 'keep' or 'retain'. In the sense 'to make a remark', to 'remark' (v.t.), it is not incorrect but merely feeble.

obtain is incorrect when used for *to effect*. It seems to have arisen from a confusion of two senses, 'to gain or acquire'; and 'to reach'. George Parker, *A View of Society*, 1781, 'A very small boy is carried by a gang ... in the dead of night to a house. ... When this gang is pretty certain that the family is in bed, they despatch ... the boy, or Little Snakes-man, to obtain their admittance.' See also **procure and secure.**

obtrude. See **protrude.**

obverse. See **converse.**

obvious. See COMPARATIVES, FALSE.

OBVIOUS, THE. *Punch* (16 Aug. 1938) quotes from *The Rugeley Mercury*: 'One effect of the better lighting' (of a church) 'is the improved visibility.'

occupy for *run to*, or *have*, or *comprise*, is loose. 'Such preparation may occupy six or seven stages' (Nigel Morland, *The Conquest of Crime*).

octopi, a mistaken plural of *octopus* by those who suppose it to be from Latin. The English termination should be used, *octopuses*; the pedantic prefer *octopodes*.

odd, 'strange', and **odd,** 'and a few more' (300 *odd*), must not be allowed to set up ambiguity, as in 'These 300 odd pages'. Write 'These 300-odd pages' or 'These 300 and odd pages'.

odd number (or **odd-number**) is incorrect for *odd-numbered* in 'the odd-number tickets'.

odious and **odorous**. The former = 'hateful or detestable'; the latter = 'having a smell', i.e. *odoriferous*, which is generally used in the favourable sense, 'sweet-smelling, fragrant', the opposite being *malodorous* ('evil-smelling'). *Odorous* is never a pejorative.

of, carelessly omitted. This happens especially in *of which* clauses; e.g. 'The Colonel ... departed to make arrangements, the exact nature of which Topper decided he would be more comfortable to remain in ignorance' (Thorne Smith, *Topper Takes a Trip*), where *the exact nature of which* should be *of the exact nature of which*.

of for *have* is a gross solecism, as in 'If I had of done it', where, moreover, *have* itself would be an illiterate intrusion.

of, for *in*, is careless. 'The task of finding concepts which shall adequately describe nature and at the same time be easily handled by us, is the most important and difficult of physics', cited (from whom?) by Stuart Chase in *The Tyranny of Words*.

of in *doing of* ('What are you a doin' of?') is common only in vulgar speech, especially Cockney.

of in *off of* is also a Cockneyism and incorrect. *Off from* may in certain cases be allowed, but *away from*, *down from*, would always be better. [In American English *off of*, *inside of*, and *outside of* are somewhat colloquial but more acceptable than in British usage.]

of, preposition. Incorrect uses of both *of* and *for* are exemplified in the following sentence (from *Swift or the Egotist* by M. M. Rossi and J. M. Hone), 'Even the very recent explanation of Mr Aldous Huxley for Swift's misanthropy is influenced by the theory of psycho-analysis.' Here 'of' should be 'by' and 'for' should be 'of'.

of all others. See **others, of all.**

of her – of hers; of his (+ noun) – **of his; of my – of mine; of your – of yours.** 'Note that "These are three friends *of mine*" and "These are three of *my friends*" have different implications; the second implies that I have more than three friends; the first does not' (Onions), though it does not exclude that possibility. There is, however, a further difference: 'A friend of the King' connotes dignity, whereas 'a friend of Bill Brown's' connotes familiarity in speech.

Certain writers have sought to confuse the issue by asking, 'What about *that long nose of his*?'; they point out that *his* cannot refer to more noses than one. Jespersen, in his admirable SPE tract *On Some Disputed Points in English Grammar*, deals fully with the entire *of my – of mine* question, and he shows that *that long nose of his* = *that long nose which is his*; he calls 'of his' (in *that long nose of his*) an appositional genitive.

Dr George O. Curme, in *Syntax*, shrewdly remarks that 'There has become associated with the double genitive a marked liveliness of feeling, so that it now often implies praise or censure, pleasure or displeasure: "that dear little girl of *yours*", "that kind wife *of yours*", "this broad land *of ours*", "that ugly nose of *his*". "Thus Professor Blackie, in that vituperative book *of his*, *The Natural History of Atheism* ... says" (John Burroughs, *The Light of Day*, Ch. vi).' For the difficulties of this double genitive when a noun, not a pronoun is involved, see **GENITIVE, VAGARIES OF THE,** at the paragraph on the double genitive.

of old, as in 'A boy of twelve years old', is incorrect for *of age*. Or rewrite thus, 'A boy twelve years old', or 'a boy of twelve'.

of the name of. See **by the name of.**

of whether. See **whether, of.**

of which. See **whose.**

off of. See **of in** *off of.*

off-handed (adj.) is unnecessary for *off-hand*; *off-handedly* (adv.) is unnecessary for *off-hand.* These terms may be written as one word.

official = 'of, pertaining to, characteristic of office; authoritative; governmental'; whereas *officious* = 'meddlesome, interfering, obtrusive, pettily fussy'.

OFFICIALESE, JOURNALESE, COMMERCIALESE. Perhaps the most sensible order is Journalese, Officialese, Commercialese.
1. *JOURNALESE.* 'The style of language supposed to be characteristic of public journals; "newspaper" or "penny-a-liner's" English' (*OED*). *Webster's* defines it more fully and exactly thus: 'English of a style featured by use of colloquialisms, superficiality of thought or reasoning, clever or sensational presentation of material, and evidences of haste in composition, considered characteristic of newspaper writing.'
  Today, these characteristics may entail the use of headline language (see NOUN ADJECTIVES), which is often confusing enough in headlines but should certainly not be allowed to encroach upon the general text; the use of special vocabulary, or words used in special senses, such as *ban, bombshell, pact, pledge, probe, quiz, slash, slay, soar*; the use of favourite clichés, such as *carbon copy, mercy dash, rags to riches*; and the creation of 'false titles', as in 'famous British cricketer George Stubbs' rather than 'George Stubbs, the famous British cricketer'.
  Needless to say, the more serious newspapers are not guilty in these respects, and indeed many of them set excellent examples of style and usage.
2. *OFFICIALESE* is that type of wordy English which has been – often justifiably – associated with Government offices. See esp. 'Vigilans', *Chamber of Horrors*, 1952, a

glossary with an introduction by EP, and Sir Ernest Gowers, *The Complete Plain Words*, 3rd edition, 1986.
  In *The Star* of 11 Feb. 1938, we find this piece of news: 'The Central News reports that unrest prevailed among certain "military and political elements". The elements, it was added, were being "energetically suppressed" ': which sounds very totalitarian.
  The Evening News, 25 Feb. 1938, gives the following instance:

'WORK THIS ONE OUT!

'What is the position now? Reduced to simple terms, it is this:
  'If A has a small business, he may open his shop for the sale of the goods specified in the schedules to the Act – and none other – during the permitted hours.
  'If, however, he cares to place his goods (without restriction as to quality or variety) on a barrow or in a cart and perambulate the streets on Sunday, he is outside the scope of the Act, for in the words of Lord Hewart he is using " a movable and peripatetic apparatus by means of which sales are enabled to be made at every sort of point in streets and roads over a large area – no fixed locality, no identifiable place".
  'Apart from avoiding the heavy penalties provided for an infringement of the Act, such a person will be freed from many burdens – not the least of which is to understand provisions in the statute such as this: "… *the following provisions of this Act shall extend only to shops that is to say those provisions of section six and section eight which relate to the approval by occupiers of shops of orders made under those sections the provisions of paragraph (c) of sub-section (1) of section seven and the provisions of paragraph (a) of section twelve."* '
  In *The Times* of 8 Aug. 1939, occurs this letter (which contains examples of both officialese and elegancies):

'PLAIN ENGLISH

'To the Editor of *The Times.*
'Sir – May I contribute an example to Mr Herbert's instances of deviations

from "plain verbiage"? I had occasion some time since to ask a Government Department to supply me with a book for official use. I was informed in reply that, although the Department was not in a position to meet my request, I was "authorized to acquire the work in question by purchase through the ordinary trade channels". Or, as we should say, "buy it".

'It would be easy to add to Mr Herbert's list of words which mark the tendency he deplores. "Assist" for "help", "endeavour" for "try", "proceed" for "go", "purchase" for "buy", "approximately" for "about", "sufficient" for "enough", "attired" for "dressed", "inquire" for "ask", are general in speech as well as print. I have noticed that whereas the waste in old lavatory basins is marked "Shut", the up-to-date ones prefer the more refined "Closed". And, no doubt, some of these words and expressions are what Mr Fowler, in his *Modern English Usage*, aptly termed "genteelisms". But others seem not to have even this justification.

'Mr Herbert says with truth that even the Fighting Services have been corrupted. I have known one of them to be responsible for the use of "nomenclature" as a preferable equivalent for "name".

'August 3. Your obedient servant,
Claude Russell'

In *The Listener* of 10 April 1947, the reviewer of the first edition wrote most pertinently thus:

'Mr Partridge might have said more about officialese. ... This demon grows steadily more formidable as the Ministries multiply their number and their lists and schedules. They "initiate organizational preliminaries" instead of making preparations. They "integrate the hospitalization services for the rehabilitation of mentally maladjusted persons". No doubt Mr Partridge is now lined with Sir Alan Herbert, MP, and Mr H. G. Strauss MP, to keep up the battle against the odious "Barnacular"

of the Whitehall limpets.

'One notes that the adjective "overall", which now appears in every paragraph of every Government report and is very dear to political journalists, had not cropped up in time for note. Apart from its sensible and proper application to certain garments, it can be rightly used of overriding authorities. But the word has now become a vogue word, as Mr Partridge would say, and is applied recklessly to figures and even situations. Inclusive figures are now always called "overall figures", which they are not. And how can a situation be overall? Another vogue word for him to watch is "bracket" to signify group. "The overall figures of the lower-income brackets" is typical economists' English today. "Economese" is a theme well worth his attention.'

(Note that the work of the Plain English Society, and the efforts of the Civil Service itself, have considerably improved matters since these words were written, particularly in the important area of communication with the public.)

3. *COMMERCIALESE OR BUSINESS ENGLISH* (or, as Sir Alan Herbert calls it, *Officese*).

A few examples of words and phrases used in old-fashioned commercial offices – and avoided by all self-respecting persons: *advise* (inform), *as per, be in receipt of* ('We are in receipt of your letter'), *beg* ('We beg to bring to the notice of ...'), *duly noted, esteemed favour* and *esteemed order*, (of) *even date, favour* (letter), *friends* (competitors: 'Our friends in the trade have been guilty of price-cutting'), *kindly* (for *please!*), *per, proximo, re* (of) *recent date, same* (for *it*: 'We have received same'), *service* (v.), *shop-lady, state* (for *say*), *a substantial percentage* (much; or merely some), *thanking you in advance, transportation* (a ticket), *ultimo, under one's signature, valuable asset, valued favour, your good self* (or *selves*).

Sir Alan Herbert, *What a Word!*, has, at pp. 69–87, a delightful section on commercialese. To those lively pages we send all those who wish a wittily scathing attack on the sort of English affected by businessmen (at least, in their offices). Sir Alan gives one example that simply cannot be omitted:

'Madam,

We are in receipt of your favour of the 9th inst. with regard to the estimate required for the removal of your furniture and effects from the above address to Burbleton, and will arrange for a Representative to call to make an inspection on Tuesday next, the 14th inst., before 12 noon, which we trust will be convenient, after which our quotation will at once issue.'

Taking that letter as it stands, Sir Alan reduces it thus:

'Madam,

We have your letter of May 9th requesting an estimate for the removal of your furniture and effect to Burbleton, and a man will call to see them next Tuesday forenoon if convenient, after which we will send the estimate without delay': not counting 'Madam', we notice that the revised letter contains 42 words instead of 66. But Sir Alan goes further, by recasting, thus:

'Madam,

Thank you for your letter of May 9th. A man will call next Tuesday forenoon, to see your furniture and effects, after which, without delay, we will send our estimate for their removal to Burbleton' (or 35 words against the original 66; or 157 letters against 294 letters).

Business English, in short, is extremely un-businesslike.

officious. See **official.**

offspring is properly used as a plural ('What offspring have you?'); as a singular it may have a curious ring, as in 'Here is my offspring, what do you think of him?'

oft is to be avoided as an archaism; *many times and oft,* as a cliché.

often. The *t* is either pronounced or (more often) silent. It is decidedly old-fashioned to pronounce the first syllable as 'awf'.

To use *often* for *in many instances* sets up an ambiguity, as in 'A Danish house is often thatched with straw' (cited by Weseen).

oftener, oftenest are, by current usage, regarded as no less correct than *more often* and *most often.*

Oh. See **O.**

old age, at an. Incorrect – or rather, un-idiomatic – for *at an advanced age.*

older. See **elder and older.** Only *elder* is now used as a noun.

ology. See **ism.**

omission. See **oversight.**

omnibus. See **bus.**

omnipotent; omniscient. See COM-PARATIVES, FALSE. – The former = 'all-powerful'; the latter, 'all-knowing'.

on is often used unnecessarily, as in *earlier on, from that moment* (or *time*) *on, later on.*

on, used for *for,* is an error. 'To lay down the concept of free speech as practised in America *on* Asiatic peoples ... is consistent if you like, but meaningless' (Stuart Chase, *The Tyranny of Words*).

on, misused for *on to,* e.g. 'I never notice what happens on the road, hanging on the back takes me all my time', a pillion passenger in a motoring case at Willesden (*The Evening News,* 13 Dec. 1937). The first 'on' is correctly used, the second incorrectly; to *hang on* anything is literally to be suspended, but to *hang on to* something is to cling or hold on with difficulty. This misuse, in such a phrase as 'The cat jumped on the table', was obstinately defended by Dean Alford in *The Queen's English,* after much argument; despite the popular use of *on,* I believe his defence is indefensible. There is, of course, a real difference of meaning between 'drive on the pavement' and 'drive on to the pavement'.

on and **upon.** See **upon and on.**

on account of is unnecessary after *cause* or *reason*. For 'The reason is on account of (something or other)' read, 'The reason is that ...' or 'On account of something or other, something else happened.'

on behalf of. See **behalf of.**

on time; in time. *In time* = 'soon enough'; *on time* = 'punctually'.

on to. See **onto.**

one is often used unnecessarily or, at best, verbosely, as in 'If the opinion expressed is not one worthy of repetition, circulation should be restricted accordingly' (examination essay script).

one, use of pl. in v. after. The rule is that the formula, *one of* + plural noun or pronoun, requires the ensuing verb to be in the plural. Thus 'He's one of those chaps who plays a lone hand' (E. R. Lorac, *Death of an Author*) should be '... play a lone hand'. The use of the singular for the plural appears strangely inept when a subtle and notable writer employs it, as in 'We got out at one of those small country towns which is growing fast, but has not yet lost its character' (Joyce Cary, *To Be a Pilgrim*). The rule becomes clear from an equation:

The cows
The red cows
The cows that *are* red in colour
One of the cows that *are* red in colour
It is one of the cows that are red in colour

But where *one* is the true subject, it requires a singular verb:

One of the cows that *are* red in colour *is* for sale.

one and **he.** In British usage, *one* is correctly followed by *one, one's, oneself,* as in 'One should do one's best.' American English more readily accepts 'One should do his best.'

In certain circumstances, *one ... he ... his* is even ambiguous. Compare 'One readily admits that one may be wrong' (unambiguous) with 'One readily admits

that he may be wrong'; in the latter it is not clear whether *he* refers to *one* or to a third person. Perhaps the simplest procedure is to determine whether the *one ... one* or the *person ... he* or the *you ... you* mode is to prevail in the expression of your thought, and then to adhere to the mode chosen.

ONE and YOU modes (with a note on the *we* mode).

The *we* mode is – or should be – left to royalty, the Vatican, and editors of newspapers and other periodicals; the popularity of 'We are not amused' has waned. Queen Elizabeth II says 'My husband and I'.

In friendly or familiar speech and in familiar writing, the *you* mode is permissible and often preferable: but care must be exercised against confusing the personal *you* ('When are you going to Town?') with the generic or impersonal *you* ('When you're dead, you're a long, long time dead').

In formal speeches and addresses, as in formal and literary writing, the *one* mode is preferable ('One does one's best to live the good life; but that best may fall so far short of merit as to seem, in the result, evil; nevertheless, it is one's effort which counts as virtue'). To employ the *one* mode in conversation, unless one does it with consummate skill, may produce a comic effect ('If one does one's best, one does all that one can be expected to do, doesn't one?). It is a popular affectation among public figures today to use *one* for *I*, as in 'One learnt to ride as a child.'

one for *a* or *any*. 'Never has there been one complaint of any person having been robbed there' (John G. Brandon).

one another and **each other.** See **each other and one another.**

one in (two ... five, etc.) ... takes a singular verb, and *two* (or *three* or *five*, etc.) *in* ... takes a plural verb. The subjects respectively are simply *one* (amplified) and *two*, etc. (amplified), precisely as in *one horse in a million*, *one horse* is singular, and in *two horses in a thousand*, *two horses* is plural. In *John o' London's Weekly*, 6 Jan. 1939, 'Jackdaw' defends the advertising slogan 'Only one in five *clean* their [properly *his*] teeth ...' on the unconvincingly ingenious grounds that ' "one-in-five" contemplates not *one*, but as many *ones* as there are *fives*'. Am I, then, to presume that 'One horse in a million has a purple coat' should be '... have ...' on the ground that there are as many *ones* as *millions*! Compare 'In every five [i.e. in every set of five persons], only one cleans his teeth' and 'Of every five, only one cleans his teeth.'

ones for *those* is not wholly wrong, but it is loose and unidiomatic, as in 'Eminence is an accident in [the United States of] America, and it might befall anyone. It does befall the most unlikely ones. *Ones* who are not prepared for it. ... Ones who hoard fame and batten on it' (Paul Horgan, *A Lamp on the Plains*).

oneself and **one's self.** The difference between these two forms is precisely that between *myself* and *my self*, *yourself* and *your self*, *herself* and *her self*, *himself* and *his self*, *ourselves* and *our selves*, *yourselves* and *your selves*, *themselves* and *their selves*. The *oneself*, *yourself*, *themselves* form is that of the reflexive pronoun ('He hurt himself'), the appositive pronoun ('I myself did not understand what was happening'), and – in poetry – the emphatic pronoun ('Myself would work eye dim and finger lame', Tennyson – cited by Onions). In the *my self*, *their selves*, form, *self* is synonymous with 'personality or personal entity'.

ongoing. See VOGUE WORDS.

only, misplaced. Jespersen, *The Philosophy of Grammar*, 'The plural *feet* from *foot* was formerly only mentioned as one of a few exceptions to the rule that plurals ... were formed in *-s*'. Not 'only mentioned' but 'mentioned only as one, etc.': 'We only heard it yesterday' should be 'We heard it only yesterday.' Shakespeare makes this mistake in

The summer's flower is to the
   summer sweet
Though to itself it only live and
   die.

There is also ambiguity in the use of *only* where *alone* would be clearer, as in Nesfield's example from Johnson (*Letter to Rev. Mr White*), 'No book has been published since your departure of which much notice is taken. Faction only fills the town with pamphlets, and greater subjects are forgotten.' Nesfield takes 'only' to be an adjective qualifying 'faction', but might it not be an adverb qualifying 'fills'? Coleridge, a careful writer, at least once committed a misplacement: 'The wise only possess ideas; the greater part of mankind are possessed by them' ('Notes on Robinson Crusoe', 1830): properly, 'only the wise'. Even G. K. Chesterton fell into the error of a misplaced *only*, as in 'His black coat looked as if it were only black by being too dense a purple. His black beard looked as if it were only black by being too deep a blue' (*The Man Who Was Thursday*). Nor are philosophers exempt: 'We can only substitute a clear symbolism for an unprecise one by inspecting the phenomena which we want to describe' (read '... one only by inspecting'), Ludwig Wittgenstein, 'Logical Form', in *The Aristotelian Society: Supplementary Volume* ix, 1929. – *Merely* is subject to the same vagaries. These examples, all taken from the work of good writers, show that the natural place for *only* is usually next to the verb. This positioning is perfectly appropriate in speech and even in informal writing, but one must be ceaselessly on one's guard against ambiguity.

only and **only not** for *excepting* or *but*. 'But for all 'is bein' nothink only a stoker, the contractors would at whiles put 'im on for boss', (Henry Nevinson); and again from the same author, 'Mrs Simon would 'ave 'eaved at 'er 'ead whatever else she'd 'ad in 'er 'and, only not the baby.' These examples are both illiterate and colloquial, especially Cockney. Cf. 'He never drinks, only when it's somebody's birthday', where *only* should be *except*.

only too is defensible when it is used literally, as in 'One who has committed murder once is, as a rule, only too ready to commit it again.' But it should be avoided as a loose synonym of *very*: for instance, 'Only too pleased to help in a good cause' is absurd. Ths point is that *only too* carries the idea of excess.

onomatopoeia. See **echoism.**

onset should not be used for (first) *sign* as it is in E. R. Lorac, *Death of an Author*, 'I'm getting stylized, and that's the onset of fossilization via coagulation.'

onto is misused for *on to* in such a phrase as 'to walk onto the next station'. Wherever the *on* is simply an adverb, *on to* is the correct form. But 'in the sense in which it corresponds to *into*, *onto* is a real compound', pronounced differently from *on to* (*on' to'*), for *onto* is a trochee (*on' to*), as *OED* points out.

onus and **gravamen.** The former is 'a burden or charge, a duty or responsibility'; the latter is 'that particular part of an accusation which bears most heavily on the person accused' (*OED*). The *onus of proof* (L. *onus probandi*) is the accuser's obligation to prove the accusation he or she has made. The 'grievance' sense of *gravamen* is obsolescent.

op. cit. See **ib.**

operative (adj.). See VOGUE WORDS.

operative and **operator** (nn.). *Operative* is now chiefly confined to factory workers, but in American usage it also means a private detective.

An *operator* may be a surgeon or a dentist, a telephone or telegraph operator, or someone such as a tour operator who is engaged in a business; of a workman or mill-hand, it is to be avoided.

ophthalmologist is a person versed in the structure and functions of the eye; an *optician* is a maker of or – the usual current

sense – a dealer in optical instruments; an *optometrist* is one who measures and tests vision (without the use of drugs) and adapts lenses to the patient's vision (*OED*).

opinion, in my; I (myself) think, etc. Frequently, these phrases are unnecessary: usually, the context and the circumstances of one's statement make it clear that it is only an opinion; and if one wishes to stress *I*, it is enough to write (or say) '*I* think'.

opinion that, ... to be of the, is very wordy for *to think that* ...

opponent. See **antagonist.**

opposite (adj.) takes *to*, as in 'His house is opposite to mine'; the noun takes *of*, as in 'His is the opposite of that.' Incorrect are 'This is the opposite to that' and 'His house is opposite of mine.' ('His house is the opposite of mine' means something different and requires a particularization.) The word is also used as a preposition, as in 'His house is opposite mine.'

opposite (n. and adj.). Sometimes mispronounced with long *i*, the correct pronunciation is *oppozit*. See **-ile and -ine.** [The pronunciation with long *i* is not heard in American English.]

opposite and **contrary.** See **contrary and opposite.**

optimistic, 'inclined to optimism, i.e. to take a favourable view of circumstances and therefore to hope for the best', should not – as Weseen very properly remarks – be debased to equivalence with *hopeful* on the one hand nor with *cheerful* (or *sanguine*) on the other.

optimum, as both adjective and noun, means not merely 'the best', but 'the best compromise between opposing tendencies'. So does the adjective *optimal*. See VOGUE WORDS.

option, have no. This should be avoided, especially in 'I have (or, had) no option but to go'; 'I had to go' is infinitely better.

or and **nor**. Both *or* and *nor* are dissociative, not associative; these conjunctions 'do not link words so as to form a Compound Subject. The Verb is therefore not necessarily Plural.

'Either he or she *is* at fault. ...
Constructions like the following should be avoided: "Neither death nor fortune *were* sufficient to subdue the mind of Cargill" (Fox, *History of James II*).'

If either of the two subjects joined by *or* or by *nor* is plural, the ensuing verb must be plural; stylistically, it is advisable to set the plural subject the nearer to the verb, as in 'Neither Britain nor the Dominions desire war.'

In sentences where the subjects are of different persons (*he* and *I*, *I* and *the dog*, *you* and *your brother*, *you* and *I*), the verb should agree with the subject nearer to it, as in

'Either my brother or I *am* going';
'Neither you nor he *is* in fault';
'Neither he nor we *have* any doubt of it.'

These examples have been taken from *An Advanced English Syntax*, by Dr C. T. Onions, who adds: 'In the majority of cases, however, this form of expression is awkward, and is especially so when the sentence is a question, e.g. "Is he or we wrong?" Avoid the difficulty by saying:

Either my brother is going, or I am.
You are not in fault, nor is he.
He has no doubt of it, nor have we.
Is he wrong, or are we?'

As a general caution: Where *nor* is preceded by *neither* (whether explicit, or, as in 'Friend nor foe can help me now', implicit), *nor* presents no difficulties; in all other instances, *nor* is – or should be – synonymous with *and not*; but if it isn't, then be careful!

or for *and*. 'As matters stood, no power the police had, or' – properly 'and' – 'no action they could take, could prove Granadi to be lying' (John G. Brandon).

oral. See **aural.**

oral and **verbal**. In its general sense, *oral* is applied to that which is 'communicated in or by speech', i.e. 'spoken', as in 'Oral teaching is the best' and 'oral evidence'; it has two technical senses: (a) in Physiology and Medicine, 'of the mouth', 'pertaining to the mouth', the *oral cavity* being the cavity of the mouth; (b) in Theology, 'by or with the mouth', as in *oral communion* (the partaking of bread and wine at the Eucharist).

Verbal is applied to all words, not merely to spoken words, and it emphasizes the letter as opposed to the spirit as in 'a verbal translation', 'verbal criticisms' (criticism rather of the words than of the ideas and sentiments), 'a difference that was verbal rather than real'; a *verbal agreement*, however, is simply an agreement in speech only. In the sense 'verbatim', it is obsolescent. In Grammar, it is the adjective corresponding to the noun (and notion), *verb*.

orate for 'deliver a speech', 'to speak (in public)', is now either facetious or sarcastic – or both.

orchestrate. See VOGUE WORDS.

order, of an, adjectival, is weak for that adjective, as in 'ability of an unusual order' for 'unusual ability'. See ABSTRACT NOUNS.

ORDER OF SENTENCES AND CLAUSES. There is no point in theorizing on this subject. And no use. Sentences and clauses follow – or should follow – the natural flow of effective presentation: the minor is subordinated to the major: clarity is preserved, ambiguity avoided.

ORDER OF WORDS. Wrong order leads to ambiguity. 'All persons, events and places on the journey as far as Trieste, are entirely fictitious', author's note to Ethel Lina White's *The Wheel Spins*. Better: 'All persons, events and, as far as Trieste, places, are entirely fictitious.'

'An inquest was held only when the corpse existed, nor merely where one was suspected' should read 'not where one was merely suspected' (Milton Propper, *The Great Insurance Murders*).

'… She said, as she made room for him on a settee beside her' (Humfrey Jordan, *Roundabout*), should be '… made room for him beside her on a settee'.

'I saw a man in the room, who looked very ill' should be 'I saw, in the room, a man, who [or a man that] looked very ill' or 'In the room I saw a man, who [or, a man that] looked very ill.'

A. After those examples, which may serve as a warning to the incautious, we shall proceed to a few general remarks, based on ch. xvii, 'Word-Order', in vol. iii of Curme's *A Grammar of the English Language*.

'In English', says Dr George O. Curme, 'there are three word-orders: the verb in the second, the third, or the first place.'

1. *Verb in Second or Third Place*

'The most common order is: subject in the first place, verb in the second: "*The boy loves* his dog." This is called *normal order.*' A sentence may be inverted for varius reasons: to convey interrogation; to ensure emphasis; after *neither, nor,* and other introductory negatives, and for 'reporting' clauses in direct speech. 'Bitterly did we repent our decision', 'Never had I dreamed of such a thing', 'Only two had merciful death released from their sufferings', 'When did you meet him?', 'Where did you say she put it?', 'Only when the artist understands these psychological principles can he work in harmony with them' (Spencer).

'When the principal proposition' – i.e. the principal clause – 'is inserted in a direct quotation or follows it, the principal verb may sometimes still, in accordance with the old inverted order, … stand before the subject, but it is now more common [? usual] … to regulate the word-order by the modern group stress, so that the heavier word, be it subject or verb, stands last in the group.' Contrast: ' "Harry", *continued the old man*, "before you choose a wife, your must know my position" ' with:

' "George", *she exclaimed*, "this is the happiest moment of my life." ' Contrast also: ' "You have acted selfishly", *was her cold retort*' with: ' "You have acted selfishly", *she replied.*'

Compare too: 'The wind whistled and moaned as if, *thought Michael*, all the devils in hell were trying to break into the holy building' (Compton Mackenzie) and 'The wind whistled and moaned as if, *it sounded to him*, all the devils in hell …'. To the latter arrangement, which Sir Compton Mackenzie would never have tolerated, it must, however, be objected that it is ambiguous.

Another type of inversion is that in which the subject comes at the end for emphasis. 'Now comes *my best trick*', 'To the list may be added *the following names*', and from Galsworthy's *The Man of Property*, 'Fast into this perilous gulf of night walked *Bosinney* and fast after him walked *George*', where there is a lesser stress on 'fast' (in both instances).

Inversions are the usual reason for a verb to go into the third place, as in 'Very grateful they *were* for my offer', 'Lucky it *is* that we know her name', 'This threat he *was* unable to carry out.' The verb goes into the third place also in exclamations. Thus, 'What cheek he *has*!', 'What good friends horses *have been* to us for thousands of years!' The old inverted order, however, is retained in 'How pleasant *is* this hill where the road widens!'

Dr Curme sums up in this way: 'The normal word-order [i.e. the subject before the verb, with the complement, adverb, or object after the verb] has become the form of expression suited to the mind in its normal condition of steady activity and easy movement, from which it only departs' – better, 'departs only' – 'under the stress of emotion, or for logical reasons, or in conformity to fixed rules.'

2. *Verb in the First Place*

In modern English the first place in the sentence – an emphatic position – is occupied by the verb 'in expressions of will containing an imperative and often in those containing a volitive subjunctive, also in questions that require *yes* or *no* for an answer', as in:

> '*Hand* me that book!'
> '*Were* he only here!'
> '*Come* what will.'
> '*Did* he go?'

B. From these generalities, let us pass to the position of the adverb in the sentence or clause and to the order of adverbs or adverbial phrases when there are two or more.

For the splitting of the infinitive (*to earnestly pray*), see SPLIT INFINITIVE, THE.

The fear of an imaginary split infinitive has caused this monstrosity (cited by Fowler): 'The awkward necessity for getting to work and working as hard as possible and with hearty goodwill *altogether* seems to be forgotten', for '... sec.ns to be altogether forgotten'.

'Spare the infinitive, split the verb', as Wilson Follett says. In a compound verb (*have seen*) with an adverb, that adverb comes between the auxiliary and the participle ('I have *never* seen her'); or, if there are two or more auxiliaries, immediately after the first auxiliary ('I have *always* been intending to go to Paris'); that order is changed only to obtain emphasis, as in 'I never have seen her' (with stress on 'have') or 'Never, never have I seen her.' Failure to ensure the necessary emphasis accounts for such an infelicity as '*No one has probably seen you* – so you can go home in peace' (a detective novel, 1937), instead of '*Probably no one has seen you. ...*' There is, however, a tendency to move an adverb from its rightful and natural position for inadequate reasons, as in 'Oxford must *heartily* be congratulated on their victory', where 'heartily' modifying 'must' instead of 'be congratulated' is as absurd as – if 'certainly' was substituted for 'heartily' – 'certainly' would be if placed after 'be': logically, 'must *heartily* be congratulated' (instead of 'must be *heartily* congratulated') is no less absurd than 'must be *certainly* congratulated' (instead of 'must *certainly* be con-

gratulated'). Or as in 'The importance which *quite rightly* has been given to their meetings', instead of 'The importance which has quite rightly been given ...'.

On the same footing are the errors in 'It would be a different thing if the scheme had been *found fundamentally to be faulty*, but that is not the case' (where '... *found to be fundamentally faulty* ...' would be correct) and 'In these times it is rare that the First Lord of the Treasury *also is* Prime Minister' (where *is also* would be correct).

To separate a transitive verb from its object leads to awkwardness and generally discomfits the reader. 'I had to *second by all the means in my power diplomatic action*' should be 'I had, by all the means in my power, to second diplomatic action' or, less forcibly and less happily, 'I had to second diplomatic action by all the means in my power.' There the adverbial phrase is long and the error glaring. (Cf. 'How right were those people who *filled with lamentations the house* when a female child was born', Richard Aldington, *Women Must Work* – a passage exemplifying Gallic influence, English idiom demanding 'filled the house with lamentations', which is also euphonious.) But the rule holds good, however short the adverb. 'Have you *interpreted rightly the situation?*' should be 'Have you rightly interpreted the situation?' 'I should *advise, then, the boy* to take plenty of exercise' should be 'I should, then [better: therefore], advise the boy to take plenty of exercise.' 'It is probable that the Allies will *regard favourably Belgium's request*' should be 'It is probable that the Allies will favourably regard Belgium's request.'

'There are', Fowler cautions us, 'conditions that justify the separation, the most obvious being when a lengthy object would keep an adverb that is not suitable for the early position too remote from the verb ... But anyone who applies this principle must be careful not to reckon as part of the object words that either do not belong to it at all or are unessential to it.' In 'These men are *risking every day with intelligence and with shrewdness fortunes on what they believe', fortunes* is the object; not *fortunes on what they believe.* Put *fortunes* immediately after *risking.* But the sentence needs re-ordering: 'Every day, though with intelligence and shrewdness, these men are risking fortunes on what they believe.' In 'I can set most of the shocks that flesh is heir to at defiance' (Joan Jukes, 'On the Floor', in *New Stories*, 1934), *at defiance* should follow *set*, not only because it is too far separated from its verb but also because *set at defiance* is a verbal unit – *defy.* In 'Failure of the Powers to enforce their will as to the Albanian frontier would expose to the ridicule of all the restless elements in East Europe their authority, which, as it is, is not very imposing', *their authority, which, as it is, is not very imposing* should immediately follow *expose.* But had *to the ridicule ... East Europe* been *to ridicule* (two words instead of eleven), then the sentence would properly have read 'Failure of the Powers to enforce their will as to the Albanian frontier would expose to ridicule their authority, which, as it is, is not very imposing', for to put the very long object in front of the short adverbial phrase would be to remove the adverb too far from the verb.

The fear of splitting the infinitive has been so insidious that it has become a fear of 'splitting' even a gerund as in 'To reduce the infantry for the sake *unduly of increasing* the artillery', where the sensible (and correct) order is '... sake of unduly increasing'.

Many of the preceding examples seem to have sprung from wrong ideas of correctness. Probably, however, the most frequent cause of error is that which one would expect: carelessness. (For the misplacing of *only*, see '**only,** misplaced'.) 'The Freudian theories in the last few years have influenced the novelists greatly' should be 'In the last few years the Freudian theories have greatly influenced the novelists', for the original position of *in the last few years* makes it appear that the Freudian theories began to exercise an influence not until the middle 1930s; *greatly* was also out of

position. 'It has been implied that Germany is a collectivist State, or, if not, that it has at least far advanced in Socialism' should be '... has at least advanced far in Socialism'.

See, too, the four examples set at the head of this article: all four result from carelessness, although the fourth might have been given in the FALSE AGREEMENT article.

These misplacings of the adverb (or the adverbial phrase) exemplify the need of caution. But all errors exemplify that need: and errors of word and errors of syntax are instructively frequent in the work of those popular authors who turn out three or four or five books a year – often under two (or even three or more) names.

But adverbs may depart from the positions recommended in the foregoing paragraphs if there is a good reason. The best reason of all is clarity: but then, we hardly need give examples of this. The reason next in importance is that of emphasis. 'I met your father *yesterday*' is the normal order; 'I met *yesterday* your father', as we have already seen, is abnormal and unidiomatic in English (though correct in French); '*Yesterday* I met your father' stresses the day – the time – *yesterday*; 'I *yesterday* met your father' is now affected, although it was common enough in the 18th century ('The jury now will examine the [article]', *The Sessions Papers of the Old Bailey*, 1751).

The *yesterday* example comes from Geo. O. Curme's *Syntax*, where it is also pointed out that sometimes the adverb (or adverbial phrase) modifies, not the verb alone but the sentence as a whole. 'In this case the adverbial element usually precedes the verb, verbal phrase, or predicate noun or adjective' (i.e. the object or the complement), as in 'He *evidently* thought so' or, more strongly, '*Evidently* he thought so'; 'He not only believes in such books, but he *even* reads them to his children'; 'He *absolutely* lives from hand to mouth', where 'lives *absolutely*' would, at best, change the sense or, at worst, create confusion; 'She *always* lets him have his own way' or, more emphatically, '*Always* she lets him have his own way.'

For adverbs such as *not, never, nowhere,* see NEGATION.

ordinance; ordnance; ordonnance. An *ordinance* is a regulation, by-law, rule, that is less permanent, less constitutional, less general than a law or a statute; especially a municipal or other local enactment; also it is a religious observance, and a decree, and a dispensation of Providence or merely of destiny.

As a military term, *ordnance* = 'cannon' (mounted guns); but the chief sense of the term is, 'the public establishment concerned with the military stores and materials, the management of the artillery, etc.'.

Ordonnance is a systematic arrangement, e.g. of parts or features in a piece of architectural or artistic work, or of literary material; Sir Joshua Reynolds spoke of 'disproportionate ordonnance of parts' (*OED*).

organic. See VOGUE WORDS.

organizational preliminaries = preparations.

orient (v.). See **orientate.**

Oriental and **Eastern.** *Eastern* refers to the East portion (or part or region or land) of any part of the world; *Oriental* only to the countries, regions, etc., lying to the east of the Mediterranean, and especially to Asia or rather to Asia-without-Siberia. *Eastern Europe, the Orient, Oriental lands, Oriental drugs,* and similar expressions require a capital letter, but one may with propriety drop the capital both in 'the eastern part of the island', 'the eastern extremity of Great Britain', and in *oriental* as an adjective in astrology or astronomy, or in *oriental stitch* (a technicality in needlework).

orientate and **orient** (v.). (n.: *orientation*). *Orient* is the main form, with *orientate* as a British (rather than an American) variant. (See also **disorient.**) One can *orient* one's behaviour, one's conscience, one's ambition, or another person, or one can,

reflexively, *orient oneself*; i.e. guide or direct it, him, her, oneself, or to get one's bearings, put another on the right path or track. [*Orientation course,* American pedagoguese for an introductory, general, or historical study, usually of the social sciences designed for college freshmen or sophomores.]

osmosis. See VOGUE WORDS.

ostensible and **ostensive.** The former = 'declared, avowed; pretended or merely professed', as in 'Her ostensible demand was for English aid in her restoration to the throne' (J. R. Green), 'His ostensible reason was that ...'. In Philosophy, *ostentive* = 'declarative', as in 'Reason is heuristic, not ostensive: it asks questions but does not supply the answers'; applied to a proof, it means 'specious'; in Logic it = 'directly demonstrative', 'setting forth a general principle manifestly including the proposition to be proved' (*OED*). So an *ostensive* definition 'shows' the meaning of what it describes.

other, omitted after *any.* See GENITIVE, VAGARIES OF THE, last paragraph.

other, used intrusively. *Other* is incorrectly and ambiguously introduced in the following (quoted by Nesfield from *The Daily Telegraph* in August 1900): 'The Jingo element is strong in London, stronger than it is in the *other* provincial towns.'

other, the. Avoid clumsy use. How awkward is the following! 'While one man was baling out the water from his canoe, another tipped up the boat so that it shipped bucketsful. It was the fun-maker who suffered, for *the other* man got out and landed while *the other* sank with the canoe' (Violet O. Cressy-Marcks, *Up the Amazon and over the Andes*).

other ... except. An article in *The News Chronicle,* 4 March 1938, speaks of 'every other country except ours'. Our country, to be excepted from, must first be one of those 'others', which is absurd. The sense is expressed either by 'every country except (or, but) ours', or by 'every other country than ours', which is correct but clumsy.

other than is the correct form (as also the similar combinations, *different from*, *opposite to*, *contrasted with*). Writers occasionally forget that *other* in *other than* is an adjective or a pronoun, not an adverb. Thus *other than* should be *apart from* in this sentence by C. G. Macartney: 'Other than that' – a missed catch – 'the batsmen were quite comfortable.' For the meaning 'in any other way than', the correct choice is *otherwise than*, as in 'We can't get there otherwise than on foot.' But see **otherwise.**

other than that, misused for *apart* (American: *aside*) *from that.* 'A particularly smart job – with the exception of the murder of this poor fellow. ... Other than that, I'm bound to say that I quite appreciate a neat bit of work' (John G. Brandon).

other to. *Other to* is occasionally misused for *opposite to* or *across from*, as in 'On the other side to mine', 'In the other room to mine'.

others, of all, is a form of false comparison. The 'he' referred to in 'he was the best (cricketer) of all others' is *not one of the others*, but *best of all* (the cricketers), or *better than any of the others*. This illogicality was frequently committed by Southey, Thackeray, and many other esteemed writers, but it is unjustifiable. Nesfield (*Errors in English Composition*, 1903) puts it thus: 'The thing to which the Superlative refers must be *included* amongst things of its own class, otherwise no such comparison can be made.' E.g. 'The place which of all others in the wide world she had wished most to see' (Southey, *The Doctor*).

otherwise for *other* is misused. 'What he expected from life, otherwise than a day-by-day relish of experience and some eventual recognition of his disinterestedness, could not be seen' (Frank Swinnerton, *Harvest Comedy*).

ought (n.). See **aught.**

ought is stronger than *should*. 'You ought to do it' is stronger than 'You should do it.' See also the entry, PAST MODAL.

ought, didn't – hadn't – shouldn't. ' "He shouldn't ought to behave like that. It's hardly decent" ', for 'He ought not to behave like that.' *Ought* never requires the auxiliary, the use of which can lead to the most ridiculous grammatical confusion, as in: 'He didn't ought to have done it, had he?' or 'He hadn't ought ..., did he?'

-ourous for **-orous**, as in Galsworthy, *The Silver Spoon*, 'The rumourous town still hummed', is incorrect.

our's is incorrect for *ours*.

ourselves. See **myself and oneself.**

out loud, colloquial, is stylistically inferior to *aloud*, as in 'She sobbed out loud'; also it tends to be ambiguous.

outcast (one who has suffered expulsion from society) and **outcaste** (one who has lost caste or has no caste) have often been confused.

outdoor is the adjective, **outdoors** the adverb, as in 'She put on her outdoor clothes to go outdoors into the rain and wind.' Oddly enough, the corresponding noun is *outdoors*, as in 'The outdoors is stimulating' although *out-of-doors* is perhaps more usual ('He prefers the out-of-doors to the most comfortable house').

outline is a skeleton preliminary plan; **summary** an abridged restatement.

outside of is incorrect in 'Outside of the house, he could see quite well; inside of the house, he could hardly see.' Read 'Outside the house ..., inside the house ...', for the prepositions are *outside* and *inside*. [In American usage, *outside of* and *inside of* may occur in informal writing as well as in conversation.]

outward and **outwards.** The latter is only adverb; the former is chiefly an adjective ('the outward voyage') but often functions as an adverb in American English, in older British writing and in the phrase 'outward bound'.

over for *about* or *concerning* is catachrestic or, at best, very colloquial, as in 'He was anxious over your misfortune', 'He was happy over your good fortune.'

over should, to avoid ambiguity, be *for* over in the following: 'It was audacious, perhaps foolhardy. But not too daring for a determined man who at last had an opportunity to satisfy a grudge he had nursed over a decade' (actually, thirteen years at least; Milton Propper, *Murder at the Polls*). *Over* in the time-sense is normally 'for the duration of', or 'spread over', not, as in the example, 'more than'. But it is reasonable to use *over* elsewhere with numbers, as in 'collected over £20' and 'He is over 18.'

over and **above**. See **above and over.**

over-all, overall, (as adj.) See OFFI-CIALESE, last paragraph. A VOGUE WORD.

over-availability is nauseating officialese for *glut*.

OVER-EMPHASIS,   OVER-STRESSING, etc. See TAUTOLOGY. But we give one example here, just to show what we mean: 'The general appearance of the road – as regards traffic and pedestrians – presented quite a usual aspect' (John Ross, *The Moccasin Man*, 1936). But the more usual kind of over-stressing is that which is present in HYPERBOLE.

overflowed; overflown. The preterite of *overflow* is *overflowed*; so too is the past participle, in current usage. Reserve *over-flown* for *overfly*, 'to fly over', hence 'to surpass in flight' (i.e. to fly faster or further or higher).

overkill. See VOGUE WORDS.

overlay and **overlie**. The latter = 'to lie over or upon', lit. (as in Geology) or fig.; hence, 'to smother by lying upon', more generally *overlay* ('She overlaid her child'). *Overlay* is much wider in its application: e.g. 'to cover *with*', 'to deck all over', 'to conceal or obscure as if by covering up', 'to overburden'. Do not use *overlay* in the first sense of *overlie*. *Overlay – overlaid – overlaid; overlie – overlay – overlain*.

overlook and **look over**. The latter = 'to look at, to inspect, to read through'; the former = 'to look over the top of', 'to look down upon', (of a place) 'to command a view of'; also, 'to disregard, to ignore; to fail to see'; also, and confusingly, 'super-vise'. It is best not to use *overlook* at all if there is danger of confusion between these last two often opposed senses.

overly (for *excessively*, as in 'overly enthu-siastic') is either Scottish or an American-ism; *over* ('over ready to …') or *excessively* is preferred in British usage.

oversight; omission; supervision. *Oversight* = 'supervision, superintendence; care or management', but is slightly obso-lescent in this sense. Its dominant current sense is 'failure or omission to see', hence 'inadvertence', hence 'a mistake of inad-vertence', as in 'It may have been an over-sight' (*OED*).

overtone and **undertone**. *Overtone* is a technical term in music, 'a tone other than the lowest in a harmonic series'. Other-wise, both words mean that something has more in it than is apparent. An *overtone* is a subtle, elusive implication, an additional secondary effect. 'Their·friendship had been a light amusing lyrical affair, with no overtones or implications' (Claude Houghton, *Strangers*, 1938). An *undertone* is an underlying quality or undercurrent of feeling; often an unexpressed communal state of mind, as in 'undertones of pessimism in the City'.

overwhelming is misapplied when it is used as a mere synonym of *vast*, as in 'Though it can be said that, in the over-whelming majority of cases, secret mes-sages can be deciphered and read by the trained expert, the fact remains that the time factor may make the decipherment valueless' (Nigel Morland, *The Conquest of Crime*). So, too, *an* (or, *the*) *overwhelming proportion of* is infelicitous for *by far the larger part of* or *the vast majority of*.

owing to. See CONJUNCTIONS, DISGUISED, and **due to.**

oxidation, oxidize, etc., form a group that requires careful discrimination.

ozone should be used neither as a synonym of *air* (especially, good or healthy air), as so many advertisers use it; nor of *oxygen*, for properly it = 'an altered condition of oxygen, existing in a state of condensation, with a particularly pungent and refreshing odour'. Mortimer Collins employed it correctly in 'Exhilarated by the fresh ozone of the mountains', though he need not have used *fresh* at all (*OED*). It is the *ozone layer* in the stratosphere that usefully absorbs most of the sun's ultraviolet radiation.

P

pact is 'an agreement made between persons or parties, a compact' (*OED*): a dignified word, it should not be debased to trivial uses. Properly, it is applied to *formal* agreements; to solemn or weighty or important or significant agreements.

palate; palette; pallet. *Palate* is 'the roof of the mouth', hence one's sense of taste; *palette*, that tablet of wood (or occasionally porcelain) on which an artist lays and mixes colours; *pallet* is a straw bed, hence a mean or humble bed or couch, or a platform for storing and moving loads in a warehouse.

Pall Mall. See **Mall and Pall Mall.**

palpable. See VOGUE WORDS.

panacea should not be used for a cure for a particular ill, for *panacea* means 'a catholicon', i.e. 'a universal remedy'. Therefore to speak of 'a panacea for gout' is absurd.

panegyric is not merely *praise*, but either a public speech or a public writing, in praise of a person, thing, achievement; a laudatory discourse; 'a formal or at least an elaborate eulogy', or, derivatively, 'laudation' or any 'elaborate praise' (*OED*).

panic (v.i. and v.t.) has present participle *panicking* and past participle (and tense) *panicked.*

parable. See ALLEGORY.

paradigm. See VOGUE WORDS.

PARAGRAPHING. In the words of that eminent philosopher and rhetorician, Alexander Bain (1818–1903), 'The division of discourse next above the Sentence is the Paragraph. It is a collection, or series, of sentences, with unity of purpose' – an orderly collection, a natural sequence.

'Between one paragraph and another, there is a greater break in the subject than between one sentence and another. The internal arrangement comes under laws that are essentially the same as in the sentence, but on a greater scale.

'The Paragraph laws are important, not only for their own sake, but also for their bearing on an entire composition. They are the general principles that must regulate the structure of sections, chapters, and books. The special laws applying to different kinds of prose composition – Description, Narrative, Exposition, and Persuasion – cannot supersede those general principles; they only deal with the matter in hand from a higher point of view. Apart from the application of these higher laws, we may adapt an old homely maxim, and say, "Look to the Paragraphs, and the Discourse will take care of itself" ': each paragraph (or, on a large scale, each section of a chapter) corresponds to a point to be made, described, narrated; to a head of discourse, a topic, an aspect. If you establish the ordonnance of your theme, you will find that there is one order superior to all others; in establishing the order in which you desire to make the points of your exposition or your argument, to set forth the incidents in your narrative, the aspects in your description, you simultaneously and inevitably establish the division into paragraphs and the order of those paragraphs. That is the nearest sensible thing to a general rule.

But here are several minor precautions.

I. If a paragraph shows signs of becoming tediously long, break it up into two or three or even four parts, linked one to another and casting back to the first head by such a conjunction or such a conjunctival phrase (e.g. 'in such circumstances as these, it was natural that ...') as indicates the dependence of the second, third, fourth of the theme-involved paragraphs on the first and the relation of the second to the first, the third to the second, the fourth to the third. Modern taste favours shorter paragraphs than were advocated in the past, as providing more resting-places for the reader. But although a single topic may extend over two or more paragraphs, a single paragraph should never deal with two or more unrelated topics.

II. Do not shred the story or the discourse, the essay or the whatnot into a sequence of very short paragraphs, for this is an irritating trick beloved of slick journalists.

III. But to interpose a one-sentence paragraph at intervals – at longish intervals – is prudent. Such a device helps the eye and enables the reader (especially if 'the going is heavy') to regain his or her breath between one impressive or weighty or abstruse paragraph and the next.

IV. If the development of the theme is logical, natural, easy, one paragraph follows on its predecessor so inevitably that a conjunction may often be unnecessary. A long procession of *but, however, nevertheless, therefore, moreover* can become a weariness – and generally does.

V. Examine the paragraphing in the longer articles of this book. I do not pretend that it is perfect, but I believe that it is both simple and adequate.

[An interesting treatise is E. H. Lewis, *The History of the English Paragraph* (Chicago, 1894), referred to by Perrin.]

parameter. See VOGUE WORDS.

paramount (either 'superior' or in modern usage, 'supreme' in rank or authority; hence, 'pre-eminent'), as in 'of paramount importance', is sometimes misused for *tantamount* (to), 'equivalent (to)'.

paranoid. See VOGUE WORDS.

parasol is a (carried) sunshade; an *umbrella* is a (carried or not carried) protection against rain or sun. The distinction between *parasol* and *sunshade* (*q.v.*) is that the former is small and umbrella-shaped; the latter may be anything designed to protect against the sun's rays, be it a visor, large umbrella, lattice, or awning.

parentheses. See **bracket.**

PARENTHESIS, USE AND DANGERS OF. The danger of losing the thread of grammatical sequences is illustrated by the following sentence from Sir Arthur Evans's lecture, 'The Minoan World', 16 Oct. 1936:

'But the present Exhibition, arranged by him in connexion with the Jubilee of the British School of Athens (though the results of the discoveries at Knossos itself naturally still form the main theme on an amplified scale), the object has been to supply as far as possible the materials for a general survey of the Minoan culture in its widest range, etc.'. Charles C. Boyd, in *Grammar for Great and Small*, hit the nail on the head when he remarked that, 'The test of a parenthesis is whether the other words make sense without it.' See also PUNCTUATION.

parson, technically, is 'a holder of a parochial benefice in full possession of its rights and dues; a rector'. Hence, colloquially, any beneficed clergyman – any (Protestant) clergyman, whether Anglican or Nonconformist: but in this extended, this colloquial sense, it is – except in rural use – slightly, occasionally very, depreciatory ('dyslogistic', as the philologists and grammarians have it). In favourable or neutral contexts, therefore, *parson* is to be avoided, as of course it is also in formal speech or writing except in its technical sense (based on *OED*). [In American usage, *parson* may have a familiar, affectionate connotation. *Parsonage* is in more regular use.]

part; whether singular or plural. See **number.**

part, misused for *some*, as in 'Part of the students fail their examinations.' See also **portion** and **share.**

partake of is not simply 'to *take*': it means 'to take one's share of', 'to share in'. 'Being alone, I consoled myself by partaking of a glass of stout' is silly: 'Your papa invited Mr R. to partake of our lowly fare' (Dickens) is sensible.

partiality. See **prejudice.**

partially, wrongly used for *partly*. Harold Herd in *Watch Your English* gives an excellent example of the ambiguity caused by this misuse: 'The appeal was partially heard before the Lord Chief Justice ... yesterday', where 'partially' might mean *unfairly*, with a bias towards one side. However, the adjective *partial*, 'incomplete', as in *a partial success*, can hardly be avoided. Both *partially* and *partly* may mean 'in part'; but *partially* is more suitable for the meaning 'not fully (of conditions)' as in 'partially blind', and *partly* for 'to some extent (of things and places)' as in 'a shack made partly of tarpaulin' or 'They live partly in Rome and partly in London.'

PARTICIPAL PHRASES, DISCONNECTED. 'Upon landing at the quay the little town presented a strong contrast in styles' (Hulbert Footner, *The Obeah Murders*). 'Listening, there was much to stimulate both mind and imagination' (Arthur Bryant). 'After walking about two miles from Llangollen, a nar-

row valley opens on the right' (W. W. Davies, *A Wayfarer in Wales*).

See **CONFUSED PARTICIPLES.**

PARTICIPLES, FUSED. See **FUSED PARTICIPLES.**

party should not, in formal English, be used for *person*: 'The old party looked ill' should be 'The old man' – or 'woman' – 'looked ill'. A *party* is a group or body of persons; in legal phraseology, *party* does not denote 'one person': it denotes each side (one or more persons) in a contract or an action. [With acknowledgements to Harold Herd.]

pass, misused for *meet*. A train *passes* another going in the same direction; *meets* one that is coming in the opposite direction. But a train can either *pass* or *overtake* one going in the same direction; it can also *pass* one that is stationary. Obviously a train can *meet* another only if the two are travelling in opposite directions; but one *passes*, rather than *meets*, another vehicle going in the opposite direction and on the other carriageway of a motorway.

passable and **passible.** The former = 'traversable or viable', hence 'tolerable', '(almost) satisfactory'; the latter is a theological technicality, meaning 'capable of suffering', 'exposed to suffering'.

passed and **past.** *Past* was formerly the common spelling of the past participle of *pass*, but this use is now obsolete and confusing: *passed* is the preterite and past participle, *past* is adverb or adjective or noun or preposition. We write 'the past month', 'in the past', but 'the month has passed quickly.'

PAST MODAL FOR PRESENT 'softens the form of the expression', as in 'You *should*' for 'It is your duty to' (do something); '*Would* you help him?' for *Will* you help him?'; '*Might* I say what I think?' for '*May* ...?'; '*Could* you come a little earlier than we arranged?' for '*Can* you ...?' The same applies to 'You *should* not speak so disrespectfully of your parents' for 'You *ought* not to speak ...' (based on *OED*'s remarks at *ought*, v, iii, 5b).

pastor should not be used as an exact synonym of *minister* or *clergyman*; it should be restricted to a 'minister in charge of a church or congregation, with particular reference to the spiritual care of his "flock"' (*OED*). Methodists and Baptists seem to prefer *pastor* or, old style, *preacher*; Presbyterians, *minister* or *pastor*, Congregationalists, *minister*; Episcopalians, *minister* or *rector* (High Churchmen, sometimes, *priest*); Roman Catholics, *priest*. *Preacher* and *parson* (Protestant) are now old-fashioned. *Clergyman* is usually Episcopalian, though *clergy* is a common term. The Methodist pastor lives in a *parsonage*; the Presbyterian and the Congregationalist minister in a *manse*; the Episcopalian rector and the Catholic rector (priest in charge, sometimes *pastor*) in a *rectory*.

pastoral; pastorale. The second is a noun only, *pastorale* being a musical term for an instrumental composition in rustic style or of pastoral scene, or an opera or cantata with a rustic subject; *pastoral* = 'used for pasture' ('Epirus is essentially a pastoral country', Grote), and also 'of or pertaining to shepherds; relating to, occupied in, consisting of (the care of) flocks and/or herds', as in 'pastoral farms', 'Agricultural and Pastoral Show', hence 'of a Church pastor' or 'relating to the guidance of a "flock" of Christians', and as a term in music, art, literature, 'setting forth the shepherd's life', with the corresponding noun *pastoral*; (Literature) 'a play, a dialogue, a poem, dealing with the life of shepherds, or, more widely, the rural life', and (Art) 'a picture of the same or a similar kind' (*OED*).

pathos. See **bathos.**

'**patron** of the arts', but not of a green-grocer or a bookmaker. Tradesmen have *customers*, professional men have *clients* – though doctors have *patients*.

See also **client and customer,** and cf. the following entry.

patronize for *trade with* (a grocer) or *at* (his shop) is commercial pretentiousness.

pavement is the usual British, *sidewalk* the usual American term for 'the paved footway at the side of a street, as distinct from the roadway' (*OED*). If at the side of a country road, it is a *footpath* in Britain, a *path* in America.

pay away; pay down; pay off; pay out; pay over; pay up. To *pay down* is to pay part of a due or debt, also to pay on the spot or immediately; *pay off* is to pay a person in full and discharge him or her, whereas *pay up* is to pay in full for something or to discharge a debt in full; to *pay over* is to hand money (*to* a person) either in part or, less generally, in full; *pay away* is pay unexpectedly or reluctantly or with difficulty or (e.g. of a bill) to a third party; and *pay out* is to pay a sum from one's account or a fund, or to get rid of a person (e.g. an undesirable partner) by paying (e.g. his share of the capital).

peaceable and **peaceful.** The former is now restricted to persons, their character, their actions, their feelings, etc., as in 'She shall give security for her peaceable intentions' (Goldsmith) and 'The inhabitants are shepherds ... simple, peaceable, and inoffensive' (Elphinstone). *Peaceful*, 'full of or characterized by peace; undisturbed, untroubled, quiet', is applied to periods, occasions, countries, scenes, parties, states of mind, appearances, faces, as in 'The Thames Valley affords many peaceful scenes and vistas', 'In death, peaceful is the face that in life was either anxious or stormy', 'Peaceful Italy involv'd in arms' (Dryden) (*OED*).

peak. See VOGUE WORDS.

peculiar(ly) is better avoided in the sense of *particular(ly)* or *especial(ly)*; e.g. Helen Harris, 1891, 'The Arabs regard the spot as peculiarly sacred' (*OED*).

-ped, as in the adjectives (hence nouns) *biped*, *triped*, *quadruped*, means 'footed' (*biped* = two-footed); 'five=footed' is *quinqueped* (n.) or *quinquepedal* (adj.), 'eight-footed' is *octoped*, 'ten-footed' is *decapod*. The series extends to *multiped* (many-footed), which may be more or less than *centiped* (hundred-footed, the insect being a *centipede*) and is generally less than *milliped* (thousand-footed, the insect being a *millipede*). But *centipede* and *millipede* are also adjectives. In -*ped*, the *e* is short; in -*pede* it is long.

PEDANTRY. 'O, in what a mightie vaine am I now against Horn-bookes! Here before all this companie, I professe myself an open enemy to Inke and paper. Ile make it good upon the Accidence body, that in speech is the devils Pater noster: Nownes and Pronounes, I pronounce you as traitors to boyes buttockes, Syntaxis and Prosodia, you are tormentors of wit, and good for nothing but to get a schoolmaster two pence a weeke. Hang copies, flye out phrase books, let pennes be turned to picktooths: bowles, cards, and dice, you are the true liberal sciences, Ile ne're be Goosequil, gentlemen, while I live' (Thomas Nashe, *Summers last Will and Testament*, written in 1593).

Pedantry, says *OED*, is 'the character, habit of mind, or mode of proceeding, characteristic of a pedant' (one who overrates book-learning or technical knowledge); 'mere learning without judgement or discrimination; conceit or unseasonable display of learning or technical knowledge'; hence 'undue insistence on forms or details; slavish adherence to rule, theory, or precedent, in connection with a particular profession or practice'. An alternative definition is the Viscount Stranford's (*c.* 1869), 'Undue stress laid on insignificant detail, and over-valuation of petty accuracy'.

The pedant, then, maintains tradition against usage in speech and in writing; he is the trouble-feast at every linguistic banquet, the spoil-sport in all word-fun, the wet blanket on all stylist ardour, the killjoy of every verbal or syntactical exuberance, the 'sour-graping' *écrivain manqué* that crabs the work of the successful or the copious creative writer; the scholar that

believes scholarship to be a close corporation of university professors, readers, lecturers, lectors, demonstrators, and what have you, and denounces all outsiders as 'unscientific' or 'brilliant but not sound', their work as 'spectacular but not scholarly', 'interesting but untrustworthy', and drags in irrelevance to prove the charge; the research student that believes research superior to creation, the history of the vowel *e* from Noah's stepping into the Ark to Norma's stepping into the Austin to be more important than *Tom Jones*; the sort of person who calls Shakespeare a bad writer because he breaks so many rules; who prefers Whittier to Whitman; who thinks *aggravation* (annoyance) a crime and *psychological moment* a sin, *different to* a solecism, and *under the circumstances* an impossibility. But why allow oneself to grow angry? for pedants, like the poor, are always with us. (See also **PLURALS, UN-ENGLISH.**)

peer, misused for (a person) *superior*. 'He is the equal if not the peer of anyone in the club' (vouched for by Weseen). [The belief that *peer* means superior or at least connotes *superiority* is exceedingly common among Americans – so common and so strong that it actually has this meaning more often than not. And unfortunately, correction at school only drives the word from the vocabulary of expression (as opposed to the vocabulary understood).]

pence is the collective, **pennies** the distributive (or separative) plural of *penny*. Thus, 'The fare was fivepence', 'Two insular and pence-paying realms' (*OED*); 'I gave him three pennies', three coins, whereas 'I gave him threepence' refers to the sum, paid in three separate pennies; 'The miser counted his great heap of pennies'; 'Pennies are brown, pence are money.' [In American English, *penny* colloquially = cent; pl. *pennies* (*pence* does not occur).]

pendant, -ent. See **dependant.**

pending. See **CONJUNCTIONS, DISGUISED.**

penetrant, for *penetrating* (of mind: 'subtle', 'acute') is not wrong; but it is disappearing from general use. It should be reserved for 'physically penetrating or trenchant', 'deeply cutting', or 'entering deep'.

penultimate is the last but one; **antepenultimate,** the last but two. Noun and adjective.

people, 'a nation, race, tribe, community', is singular, with plural *peoples*; *people*, 'persons', is plural, as is *the people*, 'the laity', and *the people*, 'the common people', i.e. those who do not belong to the nobility or the ruling (or official) classes. See also **persons.**

per is commercialese – and permissible in a Latin phrase, *per annum*, or in 'miles per gallon', '32 feet per second per second'. But where possible, use *a* – 'five times a year' rather than 'per year'. It should not be used, outside commercial contexts, for 'by means of', as in 'Mr Chamberlain went to Munich per aeroplane.'

per cent is occasionally misused for *percentage*; properly, *per cent* is used after a numeral. [American usage prefers *percent*.]

percentage for *proportion*. 'In motor racing, the machine – not the man – does the larger percentage of the work.' Idiomatically, one would go a step further and write, 'In motor racing, the machine does most of the work.'

perceptible; perceptive; perceptual. In current usage, *perceptible* is 'able to be perceived by the senses or the mind; observable'; 'a perceptible difference' is a difference that can be seen, felt, or understood, but it is not synonymous with *considerable*, as certain careless writers have supposed. *Perceptive* is 'capable of perceiving, belonging to or instrumental in perception', as in 'perceptive faculties'; hence, 'quick in perception, quick to notice; intelligent', as in 'Dickens was a most perceptive man.' *Perceptual* is a learned term, meaning 'of or belonging to perception; consisting in, or of the nature of, percep-

tion or the things perceived', as in 'perceptual images' (*OED*).

perennially = 'permanently', 'constantly', 'perpetually', not 'year after year' as in 'Perennially subject to attacks of gout'. The same applies to the adjective, which does not = 'recurring year after year'.

perfect, more, most; less, least; all these are inadmissible. See COMPARATIVES, FALSE. Used for *complete*, it is incorrect, as in 'The ship is a perfect loss.'

PERFECT INFINITIVE, wrongly used. The perfect infinitive seems to unpractised writers to accompany 'I (or you or he) should, or would, have liked', or 'He had intended', as in 'They would have liked to *have been* there, I'm sure', 'I should have liked to *have gone* to the cricket match', 'If he had intended to *have done* that, he might at least have told me': whereas the correct forms are 'They would have liked to *be* there', 'I should have liked to *go*', 'If he had intended to *do* that'. Compare 'If he had intended *doing* that'. The idea of the past is already in the finite verb ('would have liked', 'should have liked', 'had intended'): why repeat it? To good sense as to logic, the repetition is always irritating and occasionally confusing (based on Onions, *An Advanced English Syntax*,§ 179).

perform one's ablutions. See **ablutions.**

permissive. See VOGUE WORDS.

permit; allow. The former is active, the latter neutral; the latter is the more formal; the former connotes forbearance, sufferance, mere toleration, whereas the latter connotes approval and denotes sanction. One *allows* a thing by default or out of weariness; one *permits* it by express action – one states or even legalizes (certainly one formalizes) it. 'I allow him to come here; I permit him to stay past the agreed time.' 'That may be tacitly allowed which is not expressly permitted' (*Webster's*).

permit of. See **admit, admit of.**

perpetually and **continually**. In current usage, *perpetually* means 'incessantly; persistently; constantly recurrent; continually'; – not necessarily 'eternally' nor 'for the rest of one's life'.

perquisite; prerequisite. A *perquisite* is an incidental extra advantage, privilege, or 'fringe benefit' – colloquially, a 'perk'. A *prerequisite* is a requirement to be satisfied in advance, a necessary precondition.

persecute and **prosecute** are occasionally confused. The former is to 'pursue with malignancy or with enmity and injurious action'; to *prosecute* is 'to institute legal proceedings against' (a person). *Persecute* used to mean 'prosecute at law'; a sense now obsolete except in dialect and in humorous writings or speech.

persistently. See **consistently**.

-person. See SEXISM.

personage, misused for *person*. 'She looked exactly the same cool, cynical personage as when she had spoken to him at the bank that morning' (John G. Brandon, *The Dragnet*). 'That entirely mythical personage, "the man in the street" ' (from an essay script). A *personage* is somewhat important.

personal and **personally.** 'My personal opinion', 'I personally think', 'to pay a personal visit' are excessive – not to say absurd – for 'my opinion', 'I (or *I*) think', 'to pay a visit'. If you must have emphasis and wish to avoid italics, you can say 'my own opinion', 'I myself think'; and for 'to pay a personal visit' (as though one could visit otherwise than in person!) it is best to substitute some more sensible phrase. Instead of saying, 'Tom Mix paid a personal visit to London', say 'Tom Mix paid a visit to London' or, if you consider that event to be remarkable, 'Tom Mix actually paid a visit to London' – although 'actually visited' is more economical and telling than 'paid a visit to'.

personal is an adjective; **personnel** (stress on last syllable) is a noun, meaning 'the body of persons working in an establishment', and in its military sense often opposed to *matériel*. (It also means the department within an organization concerned with the welfare of the employees.) *Personnel* is often used with a plural verb; but it is in any case rather a stiff word for 'staff' or 'employees'. It should not be used with a number, as in 'two or more personnel'.

PERSONAL REMARKS, or PERSONALITIES as they are sometimes called.

Personality is 'the quality of being directed to or aimed at an individual, especially in the way of disparagement or unfriendly reference'; e.g. 'Personality in his satires ... accorded with the temper and the talent of Pope', as Disraeli the Elder suggested. That sense leads to and merges with this: (Generally in plural) 'A statement or remark aimed at or referring to an individual person, usually of a disparaging or offensive kind'; e.g. 'The Court cannot and will not stand journalistic personalities about its members' (C. Lowe). [With thanks to *OED*.]

Avoid personalities except when they are *not*, in the usual sense, personalities: be personal only in a friendly, pleasant, or respectful way. It is easy to give offence unwittingly. the loss of a friend is too high a price to pay for a witticism at his or her expense; the enmity of a stranger outweighs the pleasure of relieving oneself of a brilliant *mot*.

And in any event, remember that in these polite days, it is dangerous to put personalities into print. Cases of libel are distressingly frequent, and even though that person who is the object of a personality may not take offence (at least to the extent of instituting a lawsuit), his or her friends may say, 'Look here, A., this is going too far: you *can't* lie down under that, you know.' Or one of the sharking firms of shady solicitors that specialize in libel – and keep someone constantly on the watch for potential libel – will offer to take up the matter in the courts or obtain a fat sum out of court.

personality. In addition to retaining the basic sense, 'the fact (or the quality) of being a person, not, e.g. a thing', and the sense 'personal existence or personal identity', *personality* is now used chiefly in the sense 'distinctive personal or individual character, especially when *of a marked or notable kind*' (*OED*; italics mine); but that kind need not necessarily be *a pleasing* (attractive) *personality*; therefore a modifying word is advisable – e.g. *attractive, lovable, remarkable*. See also the following entry.

personality and **personalty** are occasionally confused. *Personalty* is a legal term for 'personal estate'; or, as Henry Stephen defines it in his famous *New Commentaries on the Laws of England*, 1841–5, 'Things personal (otherwise called personalty) consist of goods, money, and all other moveables, and of such rights and profits as relate to moveables.' *Personality* = 'personal existence, a distinctive personal character' (Harold Herd); it also means 'famous person', as in 'TV personality'. For the literary or grammatical sense of *personality*, see **personal remarks**.

PERSONIFICATION. In personification, a quality is represented as a person: 'Confusion spoke', 'Vice is a monster', 'Poetry is a mellifluous rhetorician.' Or, more fully: 'The attribution of personal form, nature, or characteristics; the representation of a thing or abstraction as a person, especially as a rhetorical figure' (*OED*).

Once so common, especially in poetry and perhaps above all in odes, personification is now suspect. When writers personify, they are looked at askance: 'He's ranting', say the critics; 'Getting a bit above himself', say his friends; and maybe he feels not too comfortable about it himself.

But in impassioned verse and poetic prose, personification is permissible. It is, however, to be used sparingly and with the nicest discretion. If done, it should be done consistently. Write either 'France, who modified her policy ...' or 'France, which modified its policy', but not 'who ... its' or 'which ... her'.

personnel. See **personal ... personnel.**

persons is now less usual than *people* except in formal or legal contexts. [American writers on the whole prefer to use *persons* after a numeral, as in 'eighty persons were present'.]

perspective and **prospective.** Except in heraldry, *prospective* is obsolete or rare as a noun; as an adjective, it means, on the one hand, 'regarding or concerned with or operative in the future', and on the other, 'future; expected or hoped for'. *Perspective* = 'of or belonging to perspective', i.e. to a particular 'art of delineating solid objects on a plane surface', hence, 'the relation – especially the proportion – in which the parts of a subject are viewed by the mind; the aspect of an object of thought', and several technical senses. See also **VOGUE WORDS**.

perspicuity, 'clearness of statement' (*OED*), and **perspicacity,** 'clearness of understanding' (*ibid.*), are easily and often confused. Perspicacity is required to grasp the distinction, and perspicuity to explain it. The same applies to the adjectives, *perspicuous* and *perspicacious*.

PERSPICUITY. In general, this subject is treated at **OBSCURITY.** Very little, therefore, needs to be said at this point.

Within the scope of the sentence, perspicuity is clear statement, viewed more broadly, it is clear ordonnance in composition: in either case, lucidity is attained not only negatively by freedom from the ambiguous and the obscure but, positively, by an unassailable univocality.

perspiration and **perspire.** See **sweat.**

persuasion. Correctly used for 'religious (and less often political) beliefs or opinion', it is classified by *OED* as 'slang or burlesque' when used for nationality, sex, kind, sort, description, as in 'She said she thought it was a gentleman in the haircutting persuasion' (F. Anstey, *The Tinted Venus*).

perturb and **disturb** alike mean 'to agitate'; in current usage, the former is reserved for mental and spiritual agitation, whereas the latter tends to be used of physical discomfort; and certainly *perturbation* is now applied only to the non-physical, *disturbance* rarely to other than the physical. 'Disturbed at my studies, I fell into a vague perturbation of mind and even of spirit.'

peruse is not synonymous with 'to *read*', for it means to read thoroughly, read carefully from beginning to end. One *peruses* a contract, one *reads* an (ordinary) advertisement – that is, if one does not merely glance at it.

pessimistic is 'pertaining to or like or suitable to pessimism'; hence, 'disposed to take the gloomiest view of circumstances and therefore to expect the worst': but do not debase it to meaning nothing more than 'gloomy'.

petit; petite. The English adjective *petit* is obsolete except in legal cases; *petite* is now applied to a woman, a girl, or rarely a female child, of small size or stature, and it has a connotation of daintiness of figure.

phantasy. See **fantasy.**

phenomena is plural (see **phenomenon**), not singular as it is made to be in 'The phenomena will not have been considered in all its bearings unless I add …' (M. D. Eden, translation of Freud, *On Dreams*, 1914).

phenomenal should not be debased to equivalence with *unusual*; it may, however, be used as a synonym of *prodigious*, as in 'The success of Miss Kate Greenaway's *Birthday Book* was phenomenal' (*The Athenaeum*, 7 Jan. 1882).

phenomenon; scientific plural, *phenomena*; ordinary plural, *phenomenons*; incorrect plural, *phenomenas* (cf. **stratas** and **datas**). In the sense 'a prodigy', it is a colloquialism. Not to be used of anything unremarkable, nor to be confused with *feature* or *quality*. And see **phenomena.**

philology. See **linguistics.**

phoney (superior to *phony*) is a colloquialism. (See esp. 'Spivs and Phoneys' in my *Here, There and Everywhere.*) The word is to be avoided in serious writing and dignified speech.

phonograph. See **gramophone.**

phosphorous (adj.) is a not infrequent misspelling of *phosphorus* (n.).

photo is a somewhat colloquial abbreviation of *photograph*. It may be used, with lamentable ignorance or levity, for any *portrait* (drawn or painted). [In the USA this usage is not known.] A young lady who is supposed to be well educated and is herself an instructor of youth, speaks of a friend of the family who 'had his photo in the Academy last year'.

PHRASAL VERBS, CHANGEABLE POSITION OF ADVERBS IN. Dr Harry Schnur asks, 'What rule governs "Take your hat off" and "Take off your hat"; "He laid his rifle down" and "He laid down his rifle", etc.?'

It seems to depend upon the length of the object. Nobody would say 'Take that ridiculous great big hat with the red tassels off'; there, 'Take off' must precede the rest of the sentence.

phrenetic, 'delirious, crazy', and *phrenic*, a scientific term for 'pertaining to the diaphragm' (*OED*), are sometimes mistaken, the one for the other.

picture is colloquial (and trivial) for 'a (very) beautiful or picturesque object', as in 'The room, when decorated, was a picture', 'The child was a picture.'

pictures. See **motion pictures.**

piece is now dialectal only, in the sense 'a portion of space', i.e. a short distance, a part of the way, or 'a portion of time', i.e. a while, especially a short while. As applied to a woman or a girl, it is depreciatory, or, at best, trivial.

pinchers is American for *pincers*. But whereas *pincers* has no singular, *pinchers* has a technical singular: '*Pincher* … a nipping tool fitting the inside and outside of a bottle, in order to shape the mouth' (Knight's *Dictionary of Mechanics*, Supplement, 1884) (*OED*). [In American English small pinchers are nowadays called *pliers* and *nippers*. These are the terms used in the catalogues of Sears, Roebuck and Co. and Montgomery Ward and Co.]

pistol is the weapon, **pistole** (accent on second syllable) an obsolete Spanish or French gold coin.

piteous; pitiable; pitiful (and the corresponding adverbs in -*ly*). They can all mean 'deserving or causing pity'. In addition, the rarer *piteous* can mean 'appealing for pity' ('piteous cries'). *Pitiable* may mean 'contemptible', which is now probably the chief meaning of *pitiful* ('A pitiful attempt to ape Royalty'). An older meaning of *pitiful*, 'feeling pity; compassionate' is now archaic.

placable, for *quiet*, *peaceable*, is misused; its true sense, *easily appeased*, *forgiving*, is distinct.

placable, placeable; placatory, placating. *Placeable* = 'capable of being placed'; *placable* = 'gentle, mild, forgiving; esp. easily pacifiable or appeasable', as in 'Though irritable, he was placable.' *Placatory* (rarely of persons) = 'conciliatory or propitiatory', as in 'a reply both dignified and placatory', 'a placatory offer or offering'. As an adjective, *placating* is a synonym of, and less formal, less literary than, *placatory*; like *placatory*, it is not used of persons themselves.

The respective adverbs are *placably*, (*placeably* doesn't exist), *placatorily*, *placatingly*.

The respective opposites are *implacable*, *unplaceable*, *unplacatory*, *unplacating*, but the third and fourth are not much used (*OED*).

place is a somewhat colloquial US replacement for *where* in *anywhere*, *everywhere*, *nowhere*, *somewhere*.

plain, like homely, is to be avoided in descriptions of women, for, there, it is a euphemism for *ugly* or, at best, *unbeautiful*. *Homely*, however, is inoffensive (or it should be!) in Britain, where it has the connotation of 'home-loving', 'unpretentiously housewifely'. [In American usage *homely* usually means plain and even unattractive when applied to persons and things. *Homelike* and *homey* (colloquial) preserve the connotation of affectionate welcome and comfortable ease.]

plain; plane. The spellings are often confused. As nouns, both = 'a flat surface', but a *plain* is a stretch of flat country, while a *plane* is either a level surface in mathematics or a 'level' in the abstract ('on a lofty intellectual plane'). *Plane* has many other noun senses, but as an adjective means only 'flat'. *Plain* has only one other noun sense, 'a stitch in knitting', but many adjectival senses.

plane sailing; plain sailing. The former was the original spelling, but is now restricted to a nautical sense. *Plain sailing* is the usual form for 'an uncomplicated course of action'.

PLATITUDES are, to thinking, what clichés are to writing. 'The platitude is the prince of spiritual peace; his yoke is easy, his burden is light' (Frank Binder, *Dialectic*).

plead – preterite and past participle *pleaded* (American and Scottish : also *pled*).

PLEONASM. See VERBOSITY.

PLEONASTIC NEGATION. See NEGATION, Section *C* (b).

plethora is not mere *abundance*, but *superabundance*.

PLURALS, SNOB. Big-game hunters are in the habit of speaking of a *herd of antelope* or *giraffe* or *elephant*, a *troop of lion*, a *crash of rhinoceros*, *three tiger*, and *five leopard* (the numbers are arbitrary), and so forth. Perhaps on the analogy of a *herd of deer* or *three deer*, a *flock of sheep* or *five sheep*, a *hover of trout* or *eight fine trout*.

This sort of thing is all very well at 'The Travellers', on safari, and in the best lounge at Nairobi: after all, minorities have their rights. But when, at the zoo, you hear a man, who doesn't know the difference between a jaguar and a cougar, say to his son, aged seven, 'Just look at those two lion, Willie!', you feel that snobbery has become a symptom of 'the larger lunacy'.

PLURALS, UN-ENGLISH. Jespersen, in *Growth and Structure of the English Language* (sec. 141), speaks of those 'abnormal plurals which break the beautiful regularity of nearly all English substantives – *phenomena, nuclei, larvae, chrysalides, indices,* etc. The occasional occurrence of such blundering plurals as *animalculae* [the correct plural is *animalcula,* singular *animalculum*; the English is *animalcule,* plural *animalcules*] and *ignorami* [as if from a Latin noun, *ignoramus,* "an ignorant person", whereas *ignoramus* = "we are ignorant": English usage has given us *ignoramus,* singular, with plural *ignoramuses* (against which pedants inveigh)] is an unconscious protest against the prevalent pedantry of schoolmasters in this respect.' But usage has consecrated *strata* as the plural of *stratum*

The general rule is: Add *s* (or, to nouns ending in *s* or *x* in the singular, *es*). Therefore *nucleuses* and *chrysalises. Indices* differs from *indexes* – see the separate entry. For *phenomena,* see **phenomenon.** The plural of *formula* is *formulas* or *formulae* – see separate entry. The 'Greek' scientific singulars, *electron, ion, neutron,* and the rest take the normal English plural, as in R. A. Millikan's learned book, *Electrons, Protons, Photons, Neutrons, and Cosmic Rays.* This rule applies not only to Greek and Latin words (*octopus* – *octopuses; rhinoceros* – *rhinocersoses*), but to words from modern languages: thus, the plural of *stiletto* is *stilettos*; not, as in Italian, *stiletti.* For those who wish to go further into the matter, there is no better authority than *A Grammar of Contemporary English* (Quirk, Greenbaum, Leech, & Svartvik), latest edition, 1985.

plus as a preposition meaning 'together with' does not affect the plurality of a following verb. The verb agrees with the

noun before *plus.* 'His experience plus his qualifications makes him the best choice', 'his qualifications plus his experience make ...'. The use of *plus* as a conjunction, meaning 'and furthermore', as in 'She can drive, plus she's attractive' has no place in serious writing.

p.m. See **a.m.**

Poet Laureate. The correct plural is *Poets Laureate.*

poetess. She would rather be called a *poet.* See SEXISM.

POETIC PROSE. Poetic or imaginative prose is prose that so far partakes of the nature of poetry as to possess the vocabulary – the words and the phrasing – of poetry and some of its rhythms. But it is not – or should not be – metrical, except sequences of not more than (say) eight syllables: the metrical character should be broken up.

Poetic prose is out of fashion. Yet it may be found in such earlier twentieth-century writers as G. K. Chesterton, Hilaire Belloc, Santayana, Frank Binder. The golden age of poetic prose was the approximate period, 1810–50; perhaps the greatest master was De Quincey. Both Walter Savage Landor and Robert Eyres Landor occasionally wrote pages of splendour in a genuinely poetic prose; William Sharp, a lesser man, employed poetic prose in most of his imaginative work.

To those who would essay this difficult and demoded genre, I recommend a study of all the writers I have named; to these names I add those of Shelley (*The Defence of Poetry*), Edgar Allan Poe, and the two-centuries-earlier Thomas Browne (*Urn Burial, The Garden of Cyrus, Religio Medici*), who sometimes achieves effects unsurpassed by even De Quincey.

POETS' LICENCE. A learned professor objected to A. E. Housman's 'The bells, they sound on Bredon' that the 'they' is superfluous and the line ungrammatical, and went so far as to say that 'a man who cannot write better English than that has no business to write at all'. Such a rash judgement would condemn most of our greatest writers, for they have all made such 'mistakes'. Indeed, as Flaubert remarked in a letter to Turgenev, it is not to the greatest, but to lesser masters that we look for models of style. The pedant critic overlooked the fact that this ungrammatical construction is an idiom so characteristic of English ballad poetry that modern poets writing in that style have adopted it as a matter of course.

> He rendered Tunstal all his right,
>> Knowing his valiant blood unstained,
> The king he caused this trusty knight
>> Undefiled Tunstal to be named.
>>> (An Elizabethan ballad of
>>> the Battle of Flodden)

> The silly buckets on the deck,
>> That had so long remained,
> I dreamed that they were filled with dew,
>> And when I woke it rained.
>>> (S. T. Coleridge, *Ancient Mariner*)

> Lars Porsenna of Clusium,
>> By the nine gods he swore,
> That the great house of Tarquin
>> Should suffer wrong no more.
>>> (T. B. Macaulay, *Lay of Horatius*)

> 'Last night the moon had a golden ring
>> And tonight no moon we see.'
> The skipper he blew a whiff from his pipe
>> And a scornful laugh laughed he.
>>> (Longfellow, *The Wreck
>>> of the 'Hesperus'*)

> The fays that to my christening came, –
>> For come they did, my nurses taught
>> me, –
> They did not bring me wealth or fame,
>> 'Tis very little that they brought me.
>>> (Andrew Lang)

> Mrs Jones gave a musical party,
>> Her friends she invited them all;
> There was old Mr Jenkins so hearty
>> And young Mr Jenkins so tall.
>>> (Mid-Victorian comic song)

This idiom is particularly common in rustic speech, to which ballad poetry always tends, and sometimes, as in the line of Housman quoted above, serves to suggest the homely character of the person speaking. It also falls naturally from the lips of a Shakespearean character of the utmost beauty and dignity, Viola (*Twelfth Night*), when on learning that the coast on which she has been shipwrecked is that of Illyria, she says meditatively, 'My brother, he is in Elysium.' It is a matter of emphasis and of the subtle process of thought. Nevertheless, this construction is strictly incorrect and should not be used in mere imitative carelessness, but only when it is necessary to the expression of a shade of meaning.

Within an hour or two of writing the above I had occasion to buy some flowers in Holborn from a man who complained, 'The growers and the dealers, they fix the price between 'em.'

An error of a different and more serious kind is that of Shakespeare in the song:

> Hark, the lark at heaven's gate sings,
>> And Phoebus 'gins arise
> His steeds to water at those springs
>> On chaliced flowers that lies.

But Shakespeare wanted his rhyme, and the words were to be sung to the accompaniment of music; the error would pass unnoticed. Scholars suggest that *lies* is here a plural form borrowed from the Northern dialects.

There are grave blemishes in Keats's famous odes. Take the first stanza of *To a Nightingale*, which stanza it is necessary to quote in full:

> My heart aches, and a drowsy numbness pains
> My sense, as though of hemlock I had drunk
> Or emptied some dull opiate to the drains
> One minute past and Lethewards had sunk.
> 'Tis not through envy of thy happy lot,
>> But being too happy in thy happiness
>>> That thou, light-wingèd dryad of the trees,
>>> In some melodious plot

Of beechen green and shadows
    numberless
Singest of summer in full-throated
    ease.

It may be mentioned first that the idea of *emptying ... to the drains* is too suggestive of the kitchen-sink; and again, that one does not *empty* a liquid, but a vessel containing it. The latter part of the stanza, however, is mainly in question; for the grammatical skeleton of the long unbroken sentence is ' *'Tis not through envy of thy happy lot ... that thou ... singest of summer*', which is mere nonsense. It is to his own 'envy', to himself as 'too happy', that the poet means to refer, but grammatically the words can apply only to the bird itself.

The *Ode on Melancholy* is addressed to a hypothetical listener: *Go not to Lethe ...*; *Make not thy rosary of yew-berries ...* and Keats ends the second stanza with:

Or if thy mistress some rich anger shows,
    Emprison her soft hand and let her
        rave,
    And feed deep, deep, upon her
        peerless eyes.

Then immediately he begins the third: *She dwells with beauty ...* Who can 'she' be but the lady with the peerless eyes? It is only in the sixth line, with,

Ay, in the very temple of delight
    Veil'd Melancholy has her sovran
        shrine ...

that we first hear of the personified subject of the title.

These are the errors of a concentrated passion, knowing its own meaning too well to see that the chosen words and images are not clear to another.

Common in 18th-century poetry is the use of *thou* and *you* (singular) indifferently in the same poem; a typical example is this from a political poem against Defoe, about 1703:

When you and I met slyly at the *Vine*,
To spin our Legion-letters o'er our
    wine,

These were the useful flams and shams,
    thou know'st,
Which made thy passage easy to thy
    post.

Probably both usages were at that time colloquially current, and the employment of both seemed to a writer to bring variety to his verse. Today there is a certain remote dignity in the use of 'thou', which if chosen must be maintained.

Byron, with all his rhetorical splendours, was not impeccable. Notorious is his ... *there let him lay*, in the address to Ocean (*Childe Harold*, IV), which is thrown into greater prominence by his correct – *where haply lies* two lines earlier. Elsewhere he writes, *Awakening with a start, The waters heave around me*; an instance of false agreement; as also is:

The thunder-clouds close o'er it, which
    when rent
The earth is covered thick with other
    clay,
Which her own clay shall cover ...
             (*Childe Harold*, III)

Swinburne, a great scholar, who wrote well in Greek, Latin, Italian, and French, is seldom at fault, but perpetrates a grammatical offence in writing, 'woe are we that once we loved and love not'. *Woe is me* meaning *woe is to me* or *woe is mine*, the plural form must be *Woe is us*. But Swinburne, perhaps unconsciously, preferred euphony to sense.

Not a misuse of words but a confusion of his metaphor is Tennyson's 'Then I shall see my pilot face to face when I have crossed the bar.' The poet's image is of a divine guide who takes him in charge when, having passed the dangers of mortality, he reaches the open sea; whereas the marine pilot steers the vessel past those dangers and, when the open sea is reached, turns his back on it and leaves it.

It is risky to base one's poetical imagery on objects or actions requiring technical knowledge.

That singular genius, Gerard Manley Hopkins, whose poems, though written in the 1880s, were first published in 1918 and have strongly influenced contemporary writers, allowed his search for novel and individual forms of expression to draw him into strange and inexcusable distortions of syntax:

What life half lifts the latch of!
What hell stalks towards the snatch of,
Your offering, with dispatch, of!
(*Morning, Midday and Evening Service*)

Recorded only, I have put my lips on pleas
Would brandle adamantine heaven with ride and jar, did Prayer go disregarded:
Forward-like, but however, and like favourable heaven heard these.
(*The Bugler's First Communion*)

When will you ever, Peace, wild wood one shy wings shut,
Your round me roaming end, and under be my boughs? (*Peace*)

Thou knowest the walls, altar and hour and night:
The swoon of a heart that the sweep and the hurl of thee trod
Hard down with a horror of height:
And the midriff astrain with leaning of, laced with fire of stress.
(*The Wreck of the 'Deutschland'*)

Patient analysis may reveal the meaning of the poet, but his experimental eccentricities are no safe guide to lesser men.

(Written for this book by Wilson Benington, who, himself a delicately lyrical minor poet, died in April 1942.)

point of view. See **standpoint.**

policy and **polity.** The latter means 'civil organization; civil order', also 'civil government' or 'a particular form of government', 'a state': it is no longer used synonymously with *policy*, 'a *course* of action intended, or adopted and pursued by a ruler or a government'. Weseen gives a good example in 'The United Kingdom is democratic in polity, but each party has its own policy, and so has each cabinet' (adapted) (*OED*).

Political Economy. H. D. Dickinson, in his review of *Political Economy and Capitalism*, by Maurice Dobb, in *The Modern Quarterly* of January 1938, writes:
'Sixty years ago "economics" began to supplant "political economy" as the name of the science that studies the material conditions of social well-being. This change in linguistic habits reflected a profound change in the method of the science itself. Instead of studying the *productive* relations of a human *society*, as Adam Smith and the classical economists had done, the vulgar economists (to give them Marx's designation) studied the *market* relations of isolated *individuals*. Dobb's use of the almost obsolete term "political economy" in the title of the present work is a banner of revolt against contemporary individualist tendencies and marks a return to the methods and outlook of the classical economists.'

politician and **statesman.** In the USA, *politician* has a connotation of intrigue and jobbery; in Great Britain, where it is not so sinister a word, it means 'one skilled – or engaged – in politics', all MPs being politicians. A *statesman* is a Cabinet Minister – a good one – or, at the least, an MP that has much influence and uses it sagaciously.

populace is a noun, *populous* an adjective. *Populace* is now, for the most part, derogatory: instead of meaning 'the common people', as it used to do, it = 'the mob' or even 'the rabble'.

pore; pour. One *pores* over a book, but *pours* liquids.

portentous for *portentous* is seldom written but often uttered: cf. **presumptious** for *presumptuous*. Probably on the analogy of *pretentious*.

portion and **part.** *Portion* = 'share' (one's portion of food; of an estate); it is short for *marriage portion*; it is one's lot or fate ('Brief life is here our portion', Neale); a (limited) quantity; not now used often for 'a part of *any* whole'. Roughly, a *portion* is an entity cut or taken from a mass or conglomerate, whereas a *part* is a fraction or a constituent ('part of a house, a pen, a body, a country, etc.'), as in 'Five portions cut from that cake will leave only a small part' (*OED*).

PORTMANTEAU WORDS. These are coinages such as *motel* or *Oxbridge*, sometimes also called 'blends'. The coining of these should be done with care – and with especial attention to the avoidance of ambiguity. When in Robert Carson's very fine novel, *The Revels Are Ended*, I read that a man breathed 'stentoriously' I thought, 'Oh, he means *stertorously*.' But Carson writes so well that I then reflected that he intended a portmanteau, or a blend, of *stentorianly* and *stertorously*, for he wishes to convey the senses of an extremely noisy stertorousness.

See especially 'Word-Making' in my *For These Few Minutes*, 1938.

POSITION OF WORDS. See ORDER OF WORDS.

position to do (something), **not to be in a.** Extremely wordy for *be unable to do* or, in sentences, *cannot do*. See ABSTRACT NOUNS.

positive for 'merely *sure*' or 'merely *certain*' is hyperbolical and misused; the correct nuance is 'quite sure' or 'dogmatically (or assertively) sure'. There is something odd about this sentence from Stuart Chase's *The Tyranny of Words*: 'The scientist finds his referents and makes positive that others can find them in the dark': despite the fact that *positive* is used as = 'quite sure'. Idiom demands 'makes certain that …'.

For 'thoroughgoing', 'complete', as in 'He's a positive fool', *positive* is a colloquialism.

possess is stronger than *have*. Where the two words are synonymous, euphony or dignity will decide which is the better. *Possess* is, for instance, never derogatory: one *has* faults, one does not possess them.

Usually, however, these two words are not synonymous.

POSSESSIVE, DUPLICATED. 'Seyss-Inquart's sentimental contact with Austria has been very different from that of Hitler's', should be either '… different from that of Hitler' or '… different from Hitler's' (G. V. Carey, *Mind the Stop*).

POSSESSIVE CASE. See GENITIVE, VAGARIES OF THE.

POSSESSIVE NOUN, unnecessary. 'Mr Garston's, the pawnbroker's, voluntary contribution' (Cecil Freeman Gregg, *Tragedy at Wembley*).

POSSESSIVE PRONOUN, agreement. Arthur Bryant, *The Illustrated London News*, 27 Nov. 1937, '… the sound of martial music would be borne to eager … ears as regiment after regiment made their way', etc. The nominative 'regiment' is in the singular and the pronoun should be *its*.

POSSESSIVE PRONOUN, omission of. Alexander Smith, in *The History of the Highwaymen*, 1714, begins the chapter on 'Tom Sharp, Murderer and House-Breaker', thus: 'He was not only *Sharp* by name, but also sharp by Nature, as appears by dressing himself in an old suit of black clothes …', where 'by his dressing himself' would be correct.

possibility is sometimes misused for *chance*. 'I had no possibility to eschew the confusion' (a detective novel). The author might, however, have written, 'There was no possibility of my eschewing the confusion' – but the sense would have been slightly changed. And sometimes for *potentiality*, as in 'The main theme … is … the vision which revealed men and women as they are in actuality and, simultaneously, … as they would be if all their stunted possibilities had attained maturity' (Claude Houghton, *Six Lives and a Book*).

possible. See COMPARATIVES, FALSE. Cf. **impossible.**

possible for *necessary* or *unavoidable* would seem to be an improbable error. Nevertheless, it occurs – surprisingly often. In *Mr Pendlebury Makes a Catch*, Anthony Webb permits an educated character to say, 'They [the police] have their duty to do, but I am sure they will do their best not to make things more difficult for you than possible' (for 'than necessary' or 'than is unavoidable').

possibly for *perhaps*. In conversation it is both permissible and, in general, clear, but in writing it is sometimes ambiguous. Consider 'He cannot possibly do it' and 'He cannot, possibly, do it': the first is clear, the latter becomes ambiguous if a careless writer omits the commas.

post. In North America, one *mails* a letter; in Britain, one *posts* it.

postcard; postal card. In Britain, a postcard may be already postage-stamped or it may require a postage stamp; in the USA, it requires one, an already postage-stamped card being in the States a *postal card*.

posterior to = after. (Esp. in gobbledygook.)

postscript and *PS*. Strictly, the latter is an abbreviation of the former; to say *PS* is to speak colloquially, but it is not reprehensible. The plural of the word *PS* is *PSS*; but in a letter one's second *PS* is generally written *PPS*, one's third *PPPS*.

potable and **drinkable.** See **eatable.**

potent and **potential.** *Potent* is 'powerful', whether of person or liquor; *potential* is 'possible as opposed to actual; latent'. A potential statesman is one who has the ability: all he needs is the opportunity.

pother is a literarism; it is now pronounced to rhyme with *bother*.

pot-herb, mistakenly supposed to be a plant growing in a pot, is one growing in the kitchen-garden, *for the pot*.

pour. See **pore.**

practical, misused for *practicable*. 'She tried to open the window on the right, but it didn't seem practical' (G. M. Marlow, *Pictures on the Pavement*).

practical, when misused for *virtual*, leads to strange ambiguities; this misuse springs from that *practically* which means, not 'in a practical manner', but 'almost', 'virtually'. 'It provides proof positive that forgery by typewriter is a practical impossibility' (Nigel Morland, *The Conquest of Crime*), a very odd statement indeed. (Here, exaggeration or overstatement may have originated the error, '... is an impossibility' being all that was required.)

practically. In *What a Word!*, Sir Alan Herbert – that intellectual swash-buckler in, and sturdy champion of, the cause of good English – writes thus: 'As a rule, "practically" means "*Not* practically" or "Nearly". For example, we [foolishly] say of a reluctant engine that it "*practically* started" when it did not start but made a bronchial sound and is now silent. – Do not misunderstand me. ... Life would be impossible if we never said "practically". You may say that a family is "practically extinct" when the only survivor is a dying old man', although a stylist would much prefer '*virtually* extinct'. 'But', Sir Alan Herbert resumes, 'it would be silly to say that the horse placed second "practically" won the Derby. A boxer may be "practically" knocked out, though still on his feet: but you cannot "practically" hit the bull's-eye, unless you do hit it. It is not the word but the habit that is bad.' I should go further and say: Avoid the word when it synonymizes *almost* or *virtually* – *as good as* – *to all intents* – *in effect* – *though not formally* (or *explicitly*), and select whichever of those seven synonyms is the most suitable to the context. [Since Herbert wrote, the use of *practically* for 'in effect' has become widely accepted, although careful writers still avoid the more questionable sense of 'almost'. The distinction is clearly observable in his examples.]

practice (n.), **practise** (v.), are often confused in spelling. [*Webster's*: *practice* also *practise* (n.); *practice* or *practise* (v.).]

precedence, precedent. *Precedence* means superiority, especially socially, as in 'An earl takes precedence of a baronet'; cf. 'The moral always takes precedence of the miraculous' (A. Davidson, quoted by *OED*). A *precedent* is a previous example or case that establishes a moral, social, or legal ruling; a lawyer has virtually won a case when he or she has found a precedent. *Precedence* is wrongly used in this sentence, 'There is, he thinks, no precedence for the admission of such evidence' (Anthony Weymouth, *Tempt Me Not*). (*Precedence* and *precedent* (n.) are both stressed on the first syllable in British English, but the Americans sometimes stress *precedence* on the second.)

precession and **procession.** The former implies, a *going before*, the latter a *going forward*, but is usually applied to a body of persons marching in ceremonial order. The man in the street knows *precession* only in *the precession of the equinoxes*; that is, if he knows it at all!

PRECIOUSNESS (or Preciosity). See also AFFECTATION.

OED's definition is 'affectation of refinement or distinction, especially in the use of language; fastidious refinement in literary style' and one of that dictionary's quotations is, 'this ... may be described as the *reductio ad absurdum* of the preciosity of Pater and Stevenson'. It is at times difficult to distinguish between art, artifice, and affectation: preciosity ensues when subtlety or delicacy or both subtlety and delicacy are employed in contexts that do not call for them.

Here are several brief examples. Preciousness can be satisfactorily judged only in long passages; but long passages cannot be quoted here; therefore I recommend that those who wish to go further into the subject should read extensively in Pater, Symonds, Hewlett (the romantic novels).

From Pater's essay, 'Aesthetic Poetry' in *Appreciations*, 1889, comes this: 'The choice life of the human spirit is always under mixed lights, and in mixed situations, when it is not too sure of itself, is

still expectant, girt up to leap forward to the promise. Such a situation there was in that earliest return from the overwrought spiritualities of the Middle Age to the earlier, more ancient life of the senses; and for us the most attractive form of the classical story is the monk's conception of it, when he escapes from the sombre atmosphere of his cloister to natural light. Then the fruits of this mood, which, divining more than it understands, infuses into the scenery and figures of Christian history some subtle reminiscence of older gods, or into the story of Cupid and Psyche that passionate stress of spirit which the world owes to Christianity, constitute a peculiar vein of interest in the art of the fifteenth century.'

John Addington Symonds, usually ornate, is, at times, precious, as in the following reference* to a passage ('*L'altra mattina in un mio piccolo orto ...*') in Lorenzo de' Medici's *Corinto*: 'Here we have the *Collige virgo rosas*, "Gather ye roses while ye may", translated from the autumn of antique to the April of modern poetry, and that note is echoed through all the love-literature of the Renaissance. Lorenzo, be it observed, has followed his model, not only in the close, but also in the opening of the passage. Side by side with this Florentine transcript from Ausonius I will now place Poliziano's looser, but more poetical handling of the same theme, subjoining my version of his ballata.'

And now three examples from Maurice Hewlett, *The Forest Lovers*, 1898:

'The time of his going-out [*departure*] was September of the harvest: a fresh wet air was abroad.'

'There was a tall lady. ... She was dainty to view, her hands and arms shone like white marble; but apart from all this, it was clear to Prosper that she lacked the mere strength for the office she had proposed herself.'

'Next day he rode fast and long without meeting a living soul, and so came at last into Morgraunt Forest, where the trees

---

*Page 210, vol. ii, *Essays Speculative and Suggestive*, 1890; Essay on 'The Pathos of the Rose in Poetry'.

shut out the light of day, and very few birds sing. He entered the east purlieus in the evening of his fifth day from Starning, and slept in a rocky valley. Tall black trees stood all round him, the vanguards of the forest host.'

In Robert Louis Stevenson also are there examples of preciosity; for instance, in *Markheim*.

precipitate and **precipitous**. See following entry.

precipitously is erroneously used for *precipitately* in 'She looked around her wildly, and precipitously left the room' (Peter Traill, *Half Mast*); *precipitous* meaning 'very steep', and *precipitate* 'violently hurried'. One might leave a room 'precipitously' by jumping out of the window or falling downstairs.

PRÉCIS WRITING. 'If we try to analyse any given propositions we shall find in general that they are logical sums. ... But our analysis, if carried far enough, must come to the point where it reaches propositional forms which are not themselves composed of simpler propositional forms. We must eventually reach the ultimate connexion of the terms, the immediate connexion which cannot be broken without destroying the propositional form as such. The propositions which represent this ultimate connexion of terms I call, after B[ertrand] Russell, atomic propositions. They, then, are the kernels of every proposition, *they* contain the material, and all the rest is only a development of this material. It is to them that we have to look for the subject matter of propositions' (L. Wittgenstein, 'Some Remarks on Logical Form' in *Knowledge, Experience and Realism*, 1929).

COD spells the word 'précis' with an accent, but no longer in italics, regarding it as now naturalized. The plural is the same as the singular. The verb 'précis', to make a précis of, forms the parts 'précises, précising, précised'; I must say that I prefer 'précis'ing' and 'précis'd'.

By the same authority, the term 'précis' is defined as 'a summary or abstract, esp. of a text or speech'. My impression is that *summary* is an exact synonym of *précis* and that *abstract* might be usefully restricted to a summary or epitome of scientific or technical information – above all, of figures (e.g. statistics). One might also mention *abridgement*, which is also either a compendium or an epitome: but the terms are not interchangeable at will, and it is better to maintain distinctions than to destroy them. From *COD*'s definition it would be dangerous to deduce that *abridgement* and *précis* are synonymous: one makes a précis of a paragraph, a passage, even a chapter, or of a letter, a report, a document; not of a book of any considerable size, the summary of a book being either (large scale) an abridgement or a compendium, or (small scale) a synopsis. An *abridgement* (which form I prefer to *abridgment*), as *OED* says, is either 'a compendium of a larger work, with the details abridged, and less important things omitted, but retaining the sense and substance' or 'an epitome or compendium of any subject that might be treated much more fully'; it is also, *OED* allows, a synopsis – but that is a sense we should do well to ignore, at least to the extent of avoiding it. [The term *digest*, as synonymous with *abridgement* and *abridge*, has been popularized by the magazines *The Literary Digest* (now defunct) and *The Reader's Digest*. The term was borrowed from the Law, where it means a compilation, systematically arranged, of legal rules, decisions, and statutes.]

There are four main ways in which a précis can be made:

I. To summarize in one's own language and to cast the summary into Reported Speech (*oratio obliqua*) – or to retain reported speech if the original itself is oblique.

II. To summarize in one's own language and, unless the original is itself in Reported Speech, ignore the convention of reported speech – i.e. leave the summary in Direct Speech.

III. To retain, so far as possible, the language of the original and, unless the original is already oblique, to cast the summary into Indirect or Reported Speech.

IV. To retain, so far as possible, the language of the original, but to ignore the convention of Reported Speech – unless the original is in Reported, in which case there is no sense in turning the Indirect into the Direct mode.

A certain Examining Board (one of whose revisers I had the honour – and I mean 'honour' – of being) says, in its instructions concerning précis, that 'generally the recognized technique of "reported speech" should be expected, together with a formal title, and the date if relevant'; but it does not insist on Reported Speech. The custom of putting a précis into Reported Speech is an old one. That something is to be said for it – e.g. that the précis gains in impersonality (if that *is* a gain) – I admit. But much more can be said against it: one takes longer to cast a précis into Indirect Speech than into Direct, unless the original is in Indirect Speech; a précis in Indirect is more difficult to make; therefore, the proportion of errors will be larger in an Indirect than a Direct précis; and the potentiality of ambiguity is much higher in Indirect than in Direct Speech. As a school exercise, Reported Speech has its intellectual value; but in the practical world, to turn Direct into Indirect Speech is a waste of time. Moreover, it is a relic of a rigid Classicism: why should we be forced to imitate Livy?

Examining Boards, in general, have traditionally recommended Method I: a summary couched in one's own words and cast into Reported Speech. Failing that, they tolerate Methods II and III: III, a summary that, cast into Reported, retains much or even most of the wording of the original; II, a summary not in Reported, yet written in one's own words. But they frown on IV, which, abandoning the convention of Reported, yet sticks as close as possible to the wording of the original.

Now I plead for the abolition of Reported Speech (unless the original is Indirect) from précis writing. Which, then, of Methods II and IV do I prefer?

As a literary exercise, as a training in composition, Method II (one's own language, in Direct Speech) is superior to Method IV; but as précis *qua* précis, IV (Direct Speech in words keeping as close as is idiomatically possible to those of the original) is superior, for this is the method that precludes error more than any other method does.

In short, there is précis by recast and there is précis by reduction; the *literary* ideal is a recast of the reduction. If the reduction is carefully made, it will require only a slight recasting.

For easy reading, it is advisable to break a long, unparagraphed passage into paragraphs – not arbitrarily but according to the divisions of the subject. (Do not tinker with an already satisfactory paragraphing.) And do not alter the order of the narrative or the discourse unless the order is faulty: remember that you're not supposed to be presenting yourself; you are required to represent the author in brief. Don't show off by changing the ordonnance of good writers: they know better than you do how *they* wish to set forth their subject.*

Here follow three passages set in a certain School Certificate examination. Before each of the to-be-précis'd passages come these instructions: 'Write a Précis giving clearly the substance of the following passage and presenting *in a consecutive and readable shape*, briefly and distinctly expressed, the main points of the argument, so that anyone who has not time to read the actual passage may learn the substance of it from the Précis.'

The Functions of a Cabinet
(to be reduced to 280–300 words)

A German professor in a lecture on anatomy is reported to have said to his

---

*See also my *Précis Writing* (Routledge, London).

class, 'Gentlemen, we come now to the spleen. About the functions of the spleen, we know nothing. So much for the spleen.' It is with much the same feeling that one enters upon the task of writing a chapter upon the cabinet: although that body has become more and more, decade by decade, the motive power of all political action. The fact is that the cabinet from its very nature can hardly have fixed traditions. In the first place, it has no legal status as an organ of government, but is an informal body, unknown to the law, whose business is to bring about a co-operation among the different forces of the state without interfering with their legal independence. Its action must, therefore, be of an informal character. Then it meets in secret, and no records of its proceedings are kept, which would in itself make very difficult the establishment and preservation of a tradition. This could, indeed, happen only in case of a certain permanence among the members who could learn and transmit its practice. But a new cabinet contains under ordinary circumstances none of the members of its predecessor. A Conservative minister knows nothing of the procedure under Liberal administrations; and we find even a man of the experience of Sir Robert Peel asking Sir James Graham about the practice of a Liberal cabinet, of which that statesman – who at this time changed his party every decade – had formerly been a member. No doubt the mode of transacting business varies a good deal from one cabinet to another, depending to a great extent upon the personal qualities of the members. Still, the real nature of the work to be done, and hence the method of doing it, have changed during the last half century less in the case of the cabinet than of any of the other political organs of the state, and one can observe certain general characteristics that may be noted.

The conventions of the constitution have limited and regulated the exercise of all legal powers by the regular organs of the state in such a way as to vest the main authority of the central government – the driving and the steering force – in the hands of a body entirely unknown to the law. The members of the cabinet are now always the holders of public offices created by law; but their possession of those offices by no means determines their activity as members of the cabinet. They have, indeed, two functions. Individually, as officials, they do the executive work of the state and administer its departments; collectively, they direct the general policy of the government, and this they do irrespective of their individual authority as officials. Their several administrative duties, and their collective functions are quite distinct; and may, in the case of a particular person, have little or no connection. The Lord Privy Seal, for example, has no administrative duties whatever; and it is conceivable that the work of other members might not come before the cabinet during the whole life of the ministry.

The essential function of the cabinet is to co-ordinate and guide the political action of the different branches of the government and thus create a consistent policy. Bagehot called it a hyphen that joins, a buckle that fastens, the executive and legislative together; and in another place he speaks of it as a committee of Parliament chosen to rule the nation. More strictly it is a committee of the party that has a majority in the House of Commons. The minority are not represented upon it; and in this it differs from every other parliamentary committee. The distinction is so obvious to us today, we are so accustomed to government by party wherever popular institutions prevail, that we are apt to forget the importance of the fact. Party government as a system has developed comparatively recently; but it has now become almost universal.

(Lowell, *The Government of England*)

Here is a précis by reduction, with a few slight recastings that are demanded by the laws of composition, logic, good sense.

Functions of the Cabinet

The Cabinet has become, increasingly, the motor of all political action. The Cabinet* can hardly have fixed traditions. Firstly, it has no legal status as an organ of government, but it is an informal body, unknown to the law; its business is to co-operate the different forces of the state without interfering with their legal independence. Its action, therefore, is informal. It meets secretly; no records of its proceedings being kept, the establishment and preservation of a tradition is difficult. This could, indeed, happen only with permanent members. But a new Cabinet normally contains none of the members of its predecessor. A Conservative minister knows nothing of the procedure under Liberal administrations; and vice versa. The transaction of business varies from one Cabinet to another, according to the members' personalities. Still, the nature of the work to be done, hence the method, have changed during the last half century less in the Cabinet than in any other political organ: one can observe certain general characteristics.

The conventions of the Constitution have so limited and regulated the exercise of all legal powers by the regular organs of the state as to vest the main authority of the central government in a body unknown to the law. The members of the Cabinet are the holders of public offices created by law; but their possession of those offices by no means determines their activity as members of the Cabinet. They have two functions. Individually, they do the executive work of the state and administer its departments; collectively, they direct the general policy of the government, irrespective of their individual authority as officials.

The Cabinet's essential function is to co-ordinate and guide the political action of the different branches of the government. It is a committee of the party that has a *majority* in the House of Commons;

in this it significantly differs from every other parliamentary committee. It affords a remarkable illustration of party government, which, though developed comparatively recently, is now general.

The Capture and Defence of Arcot
(to be précis'd in 280–320 words)

Clive was now twenty-five years old. After hesitating for some time between a military and a commercial life, he had at length been placed in a post which partook of both characters, that of commissary to the troops, with the rank of Captain. The present emergency called forth all his powers. He represented to his superiors that, unless some vigorous efforts were made, Trichinopoly would fall, and the French would become the real masters of the whole peninsula of India. It was absolutely necessary to strike some daring blow. If an attack were made on Arcot, the capital of the Carnatic, and the favourite residence of the Nabobs, it was not impossible that the siege of Trichinopoly would be raised. The heads of the English settlement, now thoroughly alarmed by the success of Dupleix, and apprehensive that, in the event of a new war between France and Great Britain, Madras would be instantly taken and destroyed, approved of Clive's plan, and intrusted the execution of it to himself. The young captain was put at the head of two hundred English soldiers, and three hundred Sepoys armed and disciplined after the European fashion. Of the eight officers who commanded this little force under him, only two had ever been in action, and four of the eight were factors of the company, whom Clive's example had induced to offer their services. The weather was stormy; but Clive pushed on, through thunder, lightning, and rain, to the gates of Arcot. The garrison, in a panic, evacuated the fort, and the English entered it without a blow.

The intelligence of these events was soon carried to Chunda Sahib, who, with his French allies, was besieging Trichinopoly. He immediately detached an army of ten thousand men, under his son, Rajah

---

*Not *it*; *it* would be ambiguous.

Sahib, to invest the fort of Arcot, which seemed quite incapable of sustaining a siege. The walls were ruinous, the ditches dry, the ramparts too narrow to admit the guns, the battlements too low to protect the soldiers. The little garrison had been greatly reduced by casualties. It now consisted of a hundred and twenty Europeans and two hundred Sepoys. Only four officers were left; the stock of provisions was scanty.

During fifty days the siege went on. During fifty days the young captain maintained the defence, with a firmness, vigilance, and ability, which would have done honour to the oldest marshal in Europe. The breach, however, increased day by day. The garrison began to feel the pressure of hunger. Under such circumstances, any troops so scantily provided with officers might have been expected to show signs of insubordination. But the Sepoys came to Clive, not to complain of their scanty fare, but to propose that all the grain should be given to the Europeans, who required more nourishment than the natives of India. The thin gruel, they said, which was strained away from the rice, would suffice for themselves.

An attempt made by the government of Madras to relieve the place had failed, but Rajah Sahib learned that the Mahrattas were in motion; their chief, Morari Row, roused by the fame of the defence of Arcot declared that he had never before believed that Englishmen could fight, but that he would willingly help them since he saw that they had spirit to help themselves. It was necessary to be expeditious. Rajah Sahib offered large bribes to Clive; they were rejected with scorn, and he determined to storm the fort.

The enemy advanced, driving before them elephants whose foreheads were armed with iron plates. It was expected that the gates would yield to the shock of these living battering-rams. But the huge beasts no sooner felt the English musketballs than they turned round and trampled on the multitude which had urged them forward. The rear ranks of the English kept the front ranks supplied with a constant succession of loaded muskets, and every shot told on the living mass below. After three desperate onsets, the besiegers retired.

The struggle lasted about an hour. Four hundred of the assailants fell. The garrison lost only five or six men. The besieged passed an anxious night, looking for a renewal of the attack. But when day broke, the enemy were no more to be seen. They had retired, leaving the English several guns and a large quantity of ammunition.

(Lord Macaulay)

My version (by reduction and slight recasting) is this:

The Capture and Defence of Arcot

Clive, promoted commissary captain at 25, represented that, unless vigorous efforts were made, Trichinopoly would fall: the French become masters of India. If an attack were made on Arcot, capital of the Carnatic and residence of the Nabobs, the siege might be raised. The heads of the English settlement approved of Clive's plan. He was put in command of 200 English soldiers and 300 Sepoys, with eight officers. Clive pushed on, through storms, to Arcot. The garrison, panicking, evacuated the fort; the English entered.

Intelligence was soon carried to Chunda Sahib, who, with French allies, was besieging Trichinopoly. He immediately detached 10,000 men, under his son, Rajah Sahib, to invest Arcot fort, which seemed incapable of sustaining a siege. The garrison now consisted of 120 Europeans and 200 Sepoys with four officers and scanty provisions.

During fifty days Clive maintained the defence like a veteran. The breach, however, increased. The garrison began to feel hunger. But the Sepoys proposed that the grain should be given to the Europeans, who required more nourishment: the thin gruel strained from the rice would suffice for themselves.

An attempt by the Madras government to relieve Arcot had failed, but Rajah Sahib learned that the Mahrattas were moving; expedition was necessary. Rajah offered bribes to Clive; they were rejected; he determined to storm the fort.

The enemy drove before them elephants forehead-armed with iron plates: battering-rams. But the huge beasts, feeling the English bullets, trampled on the multitude behind; every shot told on the living mass below. After three desperate onsets, the besiegers retired.

There fell 400 assailants, only six defenders. The besieged passed an anxious night, but when day broke, the enemy had retired, leaving several guns and much ammunition.

Here is a passage to be précis'd in 260–300 words.

The Pitt-Newcastle Coalition

The two most powerful men in the country were the Duke of Newcastle and Pitt. Alternate victories and defeats had made them sensible that neither of them could stand alone. The interest of the State, and the interest of their own ambition, impelled them to coalesce. By their coalition was formed the ministry which was in power when George the Third ascended the throne.

The more carefully the structure of this celebrated ministry is examined, the more shall we see reason to marvel at the skill or the luck which had combined in one harmonious whole such various and, as it seemed, incompatible elements of force. The influence which is derived from stainless integrity, the influence which is derived from the vilest arts of corruption, the strength of aristocratical connection, the strength of democratical enthusiasm, all these things were for the first time found together.

Newcastle brought to the coalition a vast mass of power, which had descended to him from Walpole and Pelham. The public offices, the church, the courts of law, the army, the navy, the diplomatic service, swarmed with his creatures. The great Whig families, which, during several generations, had been trained in the discipline of party warfare, and were accustomed to stand together in a firm phalanx, acknowledged him as their captain. Pitt, on the other hand, had what Newcastle wanted, an eloquence which stirred the passions and charmed the imagination, a high reputation for purity, and the confidence and ardent love of millions.

The partition which the two ministers made of the powers of government was singularly happy. Each occupied a province for which he was well qualified; and neither had any inclination to intrude himself into the province of the other. Newcastle took the treasury, the civil and ecclesiastical patronage, and the disposal of that part of the secret-service money which was then employed in bribing members of Parliament. Pitt was Secretary of State, with the direction of the war and of foreign affairs. Thus the filth of all the noisome and pestilential sewers of government was poured into one channel. Through the other passed only what was bright and stainless. Mean and selfish politicians, pining for commissionerships, gold sticks, and ribands, flocked to the great house at the corner of Lincoln's Inn Fields. There, at every levee, appeared eighteen or twenty pair of lawn sleeves; for there was not, it was said, a single Prelate who had not owed either his first elevation or some subsequent translation to Newcastle. There appeared those members of the House of Commons in whose silent votes the main strength of the Government lay. One wanted a place in the excise for his butler. Another came about a prebend for his son. A third whispered that he had always stood by his Grace and the Protestant succession; that his last election had been very expensive; that he had been forced to take up money on mortgage; and that he hardly knew where to turn for five hundred pounds. The Duke pressed all their hands, passed his arm round all their shoulders, patted all their backs, and sent away some with wages, and some with promises. From this traffic Pitt stood haughtily aloof. Not only was he himself incorruptible, but he shrank from the loathsome drudgery of corrupting others. He had not, however, been twenty years in Parliament, and ten years in office, without discovering how the Government was carried on. He was perfectly aware that bribery was practised on a large scale by his colleagues. Hating the practice, yet despairing of putting it down, and doubting whether, in those times, any ministry could stand without it, he determined to be blind to it. He would see nothing, know nothing, believe nothing.

It may be doubted whether he did not owe as much of his popularity to his ostentatious purity as to his eloquence, or to his talents for the administration of war. It was everywhere said with delight and admiration that the Great Commoner, without any advantages of birth or fortune, had, in spite of the dislike of the Court and of the aristocracy, made himself the first man in England, and made England the first country in the world; that his name was mentioned with awe in every palace from Lisbon to Moscow; that his trophies were in all the four quarters of the globe; yet that he was still plain William Pitt, without title or riband, without pension or sinecure place. Whenever he should retire, after saving the State, he must sell his coach horses and his silver candlesticks. Widely as the taint of corruption had spread, his hands were clean. They had never received, they had never given, the price of infamy. Thus the coalition gathered to itself support from all the high and all the low parts of human nature, and was strong with the whole united strength of virtue and of Mammon.

(Lord Macaulay)*

The following is my suggestion:

*This passage is reprinted, as are the preceding passages, with the very kind permission of the Oxford and Cambridge Schools Examination Board.

The Pitt-Newcastle Coalition

The most powerful men were the Duke of Newcastle and Pitt. Alternate victories and defeats had made them sensible that neither could stand alone. The interest of the State, and their own ambition, impelled them to coalesce, in the ministry that was in power when George the Third became king.

The more carefully the structure of this celebrated ministry is examined, the more we marvel at the skill or the luck that had harmoniously combined such various and seemingly incompatible forces. The influences deriving from stainless integrity and from the vilest arts of corruption, the strength of aristocratical connection, and democratic enthusiasm, all merged for the first time. Newcastle brought a vast mass of power; the public offices, the church, the courts of law, the army, the navy, the diplomatic service, swarmed with his creatures. The great Whig families, trained in party warfare, acknowledged him as their captain. Pitt had what Newcastle lacked, an imaginative and passionate eloquence, a high reputation for purity, and the confidence and ardent love of millions.

The partition of government was singularly happy. Each man occupied a province for which he was well qualified; and neither wished to intrude into the other's. Newcastle took the treasury, the civil and ecclesiastical patronage, and the bribing of members of Parliament. Pitt was Secretary of State, with the direction of the war and of foreign affairs. Thus all the filth was poured into one channel. Through the other passed only what was bright and stainless. Mean, selfish, self-seeking politicians flocked to Newcastle's great London house. There appeared ambitious Prelates and those MPs in whose silent votes the strength of the Government lay – one wanting this; another that. The Duke pressed all their hands, and sent away some with wages, some with promises. From this traffic Pitt stood haughtily aloof. Incorruptible, he shrank from the drudgery of corrupting others. He inevitably knew, however, how the Government was carried on; that bribery was practised on a large scale: but doubting whether any ministry could stand without it, he determined to be blind to it. He would know nothing.

Perhaps he owed as much of his popularity to his ostentatious purity as to his eloquence, or to his talents for the administration of war. It was everywhere said with delighted admiration that the Great Commoner had, in spite of the Court and the aristocracy, made himself the first man in England, England the first country in the world; that his name was mentioned with awe in every Palace of Europe; yet that he was still plain William Pitt, without title, pension, or sinecure. Whenever he should retire, after saving the State, he would be poor. Widely as corruption had spread, *his* hands were clean. Thus the coalition was strong with the united strength of virtue and of Mammon.

precisian (not *precision*); **precisionist** (not *precisianist*). A *precisian* is a person rigidly precise; but one who makes a profession or practice of precision is a *precisionist*. Hence, *precisianism*, the abstract noun corresponding to *precisian*; *precisionism*, to *precisionist*.

predicate is occasionally misused for *predict*; and vice versa. The former = to declare, assert, affirm; the latter = to foretell.

predominant. See **dominating.**

prefer ... than. See **than.**

preferable, more. See COMPARATIVES, FALSE.

pregnant of. See PREPOSITIONS WRONGLY USED.

prejudice (v.) and **prejudicial** are usually inferior to 'to *harm*' and *harmful*. To use the longer words, one needs a good reason.

prejudice (n.) **against,** but *partiality for.* The former word (except in legal termi-

nology) is now usually pejorative, the latter favourable.

preliminary. See COMPARATIVES, FALSE.

premise, misused for *presumption, assumption.* 'Since then, nothing has been seen or heard of him, and as that is the case, the premise is that he's still there' (John G. Brandon, *The Dragnet*). The author here misunderstands the meaning of *premise*, a term in Logic for 'the previous statement from which another is inferred' (*COD*); the assertion that 'nothing has been seen or heard of him' is the premise from which it is inferred that 'he's still there'.

premiss is, in Logic, preferable to *premise.*

prepared to admit, confess, state, etc., **be.** 'I am prepared to confess that I am the culprit' is absurd; the verbosity is undignified; one confesses, or one doesn't. (Sir Alan Herbert attacks *prepared to admit*.)

PREPOSITION AT END. Instances of the extreme awkwardness, and even ambiguity, of this construction, are the following: 'The paper so praised Boswell himself was the author of' (J.Timbs, *The Romance of London*, 1865); the writer should rather have said 'Boswell ... was the author of the paper ...'. 'When she prattles about herself and her admirers, she makes the reader blush for the shamefacedness she evidently does not even guess at the lack of' (quoted by Nesfield from *The Spectator*, 31 Jan. 1903); here one cannot be sure whether 'the reader' blushes for (but why *for*?) his or her own shamefacedness or the prattler's lack of it.

Yet too great a fear of putting the preposition at the end sometimes leads to even worse errors. Thus, a certain author has written, 'They who come here see it as though it were a place of earth records, in the form that in their own countries such things are kept', meaning 'are kept in', or, better, 'the form in which such things are kept'; here the writer shirks the necessary repetition of *in*, and writes ungrammatically. The same error, and for the same reason, occurs in the inscription on the monument to John, Duke of Argyle, in Westminster Abbey: 'A General and Orator exceeded by none in the Age he lived [in]'.

Dr Pearsall Smith, in *English Idioms*, called the preposition at the end of a clause or a sentence an Anglicism; he added that it should not be discouraged. In SPE Tract No. xiv, the late H. W. Fowler wrote thus:

'It is a cherished superstition that prepositions must, in spite of the ineradicable English instinct for putting them late ("They are the fittest timber to make great politics of" said Bacon; and "What are you hitting me for?" says the modern schoolboy), be kept true to their name and placed before the word they govern. ... The fact is that the remarkable freedom enjoyed by English in putting its prepositions late and omitting its relatives is an important element in the flexibility of the language. The power of saying *A state of dejection such as they are absolute strangers to* (Cowper) instead of *A state of dejection of an intensity to which they are absolute strangers*, or *People worth talking to* instead of *People with whom it is worth while to talk*, is not one to be lightly surrendered. ... *That depends on what they are cut with* is not improved by conversion into *That depends on with what they are cut*; and too often the lust of sophistication ... becomes uncontrollable, and ends with *That depends on the answer to the question as to what with they are cut*. Those who lay down the universal principle that final prepositions are "inelegant" are unconsciously trying to deprive the English language of a valuable idiomatic resource, which has been freely used by all our greatest writers, except those whose instinct for English idiom has been overpowered by notions of correctness derived from Latin standards. The legitimacy of the prepositional ending in literary English must be uncompromisingly maintained; in respect of elegance or inelegance, every example must be judged not by any arbitrary rule, but on its own merits, according to the impression it makes on the feeling of educated English readers.'

PREPOSITION REPEATED UNNECESSARILY. 'An order, this, at which the taximan would have jibbed at violently ...' (John G. Brandon, *The Dragnet*); 'The weak estate in which Queen Mary left the realm in' (Milton: cited by Onions).

PREPOSITIONS, DISGUISED. See CONJUNCTIONS, DISGUISED.

PREPOSITIONS WRONGLY USED. The idea is owed to Charles Boyd's very useful book, *Grammar for Grown-Ups*; Boyd gives a tabulated list of words, with the wrong and the right prepositions to accompany them. I have drawn a few examples from his valuable list, and added a few of my own. For a fuller list than mine, see Nesfield's *English Composition*, ch. on 'Errors in Prepositions', and his *Errors in English Composition*, pp. 178–87. Here, the error precedes the correct use.

acquiescence to for *acquiescence in*
adherence of for *adherence to*; *an adherent to* for *an adherent of*; *adherent* (adj.) *of* for *adherent to*
assist (him) *to do* for *assist* (him) *in doing*
(one's) *belief of* (e.g. *revelation*) for *belief in*
(one's) *character of honesty* for *character for honesty*
comment (n. and v.) *to* (a thing) for *comment on*
conducive of for *conducive to*
consequent to for *consequent on*
end by for *end with*, as in 'The service ended by a prayer'; or for *end in* (as in 'It all ended by his going off in a huff ')
favourable reception with (the public) for *favourable reception by*
forbid (someone) *from doing* it for *forbid* (someone) *to do* it
in comparison of for *in comparison with*
in respect to for *in respect of*
in search for for *in search of*
in support for for *in support of*
inferior than for *inferior to*
involved by for *involved in*

judged on (certain standards) for *judged by*
knowledge on for *knowledge of*
listen at for *listen to*
oblivious to for *oblivious of*
prefer (something) *than* for *prefer*
  (something) *to*
pregnant of for *pregnant with*
(one's) *relations towards* (another person)
  for *relations with*
sensible to for *sensible of*; contrast
  sensitive of, which is incorrect for
  sensitive to
superior than for *superior to*
tendency for for *tendency to*
tolerant to for *tolerant of*
with a view of for *with a view to*

prerequisite rarely means more than *re-quisite* (adj., n.); the latter, rarely more than *needful*, *need*, or *necessary*, *necessity*. See also **perquisite** and **requirement**.

prescience, misused for *presentiment*. (With reference to 1936) 'The prescience [his own] of another European War harassed him' (Gilbert Frankau, *Royal Regiment*, 1938); the error occurs at least three times in the book. *Prescience* is 'foreknowledge', a *presentiment* is 'a foreboding'.

prescribe and **proscribe** are sometimes confused. The former, 'to recommend, advise, order', is not to be confused with the latter, which has an opposed meaning: to *prohibit* or *condemn*.

present-day for *present* or *contemporary* is an unnecessary synonym; and why use two words for one? 'The present-day system in politics' drew my attention to this particular piece of ineptitude.

present writer, the, is inferior to *the author* in the sense 'I (or me), the writer'; and usually *I* is preferable to either.

presentiment. See **prescience**.

presently means 'soon' in Southern British English. Its use to mean 'now' (as in 'She is presently in Thailand') is equally ancient, is current in both Scottish and American usage, and is coming back into England. Replace this second sense by 'currently' or 'at present' if there is any danger of ambiguity; which might arise in 'She is presently coming home from Thailand.'

preserve. See **reserve**.

president for *presidency* or *Presidency*. The American *run for president* (properly *President*) and *candidates for President* are colloquialisms for *run for Presidency*, *candidates for the Presidency*.

prestigious today means 'having or conferring prestige'. An older sense 'marked by illusion or trickery' is now archaic. See VOGUE WORDS.

presume. See **assume**.

presumptive for *presumptuous*: 'If I am unhappy it is my own fault for being a presumptive fool' (from novel read in typescript): in this sense never correct and now obsolete. *Presumptive* is defined as 'giving grounds for presumption', and *presumption* as either 'arrogance' or in Law as 'an inference from known facts' (*COD*). Thus, *presumptive* is related to this second sense of *presumption* ('presumptive evidence') and *presumptuous* to the first, and now chief, sense.

pretend dominantly = 'to feign, represent falsely', and, although the sense 'to profess' is admissible, it is better to use the word *profess*.

preventitive, preventative, preventive, are easily confused. The first is incorrect for either of the other two; *preventive* is the best form, whether for the noun or for the adjective.

previous to for *before* or *until* is commercialese.

previously to this is catachrestic for *previous to this*, which is itself verbose for *before this* or *previously*. 'Previously to this we could toy with various ideas' (E. R. Lorac, *Death of an Author*). Perhaps the author hesitated between *previously* and *prior to this*.

priceless. See **invaluable**.

primary. See COMPARATIVES, FALSE.

primeval (now held to be preferable to *primaeval*) and **primitive**. Both words = belonging to or characteristic of the first age of the world or of anything ancient. But only *primitive* = rough, elementary; old-fashioned. *Primitive*, moreover, has learned senses (in, e.g. anthropology, medicine, and philology) not possessed by *primeval*.

primordial; principal. See COMPARATIVES, FALSE.

principal, confused with *principle*. F. R. Burrow, *The Centre Court*, writes, 'On the principal of taking the biggest first, I will begin with Eastbourne.' *Principle* is only a noun. *Principal* is either an adjective meaning 'main, chief' or a noun meaning 'head of a college', 'leading performer' or 'capital sum of money'.

priority has been foisted upon us by the Services, including the Civil Service, as a synonym for 'urgency', 'a matter of urgency', 'an essential', 'a prime necessity', as in 'The man-power of industry has become No. 1 priority.' Like *ceiling* it is to be treated with great disrespect.

prise; prize; pry. The verb meaning 'force open or out' is spelt *prise* (or sometimes *prize*) in Britain, with *pry* as an American variant. The verb meaning 'value' is always *prize*.

pristine, which formerly meant 'in an original unspoilt condition', is now often used in the sense 'spotless, unsullied', even 'brand-new'. Although reputable writers are beginning to use it like that, the sense is not yet acceptable in more conservative circles.

problem is euphemistic for 'self-willed, bad-tempered, ill-trained' (a *problem* child) or 'distressed, poor' (a *problem* area). But why use *problem* as an adjective at all? See also ABSTRACT NOUNS.

proceed, for mere *go* or *walk* or *march* or *travel* is pompous and silly.

procession. See **cavalcade** and **precession.**

procure and **secure.** To *procure* is 'to gain or win; to obtain by care or effort'; to *secure* is 'to obtain for certain; to obtain for safe possession'. *Procure* and *secure* should not be so weakened that they become synonymous with the neutral *obtain* or with the simple *get*.

productivity is a horrible word; use *output*.

professor is illicitly used by pill-vendors, mountebanks, showmen of all sorts. To speak of a *professor of music* (or of *singing*) is permissible, if he or she be prominent or very capable in that profession. In general, it is best to reserve the term for university professors.

proficiency. See **efficiency.**

profile. See VOGUE WORDS.

PROGRESSIVE (OR CONTINUOUS) TENSES are often, by stylists, employed to avoid ambiguity: 'Fruit was eaten in large quantities' may refer either to habitual action or to a certain occasion. 'Fruit was being eaten in large quantities' is – or *should* be – applicable only to continuous action on a certain occasion. Based on Onions.

prohibit. See **inhibit.**

prohibit (a person) to (do something) is archaic. Either one *prohibits* a person *from* doing something, or one prohibits the thing in question: thus, 'The Prime Minister prohibits them from discussing the matter in public' or 'The Prime Minister prohibited public discussion of the matter.'

prolific is often misused for *profuse*. The former = 'fertile; producing abundantly', and is properly used of the producer but not of the product.

PROLIXITY. See VERBOSITY.

promote should not be used with bad or evil things, for it means 'to further, to advance'. Do not say 'Drink promotes idleness' but 'Drink increases (or leads to) idleness.'

prone and **supine**. 'To lie *prone*' is to lie, face downwards, on one's belly, as in (normal) rifle-shooting: 'to lie *supine*' is to lie flat on one's back, face to the zenith. Both of these words may be applied to the person or to the position.

PRONOUN, POSSESSIVE. See POSSESSIVE PRONOUN.

PRONOUNS, CONFUSED. In *The Queen's English*, Dean Alford writes: 'The following note has been sent me, received' – wrong agreement, Dean! – 'after a tithe dinner in Devonshire: "Mr T presents his compliments to Mr H, and I have got a hat that is not his, and if he have got a hat that is not yours, no doubt they are the expectant ones."'

See also **AMBIGUITY**, towards end (particular examples: pronouns group).

PRONOUNS JOINED by *and* or dissociated by *or* must not be in different cases, as they are in 'He and me will go now'; 'She didn't hit him or I.'

PROOF CORRECTING, HINTS ON. Not a subject to be treated in this book. But the curious – and the inexperienced – should consult G. V. Carey, *Mind the Stop*, last chapter.

propaganda is a singular (not, like *data* and *strata*, a plural); it has no plural. See also **publicity.**

propellant and **propellent; propulsion; propulsive.** 'Wind is a propellant, that is to say, a propellent [= driving] force', Weseen; but *Webster's* has both spellings for both noun and adjective.

Propulsion is the action of driving or pushing forward or onward, or the being so driven, or the effort required therefor; *propulsive* is its adjective.

properly so called is needed in contradistinction to 'falsely (or improperly) so called' but generally it is a wordy synonym for *proper* (after, not before, the noun it qualifies). Thus 'The dialects

properly so called' are merely 'The dialects proper'.

prophecy and **prophesy.** The latter is the verb, the former the noun, *the thing prophesied.*

proponent (opp. *opponent*) is a proposer or propounder; the term, therefore, is not – as it is sometimes supposed to be – synonymous with *supporter*. 'The proponents of the President called at noon.'

proportion should not be used for *portion* (or *part*), or *number*, as in 'The greater proportion of journalists are men.' Confine the word to contexts with a strong sense of 'ratio', and compare **percentage.**

proportion of, a = *a part of* or simply *some.*

proportions is commonly used for *size* in such a sentence as 'the chair is not suited to a man of his proportions'; but prefer *size, extent,* etc.

propose and **purpose.** To *purpose* is 'to set before *oneself* for accomplishment', as in 'My friend purposes to open an office' (Johnson), 'His mother purposed that he should be a preacher' (Lynch), 'I purpose ... keeping a sort of journal' (Francis Kemble); also in the passive (though this is obsolescent), as in 'I am purposed instantly to return' (Scott) and 'The whole nation was ... fully purposed that the next brood of Æthelings ... should be ... Englishmen' (Freeman). In short, *propose* is encroaching far too freely on the territory of *purpose* (*OED*).

proposition, fast becoming a passe-partout word, is in constant misuse. A *proposal* of marriage is not a 'proposition', but the word is properly applied to a draft of the terms for a business agreement. *Proposition* is not synonymous with *affair, matter, task, undertaking.* For a slashing attack on the word see Fowler's *Modern English Usage*; consult also Horwill's *Modern American Usage.*

proprietrix for *proprietress* is absurd. Nor is *proprietress* necessary, unless one wishes to draw attention to the sex of the *proprietor*.

prosaic and **prosy**. Both = 'commonplace, matter-of-fact', but *prosy* has the connotation of tedious, so that its sense is 'commonplace *and* tedious; dull and wearisome'. Neither is now used for 'consisting of, or written in prose', *prose* being the current adjective.

proscribe. See **prescribe**.

prosecute, confused with *persecute*. See **persecute and prosecute**.

proselyte, a noun, is used as a verb by Don Marquis (*The Almost Perfect State*): 'It is far from our purpose to proselyte.' He is an American writer. The British verb is *proselytize*.

prospective. See **perspective and prospective**.

prostrate (adj.) and **supine** are sometimes inexactly used. The former is lying face downwards, the latter face upwards, on the back. Two different states of mind or feeling may be expressed in these attitudes. See also **prone and supine**.

prosy. See **prosaic and prosy**.

protagonist is occasionally confused with *antagonist*, which is almost its opposite. In literary terminology, *protagonist* (Greek *protos*, 'first', and *agonistes*, 'a contender for a prize') means 'the chief character in a drama; hence in a novel, a story', etc.; derivatively, 'a person prominent in any contest or cause; a champion of a cause' (*OED*).

Protagonist should not be used loosely for any *supporter* (or *partisan*) or *upholder*, for in its derivative sense it means 'a *prominent* supporter or champion of any cause' (*OED*). It is tautologous to speak of 'a chief' or 'the leading' *protagonist*.

protest may be used for *protest against* in American, but not in British, usage. 'They bitterly protest attempts by the Government to aid stability' (Stuart Chase, *The Tyranny of Words*).

Protestant and **protestant**. The former is the opposite of a Roman Catholic, the latter is a protester – and the term is so obsolescent as to be virtually obsolete.

prototype, misused for *predecessor* or *similar*. 'The book ... would have passed into the limbo of the remainder lists with thousands of its prototypes had not the quality of one of the wilder anecdotes ... earned it a place in the news columns of a Sunday paper' (Margery Allingham, *Dancers in Mourning*). There can be only one prototype.

protrude, obtrude, intrude. 'I hope I don't protrude', said the foreign gentleman, joining the company uninvited. To *obtrude* (a thing) is to force it on a person's attention; *intrude* may also be used in that transitive sense. However, *protrusive* is literal, *obtrusive* is 'too noticeable', and *intrusive* is particularly 'redundant, unwanted'.

prove, in 'the exception proves the rule', is used in its primary sense, 'to test; to make trial of', as in the biblical 'Prove all things and hold fast to that which is good' (Weseen).

provenance is a literary word, not to be used for everyday *origin* or *source*.

provide, misused for *form* or *constitute*, as in 'Darts provides one of the most interesting games of skill and can be played almost anywhere' (examination essay script).

provided and **providing** are used as conjunctions in the sense 'on condition that; in case that; if only' as in 'Provided the temperature remains the same, the volume which a gas occupies is ...' and 'Freytag proposes a concert, providing somebody will pay for it' (based on *OED*). See CONJUNCTIONS, DISGUISED.

prox. See **ult**.

pry. See **prise**.

PS. See **postscript**.

psychic, esp., and **psychological** are, perhaps mostly in gobbledygook, being overworked for *mental* or *emotional*. A *psychological disturbance* = a (strong) emotion – no more than that.

psychological moment, at the, is a mere synonym – and how pompous! – for *in the nick of time*. In the sense 'at the psychologically most favourable moment', it is permissible, though hackneyed. It came into English as the translation of a French mistranslation of the German *das Moment*, which = 'momentum', not 'moment of time'. See especially Fowler's *Modern English Usage*.

psychology. Be sure to use this vague term so precisely that its volatility is crystallized, for it can be distressingly ambiguous. E.g. 'Shakespeare's psychology' has at least four meanings, the two most obvious being: 'Shakespeare's opinion of or theories about the mind' and 'the way in which Shakespeare's mind worked'. In *The Philosophy of Rhetoric*, p. 82, Dr I. A. Richards has a most illuminating paragraph on the subject.

publicity; propaganda. The latter is 'any association, systematic scheme, or concerted movement for the propagation of a particular doctrine or practice' (*OED*), whereas *publicity*, in its 20th-century sense, is 'the business [or the practice] of advertising or making articles, schemes, or persons publicly known' (*ibid.*). *Propaganda* cannot be applied to the advertising of articles (goods), being used chiefly in a political context and in a disparaging sense.

puerile. See **juvenile.**

punctilious and **punctual.** A punctilious person – one who is scrupulously observant of fine points, or of details of action or behaviour – is always *punctual*, i.e. scrupulously observant of an appointed time (or, of trains, 'not late').

PUNCTUATION. In a curious little treatise published in 1644, *The English Primrose*, by one Richard Hodges, a schoolmaster in Southwark, occurs this sentence: 'Great care ought to be had in writing, for the due observing of points:

for, the neglect thereof will pervert the sense. As for example, My Son, if sinners intise thee consent thou, not refraining thy foot from their way. Which ought to be written thus, My son, if sinners intise thee consent thou not, refraining thy foot', etc.

Here is a newspaper article that calls attention to the importance of punctuation:

PUNCTUATION AND SPELLING
—
Dr Temple's Views
—
A Word to 'Idle Examiners'

The Archbishop of York, Dr Temple, thinks that correct punctuation is more important – intellectually – than correct spelling. He said so yesterday when he presented the school prizes at the Royal Infant Orphanage at Wanstead.

'In writing essays,' said Dr Temple, 'there are two things one has difficulty with – spelling and stops. Nearly everybody says it is the spelling that matters.

'Now spelling is one of the decencies of life, like the proper use of knives and forks. It looks slovenly and nasty if you spell wrongly, like trying to eat your soup with a fork.

'But, intellectually, spelling – English spelling – does not matter. Shakespeare spelt his own name at least four different ways, and it may have puzzled his cashiers at the bank.

'Intellectually, stops matter a great deal. If you are getting your commas, semicolons, and full-stops wrong, it means that you are not getting your thoughts right, and your mind is muddled' (*The Observer*, 23 Oct. 1938).

Before making a few remarks on punctuation in general and then giving some significant examples of mispunctuation, I shall refer the reader to certain authorities to be studied:

Dean Alford (Henry Alford), *The Queen's English*, 1863 (7th ed., 1888), pp. 124–5, 130–1.

Alex. Bain, *English Composition and Rhetoric*, 2 vols., 1887–8, at I, 89–90.

Alex. Bain, *A Higher English Grammar*, 2nd ed., 1897, at pp. 335–9.

F. Howard Collins, *Authors' and Printers' Dictionary*, 1905; 10th ed., 1956.

F. G. & H. W. Fowler, *The King's English*, 1906; 3rd ed., 1931, at pp. 228–9 (excellent).

Maurice H. Weseen, *Everyday Uses of English*, 1922, pp. 313–33 (useful).

H. W. Fowler, *Modern English Usage*, 1926 (excellent). Revised, 1965.

W. Whitten & F. Whitaker, *Good and Bad English*, 1939 (short but valuable).

The best short book. G. V. Carey, *Mind the Stop*, 1939.

The fullest and most systematic guide to punctuation and its allies is EP, *You Have a Point There*, 1952. American punctuation is covered in a chapter by John W. Clark. For a very concise, practical summary: my *Notes on Punctuation*, 1955.

See also Sir Ernest Gowers, *The Complete Plain Words*, revised by Sidney Greenbaum and JW, 1986.

Before coming to intrinsic punctuation let us for a moment consider extrinsic punctuation – punctuation in reference to quotation marks. There is a tendency among printers to put the period (full-stop) and comma inside the 'quotes', but the semicolon and colon outside (though one often sees this sort of monstrosity: 'He was "hot-stuff;" he was "no fool:" he was formidable'), as in:

'The word "breakfast," now always written as one word, was, before that, a hyphenated word, "break-fast." The natural course is for such words to begin as two vocables, "care free"; to become hyphenated words, "care-free": and to end up as single words, "carefree." '

But careful printers are beginning to follow the more logical rule of putting punctuation inside the 'quote' only when the punctuation mark is actually *part* of the quotation and also serves to round off the entire phrase or sentence that is concluded.

A good writer will punctuate the above example thus:

'The word "breakfast", now always written as one word, was, before that, a hyphenated word, "break-fast". The natural course is for such words to begin as two vocables, "care free"; to become hyphenated words, "care-free"; and to end up as single words, "carefree".'

If one is quoting a person's actual words, the same rule should be observed as is observed in that example: with the caution that 'he said', 'as he said', etc., are to be treated as parenthetical; indeed, if you are in doubt, use parentheses.

'It was', he remarked, 'easy enough to find her.' Or 'It was' (he remarked) 'easy enough to find her.' In such an example, the quotation marks come *inside* the comma and *outside* the period, for the statement is obviously more important than the 'he remarked'. (In the English Bible (AV), there are no quotation marks.)

In support of Dr Temple (as cited early in this article), I quote from Frank Whitaker's practical, sane, suggestive address in the *JIJ*, January 1939: 'Of punctuation I have time only to say this: that we ought to deplore the growing tendency to use only full-stops and commas. Punctuation is an invaluable aid to clear writing, and I suggest that far too little importance is attached to it by many journalists.'

In very short sentences, the period (which marks the end of a statement) and the comma (which signifies apposition, as in 'Edward VII, King of England', or divides principal from subordinate clauses, as in 'When the girl arrived, the boy sat down') can – though not always happily – be made to suffice; but once you begin using long sentences, you need either the semi-colon, for a pause – a break – more important than that which is marked by a comma, as with the semi-colon in this sentence, or the colon, for a counterbalancing or poising of the importance-stresses or significance-divisions: or for an addition that is too immediate to be marked by so definite and so final a stop as the period –

such an addition as you will have noticed in this, my rather long sentence, which (as at '... for a pause – a break – more important ...') exemplifies the dash. The stop written ':–' is the colon-dash; it serves to introduce a list or anything else that has been formally announced; it might, in short, be defined as 'annunciatory'. Nowadays, however, the colon-dash usually gives way to the simple colon, especially when the list or more especially the illustrative sentence or passage (e.g. 'The word "breakfast", now always written as one word ...' earlier in this article) begins on a new line.

There are fine shades of distinction between the following:

(a) 'The man rose to his feet, his opponent rushed at him, and both fell heavily to the ground.'

(b) 'The man rose to his feet; his opponent rushed at him; and both fell heavily to the ground.'

(c) 'The man rose to his feet: his opponent rushed at him: and both fell heavily to the ground.'

I think that, here, (c) is affected, for it is too literary for the context. In (a), the first comma is perhaps too weak to mark adequately the ensuing pause. Of these three, (b) is the best: but better still is the more varied:

'The man rose to his feet; his opponent rushed at him, and both men fell heavily to the ground.'

If, however, 'and' were omitted, the most effective and suitable punctuation would be

'The man rose to his feet; his opponent rushed at him; both fell heavily to the ground',

although some writers might prefer

'The man rose to his feet. His opponent rushed at him; both fell heavily to the ground', or

'The man rose to his feet; his opponent rushed at him. Both fell heavily to the ground.' The objection to

'The man rose to his feet. His opponent rushed at him. Both fell' – but certainly not 'And both fell' – 'heavily to the ground' is that the sentences are too nearly equal in length for so sharp a dissection as that which is given by three periods.

At this point, I should like to draw attention to the recent revival, in literary prose, of the 18th-century use of the semicolon: that use which produces the effect of a stressed pause or of a rhetorical break, as in the following example from Michael Harrison's novel (or rather, one of his novels), *When All the Trees Were Green*, 1936: 'And now we are coming to a clearing in the woods; a little glade, bright green with the soft moss-grass; in the centre of which glade a stream ran between deep banks ...'

There are, in fact, five ways of indicating a break or a pause.

(1) Parentheses, as in 'He was (God forgive him!) a scoundrel.'

It is worth one's while to remember that the contents of a parenthesis (the words between parentheses) must be such that their omission would neither alter the syntactic flow nor materially affect the sense.

(2) Dashes, as in 'He was – God forgive him! – a scoundrel.' This is stronger than (1).

(3) Commas, as in 'He was, God forgive him!, a scoundrel': but there the exclamation mark virtually precludes the use of the second comma.

(4) Semi-colons, as in 'He was; God forgive him!; a scoundrel!' though here, too, an exclamation mark is wrong in conjunction with a semi-colon.

But (3) and (4) are viable in: He was, as all men knew, a scoundrel' and 'He was; as all men knew; a scoundrel', the latter being very literary.

(5) Colons, as in 'He was: God forgive him!: a scoundrel', where, again, the exclamation mark induces a feeling of discomfort; a discomfort absent both from 'He was: as all men knew: a scoundrel' and from the preferable 'He was: all men knew [*or* knew it]: a scoundrel', which is perhaps even more literary than (4).

The importance of punctuation – an importance that could hardly be over-emphasized – may be illustrated by the following example: the letter of invitation to Jameson at the time of his raid into the Transvaal. In telegraphic form, the text runs thus: 'It is under these circumstances that we feel constrained to call upon you to come to our aid should a disturbance arise here the circumstances are so extreme that we cannot but believe that you and the men under you will not fail to come to the rescue of people who are so situated.'

If you put a full-stop after 'aid', the message contains an unequivocal invitation ('Come at once!'). But if you put the full stop, not after 'aid' but after 'here', the message becomes merely a conditional invitation depending on a circumstance arising at some indefinite time in the future.

Now, it is believed that the authors meant it to be conditional. But when it was cabled to *The Times*, the period was inserted after 'aid': as a result, the message was made to appear to justify Jameson's precipitancy.

[With thanks to Professor A. W. Stewart, who was, to many, better known as J. J. Connington.]

Now for some examples, this article being but short and readers desirous of detail being recommended to refer either to *The King's English* or to *Mind the Stop*.

In a publisher's list of books there appears:

'ANARCHY or HIERARCHY

by S. de Madariaga

Author of *Englishmen, Frenchmen, Spaniards, Disarmament, The Genius of Spain*, etc.'.

Very confusing, that list of the author's works! Read, 'Author of *Englishmen, Frenchmen, Spaniards*; *Disarmament*; *The Genius of Spain*; etc.'.

'The only student I have ever met who ever believed his ears was blind': the lack of punctuation is defensible on the score of fluency; but 'The only student I have met who ever believed his ears, was blind' does away with that ambiguity which may strike others as it did me – with a jar. The sentence needs to be rewritten, perhaps in the form, 'Of all the students I have met, only one believed his ears: and he was blind' or '...; and he was blind.'

From the same author (Frank Binder, *Dialectic*) comes 'It is not enough to lead a student by the still waters, one must lose him at last in the stormy ones.' The comma is inferior to a semi-colon or, as this example occurs in literary English, a colon.

'Bush and Brown slept in cloak and blanket on the bare soil, probably, Hornblower anticipated, most uncomfortably' (C. S. Forester, *Flying Colours*). The comma after 'soil' is too weak; I suggest, 'B. and B. slept ... on the bare soil; probably (Hornblower anticipated) most uncomfortably.'

In the British Museum copy of H. A. J. Munro's *Criticisms and Elucidations of Catullus*, someone has, against the sentence 'The latest editor of the text Baehrens believes it like me to be one poem', the criticism, 'not grammatical'. (Munro had very odd ideas about punctuation; usually, he eschewed it – except for the period.) Rewrite, 'The latest editor of the text, Baehrens, believes it, like me, to be one poem' or, better, 'The latest editor of the text, Baehrens, like me believes it to be one poem' or 'Like me, the latest editor of the text, Baehrens, believes it to be one poem.'

'There was no villa to be seen. ... As they drew near it became evident that the narrow road ended by the villa itself' (Louis Bromfield, *The Strange Case of Miss Annie Spragg*). This passage obviously requires a comma after 'near'.

'For all the Loyalist Party know the girl may turn up at any second' (Laurence Meynell, *The House in the Hills*). Punctuate, 'For all the Loyalist Party know, the girl ...'.

'The crowd was thinning, many of the girls, among them Joan and Valerie, finding it chilly standing about in their scanty costumes, had gone up to dress' (W. H. Lane Crauford, *Murder to Music*). Anyone would feel chilly if he (or she) were stranded in such a sentence as that! Repunctuate in some such fashion as this: 'The crowd was thinning; many of the girls (among them Joan and Valerie), finding it chilly standing about in their scanty costumes, went up to dress.'

'The night it all began torrential rain fell' (Dale Collins, *Lost*): insert a comma after 'began'.

' "You don't really like it, you're only pretending to please me" ' (Muriel Hine, *Clear as the Sun*): a comma is required after 'pretending'; but that insertion weakens the comma after 'it'. Punctuate, 'You don't really like it; you're only pretending, to please me.'

'If there was any previous connection between Bennett and the Oultons that, and not Mrs O'Brien's name and address on their back, might account for Bennett's interest in Miss Molly's sketches' (E. R. Punshon, *The Dusky Hour*): put a comma after 'Oultons'.

'Can he, he has admittedly made money in America, be the confidence trickster ...?' (*ibid.*): not commas but dashes are required; parentheses would destroy the inference.

'And once I had discovered that there was no longer any doubt as to whether a spark of life still lingered in him' (Stephen Maddock, *Doorway to Danger*). I had reached the end of the sentence before I realized that not the whole sentence but only 'once I had discovered that' is an adverbial clause; a comma is needed after 'that', which is pronoun, not conjunction.

'He trod over to the window. ... His torch explored the shadows cast by the flowering shrubs without, however, revealing anything but a nondescript cat' (Georgette Heyer, *A Blunt Instrument*). When I came upon this sentence, I read 'the flowering shrubs without' (i.e. outside the house) and was then pulled up with a jerk. After 'shrubs', either a comma or, better, a semi-colon is required.

'Shall we borrow one of Torquemada's witticisms and call them four more "little grey sells!" ' (publisher's foreword to Agatha Christie's four stories in one volume, *Murder in the Mews*). Instead of '... "little grey sells!" ' we require '... "little grey sells"!'; and a question mark would have been preferable to the exclamation mark.

In 'When the dreadful plague was mowing down the terrified people of London in great swathes, this brave man, instead of flying quietly, remained at his house' (Walter Thornbury), it is obviously the printer, not the author, who has erred by putting a comma after 'quietly' instead of before it.

'He had opposed the policy of alliance with Egypt against Assyria, ... but when war came, in spite of his efforts, he heartened the spirit of King Hezekiah to fight to the death' (Introduction to Isaiah, in *The Bible as Literature*). Remove the comma from after 'came'. Better rewrite thus, '... but when, in spite of his efforts, war came, he heartened ...'.

And, finally, two examples from Stuart Chase's *The Tyranny of Words*:

'What is the ultimate nature of matter? The question we know by now is meaningless.' Punctuate thus: '... The question, we know by now, is meaningless.'

'A bank studied on the basis of what is going on inside without recourse to abstractions like "credit", "liquidity", "soundness", is a pretty whimsical thing.' A comma after 'inside' would remove an ambiguity.

[To American readers Mr Partridge's recommendations of the colon may seem strange, though perhaps in his examples the colon has 'a more elegant effect'. Certainly it should remind readers of the punctuation in their Bibles. For American usage an important authority is the University of Chicago Press's *A Manual of Style*. Many American printers prefer a general practice of setting all periods and commas within the quotation marks, all semi-colons and colons outside the quotation marks. The small points dangling after the broad double quotes of American use are curious-looking. However, in typescripts, where every symbol takes an em space, double quotes after period or comma may jut out ridiculously, especially when only the last word is quoted. Mr Partridge's account of punctuation shows by its wealth of possible effects that punctuation can be made a part of the art of writing – instead of the simple, almost mechanical routine that American schools recommend.]

PUNCTUATION AND QUOTA-TION MARKS.

The very tricky relationship between these two is fully treated in *You Have a Point There* (3rd edition, revised, 1955).

PUNS. The pun is the lowest form of wit.

'... the universal Elizabethan habit of punning, which pervaded conversation and literature alike. Every kind of play on words was common, from the merest jingle in sound to the most elaborate calembour. Puns are now out of favour, probably because we think that the punster wishes us to laugh at them. We should be careful, however, not to take the punning habit of the Elizabethans too seriously. Clearly the Elizabethans did not laugh at puns, unless they were peculiarly amusing. They got merely a certain intellectual titillation out of the grotesque association of ideas which punning induced (Greenough and Kittredge, *Words and Their Ways in English Speech*).

Briefly, a pun is 'a play upon words'; more fully and more precisely, 'the use of a word so as to suggest two or more meanings or different associations, or the use of two or more words of the same or nearly the same sound with different meanings, so as to produce a humorous effect' (*OED*).

Despite the epigraph, many puns are far from being 'the lowest form of wit': superficially these superior puns are mere puns (why *mere*?); but they may comport a wealth of connotation that raises them to the upper regions of wit and they may

have undertones and (to the ordinary reader) buried meanings that spring – can spring – only from profundity. From William Empson's acute and provocative *Seven Types of Ambiguity*, I select a few examples.

In *Macbeth* we have the verses,

Augurs, and understood relations, have
By maggot-pies, and choughs, and rooks, brought forth
The secret'st man of blood (III, iv.125–7).

Set beside this passage the significant

Light thickens, and the crow
Makes wing to th' rooky wood (in III, ii).

'Macbeth looked out of the window because Banquo was to be killed soon after dusk, so he wanted to know how the time was going. ... The peaceful solitary *crow*, moving towards bed and the other crows, is made unnaturally like Macbeth and a murderer who is coming against them; this is suggested ... mainly, I think, by the use of the two words *rook* and *crow*. *Rooks* live in a crowd and are mainly vegetarian; *crow* may be either another name for a *rook*, especially when seen alone, or it may mean the solitary Carrion crow. This subdued pun is made to imply' this, that and the other.

Having mentioned euphuistic conceit and the paradoxes cultivated in the 1890s, 'which give a noun two contradictory adjectives and leave it to the reader to see. how the adjectives are used', Empson subtly continues thus: 'In an extended sense ... this in itself is an ambiguity, just as a pun may repeat its key word once in each sense and be not less a pun. These tricks demand some thought and much awareness of the nature and pitfalls of language; it is not altogether a good sign when they are despised.'

Remembering that, in Shakespeare's day, *quibble* meant 'a pun', and that, in 1711, the swift-minded Shaftesbury could write, 'All humour had something of the quibble. The very language of the court was punning', we may, after Empson, quote from Johnson: 'A quibble is to Shakespeare what luminous vapours' – probably mirages; possibly mists sun-thinned – 'are to the traveller; he follows it at all adventures; it is sure to lead him out of his way and sure to engulf him in the mire. It has some malignant power over his mind. ... A quibble was for him the fatal Cleopatra for whom he lost the world, and was content to lose it.' Empson's comment is, 'Nor can I hold out against the Doctor, beyond saying that life ran very high in those days, and that he does not seem to have lost the world so completely after all.' But he deplores the fact that Shakespeare was 'so fearfully susceptible to puns'. I merely add the well-known facts that punning was in the literary air, a literary exercise, a Court exercise, of Shakespeare's time, and that he wrote not merely for himself but also for his audiences; even the groundlings expected puns and enjoyed them.

And Milton punned – punned even in the bare and virile *Samson Agonistes*, where, at least once, there occurs a weighty and effective pun-by-etymology; Delilah is, in Samson's words,

> 'That specious monster, my accomplished snare'.

As Empson points out, the pun or rather puns are worked out thus: '*Specious*, "beautiful and deceitful"; *monster*, "something unnatural and something striking shown as a sign of disaster"; *accomplished*, "skilled in the arts of blandishment and successful in undoing her husband". The point here is the sharpness of distinction between the two meanings [of each of the three words, *specious, monster, accomplished*], of which the reader is forced to be aware; they are two pieces of information, two parts of the narrative; if ingenuity had not used an [etymological] accident, they would have required two words [each].' This quotation from Milton prompts Empson to laugh quietly – or so I gather

– at those who are 'mainly conscious of the pun' – any pun – 'not of its consequences'.

He then adduces, from *Paradise Lost* (vi, 565–7), the words,

> Ye, who appointed stand,
> Do as you have in charge, and
>   briefly touch
> What we propound, and loud that
>   all may hear,

and comments thus: 'It is a bitter and controlled mood of irony in which Satan gives this address to his gunners; so much above mere ingenuity that the puns seem almost like a generalization. But here, as for ironical puns in general, to be put into the state of mind intended you must concentrate your intention on the ingenuity; on the way the words are being interpreted both by the gunners themselves and by the angels who have not yet heard of artillery; on the fact that they are puns.'

He goes on to note that the pun has become more obvious; has become overt; has become 'less intimately an expression of sensibility'. (Here I interpolate a wish that the Miltonic puns and the subtler of the Shakespearean puns, in their essence, their principles, their dignity, their verbal richness, their sophistication and depth and variety of meaning, should be revived.) 'Thus', Mr Empson continues, 'its most definite examples are likely to be found, in increasing order of self consciousness, among the seventeenth-century mystics who stress the conscious will, the eighteenth-century stylists who stress rationality, clarity and satire, and the harmless nineteenth-century punsters who stress decent above-board fun.' He then, sarcastically, analyses the kinds of pun that are deemed, by the ordinary person, to be justifiable – puns for which the reader or the auditor has been prepared; puns so obvious that no preparation was necessary; puns that 'demand an attention ... not absorbed into the attention demanded by the rest of the poem, and are a separate ornament on their own'; puns that are explicit only, not puns that are both explicit and implicit; puns that pose no strain on the intellect, no premium on imagination, no price on aesthetic awareness. In his implicit defence of the stronger, subtler, richer pun, he is, perhaps unconsciously, pleading for a departure from the standard of nit-witticism, for a proper contempt of the non-compulsive prohibitions set up by morons. (Not that Empson is wholly contemptuous of the 'curiously worldly' use of the pun in the 18th century; he admits its virtues, as he admits the virtues of the 19th-century pun.)

Yet even the simple, obvious puns of the 19th century are not always either obvious or simple – except to the cultured and intelligent reader or auditor. As exercises of wit, many are salutary; nor, all of them, the worse for the fact that, abstracted from their context, they can 'stand on their own feet' – no inconsiderable feat for a pun.

Charles Lamb, who once said 'May my last breath be drawn through a pipe, and exhaled in a pun', punned inveterately. Here are several of his witticisms, culled from Walter Jerrold's *Bon-Mots of Charles Lamb and Douglas Jerrold*, 1913. 'Charles Lamb and Ayrton were playing at whist, when Ayrton took a trick by trumping.

' "Ah!" said he, "when Greek meets Greek" [Jerrold failing to indicate that here is a goodish pun on *Greek*, 'a cardsharper'] "then comes the tug of war."

' "But, when *you* meet Greek," retorted Lamb, "you can't read it." '

'An old lady, who was fond of her dissenting minister, once wearied Lamb by the length of her praises.

' "I speak because I *know* him well," said she.

' "Well, I don't," replied Lamb; "I don't, but damn him! at a venture." '

'You have no mock modesty about you – no, nor real either.'

From the same small volume, I take a few puns made by Douglas Jerrold (1803–57).

'Someone praised the *mise en scène* at one of Kean's revivals at the Princess's Theatre, to which Jerrold retorted, "Oh yes, it is all scenery and Keanery." '

'A friend was one day reading to Jerrold an account of a case in which a person named Ure was reproached with having suddenly jilted a young lady to whom he was engaged.

' "Ure seems to have turned out to be a base 'un," said Jerrold.'

'Jerrold said to an ardent young gentleman, who burned with a desire to see himself in print: – Be advised by me, young man – don't take the shutters down before there is something in the window.'

'Discussing Mrs Grundy and her "set", a member of the same club said, "They'll soon say marriage is improper."

' "No, no," said Jerrold, "they'll always consider marriage good breeding." '

'A lawyer's smile Douglas Jerrold described as "dirt cheap at six and eightpence".'

'He kissed her and promised. Such beautiful lips! Man's usual fate – he was lost upon the coral reefs.'

'To a very thin man, who had been boring him, Jerrold said: "Sir, you are like a pin, but without either its head or its point." ' [Sharp as a needle, in fact.]

'A certain pretty actress being mentioned, Douglas Jerrold praised her early beauty. "She was a lovely little thing," he said, "when she was *a bud* and" – (a pause) – "before she was *a blowen*." '

'On the carrying of Free Trade, Douglas Jerrold, an earnest free trader, immediately proposed the following epitaph for Protection:

Here Lies

PROTECTION

It lied throughout its life
and now
Lies Still.'

Which reminds one of the epigram,

And in her wondrous eyes
Love lies – and lies and lies

(or words to that effect).

Let us pass from the two wisely-simple, not-so-simple, witty Charles Lamb and Douglas Jerrold to the sophisticated James Abbott McNeill Whistler (1834–1903) and Oscar Wilde (1856–1900). Here I draw upon Walter Jerrold's *A Book of Famous Wits*, 1912. Whistler, however, was not a frequent punster; he was a frequent wit. But we may record that, Whistler 'having made some happy remark, Wilde showed his appreciation by saying, "I wish I had said that, Whistler." "You will, Oscar; you will," said Whistler dryly. ... One of Wilde's retaliations may perhaps be recognized in his remark that "Whistler, with all his faults, was never guilty of writing a line of poetry." '

Sir Lewis Morris (author of *The Epic of Hades*), feeling disgruntled by the neglect with which he met while successors to the Laureateship were being discussed after Tennyson's death; 'It is a complete conspiracy of silence against me! What ought I to do, Oscar?' 'Join it,' said Wilde.

' "It appears that I am dying beyond my means", was his whimsical comment on the straits to which he was reduced in his last illness.'

Of recent punster-wits, I shall cite only Humbert Wolfe (poet and wit and able Civil Servant). Of a certain intellectualist critic of poetry, he remarked that he spoke on the subject as a professor *ex cathedra ignorantiae*. Asked how a woman politician, not long inducted into office, was progressing, he said, 'Oh, she's still *virago intacta*.'

pupil and **student.** In older British usage it was a *pupil* at a school, a *student* at a university. In America and now increasingly in Britain we cater to the young people and speak of *high school students* as well as *college* and *university students*. But a professor may talk of 'a former pupil of mine'. Musicians and painters have *pupils*, not *students*, though these are 'students of painting or of music' and some of them may study at 'the Art Students League'.

puppet and **marionette.** A puppet is the kind that fits over your hand, or that is moved on rods from behind or appears as a shadow on a screen. The word is also used of the ones moved from above on strings or wires; but these, strictly speaking, are *marionettes*.

purchase is usually inferior to *buy*.

pure does = *mere*, but avoid it if, as in 'pure Nudism', it sets up an ambiguity. See also COMPARATIVES, FALSE.

Puritan and **puritan.** A *Puritan* is a member of that party of English Protestants who, from late 16th to mid 17th century, desired a further purification of the Church and, especially, a simpler form of worship. A *puritan* is 'one who is, affects to be, or is accounted, extremely strict, precise, or scrupulous in religion or morals' (*OED*); it is now a pejorative term.

purport in the sense of 'purpose' is now so rare – so nearly obsolete – as to make its employment inadvisable: see the passage quoted at **malapropisms.** The general sense of the noun is 'meaning' or 'tenor'; and, properly used, the word is restricted to documents and speeches. As a verb it signifies 'to be intended to seem', 'to be made to appear', as in 'He received a letter purporting to be written by me and to contain my decision on an important matter.' (Adapted from *COD*.) The verb can be used of persons who 'are reputed to be' something ('men purporting to be shepherds'); but not where a verbal 'claim' is made, as in 'He purports to have discovered the answer.'

PURPOSE. See FINAL CLAUSES.

purpose (v.). See **propose and purpose.**

purposely. See **advisedly.**

pursuant to is officialese for *according to* (an agreement, etc.).

putter and **potter** (v.). The latter is Standard British and American, the former is British dialectal and American Standard.

putting. See CONJUNCTIONS, DIS-
GUISED.

puzzle. See **riddle.**

Q

qua means 'in the role of'. It is used when
something or someone is to be considered
from a particular point of view, as in
'Money, qua money, does not bring happiness.' It does not mean 'as regards', as in
'Our situation qua money is deplorable.'

quaint is 'unusual, uncommon, or even
odd', but at the same time either 'attractive' or 'agreeable' esp. if it is either 'pretty
or dainty in an old-fashioned way'. Do not
use it to mean either 'merely odd' or
'amusing (or droll)'; those are a slangy or,
at best, a colloquial usage.

Quakers. See at **Mormons,** where it
occurs, not by association of ideas (no
association is possible), but for the sake of
convenience.

qualitive is incorrect for *qualitative* (referring to quality) which is often contrasted
with *quantitative* (referring to quantity).

quality of is correct in 'a certain quality
of paper' but wrong in 'To finish up in
some club of the same quality of his own'
(John G. Brandon, *The Mail-Van Mystery*),
where the first 'of' seems to have led the
author astray.

quantative is incorrect for *quantitative* or
quantitive. Cf. **qualitive.**

quantity and **number.** It is better not to
speak of *a large* (or *a small*) *quantity* of things
or persons when one means *a large* (or
small) *number*, but in familiar (though not
in literary) Standard English, a *quantity*
may be used of an indefinite, i.e. of a fair

or considerable, number of persons or
things, as in 'Four chairs and a quantity of
pillows' (Mrs Carlyle, 1852). But avoid it
if it leads to ambiguity; it is better to differentiate, as in 'It takes a large number of
nuts to make such a quantity as there is in
this bag' and 'He gave away a large quantity of canned goods but still has a number
of cans' (*OED*).

quantum leap. See VOGUE WORDS.

quarter after, a. See **half after, a.**

query and **inquiry; quest.** A *query* is a
specific question, a question of limited or
particular or *singular* reference, whereas an
inquiry, though it may simply mean 'a
question', more usually means a set or a
series of questions, an investigation, as in
'an official inquiry into the fate of *The
Thetis*'. A *quest*, in current usage and apart
from technicalities, is a search or pursuit,
especially of something remote, or figuratively; e.g. 'the quest of the Holy Grail'.
See also **enquire.**

question (v.) is used in a misleading manner in the following from Eric Partridge,
*The French Romantics' Knowledge of English
Literature*, 1924, 'Despite his popularity,
Scott was questioned as to whether he was
a suitable source for dramatists.' The
meaning is not that someone asked Scott
this question, but that *the question was raised*
or *the suitability was called in question.*

question (n.) can mean 'doubt', as in
'There was some question as to their
honesty', or 'Their honesty is beyond all
question.' The combination *no question* is
ambiguous: it may mean that something is
certainly true or that it is certainly false. To
resolve the ambiguity of such sentences as
'There is no question that you have been
cheated', prefer 'no question but that'
or replace *question* by either *doubt* or
possibility.

quiescent; quiet. *Quiescent* means 'inac-
tive, at rest, motionless', as in a 'quiescent
star', 'He lay quiescent', and, in Philology,
(of a letter that is) 'silent, not sounded'
(*OED*).

quit – quitted. Of these alternative forms of the preterite and past participle, *quit* is the American preference and is becoming increasingly common in British usage.

quite has two Standard senses: (i) 'completely, wholly, entirely, to the fullest extent', as in 'Haws ... which often quite cover the hawthorn bushes' (Jefferies), 'Here have I sat ... quite by myself'; 'quite certain', 'a quite separate question' or 'quite another question (or, thing)'; and
(ii) 'somewhat, rather, to some extent', as in 'quite pleasant', 'I quite enjoyed it.' When *quite* is used with 'absolute' adjectives (see **COMPARATIVES, FALSE**) there is no danger of confusion: one cannot be 'rather immortal' or 'somewhat dead'; and there is no confusion over negatives, since 'not quite cold' must mean 'not completely'. But 'quite cold' might mean either 'rather chilly' or 'completely cooled'. If the context does not clarify the matter, replace *quite* by *rather, absolutely,* etc.

quite a is correctly used before adjectives when *quite* = 'somewhat' (see above), as in 'quite a long time'; but when *quite* = 'completely', only *a quite*, as in 'a quite impossible task', is permissible. Permissible also, though not very formal, are 'quite a few', 'quite a while'. But the use of *quite a* (for *quite some*) before other nouns with no intervening adjective, as in 'quite a story', is distinctly colloquial.

QUOTATION. See **MISQUOTATIONS.**

QUOTATION MARKS, unnecessary use of; e.g. in 'It would seem that over all was hanging some menace which was real but intangible, something against which the sling-shots, the knives, the "silenced" automatics of gangdom, could not prevail.' The quotation marks would be appropriate only if the word *silenced* were a technical or slang term of which the reader was presumably ignorant.

QUOTATION MARKS TO INDICATE SLANG. See **SLANG,** Section III, last paragraph.

quote. See **cite.**

R

rabbit, Welsh, generally supposed to be a corruption of *rarebit,* is in fact 'a slang nickname for a local dish, similar to "Norfolk Capons" for red herrings, "Irish apricots" for potatoes, etc.' (Ackermann). The form *rarebit* is incorrect.

racism; racialism. The two words seem to be used indiscriminately, the former being now the more common; though some writers try to distinguish between *racism* as a scientific theory and *racialism* as racial prejudice.

racquet, a frequent spelling of (tennis-) *racket,* is quite incorrect though now well established; 'in some mysterious way', says Sir Gordon Lowe (*Lowe's Lawn Tennis Annual,* 1935), 'it has got mixed up with the French spelling "raquette" '.

radical, Radical; radicle. A *Radical* is 'one who advocates sweeping changes, esp. in government and the social order'; *radical* means 'basic, fundamental'; but a *radicle* is, in Botany, an embryonic primary root, or, more generally, a rootlet; in Philology, however, a root or stem is a *radical,* not a *radicle.* The noun *radical* has also technical senses in Chemistry.

radio has virtually superseded the older British *wireless.* It functions as both noun and verb.

railroad is the usual term in the USA, **railway** the usual term for Britain. But *railway* is much more widely used (witness Weseen) in the States than is generally believed in Britain, and in Britain *railroad* was, until *c.* 1900, at least as common as *railway*. [*Webster's* states a distinction often made in American English: *railroad* for heavy steam transportation; *railway* for the lighter street-car (or tram) lines, for shop railways, crane railways, or any way for wheels. *Webster's* admits *railway* for *railroad* as defined above; but by some opinions it is old-fashioned and probably obsolescent.]

raise is transitive, *rise* is intransitive. The noun is *rise* in the sense 'upward slope' or 'increase', but *raise* in cards for an increase in a stake or bid. An increase in salary is usually a *rise* in Britain and a *raise* in America.

raise and **rear.** The British on the whole *rear* (or 'bring up') children, and *rear* or *raise* (or 'breed') animals. The Americans *rear* or *raise* children and *raise* animals. Everyone *raises* (or 'grows') crops.

raison d'être is a wholly unnecessary Gallicism for *reason*, or, occasionally (and incorrectly), *explanation*.

ranch and **rancho; range; hacienda.** A *range* is 'the region in which cattle or sheep may pasture' (but chiefly the former), or, without *a* or *the*, 'grazing ground'. A *rancho* is 'a large grazing farm; a ranch; distinguished from *hacienda*, a *hacienda* being a Spanish American term (*rancho* is Spanish American too, but also Southwestern US) for 'a cultivated farm, with a good house, in distinction from a farming establishment with rude huts for herdsmen, etc.', i.e. a *rancho*. In Western USA and Canada a *ranch* is 'an establishment, with its estate, for the grazing and rearing of horses, cattle, or sheep' (not cattle only, as *OED* has it); especially 'the buildings occupied by owner and employees, with the adjacent barns, corrals, etc.; also, the persons on the estate collectively'. Loosely (and commonly) any farm in the West, esp. if large.

rang. See **ring.**

range (n.). See **ranch.**

rapt. See **wrapt.**

rare and **scarce.** Weseen has neatly established the difference, thus: 'The adjective *rare* is often misused for *scarce*, as "Potatoes are rare this winter." *Rare* applies properly to things that are infrequent at all times and usually to things that have superior qualities, as "Great leaders are rare." *Scarce* applies to ordinary things that are temporarily not plentiful, as "Jobs are scarce this winter." '

rarely or ever. See **seldom or ever.**

rat race. See VOGUE WORDS.

rather, had; rather, would. In the first person, *had rather* is legitimate, as in 'I had rather oppose prejudices than confute arguments'; but *would rather* when a hypothesis is expressed; e.g. 'Were a patriot reduced to the alternative of death or political slavery, I am confident he would rather die than live' (or 'he would, I am confident, rather die than live'). But this distinction is now almost dead, owing to the virtual disappearance of *had rather*. The contraction *I'd* (or *he'd, they'd*) *rather* does duty for both. See also **would rather.**

rather a ..., misused for *a rather ...* 'He was rather a dandy' is correct, for 'a dandy' is, here, indivisible in the sense that one cannot say 'a rather dandy'; but where an adjective intervenes, 'He was rather a conceited dandy' is incorrect for '... a rather conceited'; cf. 'a very conceited dandy'.

rather than for *than.* 'All this was new to him, his experience having made him more knowing about bookies rather than books' (John Ferguson, *Death of Mr Dodsley*). To correct this sentence, omit 'rather', or write '... having made him knowing about bookies rather than about books'.

ratiocination usually signifies *reasoning*: when it does, *reasoning* is preferable.

rational ('endowed with reason'), hence 'sane, sensible, reasonable', is now rare as a noun; *rationale*, 'a reasoned exposition of principles; hence, an explanation', also 'the logical or the rational basis (*of* anything)', is only noun (*OED*).

rationalize, rationalization, as applied to e.g. a factory, mean *modernize, -ization,* or *manage sensibly* (*run well*), *good management.*

re from *in re* (Latin), 'in the matter of', which is supposed in commercial offices to be an abbreviation of 'referring to', can be properly used only in the driest of business communications.

re- and **re** (v.). Most compounds with *re-* are spelt as one word; but hyphenate when the following word begins with *e,* as in *re-elect* and *re-enact,* or when the resultant compound must be distinguished from a more familiar form, as with *re-count,* 'to count again', and *recount,* 'to narrate', or *re-cover,* 'to cover again', and *recover,* 'to have good health again'.

re- verbs and their corresponding nouns are being run to death by bureaucracy: *re-categorize, re-validate,* etc.

reaction is correctly used in *one's reaction to,* 'one's response (whether conscious or subconscious) to' or 'one's behaviour in relation to an influence (actual or presumed)', as in 'His reaction to the doctor's treatment was, all in all, satisfactory' or 'I fear that my reactions to his proposal were not quite what he expected.' In technical use, a stimulus (not a person) has a *reaction on* something, as in 'The reaction of the doctor's treatment on the patient was alarming'; and when the word means something like 'backlash', it is often used with *from* or *against,* as in 'There has been a widespread reaction against the permissiveness of his views on education.' A VOGUE WORD.

reactionary. Says Sir Alan Herbert: 'The word is not needed. Speak, if you like, of the forces of Obstruction, the foes of Change, the apostles of Privilege, the enemies of Reform and Progress (though Progress is another "Question-Begger"); but kill this mean and imbecile sneer-

word, whose history is a long procession of errors' (*What a Word!,* p. 28).

real is often unnecessary. Particularly unnecessary in the phrase in which it so often occurs; *in real life,* as, e.g. in 'Very often in fiction, as in real life, one is appalled ...', where *in life* (or *in reality*) would be much superior to *in real life.* That example occurs in a review written by a novelist that prides himself on his economical style.

Always ask yourself whether *real* or *mere* or *actual* is necessary [not '*really* necessary']: if it is not, then omit the excrescential word. And cf. **really.**

realism, realist, realistic. See VOGUE WORDS.

really, actually, and **definitely** are generally unnecessary. The frequent use of 'really', 'definitely', 'actually', 'as a matter of fact', 'to tell you the truth', etc., shows the speaker's lack of confidence in his own credibility; he seems to need additional assurance that what he asserts is not a fabrication or a mere conjecture. Those whose Yea is Yea and their Nay Nay have no need of these adverbial supports. Mgr Ronald Knox, in *Double Cross Purposes,* says that 'They found Victor Lethaby a tornado of well-bred apologies, all punctuated with an irritating repetition of the word "actually" – a habit of modern youth, particularly when he is lying.' It is a well-known fact that *as a matter of fact* often prefaces either a lie or a deliberate half-statement.

realm. See **sphere.**

realty is the legal term for 'real property', 'real estate': it can never be used as a synonym of *reality.*

reason. See **cause.**

reason ... because, or **why ... because,** is often used redundantly for *reason ... that,* as in 'The reason he does this (or, why he did this) is because he knows no better.'

rebound; redound. To *rebound* is literally 'to bounce back', or figuratively 'to recoil adversely on the doer', as in 'This legislation has rebounded on those who agitated for it.' To *redound* is either 'to contribute to', as in 'This action redounded to his advantage', or 'come as the final (not necessarily adverse) result to (not necessarily the doer)'. 'The minister's action redounds on her party.' The second senses of the two verbs are thus barely distinguishable.

receipt of, be in = to *receive* or to *have received*. (Officialese.)

RECEIVED STANDARD. See STANDARD ENGLISH, II.

receptacle, of a thing; **recipient,** of a person. 'The recipient of the ornate receptacle was less pleased than its donors had hoped he would be.'

recollect and **remember.** The former may be synonymous with the latter; but discriminating writers and speakers – discriminate. '*Recollect* when distinguished from *remember*, implies a conscious or express effort of memory to recall something [that] does not spontaneously rise in the mind' (*OED*), as in 'At last I recollected what, during my illness (lasting, you may recall, some nine weeks), I had failed to remember, important though it was.'

record-player. See **gramophone.**

recountal occurs in *OED* with the implication that its use is mainly journalistic. There can be little doubt that it arose through a confusion of *account, recounting, recital*, and it jars one to find it in a reputable novelist such as Georgette Heyer: 'She chose the luncheon hour as a suitable time for the recountal to Jim of the whole affair of the letter (*They Found Him Dead*).

recourse. See **resource.**

recreation and **re-creation** are to be kept distinct: the latter = 'creation anew', the former = 'refreshment, physical or mental or spiritual'. In 'This was a temperament singularly fitted for the recreation of life's little comedies and tragedies'

(John Galsworthy, Preface to Stacy Aumonier's *Ups and Downs*), *re-creation* is the word required. The corresponding adjectives are *recreational* and *re-creative* (generally written *recreative*).

recrudescence has been so strongly and wittily condemned by Fowler that I, who have sinned but do not repent, need only point out that, etymologically, it = 'a breaking out again of a wound', 'a becoming raw of the flesh'; hence, it is used of a disease, a sore, an epidemic. Hence, figuratively, a renewal or a return of a quality, or a state of things, especially and *properly* if they are regarded as evil or objectionable, as in 'a recrudescence of calumny', 'the recrudescence of a metaphysical Paganism' (*OED*), and 'His headaches were less frequent and there had been no recrudescence of the [mental] blackouts' (Ngaio Marsh, *Died in the Wool*). Any extension of that 'figuratively' leads inevitably to absurdity.

rectify. See **justify.**

recto. See **verso.**

rector and **vicar.** A *rector* was a parson whose tithes formerly passed directly to him; a *vicar* never held tithes – the tithes being held by others, who paid him either a part or a salary. The distinction is no longer relevant.

recumbent and **incumbent; super-incumbent; decumbent.** *Recumbent* is 'lying down'; 'reclining' ('His recumbent form was scarcely visible'); so too is the now rare *decumbent* ('The advantages of a decumbent' – now preferably *recumbent* – 'position', which has in Botany the technical sense, (of plants) 'lying or trailing upon the ground, but with up-pointing extremity'. In *incumbent*, the stress is on the weight of the 'lier'; cf. the figurative *incumbent on* ('obligatory upon'), as in 'It is incumbent on him to look after his aged mother.' In Geology, *incumbent* has, like *superincumbent*, the sense, 'overlying'; *superincumbent*, however, is not properly a geological term, though it is applied, in a general way, to overhanging rocks (*OED*).

recurring for *frequent* is wholly unnecessary; and it is also catachrestic, for, as an adjective, it should be applied to that which recurs either at irregular intervals or, as in *recurring decimals*, to infinity, and for irregular recurrence the correct adjective is *recurrent*; 'It might well be that here the scientific criminologist will find one more means of dealing with a problem that is one of the most recurring in his work' (Nigel Morland, *The Conquest of Crime*).

redound. See **rebound.**

reduce. See **deplete.**

REDUNDANCY. See **VERBOSITY**, last paragraph.

redundant, at first Service, then Whitehall jargon, is threatening to displace *unnecessary* things and *superfluous* staff. The (British) sense 'unemployed because one's job has been eliminated' is now of course very common; and the word is coming up in the world, having gained the non-pejorative technical sense of 'serving as a duplicate in case of the failure of a component'.

refer to. See **allude.**

reference has (already) been made, to which – *already mentioned.* (Officialese.)

referring. See **CONJUNCTIONS, DISGUISED.**

reflection and **reflexion.** See **-ection.**

refute and **deny.** To *deny* an accusation is merely to assert that it is false; to *refute* an accusation is to prove that it is false. One can also *refute* (or *confute*) the accuser; and one may *confute* an accusation. Perhaps it would be wise to reserve *confute* for proving accusers and arguers to be wrong, and *refute* for proving accusations, arguments, theories to be wrong; certainly *refute* is much the more common in the latter application. A further distinction between *confute* and *refute* is that the former is the stronger word.

regal. See **kingly** ...

regalia, 'emblems (or insignia) of royalty', is a plural.

regard. One says *in regard to* and *without regard to*, but *as regards*.

regarding. See **CONJUNCTIONS, DISGUISED.**

regime is an English word. It is not italicized, though it sometimes bears an accent: 'régime'; cf. **role.**

REGIONAL DIALECTS. See **DIALECT** and **STANDARD ENGLISH, II.**

regret (v.) is frequently ambiguous; as in 'For an instant Mr Pendlebury regretted the freshness of Berkshire. Then his natural buoyancy reasserted itself. After all, though it was hot here ... Central London must be an inferno' (Anthony Webb, *Mr Pendlebury's Second Case*). The meaning is that Mr Pendlebury, who was not in Berkshire at the time, longed for – *not* 'was repentant (or apologetic) about' – the pleasant county of Berkshire.

regulate and **relegate** are often confused by those who know the former but have merely heard the latter. *Relegate* is 'to consign to an inferior position, or to hand over to another to deal with'.

rehabilitate; rehabilitation = to cure or heal; a cure or healing. Mostly officialese.

Reims for *Rheims.* See **Bruxelles** ...

rejoinder is either 'the reply to a charge or pleading in Law' or, in general usage, 'an answer to a reply': it is a pity to weaken it to synonymity with '*any* reply' (*OED*).

relate. See **VOGUE WORDS.**

relating to is longwinded.

relation and **relative.** The writer is one of those who prefer *relative* to *relation* in the sense 'kinsman'.

relations towards. See **PREPOSITIONS WRONGLY USED.**

RELATIVE CLAUSES. For the use of *that, which, who* (the why and the when), see **which and that.**

'A moderate number of relative clauses may give charm and ease to the style, many consecutive ones are often felt as heavy and cumbersome', writes Otto Jespersen in *Notes on Relative Clauses* (SPE Tract No. xxiv). He gives an excellent example from Medwin's *Life of Shelley*, 1847:

'Lewis told that [i.e. the story] of Minna, *which* first appeared in *The Conversations of Lord Byron*; and one also sketched there, *which* is more stirring, of a haunted house, at Mannheim, *which* he had inhabited, *that* had belonged to a widow, *who* to prevent the marriage of her only son with a poor but honest maiden, had sent him to sea, *where* he perished in a wreck.'

The sentence might be rewritten thus:

'Having told the story of Minna which first appeared in *The Conversations of Lord Byron*, Lewis went on to relate another and more stirring story, which had been briefly outlined there. It concerned a haunted house, which, inhabited later by Lewis, had belonged to a widow. This widow, to prevent her son's marriage with a poor but honest maiden, had sent him to sea – and to his death in a wreck [*or*, to sea, where he perished in a wreck].'

RELATIVE CLAUSES, WRONG POSITION OF. See AGREEMENT, FALSE.

RELATIVE PRONOUN, attached to wrong noun. See AGREEMENT, FALSE.

RELATIVE PRONOUN, omitted. In many instances, the omission of the relative pronoun leads to 'a form of expression which can hardly be matched for conciseness in English or any other language' (Onions), although this omission is generally avoided in dignified or literary writings. Thus 'The man I was talking about is a well-known author', *that* being omitted and this shorter form being preferred to 'The man about whom I was talking'; 'The etymology (*that*) you met with' rather than 'The etymology with which you met'. As Jespersen has

remarked, this omission of the relative pronoun, so far from being a fault, 'is a genuine English idiom of long standing' (*Growth and Structure of the English Language*, p. 118).

relative to is gobbledygook; cf. the barnacular *relating to*.

relatively is usually superfluous. See **comparative.**

relegate. See **regulate.**

relic is incorrect for *relict*, an archaic word for 'a widow'. *Relict* also has technical senses in geology and ecology, but use *relic* elsewhere.

remediable; remedial. The former is passive, 'able to be remedied or redressed; curable', as in 'Where injustice, like disease, is remediable, there the remedy must be applied in word or deed' (Jowett); the latter is active, 'affording or constituting a remedy, tending to remedy, relieve, or redress; potentially curative, potentially effective in providing a remedy', as in 'The remedial part of a law' (Blackstone).

'Every good political institution must have a preventive operation as well as a remedial' (Burke), and 'Tribulation is a remedial (though bitter) pill.' The adverbs are *remediably* and *remedially*; the opposites of the adjectives are *irremediable* (adverb in *-bly*) and – what? Perhaps *inefficacious* and *ineffectual*. There seems to be no such adjective as *irremedial*, though it is hard to see why there shouldn't be one! (Based on *OED*).

remember. See **recollect.**

remembrance and **reminder.** Either word is in use for 'memento, keepsake'. Anything else (a letter, a mention, a knotted handkerchief) that reminds one is a *reminder*.

reminisce has now been adopted as Standard English, for it is so very convenient for 'to indulge in reminiscences; (of a person) to be reminiscent'; in the sense 'to recollect or remember', it serves no useful purpose and is already obsolescent.

reminiscent of for *indicative of* or *redolent of* is feeble: and incorrect.

remit and **send**. Remit = 'to *send*' only in the specific sense, 'to send or transmit (money or valuables) *to* a person or a place'. In any other sense of *send*, *remit* is either incorrect or unthinkable.

remunerate. See **renumerate**.

Renaissance and **Renascence; renaissance** and **renascence**. As a synonym of 'rebirth', only *renascence*; for a revival, e.g. in art or literature, either *renaissance* or *renascence* though preferably the latter. For that great European revival of art and letters which began in the 14th century and reached its English peak in the 16th century, or the period itself or its architecture, *Renaissance* is the more usual, the other being literary and perhaps a trifle affected: the adjectives are *Renaissance* or *Renascence*, preferably the former. The adjective corresponding to the 'rebirth' sense of *renascence* is *renascent*; there is no such adjective as *renaissant*, and *Renaissant* is virtually obsolete.

rend, 'to tear, to tear apart'; preterite *rent*; past participle, *rent*.

render a decision and **render decisions** are inferior to *make a decision* and *make decisions*.

render a return (list, report, etc.) is an example of inept officialese and fatuous tautology; to *make a return* suffices; cf. *rendition*.

render inoperative. Use *disable* or *supersede*, whichever suits; preferably the former.

rendition is 'a performance' or 'a translation', but *rendering* is preferable; *rendition of returns* or *reports* is – whatever strong adjective comes to mind.

rent (v.). See **hire**. And cf. the entry at **rend**.

renumerate, 'enumerate again', is obsolete; *remunerate* = 'to repay or requite; to reward'. But people that have never heard of *renumerate* (and, if they did, wouldn't know what it meant), often allow their undisciplined tongues to say *renumerate* when they intended *remunerate*.

reoccurrence is rare for *recurrence*; *reoccur* is rare for *recur*.

repairable can be used for *reparable* only of material things (buildings, roads, boots); in the sense 'falling due to be repaired, due (if occasion arises) to be repaired', either form is correct, but for material objects, *repairable* is to be preferred.

repast. See ELEGANCIES.

repellent and **repulsive**. In the sense 'disgusting', either word may be used with any noun, although *repulsive* is stronger. Fabrics that 'ward off' moisture etc. are *repellent* not *repulsive*.

repent for *regret* or *resent* is a misuse. 'She had treated them well and he no longer repented her coming to Grakenhill' (H. W. Freeman, *Joseph and His Brethren*).

repercussions is being overworked by the Press and by Civil Servants. See VOGUE WORDS.

repertoire and **repertory**. The latter is a storehouse (lit. or fig.) where something may be found, as in 'The established repertory of our statutes and usages' (Milman); it may be, but is better not, used as a synonym of *repertoire*, 'a stock of plays or musical pieces which either a company or a player is accustomed – or prepared – to perform'; hence one's stock of, e.g. stories; the adjective of *repertoire* however, is *repertory*, as in *repertory company* and *repertory theatre* (OED).

REPETITION, needless, has been described as 'a mark of illiteracy – or of a minor intelligence'. 'It looked bad, that it did! With all the ... Very bad, it looked. Hersey wouldn't half be interested, he wouldn't!' (Freeman Wills Crofts, *Sudden Death*). Nor is repetition particularly effective or even useful in 'Denis had met the girl at Stern Bridge, and had gone there without going through Isle by going some roundabout way' (John Newton Chance, *Wheels in the Forest*): which is, moreover, an ambiguous sentence.

Words or phrases should be repeated only if the repetition is effective or if it is essential to clarity: two occasions that occur often enough. Macaulay is an excellent writer to study in this respect.

replace, lit. 'to put back (in place)', also means 'to displace, supplant, supersede, take the place of, serve instead of' or 'find a substitute for': where, however, one of those verbs can be used without impropriety or awkwardness, use it! In all the noted senses, *replace* has become part of usage. What, after all, could we say instead of 'The lost book is *irreplaceable*'?

replete is debased to mean *complete* or *furnished with*, in the announcement, by a catering firm, of a branch café 'replete with every modern convenience'; *replete* means 'quite full', 'full to overflowing'. See also COMPARATIVES, FALSE.

replica should not be used as a synonym of *repetition*, as it is in 'His speech was an almost exact replica of one delivered by Disraeli.' Be careful with *replica*, which might well be restricted to its use as an art term; and as an art term, it is properly 'a copy, duplicate or reproduction … made' – not by another but – 'by the original artist' (*OED*).

reported. See **reputed and reported.**

REPORTED SPEECH. One excuse for reported speech is a desire to break up the monotony of verbatim dialogue by making it impersonal: but reported or indirect speech (*oratio obliqua*) is, because of its artificiality, more apt than direct speech (*oratio recta*) to become monotonous. What, in 'They declare that they refuse to fight' or 'They declared that they refused to fight', is there that is preferable to ' "We refuse to fight", they declare' or 'They declare: "We refuse to fight"'?

The Classics started this cumbrous metamorphosis of the speaker's actual words, and despite the fact that the Romans often made a sad mess of it, we stick to an outmoded vehicle of thought. Newspaper reporters of Parliamentary (and other) speeches continue to use it; examiners of the young still set questions on it. The best justification is that it exercises the wits; but why exercise the wits in steering one's verbal craft between the Scylla of pedantry and the Charybdis of unwieldiness?

Nevertheless, for the sake of those who contrive to believe in the virtues of reported speech, perhaps I ought to say that an excellent exposition is made by Dr Onions in *An Advanced English Syntax*. Of the different kinds of reported speech, he gives an illuminating example.

He points out that the passage: 'Croesus, king of the Lydians, said to Solon, the Athenian: "My Athenian guest, *your* great fame has reached even to *us*, as well of *your* wisdom as of *your* travels, how that as a philosopher *you have* travelled various countries for the purpose of observation. *I am* therefore desirous of asking *you* a question. *Tell me*, who *is* the most happy man *you have* seen?" ' – can be reported in three different ways, i.e. from the viewpoint of Croesus, from that of Solon, and from that of an outsider.

I. Croesus would say:

'I said to Solon that *his* great fame *had* reached even to *us*, as well of *his* wisdom as of *his* travels, how that as a philosopher *he had* travelled through various countries for the purpose of observation. *I was* therefore desirous of asking *him* a question. *I asked him to tell me*' – or *would he tell me* – 'who *was* the most happy man *he had* seen', the *would he tell me* representing a possible 'Will you tell me?'

II. Solon would say:

'Croesus told me that *my* great fame *had* reached even to *them*, as well of *my* wisdom as of *my* travels, how that as a philosopher I *had* travelled through various countries for the purpose of observation. *He was* therefore desirous of asking *me* a question. *He asked me to tell him*' – or *would I tell him* – 'who *was* the most happy man I *had* seen.'

III. An outsider's account (being in the third person throughout, this is the most usual form of reported speech) would run:

'Croesus, king of the Lydians, said to Solon, the Athenian, that *his* (Solon's) great fame *had* reached even to *them* (the Lydians), as well of *his* wisdom as of *his* travels, how that as a philosopher *he had* travelled through various countries for the purpose of observation. That *he* (Croesus) *was* therefore desirous of asking *him* (Solon) a question. *Would he tell him*, who *was* the most happy man *he had* seen?'

[For an excellent grammatical survey of reported speech, see Jespersen's *A Modern English Grammar on Historical Principles*, Part iv, ch. xi, 'Indirect Speech'.]

I am willing to admit that there may be occasions when reported speech is a convenience; but is that convenience sufficiently great to outweigh the consequent lack of clarity and brevity? In brief, reported speech may serve to introduce variety; but variety – especially, as here, a very limited variety – cannot compensate for ambiguity, ponderousness, and verbosity. Moreover, it is slowly becoming recognized that it is important, often indeed essential, to have the speaker's exact words: and quite apart from the fact that reported speeches sometimes misrepresent, carelessly or unthinkingly, the actual speech, it does seem unnecessary that we should be forced to view words (elusive enough, ambiguous enough, at the best of times) through a blur-glass darkly.

reprehend, 'to reprove, rebuke, find fault with', is occasionally confused with *apprehend, comprehend*, and even *represent*; *apprehend* is 'to seize or grasp' (physically or mentally); *comprehend* is 'to understand'.

reprint. See **edition.**

repulsive. See **repellent and repulsive.**

reputed and **reported.** The former is occasionally misused for the latter (or for *said*), as in 'It is reputed that he tried to escape.'

required information, the = the facts you need.

requirement and **requisite.** A *requirement* is 'a want, a need; that which is needed', as in 'the requirements of a hospital', '£10,000 would meet the requirements of capitalization'; also 'a condition that must be fulfilled', as in 'The other professors are under more stringent requirements to teach' (Mark Pattison). A *requisite* is 'something indispensable, especially an indispensable quality or property', as in 'The form of febrifuge which combines ... the two requisites of efficacy and economy' (C. R. Markham, concerning Peruvian bark). Sometimes the two words are interchangeable; but demands to be met are always *requirements*, and necessary physical objects are always *requisites* ('toilet requisites'). A *prerequisite* is 'something required beforehand' (there being no such term as *prerequirement*) or 'a condition previously necessary' (as in 'The ... prerequisites of success are ability, courage, and luck'): there is, in the latter sense, very little difference between *requisite* and *prerequisite*; the latter does, however, stress the fact that before anything can be done at all, certain conditions must already have been complied with (*OED*).

research (n.). There has, since about 1930, been a growing tendency to speak of research *on* a subject. But surely one does research – or one researches – *in* a subject and *into* a special aspect of a subject? Thus, 'His researches have been in history and in geography; especially into certain problems of historical geography.'

reserve and **preserve.** A *reserve* (in addition to non-competing senses) is 'something set apart for a specific purpose', including a district or a place; if for a native tribe, it is often called a *reservation*; the word is also used for the strip of land between the carriageways of a British road. A *preserve* is 'a piece of ground, especially a wood, set apart for the rearing (and protection) of game', also 'a pond for fish; a vivarium'; often figurative, as in *to poach on a person's preserves*.

reside and **live; residence** and **house.** To *reside* is to live permanently or at least for some considerable time *in* or *at* a particular place; to live officially (i.e. *to be in residence*) at a place. One's *residence* or, less formally, *dwelling*, is one's settled abode, especially the house or mansion of a person of rank or distinction: you and I have a *house*, the President or the Prime Minister has a *residence*.

residuum is a legal and scientific variant of *residue*, which is for general purposes much the more serviceable and unaffected.

resin and **rosin.** *Rosin* is natural *resin* 'in a solid state obtained as a residue after the distillation of oil of turpentine from crude turpentine' (*OED*). There is also synthetic resin, 'an organic compound made by polymerization'.

resolve (n.); **resoluteness; resolution.** As 'steadfastness of purpose', *resolve* is archaic, as in the set phrase, *of high resolve*; *resoluteness* is now the usual word in this sense. The dominant sense of *resolve* is 'a (specified) resolution or determination', as in 'She made up her mind never to marry again, and she kept her resolve' (Jessopp); as 'a formal resolution of a deliberative body', it may occur in American English, though *resolution* is the common term. As an abstract, *resolve* = 'determination'; cf. *resoluteness* above. But as a scientific, medical or musical term, *resolution* has no rivals (*OED*).

resource; recourse. They both suggest turning for help; some common phrases are *have* (or without) *recourse to*, and *as a last resource*. 'Flight was our only resource.' You examine your *resources* (stock that can be drawn on to supply some need), and decide which of them *to have recourse to*, i.e. to adopt as means of help.

respectable, 'worthy of respect'; **respectful,** 'showing respect'; **respective,** as in 'The practical sovereignty of all three brothers was admitted in their respective territories' (Bryce: in *OED*). These adjectives and their adverbs are occasionally confused by the slovenly.

respecting. See CONJUNCTIONS, DISGUISED.

respectively, misused for *both*. In 'He is a member of the hockey eleven and the rugger fifteen respectively', omit *respectively*; or rewrite thus, 'He is a member of both the hockey eleven and the rugger fifteen.' It is often used unnecessarily.

responsible should be restricted to human beings. Usage now permits such sentences as 'Great heat is responsible for many deaths', but here *responsible* is inferior to *the cause of*. *Responsible* is wrongly used also in 'The same year was responsible for a thoroughly Classic attack on Shakespeare' (E. Partridge, *The French Romantics' Knowledge of English Literature*, 1924). Surely the responsibility rested on those who made the attack in that year!

restive and **restless.** Of horses, *restive* = 'refractory' or 'intractable'; the same applies to human beings. *Restless* = 'averse to being still, settled or quiet', or 'deprived of rest; hence, uneasy' (*OED*).

restrain. See **constrain.**

result for *fact* is feeble, as in 'The autopsy shows the curious result that Jensen was dead before the shot that was supposed to have killed him had been fired' (Cameron McCabe).

NB: an action, process, etc., *has a result* or *shows* (or *discloses* or *proves*) *a fact*.

resurrect is occasionally misused for 'to *find*' as in 'Where did you resurrect that hat?', when the hat is new; but if the speaker says 'When did you resurrect that hat?' and means 'When did you rescue it from the rubbish-heap?' he is simply using *resurrect* figuratively in the sense, 'restore to life, or to view again' ('Slavery is already dead, and cannot be resurrected') (*OED*).

retort and **riposte** should not be used as colourless synonyms of *reply*; *retort* is to reply sharply; *riposte* (a term from fencing) is to reply sharply and wittily. ' "I love you", he said ardently. "I love you too", she retorted [or riposted]' shows up the absurdity.

returnee is gobbledygook for a serviceman returning from abroad. See **-ee.**

re(-)validate is 'pure' Whitehall for *renew* or *re-issue.*

revelation for *disclosure* – a strong word for a weak one – is not to be overworked. (Journalists are a shade too fond of it.)

Revelations is incorrect for *Revelation* as the short title of *The Revelation of St John the Divine*. *Revelation* is lit. 'a drawing back of the Veil', whereas *Apocalypse* (as in the Vulgate) is 'an uncovering'.

revenge and **avenge** (vv.); **revenge** and **vengeance** (nn). See **avenge.**

reverent must not be confused with *reverend*; the former applies to the worshipper, the latter to the object of worship (or reverence), and now chiefly, as a title, to clergymen.

reversal; reversion. The former is the noun corresponding to *reverse* ('to reverse the order'). *Reversion* is a legal term, but it also = 'the right of succession to a thing or an office'; and it is used in insurance and in biology.

reverse (n.). See **converse.**

review; revue. A *review* is an inspection (military, legal) or a published critique. A *revue* is an entertainment with songs and usually satirical sketches.

revolutionist (n.) is an unnecessary variant of *revolutionary*, which serves very well as both noun and adjective. This variant is surprisingly common.

revue. See **review.**

rewarding. See VOGUE WORDS.

RHETORICAL, THE. Rhetoric, as Lord Baldwin of Bewdley once remarked, is the harlot of the arts.

There are two Rhetorics: the old and the new. Of the old, a typical expositor is Alexander Bain, who died early in the present century; of the new, the best expositor is Dr I. A. Richards, whose *The Philosophy of Rhetoric*, 1936, has done so much to rehabilitate both the art and the study thereof.

In *English Composition and Rhetoric*, enlarged edition, Part II, 1888, Bain says in the Preface: 'I do not here enter on a defence of the utility of Rhetoric in general, though many persons are still disposed to question it. Since the art first took form in Greece, it has seldom been neglected by writers aiming at superior excellence of style. In order to vanquish the difficulties of the highest composition, it is necessary to attack them on every side. ...

'The direct bearing of the Rhetorical art is, of course, not Invention, but Correctness, in other words, polish, elegance, or refinement. It deals with curable defects and faults, and with such merits as can be secured by method. It aids, without superseding, the intuitive perception of what is excellent in a literary performance.

'There is not wanting, however, a possibility of rendering assistance to invention proper; somewhat similar to the contribution of Logic to the Art of Discovery. All right criticism, in helping to reject the bad, urges to renewed search for the good. Nor is this all. By taking a broad and systematic view of the possibilities of style, Rhetoric prevents the available means of effect from being overlooked, and draws attention to still unoccupied corners of the literary field.'

There you see – or can at least perceive – the defects of the old Rhetoric: it is, in the best sense of the word, superficial: on the one hand, it is a superior art of composition; on the other, it is a means of exciting certain emotions in an audience.

'I need spend no time, I think, in describing the present state of Rhetoric. Today it is the dreariest and least profitable part of the waste that the unfortunate travel through in Freshman English [especially in the United States]! So low has Rhetoric sunk that we would do better to dismiss it to Limbo than to trouble our-selves with it – unless we can find reason for believing that it can become a study that will minister successfully to important needs.

'As to the needs, there is little room for doubt about them. Rhetoric ... should be a study of misunderstanding and its reme-dies ... "How much and in how many ways may good communication differ from bad?" '

In reference to the traditional expositors of Rhetoric, Dr Richards says that, 'instead of tackling, in earnest, the prob-lem of how language works at all, they assume that nothing relevant is to be learnt about it; and that the problem is merely one of disposing the given and unques-tioned powers of words to the best advan-tage. Instead of ventilating by inquiry the sources of the whole action of words, they merely play with generalizations about their effects.

'To account for understanding and mis-understanding, to study the efficiency of language and its conditions we have to renounce, for a while, the view that words just have their meanings and that what a discourse does is to be examined as a com-position of these meanings – as a wall can be represented as a composition of its bricks. We have to shift the focus of our analysis and attempt a deeper and more minute grasp and try to take account of the structures of the smallest discussable units of meaning and the ways in which these vary as they are put with other units. ... Most words, as they pass from context to context, change their meanings; and in many different ways. It is their duty and their service to us to do so.'

Dr Richards then touches on one of his main theses: 'the Proper Meaning Super-stition ... the common belief ... that a word has a meaning of its own (ideally, only one) independent and controlling its use and the purpose for which it should be uttered'.

'A revived Rhetoric', he says, returning to the attack, 'or study of verbal under-standing and misunderstanding, must itself undertake its own inquiry into the modes of meaning – not only, as with the old Rhetoric, on a macroscopic scale, dis-cussing the effects of different disposals of large parts of a discourse – but also on a microscopic scale by using theorems about the structure of the fundamental conjec-tural units of meaning and the conditions through which they, and their inter-connections, arise.'

One of these theorems is 'the context theorem of meaning', which he says, 'pre-vents our making hundreds of baseless and disabling assumptions ... about meanings, over-simplifications that create false prob-lems. ... Pre-eminently what the theorem would discourage, is our habit of behav-ing as though, if a passage means one thing it cannot at the same time mean another and an incompatible thing. ... This theo-rem goes further, and regards all discourse – outside the technicalities of science – as over-determined, as having multiplicity of meaning.

'The next problem concerns what hap-pens when we put words together in sen-tences. ... The theorem recommends us rather to turn the problem round and ask what happens when, out of the integral utterance which is the sentence, we try to isolate the discrete meanings of the words of which it is composed. ... It is there that the most deep-rooted, systematic and persistent misunderstandings arise': to Richards the sentence, not the word, is the unit of speech.

'The context theorem of meaning will make us expect ambiguity to the widest extent and of the subtlest kinds nearly everywhere, and of course we find it. But [whereas] the old Rhetoric treated am-biguity as a fault in language, the new Rhetoric sees it as an inevitable conse-quence of the powers of language and as the indispensable means of most of our important utterances – especially in Poetry and Religion.

'The extra meaning that comes in when a sentence, in addition to making a state-ment, is meant to be insulting, or flatter-ing, or is interpreted so – we may call it emotive meaning – is not so different from plain statement as we are apt to suppose. As the word means the missing part of its contexts and is a substitute for them, so the insulting intention may be the substitute for a kick. The same general theorem covers all the modes of thought.

'There is a progression of some sort in every explicit sentence [e.g. in "The cat is on the mat", to take the simplest sentence-type]. but in the strictest prose the meanings of the separate words theoretically stay put and thought passes from one to another of them. At the other end of the scale the whole meaning of the sentence shifts, and with it any meanings we may try to ascribe to the individual words. In the extreme case it will go on moving as long as we bring fresh wits to study it. When Octavius Caesar is gazing down at Cleopatra dead, he says,

> she looks like sleep,
> As she would catch another Antony
> In her strong toil of grace.

"Her strong toil of grace". Where, in terms of what entries in what possible dictionary, do the meanings here of *toil* and *grace* come to rest? ... In most prose ... the opening words have to wait for those that follow to settle what they shall mean – if indeed that ever gets settled.

'All this holds good not only as to the *sense* of the waiting words but as regards all [those] other functions of language which we can distinguish and set over against the mere sense. It holds for the *feeling* [of my audience] towards what I am talking about, for *the relation towards my audience* I want to establish or maintain with the remark, and for the *confidence* I have in the soundness of the remark – to mention three main sorts of these other language functions. In speech ... I have the aid of intonation for these purposes.

'... In writing we have to [substitute for] intonation as far as we can. Most of the more recondite virtues of prose style come from the skill with which the rival claims of these various language functions are reconciled and combined.'

We pass to the essence of Dr Richards's attack upon 'the Usage Doctrine': 'Its evil is that it takes the sense of an author's words to be things we know before we read him, fixed factors with which he has to build up the meaning of his sentences as a mosaic is put together of discrete independent tesserae. Instead, they are resultants which we arrive at only through the interplay of the interpretative possibilities of the whole utterance. In brief, we have to guess them and we guess much better when we realize we are guessing, and watch out for indications, than when we think we know.'

No less acute, illuminating, and, in its dignified sense, entertaining is his arraignment of what he calls 'the Club Spirit'; but for this I must refer the reader to pp. 77–80 of *The Philosophy of Rhetoric*.

And with the conclusion of Dr Richards's own eloquent peroration, this faulty gist of some of his views on Rhetoric may fittingly end: 'It is an old dream that in time psychology might be able to tell us so much about our minds that we would at last become able to discover with some certainty what we mean by our words and how we mean it. An opposite or complementary dream is that, with enough improvement in Rhetoric we may in time learn so much about words that they will tell us how our minds work. It seems modest and reasonable to combine these dreams and hope that a patient persistence with the problems of Rhetoric may, while exposing the causes and modes of the misinterpretation of words, also throw light upon and suggest a remedial discipline for deeper and more grievous disorders; that, as the small and local errors in our everyday misunderstandings with language are models in miniature of the greater errors which disturb the development of our personalities, their story may also show us more about how these large-scale disasters may be avoided.'

[I take the greater pleasure in recommending all serious students of semantics and of the art of writing to read and ponder *The Philosophy of Rhetoric* for the very reason that Dr Richards and I do not always agree on literary and linguistic questions. I do not agree with everything in the foregoing abstract, but his provocativeness is so tonic and bracing that I do not wish to obscure the issue with demurrers, modifications, precautions.]

rhyme and **rime**. Although the former is the usual spelling, the latter is not incorrect (though archaic) and has historical justification; it has of late years been to some extent revived to make clear its distinction from *rhythm*. When *rime* = frost, it is always spelt thus.

rich. See **affluent**.

rid – preterite, *rid* – past participle, *rid*; *ridded* is permissible but now archaic in both preterite and past participle.

riddle should not be used as a co-extensive synonym of *puzzle*. A *riddle* is an enigma or dark saying ('When is a door not a door?'), *puzzle* being no longer used in this sense; a mystery (*The Riddle of the Sands*), hence a mysterious person. On the other hand, *puzzle* may be applied to a person or a thing that puzzles us ('He's a bit of a puzzle'), though not with quite the sense of 'mystery'; and whereas a *puzzle* is used of any toy, device or (non-verbal) problem designed to exercise the brain, *riddle* is applied only to a verbal problem. Sir Winston Churchill perhaps used the word a trifle loosely, when he spoke of Russia as 'a riddle wrapped in a mystery inside an enigma'.

ride – preterite, *rode* – past participle, *ridden* (rarely *rid*).

rife. See COMPARATIVES, FALSE.

right of ways is incorrect for *rights of way*.

right to, have a. See **have a right to.**

rigorous. See at **vigour**.

rime. See **rhyme**.

ring (of bells) – preterite, *rang* (or *rung*: but avoid it) – past participle, *rung*. But 'to

ring' a tree or a bull has both preterite and past participle *ringed*.

riposte. See **retort**.

rise. See **raise**.

role, without accent or italic, is correct; so is 'rôle', with accent but without italic; cf. **regime.**

Roman Catholic; Catholic; catholic. The first two are both noun and adjective; the third, adjective only. In the sense 'universal', *catholic* is obsolescent. The prevailing nuances of *catholic* are 'of universal human interest or use'; 'touching the needs, interests, or sympathies of all men', as in 'What was of catholic rather than national interest' (Froude); (of persons) 'having sympathies with all' ('He is catholic in his tastes'), (of things) 'embracing all' ('The sun poured its clear and catholic looks', Stevenson). *Catholic Church* or *Church Catholic* formerly meant 'the Church universal, the entire body of Christians'; but since the Reformation it has also and more usually meant 'the Church of Rome', often designated *the Roman Catholic Church*; *Catholic* suffices in opposition to *Protestant* or to *Anglo-Catholic*; in short, it always suffices.

Romania is correctly so spelt; not *Roumania* or *Rumania*.

rosin. See **resin and rosin**.

rotary, rotatable; rotating; rotational; rotative; rotatory.
Rotary (adj.): (of motion) circular, i.e. taking place round a centre or axis; also, operating by means of rotation, especially in reference to that large class of machines in which the main action is dependent on the rotation of an importantly operative part; also as in 'Storms that are cyclonic; i.e. rotary and progressive'; (of persons) acting in rotation – for which the dominant adjective is *rotational*. As a noun, it is short for Rotary International, a worldwide charitable society of businessmen.
Rotatable: capable – or admitting – of a rotatory movement, as in 'a sounder [a

surgical instrument], rotatable on a long shaft'.

Rotating (adj.): (*a*) turning round a centre (or an axis) – for which *rotatory* is commoner; (*b*) causing rotation – for which *rotatory* is more usual and less ambiguous.

Rotational: acting in rotation, as in 'rotational members'; also of or belonging to rotation, as in 'motion, whether orbital or rotational', *rotatory* being the dominant adjective.

Rotative: turning round like a wheel, acting by or operating in circular motion: a sense in which *rotary* and *rotatory* are more strongly established. Producing – or produced by – rotation, as in the astronomical 'rotative forces'; hence, connected with rotation; in these three nuances, *rotatory* is at least equally common; in the 'of the nature of rotation' sense of *rotative*, *rotatory* is more usual. But a useful sense is 'recurrent', as in 'Cotton was cultivated in India as a rotative and not as a special crop' (Sir R. A. Arnold, *The Cotton Famine*, 1864), a further synonym being 'seasonal'.

Rotatory: in rotation, *rotational* being preferable. Causing rotation (cf. *rotative*), especially in *rotatory apparatus*. Working by means of rotation; and of things that *rotate* (v.i.): as in 'rotatory storms' and 'cruel rotatory spurs' (Stevenson). Of the nature of, or connected with, rotation, as (of a wheel) 'having a rotatory motion', 'a rotatory velocity'.

Rotation, basically, is either the action of moving or turning around a centre or axis (or on an axis), or the action of producing such a movement (*OED*).

round. See **around.**

round house; roundhouse. The former is any house that is circular, whereas a *roundhouse* is 'a circular shed for locomotives, with a turn-table in the centre', and either a cabin – or a set of cabins – on the afterpart of a ship's quarter-deck, a blow in boxing, a pitch in US baseball, or, though now only historical, a lock-up, or a place of detention for arrested persons –

but all senses have the alternative forms *round-house* and *round house*.

route is occasionally misused for *method* or *manner* or *procedure* or *process*, as in 'attaining fame by the political route'. [*Route* is generally pronounced *root*, but the pronunciation with the diphthong of *out* survives in military use, and in the USA in railroad use, and often in business ('milk route', 'bread route', 'paper route'). *Webster's*.]

royal. See **kingly.**

royal tennis. See **tennis.**

rung. See **ring.**

rush (n. and v.) is being overworked by journalists: on 18 Dec. 1938 Frank Whitaker included it in his list of 'rubber-stamp words' (see **amazing**). It is not an exact synonym of *haste*.

S

Sabbath, the, and **Sunday.** But the better word is *Sunday*, *the Sabbath* being slightly affected where it is not Scottish; in good, normal English, *sabbath* is short for *witches' sabbath* (a midnight meeting of demons, wizards, witches, Devil-presided). *Sabbath* is, of course, correctly used of the day (Saturday) observed by Jews, and (Friday) by Muslims.

sabotage, used as verb, for *to wreck*, is unhappy and introduces a mechanical note that is out of keeping. In *What a Word!* Sir Alan Herbert attacks it and quotes, as an example of its misuse, 'Sabotaged the Peace issue'. See also **COMPARATIVES, FALSE.**

sacrosanct and **sacred.** The former is, stylistically, an intensive of the latter;

prudent writers, however, use it only in the specific sense (of persons; laws, customs, obligations, authority) 'secured by a religious sanction from violation, infringement, or encroachment', as in 'Truth, which alone of words is essentially divine and sacrosanct' (John Morley, 1871) (based on *OED*). See also COMPARATIVES, FALSE.

sadism and **masochism.** In generalized and (at first) loose usage, the former is desire to hurt others and the ability to enjoy their pain; the latter is the desire to be hurt and especially the enjoyment derived from being hurt. But in medical and strictly correct usage, *sadism* is 'a form of sexual perversion marked by a love of cruelty' (*OED*), the name deriving from the Comte (*not* Marquis) de Sade (†1814); and *masochism*, from the Austrian novelist, Sacher-Masoch, is 'sexual perversion, in which a member of one sex takes delight in being dominated, even to the extent of violence or cruelty, by one of the other sex' (Dunglison). Both are morbid faults: the former is dangerous, the latter pathetic.

said, the ('the said act'), is permissible for *this* in legal phraseology – and nowhere else. See also **the said.**

sailer is either *a sailing ship*, or a ship (or vessel) with reference to her sailing powers ('A very strong tight ship, and a pretty good sailer', Defoe); a **sailor** is a seaman, a mariner.

sake and **sakes.** 'When the preceding genitive is plural, the plural *sakes* is often used', as in 'For both our sakes, I would that word were true' (Shakespeare), 'Put yourself to no further trouble for our sakes' (Addison) (*OED*). True; but there are two points to be made: (i) '"For our sake" implies a common concern or purpose. "For our sakes" implies a difference of concern or purpose' (Weseen): a valid and valuable distinction. But (ii) except where metre needs *both our* (or *your* or *their*) *sakes*, a good writer would today write 'for the sake of both of us' (jointly) and 'for the sakes of both of us' (separately).

salary. See **honorarium** (and also **wage**).

salon and **saloon.** *Saloon* is American for a bar-room, and general for a public room on a passenger boat; American for a drawing-room (especially a large one); and general for a large apartment or hall in a hotel or restaurant; also British for a closed car, and for the more comfortable bar in a public house. *Salon* is a reception-room of a Parisian lady of fashion, hence a gathering (more or less recurrent) of notabilities at her house; hence, either the room or the gathering in other capitals. Also, a drawing-room on the continent, especially in France; also the establishment of a hairdresser or beautician.

salubrious; sanitary; salutary. They all 'promote health'; but air and climate are *salubrious*, while *sanitary* things are hygienic and free from infection, and *salutary* is now chiefly used in the figurative sense 'morally beneficial', and often of something unpleasant, as in 'a salutary shock'.

same (adj.) – used tautologically. 'The comedian has repeated the same joke at least a thousand times.'

same (n.). 'We are in receipt of your favour of the 2nd inst, and thank you for same'; *the same* would be correct, but it is stilted and too commercially conventional; *it* would be better.

same and **similar.** The former denotes identity; the latter implies mere likeness. 'He was positive it was the same man.' 'It is a house of similar design to ours' (or 'It is a house of a design similar to that of ours') (Harold Herd, *Watch Your English*).

same, the, is incorrectly followed by *which* in such a sentence as 'Is the agency referred to the same agency which the honourable gentleman repudiated the other day?' The correct form would be 'the same agency as that which' or 'as the one which'; but 'the same' is itself unnecessary, and the hon. member would have better expressed his meaning, 'Is the hon. gentleman referring to the agency which he repudiated the other day?' Cf.

'The post which the judge subsequently received is not the same that he was originally offered' (C. Daly King, *Arrogant Alibi*): where 'not the same that' should be 'not the same as that which' or 'not the one that' or, better, 'not that which'.

same ... of, incorrect for *same ... as that of.* 'It was the same colour of' – properly *same colour as that of* – 'the moundy platform where they stood' (Paul Horgan, *A Lamp on the Plains*).

sanatorium; sanitarium; sanitorium. The second and third are US variants of the first. The conventional plurals are either *-iums* or *-ia*, but soon the plurals in *-iums* will (as they should) oust the others.

sang. See **sing.**

sanitary convenience is an entire lavatory or a water-closet or a urinal. (Local Government officialese.)

sank. See **sink.**

SARCASM. See IRONY, last paragraph.

sateen and **satin.** *Sateen* is a cotton (or woollen) fabric that has a glossy surface like that of satin; but sateen is to satin what *near silk* is to (*sheer*) *silk*. *Satin* is a silk fabric that has on one side a glossy surface produced by such a method of weaving as ensures that the warp threads are 'caught and looped by the weft only at certain intervals' (*OED*).

SATIRE. 'Satire, in its literary aspect, may be defined as the expression in adequate terms of the sense of amusement or disgust excited by the ridiculous or unseemly, provided that humour is a distinctly recognizable element, and that the utterance is invested with literary form. Without humour, satire is invective; without literary form, it is mere clownish jeering' (Richard Garnett, in *The Encyclopaedia Britannica*, 1911).

satire; satyr. *Satire* is that which has been briefly treated in the preceding entry; a *satyr* is a woodland god (in form: part man,

part beast) that tends to Bacchic revelry and sexual pursuits.

satisfied that, (not) to be = *to believe* or *not to believe*. Mostly officialese; and unattractive when used of something distressing, as in 'if you are satisfied that they are dead ...'.

save is obsolete for *unless*; 'elegant' for the preposition *except*. The conjunctival *save that* ('Then all was still, save that a vast gush of fire rose up for a moment', R. I. Wilberforce, 1842) is archaic in prose, literary in verse (*OED*).

saw – preterite, *sawed* – past participle, *sawed* or *sawn*. The past participle used predicatively is either *sawed* or *sawn*, but preferably *sawed* ('The wood to be sawed is in the yard, over there'); attributively in Britain always *sawn* ('Sawn wood is easier to handle') [in the USA *sawed* or *sawn*].

says for *say* is illiterate, as in 'I says, says I' and 'Says you' (generally spelt *sez*), which, by the way, is fly-blown.

scan means either to 'glance through casually' or 'to examine minutely'. Make sure the word is not ambiguous in the context. When one scans verse, one metrically analyses it.

scarce. See **rare.**

scarcely. See **hardly.**

scarcely ... than. See **hardly ... than.**

scarify means 'scratch the surface', as of the skin for vaccination. It has nothing to do with *scare*.

scatheless and **unscathed.** *Scatheless* = 'without scathe', i.e. without harm or injury, as in 'It is a game from which you will come out scatheless, but I have been scalded' (Trollope). *Unscathed* = 'unharmed, uninjured', as in 'Whatever his experiences of this kind may have been, he passed unscathed through them' (A. W. Ward) (*OED*). The distinction, therefore, is very fine; but clear.

scenario. See VOGUE WORDS.

Sceptic is not synonymous with *infidel*, and its use for 'one who maintains a doubting attitude with reference to some particular question or statement' is a popular looseness that is so very loose as to deserve the stigmatic label, 'catachresis'. In Philosophy, a *Sceptic* is one who doubts – or even denies – the possibility of real knowledge of any kind; also (but not of Pyrrho or his disciples) one who denies the competence of reason, and the possibility of certitude, in all matters that lie outside the bounds of experience – and he is in lower case (*s.* not *S.*).

In theological and other religious writings, a *sceptic* is one who doubts – but will not absolutely deny – the truth of Christianity or, at the least, of one or more of the important among the Christian dogmas. (Cf. *agnostic, q.v.* at **agnostic and atheist**.)

Among etymology-worshippers, a *sceptic* (late Latin *scepticus*, 'inquiring', from Greek *skeptikos*, akin to *skeptesthai*, 'to look out; to consider') is a seeker after truth.

But in general (and, of course, correct) use, a *sceptic* is one who, in reference to a department of inquiry (e.g. natural science, spiritualism, psychology), doubts the validity of what is there set forth, or claimed, as knowledge. Hence, a person that, by habit, tends rather to doubt than to believe any apparent fact, any assertion, that comes to his or her attention. (With due acknowledgements to *OED*.)

sceptic, sceptical; skeptic, skeptical. The *sk-* forms are the usual ones in the USA; *sceptical* is preferred to *sceptic* for the adjective. (The *sc* is pronounced as *sk*; there is an ancient pun about *sceptics* that are *septic*.)

scheduled for discontinuance, be, is officialese for be doomed to disappear.

schizophrenia (adj. **schizophrenic**). The name of this 'hysterical dissociation of personality', characterized by withdrawal from the reality of the outside world, is frequently misused; with the misuse of the adjective, compare that of *allergic* (with

noun *allergy*). Pronounce *skĭt-za-free-nĭ-a*, primary accent falls on *-free-*, a secondary on the first syllable.

Scot, Scotch, Scots, Scottish (adj.); **Scotsmen** (or **-women**), the **Scots** and a **Scot** (nn.).

Since about 1870, there has, in Scotland, been an increasing tendency to discard *Scotch* and to use *Scottish* or, less frequently, *Scots*; good writers prefer *Scottish* in reference to the nation (*the Scottish people*), the country at large (*Scottish scenery, the Scottish border*), its institutions and characteristics (*a Scottish lawyer, the Scottish character, Scottish poets*); nevertheless, there simply isn't an alternative for *Scotch whisky* and *Scotch broth*. Usage – that is, current usage – favours *Scots* in *Scots law*, and *Scots* is obligatory in *a pound Scots, a shilling Scots, a penny Scots*, and in such variations from English weights and measures as *Scots acre, Scots mile, Scots pint, Scots stone*; moreover, in language contexts, we say *a Scots dialect* or *phrase*, although a *Scottish dialect* or *phrase* would not be incorrect; as a noun, *Scots* = the language spoken by the inhabitants of the Lowlands. *Scots* is invariable in such regimental names as *Scots Guards* and *Scots Greys*, and for those bodies of mercenaries serving abroad, *the Scots Brigade* and *the Scots Dutch*. For fuller details, see *OED*.

scrip and **script.** 'In loose or popular language', *scrip* is 'applied to share certificates in general'; properly, it is 'a provisional document entitling the holder to a share or shares in a joint-stock undertaking, and exchangeable for a more formal certificate when the necessary payments have been completed'; it is 'short for the obsolete *subscription receipt*'. But *script* is handwriting ('His is a beautiful script'), hence a kind or system of writing ('a cuneiform script', 'the Babylonian script', 'the complicated Japanese scripts'); in Law, it is the original document in opposition to a counterpart (or *rescript*) (*OED*). *Script* in theatre, movie, and radio jargons = manuscript or typescript – for theatre and radio, the play; for motion pictures, the synopsis, scenario, dialogue, etc. [In

American usage *scrip* may also = a certificate of indebtedness used in place of government currency.]

Scylla and **Charybdis** constitutes a cliché when the two names are used in combination to signify the danger of running into an equal or greater evil or peril in the (hasty) avoidance of its opposite. But many who use the cliché forget the origin: Scylla is a rock (personified as a horrible and dangerous sea-monster) on the Italian side of the Straits of Messina; opposite is Charybdis, a once-dangerous whirlpool on the coast of Sicily.

seamstress. See **sempstress.**

seasonable is 'suitable to or to be expected in the season referred to': 'It's seasonable weather' is that infuriating remark for which we must be prepared when, in winter, one experiences weather that might be more aptly described as a blight. *Seasonal*, however, means 'in season', 'characteristic of the seasons or, especially, of a particular season' ('seasonal variations of weather'); hence (of trades) 'dependent on the season' or (of employees) 'engaged only in or for a particular season' ('Seaside-hotel waiters are mostly seasonal'); applied to diseases, it = 'recurrent' or 'periodical', as in 'Hay fever, fortunately, is a seasonal complaint.' *Seasoned* is 'matured' (worked on by the season) or (of wood) 'dried – hence, hardened – by keeping'; of persons or animals it = 'acclimatized', 'fortified by habit, especially familiarized with a certain occupation' ('4,000 seasoned troops') (*OED*).

secretarial is the adjective corresponding to *secretary*; **secretariat** is the official, especially governmental, establishment of a secretary, hence the staff and the place where a secretarial department works or records are preserved. The position of a non-official secretary is a *secretaryship*.

sector is a technical term in mathematics, though now sometimes used for 'a distinct branch of an enterprise, the economy, etc.'; **section** is (for the most part) a general one ('part, portion, division, subdivision, and slice'). The only sense in which they are confused the one for the other is the military one, 'a portion or section of a front, corresponding generally to a sector of a circle the centre of which is a headquarters', the correct term being, not *section* but *sector*. A sector was that portion of the front which was, in practice during the First World War, occupied by a division (*OED*; *Larousse du xxᵉ siècle*).

secure (v.). See **procure and secure.** It is misused for *ensure* (or *effect*) in 'The police have got frightfully swollen heads; the conditions of the modern world all tend to secure that' (Laurence Meynell, *The Dandy*). The adjective and the noun tend to displace the preferable *safe* and *safety*.

see, do you. The frequent introduction, in conversational narrative and description, of *d'you see?*, *you see?*, or *see?*, is a bad habit with very many people, and is always a sign of uncertainty and a lack of clear thinking. It is no new fault, for it was censured in 1789 by 'Aristarchus', who says 'would it not be somewhat extraordinary if I asked him at every third word – *Are you blind?* [*Listen!* as well as *See?* is a frequent interjection in low colloquial American.]

see one's way to, not to. To refuse. (Mostly officialese.)

see where is incorrect for *see that* (and an astonishingly common error it is!), as in 'I see where they've had another storm at home', for 'I see' – i.e. have read in the newspaper – 'that they've had another storm.'

seeing. See CONJUNCTIONS, DISGUISED.

seldom is not now to be used as an adjective, though it was formerly so employed by good writers; e.g. Thackeray (in *Esmond*), 'My Lord Duke's entertainments were both seldom and shabby.'

seldom ever is pleonastic for *seldom* in such a sentence as 'I seldom ever go to town nowadays.' Cf. the following entry.

seldom or ever, like *rarely or ever*, is a not uncommon error for *seldom or never* (or for *seldom if ever* in the same sense). Thus, George Parker, *A View of Society*, 1781, 'Red Sail-Yard Dockers [a cant term] are people who live by buying and selling the king's [naval] stores, and who are seldom or ever detected, from the king's mark not being commonly known'; (with reference to a trencher) 'That is, a square piece of deal board, seldom or ever scraped, (never wash'd) off which the younger part of the University dine' (Anon., *A Day in Vacation at College*, 1751). Nesfield finds this error committed by Sydney Smith: 'Those who walk in their sleep have seldom or ever the most distant recollection that they have been dreaming at all.'

selection and **composition.** *Selection* = an (or the) art of selecting or choosing, or a thing selected. Therefore, it should not be employed where there is no idea of selecting or choosing, as in 'What selection of Bach's do you like best?' Weseen pertinently remarks that 'When the reference is to a programme [or, e.g., an anthology] some other word such as *number*, *piece*, *composition*, or a more specific word such as *waltz*, *poem*, *essay* is always preferable to *selection.*'

self is incorrect for *I* in, e.g. 'Self and family desire to extend to you our sympathy.' The plural is *selves* ('their dead selves'), not *selfs* as so often in A. S. M. Hutchinson's novel, *As Once You Were*.

semi. See **demi.**

semi-monthly; semi-weekly. See **bimonthly.**

semi-yearly is a hybrid for either *semi-annual* or the more English *half-yearly*. (Advs.: *semi-annually, half yearly*.)

seminar and **seminary.** The former is a university technicality for 'a select group of advanced students associated for special study and original research under the guidance of a professor' (or other head of department); hence, 'a class that meets for systematic study under the direction of a teacher', or 'a conference of specialists'.

A *seminary* is any place of secondary education; and specifically 'an institution for the training of those destined for some particular profession' – in the Catholic Church, a college for training youths and young men to become priests.

The learner in either a seminar or a seminary is a *seminarist* or a *seminarian* (*OED*).

Semitic; Hebraic, Hebrew. *Semitic* = 'belonging to or concerned with the Semitic group of languages' (Hebrew, Aramaean, Arabic, Ethiopic, Ancient Assyrian), as in 'a Semitic verb', 'a Semitic scholar', 'Semitic studies'; as a noun, *Semitic* is the Semitic family of languages; *Semitics* is a study thereof, or of the Semitic peoples.

Hebraic = 'of, concerning or characteristic of the Hebrews or their language. A *Hebraist* is one versed in the Hebrew language, a Hebrew scholar.

Hebrew (n.) is an Israelite; historically, it is 'applied to the early Israelites'; also the language spoken by the Hebrews. As an adjective, it = 'Israelitish, Jewish', and 'of, concerning, like or characteristic of the Hebrew language'. See **Jew.**

sempstress and **seamstress.** The former is obsolescent; the latter, almost literary. *Sewing woman* or *sewer* is rather more common in general use for a professional, *needlewoman* for a non-professional 'woman that sews'. The male is *seamster* or *sempster:* but both are archaic.

send a remittance is inferior to *make a remittance*.

senior. See **junior.**

SENSE-CONSTRUCTIONS. Sense-constructions are those in which – according to their upholders – grammar (whether accidence or syntax) is set aside in the interest, and to the increase, of ready understanding. Rarely are they justifiable: for, in almost every instance, the breaking of the rule tends to set up or does actually set up an ambiguity, or else it so shocks the cultured reader (or listener) that the intended advantage is wholly lost.

For three excellent examples, see **between you and I, anyone ... they** and **friends with.**

For the second, see the following extract from a letter that appeared in *The Observer* of 12 March 1939: ' "Anyone can call *their* house a hall" is a subtle recognition of the virtual plural in "anyone" ' (H. B. Bullen): but has not almost every noun or pronoun a virtual plural? Can that virtuality (so far taken for granted that one never thinks of it) be held to be a sufficient reason for dispensing with a simple and sensible rule? I think not.

Where sense-construction is idiom, it is folly and presumption to meddle with it. Here is another example.

'Of clearing or settlement or homestead, white man or blackfellow, there was no slightest sign' (Michael Innes, *Lament for a Maker*). *No slightest sign* follows a formula; it = 'no sign, not even the slightest'. Literally, *no slightest sign* = 'no very slight sign' (but, on the contrary, an important sign); but actually (or idiomatically), it is a sense-construction for *no sign at all.*

See also COLLECTIVE NOUNS; collectives afford an example of legitimate as opposed to illegitimate or, at best, disputed sense-constructions.

sensible and **sensitive.** The former is now obsolete for the latter in the nuances, 'having more or less acute power of sensation or feeling', 'apt to be quickly or acutely affected by some object of sensation', 'capable of delicate or tender feeling' and 'readily accessible to some specified emotional influence' (*OED*). Jane Austen's title *Sense and Sensibility* exemplifies the use of two nouns, the one related to *sensible* in the sense of 'reasonable', the other to its now obsolete sense. Those persons who have some French (but not enough) are misled by the French

sensible, which = 'sensitive'. The English *sensible* is the French *sensé*; the English *sensitive* is the French *sensible*. See also PREPOSITIONS WRONGLY USED.

sensitiveness and **sensitivity.** The former is the general, the latter is the psychological term (as in 'sensitivity to stimuli', 'cutaneous sensitivity'). Therefore, *sensitivity* is merely the psychological version of *sensitiveness*, which is both 'the power or the capacity of sensation (feeling)' and especially 'a highly developed capacity or power of sensation; keen or delicate susceptibility to outward impressions'; hence, '(excessive) touchiness', also 'the quality of being easily affected by or quickly indicating changes of condition', as in photography (*OED*).

sensual, sensuous, sensory. *Sensory*, being the most technical of these three terms, is much less likely to be confused with either of the other two than *sensual* is with *sensuous* or vice versa. *Sensory* = 'of or relating to the sensorium' (physiology) or 'relating to sensation or sense-impressions' (psychology).

Sensual is obsolete in the nuances 'sensory; pertaining to physical sensation; perceptible by the senses'. As 'physical' (or 'sensuous') it is so moribund that it should be avoided − all the more that to use this sense is to confuse the issue. Its predominant senses are 'lewd' or 'unchaste', and 'voluptuous' (as in *sensual pleasure*) or 'excessively inclined to the gratification of the senses' (especially in sexual activities). In philosophy it = 'materialistic'.

Sensuous should be avoided in the now rare, almost dead sense 'excessively addicted to the pleasures of the senses, especially to sexual pleasure'. Its nuances are these: 'Of or pertaining to the senses', 'derived from or perceived by or affecting the senses', 'concerned with sensation (feeling) or sense-perception'; (of pleasure) 'received through the senses' and 'sensitive, or keenly alive, to the pleasures of sensation'. Thus, a *sensuous* artist is not necessarily a *sensual* man; the pleasure derived from music is *sensuous*, not *sensual* (definitions: *OED*).

separate for *dissociate* is incorrect, as in 'It was intolerably easy to separate mentally the academic theories of war from the human side of it, even when one was engaged in it oneself' (C. S. Forester, *A Ship of the Line*).

separate between. Freeman Wills Crofts, *Mystery in the Channel*, 'He had to separate between what was essential and what was accidental', where *distinguish between* or *separate ... from* is meant.

separate cover, under. Separately.

SEQUENCE OF TENSES. See TENSE-SEQUENCE.

sergeant; serjeant. The former is in the army or police, but the latter is the official spelling in legal, and British parliamentary, contexts.

seriatim. Serially.

series, 'one set of ...', is occasionally mis-used as a plural. Thus, 'A series of cellars provide the various parts of our dressing-station.'

serried, 'closely ranked', and **serrated,** 'saw-toothed in shape', are sometimes confused.

serve the purpose of usually means *serve* or *serve as.*

service (n.) is, as Weseen has remarked, 'a much overworked word', especially in commercialese; *duty* is, in many contexts, preferable, and in others *expert advice* or *expert assistance* or *expert attendance.*

service (v.) should not be loosely used for *to serve.* One *services* a machine, or a debt, and a bull may be said to *service* a cow, but that is where it stops.

session and **cession.** The former = a sitting, a séance; the latter, a surrendering, a surrender (of territory or rights).

sestet; sextet. A *sestet* is the last six lines of a sonnet. Use *sextet* for six musicians, or a composition written for them.

set for 'to *sit*, be seated' is now a solecism – when it's not dialectal. The same remark applies to figurative uses ('The matter sets heavily on her mind'; 'The food does not set well on her stomach').

sets-off, sets-out, sets-to. Incorrect for *set-offs, -outs, -tos*; but these awkward com-binations should be avoided.

sew – sewed – sewed or, archaically, **sewn.** *Sewn* survives in *hand-sewn* and *machine-sewn.*

sewage; sewerage. *Sewage* is refuse mat-ter conveyed in sewers; *sewerage* is 'drainage or draining by means of sewers; a system, a method, of draining by sewers', hence 'sewers collectively; the system of sewers belonging to a particular locality'. Although *sewerage* can be used in the sense of *sewage* as here defined, careful writers do not so use it (*OED*).

sewn. See **sew.**

sex. See **gender.**

SEXISM. Since this book was first pub-lished, there has been increasing concern to avoid a masculine bias in the use of lan-guage. The chief grammatical problem is that English lacks a third person singular pronoun, or possessive adjective, referring to both men and women. (For further dis-cussion of this point, see **they, their.**)

In general vocabulary, the modern ten-dency is to replace such specifically femi-nine forms as *authoress* and *editress* by *author* and *editor*. Such adjustments are not always possible, since for instance a *governor* (who might be male or female) is obviously dif-ferent from a *governess*; but you could always call her a *teacher*. One may avoid sexual stereotyping by the use of these sex-ually neutral words, replacing *foreman* by *supervisor* and *charwoman* by *cleaner*, and may speak of *staffing* rather than of *manning* an office. Similarly, it is better not to refer to a person's sex by using such expressions as *woman driver, female lawyer,* or *male nurse,* unless it is really relevant. See also **Ms.**

sez. See **says.**

shadow in the sense of *reflected image* and conveying the idea of *an exact likeness* was at one time common, but is incorrect and can be confusing; the latest example quoted by *OED* is from Scott, 1823, 'The planets which shine above us as little influential of our destiny as their shadows, when reflected in the river, are capable of altering its course' – in which Scott was doubly wrong, for it is 'the planets' themselves that are 'reflected', not 'their shadows'.

To modern readers for whom a shadow is the dark figure thrown by a body intercepting light, a figure whose likeness to that body is often grotesquely distorted, certain passages of literature are puzzling until they realize that 'shadow' is used in the sense of 'reflection', as in Shakespeare's Sonnet LIII:

What is your substance, whereof
    are you made
That millions of strange shadows on
    you tend?

shake – shook – shaken. *Shook* as past participle is solecistic when not dialectal.

shall and **will.** 'Shall the material universe be destroyed?' was the subject of debate in a young men's institute in Scotland, according to a correspondent of Dean Alford in 1870, who, seeing that the universe remains intact, concludes that the decision must have been 'No'.

'The faultless idiomatic use of *shall* and *will* is one of the points which are regarded as infallible tests of the correct English speaker; it offers peculiar difficulties to Scots, Irishmen, and Americans', says Dr C. T. Onions in *An Advanced English Syntax*. He refers to traditional usage south of the Border.

The same rules affect all three kinds of future tense: the simple, 'I shall go' – the progressive, 'I shall be going' – and the perfect, 'I shall have gone.' Indeed they affect also the corresponding pasts, *would* of *will,* and *should* of *shall*; but for the purpose of reference, *should* and *would* are in the present work treated separately.

Mere futurity was traditionally expressed by *shall* in the first person ('I shall go', 'We shall go') and by *will* in the second and third persons ('You *or* he will go', 'They will go'). In this usage *shall* and *will* are mere indications of time – formulas expressive of futurity – auxiliaries of tense.

The chief modification of that general rule is a survival of the original (the Old English) senses of *shall* and *will.* Dr Onions summarizes thus: '*Shall* denoting obligation, necessity or permission; *will* denoting resolve or willingness'. And the following are his examples:*

(1) 'I *will* (= am resolved to) live a bachelor.'

(2) '*Will* you (= do you intend or wish to) take it with you, or shall I (= am I to) send it?'

(3) 'We *will* send someone to fetch you.' [= 'We are resolved to send someone to fetch you'; mere futurity would require 'shall'.]

(4) 'He *will* (= is determined to) go, say what you may.' [But if *will* be employed, it must be stressed; otherwise 'is. determined *or* resolved to go' is usual.]

(5) 'Thou *shalt* not steal'; 'You (he, they) shall go this instant.' [With the latter might be compared this: 'Westwood said, *hale him away, dead or alive, for go he shall*' (*The Sessions Papers of the Old Bailey,* 1741).]

(6) 'Where the tree falls, there it *shall* lie.' [I.e. 'it must lie'.]

(7) 'He found the country in a state of unrest, for reasons which you *shall* hear.' [I.c. 'for reasons which you will be per-

---

*The parentheses *within* the example-sentences are Dr Onions's; the square brackets following the example-sentences are mine.

mitted to hear'. This usage is now a literary, not a spoken one.]

(8) 'You *shall* repay me at your convenience.' [This stresses the obligation or the permission, according as the speaker intends his statement to be understood. More gracious is, 'You will, please, allow me to add (or, I should like to add), repay me at your convenience.']

(9) '*Wilt* thou have this woman to be thy wedded wife?' Answer: 'I *will*.' [I.e. 'Do you wish to have …?' Answer: 'Yes, I do wish to …'.]

Dr Onions modifies his general modification, thus: '*Shall* is sometimes stronger than *will*; e.g. "You will not go away?" – "I *shall*." *Will* is occasionally used to express command; e.g. "You *will* not go out today; you *will* stay in and work."' Closely connected with this use of *will* is that use whereby *will* serves to soften a request in the interrogative. '*Will* you tell me the time, please?' which is rendered still more polite by substituting *would* for *will*.

Dr Onions notes that the future tense is not uncommonly employed to express an inferential fact of the present: 'This *will* no doubt be the book he referred to.' But such an inferential fact is equally well and idiomatically expressed by '*This*, doubtless, is the book he referred to.' Compare the tense but contrast the usage in Sheridan's 'Courage *will* come and go', where *will* connotes (rather than expresses) tendency or present habitual action: an even better example is 'These things *will* happen' for it shows that 'courage' and 'these things' are invested with will-power, intention, determination (cf. the thought behind 'The cussedness of the universe tends to a maximum'). The past of this *will* is *would* (see **would and should**).

He further notes that in independent questions, the rule for the employment of *shall* and *will* is the same as in independent statements; 'but in the 2nd person that auxiliary is used which is expected in the answer:

' "*Shall* you go to London tomorrow?" (The expected answer is "I *shall*.") The substitution of *will* would convert the sentence into a kind of request.' But not if the progressive tense be used, for '*Will* you be going to London tomorrow?' asks what the addressed person intends to do on the morrow, and 'Are you going to London tomorrow?' stresses not so much intention as futurity.

Literary uses of *shall* for all three persons are these:

(*a*) In those clauses in which the action is mentioned or implied as being under consideration or in prospect: 'Permission to use the reading-room will be withdrawn from any person who *shall* write on any part of a printed book.' (This might have been included under OFFICIALESE; logic and good sense and idiomatic usage would seem to prefer 'Permission … will be withdrawn from any person who [or that] writes on any part of a printed book.') 'There will I hide thee, till life *shall* end.' (I.e. 'There am I resolved to hide thee …'. The corresponding past is 'There did I' – or, 'was I resolved to' – 'hide thee, till life should end.')

(*b*) In implied commands, e.g. 'My aunt intends that you *shall* accompany us.' Current idiom, however, prefers 'My aunt intends you to accompany us.'

In colloquial and indeed all spoken English, however, *will* is fast displacing *shall* in all cases in which *shall* was formerly used and in which we are recommended to use it. That there should be this tendency is a pity, for once *shall* has disappeared, we shall have lost many subtle and useful distinctions. It survives chiefly in first person questions, where it usefully distinguishes 'Shall I open the window?' (as an offer or proposal) from 'Will I need a towel?' (= will it be necessary). It is useful that the contraction 'll stands for both *shall* and *will*.

share and **part.** Cf. the entry at **portion and part**. Do not misuse *share*, 'an *allotted* *portion*', for *part*, as in 'A large share of the meadow'.

shave – shaved – shaved. The past participle *shaven* survives as an adjective.

she. See **they, their.**

sheared. See **shore** (v.).

shekels is used facetiously for 'money'; but it should probably not be so used, now that the *shekel* is the official monetary unit of modern Israel.

shew; show. The latter is now the usual spelling. Don't show off by using *shew*. (But *shewbread* has survived.)

shine (v.i.); preterite *shone*; past participle, *shone*. But the transitive verb has preterite and past participle *shined*. 'The sun shone yesterday', 'The sun has not shone the last few days'; 'He shined (*or* has shined) my boots'; these are correct. [The old-fashioned *shined* for *shone* may occur in American usage.]

shipment. See **cargo.**

shook. See **shake.**

shore of an ocean, a sea, a lake, or even of a great river; *bank* for all other rivers.

shore is archaic for *sheared* as the preterite of 'to *shear*'; the past participle is either *sheared* or *shorn*, the former only as a verb, the latter as both verb and adjective ('the shorn lamb').

short. See **brief.**

short supply, in = *scarce*. (Officialese.)

shortly is to be avoided as a synonym of *briefly* in such a sentence as 'She spoke shortly', which conveys the idea of curtness or abruptness. Still more ambiguous is 'She will speak shortly', which conveys that 'She will speak before long.'

should and **would.** See **would and should.**

shouldn't ought. See **ought, didn't ...**

show. See **shew.**

show – showed – showed or, preferably, **shown.** In the passive, *shown* is obligatory ('He was shown to be a thief'); in the active, *showed* is less common than *shown* (*OED*).

shrink – shrank – shrunk. The past participle *shrunken* is adjectival as in 'shrunken heads'.

shut. See **close.**

sic means 'intentionally so written', and is printed in italics and between square (or sometimes round) brackets. It is properly used to assure the reader that quoted words, though unlikely, are accurately reproduced. It should not be used to scoff at unintentional error or at illiteracy.

sick. See **ill and sick.**

sick and sickly. The former refers to temporary, the latter to habitual illness; *sickly*, to be more precise, means 'habitually ailing'.

sick of, 'ill with', is now *sick with*; *sick of* is familiar (not slangy) for 'thoroughly weary of', with intensive *sick and tired of.*

sidewalk. See **pavement.**

significant. See **VOGUE WORDS.**

sillily may be difficult to pronounce, but it is easy to write and so much more economical than *in a silly manner*. One might, however, prefer *foolishly*.

silly (n.). See at **stupid person.**

similar, exactly, is a misuse for either *same* or *very closely resembling*; 'similar' is too vague to be made 'exact'. *The Daily Express* often uses it: and on 27 Nov. 1937, it defended the sentence, 'This thing is exactly similar to that.'

similar and **analogous.** *Similar* is 'having a marked resemblance or likeness; of a like nature or kind' ('We are on our guard against similar conclusions', Burke); constructed with *to* ('This is similar to that'). It has technical senses in mathematics and music. *Analogous* is 'having – or, characterized by – analogy*; similar in certain attributes, circumstances, relations, or uses; having something parallel'; it is constructed with *to*; 'Disorders analogous to those of Syracuse' (Grote). It has a technical sense in Natural History. In the sense 'expressing an analogy', it is inferior to *analogical*.

similar and **same.** See **same and similar.**

similar as for *similar to* or *same as* is probably caused by a confusion between those two phrases. It is an odd mistake to find in so able a writer as Nicholas Blake, yet in *There's Trouble Brewing*, we come on: 'The remains appear to be of similar height and physique as Bunnett': either for 'of height and physique similar to Bunnett's' or, more probably, for 'of the same height and physique as Bunnett [was]' or 'as Bunnett's'.

similar to, misused for *the same as.* J. H. Vaux, the convict, writing from Newcastle (New South Wales) and speaking of robbery with violence, says, in 1812, 'This audacious game is called by *prigs* [i.e. thieves] *the ramp*, and is nearly similar to *the rush*'. (Or is it possible that by 'nearly' Vaux meant 'closely'? In that now obsolete sense he would have been correct.) Cf. preceding entry.

SIMILES, BATTERED. Here is a short list of similes that have been – and still are – working overtime. Think twice before you use any of the following.

as similes: see the keywords
aspen leaf, shake (or *tremble*) *like an*

bad shilling (or *penny*), *turn up* (or *come back*) *like a*

bear with a sore head, like a
behave, see *bull* ...
black as coal – or *pitch* – or *the Pit, as*
blush like a schoolgirl, to
bold (or *brave*) *as a lion, as*
bold as brass, as
bright as a new pin, as [obsolescent]
brown as a berry, as
bull in a china shop, (*behave*) *like a*

cat on hot bricks, like a; e.g. *jump about*
caught like a rat in a trap
cheap as dirt, as
Cheshire cat, grin like a
clean as a whistle, as
clear as crystal (or *the day* or *the sun*), *as*; jocularly, *as clear as mud*
clever as a cart- (or *waggon-*) *load of monkeys, as*
cold as charity, as
collapse like a pack of cards
cool as a cucumber, as
crawl like a snail
cross as a bear with a sore head (or *as two sticks*), *as*

dark as night, as
dead as a door-nail, as
deaf as a post (or *as an adder*), *as*
different as chalk from cheese, as
drink like a fish, to
drop like a cart-load of bricks, to
drowned like a rat
drunk as a lord, as
dry as a bone (or *as dust*), *as*
dull as ditch-water, as
Dutch uncle, talk (to someone) *like a*
dying duck; see *look like* ...
dying like flies

easy as kiss (or *as kissing*) *your hand, as*; also *as easy as falling off a log*

fight like Kilkenny cats
fighting cocks: see *live* ...
fit as a fiddle, as
flash, like a
flat as a pancake, as
free as a bird, as; as free as the air
fresh as a daisy (or *as paint*), *as*

good as a play, as; i.e. very amusing
good as gold, as; i.e. very well behaved

**Analogy.* Apart from its technical senses in Logic, Philology, Natural History, and its loose sense, 'similarity', it = 'resemblance of things with regard to some circumstances or effects', 'resemblance of relations'. 'Knowledge is to the mind, what light is to the eye' is an excellent example of analogy.

good in parts, like the curate's egg
green as grass, as
grin: see *Cheshire cat*

hang on like grim death
happy (or jolly) as a sandboy (or *as the day
    is long*), as
hard as a brick (or *as iron* or, fig., *as nails*),
    as
hate like poison, to
have nine lives like a cat, to
heavy as lead, as
honest as the day, as
hot as hell, as
hungry as a hunter, as

innocent as a babe unborn (or *as a new-born
    babe*), as

jolly: see *happy*

keen as mustard, as
Kilkenny cats: see *fight*

lamb to the slaughter, like a
large as life (jocularly: *large as life and twice
    as natural*), as
light as a feather (or *as air*), as
like similes. see the keywords
like as two peas, as
like water off a duck's back
live like fighting cocks
look like a dying duck in a thunderstorm
look like grim death
lost soul, like a

mad as a March hare (or *as a hatter*), as
meek as a lamb, as
memory like a sieve, a
merry as a grig, as [obsolescent]
mill pond, the sea [is] like a

nervous as a cat, as

obstinate as a mule, as
old as Methuselah (or *as the hills*), as

plain as a pikestaff (or *the nose on your face*),
    as
pleased as a dog with two tails (or *as Punch*),
    as
poor as a church mouse, as
pretty as a picture, as
pure as the driven snow, as

quick as a flash (or *as lightning*), as
quiet as a mouse (or *mice*), as

read (a person) like a book, to (be able to)
red as a rose (or *as a turkey-cock*), as
rich as Croesus, as
right as a trivet (or *as rain*), as
roar like a bull
run like a hare

safe as houses (or *as the Bank of England*),
    as
shake: see *aspen leaf*; also shake like a jelly
sharp as a razor (or *as a needle*), as
sigh like a furnace, to
silent as the grave, as
sleep like a top, to
slippery as an eel, as
slow as a snail (or *as a wet week*)
sob as though one's heart would break, to
sober as a judge, as
soft as butter, as
sound as a bell, as
speak like a book, to
spring up like mushrooms overnight
steady as a rock, as
stiff as a poker (or *as a ramrod*), as
straight as a die, as
strong as a horse, as
swear like a trooper
sweet as a nut (or *as sugar*), as

take to [something] like (or *as*) a duck to
    water
talk like a book; and see *Dutch uncle*
thick as leaves in Vallombrosa as [Ex.
    Milton's 'Thick as autumnal leaves
    that strow the brooks In Vallombrosa']
thick as thieves, as
thin as a lath (or *as a rake*), as
ton of bricks, (e.g. *come down* or *fall*) like a
tough as leather, as
true as steel, as
turn up: see *bad shilling*
two-year-old, like a

ugly as sin, as

warm as toast, as
weak as water, as
white as a sheet (or *as snow*), as
wise as Solomon, as

simpleness is being superseded by *simplicity*, except in the sense, 'foolishness; lack of intelligence; lack of shrewdness'.

SIMPLICITY. Simplicity of language or style is 'absence or lack of elegance or polish' or, in the modern acceptation, 'freedom from ornateness or over-elaboration; plainness or directness of an attractive kind' (*OED*); also 'freedom from or lack of obscurity or abstruseness'.

Simplicity is an admirable ideal; it can, however, be pushed to that extreme wherein the style becomes inadequate to the subject.

This is not a theme that can be satisfactorily treated within the limits of an article. But to those who feel that any guidance is better than none, I recommend 'Simplicity' in Alexander Bain's *English Composition and Rhetoric*, 1887–8, at I, 247–8; and to those who prefer example to precept, I suggest a perusal of my *English Prose: 1700–1914*, to which must be added a patient study of the Bible in the Authorized Version.

simplistic means 'too simple, oversimplified'. It is thus pejorative, and not a synonym of the often appreciative word *simple*. Since *simplistic* itself denotes excess, it is tautologous to call things 'too simplistic' or 'oversimplistic'.

simply should, in many contexts, be avoided in the sense of *merely* (as in 'He is simply careless'), for it often sets up an ambiguity. Note, too, that 'He spoke simply' = 'in simple, unaffected, sincere manner', whereas 'He simply spoke' = 'He only spoke; he spoke but did not act, sing, etc., etc.' As an intensive, *simply* is familiar English – not quite reprehensible, but to be avoided in good writing or dignified speech; 'simply too lovely for words' may be amusing, but it is also trivial.

simulate and **dissimulate.** See **dissimulate and simulate.**

simultaneous. See COMPARATIVES, FALSE.

since (adv.) for *ago*, is, says Weseen, 'incorrectly used … in such expressions as "It was a long time since" and "I was there two weeks since" '; but *OED* makes no discouraging remark concerning this usage and gives these examples: 'A merchant … bespoke it not half an hour since'; 'Literati long since defunct' (De Quincey: *long ago* would be contrary to usage); 'He went out a little while since' (T. L. Peacock): nevertheless, in Weseen's second example, *ago* would be much superior to *since*, and in the first, rather better. Weseen makes an excellent point when he says that '*since* carries the mind forward from a starting point in the past to the present and applies to the intervening period', whereas '*ago* refers to a point in past time and carries the mind back from the present'. See also **ago.**

since (conj.) leads to errors in the use of tense. It is obviously incorrect to write 'He is a notability since he has written that book'; less obviously incorrect is 'He has been a notability since he has …', the logical (and correct) form being 'He has been a notability since he wrote …'.

The rule is that a verb in the main clause should be in the perfect tense, although one may say 'It's a long time (= present tense) since her birthday.' A verb in the clause introduced by *since* is normally in the preterite; but a delicate nuance is conveyed by 'Since we have owned a car (= we still own one) we have gone camping every year.' (Example from *A Grammar of Contemporary English*, Quirk *et al.*). And see **as.**

sine die; sine qua non. For these Latin phrases use *indefinitely*; *necessity* or *essential*.

sing – preterite *sang* – past participle *sung*. *Sung* is the only form possible for the participle, and *sang* (not *sung*) for the preterite.

Sinhalese is now the right word for the people and language of Sri Lanka, formerly Ceylon.

sink – sank – sunk are the usual forms in current speech and in prose. The preterite *sunk* is becoming rare. The alternative past participle *sunken* is attributive, as in 'a sunken road', 'sunken cheeks', 'sunken rocks': yet *sunk* is preferred where (deliberate) human agency is implied, especially in certain technical senses, e.g. in architecture: 'a sunk ditch' 'sunk [= submerged] lands', 'sunk carving', 'sunk cistern', 'sunk panel', etc. (*OED*).

sinus; plural sinuses.

situate; situated. In general, *situated* is to be preferred; in legal phraseology, *situate* is sanctified by custom, but elsewhere it is an absurd affectation, much affected by estate agents.

situation. See ABSTRACT NOUNS and VOGUE WORDS.

size; sized. *Every-size, fair-size, medium-size, middle-size, small-size, large-size,* etc., as adjectives are incorrect for *fair-sized, medium-sized, middle-sized, small-sized, large-sized; every-sized* seems illogical, and *of every size* (after the noun) is preferred. So too *larger-sized, smaller-sized* are correct – but unnecessary – for *larger* and *smaller*. Note, however, *outsize*.

size of, the, as in 'That's the size of it' (= that is what it amounts to, that is what it signifies), is a colloquialism; it rings oddly in formal, impressive, or beautiful contexts.

skilful; skilled. Possessing skill; showing skill. Usage, however, restricts *skilled* to labour – to craftsmen or technicians – and to their work. E.g. 'a skilled wool-sorter' but 'a skilful batsman' (Harold Herd).

slack is, in the sense 'to *slake* (one's thirst)', said by Weseen to be incorrect; but one may *slack* or *slake* lime.

slander. See at **libel.**

slang is incorrect for *slung* (preterite of *sling*); the past participle is *slung*.

SLANG.

I. DEFINITIONS; EXAMPLES

OED – that ever present help in time of doubt, and that *monumentum aere perennius* – defines the almost undefinable

slang as 'language of a highly colloquial type, considered as below the level of standard educated speech, and consisting either of new words or of current words employed in some special sense'; H. W. Fowler, as 'playing with words and renaming things and actions; some invent new words, or mutilate or misapply the old, for the pleasure of novelty, and others catch up such words for the pleasure of being in the fashion'; *Webster's*: 'Language comprising certain widely current but usually ephemeral terms having a forced, fantastic, or grotesque meaning, or exhibiting eccentric or extravagant humor or fancy'.

It stands below colloquialisms, but above cant: it excludes dialect; and it is now improperly applied to solecisms, illiteracies, pidgin English, and all jargons. If a cant word gains wider currency, it is by its admission to the vocabulary of slang; if a slang word is promoted, it is to the ranks of colloquialism. [See the articles CANT, COLLOQUIALISMS, DIALECT, JARGON and SOLECISMS.] That, in the past, *slang* was applied, at different times, to all of these grades except dialect is no reason for so using it now. Moreover, don't call slang *cant*, nor *lingo*, nor *argot*.

In the matter of fine distinctions, example, as the worthy proverb assures us, is better than precept.

Here are a few examples exhibiting the difference between slang and colloquialism and Standard English. Standard *man* is colloquial *chap* and slang *bloke* or *cove* or *cully* or *guy* or *stiff* or *bozo*, of which slang terms the first three were originally cant; and *old man* is colloquial *old* (or *ancient*) *chap* (or *fellow*) and slang *old buffer* or *old geezer*, *money* is colloquial *wherewithal* or *shekels* and slang *spondulicks* (originally American) or *tin*; *doctor* becomes the colloquial *doc* and the slang *vet, croaker, pill-shooter*, *lawyers' clerk* becomes colloquial *limb of the law*; *lawyer*, colloquially *pettifogger*, becomes in slang, *landshark* (British), *mouthpiece* (British and American), *fixer* (American); a clergyman is colloquially *parson* and slangily *amen wallah, fire escape, holy Joe, sky pilot*.

Or consider this piece of British race-course dialogue,* in which Gus is a book-maker; 'Fairy' Smith is his clerk; 'Fat' Wilkins is his 'tictac man' or signaller; a 'shark', 'squib', and 'knowing one', or professional punter, and a 'steamer' or ordinary punter, are participants.

Gus (to the public at large). Pick where you like; I don't care. Shoot it in; shoot it in! It won't grow in your pockets, my lads. The jolly old favourite at two to one before he's a lot less.

Fat. Finith to fere! Finith to fere [Five to four].

Gus. Evens on the field – what did I tell you? Bet levels, you devils. Shoot it in! Shoot it in!

Shark. Cow's calf [ten shillings] on *Fish*.

Gus (interpreting to 'Fairy'). Three halves on *Physic*. [*Psyche* is the horse's name.]

Steamer. Three tossaroons [half-crowns] each way on *Treacle Tart*.

Gus (to 'Fairy'). *Treacle Tart*: seven and six at fours to win; evens a place.

Fat (in a hoarse stage whisper). Scrub [cancel the previous odds on] *Treacle Tart*. A bice [two] and a half is the best. [I.e. 2½ is the best odds.]

Gus (incredulously). Come orf it!

Fat (waving as if demented). Scrub it! You'll do your dough. *Treacle Tart*'s a springer [a dark horse]. It's deuces [odds of two to one]; it's exes to fere [six to four].

Gus (altering his board). Too late will be the cry. Shoot it in!†

II. ORIGIN; REASONS FOR USE

‡Slang, being the quintessence of colloquial speech, is determined by convenience and fancy rather than by scientific laws, philosophical ideas and absolutes, and grammatical rules. As it

---

*The basis is slang, but some of the words are cant.

†The rest of this delectable dialogue, which is six times as long as this excerpt, will be found in my *Slang Today and Yesterday*.

‡The ensuing paragraphs represent a condensation and modification of chapters II-IV of my *Slang Today and Yesterday*, revised 3rd edition, 1949.

---

originates, so it flourishes best, in collo-quial speech. 'Among the impulses which lead to the invention of slang,' Henry Bradley remarked, some years ago, 'the two most important seem to be the desire to secure increased vivacity and the desire to secure increased sense of intimacy in the use of language.' The most favourable conditions of growth are those of 'crowd-ing and excitement, and artificial life. ... Any sudden excitement or peculiar cir-cumstance is quite sufficient to originate and set going a score of slang words', said John Camden Hotten in his dictionary of slang. Its origin and its use become more interesting as we bear in mind one of its primary laws: slang is not merely employed as a means of self-expression: it connotes personality: 'its coinage and cir-culation comes rather from the wish of the individual to distinguish himself by oddity or grotesque humour' (Greenough and Kittredge). Another aspect is presented in Earle Welby's dictum that 'some slang originates in an honourable discontent with the battered and bleached phrases in far too general use', his fresh slang being 'the plain man's poetry, the plain man's aspiration from penny plain to two-pence coloured'.

One of the most interesting pro-nouncements on the origins and uses of slang is that made by H. L. Mencken in his invigorating *The American Language*. 'What slang actually consists of doesn't depend ... upon intrinsic qualities, but upon the sur-rounding circumstances. It is the user that determines the matter, and particularly the user's habitual way of thinking. If he chooses words carefully, with a full under-standing of their meaning and savor, then no [?] word that he uses seriously will belong to slang, but if his speech is made up chiefly of terms poll-parroted, and he has no sense of their shades and limitations, then slang will bulk largely in his vocabu-lary. In its origin it is nearly always respectable; it is devised not by the stupid populace [Cockneys are certainly not stupid], but by individuals of wit and ingenuity; as Whitney says, it is a product of an "exuberance of mental activity, and the natural delight of language-making". But when its inventions happen to strike the popular fancy and are adopted by the mob, they are soon worn threadbare and so lose all piquancy and significance, and, in Whitney's words, become "incapable of expressing anything that is real". This is the history of such slang phrases as ... "How's your poor feet?" ... "Have a heart!", "This is the life." '

But why is slang used at all?

Slang, I believe, is employed for one, or several, of the following sixteen reasons – and there are doubtless others.

(1) In sheer *joie de vivre*, by the young in spirit as well as by the young in years; 'just for the hell of it'; playfully, waggishly.

(2) As an exercise either in humour or in wit and ingenuity. The motive is usually self-display, snobbishness, emulation; or responsiveness; or a quasi-professional delight in virtuosity.

(3) To be different from others; to be novel.

(4) To be picturesque – either from a positive desire or, as in the wish to avoid insipidity, from a neutral or negative volition.

(5) To be arresting, striking, or even startling. (*Épater les bourgeois.*)

(6) To avoid clichés.

(7) To be brief, concise.

(8) To enrich the language. This purposiveness and deliberateness are rare except among the well-educated, Cockneys forming the most important exception; in general, therefore, it is literary and pondered rather than popular and spontaneous.

(9) To impose an air of solidity and concreteness on the abstract; of earthiness on the idealistic; of immediacy and appositeness on the remote. (In the cultured the effort is usually premeditated; in the uncultured it is almost always unconscious or perhaps rather subconscious.)

(10) To lessen the sting of, or on the other hand to give additional point to, a refusal, a rejection, a recantation; to reduce, perhaps also to disperse, the solemnity, pomposity, or excessive seriousness of a conversation – or on rare occasions, of a piece of writing; to soften the starkness, to lighten or to prettify the inevitability of death, the hammer-blow of madness, or to mark the ugliness or the pitiableness of profound turpitude (e.g. treachery, barbarous ingratitude); and thus to enable the speaker, or his auditor, or both, to endure, to 'carry on'.

(11) To talk, or to write, down to an inferior, or to amuse a superior, public; or merely to be on the same speech-level with one's audience or one's subject-matter.

(12) For ease of social intercourse: an affable attitude, this.

(13) To induce friendliness or intimacy of a deep or durable nature.

(14) To show that one belongs to a certain school (especially if it be Public or fashionable), trade or profession, artistic or intellectual set, a social class; in brief, to establish contact or to be 'in the swim'.

(15) To show or prove that someone else is not 'in the swim'.

(16) To be secret – not understood by those around one. (Children, students, lovers, members of forbidden political societies are the chief exponents.)

III. ATTITUDES TO SLANG

Slang now excites less disapprobation than was its lot before the present century; disapproval, indeed, had coloured the views of some notable 19th-century philologists and grammarians; nor is the condemnatory attitude yet dead. In 1825 J. P. Thomas, in *My Thought Book*, bluntly declared that 'the language of slang is the conversation of fools'; O. W. Holmes was scathing at its expense. Greenough and Kittredge condemn it on the ground that, being evanescent, vague, and ill-defined, slang has a deleterious effect on those who use it often, for it tends to destroy all those delicate shades of meaning which are at the root of a good style; they hold that it is the speech of lazy persons; and assert that when a slang word becomes definite in meaning it has almost ceased to be slang,

– which is manifestly false, for most slang words are unconventional synonyms of conventional words. A fairer view is that expressed by Professor H. C. K. Wyld; 'While slang is essentially part of familiar and colloquial speech, it is not necessarily either incorrect or vulgar in its proper place', which, the Fowler brothers assert in *The King's English*, 'is in real life' – that is, in conversation. The Fowlers continue by saying that, 'as style is the great anti-septic, so slang is the great corrupting matter; it is perishable, and infects what is round it'. The same thought is conveyed from a different angle by Professor G. H. McKnight, who remarks that, 'originating as slang expressions often do, in an insensibility to the meaning of legitimate words, the use of slang checks an acquisition of a command over recognized modes of expression … [and] must result in atrophy of the faculty of using language'. This applies mainly to authors and orators. But no stylist, no one capable of good speaking or good writing, is likely to be harmed by the occasional employment of slang; provided that he is conscious of the fact, he can even employ it freely without stultifying his mind, impoverishing his vocabulary, vitiating the taste or impairing the skill that he brings to the using of that vocabulary. Except in formal and dignified writing and in professional speaking, a vivid and extensive slang is perhaps preferable to a jejune and meagre vocabulary of Standard English; on the other hand, it will hardly be denied that, whether in writing or in speech, a sound though restricted vocabulary of Standard English is preferable to an equally small vocabulary of slang, however vivid that slang may be.

With regard to the use of slang, the Fowlers raise an important point when they say that 'foreign words and slang are, as spurious ornaments, on the same level. … The effect of using quotation marks with slang is merely to convert a mental into a moral weakness.' But there I must join issue with the authors of *The King's English*. They say that if a man uses slang at all (they advise him not to use it) in writing, let him do so in a courageous, not a cowardly manner: let him use it frankly, without quotation marks. So far as it goes, that is admirable; it does not go far enough. A good writer wishes to indicate that the word or phrase he puts into inverted commas is *not* Standard English, is not pure English, is not to be aped by the young nor unreflectingly copied by a foreigner; its status, he implies, is suspect, but he is using it because it is necessary to the atmosphere or to the characterization he wishes to make. True; he will use slang sparingly; he will use it only when it is necessary to the effect he is desirous of creating: but, precisely because he employs words scrupulously and precisely because he is anxious to avoid being taken as an exemplar of slang, a supporter of this particular word or phrase, he fences it off with quotation marks. 'This is not Standard English; I am using slang with the reservation that a Standard English term might, after all, have been preferable; however justifiable it is here, it is not always justifiable.'

IV. THE ROLE OF SLANG

'An analysis of modern slang', wrote Brander Matthews in 1893, 'reveals the fact that it is possible to divide [it] … into four broad classes, of quite different origin and very varying value. Two unworthy, two worthy. Of the two unworthy classes, the first is that which includes the survivals of "thieves' Latin". … Much of the distaste for slang felt by people of delicate taste is, however, due to the second class, which includes the ephemeral phrases fortuitously popular for a season [e.g. *Where did you get that hat?*] … The other two classes of slang stand on a different footing … They serve a purpose. Indeed, their utility is indisputable, and it was never greater [the remark is still valid] than it is today. One of these consists of old and forgotten phrases and words, which, having long lain dormant, are now struggling again to the surface. The other consists of new words and phrases, often vigorous and expressive, but … still on probation':

these two classes help to feed and refresh the vocabulary. 'It is the duty of slang to provide substitutes for the good words ... which are worn out by hard service.' Of the fourth class – vigorous new slang – he goes on to say that it is 'what idiom was before language stiffened into literature'; compare Lounsbury's description of slang as 'the source from which the decaying energies of speech are constantly refreshed'.

V. THE ESSENCE OF SLANG

Two writers have been particularly successful in attempting to set forth the essentials of slang. Professor Albert Carnoy, very briefly in *La Science du mot*, 1927; Frank Sechrist, at some length, in 'The Psychology of Unconventional Language' (*The Pedagogical Seminary*, December 1913). 'L'argot', writes Carnoy, 'est constitué par un vocabulaire particulier dans lequel la fantaisie intentionnelle joue un rôle dominant. Il tend à produire une sensation de nouveauté, d'imprévu, d'ingéniosité en donnant à certains mots un sens inusité et "piquant". Les procédés employés à atteindre à ce but sont analogues à ceux qui président en général à l'évolution du sens, ceux notamment qui produisent le langage "image", "expressif" et "affectif". Toutefois dans l'argot, la part de la conscience [consciousness] est plus grande, et toujours se fait sentir un effort pour parler autrement que la façon naturelle, pour être drolatique, contourné ou ironique. L'argot correspond à un état d'esprit dédaigneux ou bon enfant qui ne prend pas trop au sérieux les choses dont on parle.'

To précis and paraphrase Sechrist is difficult. Here, however, are a few of his remarks:

'[Slang] is purely unsentimental.'

'It is superior to accepted use through its emotional force.'

'Slang phrases often possess a greater wealth of association than others because they appeal to recent experiences rather than to dim memories.'

'The emotional tension produced by slang is greater than that of more custom-ary and conventional language, and the mind in time seeks a relief from it.'

'Slang is radical. It looks to the present, puts off restraint, and does not concern itself with limits in speech.'

'[It] keeps close to the objective world of things. ... It is the language of reality as common sense.'

'Slang will often be clear, even though it must be distasteful; it will be familiar, even though it must be coarse. It is realistic, naturalistic, unromantic.'

Anthropomorphically considered, slang 'is the individual speaking from the racial substratum, while conventional language is the language of expedience, of social deference, and reverence for the past'.

Sechrist's long article, which was reprinted in book form, should be read by all those who are interested in the psychology of language. To his illuminating remarks, I add a summary of my own views:

Slang tends to be 'Saxon' rather than 'Latin-Greek' – native rather than learned in its elements; except among the very cultured and the innately supple and subtle, it is simple and direct rather than complex and concealed or insinuatory; it reduces the peculiar and the particular (in which, nevertheless, it rejoices and is, on occasion, 'at home') to the level of general comprehension; it abridges rather than develops or elaborates; so far from padding, it omits the incidental and the contingent; rather than divest them of colour, it renders them pictorial and metaphorical; except in humour and wit, it eschews sentimental hyperbole and philosophical highfalutin'; it takes nothing too seriously, yet (very faintly) it implies a moral or an intellectual standard, usually at the level of good sense or, at the lowest, of common sense; it universalizes words and phrases rather than exclusively or snobbishly confines them to one social class; it refers itself to human nature rather than to Nature; it dispels hypocrisy and humbug; in short, it is catholic, tolerant, human, and, though often tartly, humane.

Inherent in human nature as a psychological tendency and potentiality, slang is indicative not only of man's earthiness but of his indomitable spirit: it sets him in his proper place: relates a man to his fellows, to his world and the world, and to the universe.

(My *A Dictionary of Slang and Unconventional English* appeared in 1937; 3rd edition, very much enlarged, 1948.)

[Note: It would be impertinent to modify what EP, a well-known authority on the subject, has to say about slang. We therefore merely add a few examples current at the end of the century: *bird* (British, girl), *bread* (money), *crash out* (to sleep), *fuzz* (police), *grotty* (British, unpleasant), *jerk* (fool), *snafu* (confusion, chaos), *zap* (to kill, destroy).]

slant (n.). See **standpoint**.

slattern. See **sloven**.

slayed is incorrect for *slew*, the preterite of *slay*; the correct past participle is *slain*. *Slayed* however, is common in the slang sense 'convulsed', as in 'Her jokes really slayed them.'

sled, sledge, sleigh, as vehicles. As 'a vehicle running on ice or snow', the three terms are synonymous, *sledge* being in the USA the least used, *sled* the most; in British usage, *sledge* is the most used, *sled* the least. In American and Canadian usage a *sled* is a small downhill toboggan, and a *sleigh* is the larger affair with seats, pulled by a horse.

sleuth for *detective* should be employed only in a facetious way: used seriously, it is journalese.

slippy for *slippery* is described as 'colloquial' (*COD*); and *look slippy*, for *be quick*, as British.

sloven and **slattern.** The former is common to the two sexes; the latter is used only of the female – 'a woman or girl untidy and careless in clothes and cleanliness (and other habits) and also in housework'. A *sloven* is any untidy or dirty

person; hence also a careless, slipshod workman, craftsman, or writer. *Slut*, by the way, is stronger than *slattern*: a *slut* is a foul *slattern*; hence, a low or loose woman or girl, or a forward, impudent one (especially of a girl); and, unlike *slattern*, it may be used playfully ('Ah! you're a wheedling slut', Swift) (*OED*).

slow; slower. *Slow* often replaces *slowly* as an adverb in less formal contexts, and particularly in commands, compounds, and some fixed phrases: 'drive slower/more slowly'; 'slow-moving traffic'; 'Dead Slow (road sign)'; 'a go-slow'.

slut. See **sloven**.

small fry is occasionally misused as a singular. 'Garston takes your overcoat on Monday and lets you have it back again on Saturday night – for a consideration. Or will buy it for that matter. Small fry' (Cecil Freeman Gregg, *Tragedy at Wembley*).

smell – smelled, smelt – smelled, smelt; but in both preterite and past participle, *smelt* is now the preferred British form, and *smelled* the American.

snicker is obsolescent or American for 'to *snigger*', to laugh in a half-suppressed manner. *Snigger* has a connotation of slyness in the laughter and of fault or absurdity in the object. To say, as Weseen does, that *snicker* and *snigger* are 'colloquial substitutes for *giggle*' is not only to classify them wrongly but also to misunderstand them.

SNOB PLURALS. See **PLURALS, SNOB.**

snout is obsolescent for the trunk of an elephant, pejorative for the nose of a man. Properly it is the projecting part of an animal's head; it includes nose and mouth, and is applied also to insects and fishes.

so (adv.), emphasizing the adjective following, as in *I was so pleased*, is a weak and slovenly form of expression. *Much* or *very* is preferable.

so, ambiguous, 'A prosperous, carefree foreigner, probably visiting Monte Carlo for the first time in his life, and so eager for adventure' (Mrs Belloc Lowndes, *The House by the Sea*). Should not *so* be *therefore*? *So* for *therefore* or *accordingly* is much overworked.

so for *so that* or *in order that* is always colloquial and sometimes ambiguous, as in 'I don't know why I did that exactly' [he means, 'I don't precisely know why' or 'I don't know precisely why ...'] – 'Perhaps a kind of dim hope that I'd find something ..., but more to be alone and quiet – *so* I could think' (Inez Irwin, *The Poison Cross Mystery*). (It is but fair to the author to add that she puts this statement into the mouth of a youngish detective who is better at detecting than at talking.) 'I do not ask you to believe these things, but I will give you proof, so you can judge them for yourself' (novel published in 1937).

so in *do so* is frequently misused; sometimes because it is asked to do too much. In *The World of Words* I found that I had written: 'A young child is not told, "The subject usually precedes the verb", yet that child has no difficulty in learning to do so', instead of the correct ... 'yet that child has no difficulty in learning to set [or, place] the subject before the verb'. There is a considerable strain on *so* in 'King Carol today ... proclaimed to his people: "Rumania must be saved, and I have decided to do so"' (*The Star*, 11 Feb. 1938); and here is a parallel misuse in *The Daily Herald* of the same date, 'Mr B said later: "Much as we hate doing so, we are reconciled to the fact."'

so, superfluous. As e.g. in 'Both Karl and his mother discussed the crisis with Sir Oscar Bloom, but separately so, and from different viewpoints' (Warwick Deeping, *Sackcloth and Silk*).

so as for *so that*, in the sense *in order that*, should be followed by *to* + the infinitive. Therefore 'He did this so as he might win the prize' is unfortunate. 'He did this vigorously – so as to fall down exhausted' (result) is not incorrect; but it is clumsy for

'He did this so vigorously as to fall down exhausted.'

so that = *with the result that* (generally) and *in order that*. These senses are distinguished by the tense of the following verb, as in 'He came home late, so that he missed me', and 'He came home early, so that he would not miss me.' But its use is occasionally ambiguous.

sociable and **social.** *Sociable* is 'naturally inclined to be in company with others', hence 'inclined to seek their company and to enjoy it', 'affable'; hence of occasions, 'of or characterized by companionship, especially friendly or at least pleasant companionship' (*sociable habits* or *manners*, *sociable life*, *sociable talk*). *Social* = 'of or like, connected with or due to society as an ordinary condition of human life' (*social usefulness, social sympathy, the social order* or *state, social rank*); 'concerned with or interested in the constitution of society and its problems' (*a social reformer, social reform*) (*OED*). Thus, a *social evening* or a *social club* involves the society of other people, but it may or may not be *sociable*.

SOCRATIC IRONY. See IRONY, third paragraph.

solar topi is incorrect for *sola topi* (or *topee*). The pith helmet formerly used in India was so called from the sola, a swamp plant producing the pith, and is misspelt *solar* from the mistaken idea that the adjective refers to the *solar rays* (the rays of the sun, from which the helmet protects the wearer's head) (Ackermann, *Popular Fallacies*).

sole is obsolescent in the following senses: (Of places) 'lonely or secluded'; 'unique, unrivalled'; (of actions) 'exercised by one person only'; 'uniform or unvaried' (as in 'a sole colour'). In Law, it = 'unmarried'; a *corporation sole* is vested in one person (e.g. 'a parson is a corporation sole'). It is rare in the sense 'alone or solitary', and mostly attributive. The two commonest senses in non-technical English are 'one and one only', as in 'the sole support of his mother; 'the sole manager of these estates'; and (of properties, rights, privileges, duties, obligations) 'exclusive', as in 'A theory of which he claims the sole invention', 'This is a task in which he has the sole obligation' (*OED*).

SOLECISM AND SOLECISMS.

Solecism, the Greek *soloikismos*, derives from the offensive and illiterate corruption of the Attic dialect as spoken by those Athenian colonists who settled at *Soloi* (Soli), in Cilicia, a province of Asia Minor. (The Greek word was probably slang, originally.)

OED defines it, in the social sense, as 'a blunder or impropriety in manners'; in the linguistic sense, as 'an impropriety or irregularity in speech or diction' – a gross mispronunciation, a stress wrongly placed (especially in a well-known word); 'a violation of the rules of [accidence] or syntax; properly, a faulty concord', or, as Bentley had it, 'The last part of the sentence not agreeing nor answering to the first; which is the proper definition of a Solœcism': such a faulty concord as, e.g., 'He and I was in town.' In the 20th century, however, its linguistic sense is generally taken to be a faulty pronunciation, an ignorant syntaxis, a gross fault in accidence ('two mans').

In short, it is approximately synonymous with *illiteracy*, which, however, includes also misspellings. "'E ain't a-comin' 'ere' contains three solecisms ('*E*, *comin'*, '*ere*) and five illiteracies ('*E*, *ain't*, *a-*, *comin'*, '*ere*).

solicitor. See **lawyer.**

solidity should not be made synonymous with *solidarity* ('community or perfect coincidence *of* (or *between*) interests'), as Graham Seton makes it in *The K. Code Plan*, nor with *stolidity*, which is 'dull impassiveness' or 'a natural incapacity for feeling', the former sense being favourable, the latter unfavourable (*OED*).

soliloquy. See **dialogue.**

some, ambiguous. 'In particular propositions the adjective *some* is to be carefully interpreted as *some, and there may or may not be more or all.*' An interpretation *some, not more nor all* often leads to trouble. 'If I say "some men are sincere", I must not be taken as implying that "some men are not sincere"; I must be understood to predicate sincerity of some men, leaving the character of the remainder wholly unaffected. It follows from this that, when I deny the truth of a particular, I must not be understood as implying the truth of the universal of the same quality. To deny the truth of "some men are mortal" might seem very natural, on the ground that not *some* but *all* men are mortal; but then the proposition denied would really be *some men are not mortal*. ... Hence, when I deny that "some men are immortal" I mean that "no men are immortal"; and that when I deny that "some men are not mortal" I mean that "all men are mortal"' (Jevons and Hill, *The Elements of Logic*).

some for *about, approximately, nearly, not many more than* is condemned by a rhetorician, who cites 'Some sixty men were present': but this is impeccable English. It should, however, be used only with round numbers, not as in 'Some sixty-three men ...'.

some for *part* is a misuse, as in 'I shall spend some of the day in Town.'

some for *somewhat* (or *rather*) is an Americanism ('He is some better today'); for *very* (or *much*), *very pleasant, large*, it is slang ('He speeded some'; 'We had some holiday'). See especially my *A Dictionary of Slang*.

some few. See **few and a few.**

some reason or another. See **some way or another ...**

some thing and **something; some time** and **sometime.** Written as separate words, these two expressions are dissociative ('I'll see you at some time before midnight'; 'Some thing, not some person, was revealed'). When units are required, *something* and *sometime* are required. In current usage, *sometime* has two main senses, 'at some future time' ('Will you tell me?' – 'Yes, sometime') and 'at some indefinite or indeterminate point of time; at some time or other' ('The prisoner escaped, sometime after nightfall'); in the sense 'now and then; occasionally', *sometimes* is the right word (*OED*). Note also 'The job will take some time (= an appreciable length of time)', and the adjectival use of *sometime* in 'the sometime (= former) bishop'.

some way or another; some reason or another. These are inferior to – indeed, wrong for – *some way or other, some reason or other*, e.g. 'In some way or other they escaped', 'For some reason or other, he left home.'

somebody (or someone) … they. See **anyone … they.**

somebody's (or someone's) else. See **else's.**

someplace is US colloquial for *somewhere*, as in 'The enemy was someplace near', 'The jar is obviously someplace else.'

something of that extent is misused for *something of that kind* or *sort*.

somewhat the same. Eric Partridge in *The French Romantics' Knowledge of English Literature*, 1924, speaks of 'a group of critics … possessing similar literary opinions as well as ability of somewhat the same high standard', but his subsequent study of English leads him to condemn this use of *somewhat* in the sense of *approximately* or *nearly* or *the like*.

somewhere near is infelicitous and slovenly for *somewhere about*, 'at (or in) approximately' (a specified period or date), as in 'I woke up somewhere about five o'clock', and also for *approximately*, as in 'He was ill somewhere about a month.' Note, too, that *somewhere about*, in these two nuances, is a trifle clumsy for *about* or *approximately* (*OED*).

somewheres is solecistic (when not dialectal) for *somewhere*.

son-in-laws is incorrect for *sons-in-law*. See **daughters-in-law.**

sooner is familiar but good English for *rather* in 'He'd sooner play than work'; not a colloquialism. One would not, however, employ it in formal or lofty prose.

sophisticate (adj.) is obsolete for *sophisticated*. But *sophisticate* (n.) is both convenient and justifiable for *sophisticated person*; *Webster's* recognizes it as unexceptionable.

sophisticated. See VOGUE WORDS.

sort of for *rather, somewhat*, is generally regarded as vulgar or low colloquial. At the end of a sentence and usually following an adjective, it is a slovenly form of modification. 'He is queer, sort of.' 'He is rather queer' or 'He is, in a way, queer' is much to be preferred. Cf. **kind of.**

sort of, these or **those.** In 'these sort of things are done by conjurers' (well-known novelist) there is a confusion between 'this sort of thing is done …' and 'these sorts of things are done …' (Baumann). Cf. **kind of, all.**

SOULFULNESS. The only profitable thing to say about soulfulness is: avoid it in speech, if you wish to retain your self-respect and your friends; avoid it in writing if you wish to be ranked as a writer at all or if you have any regard for your correspondents. (I use the term in its modern sense, 'undue or affected emotionalism'.) Perhaps the best – or should I say the worst? – example of soulfulness is afforded by the more emotional novels of that almost forgotten best-seller, Marie Corelli: *God's Good Man, The Sorrows of Satan, Wormwood*, and the others.

sound (v.). One may say that 'A thing sounds all right' (which is rather colloquial, of course), but *sound* is misused in 'In a moment or two blows would be exchanged and after that anything might happen, but most likely a miniature razor battle, particularly as the voices of both parties sounded to be of foreign origin' (John G. Brandon), where 'seemed to be' would be better, as also would 'the voices ... sounded like those of foreigners'.

SOUND AND SENSE. In his *English Composition and Rhetoric*, 1887–8, Alexander Bain treats this subject under two headings: Melody and Harmony. But there are at least two other things to be taken into consideration: (1) alliteration; (2) adequacy of sound to sense.

'The Melody or Music of Language involves both the Voice and the Ear. What is hard to pronounce is not only disagreeable as a vocal effort' – though, to some authors, easy enough to write – 'but also painful to listen to': and hardly less painful to those of us who read with the inner ear.

Bain examines certain sound-combinations that are melodious, others that are harsh, unmusical (see II, 280–90); but his findings are so obvious, his remarks so unilluminating (because so trite), that they are useless to the learner and extremely tedious to the student: and both useless and tedious to anyone who is interested in the subject. But perhaps we may quote his summary. 'The melodious flow of speech', he says, 'is dependent upon the lengthening out of the pronunciation through the presence of long vowels and continuing consonants. Rapidity and ease can be given by the alternation of abrupt consonants and short vowels; but it is hardly possible to introduce musical tone without the means of delaying and prolonging the vocal strain.'

At 'Harmony of Sound and Sense', Bain says, 'It is possible to make the Sound of the language an echo to the Sense', and first of all considers echo-words and echoic collocations – also called onomatopoeia (see **echoism**).

Passing over such obviousness as *bang*, *crash*, *hiss*, *munch*, *thunder*, *whirr*, and *whizz*, we see that imitation is most effective when the echoism and sound-effects

extend over a succession of words. Milton excels at such effects, as in

> The hoarse Trinacrian shore;

Hell's gates open thus harshly:

> > On a sudden open fly
> With impetuous recoil and jarring
>   sound,
> The infernal doors; and on their
>   hinges grate
> Harsh thunder;

whereas of Heaven's, he says that

> > Heaven opened wide
> Her ever-during gates, harmonious
>   sound,
> On golden hinges turning;

a battle:

> Arms on armour clashing, bray'd
> Horrible discord; and the
>   maddening wheels
> Of brazen fury raged;

compare the meagre discordance of

> Grate on their scrannel pipes of
>   wretched straw.

The use of sibilants constitutes perhaps the most obvious echo-effect, especially as *s* is so seldom missing in a sound-collocation of any length greater than half a dozen syllables. Whittier ripples thus the seashore:

> And so beside the silent sea
> I wait the muffled roar;

and Poe achieves a rustling in

> And the silken sad uncertain
>   rustling of each purple curtain.

But language can by imitation represent more impressive or more cumulative movement; 'a series of long syllables, or of words under accent [i.e. stressed words], with the frequent occurrence of the voice-prolonging consonants, being necessarily slow to pronounce, is appropriate to the description of slow and laboured movement. As in Pope's couplet on *The Iliad*:

When Ajax strives some rock's vast
   weight to throw,
The line too labours, and the words
   move slow.

... The opposite arrangement – that is
to say, an abundance of short and unaccented syllables, and the more abrupt
consonants alternated with the vowels –
by making the pronunciation rapid, light
and easy, corresponds to quickness of
motion in the subject', as in Gray's *Ode on
the Spring*:

Yet hark! how through the peopled
   air
The busy murmur glows!
The insect youth are on the wing,
Eager to taste the honied Spring,
And float amid the liquid noon;
Some lightly o'er the current skim,
Some shew their gaily-gilded trim,
Quick-glancing to the sun.

Of the numerous special effects, we
shall note several. Keats is a master of
drowsy, headily sensuous effects, but he
can, when he wishes, be admirably precise,
even where precision is not the quality
that one would most expect – or expect at
all – as when, by using liquid consonants,
he brings before our eyes 'the gliding
motion of the clouds' (Bain), in

And let the clouds of even and of
   morn
Float in voluptuous fleeces o'er the
   sea.

Compare a similar use of liquids here:

O what can ail thee, knight-at-
   arms,
Alone and palely loitering?

... Tennyson's ingenuity is conspicuous.
The movement of a wave at the beach is
described –

Till last, a ninth one, gathering half
   the deep
And full of voices, slowly rose and
   plunged
Roaring.

But then, Tennyson is perhaps as skilful, subtle, and delicate as anyone in the
entire range of English poets in the suiting
of sound to sense. So well known, so often
quoted is his subtle skill, that only two
other examples need be given here –

The moan of doves in immemorial
   elms;

and, to express the feeling of hopelessness,
a harsh rhythm with alliteration magistrally
employed to heighten the effect –

And ghastly through the drizzling
   rain
On the bald streets breaks the blank
   day.

Obstructed movement, toilsome striving
are characterized in the following description of Sisyphus at his task (Pope's *The
Iliad*):

With many a weary step, and many
   a groan,
Up the high hill he heaves a huge
   round stone;
The huge round stone resulting
   with a bound,
Thunders impetuous down, and
   smokes along the ground.

Huge, unwieldy *bulk* implies slowness
of movement, and may be expressed by
similar language:

            O'er all the dreary coasts
So stretch'd out, huge in length, the
   archfiend lay.
But ended foul in many a scaly fold
Voluminous and vast.

But for alliteration, see the entry at that
term. And as for the psychological adequacy of sound to sense – well, that is a big
subject: see **SUITABILITY**.

sound out is tautological for *sound*, 'to
test'. Perhaps on the analogy of *try out*.
'President is sounding out sentiment by
undercover [= secret] observers in European capitals', cited – from an American
financial weekly market letter – by Stuart
Chase in *The Tyranny of Words*.

source and **cause.** *Source* cannot be used indiscriminately for *cause*, as in 'The source of his injury was a motor collision', but, despite Weseen, it is permissible in 'The source of many failures is neglect of duty.' *OED* makes it clear that a *source* is 'the chief or prime cause *of* something of a non-material or abstract character', as in 'The free election of our representatives … is the source and security of every right and privilege' (Junius) and 'This intellectual perversion is the source of a systematic immorality' (Manning); generally, however, there is a reference (actual or implied) to the quarter whence something non-material or abstract arises, as in 'Evil-smelling gases are a source of annoyance to all those who live within a mile of the factory' and 'One source of danger is the carelessness of the garrison.'

sourkrout is incorrect for *sauerkraut*: the German *sauer* means 'pickled' and 'sour'.

southerly and **southern.** See **easterly**.

southward; southwards. The latter is adverb only; the former is chiefly an adjective, but often functions as an adverb in American English and in older British writing.

sow – sowed – sowed (or, in poetry and as adjective before a noun, **sown**). The verbal noun is *sown*, as in 'The desert and the sown'.

spake is archaic for *spoke*.

span is archaic for *spun* (preterite).

spat. See also **spit**.

speaking. See CONJUNCTIONS, DISGUISED.

special. See **especial**.

speciality and **specialty.** A special product or line of work is a *speciality* in British usage and a *specialty* in American English. To both the British and the Americans a distinguishing characteristic is a *speciality* and a legal agreement under seal is a *specialty*.

specie and **species.** *Specie* is coined money; *in specie* = in actual coin; *specie* has no plural. *Species* is both singular and plural and it = 'a class composed of individuals [animate or inanimate] having some common qualities or characteristics, frequently as a subdivision of a larger class or genus' (*OED*).

species for *sex* is a curious error. 'It was not difficult to catalogue Miss Woods. But there was one consolation – J. L. was even more adept with her species' (Robert George Dean, *The Sutton Place Murders*). Perhaps from 'The female of the species is the more dangerous.'

spectrum. See VOGUE WORDS.

speed – sped – sped. But *speed*, 'to drive a motor-car very fast', and *speed up*, 'to hasten the acceleration or tempo of' (e.g. a business, a dance) have their preterite and past participle in the form *speeded*.

spell – spelled or **spelt – spelled** or **spelt.** *Spelt* is on the whole the preferred British form, but *spelled* is the only American one, for the verb meaning 'form words'. The other verb meaning 'relieve in turns' has only *spelled*, as in 'The two sentries spelled each other.'

SPELLING does not belong to this book. See especially G. H. Vallins, *Spelling*, 1954, an excellent account with a chapter, by Professor John W. Clark, on American spelling.

Spencer, philosopher (adj. *Spencerian*); **spencer,** a jacket or bodice, a trysail; **Spenser,** poet (adj. *Spenserian*).

sphere (or realm, or world) of (e.g. *sport*) for *sport*. 'In the sphere (or realm or world) of sport, one should play for the side, not for oneself' would not be weakened by reducing it to 'In sport, one should …'.

spill – spilled or **spilt – spilled** or **spilt.** *Spilt* is on the whole the preferred British form, *spilled* decidedly the American.

spin-off. See VOGUE WORDS.

spit, 'to expectorate' – preterite and past participle usually *spat* in British use, but often *spit* in the USA; but *spit*, 'to transfix' – *spitted* – *spitted*.

spite of. See **despite.**

splendid, 'excellent' ('He was a splendid shot with a revolver'), is not a colloquialism, but it is familiar English – much overdone, and to be avoided in reputable writing or impressive speech. *Splendacious* and *splendiferous* are to be avoided as humorous slang or colloquialisms for 'magnificent'.

SPLIT INFINITIVE, THE.

In *The Queen's English,* Dean Alford scarcely troubles to discuss the matter, but seems to raise his very reverend eyebrows in sheer astonishment at the admission of such an error.

Dr C. T. Onions, in *An Advanced English Syntax,* is much more tolerant. 'The construction known by this name consists of the separation of *to* from the Infinitive by means of an adverb, e.g. "He used *to continually refer* to the subject", instead of "He used *continually to refer*", or "He used *to refer continually*". The construction is becoming more and more frequent, especially in newspapers, but it is generally admitted that a constant and unguarded use of it is not to be encouraged; some, indeed, would refuse altogether to recognize it, as being inelegant and un-English. (Instances like "For a time, the Merovings continued *to nominally rule*" are particularly ugly.) On the other hand, it may be said that its occasional use is of advantage in cases where it is desired to avoid ambiguity by indicating in this manner the close connexion of the adverb with the infinitive, and thus prevent its being taken in conjunction with some other word' e.g. 'Our object is to further cement trade relations', is obviously preferable to 'Our object is to cement further trade relations' (which yields a sense different from the one intended), and is less obviously but no less surely preferable to 'Our object is further

to cement trade relations', which leaves it 'doubtful whether an additional object or additional cement is the point' (Fowler). H. W. Fowler writes thus: 'We maintain that a real split infinitive, though not desirable in itself' – he implies that the sentence ought to be differently constructed – 'is preferable to either of two things, to real ambiguity, and to patent artificiality' (*The Split Infinitive,* SPE Tract No. xv). As an example of patent artificiality he cites 'In not combining to forbid flatly hostilities', instead of the natural and sensible 'In not coming to flatly forbid hostilities'; 'In not combining flatly to forbid hostilities' would obviously have been ambiguous.

Fowler, we see, speaks of 'a real split infinitive'. Is there then, 'an unreal split infinitive'? I myself have used one in the preceding paragraph: 'The sentence ought *to be differently constructed*', which is as blameless as '*to be mortally wounded*' or '*to have just heard*'. There is a 'split' only when an adverb comes between *to* and an infinitive '*to clearly see*'.

Avoid the split infinitive wherever possible; but if it is the clearest and the most natural construction, use it boldly. The angels are on our side.

spoil – spoiled, spoilt – spoiled, spoilt. *Spoilt* is on the whole the preferred British form, particularly as an adjective ('a spoilt child'), but *spoiled* is more usual in American English. See also **despoil.**

spoof and its plural. A correspondent wrote as follows to *The Radio Times* of 15 Jan. 1938: 'In a recent *Radio Times* the plural of the word hoof is spelled hooves in two instances. One would not spell the plural of roof rooves, and how supremely ridiculous the plural of spoof would appear if it were spelled spooves!' *Hooves* is allowed by *OED,* though it is less commonly used than *hoofs;* but good authors have preferred it. *Rooves* also was common in our early literature, and is (like *loaf, loaves*) consistent with the genius of our language; a writer that prefers it could not be condemned for error and hardly for eccentricity. But *spoof* is quoted as analogous. Has *spoof* a plural? Originally a game, it was no more capable of taking a plural form than *cricket* or *golf*. *Spoof* is the abstract quality of jocular deception inspiring some trick or practical joke; it is in fact an adjective derived from the game. If it is to be used in such a sense that a plural is required for it, there will be nothing in *spooves* more 'ridiculous' than in *spoof*, which has a comic intention from the first (WB). See also **-f**.

SPORTING PLURALS. Sportsmen (big-game hunters, anglers, and others) tend to use the singular for the plural – *trout* for *trouts*, *lion* for *lions*, etc., etc. – and to look with scorn upon those who speak of *trouts* and *lions*. The ordinary person, unacquainted with the jargon of these very superior specialists, should not allow himself to be intimidated by the snobs of sport. If you wish to shoot three *lions* or to hunt *tigers*, do so.

SPORTS (field-sport) **TECHNICALITIES.** There are, in field sports, numerous terms that baffle or are unknown to the ordinary man and woman. The best book I know on the subject is Major C. E. Hare's *The Language of Sport*.

From Major Hare's invaluable work, to which I refer the laudably curious reader, I select a few groups: animals' footmarks; retirement to rest; cries; tails; the marks on horses. And Company (or Group) Nouns.

A. i. *Footmarks*
For the footing and treading of a hart, we say: *slot**;
buck, and all fallow deer: *view*;
all deer, when on grass and hardly visible: *foiling*;
a fox†: *print*;
similar vermin: *footing*;
an otter: *marks* or *seal*;
a boar: *track*.

---

*Also applied, derivatively, to a deer's foot.

†A fox's feet are *pads*, its face a *mask* or (rarely) *front*.

ii. *Retirement to rest*
A badger *earths*;
a boar *couches*;
a buck *lodges*;
a coney *sits* (or *burrows*);
a fox *kennels*;
a hare *seats* or *forms* or (*less generally*) *squats*;
a hart *harbours*;
a marten *trees*;
an otter *watches* or, if inland, *couches*;
a roe *beds*;
a wolf *trains*.

The corresponding nouns are:

The bed of a badger is an *earth*;
buck, a roebuck, or a hart is a *lair* (or, in English dialect, a *ligging*);
coney is a *burrow*;
fox is a *kennel* or, more usually, an *earth*;
hare is a *form*.

iii. *Cries*
A bittern *booms*;
a bull *bellows*;
a panther *saws*;
a sambur (Indian elk) *saws*;
a stag *roars* (at the end of September).

At rutting time, a badger *shrieks* or *yells*;
a boar *freams*;
a buck *groans* or *troats* (hoots);
a ferret, like a polecat and a stoat, *chatters*;
a fox *barks* (or *whines*);
a goat *rattles*;
a hare or a rabbit *beats* or *taps*;
a hart *bells*;
an otter *whines*;
a roe *bellows*;
a wolf *howls*.

iv. *Tails*
The tail of a boar is a *wreath*;
a buck, a hart, or other deer, is a *single*;
a coney or a hare is a *scut*;

a fox is a *brush* or *drag*, the tip at the end being a *chafe* or a *tag*;
a foxhound, a greyhound, a wolf, is a *stern*;
an otter is a *rudder* or a *pole*;
a roe is a *target*.

v. *The Marks on Horses*

A *blaze* is 'a white marking spread over the forehead, and sometimes down the whole width of the face. An exaggerated blaze is called "white face" ' (Hare);

flesh marks are such patches of skin as have no colouring matter;

a *list** or *ray* is that dark line which runs along the back of some horses, many mules, and all donkeys;

lop ears are such ears as are 'set on in rather a loose and pendulous manner' (Hare);

a *race* or *stripe* is a white marking – it is a thin line – that runs down the nose;

a *snip* is a white or pink patch on nostril or lip;

sock; see *stocking*;

a *star* is a small white patch in the centre of the forehead;

a *stocking* is such an area of white on the leg as extends from the coronet (the lowest part of the pastern) to the knee or hock, but when the white ascends for a short distance only it is called a *sock*;

a *wall-eye* is an eye that has a bluish-white appearance (caused by lack of pigment);

white face: see *blaze*;

. a *zebra mark* is any stripe (but generally applied when there are more stripes than one) on body or limb, but, common in donkeys and mules, it is rare in horses.

B. *GROUP TERMS*: Nouns of Assemblage or Company†

---

*Perhaps from *list*, a strip (e.g. of cloth).

†See Hare's book and esp., R. J. Nicol, *A Collection of Terms, denoting Assemblages*, 1933 (privately printed).

---

i. *Birds, Mammals, Fishes, and Reptiles*
(a) *Birds*

Birds in a company are called a *flock* or a *congregation*

Bitterns or herons: a *siege*

Bustards: a *flock*

Chickens: a *brood*

Choughs: a *clattering*

Cranes and curlews: a *herd*

Crows: a *murder*

Doves: a *flight*

Ducks: (in flight) a *team*; (on the water) a *paddling*

Eagles: a *convocation*

Finches: a *charm*

Geese: (on the water) a *gaggle*; (on the wing) a *skein*

Goshawks: a *flight*

Grouse: (a single family) a *covey*; (larger band) a *pack*

Gulls: a *colony*

Hens: a *brood*

Humming-birds: a *charm*

Jays: a *band*

Lapwings; a *deceit*

Larks: an *exaltation*

Mallard(s): a *flush*

Nightingales: a *watch*

Parrots: a *flock*

Partridges: a *covey*

Peacocks: a *muster* (medievally, an *ostentation* or a *pride*)

Pheasants: (a family) a *brood*; (a large group) a *nye*

Pigeons: a *flight* or a *flock*

Plovers: a *congregation*

Poultry: a *run*

Quails: a *bevy*

Ravens: an *unkindness*

Rooks: a *clamour*

Snipe: a *walk*

Sparrows: a *host*

Starlings: a *chattering*

Storks: a *mustering*

Swallows: a *flight*

Swans; a *herd* or, less usually, a *wedge*

Swifts: a *flock*

Widgeon(s): (in the air) a *flight*; (on the water) a *bunch* or *company* or *knob*

Wildfowl(s): a *plump* or *trip*

Wrens: a *herd*

(b) *Mammals**

Antelopes in company are a *herd*
Asses: a *herd*; also a *drove* or a *pace*
Boars: a *sounder* (medievally, a *singular*)
Bucks: a *herd*
Buffaloes: a *herd*
Camels: a *flock*
Cats: (tame) a *cluster*, (young) a *kindle*
Cattle: a *herd* or *drove*; *mob* is Australian
Chamois: a *herd*
Conies: a *bury*
Cubs or whelps: a *litter*
Deer (all sorts): a *herd*
Dogs: a *kennel*
Elephants: a *herd*
Elk(s): a *gang*
Ferrets: a *business*
Foxes: an *earth* or a *skulk*
Giraffes: a *herd*
Goats: a *herd*, *flock*, or *trib* (medievally, a *trip*)
Hares: a *drove* (medievally, a *trip*)
Horses: a *herd*
Horses: (stabled) a *stable*; (stud) a *harras* (obsolete)
Hounds: a *pack*
Kangaroos: a *troop*
Leopards: a *leap*
Lions: a *flock*, *pride*, or *troop*
Mice: a *nest*
Monkeys: a *tribe*, *troop*, or *troupe*
Mules: a *barren* or a *rake*
Oxen: a *herd* or a *drove*
Piglets or pups: a *litter*
Porpoises: a *school*
Racehorses: a *field*; a *string*
Rhinoceroses: a *crash*
Seals: a *herd*
Sheep: a *flock*
Squirrels: a *dray*
Stoats: a *pack*
Swine: a *sounder*
Whales: a *school*
Whales, sperm: a *herd*
Wolves: (wild) a *pack*; also a *herd* or *rout*

(c) *Fishes, Amphibia, and Reptiles*
Eels in a company are a *swarm*

*In this list *herd* occurs 13 times; *flock*, 4; *troop*, 3; *drove*, 4.

Dogfish: a *troop*
Fishes: a *school* or a *shoal* (see also Hare's book)
Frogs: an *army*
Herrings: *army*, *glean*, or *shoal*
Mackerel and minnows, perch and pilchards: a *shoal*
Roach: a *shoal*
Sticklebacks: *a shoal*
Toads: a *knot*
Trout: a *hover*
Turtles: a *bale*
Whiting: a *pod*

The preceding lists (a), (b), (c) may be telescoped in reverse order, thus:

An *army* of frogs, herrings.
A *bale* of turtles.
A *band* of jays.
A *bevy* of quail(s).
A *brood* of chickens, or hens or pheasants.
A *charm* of finches, or humming-birds.
A *chattering* of starlings.
A *clamour* of rooks.
A *cluster* of tame cats.
A *colony* of gulls.
A *congregation* of birds in general and of plovers in particular.
A *convocation* of eagles.
A *covey* of grouse or partridge.
A *dray* of squirrels.
A *drove* of asses or cattle or hares or oxen.
A *field* of racehorses.
A *flight* of doves or goshawks or pigeons or swallows
A *flock* of birds in general; of bustards or parrots or pigeons or swifts; of camels or sheep.
A *gaggle* of geese (on water).
A *herd* of animals in general; of antelopes, asses, buffaloes, cattle, elephants, giraffes, goats, horses, oxen; of seals or sperm-whales.
A *host* of sparrows.
A *hover* of trout.
A *kennel* of dogs (a family); a large number is a *pack*.
A *litter* of piglets or pups or lions' whelps.

A *mustering* of storks.
A *nest* of mice.
A *pack* of hounds or stoats or wolves.
A *plump* of wildfowl.
A *pride* of lions.
A *run* of poultry.
A *school* of fishes in general; or
  porpoises or whales.
A *shoal* of fishes in general; of
  herrings, mackerel, minnows,
  roach, sticklebacks.
A *siege* of bitterns or herons.
A *skulk* of foxes.
A *sounder* of boars or swine.
A *string* of racehorses.
A *swarm* of bees or eels.
A *team* of ducks.
A *tribe* of monkeys.
A *trip* of wildfowl.
A *troop* of kangaroos or lions or
  monkeys; of dogfish.
A *watch* of nightingales.
A *wedge* of swans.

ii. *Persons – and Objects*

Apart from generally accepted terms
like *crowd* and *host*, suggestions have, at
various times, been made for new ones, on
the lines of certain fanciful medieval Company Terms (e.g. in *The Book of St Albans*,
1486), such as a *bevy* of ladies, a *blast* of
hunters, a *blush* (or *rascal*) of boys, a *boast*
of soldiers, a *charge* of curates, a *dignity* of
canons, a *gaggle* of gossips, a *hastiness* of
cooks, a *laughter* of eggs (modern), a *skulk*
of thieves, and so on. Here are some of the
modern suggestions:

(a) *Objects*
  Aeroplanes: a *buzziness*
  Bicycles: a *wobble*
  Cocktails: a *shake* or *scatter*
  Motor-cars: a *maze* or a *stink*
  Sausages: a *sizzle*
  Whisky: a *want*.

(b) *Persons**
  Actors: a *condescension* (N)

*H = Major C. E. Hare; N = Colonel R. J. Nicol;
P = *Punch*; SD = *The Sunday Dispatch*; BD = Lt-Col.
C. Bartley-Denniss; EP = Eric Partridge.

Aldermen: a *guzzle* (P)
Americans: a *Mayflower* (EP)
Anglers: an *elongation* (EP)
Announcers (radio): an *accent* (EP)
Aunts: an *anticipation* (EP)
Autobiographers: an *excess* (EP)
Aviators: an *annihilation* or a *celerity*
  (EP)
Babies: a *dampness* (EP)
Bachelors: a *debauchery* (N)
Bandsmen: a *furore* (H)
Barbers: a *botheration* or a *loquacity* (EP)
Bathers (seaside): a *bareness* or *nudity*
  (EP)
Beggars: a *whine* (EP)
Bishops: a *psalter* (P); an *unction* (EP)
Bookmakers: a *surge* (H)
Bores (club): a *geyser* (P)
Boys: a *riot* (H)
Bridge fiends: a *post mortem* (P)
Butchers: a *bloodiness* (EP)
Children: a *scamper* (EP)
Chinese: a *jaundice* or a *piety* (EP)
Choir boys: an *angelry* (EP)
Chorus girls: a *click* (BD); a *giggle* (N)
Civil Servants: a *file* (EP)
Clergymen: an *offertory* or a *vestry* (EP)
Clerks: a *ledger* (EP)
Clowns: a *guffaw* (P)
Colonels: a *blimp* or an *explosion* (EP)
Colonials (British): a *dominion* or a
  loyalty (EP)
Commercial travellers: a *brazenness*
  (EP)
Commissionaires: a *chestiness* (EP)
Communists: an *envy* (EP)
Company promoters: a *boodle* (P)
Confidence men: a *plausibility* (EP)
Conservatives: a *stodge* (P)
Cooks: a *burning*, a *caprice*, or a *hash*
  (EP)
Councillors: a *corpulence* (SD)
Cousins: a *countryside* (EP)
Cricketers: a *pavilion* or a *grace* (EP)
Curates: a *coyness* (SD)
Damsels: a *spray* (H)
Dancers: a *clutter*, a *jazz*, a *rhythm*, or a
  swing (EP)
Daughters: a *dependence* (EP)
Débutantes: a *curtsy* or a *diffidence* (EP)
Dentists: a *removal* (EP)

Diplomats, a *suavity* (EP)
Divorcees: a *Reno* (EP)
Doctors: an *emulsion* (EP)
Dramatists: a *dialogue* (EP)
Dutchmen: a *courage* or a *comfort* (EP)
Editors (newspapers): an *erudition* (SD);
    a *rejection* (EP)
Englishmen: an *insularity* (EP)
Fairies: a *charm* (H)
Families: a *garden suburb* (EP)
Farmers: a *grousing* (EP)
Fathers: a *fatuity* (SD); an *overdraft* (EP)
Film stars: a *screen* or a *transience* (EP)
Financiers: a *corner* (EP)
Fishermen: *see* Anglers
Flappers: a *frolic* (P)
Footballers (Association): a *dribble* (EP)
Footballers (Rugby): a *tackle* (EP)
Frenchmen: a *gesticulation* (EP)
Garage-proprietors: an *Ali Baba* (EP)
Gardeners: a *growth* or *offshoot* (EP)
Generals: a *blather* (N); an *importance*
    (EP)
Germans: a *momentum* (EP)
Girls: an *evasion* (EP)
Gods: a *gatheration* (BD); an
    omnipotence (EP)
Gold-diggers: a *daddy* (EP)
Golfers: a *bogey* or a *mouth-disease* (EP)
Governesses: a *pathos* or an *effacement*
    (EP)
Grocers: an *imposition* (EP)
Highbrows: an *altitude* (P); a
    highfalutin' or a *depression* (EP)
Hikers: a *hustle* (EP)
Housewives: a *duster* (EP)
Husbands: a *futility* (N); an *unhappiness*
    (BD); a *duty* (EP)
Indians (Asian): a *pagoda* (EP)
Insurance men: a *prospect* (EP)
Irishmen: an *eloquence* (EP)
Italians: an *opera* (EP)
Japanese: an *adaptation* or a *hara-kiri* (EP)
Journalists: a *column* (EP)
Lawn-tennis players: a *service* (EP)
Lawyers: a *surplus* (EP)
Liberals: a *brace* (P)
Loafers: a *saunter* (H)
Lovers: (women) a *delight*; (men) a
    flattery or a *pressure* or a *cornucopia*
    (EP)

Lowbrows: an *earthiness* (EP)
Majors: a *Poona* (EP)
Mannequins: a *slink* (P); an *undulation*
    (EP)
Members of Parliament: a *chatter* (BD);
    a *promise* (EP)
Milkmen: a *clatter*, a *watering* (EP)
Millionaires: a *Mammon* (EP)
Miners: a *muttering* (H)
Misers: a *proximity* (EP)
Mothers: a *patience* (EP)
Mothers-in-law: an *interference* or
    management or *pestilence* (EP)
Motorists: a *licence* or a *mania* (EP)
Navvies: a *neckerchief* (EP)
Old maids: *see* Spinsters
Optimists: a *Micawber* (EP)
Pacifists: a *propaganda* (EP)
Pedestrians: a *morgue* (EP)
Peeping Toms: a *Godiva* (EP)
Pessimists: an *I told you so* (EP)
Playwrights, a *caste* (EP)
Plumbers: a *procrastination* (EP)
Poets: a *gush* (P); an *afflatus* (EP)
Policemen: a *college* or a *politeness* (EP)
Politicians (tame): a *plethora* (BD); an
    indifference (EP)
Portrait painters: a *palliation* or an
    improvement (EP)
Postmen: a *delivery* (EP)
Prohibitionists: a *gargle* (P)
Publicans: a *pint* or a *pot* (EP)
Publishers: an *optimism* (EP)
Punters: a *fleece* (P)
Racketeers: a *protection* (EP)
Rascals: a *parcel* (BD)
Readers (British Museum): a
    somnolence (EP)
Relatives: a *poverty* or an *invasion* (EP)
Russians: a *gloom*, a *lustrum*, or a *steppe*
    (EP)
Sailors: a *wave* (EP)
Saints: a *severity* (EP)
Scholars: a *collation* (EP)
Schoolteachers: an *unselfishness* (EP)
Scientists: a *quantum* (EP)
Scotches (whiskies): a *skinful* (SD); a
    headache (EP)
Scotchmen: a *generosity* (EP)
Servants: a *dearth* (ND); a *departure* (EP)
Shopkeepers: a *nation* (EP)

315

stair

Socialists: a *heckle* (P)
Soldiers: a *canteen* or a *courage* (EP)
Sons: an *independence* (EP)
Spaniards: a *discord* or a *revolution* (EP)
Spectators (at English field games): a *shiver* (EP)
Spinsters (of any age): a *flutter* (P)
Spinsters (old maids): an *anxiety* (EP)
'Stars' (cinema): a *constellation* or a *Hollywood* (EP)
Statesmen: a *pact* (EP)
Stockbrokers: a *margin* (EP)
Surgeons: a *see-saw* (EP)
Sweet young things: a *rapacity* (EP)
Tailors: a *long credit* (EP)
Taxi-drivers: a *tardiness* or an *expectation* (EP)
Telephone operators: an *apology* (EP)
Thieves: an *honour* (EP)
Topers: a *continuity* (EP)
Tourists: a *drove* (BD)
Turks: a *delight* (EP)
Tyrants: an *egotism* or a *Hit-or-Muss* (EP)
Uncles: a *disappointment* (EP)
Urchins: a *mischief* (H)
Vicars: a *vicariousness* (SD)
Virgins: a *trace* (H); a *malaise* or a *misfortune* (EP)
Waiters: a *dawdling* (BD)
Welshmen: an *eisteddfod* (EP)
Wives: a *questionnaire* or a *quo vadis?* (EP)
Women: a *millinery* (EP)
Writers: a *sufficiency* or a *vanity* (EP)
Young people: a *superiority* (EP)
Zealots: a *preachment* or a *proselytism* (EP)

Too late for inclusion in the alphabetical list are these three small sets, handed to me by friends.

(1) The late F. G. Rendall (of the British Museum): a *foozle* of golfers, a *fraud* of Freudians, a *frowst* of philosophers.

(2) Colonel C. H. Wilkinson (Worcester College, Oxford): a *cheat* of bursars, a *dread* of deans, a *lakh* (or *lac*) of principals (of colleges), a *prowl* of proctors – of which the first and last are in actual use among the dons.

(3) Sir Harry Luke, KCMG, D.Litt.: a *cuddle* of nurses, a *galaxy* of milkmaids, a *swell* of admirals.

spouse, though a silly word to use where *husband* or *wife* would do, is a necessary blanket term for 'husband or wife'.

sprain and **strain** (v.). The former is 'so to twist or wrench (a part of the body, usually a wrist or ankle) as to cause pain or difficulty in moving'. To *strain oneself* is so to exert oneself physically as to be in danger of injury.

spring – sprang, or, less generally, **sprung – sprung.**

square. An area 3 km *square* is a square whose sides are 3 km long; but 3 square km is an area, of any shape, measuring 3 km by one.

squirt. Blood *spurts*, not *squirts*, from a wound; here is an idiom that careless writers tend to ignore. Such writers appear to act, not on the epigram, 'The best is good enough for me', but on the assumption, 'Anything is good enough for the public.'

St, and **St.,** is, for a saint, the best form; *Ste* is the French form for a female saint. For *Street*, however, *St.* is obligatory.

staff of persons, (pl.) *staffs, staff,* a stick, rod, pole, (pl.) *staffs*, although the earlier plural, *staves*, is still available in the senses 'a stick carried in the hand as an aid in walking', 'a rod used as an instrument of divination or magic', 'a stick or pole used as a weapon', 'a spear- (or lance-) shaft'. In music, *staff* has plural *staffs* or *staves*, but obviously the variant *stave* has plural *staves* (*OED*).

staid and **stayed.** Reserve the former for the adjective ('of grave or dignified or sedate deportment, demeanour, conduct'), the latter for the verb. 'The staid fellow stayed at home', 'The staid girl has stayed – a girl.'

stair; stairs. A *stair* is one of a succession of steps leading from one floor to another; *stairs* means either the steps of staircases or a series or 'flight' of such steps; *staircase* is usually one flight of steps, occasionally a series of flights. *Stairs*, as the plural of *stair*, hence as '(two or more) steps', is now avoided, *steps* being used instead to mini-

stalactite 316

mize the likelihood of ambiguity. It is possible, though decidedly literary, to use *stair* for *stairs*, as in 'a steep, winding stair'.

stalactite and **stalagmite.** The former deposit of calcium carbonate is one that forms downwards from the roof of a cave or cavern; the latter, one that forms upwards from the floor.

stanch and **staunch.** For the adjective, much the commoner form is *staunch*; for the verb, *stanch* is preferable. [For verb, noun, and adjective, *Webster's* gives *stanch, staunch*.]

stand for *withstand* is, to put it mildly, unhappy. Whereas *stand* for 'tolerate, endure, bear' is a colloquialism to be avoided in good writing, *stand* for 'withstand' or 'resist' is the product of a meagre vocabulary; and it may be a rank mistake, leading to ambiguity, as in 'The avaricious man could not stand the solicitations of easy money.'

STANDARD AMERICAN. See Section V of the following entry.

STANDARD ENGLISH and **STANDARD AMERICAN.** If we take the definition, 'Standard English and Standard American are the speech of the educated classes in Britain and the United States' (when, that is, they are not speaking slangily), as sufficient for the moment, we may yet desire to know where, and how, Standard English arose. That rise* provides material for an interesting story.

I. HISTORY

Old English had a standard (witness Old English literature), but that standard dis-

*For the advanced student, Professor H. C. K. Wyld's books are inescapable and invaluable; so too is Professor G. H. McKnight's *The Making of Modern English*. But here I draw, for the most part, on McKnight's 'Standard English', the opening chapter of his *English Words and Their Background*. Another excellent book for the general reader and the less advanced student is Henry Bradley's *The Making of English*. This article follows very closely, in outline and often in detail, the 'Standard English' section of the chapter entitled 'English: Good; Bad; and Worse' in my *The World of Words*.

appeared with the Norman Conquest. In the victorious reigns of Edward I (1272–1307) and Edward III (1327–77), there was a strong growth of national feeling; national consciousness was certainly accompanied by, and probably it was in part the source of, an increasing hostility to the use of French in England and consequently an increasingly favourable attitude towards the use of English. 'In the second half of the Fourteenth Century', says McKnight, 'the English language came once more to its own, into use not only in Parliament and the law courts and in schools, but in the literary productions composed for English cultured society.'

In this revival of English as a literary language, after it had so long been a merely spoken language, the particular kind of English adopted was the East Midland dialect. The reasons for this adoption, says McKnight, are these: 'The dialect of the East Midland district lay between Northern and Southern dialects and, as the Northern differed considerably from the Southern, the Midland served as a midway compromise understandable by all; it formed the speech of Oxford and Cambridge, the two great centres of higher education and of a culture more profound and mellow than that of London; it formed also the dialect of London itself, the centre of the political, official and commercial life of the country. And thus it was the speech of Chaucer, who, the greatest English writer until the 16th century and, during the 11th to 14th centuries, the only great writer to employ English at all, passed most of his life in London; as the dialect spoken at Oxford, it was used by Wycliffe, who discarded his native Yorkshire for this smoother speech; as the dialect of London and hence of the Court, it was used by Gower, who might have been expected to employ the Kentish dialect.' Chaucer's and Gower's best work appeared in the last twenty years of the 14th century; in the 15th, their disciples – and others – followed their lead and wrote in the East Midland dialect. Standard English, then, began in the second half of the 14th century as the East Midland dialect; and in the 15th century that dialect was established as the correct one to use for general literary purposes. It was the more readily adopted because it had not the harshness of the Northern dialects, very little of the rather drawling softness of the Southern. The supremacy of the East Midland dialect was unquestioned by the dramatists and the poets of the Elizabethan age.

The language of the 16th and early 17th century, however, was far from being so fixed and regularized as that of the 19th and, though less, the 20th century. Spelling was idiosyncratic, syntax experimental, and vocabulary a glorious uncertainty; these features and tendencies were counterbalanced by 'the freedom enjoyed by the writers of that period in the adoption of new words and the combination of existing words in word-compound and in phrase'. Regularity in spelling and vocabulary, along with order in accidence and syntax, came in the approximate period, 1660–1800. 'In the 18th century, especially near the end, the influence of grammars and dictionaries made itself fully felt. Words admissible into literary use were registered with their meanings in dictionaries, which also more and more undertook to indicate the pronunciation. English grammar became a subject for school study, and conformity to the use authorized by dictionary and grammar became the test of [culture] in language.'

For more than 300 years the East Midland dialect, 'at first, no doubt, merely held to be the fashionable mode of speech, has gained in prestige, until at the present day, it is spreading all over [Great Britain], and among all classes' (Wyld, *The Growth of English*). This dialect has become Standard English: the criteria of that standard are the choice of words and phrases, the syntax, the pronunciation. Of Standard English as we know it in the 20th century, we may say that it 'is a kind of English which is tinged neither with the Northern, nor Midland, nor Southern peculiarities of speech [and] which gives no indication ... of where the speaker comes from. ... It is

the ambition of all educated persons in [Great Britain and Northern Ireland] to acquire this manner of speaking, and this is the form of our language which foreigners wish to learn' (*ibid.*).

But it is important to bear in mind that 'no form of language is, *in itself*, [originally] better than any other form. A dialect gains whatever place of superiority it enjoys solely from the estimation in which it is commonly held. It is natural that the language of the Court should come to be regarded as the most elegant and refined type of English, and that those who do not speak that dialect naturally' – that is, as birthright or as environmental training – 'should be at the pains of acquiring it. This is what has happened, and is still happening, to the dialect which is called Standard English' – although Standard English is to be no longer regarded as a dialect properly so called. [But see Note at the end of **DIALECT**.] 'Of course, since this form of English is used in the conversation of the refined, the brilliant and the learned, it has become a better instrument for the expression of ideas than any other [variety] of speech now spoken.'

'When', continues Professor Wyld, 'we speak of Good English, or Standard English, or Pure English, as distinct from ... Provincial English [the dialects proper], we must remember that there is nothing in the original nature of these ... dialects which is in itself inferior, or reprehensible, or contemptible. In a word, the other dialects are in reality and apart from fashion and custom, quite as good as Standard English [the same holds, of course, for Standard American in relation to American dialects], considered simply as forms of language; but they have not the same place in general estimation, they have not been so highly cultivated' (nor have they become so subtle and delicate), 'and they have not the same wide currency.'

II. STANDARD ENGLISH: DEGREES AND KINDS

There are, however, different kinds of Standard English: The best of these is

Received Standard,* for it fulfils all the requirements of good speech; Modified Standard is Standard English that differs from Received mainly in pronunciation; and Literary Standard lies beyond any matter of pronunciation, and is confined to written English – and should it be used in speech, it is too bookish to be Received.

Of Literary English – Literary Standard – it is necessary only to say that it is the more conventional, stylized, and dignified, more accurate and logical, sometimes the more beautiful form that Received Standard assumes, like evening dress, for important occasions; it is also more rhythmical and musical. The prose of Sir Thomas Browne, Gibbon, De Quincey, The Landors, Pater is in Literary English. With dialect, colloquialism, slang, cant, it has nothing to do unless they possess a long pedigree – and then only in rare instances.

What then of Received Standard and Modified Standard? 'It is proposed', says Wyld in his *A Short History of English*, 'to use the term *Received Standard* for that form which all would probably agree in considering the best, that form which has the widest currency and is heard with practically no variation among speakers of the better class all over the country. This type might be called Public School English.' (The stress here, you see, is on pronunciation and enunciation.) 'It is proposed to call the vulgar English of the Towns, and the English of the Villager who has abandoned his native Regional Dialect' – dialect in the ordinary sense of the term – '*Modified Standard*. That is, it is Standard English, modified, altered, differentiated, by various influences, regional and social. Modified Standard differs from class to class, and from locality to locality; it has no uniformity, and no single form of it is heard outside a particular class or a particular area.' Very obvious, as Professor Wyld

is the first to admit; very important, as he was the first to emphasize.

III. THE LIMITS OF PURE (or, RECEIVED STANDARD) ENGLISH*

There is a perhaps startling difference between pure English and the English spoken by the uncultured. In the American 'Them guys ain't got no pep' and the British 'Them blokes ain't got no go', not even a single word satisfies the standard exacted by pure English, whether American English or British English. In both versions, the first word (*them*) is ungrammatical (for 'these' or 'those'); the second is slang (for 'men'); the third (*ain't*) is illiterate; the fourth (*got*) is unnecessary – and colloquial; the fifth (*no*) is illogical, the sense demanding *any*; and the sixth (*pep*: *go*) is slang. Both versions are not merely uncultured but illiterate; yet the speech is straight from the shoulder, the meaning unmistakable.

There are, however, inestimable advantages to be obtained from uniformity of vocabulary and from regularity of syntax: that uniformity and that regularity do at least make understanding much easier: and communicability is the primary requisite of both speech and writing.

Since the 17th century, English has gained tremendously in precision. Language has not been evolved to be the sport of the illiterate, any more than to be the plaything of the highbrow or the chopping-block of the journalist. Language is a means – the chief means – of communication, not merely between two Chicago gangsters or two Soho toughs, but among all the members of a nation; internationally too. 'It is important that the language medium should offer as little as possible resistance to the thought current, and this end is attained only when the symbols of language are ones that convey precisely the same meaning to all who use the language.'

---

*'Received Standard' and 'Modified Standard' are Professor Wyld's designations, whereas 'Literary Standard' is a designation proposed – after due thought – by myself.

*In this section I draw heavily on G. H. McKnight's *English Words and Their Background*.

But we may raise a question concerning the degree to which a language can be healthily standardized. Too often are spoken British and spoken American English criticized as though it were impossible for them to have any laws of their own – a freedom not shackled at every turn by the rules explicit or implicit in Literary Standard.

A language cannot be at the same time entirely standardized and truly vital: a rigorously regimented language would die from stiffness of the joints and atrophy of the spirit. 'Ideas inherited from the past ... may find adequate expression in the idiom of the past. ... The shifting, developing forms assumed by living thought, however, demand the plastic medium of a living language.' It is only natural that new systems of thought and new modes of living should, by the very strength of their processes and by their widespread currency, generate new words, new compounds, new phrases, and even new modes of expression: in linguistics, as in politics, the will of the nation is all-powerful; it is of no use for the pedants to deplore and lament the misuses implicit in (say) *aggravating* or *the psychological moment*, for usage has consecrated the original errors and turned them into correct currency.

On this question of the limits of pure English (Received Standard), Logan Pearsall Smith, an American long resident in England, has, in 'Popular Speech and Standard English' (an admirable article to be read in full), in *Words and Idioms*, written as follows: 'Since our language seems to be growing year by year more foreign, abstract and colourless in character, it stands in greater need than ever of this vigorous and native reinforcement' which we could obtain from dialect in particular and popular speech in general. This reinforcement could be enlisted and fruitfully employed by all of us, 'were we not paralysed by that superstitious feeling of awe and respect for standard English [i.e. Received Standard] which is now [1925] spread by the diffusion of education'. We are enslaved by the tyrant Correctitude.

But why should Standard English have to resort to dialectal and popular speech for vitality and picturesqueness instead of drawing on its own resources? 'It is inevitable', Pearsall Smith continues, 'that when any form of speech becomes a standard and written language, it should as a consequence lose much of its linguistic freedom. All forms of speech have of course their rules and usages, but in a written language these rules and usages become much more settled and stereotyped': so that, finally, words and phrases are adjudged to be good or bad, not by their strength, clarity, and aptness of expression, but by the external criterion of correctness. 'Such an attitude ... tends ... to fix grammar and pronunciation, to discourage assimilation [of picturesque or vigorous outsiders], and to cripple the free and spontaneous powers of word-creation.' Then, too, 'a standard language, in modern conditions, tends to be rather a written than a spoken language. The printed word becomes more and more the reality, the spoken word an echo or [a] faint copy of it. This inversion of the normal relation between speech and writing, this predominance' – almost, tyranny – 'of the eye over the ear, of the written symbol over its audible' – i.e. spoken – 'equivalent, tends to deprive the language of that vigour and reality which comes, and can only come, from its intimate association with the acts and passions of men, as they vividly describe and express them in their speech.'

The foregoing, however, is not to be taken as an attack on, nor as a depreciation of, the *virtues and the advantages* of Standard English, for this, the accepted form of English, with its national scope and its national use, with its rich and varied vocabulary, with its often subtle and, for the most part, flexible syntax, with all the historical associations inevitably and naturally garnered in the course of centuries, and these and other associations enriched by successive generations, is the inestimably precious inheritance of the British people, as any such language is of any ancient people. The position of good (or pure) English is, in essentials, impregnable: for as it arises from, so does it serve, a social need. The danger lies, not in its being set aside (with the result of linguistic chaos, and hence of a lack of national unity), but in its being so unreflectingly and blindly respected that we may forget the very existence of popular speech and widespread colloquialism, of slang and dialect, and thus forget both their intrinsic value and their value as readily available sources of freshness and invigoration.

No standard language exists on its own capital; no standard language can thus exist – if it is to continue to be a language and not become a mausoleum. Standard English, sprung from a regional dialect, has never, for long, disregarded the other dialects, over which, by a geographical, political, and social accident, it has been exalted; those others have always had too much to offer in potential enrichment of the triumphant dialect. Like dialect, popular speech abounds in uncouth phrases and low words and absurd (or, at the least, hasty) perversions and inaccuracies; but it also abounds in vivid phrases, in racy and vigorous words, in strong monosyllables and picturesque compounds, and also in ancient words that have, unfortunately for us, dropped out of cultured speech. How useful, how valuable, how fitting it would be if many of these words and phrases were to be admitted, or re-admitted, to standard speech and were, in their turn, to become Received Standard, whence there would duly be expelled those learned terms which had become synonyms of these racier or stronger or more musical terms adopted from dialect and from the popular speech of the towns. Their adoption would not merely enrich but also improve the material stock, hence the cultural and spiritual value and potentialities, of Standard English, which they would strengthen and render less standardized.

'Human speech', as Pearsall Smith has remarked in that work which we have already quoted, 'is after all a democratic product, the creation, not of scholars and grammarians, but of ... unlettered people. Scholars and men of education may cultivate and enrich it, and make it flower into all the beauty of a literary language', but they should not, in their efforts to keep the language pure, forget that it should also be kept vigorous; they are too apt to forget that the 'rarest blooms are grafted on a wild stock, and [that] its roots are deep-buried in the common soil. From that soil it must still draw its sap and nourishment, if it is not to perish [from inanition], as the other standard languages of the past have perished, when ... they have been ... cut off from the popular vernacular.'

Nevertheless, as McKnight has excellently said in his excellent *Modern English in the Making*, 'the standardization of modern English is not as nearly complete as is sometimes supposed. The language ideal of philosophers like [Wilkins and] Locke has never been realized. Idealistic efforts ... have been only partially successful. The English language has not been subjected to absolute rule. ... In other words, English is not yet a dead language. ... "Law", said Roscoe Pound, "must be stable and yet cannot stand still." The statement applies with little modification to ... language. Language, though regulated, ... must change in company with changing conditions of life.'

Let us, therefore, have purity, so far as possible. But not to the detriment of raciness and vigour.

IV. WORLD ENGLISH

English is now a world language, spoken and written not only as a first language in the countries of the 'white' Commonwealth, but as a second language throughout the former British Empire and as a lingua franca elsewhere. World English follows one or other of the two great national standard varieties, the British and the American, with further national variations of pronunciation, grammar, and vocabulary; these being less in the case of, say, Canada and Australia and more in the second-language countries such as India and Nigeria. One must only hope that these variations will not drift so far away from the international Standard as to impede international communication.

V. STANDARD AMERICAN SPEECH AND WRITING

This is the other great national Standard variety of English.

In writing, there is an American Literary Standard, which so closely resembles British Literary Standard as to establish no basic, no important difference. But is there, in American speech, a Received Standard? Or is there nothing but a number of Modified Standards? One might, on first thought, say that there are only Modified Standards, although one might add that some of these modifications are more pleasing to the British ear or more widely used than others. But the fact remains that, although there is, in the United States, no speech that can be classified as Received Standard with the same feeling of certainty as Public School speech can be said to be Received Standard in Britain, yet the speech of the cultured elements of American society is as close to being a Received Standard as can be expected in so vast and many-peopled a land as the United States. That the criterion is neither so severe nor so rigid as that of British Received Standard does not make it any the less a genuine criterion.* But in America even more than in Great Britain, the speakers of Modified Standard are more numerous than the speakers of Received Standard.

It must, however, be remembered that the differentiation between Standard and popular speech, between Standard and slang, between slang and cant, is, on the whole, less marked in the United States than in Britain. For further discussion, see **BRITISH AND AMERICAN USAGE**.

standpoint, point of view; viewpoint; angle and **slant**. The first is a blameless variant of the second, whether literal or

figurative. *Viewpoint*, however, though admitted (without comment) by *OED*, has been deprecated by purists; not being a purist, I occasionally use it, although I perceive that it is unnecessary.

Angle, modern and permissible, is not to be used to the exclusion of *standpoint*; Americans tend to overdo *slant* in the figurative sense ('mental point of view') but in Britain it has not yet been acclimatized.

Point of view (etc.) is used unnecessarily in 'From the studying point of view, the book is excellent.' Perhaps 'For study, the book is excellent.'

stanza. See at **verse.**

starlight and **starlit**. The former is a noun, and attributively an adjective ('a starlight night'); *starlit* is only an adjective ('a starlit night'). *Starlit* = 'lit up, or lighted, by the stars' ('The whole of the starlit sky', Proctor), and so does *starlight* ('A starlight evening, and a morning fair', Dryden): in this sense, *starlit* is to be preferred. But in the transferred sense, 'bright as the stars', only *starlight* is used, as in 'starlight eyes' (based on *OED*).

start for *begin* is familiar – not literary – English, whether it is used transitively or intransitively; but where either verb will fit, *begin* is better, 'That story begins on page 79' being superior to '... starts on page 79'. (One can only, of course *start* a fire or an engine.) To *start in* to do some-- thing is an American colloquialism for 'to start [preferably *begin*] to do something'.

state (n.). See **edition**. In the sense 'alarm, fuss, anxiety, distraction', it is a colloquialism.

state and **say**. *State*, being much stronger than *say*, should be reserved for formal or impressive contexts. 'I wish to state that I like fish' is an absurd overstatement.

state-of-the-art. See **VOGUE WORDS**.

stately is now rare as an adverb; so is *statelily*. *In a stately manner* is the locution sanctified by usage.

States, the. See **America.**

---

*The best account of American pronunciation is Professor Kenyon's admirable 'Guide to Pronunciation', *Webster's New International Dictionary*, Third Edition.

statesman. See **politician and statesman.**

stationary is the adjective ('static; not moving'); *stationery*, the noun ('writing materials').

statute and **statue** are occasionally confused by the ignorant. A *statute* is a (formally enacted) law.

staunch. See **stanch.**

staves. See **staff.**

stay, in Law = 'to delay', 'to arrest (an action) for the time being' – not 'to put an end to'.

stayed. See **staid and stayed.**

steal, 'a theft', 'something stolen', 'a corrupt transaction or a fraudulent one,' is an American and Canadian colloquialism.

sticker and **stickler.** A *sticker* is a person constant to a cause or persistent (or persevering) in a task, whereas a *stickler* (for something) is a pertinacious contender for, or supporter or advocate of, a cause or a principle, a person or a party, also one who insists on the letter as opposed to the spirit of, e.g. a form of ceremony, a custom or habit.

still more yet is redundant for *still more* or *yet more*, as in 'Still more yet is to be said for a strong defensive force.' *Still* (or *yet*) *more* is an intensive of *more* and should not be used unless an intensive is required.

stimulant and **stimulus.** *Stimulant,* in medicine and physiology, is 'something that temporarily quickens some vital process, or the function of some organ', as in 'The abuse of stimulants, in the form of alcohol, tobacco, tea, and coffee'; hence, in general use, 'alcohol; an alcoholic drink', as in 'In one of his many serious illnesses he refused all stimulants' (A. C. Benson, concerning Archbishop Benson). *Stimulus* is a medical synonym of the medical sense of *stimulant,* and also, in medicine, it = 'the resulting stimulation'; in general use it is 'an agency or influence that stimulates [or excites] to action or that

quickens an activity or process'; hence, 'a quickening impulse or influence' (as in 'Difficulty is a stimulus'). Plural, *stimuli* (*OED*).

sting – stung (archaic and dialectal: **stang) – stung.**

stingy and **economical.** An *economical* person is careful of his money, but when occasion calls for liberality he may be generous; a *stingy* person is one who, too careful of his money, is always niggardly.

stipend should be reserved for magistrates and clergymen.

stolidity. See at **solidity.**

stomach. See **belly.**

stop in the sense of *stay, remain, sojourn* (at a place or with a friend), though general, is strictly a misuse of the word; *OED* allows it, only cautiously saying that *stay* 'is more correct'. *Stop* (or *stop off* or *stop over*) is, however, correctly used for a short break in a journey.

STOPS. See PUNCTUATION.

storey and **story.** In British usage it is possible and useful to reserve *story* for 'a narrative', *storey* for 'a set of rooms on (or one large room constituting) one floor or level': this is merely a matter of convenience, for etymologically *storey* is a mere variant of *story.* The use of *storey* is to be recommended on the score of clarity: 'the story of a story' is readily distinguishable from 'the story of a storey'; consider, too, 'the storey in this story is the fifth'. See also **floor and storey.** [In American English the spelling *storey* for *story* is exceedingly rare.]

strait, 'narrow, constricted', is occasionally confused with *straight,* 'direct, unswerving'.

strata is a plural ('layers') and should not be used as a singular, the correct singular being *stratum.* 'Woman, from her childhood, except perhaps in that strata of society which has divorced itself from the common cause of mankind, is ever the mother' (Graham Seton, *The K Code Plan*). 'A little learning ...': in a powerful and almost intolerably moving novel published in 1945, occurs the very odd plural *stratae*. *Data* (singular *datum*) is occasionally misused in the same way. [*Webster's* notes that *data* is 'not infrequently used as a singular'; it brings no such comfort, however, to the users of *strata* as a singular, and for good reason. It is important to distinguish one stratum from another; but *data* is usually collective.]

stratosphere. See **troposphere.**

stricken. See following entry.

strike – struck – struck (archaic, **stricken).** But *stricken* as a participial adjective is actively extant in *a stricken deer* (wounded in the chase); in the science of percussion, it = 'struck with a blow'; in music, *a stricken note* is one produced by striking a blow; *fever-stricken, poverty-stricken, sorrow-stricken*; in the sense of '(mind, heart) afflicted with frenzy or madness'; jocularly *love-stricken* (*maiden* or *swain*); *stricken measure* (a measure 'having its contents levelled with the brim'); and *stricken field*, 'a pitched battle' (*not* a ravaged field); a rare variant is *stricken battle*. The archaism *stricken hour* means a full hour (from one hour-striking to the next).

string – strung (dialectal or solecistic, **strang) – strung** (except as in next entry).

stringed, not *strung*, is the participial adjective to be used

(*a*) of musical instruments ('wind and stringed orchestras'); hence it = 'produced by strings or stringed instruments' (stringed music);

(*b*) in heraldry;

(*c*) and of a running-track divided into 'lanes'.

strive – strove – striven (solecistic: **strove).** [American English has the variant *strived*.]

STRONG VERBS. See **IRREGULAR VERBS.**

student. See **pupil.**

studio and **study.** A *study* is a room in which a student or a scholar studies or works, or a room in which a writer writes, whereas a *studio* is the work-room of a painter or a sculptor – or of a photographer; hence in cinematography, a room in which films are staged; in radio and television, a room in which items to be broadcast are produced; and a room in which recordings are made.

stupid person. See at **moron.** – By the way, the noun *stupid* (for a *stupid person*) is a colloquialism, as *silly* is for a *silly person*.

STYLE.

Le style, c'est l'homme même.

(Buffon)

An aesthetic discussion of style would be out of place in this book. Moreover, many of the practical questions of style are dealt with elsewhere: especially on the positive side, at **SUITABILITY** and, on the negative side, at **WOOLLINESS**. Particular aspects are treated here; for instance, the use of the **SUBJUNCTIVE,** **FALSE AGREEMENT, ARCHAISMS, AMBIGUITY, COLLOQUIALISMS** and **DIALECT** and **SLANG, CLICHÉ, CONFUSED PARTICIPLES** and **FUSED PARTICIPLES, ELEGANCIES, GRAMMAR AND LOGIC, JARGON, LITERARISMS, METAPHOR, NEGATION, OBSCURITY, ORDER, PRECIOUSNESS, PUNCTUATION, RHETORIC, SIMPLICITY, SOUND AND SENSE, STANDARD ENGLISH, SIMILES (BATTERED), SYNONYMS, TAUTOLOGY, TENSE-SEQUENCE.**

But it may be well to recall to the aspirant writer's as to the student's and even the critic's mind, the too often forgotten fact that style is not something that one assumes on special occasions (like dress clothes), but that which one *is* when one writes; so far from being compelled to seek it, one cannot avoid it.

In writing, hence in style, the primary consideration is comprehensibility –

therefore clarity; one's first duty is to make oneself understood.

The second is to be adequate to one's theme: the style should be thoroughly suitable to the subject.

The third, which is partly implied in the second, is to write well: forcibly when force is required; beautifully when loveliness is to be described or conveyed; concisely when concision is necessary or, at the least, advisable.

(When, in 1938, G. M. Young wrote in *The Observer*, 'Good writing is the most efficient mode of communicating in words made visible', he gave 'too bare a definition of literary style in general' as Frank Whitaker remarked in the *JJJ*, January 1939.)

'Without distinction of speech', says Frank Binder,* 'there is never much distinction of idea, and therefore it need hardly be said that in no age have men so striven [as in the 20th century] to be different and yet so frantically failed to be anything but the same. That the style is the man, we know, but this is one of those unfortunate truths which have the licence of all lips and the hospitality of few hearts, and whilst everyone is sighing for personality in others, he shuns the labour of attaining it for himself. He is pleased with such facility as he has, the facility that comes not of power but of habit, the averaging habit of familiar fluency and of the practised drumming of ordinary ideas. And the thinner the fluid the faster the flow.'

Here is a very brief list of *some* of the more important books on style.

Walter Pater: *Appreciations* (with an essay on style), 1889.

John Addington Symonds: 'Notes on Style' in *Essays, Speculative and Suggestive*, 1890.

Herbert Spencer: *The Philosophy of Style*, edited by Fred Newton Scott, 1895.

Walter Raleigh: *Style*, 1897; very strongly recommended.

Remy de Gourmont: *Le Problème littéraire*, 1902.

Robert Louis Stevenson: *Essays on the Art of Writing*, 1905.

Sir A. Quiller-Couch: *On the Art of Writing*, 1916.

Fred Newton Scott: *Contributions to Rhetorical Theory*, 1918 and after.

J. Middleton Murry: *The Problem of Style*, 1922.

Vernon Lee: *The Handling of Words*, 1923.

Joseph Warren Beach: *The Outlook for American Prose*, 1926.

Herbert Read: *English Prose Style*, 1928.

John Brophy: *English Prose*, 1932.

F. Duchiez & P. C. Jagot: *L'Éducation du style*, 1934.

Bonamy Dobrée: *Modern Prose Style*, 1934.

S. P. B. Mais: *The Fun of Writing*, 1937.*

Eric Partridge: chapter on style in Book III of *English: A Course for Human Beings*, 1948.

G. H. Vallins, *Good English, Better English, The Best English*, in the enlarged editions published in The Language Library: 1952, 1955, 1957.

Of this list, it can at least be said that every one of these works will be found to contain matter useful to the student of style, to the writer, to the critic, no matter how experienced or inexperienced, how conceited or how humble, he or she may be.

For those who wish to know something of the history of English Prose, without having to wade through ponderous tomes, an excellent book is George Philip Krapp's *The Rise of English Literary Prose*.

(For the practical side, see COMPOSITION. And for a link between the practical and the theoretical side, consult that notable book, Sir Herbert Grierson's *Rhetoric and English Composition*.)

subconscious. See **unconscious and subconscious.**

---

*In his remarkable (and remarkably unknown) *Dialectic*, pp. 21–2.

*A book for young people.

subject (n.). In 'Roberts shared in all the contraband – many and various in subject – that Smith managed to get hold of' (George Ingram, *Stir*), *subject* is misused for *kind*, *sort*. See also **topic**.

subject (v.) is occasionally used catachrestically for *subordinate*, as in '[Newspaper] editors must subject their personal interests to the interests of the community.'

subject to and **addicted to.** *Subject to* = liable to (a disease); liable to the recurrence (or merely the incidence) of an action, a process, a state or condition; exposed to, open to, liable to suffer from something damaging, harmful, disadvantageous, e.g. peril, violent treatment, bad weather, etc.: as in 'subject to social disadvantages', 'subject to insolence', 'subject to earthquakes', 'subject to epileptic fits', 'subject to exception', 'subject to personal examination'. The noun is *subject*, as in 'The poor fellow is an epileptic subject'. But *addicted to* is 'given to a harmful practice or an evil habit' (*addicted to drugs*, *addicted to alcohol*); the noun is *addict*, as in 'He is a drug addict.'

subjective. See VOGUE WORDS.

SUBJUNCTIVE. The whole vexed question of the subjunctive mood has been admirably posited and explained by Dr C. T. Onions in *An Advanced English Syntax*. That most lucid and, in the best sense, methodical grammarian gives the history of the subjunctive – a subject that would be extraneous here. But on his exposition of the nature and the uses of the subjunctive rests the whole of the following article.

'The Subjunctive is a Mood of *Will*; in its simplest uses it expresses *desire*, and all its uses can be traced to this primary meaning.'

In modern English, especially from the middle of the 17th century, the subjunctive is much less used than formerly – much less, too, than in many of the other European languages. In short, the English subjunctive is, and has long been, in a state

of decay:* partly because the English people has become increasingly careless of distinctions of thought; partly because, in subordinate clauses, *may*, *might*, *shall*, *should* have been increasingly substituted for the true or simple subjunctive. For example, *lest he die* has, for the most part, been supplanted by *lest he may die* or *lest he should die*. Actually, these modal auxiliary words (*may*, *should*, etc.) are subjunctive in origin.

But, although it is freely admitted that the use of the subjunctive has been restricted and even, in its survivals, modified, it is foolish 'to say (as is sometimes said) that the Subjunctive, except in the case of *be* and *were*, is an extinct Mood. ... A careful examination of both the [spoken] and the literary language shows that the Subjunctive is really a living Mood, and that it can never become extinct without an entire reconstruction of certain classes of sentences,· e.g. the Conditional sentences [of Group II at CONDITIONAL CLAUSES]. In these sentences we have the Past Subjunctive referring not to Past time but to Present or to Future time, which a Past Indicative could not do', as in '*Were* my brave son at home, he *would* not suffer this' (Present) and in 'If he *were* to do this (or, If he *did* this), he would sin' (Future).

Except in certain forms (e.g. *be* and *were*), the subjunctive has been *disguised*: that which, by itself, appears to be an Indicative, may, from the context, emerge clearly as a subjunctive: to the test of form and inflection must be added the test of *meaning*.

Here is a test of Mood: In 'It is necessary that I remain here', *remain* is subjunc-

*In *We Who Speak English* Professor C. A. Lloyd discusses 'the living subjunctive' and the contemporary use of the present subjunctive in substantive clauses after *beg*, *command*, *arrange*, *ask*, *warn*, *insist*, *suggest*, etc. This usage is not noticed by Jespersen or Fowler, and it seems to be an American phenomenon, though, as Professor Lloyd reports, Fowler himself uses it in the article on *foam*, *froth* (*Modern English Usage*): 'One demands of foam that it *be* white.'

tive because we can also say 'It is necessary that he *remain* here.' In 'I wish I had a violin', *had* is subjunctive because we could change the sentence to 'I wish it *were* possible for me to have a violin.'

The most important point, for practical purposes, is the uses of the subjunctive; the most difficult point is the correct tense to employ.

Let us examine the uses of the subjunctive, *A*, in simple sentences and the principal clauses of complex sentences, and *B*, in subordinate clauses.

A. In *Simple Sentences and Principal Clauses* the subjunctive is used to express 'a wish or request that something may be', as in 'God *bless* you' and 'So *be* it'; or a concession, as in '*Be* that as it may ...' These subjunctival wishes and concessions are confined to the present tense.

Also 'in the principal clause of conditional sentences implying a negative', as in 'I *would* not say, even if I knew' and 'Had we done it, we *should* have let you know.' It is worth remembering that the only verbs so used are *could*, *would*, *should*, *might*, and *must*, although in poetry and poetic prose two others are permitted – *were* (= would be) and *had* (= would have), as in 'If thou hadst been here, my brother *had* not died' (the Bible).

So, too, where the *if*-clause has been omitted, as in 'I *should* like to go' (i.e. if I could), 'How *would* you express it?' (i.e. if you were asked), and 'Anyone *might* see that he is not well' (i.e. if he looked).

B. In *Subordinate Clauses* the uses of the subjunctive are more numerous – as might be expected.

i. In conditional sentences of Group II; the tense is either the past or the pluperfect. See **CONDITIONAL CLAUSES**.

ii. In clauses introduced by *if* or *though* subordinated to *as* or *then* representing a comparative clause, as in 'I feel as if I *were* going to fall.' See **as if**, and **was or were**.

iii. In conditional sentences of Group III, 'where the Subjunctive implies *reserve*, or is *restrictive*', as in 'If it *be* so ...'. See **CONDITIONAL CLAUSES**.

iv. In noun clauses, depending on a verb of *will* or *request*. This is usual in statutes and notices. 'It is requested that letters to the Editor *be* written on one side of the paper only'; 'The regulation is that no candidate *take* a book into the examination room.' Also 'It was requested ... *should be* written ...'; 'The regulation was that ... *should take* ...', though even here the present subjunctive is more common, this present-for-past-subjunctive being a hallmark of officialese.

In noun clauses dependent on '*it is right* (or *not right*), *it is wrong*, *it is necessary*, *it is not possible*, and *is it possible?* as in 'It is right (or, not right; or, is it right?) that you *be* dismissed', 'It is necessary that he *go*.' Note, however, that the simple subjunctive is less usual than a subjunctive-equivalent, as in 'It is right (etc.) that he *should* be dismissed' and 'Is it necessary that he *should go*?' After *is it possible?* and *it is impossible* the subjunctive-equivalent, as in 'Is it possible that he *should be* such a fool?', is almost obligatory, for 'Is it possible that he *be* such a fool?' is intolerably archaic and 'It is impossible that he *be* such a fool' is almost intolerable. Where, however, 'is it possible?' is merely exclamatory, the indicative is obligatory, as in 'Is it possible that he *has* left England?'

In noun clauses dependent on *wish* and the archaic *would*, to indicate the object of the wish, as in 'I wish I *were* there' or 'had been there' or 'could have been there'; and in '*Would* that he *had* lived', where *would* = *I would*.

In noun clauses dependent on a verb of emotion, 'where the speaker contemplates the *thought* of something happening rather than its actually happening'; not the simple subjunctive but the *should*-equivalent is used here. 'I grieved that you *should* be so angry'; 'It cannot be wondered at that he *should* have been so anxious'; 'That he has acted thus is a misfortune, but that he *should* have acted thus is not surprising.'

v. In temporal clauses (clauses of time) of a certain type, i.e. when the action of the Temporal Clause is prospective; or, in other words, when the temporal clause refers to the future, whether from a present or from a past viewpoint. The simple subjunctive is now confined to poetry and poetic or, at the least, lofty prose, as in 'This night, before the cock *crow*, thou shalt deny me thrice' and 'The sun a backward course shall take ere aught thy manly courage *shake*.' But the *shall* and *should* equivalents – in which, by the way, it is *shall* or *should* in all persons and both numbers – are common in ordinary good prose as well as in lofty prose, as in 'When his eyesight *shall fail*, he will apply for a pension' and 'He decided to wait until the car *should pass* him'; here too, however, the indicative is fast becoming more usual, as in 'He decided to wait until the car passed him.' Perhaps I should have written 'apparent indicative', for is not *passed* a virtual subjunctive in this sentence, whereas it is indubitably indicative in 'He decided to wait – until the car passed him. The car's passing made him immediately change his mind, and he walked hurriedly on.' It is obvious that the discarding of the subjunctive in such temporal clauses as these would lead to ambiguity.

In vi–ix, which follow this interpolated paragraph, the subjunctive is archaic except in poetry and in poetic and other lofty prose. A good case for its retention could be argued in every instance; after all, there is no good reason why the English language should be reduced to the level of the gangster and the professional thief, the half-wit and the nit-wit; they get quite enough of their own way as it is!

vi. In final clauses (clauses of purpose) introduced by *lest*:

Lord God of Hosts, be with us yet,
Lest we *forget*, lest we *forget*

(Kipling);

the *forget* would still have been *forget*, i.e. a subjunctive, had that sinewy Imperialist been prophetically speaking of (say) the Fuchrer:

Lord God of Hosts, be with him yet,
Lest he *forget*, lest he *forget*.

vii. In concession clauses:

'Though he *do* his best, his best is bad';
'Try as he *might*, he failed'.

viii. In general relative clauses, especially in the past:

Calm, but not overcast, he stood
Resigned to the decree, whatever it *were*,

(Byron)

where it would now be avoided even in poetry: Bacon's 'However it *be* between nations, certainly it is so between man and man' is archaic, though not ludicrously so, but if we change his sentence, to 'However it *may* be ... certainly ...' we get an effect of good prose, not necessarily poetic nor even literary; the substitution of the subjunctive-equivalent for the simple subjunctive has made all the difference, as indeed it would in a general relative clause in the past tense: change Byron's two verses to prose and you get 'He stood calm, but not overcast: resigned to the verdict, whatever it *might be*', which is ordinary good prose – certainly not poetic nor (except in sentiment) lofty.

ix. In dependent questions:
'All men mused [= wondered] whether he *were* Christ' (the Bible); 'Even those who had often seen him were at first in doubt whether he *were* the brilliant and graceful Monmouth' (Macaulay).

(Note how feeble would have been the catachrestic *if* in these two examples; see **if for whether**.)

TENSES OF THE SUBJUNCTIVE. In the subjunctive, as in the indicative, the tenses are those which conform to that general and invaluable principle which is known as the sequence of tenses. This applies also to the 'modal auxiliary' subjunctive-equivalents *may*, *might*, *shall*, *should*. See TENSE-SEQUENCE.

'I have told you that you *may* know';
'The headmaster said that we *might* have a holiday';

'He took care that his form master *should* not see him';

'If you *did* it [either now or in the future], you *would* repent it' (either now or in the future);

'She looked as though she *were* fainting.'

There are, of the subjunctive, at least two forms that seem to be rather too 'refayned' for my simple taste: *I could wish* for *I wish*, as in 'I could wish that he had written a better book'; and *it were to be wished* for *it is to be wished*, as in 'It were to be wished that princes would lay aside their ambitious projects.' In this matter, it is to be remembered that the objection is being made to positive, unconditional statements, which require nothing more subtle than an indicative. Used correctly, *I could wish* refers to a wishing in past time, *could* being the past of *can*; correctly used, *it were to be wished* can occur only in subordinate clauses – e.g. 'He gently inquired whether it were to be wished that the wretched men should suffer so undignified a death', and even that is a trifle clumsy for 'whether it were desirable'.

Two errors of the same kind are made in the following sentence from John G. Brandon's *The Mail-Van Mystery*: 'The thing that struck "the Wallflower" most, was the air of furtivity [it should be *furtiveness*] with which the newcomer glanced here, there and everywhere, as though he might be fearing [i.e. as though he feared] that some entirely unwelcome person might pounce [? would pounce] out upon him from any corner at any moment.'

[Note. Since the above was written there seems to have been some increase in the use of the 'true' subjunctive, spearheaded by American practice. An American writer may well prefer 'It is necessary that he go', where British usage might choose the subjunctive-equivalent '... that he should go'. American style allows this even in the negative, which sounds odd in British ears, as in 'He took care that his form master not see him.']

sublime, sublimated; subliminal. Of these three terms, the first is the only one now in general as distinguished from psychological use. *Sublime* = 'elevated, lofty, exalted', literally and figuratively; hence 'supreme', 'perfect'; in literature and aesthetics, it = 'apt or designed to inspire awe, deep reverence, lofty emotion, by beauty or grandeur'. *Sublimated* in the sense 'lofty, sublime', is obsolescent: better discard it! In chemistry, it = 'produced by the process of sublimation'; in psychology, it = (of a primitive impulse) 'modified and adapted, especially to the needs of civilization', as in *sublimated sex, sublimated savagery*. *Subliminal* is also a psychological term; it = 'below the threshold of sensation or consciousness, pertaining to the subliminal self', as in *subliminal consciousness*, and is now used particularly of television advertising designed to influence the viewer subconsciously. The corresponding nouns are *sublimity* or *the sublime; sublimation; a* or *the subliminal*.

Note that in *sublime* and *sublimated*, the etymology is *sub*, 'up to', and *limen*, 'the head-piece or lintel'; but in *subliminal, sub* = 'below' and *limen* = 'foot-piece or threshold'.

submittance is obsolete for *submission*.

subnormal. See **abnormal.**

subsequent. See **consequent.**

subsequent to = *after*. (Officialese.)

subsist. See **exist.**

substantial and **substantive.** Apart from technical senses, these terms are synonymous except in the following senses of *substantial*: real or true in the main ('On the whole, substantial justice had been done'); of real worth, repute, reliability ('The substantial intellect of the country'); (of persons) wealthy, weighty, influential ('A substantial Scottish grazier'); (of structures) made of solid material, of good workmanship ('a substantial house'); (of food) very nutritious, (of a meal) solid. And except in these senses of *substantive*: (Of persons, nations, groups, or associations of persons) independent ('substantive inventors'); not transitory ('Let us call the resting-places the "substantive parts", and the places of flight the "transitive parts", of the stream of thought', Wm James). The chief senses in which *substantial* and *substantive* are synonymous are: Material or essential; not imaginary, not illusory, i.e. real; having a firm basis, solidly established; of considerable amount or quantity, valuable or effective because of large numbers (*OED*).

Don't use *substantial* where *big* or *large* would do.

substitute, misused. 'He must substitute sugar by saccharin' should be 'He must substitute saccharin for sugar.'

substract is a surprisingly common error for *subtract*. *Subtract* and *detract* are occasionally confused. Both mean to deduct, but *detract* is applied only to virtue, reputation, status (see **detract**), *subtract* is rare in a figurative sense, George Eliot's 'The transient pink flush ... subtracted nothing from her majesty' now seeming slightly obsolescent; indeed, *subtract* is, in current usage, confined – or virtually confined – to mathematics.

succeed and **follow** are not synonymous; the latter having usually 'a literal and physical sense' and being applicable 'to many persons or things at the same time' ('A thousand sheep followed the bell-wether'); *succeed* 'usually means to come next after and take the place of. It implies only two individuals', or two groups or bodies viewed as units, in 'Haig succeeded French', 'Winter succeeds autumn', 'A Conservative government succeeds a Labour one', 'An eldest son succeeds his father.'

successively and **successfully** are sometimes confused. The latter = 'with success', the former = 'in succession', 'consecutively'.

succubus and **incubus.** A *succubus* is a female demon supposed to have sexual intercourse with men in their sleep; hence, a demon or evil spirit or, metaphorically, a whore; *succuba*, a variant, is rare. Etymo-

logically, 'a person lying *under* another'. An *incubus* is a male demon that seeks sexual intercourse with women in their sleep; hence, a nightmare; hence, a person or thing that oppresses one as does a nightmare. Etymologically, 'a person lying *on* another'.

such is pompous for *any* or *any such* or *this* or *that* (or *these* or *those*). 'For the sake of verisimilitude the scenes of this story have been laid in real places. All the characters introduced, however, are wholly imaginary, and if the name of any living person has been used, this has been done inadvertently and no reference to such person is intended' (author's note to *The Loss of the Jane Vosper*, F. W. Crofts); 'Of the Roman's earthworks, if such were made, no traces remain' (Francis Brett Young, *This Little World*). 'No unauthorized objects or materials could ... have been included. He wished to take strong exception to the suggestion that such might have occurred' (F. W. Crofts, *The Loss of the Jane Vosper*).

such for *of them*. This odd misusage occurs in Carolyn Wells's *The Clue of the Eyelash*; ' "Will you suggest some names as possibilities?" – "No, there are too many such." '

such for *similar* should be used with caution.

such for *so* (pronoun). *The New Statesman and Nation* of 5 Feb. 1938, quotes from a Selfridge advertisement written by a public school member of the staff; it ends thus: 'With this being such he will always be an ever-awake and useful member of society.'

such may correctly mean 'such people', as in 'He was the father of such as dwell in tents' (Gen. iv. 20), but it is not to be used in the singular for *some one*. ' "Can you suggest ... anyone who wished his death?" – "Mercy, no!" "Yet there must have been such. Somebody killed him" ' (Carolyn Wells).

such for *such part* or *so much* is infelicitous. 'His eyes ran quickly over such of the interior ... as they could reach' (John G. Brandon, *The Mail-Van Mystery*). 'Then he mooched to another window and surveyed such as was to be seen of the rear of the place from that point' (John G. Brandon, *The Pawnshop Murder*).

such is either commercial or colloquial for *such things*. '... Cabalistic figures ... French kept all such, though he doubted they would be helpful' (Nigel Morland, *The Conquest of Crime*); also, 'They [500 petrol-electric sets] were to be larger than such are usually made', *ibid.*; Arthur Bryant, *The Illustrated London News*, 5 March 1938, 'We had seen enough of the folly of complete strangers maiming and slaughtering each other under conditions of extreme discomfort and degradation for the sake of national honour and glory. Like Old Caspar, we had come to recognize from bitter experience, that no good ever came of such.' Bryant so often uses 'such' in this manner that he would no doubt defend it; but brevity is its only merit.

such (or **such a**) for *very* should not be overdone; 'Such charming people!', 'Such a bright boy.' Not a colloquialism, but familiar English.

such, none. See **none such.**

such a much. 'That is why ... Rugby is such a much better game than Association' (Wodehouse, *A Prefect's Uncle*) is ugly; 'She was going to copy her stepfather, who was such a much smarter proposition than her own father' (Ernest Raymond, *The Marsh*), where 'So very much smarter a proposition' would be a way of getting round it.

such as for *as, for example* or *for instance* means 'of a kind that', not 'in the way that'. *Such* should be deleted in the following: 'When the resistance to the complex is weakened, such as in sleep, the complexes may reappear' (Isador Coriat, *The Hysteria of Lady Macbeth*). 'The same language may predominate over a very large area, such as the English language predominates in England.'

such ... that is not to be used for *such ... as*. 'He was even allowed to dust such objects of the precious collection that were not kept under glass' (Wilfranc Hubbard, *Orvieto Dust*). Cf. the next entry.

such ... which (or who) is incorrect for *such as*. 'Such trifling variations which make [Portuguese] be a mere dialect of [Spanish]', for '*such ... as*' (Letter in *The Observer*, 29 Aug. 1937); '[She had] a real compassion for such cases of hardship which were clamped [? clumped] down under her eyes' (Ethel Lina White, *The Wheel Spins*); 'Such of my acquaintances who care to submit themselves ...' (John Rhode, *The Hanging Woman*); 'The very fact that they lived in an enclosed intimacy not to be found in any ordinary road is sufficient to exaggerate such small annoyances and dissensions which from time to time arise' (John Bude, *The Cheltenham Square Murder*). The mistake probably arises from a confusion with *those ... which*. Cf. **such ... that.**

suffer with for *suffer from* a disease or disability is bad English; the 'suffering' is caused by and derived *from* the disease.

sufferance; suffering. The former is archaic as a synonym of the latter noun. Except for a legal sense, *sufferance* is extant only as = 'acquiescence, consent, sanction, permission, toleration', and mostly in the phrase *on sufferance*; 'He is on sufferance', 'liberty on sufferance', 'a Cabinet on sufferance', 'to woo on sufferance' (*OED*).

sufficient and **enough.** The main difference between them as adjectives is that, before a noun, *enough* takes no article; *sufficient* does take one, or omits it, according to the context ('a sufficient income' but 'sufficient money'). The adverbs are *sufficiently* and *enough*; noun is *enough*; *COD* does not recognize *sufficient* as a noun at all. It is, at any rate, an unnecessary ELEGANCY in 'Sufficient has been done for pride; now let us think of comfort'; 'We saw sufficient to account for the noise.' *Sufficience* is archaic; *sufficiency*, which generally takes an article (except in the sense 'adequate provision of food; adequate bodily comfort'), has three main senses: A competence ('to retire on a sufficiency'), though this is obsolescent; adequacy ('to report on the sufficiency of an examination candidate's work'); enough ('a sufficiency of wood for fuel') (*OED*). See also COMPARATIVES, FALSE.

suffragette; suffragist. The former is − or rather, was − a rabid female supporter of female suffrage (votes for women); the latter is merely any supporter (not necessarily violent or militant) of female suffrage.

suggested plan; suggestive plan. The former has been suggested by someone; the latter is 'a stimulating plan'. *Suggestive*, in this sense, is applied also to remedies.

SUITABILITY AND ADEQUACY. *Ingenium par materiae* (ability equal to one's theme).

To write satisfactorily on the subject of suitability and adequacy would be to write a treatise on style: and obviously that cannot be done here.

Broadly, adequacy* is such treatment of a theme as is felt to be not only and merely in keeping (i.e. suitable) but also worthy of it − fully worthy of it, no matter how profound, moving, subtle, or lovely the theme. To be adequate, therefore, is more than to be suitable; one may have − or adopt − a style suitable to a subject and yet one may prove to be unequal to that subject. One's conception may be excellent, but one's execution may be faulty: the road to style is paved with good intentions. Style must be clear, effective, aesthetically and emotionally adequate.

Here, more than anywhere else, practice is better than precept. And so I give a certain number of passages in which the manner suits the matter and the style is adequate to the theme. But first, one brief example on the negative side: 'And the place thereof was unknown. ... It is an

*I use the word, not as = bare adequacy (cf. the common phrase, 'barely adequate'), but as = complete adequacy.

astonishing commentary on the way man had been born and then cut down so much like grass that weeds had been his only memorial − till some explorer came along' (Violet O. Cressy-Marcks, *Up the Amazon and Over the Andes*). The inadequacy of 'came along' is pathetic; such triviality of language is one of the commonest sorts of inadequacy.

(The ensuing examples of adequacy on the positive side have been taken from Sir Arthur Quiller-Couch's *The Oxford Book of English Prose*.)

'Let us now praise famous men, and our fathers that begat us. The Lord hath wrought great glory by them, through his great power from the beginning. Such as did bear rule in their kingdoms, men renowned for their power, giving counsel by their understanding, and declaring prophecies; leaders of the people by their counsels, and by their knowledge of learning meet for the people, wise and eloquent in their instructions. Such as found out musical tunes, and recited verses in writing. Rich men furnished with ability, living peaceably in their habitations. All these were honoured in their generations, and were the glory of their times. There be of them, that have left a name behind them, that their praises might be reported. And some there be, which have no memorial, who are perished as though they had never been, and are become as though they had never been born, and their children after them. But these were merciful men, whose righteousness hath not been forgotten. With their seed shall remain a good inheritance, and their children are within the covenant. Their seed stands fast, and their children for their sakes. Their seed shall remain for ever, and their glory shall not be blotted out. Their bodies are buried in peace, but their name liveth for evermore.'

Ecclesiasticus
(Authorized Version, 1611)

That is a rhetorical style, drawing much of its beauty and effectiveness from rhythm, sense-repetition, word-repetition. Contrast it with:

'All the powder of the *Revenge* to the last barrel was now spent, all her pikes broken, forty of her best men slain, and the most part of the rest hurt. In the beginning of the fight she had but one hundred free from sickness, and fourscore and ten sick, laid in hold upon the ballast. A small troop to man such a ship, and a weak garrison to resist so mighty an army. By those hundred all was sustained, the volleys, boardings, and enterings of fifteen ships of war, besides those which beat her at large. On the contrary, the Spanish were always supplied with soldiers brought from every squadron: all manner of arms and powder at will. Unto ours there remained no comfort at all, no hope, no supply either of ships, men, or weapons; the masts all beaten overboard, all her tackle cut asunder, her upper work altogether razed, and in effect evened she was with the water, but the very foundation or bottom of a ship, nothing being left overhead either for flight or defence, Sir Richard, finding himself in this distress, and unable any longer to make resistance ...; and that himself and the ship must needs be possessed by the enemy ...; commanded the master gunner, whom he knew to be a most resolute man, to split and sink the ship; that thereby nothing might remain of glory or victory to the Spaniards ...'

(Sir Walter Raleigh, The Last Fight of the Revenge, from a Report, published in 1591.)

With this plain prose compare the following passage on death from Raleigh's *A History of the World*, 1614, concerning 'the kings and princes of the world':

'They neglect the advice of God while they enjoy life, or hope it; but they follow the counsel of Death upon his first approach. It is he that puts into man all the wisdom of the world without speaking a word. ... He tells the proud and insolent that they are but abjects, and humbles them at the instant; makes them cry, complain, and repent, yea, even to hate their forepassed happiness. He takes the account of the rich and proves him a beggar. ... He holds a glass before the eyes of the most

beautiful, and makes them see therein their deformity and rottenness; and they acknowledge it. – O eloquent, just and mighty Death! whom none could advise, thou hast persuaded; what none hath dared thou hast done; and whom all the world hath flattered, thou only hast cast out of the world and despised: thou hast drawn together all the far-stretched greatness, all the pride, cruelty, and ambition of man, and covered it all over with these two narrow words. *Hic jacet.*'

With Raleigh on death, compare Bacon:

'Men fear Death as children fear to go in the dark; and as that natural fear in children is increased with tales, so is the other. Certainly, the contemplation of Death, as the wages of sin and passage to another world, is holy and religious; but the fear of it, as a tribute due unto Nature, is weak. ... It is as natural to die as to be born; and to a little infant perhaps the one is as painful as the other. He that dies in an earnest pursuit is like one that is wounded in hot blood, who, for the time, scarce feels the hurt; and therefore a mind fixed and bent upon somewhat that is good doth avert the dolours of Death; but, above all, believe it, the sweetest canticle is *Nunc dimittis*, when a man hath obtained worthy ends and expectations. Death hath this also, that it openeth the gate to good fame, and extinguisheth envy.'

More effective is this 'Of Studies', wherein Bacon speaks with weighty and indisputable authority:

'Read not to contradict and confute, nor to believe and take for granted, nor to find talk and discourse, but to weigh and consider. Some books are to be tasted, others to be swallowed, and some few to be chewed and digested; that is, some books are to be read only in parts, others to be read but not curiously, and some few to be read wholly, and with diligence and attention. Some books also may be read by deputy, and extracts made of them by others; but that would be only in the less important arguments and the meaner sort of books; else distilled books are like common distilled waters, flashy things. Reading maketh a full man; conference a ready man; and writing an exact man; and therefore, if a man write little he had need have a great memory; if he confer little he had need have a present wit; and if he read little he had need have much cunning, to seem to know what he doth not. Histories make men wise; Poets, witty; the Mathematics, subtle; Natural Philosophy, deep; Moral, grave; Logic and Rhetoric, able to contend; *Abeunt studia in mores.*'

I have spoken elsewhere of poetic prose, but there I gave no example. Here is one, chosen from Thomas Traherne's *Centuries of Meditations* rather than from Sir Thomas Browne's more famous works.

'You never enjoy the world aright, till the Sea itself floweth in your veins, till you are clothed with the heavens, and crowned with the stars; and perceive yourself to be the sole heir of the whole world, and more than so, because men are in it who are every one sole heirs as well as you. Till you can sing and rejoice and delight in God, as misers do in gold, and Kings in sceptres you never enjoy the world. – Till your spirit filleth the whole world, and the stars are your jewels; till you are as familiar with the ways of God in all Ages as with your walk and table; till you are intimately acquainted with that shady nothing out of which the world was made: till you love men so as to desire their happiness, with a thirst equal to the zeal of your own: till you delight in God for being good to all: you never enjoy the world.'

In *Some Fruits of Solitude* (1693), William Penn, on 'The Comfort of Friends', wrote thus: 'They that love beyond the world cannot be separated by it.

Death cannot kill what never dies.

Nor can spirits ever be divided, that love and live in the same divine principle, the root and record of their friendship.

If absence be not death, neither is theirs.

Death is but crossing the world, as friends do the seas; they live in one another still.

For they must needs be present, that love and live in that which is omnipresent.

In this divine glass they see face to face; and their converse is free, as well as pure.

This is the comfort of friends, that though they may be said to die, yet their friendship and society are, in the best sense, ever preserved, because immortal.'

Let us turn to Addison and take a short passage from his paper on the Royal Exchange (*The Spectator*, 1711–14):

'Our ships are laden with the harvest of every climate: our tables are stored with spices, and oils, and wines: our rooms are filled with pyramids of China, and adorned with the workmanship of Japan: our morning's draught comes to us from the remotest corners of the earth: we repair our bodies by the drugs of America, and repose ourselves under Indian canopies. ... For these reasons there are not more useful members in a commonwealth than merchants. They knit mankind together in a mutual intercourse of good offices, distribute the gifts of Nature, find work for the poor, add wealth to the rich, and magnificence to the great. Our English merchant converts the tin of his own country into gold, and exchanges his wool for rubies. The Mahometans are clothed in our British manufacture, and the inhabitants of the frozen zone warmed with the fleeces of our sheep.'

From Chesterfield:

'London, January the 8th, O.S. 1750.
Dear Boy,

I have seldom or never written to you upon the subject of Religion and Morality: your own reason, I am persuaded, has given you true notions of both; they speak best for themselves; but if they wanted assistance, you have Mr Harte at hand, both for precept and example: to your own reason, therefore, and to Mr Harte shall I refer you, for the reality of both; and confine myself, in this letter, to the decency, the utility, and the necessity, of scrupulously preserving the appearances of both. When I say the appearances of Religion, I do not mean that you should talk or act like a missionary, or an enthusiast, nor that you should take up a controversial cudgel, against whoever attacks the sect you are of; this would be both useless, and unbecoming your age: but I mean that you should by no means seem to approve, encourage, or applaud, those libertine notions, which strike at religions equally, and which are the poor threadbare topics of half-wits, and minute philosophers. Even those who are silly enough to laugh at their jokes, are still wise enough to distrust and detest their characters: for, putting moral virtues at the highest, and religion at the lowest, Religion must still be allowed to be a collateral security, at least, to Virtue; and every prudent man will sooner trust to two securities than to one.'

From Gibbon comes this:

'It is a very honourable circumstance for the morals of the primitive Christians, that even their faults, or rather errors, were derived from an excess of virtue. The bishops and doctors of the church, whose evidence attests, and whose authority might influence, the professions, the principles, and even the practice, of their contemporaries, had studied the scriptures with less skill than devotion, and they often received, in the most literal sense, those rigid precepts of Christ and the apostles to which the prudence of succeeding commentators has applied a looser and more figurative mode of interpretation. Ambitious to exalt the perfection of the gospel above the wisdom of philosophy, the zealous fathers have carried the duties of self-mortification, of purity, and of patience, to a height which it is scarcely possible to attain, and much less to preserve, in our present state of weakness and corruption. A doctrine so extraordinary and so sublime must inevitably command the veneration of the people; but it was ill calculated to obtain the suffrage of those worldly philosophers who, in the conduct of this transitory life, consult only the feelings of nature and the interest of society. ... It was not in *this* world that the primitive Christians were desirous of making themselves either agreeable or useful' (*The Decline and Fall of the Roman Empire*, 1776–81).

With that, the grand style, contrast this simpler style of Robert Southey in *The Life of Nelson*, 1813:

'Early on the following morning he reached Portsmouth; and having dispatched his business on shore, endeavoured to elude the populace by taking a by-way to the beach; but a crowd collected in his train, pressing forward to obtain a sight of his face: many were in tears, and many knelt down before him, and blessed him as he passed. England has had many heroes; but never one who so entirely possessed the love of his fellow-countrymen as Nelson. All men knew that his heart was as humane as it was fearless; that there was not in his nature the slightest alloy of selfishness or cupidity; but that, with perfect and entire devotion, he served his country with all his heart, and with all his soul, and with all his strength; and, therefore, they loved him as truly as and as fervently as he loved England. They pressed upon the parapet, to gaze after him when his barge pushed off, and he was returning their cheers by waving his hat. The sentinels, who endeavoured to prevent them from trespassing upon his ground, were wedged among the crowd; and an officer, who, not very prudently upon such an occasion, ordered them to drive the people down with their bayonets, was compelled speedily to retreat; for the people would not be debarred from gazing, till the last moment, upon the hero – the darling hero of England.'

And now, one of the great masters of prose – Walter Savage Landor ('Aesop and Rhodope', *Imaginary Conversations*, 1824–9):

Rhodope ... Let me pause and consider a little, if you please. I begin to suspect that, as gods formerly did, you have been turning men into beasts, and beasts into men. But, Aesop, you should never say the thing that is untrue.

Aesop. We say and do and look no other all our lives.

Rhodope. Do we never know better?

Aesop. Yes; when we cease to please, and to wish it; when death is settling the features, and the cerements are ready to render them unchangeable.

Rhodope. Alas! Alas!

Aesop. Breathe, Rhodope! breathe again those painless sighs: they belong to thy vernal season. May thy summer of life be calm, thy autumn calmer, and thy winter never come!

Rhodope. I must die then earlier.

Aesop. Laodameia died; Helen died; Leda, the beloved of Jupiter, went before. It is better to repose in the earth betimes than to sit up late; better, than to cling pertinaciously to what we feel crumbling under us, and to protract an inevitable fall. We may enjoy the present, while we are insensible to infirmity and decay; but the present, like a note in music, is nothing but as it appertains to what is past and what is to come. There are no fields of amaranth on this side of the grave; there are no voices, O Rhodope, that are not soon mute, however tuneful; there is no name, with whatever emphasis of passionate love repeated, of which the echo is not faint at last.

Rhodope. O Aesop! Let me rest my head on yours; it throbs and pains me.

Aesop. What are these ideas to thee?

Rhodope. Sad, sorrowful.

Aesop. Harrows that break the soil, preparing it for wisdom. Many flowers must perish ere a grain of corn be ripened. And now remove thy head: the cheek is cool enough after its little shower of tears.

Again in contrast, an extract from that admirably lucid and effective writer, Macaulay (from his essay on Clive):

'The river was passed; and, at the close of a toilsome day's march, the army, long after sunset, took up its quarters in a grove of mango-trees near Plassey, within a mile of the enemy. Clive was unable to sleep; he heard, through the whole night, the sound of drums and cymbals from the vast camp of the Nabob. It is not strange that even his stout heart should now and then have sunk, when he reflected against what odds, and for what a prize, he was in a few hours to contend. ... The day broke, the day which was to decide the fate of India. At sunrise the army of the Nabob, pouring through many openings from the camp, began to move towards the grove where the English lay. Forty thousand infantry, armed with firelocks, pikes, swords, bows and arrows, covered the plain. They were accompanied by fifty pieces of ordnance. ... The cavalry were fifteen thousand. ... The force which [Clive] had to oppose to this great multitude consisted of only three thousand men. But of these nearly a thousand were English; and all were led by English officers, and trained in the English discipline. ... The battle commenced with a cannonade in which the artillery of the Nabob did scarcely any execution, while the few field-pieces of the English produced great effect. Several of the most distinguished officers in Surajah Dowlah's service fell. Disorder began to spread through his ranks. His own terror increased every moment. ... He ordered his army to fall back, and this order decided his fate. Clive snatched the moment, and ordered his troops to advance. The confused and dispirited multitude gave way before the onset of disciplined valour. No mob attacked by regular soldiers was ever more completely routed. The little band of Frenchmen, who alone ventured to confront the English, were swept down the stream of fugitives. In an hour the forces of Surajah Dowlah were dispersed, never to reassemble.'

Before passing to an example of contemporary prose, I should like to give John Henry Newman's definition of a gentleman (*The Idea of a University,* 1852):

'It is almost a definition of a gentleman to say he is one who never inflicts pain. ... He is mainly occupied in merely removing the obstacles which hinder the free and unembarrassed action of those about him; and he concurs with their movements rather than takes the initiative himself. ...

The true gentleman ..., carefully avoids what may cause a jar or a jolt in the minds of those with whom he is cast; – all clashing of opinion or collision of feeling, all restraint, or suspicion, or gloom, or resentment. ... He has his eyes on all his company; he is tender towards the bashful, gentle towards the distant, and merciful towards the absurd; he can recollect to whom he is speaking; he guards against unseasonable allusions, or topics which may irritate; he is seldom prominent in conversation and never wearisome. He makes light of favours while he does them, and seems to be receiving when he is conferring. He never speaks of himself except when compelled, never defends himself by a mere retort. He has no ears for slander or gossip, is scrupulous in imputing motives to those who interfere with him, and interprets everything for the best. He is never mean or little in his disputes. ... He has too much good sense to be affronted at insults, he is too well employed to remember injuries, and too indolent to bear malice. He is patient, forbearing, and resigned, on philosophical principles; he submits to pain, because it is inevitable, to bereavement, because it is irreparable, and to death, because it is his destiny. If he engages in controversy of any kind, his disciplined intellect preserves him from the blundering discourtesy of better, though less educated minds. ... He may be right or wrong in his opinion, but he is too clear-headed to be unjust; he is as simple as he is forcible, and as brief as he is decisive.'

In conclusion, I quote two extracts from Frank Binder, *Dialectic*, 1932.

'To know how a man is educated we require to know how he is examined – and no more. For it is by examinations, which are the rudder of study, that all effort to pass them is determined. Let these be altered a little and education alters in turn, adapting itself to demands which are thought to prove not only the students but the studies themselves. Indeed if the dream of Swift were true, and the highest of honours awaited him who could stunt on

the tight rope, climb the greasy pole, and chase the slippy pig with success, our schools would be closed on the instant, and with every scholar a trickster and with every university an open vanity fair we should all go pantomiming on the boards of education. For the weathercock goes as the wind blows, and students who are weathercocks in practice to much east wind of theory turn here and there and everywhere as their tails and not their heads direct them. And rightly, as students enter a higher school not to prepare for an examination but to pass it. ... All reforms of education therefore must begin where education concludes – in the examination room. It is here that attempts have been made, and whereas once we used to test for attainments we now test for potentiality. Years ago we were content to ask what a student had done, and nowadays what he is likely to do at some future date. Nowadays we seek to measure not his knowledge but his ability, not his actual possessions but his coming power to obtain, not the capital he may chance to have but the income he is certain to command. And then above the evidence of intelligence some proof of personality is required – a quality best appraised in the absence of it – and students who have impressed us by the keenness of their wits are asked to impress us still further with their independence of character and originality of thought. ... To test for intelligence is perhaps easy when the examiner has some himself, but personality, which is too often beyond the experience of both parties, is likely to prove its obscurity. For even in broad daylight it is a grand dabble in the dark to see what we have never seen or to know what we cannot recognize, and as yet we have no scales for character. We may affect the things of the spirit but we still traffic in things of earth, and candidates in examinations like the suppliants in the temple must always compact with herdsmen and changers of money. But before we test for personality we must first learn what it is and not expect teachers to impart what they do not possess themselves. In this respect we are worse than we were. With cram as our aim and with a stick as our means we at least gave what we had, but in this palaver of personality and distillation of ideals we are fast coming to a state when the deaf dun the ears of the deafened and where the blunders of a one-eyed guide are the only wisdom of his blind disciples.'

And in a loftier mode:

'Life has its alternative, the ironic one of being angled at the bank or netted at the weir. We may escape the philosophy of form with its interplay of fate and personality, of the world without and the will within, and flee to the philosophy of measures with its processes of evidence, fact and proof. Here at least we are safe, or think we are, from the flats and shifting sands of superstition, and may sail on our daylight ways, scientific, assured, and open-eyed, along the charted paths of the seas. The port is fixed, the track defined, the times determined, yet even these our modern ways, like all the wisdom of the world, are writ on water. For just as religion is fallibly poised on the floating mote of faith, so science is no less parlously embarked on the dubious bubble of a measure, on something that has no absolute standing, a something that, in want of niches in space and time, cannot be measured itself nor be assessed in ultimate units. Indeed, were the world in flux, pulsating to all sizes yet keeping the ratio in every part, or speeding and staying the flight of time with proportional pace and delay in ourselves, we should not know it, and still should deem our measures, which swelled and lapsed in concert, as fixed and final for the universe itself. And to this myth of immutable measures comes the illusion of simultaneity, since for all experiments, comparisons, and proofs, whereby a synchronism is assumed, there is a passage through space and time, the measure being brought to the object measured, the proof following by an interval of thought. Yet we are asked to believe that in transpositions from spot to spot, and in references from a moment to a

moment succeeding, there is a constancy in the object thought of, that it keeps a congruence in all its motions, and *ceteris paribus* always is what it was before. But how are we to prove this when no two points in space or time may be placed together for comparison? and since by the latest theory matter determines the space whereby it is contained, so with equal truth may space determine matter. With an equal truth we may assume that change is a change in the medium which surrounds us, that we fall like a fluid into the mould of the world, into the play of its principles and lineament of its seasons, and take on by adaptation the idiosyncrasies of time. And though we scout the thought as dialectic, how without a synchronism is this to be proved?'

A careful study of the preceding examples will show what is meant by *adequacy*, for these examples are in styles that are more than merely *suitable*.

summary; précis; abstract; abridgement. See PRÉCIS WRITING, par. 2; for *summary*, see also at **outline.**

Sunday. See **Sabbath.**

sung. See **sing.**

sunk. See **sink.**

sunlight and **sunlit** (adj.). Cf. the entry at **starlight and starlit.**

sunlight; sunshine. The former is simply the light of the sun, whereas the latter is the shining of the sun, but also 'direct sunlight uninterrupted by cloud' (*OED*). 'Sunshine peeping through some little window' (Dickens). 'There was a long fight between mist and sunshine' (Tyndall). 'He sat in the sunshine'; 'When we pass from open sunlight to a moderately illuminated room' (Tyndall), 'Sunlight is dispensed mainly from carbon' (*OED*).

sunshade. To the comment at **parasol** I must add: 'The correct, educated word for the mushroom-like diverter of the sun's rays is *parasol*.' 'To say "sunshade" is as damning', writes a correspondent, 'as to say "greatcoat" for "overcoat" or "up to Town" for "up to London".'

super, in the sense of 'very good', 'very modern', 'very efficient (or, effectual)', is becoming so general that even tolerably educated persons are beginning to forget that it is a colloquialism.

supercede is now incorrect for *supersede*.

superincumbent. See **recumbent**.

superior than. See **inferior than** and COMPARATIVES, FALSE.

SUPERIORITY. Do not be superior. No man (or woman) is entitled to take a lofty tone unless he first makes it clear that he in no way considers himself to be better than his fellows and that he offers moral advice or takes a high tone in the spirit of 'Do as I say, not as I do.' If we are better than our neighbour, the superiority may be accidental: we have been luckier, not felt the workings of some dark god.

superlative. See COMPARATIVES, FALSE.

SUPERLATIVE DEGREE. The general rule is that the superlative is to be used only when there are three or more persons or things, as in 'He is the better runner of the two', 'She was the prettiest of them all.' But the pair *the former ... the latter* ('There were two battles, A and B: the former was at X, the latter at Y') is beginning to break down – to yield to *the first ... the second*: a tendency to be resisted. Where only one of the two is mentioned, *former* and *latter* retain their potency: we say 'There were two battles ...; only the former was important' or '... only the latter can be described here'.

supernumery is a common error for *supernumerary*: cf. *tempory* for *temporary*.

supersede (to take the place of, to serve instead of) is occasionally misused for *surpass*. Weseen quotes a newspaper headline, 'Women supersede men in scholarship.'

supervision. See **oversight**.

supine. See **prone**.

supple is sometimes ignorantly confused with *subtle*. (As e.g. in Desmond Coke, *The School across the Road*.) If, greatly daring, one speaks of 'a supple mind', one means, not a subtle but an agile mind or a mind readily adapting itself.

supplement and **complement.** Whereas a *complement* is an integral second part or portion, a *supplement* is additional to something that was at first thought to be complete. To *supplement* is to augment or to add something to (to supplement something *with* something else; to supplement an income); to *complement* is to complete by adding an essential part, to supply what is (conspicuously) wanting. The adjectives are *complementary* and *supplementary*.

suppose. See **suspect**.

supposedly, misused for *presumably*. 'X is supposedly the guilty party' should be 'X is presumably the guilty party.'

supposing. See CONJUNCTIONS, DISGUISED.

suppositious and **supposititious; suppositional.** For 'supposed; based on – or at the least, involving – supposition', *suppositional* is now more common than *suppositious*. *Supposititious* (child) is one 'set up to displace the real heir or successor'; do not use it for an illegitimate child; as applied to a writing, or a passage, or even a word therein, it = spurious, counterfeit, false, forged (*OED*). *Suppositious* = 'hypothetical', as in 'a suppositious observer on the moon'.

supranational is officialese for *worldwide*.

supra-normal. See **abnormal**.

supreme. See COMPARATIVES, FALSE.

sure. See COMPARATIVES, FALSE.

surmise. See **suspect**.

surprise. See **astonish**.

surprised; astonished, amazed, astounded. As adjectives expressive of the feeling of wonder, these four are in ascending order of intensity. Originally, *surprised* meant 'suddenly attacked, assailed without warning', then 'taken unawares', hence 'detected, suddenly discovered', of which the first survives only as a military term.

suspect; surmise; suppose. 'To *suspect*' can be employed as a synonym of 'to *surmise*', but it is better to reserve it for pejorative uses. To *surmise* is 'to form a notion that the thing in question may be so, on slight grounds or without proof; to infer conjecturally', as in 'Whatever you may surmise about a future life, it is your duty to do your best by this one', 'Is it too much to surmise that he made a fortune during those prosperous years?' To *suppose* is 'to posit, for argument's sake'; especially, 'to incline to think; to entertain as an idea', as in 'Do you suppose that she wished to remain unmarried?', 'The roads were no better than the old Squire had supposed' (Violet Jacob). 'He may be supposed to have thought more than he said' (Jowett) (*OED*).

suspicion for 'to *suspect*' is to be avoided; it is dialectal.

sustain, in *to sustain a fracture*, is a bad, unnecessary word, and appears to be suggested only by an excessive sense of the gravity of the occasion or by a wish to imitate (bad) medical jargon. 'He fell from a ladder and broke his leg' says all that can be conveyed by 'sustained a fracture', and the use of *sustain* in this sense robs it of its true and fuller meaning of *to support, to uphold*. *Sustain injuries* is, by many newspaper editors in their style sheets, condemned as incorrect for *receive injuries*. Both are correct; *receive injuries* is rather less formal, less pretentious.

swang. See **swing.**

sweat (n. and v.) is a better word than *perspiration* and *perspire*. Obviously if you do not wish to offend a lady, you do not tell her that she seems to be sweating freely, but the euphemistic, mealy-mouthed days of 'Horses sweat, men perspire, and women glow' have gone; certainly, men at least prefer to sweat. *Sweat – sweated* (American often *sweat*) *– sweated* (American *sweat*); participial adjective, *sweated*.

swell – swelled – swollen, less commonly **swelled.** Prefer *swollen* for the idea of harmful excess ('her legs have swollen') and *swelled* for anything neutral or pleasant ('our numbers have swelled'). The usual participial adjective is *swollen*, except in the phrase *swelled head*.

swim – swam – swum. Not *swum* for the preterite.

swing – swung (rarely **swang**) **– swung.**

syllabification (formation of syllables; a dividing into syllables) is preferable to *syllabication*.

symbiosis; symbiotic. See VOGUE WORDS.

syndrome. See VOGUE WORDS.

synonym of and **synonym for; synonymous with** (not *of*, nor *for*). The correct use of these collocations may be exemplified in three short sentences, thus: '*A synonym of quick is fast*'; 'Synonyms for *rapid* are hard to find'; '*Mankind* is not synonymous with generic *man.*'

SYNONYMS; AND THE HERESY OF VARIETY, especially in dialogue. See also **AFFECTATION**, last paragraph.

There are extremely few exact synonyms; but here, as usually, *OED* puts the case so well that to attempt to vie with its definition is not merely ineptitude and self-conceit but a mild form (perhaps not so very mild, after all) of madness.

'Strictly, a word having the same sense as another (in the same language); but more usually, either of any two or more words having the same general sense, but each of them possessing meanings which are not shared by the other or others, or having different shades of meaning or implications appropriate to different contexts: e.g. *serpent, snake; ship, vessel; compassion, fellow-feeling, sympathy; enormous, excessive, immense; glad, happy, joyful, joyous; to kill, slay, slaughter, to grieve, mourn, lament, sorrow.*'

The educated person does not need to be told that, in the desire for variety, to consult a dictionary of synonyms (so called) and take haphazard an apparent synonym is to expose himself to the risk – almost to the certainty – of making himself ridiculous.

But as a stylistic device (for the sake of emphasis or euphony), synonyms – in the looser, more general sense – are frequently used. Some are embedded in idiom (*to have and to hold*) and cliché (*free, gratis, and for nothing*); others are stylistic (*the inaudible and noiseless foot of time; a figure, type, symbol, or prefiguration*); and both sorts are tautological.

Sound advice is this: If you are in doubt as to which of two (or more) synonyms to use, consult a good dictionary that cites abundant examples.

And this: If you wish to use two or more synonyms as a stylistic device, make sure that the choice fulfils your purpose.

It follows, therefore, that it is dangerous to achieve variety at the expense of the meaning. Do not hesitate to use the same word (or even the same phrase) twice in the one sentence, if the repetition removes an ambiguity. Such variety as is seen in 'The person did not know what to do. This individual asked someone what he should do. Indeed, the man asked several bystanders what they advised' is absurd. If you must have variety (an important but not the primary consideration), obtain it by using a wide vocabulary and a pliant, versatile style, for these will yield a profound, a structural variety as opposed to a superficial, merely verbal variety. We have passed beyond Stevenson's insistence on variety at almost any price.

SYNTAX. Whereas *accidence* is literally what happens to single words or phrasal units, *syntax* is literally the *arrangement* of words in sentences and especially the arrangement of clauses within a sentence. Accidence requires little more than a good memory; clear syntax demands a good or, at the least, a clear mind. The following works are particularly valuable:

Otto Jespersen, *Essentials of English Grammar;*

C. T. Onions, *An Advanced English Syntax* (easy enough to understand):

George O. Curme, *A Grammar of the English Language* (more advanced than the preceding);

Randolph Quirk *et al., A Grammar of Contemporary English*, 1985.

Beginners will find Jespersen particularly useful; beginners and teachers might do much worse than to use Books I and II of my *English: A Course for Human Beings.*

systematic and **systemic.** The general word is *systematic; systemic* being confined to physiology, in which it now = 'belonging to, supplying, or affecting the system or body as a whole', as in 'The … systemic sensation of hunger', 'systemic effects', 'The Systemic Circulation … divisible into Arterial and Venous'; and to pathology in which it now = 'belonging to or affecting the nervous system or special parts of it', as in 'systemic sclerosis of a small but defined tract of the spinal cord' (*OED*).

systematize and **systemize.** The latter is an inferior form. The sense is 'to arrange according to a system, especially according to the best system known or available; to reduce to system' (*OED*).

T

table (v.). To *table a motion* is to postpone consideration of it, or (in British though not in American usage) to bring it forward for such consideration. This is an obvious source of misunderstanding.

TAGS. See CLICHÉ.

take into consideration = to *consider*.

take leave, as in 'I take leave to argue the point', is inferior to *take the liberty* (of arguing the point).

take off. Witness at Highgate Police Court: 'After inquiring where the bus was bound for, I asked the conductor what time it was to take off' (*The Evening News*, 9 Feb. 1938). *OED Supplement* admits the expression as applied in aeronautics: *to start from rest, attain flying speed and become air-borne*. True, an aeroplane is often called a 'bus', so why may not a 'bus' be said to 'take off'? But 'take off' has several meanings already, both active and passive, and, unless we are to allow anything to mean anything and everything to mean everything else, some precision is advisable.

take on, in the sense of *get excited, be 'upset'* about anything, is a harmless colloquialism: 'There's Missis walking about the drawing room, taking on awful' (Whyte-Melville, 1868).

taking. See CONJUNCTIONS, DISGUISED.

talent. See **genius.**

talisman has plural *talismans* – not *talismen*, as e.g. in Robert Eton, *Not in Our Stars*. Do not confuse *talisman*, *amulet*, or charm, with *talesman* (pl. *talesmen*), one of the *tales* or persons added to a jury to make up a deficiency in number.

talk is infelicitous – too informal – for *speech* or *address* or *lecture* in such examples as the following: 'A talk on disarmament', 'Twelve talks on French Romantic Literature'.

talking. See CONJUNCTIONS, DISGUISED.

tall is opposed to *short*, as *high* is to *low*. 'A tall hill, a tall house' should ordinarily be 'a high hill', 'a high house'. But ships and trees are *tall* when they are high in proportion to their width, especially in such collocations as *a tall chimney* or *house, a tall mast* or *ship, a tall column* or *spire*. Also, *tall* is applied to things that are 'of more than average length measured from bottom to top' – e.g. *a tall hat, a tall copy* of a book. *A tall story* is a colloquialism, originally American.

tangential is gobbledygook for *irrelevant* or *insignificant*.

tankard for *mug*. 'What pseudo-ancient inns miscall a tankard – but Mr Freeman and I still call a mug – of draught ale' (R. H. Mottram, in Preface to H. W. Freeman's *Joseph and His Brethren*). Here Mottram is not sufficiently explicit. A *tankard* is a drinking-mug made of metal, usually pewter, in olden times of wood (like a barrel), but an earthenware or glass *mug* would certainly be 'miscalled' a tankard; he seems to imply that in certain inns they do not know the difference. Perhaps they don't.

tantamount. See **paramount.**

target is being overworked. See VOGUE WORDS.

Tartar, tartar; Tatar. A variant spelling of the native of Tartary is *Tatar*; the *r* crept in as a result of the influence of *Tartarian*, an inhabitant of *Tartaros*, that abyss below Hades in which the Titans were confined and, in later mythology, that part of Hades where mortals are punished. Hence, i.e. both from the ruthless *Tatars* and hell's *Tartarians*, comes *tartar*, a savage or unmanageable person – now mostly in *catch a tartar*, to encounter somebody that is more than one's match.

For the etymology of *Tatar*, see my *Name into Word*.

tasteful(ly); tasty, tastily. The former pair = 'in good taste'; the latter = 'appetizing'. Confusingly, the opposite of both is *tasteless*.

TAUTOLOGY. * Cf. and contrast VERBOSITY, *q.v.*

Tautology, as defined by *OED*, is 'a repetition of the same statement' or 'the repetition (especially in the immediate context) of the same word or phrase, or the same idea or statement in other words: usually as a fault of style'.

Before passing to a set of examples, I give a short list of very common tautological expressions, based on Maurice H. Weseen's *Words Confused and Misused* (English edition), 1932.

adequate enough
and etc.
appear on the scene
ascend up
at about (e.g. *3 p.m.*)
attach together
attached hereto
both alike (see **both for** *alike*)
burn down and burn up (see separate entry)
classified into classes
collaborate together
connect together and connect up
consolidate together
continue on and continue yet
co-operate together
couple together
debate about (v.)
descend down
discuss about
divide off and divide up
drink up and drink down
early beginnings
eat up
enclosed herewith (or herein)
end up
endorse ...: see indorse ...
equally as
file away (commercially)
final completion
final upshot
finish up (v.t. and v.i.)
first begin
flood over

follow after
forbear from
forbid from
free, gratis, and for nothing
fresh beginner
from hence
from thence
from whence
funeral obsequies
gather together
good benefit
have got (for 'have' or 'possess': see separate entry)
hoist up
hurry up
important essentials
in between
indorse on the back
inside of
join together
joint co-operation
just exactly
just merely
just recently
lend out
link together
little birdling
meet together
mention about
merge together
mingle together
mix together
more inferior
more preferable
more superior
mutual co-operation
necessary requisite
new beginner
new creation
new departure and entirely new departure
new innovation
not a one
(it) now remains
open up (v.t.)
original source
outside of
over again
over with (done, ended, finished)
pair of twins
past history
peculiar freak

---

penetrate into
plan on (v.)
polish up
practical practice
(one's) presence on the scene
proceed on(ward)
protrude out
raze to the ground
really realize
recall back
reduce down
refer back
relax back
remember of
render a return
renew again
repay back
repeat again
repeat the same (e.g. story)
(to) rest up
retire back
return back
revert back
revive again
rise up
seldom ever
(to) separate apart
settle up
shrink down and shrink up
sink down
steady on!
still continue
still more yet
still remain
study up
sufficient enough
swallow down
taste of (for taste, v.)
termed as
than what
this next week
twice over
two halves (except when from different
    wholes)
two twins (of one pair)
uncommonly strange
unite together
used to (do something) before
we all and you all
where at
where to

whether or not
widow woman
young infant

The recurrence of about, again, back, and together, is significant.

Now, certain examples; unclassified, it is true; but all of them illustrative of common tautologies.

'That should leave me with twenty houses left' (Frank Tilsley, I'd Hate to Be Dead). Read, 'That would leave me twenty houses' or 'I should still have twenty houses.'

'Count A was made the recipient of a national presentation' (TLS: cited by Sir Alan Herbert). Read, 'A national presentation was made to Count A.'

'She [a canteen assistant] set herself a standard of endurance and privation approximately as nearly as possible to that which she understood prevailed on the Western Front' (Ian Hay, The Willing Horse). Read, '... approximately that which she understood ...'.

'The first layer of cloth was plain. The second had a lovely border on' (Violet O. Cressy-Marcks, Up the Amazon and Over the Andes). Omit 'on'.

'It sounded quite natural enough' (Henry Holt, Wanted for Murder). Omit either 'quite' or 'enough', according as the other is intended.

'Treadgold gave orders that Ragusi was to be watched carefully. ... For some half an hour afterwards he sat at his desk with his head in his hands' (Anthony Weymouth, Tempt Me Not). 'Afterwards' is unnecessary; 'about' would be preferable to 'some'.

'He [a German] was a surprising contrast to some of the military police I had met in our own army, whose conduct was not always particularly edifying on all occasions' (Bernard Newman, Spy), where 'on all occasions' is redundant.

'... The pilot circling round up above' (ibid.). Omit 'round'.

'Occasionally she made a sale, but very seldom' (E. R. Punshon, The Dusky Hour) = 'She rarely made a sale.'

'We never made more than eight knots an hour' (W. H. G. Kingston, *Lusitanian Sketches*). 'An hour' is unnecessary, for a knot is a sea-mile per hour.

'Rupert Bond laughed at his friend. They were both men in their early sixties, and both had similar interests' (G. Davison, *Murder in a Muffler*). Read, 'They were in their early sixties, and they had similar interests.'

' "A canting hypocrite named Arpendrake," he began again, "has just absconded from England with the funds from an institution which really was supposed to be in the light of a great philanthropic affair" ' (John G. Brandon, *The Mail-Van Mystery*). Read, '... with the funds from a great, supposedly philanthropic institution'.

'It was a piece of ruled note-paper. ... The quality was of a very cheap, coarse nature, such as comes in thick tablets which can be bought for a trifle at any stationer's' (S. S. Van Dine, *The Kidnap Murder Case*). Read, '... It was of a very cheap, coarse quality, such as comes ...'.

'He idled along from one street to another. ... But never once, so far as we could ascertain, did he appear to glance back' (Stephen Maddock, *Doorway to Danger*): 'appear to' is unnecessary, and 'never' is enough. (And 'ascertain' should be 'see'.)

'He could form no estimate at all of with how much favour he was regarded at the Admiralty' (C. S. Forester, *A Ship of the Line*). This sentence would be improved if 'of', which rings oddly, were omitted; after 'no', 'at all' is superfluous. Rewrite thus, 'He could not estimate with what favour he was regarded at the Admiralty' – or, better still, 'He could not estimate (*or* judge) how he stood with the Admiralty.' This example merits careful consideration, for it has been taken from one of the most economical (and best) of English post-1920 novelists.

' "How I came to find the suitcase was because ..." ' (E. R. Punshon, *op. cit.*). Read, 'I found the suitcase in this way.'

'Dwarfs in all ages have ever been objects of interest' (*Tom Thumb's Diary and Proverb Book*). Omit either 'ever' or preferably – it being a phrase as opposed to a word – 'in all ages'.

'Dr T., whose knowledge of the lake and its neighbourhood can be second to that of none, pointed out to me ...' (Joseph Ll. Thomas, *Oxford to Palestine*). The cliché, *second to none*, has been enlarged with an unnecessary 'that of'.

'Further whimsicalities consist in ... demanding ... that all the books he finds in any guest-room be forthwith removed as insults to his intelligence and that the hostess see to it at once that the complete works of Maxwell Bodenheim be substituted in their stead' (G. J. Nathan, *Intimate Notebooks of George Jean Nathan*), where 'in their stead' is unnecessary after 'substituted'.

In 1852, J. H. Brodribb (a boy of 14) wrote, 'I have not been to see the Crystal Palace at Sydenham. ... The site of the old one looks quite desolate, as there is nothing left but dirt', and *The Times* (many years later) comments thus, 'The paragraph on the Crystal Palace, which seems so topical to the present time, is of course a reference to the rebuilding of Paxton's monument', where 'to the present time' is barely necessary and where 'of course' is certainly unnecessary.

teach. See at **learn.**

technic, technics; technique; technology. *Technic* is a collective term for 'technical methods and details', especially 'the formal or mechanical part and aspect of an art or science', as in 'In the technic of this art, perfection can be reached only by long training' (Lowell), but *technique* is now more general. *Technics* (as either a plural or a singular) may be used in the same sense: but here again, *technique* is more common. *Technics* in the sense 'the science or study of art or arts, especially of the mechanical or industrial arts' is inferior to the more usual *technology*. In addition to the sense noted above, *technique* means skill or ability in the formal, practical, mechanical details of one's art, i.e. mechanical skill in an art, especially in one of the fine arts, and above all 'in reference to painting or musical performance'. Likewise, *technology* has the further meaning, 'practical arts collectively' and 'technical terminology or nomenclature' (*OED*).

TECHNICALITIES. See JARGON.

TECHNOLOGY AND SCIENCE. When in doubt, the layman should consult some such dictionary as *Chambers's Technical Dictionary*, which, very good, includes scientific terms.

teeming with is incorrect for *rich in*. 'Salamanca ... a glorious old city, teeming with history' (Bernard Newman, *Death Under Gibraltar*).

temporal and **temporary** are sometimes confused; the former is 'of or belonging to this life', as opposed to *spiritual*, 'belonging to the eternal'; the latter, 'not meant to last long' 'not permanent'.

temporize and **extemporize.** In good use, *temporize* is always intransitive; as = 'to improvise or extemporize', it is incorrect. To *temporize* is to adapt oneself, to conform to time and circumstance; *temporize with* is so to act or negotiate or parley as to gain time, also to negotiate with (a person); *temporize between* is to effect a compromise between (persons). To *extemporize* (v.i.) is 'to speak extempore; in music, to improvise'; (v.t.), it is 'to compose off-hand; to compose and utter off-hand; hence, to produce on the spur of the moment, to invent for the occasion' (*OED*).

tend and **trend.** In the sense, 'to have a general tendency, to have a disposition to', *trend* is obsolescent; *tend* is the right word. *Trend*, however, is correct for 'to turn off in a specified direction; to tend to take a direction expressed by or implied in the context', and, of rivers, currents, coastlines, mountain ranges, strata, territories, or regions, 'to run, stretch, incline, bend in some direction', as in 'The coast trends to the northward', 'In its course to the

north, the Gulf Stream trends more and more to the eastward' (*OED*).

tend for for *tend to cause*. 'Dainty underwear was certainly intriguing, but tended for delay' (Cecil Freeman Gregg, *Tragedy at Wembley*): correctly, tended to cause or create delay.

tend to has become incorrect – in British though perhaps less in American usage – for *attend to*, in, e.g. 'I must *tend to* my business.' *Tend* is now used mostly in *tending herds* or *flocks*.

tendency for. See PREPOSITIONS WRONGLY USED.

tendentious means not 'prejudiced' nor 'quarrelsome', but 'having, or composed or written with a purposed tendency'. It is, however, pejorative. See VOGUE WORDS.

tennis for *lawn tennis* is a shortening. *Tennis* properly so called is that royal game which arose in the Middle Ages and from which, in the 1870s, sprang the game of lawn tennis.

TENSE-SEQUENCE. In 'Devas had struck from an angle he had not considered, though it may well have been expected' (John G. Brandon, *The Dragnet*), *may* should be *might*. 'He never has and never will mortgage the national patrimony' (*The Daily Express*, 13 Nov. 1937) should read: 'He has never mortgaged the national patrimony, and never will (do so).' 'The threat of danger gave me a fierce, triumphant determination that, come what may, one little estate would stand inviolate' (R. C. Sheriff, *The Hopkins Manuscript*) should read '... come what might'; and a careful writer would prefer *should* to *would*.

These examples will serve to indicate how necessary it is to ensure a right tense-sequence; to depart from that sequence is to produce always an effect of inelegance and often an actual ambiguity.

'The *Sequence of Tenses*', writes Dr Onions in *An Advanced English Syntax*, 'is the principle in accordance with which the Tense in a subordinate clause "follows" or is adjusted to that of the principal clause'; thus, in general, when the governing clause has a Present [e.g. 'he says'], a Present Perfect [as in 'he *has* said'], or a Future [as in 'he *will say*'], the subordinate clause has a Present (*Primary Sequence*); when the governing clause has a Past [whether progressive, as in 'he *was saying*', or preterite, as in 'he said'] or a Pluperfect [the past perfect, as in 'he *had* said'], the subordinate clause has a Past (*Secondary Sequence*). The Sequence of Tenses applies chiefly to Final and Noun Clauses.

> '*I tell*
> *have told* } you that you *may* know.'
> *shall tell*

[Here I should like to interpolate an interesting example of an error in the Historic Present (the present used, throughout a passage or a book, for the past tense): 'That night he's kind of brought up to the mark – prepared to smell a rat wherever he'll find a chance to smell one' (a detective novel): where 'prepared to smell a rat wherever he *finds* a chance' would be correct, *prepared to smell* being a virtual future.]

> '*I told*
> *was telling* } you that you *might* know.'
> *had told*

'He *has* no idea what twice two *is*', but (subject to a modification hereinafter set forth) 'He *had* no idea what twice two *was*.'

'The master *says* we *may* have a holiday' but in the past it is 'The master *said* we *might* have a holiday', the master's actual words being, 'You *may* have a holiday.'

'I *took* care that he *should* not hear me.'

If it is desired to mark something as true universally or at the time of speaking, the tense is not adjusted:

'He *had* no idea what twice two *is*.'

'Columbus proved that the world *is* round.'

'I *asked* the guard what time the train usually *starts*.'

There is no such implication of universality, no such emphasis on the time of speaking, in the following sentence (taken from Ronald Knox's *Double Cross Purposes*):

'And even if he does, I argued to myself, he would hesitate to complain of the loss, because it would involve him in some decidedly awkward explanations': clearly this should be written either 'And even if he *did*, ... he would hesitate to complain ... because it would involve him ...' or 'And even if he does, ... he *will hesitate* to complain ..., because it *will involve* him in some decidedly awkward questions.'

The tense-sequence most difficult for most persons is that which is necessitated in a long passage to be cast into indirect speech: see **REPORTED SPEECH**. In the matter of reported speech, there is one point of particular interest: 'There is ... a tendency ... to break through the old sequence when a more accurate expression suggests itself. Thus instead of [''He *said* he *was going* tomorrow''] we may with greater accuracy say: ''He *said* he *is* going tomorrow'' ' (Curme, *A Grammar of the English Language*). Dr Curme does not discuss the distinction between 'He said he *was* (or *is*) going tomorrow', where it is implied that, at the time of the reporting, he had not yet gone, and 'He said he *was* (not *is*) going on the morrow', where it is implied that, at the time of the reporting, he had already gone.

Not (or, at least, not wholly) sequence but mood is involved in the correct use of the subjunctive, but there is, obviously, a tense-sequence in the subjunctive: see particularly **SUBJUNCTIVE,** but also **CONCESSIVE CLAUSES, CONDITIONAL CLAUSES,** and **FINAL CLAUSES.**

terminal and **terminus.** In Britain, they are distinct, but in the United States they tend to overlap. A British *terminus* is the end of a route, a pipeline, etc., whereas a *terminal* is chiefly a point of access, and thus used of airline buildings and for connection with an electric circuit or a computer system.

terminate for *end, close, finish.* 'The proceedings terminated with a vote of thanks to the Chairman.' It is always worth considering whether the dignity aimed at in such formal records as the Minutes of a Meeting is not better maintained by the true English word, as 'The proceedings (or the business) *ended*, etc.' And sometimes *expire* would be preferable, as in 'His subscription terminated last month and he has not renewed it': *terminated* = ended, for good and all.

TERMS OF ADDRESS. See TITLES OF PERSONS.

testament, for *testimony,* is an occasional error caused by a misunderstanding of the two words; the former is a *will,* the latter 'an attestation in support of a fact or statement' (*OED*). Either word, however, may mean 'proof, evidence'.

testimonial on is incorrect for *testimonial to,* as in 'I dislike testimonials, but ... here is a testimonial on mathematics' (Stuart Chase, *The Tyranny of Words*).

testimony. See **evidence.**

tetralogy. See **triumvirate.**

than, misused for *as.* 'More than twice as many gliding flights had been made than in the year before' (DDC, 11 July 1938).

than, misused for *other than.* 'He disliked the clash of personality, regarding any personality than his own as an intolerable intrusion.' *But* or *differing from* might also be substituted here for *than.* Cf. 'He had scarcely won ... the place ... than his health was found shattered' (Froude), where 'when' should be substituted for 'than'. *Than* is never correct except with *other, otherwise,* or the comparative of an adjective or adverb.

than, misused for *than that.* 'We have borne so much for the peace we pray for, that I think that I would rather see all humanity lying dead like this German boy, than it should blunder blindly into a war more terrible than this has been' (Warwick Deeping, *No Hero – This*). To omit the second 'that' would not be a grave error, but a *that* is necessary after the first 'than'.

than, misused for *to.* 'Modern dictionaries are pusillanimous works, preferring feebly to record what has been done than to say' – read, *to saying* – 'what ought to be done', is an error committed by Sir Alan Herbert himself in *What a Word!* (But that entertaining book is not a grammar.) To avoid the awkwardness of having two *to*'s in the sentence, he might have written *rather than saying.*

than, misused for *when.* See **barely than** and **hardly than.**

than, different ... 'Here was quite a different kettle of fish than the one they had served up in the past' (Samuel Putnam, *Marguerite of Navarre*). The impeccably correct construction is *different ... from,* although *different to* (cf. French *différent à*) is permissible in British (though not in American) usage (see, for evidence, *OED*); if one says that 'one thing differs *from*' (never *to*) 'another', why does one not, with equal naturalness, say, 'is different from'? [*Different ... than* seems to occur more and more frequently in the New York daily and weekly press. Evidently the comparative sense of the word rather than the fact of its positive form may govern the syntax. Whether this is regrettable is a question of taste.]

than, inferior and **superior.** See **inferior than.**

than me or **than I** may occur in a sentence such as 'You are a much greater loser than *me* or *I*' (here Swift wrote *I* and was, I think, incorrect). The arguments are (1) that *than* is here a preposition and governs an object; and (2) that *than* is a conjunction introducing a clause, only the subject of which is expressed, the remainder being an ellipsis. I much prefer the use of the objective case (in this example, *me*); and all authorities agree that *than whom* (not *than who*) is correct in 'He is a king than whom there has never been a greater.'

Purists do, however, prefer the subjective case *than I* where the pronoun can reasonably be interpreted as the subject of a verb; 'They pay George more than I (do)' but 'They pay George more than (they pay) me.' If the subjective form on its own looks pedantic, supply the verb and write '... than I do'. If the objective form looks ambiguous, or indeed if a noun rather than a pronoun is involved, it may be clearer to use a full clause, since '... than me' or '... than John' may be interpreted in either way.

than what. The writer of a letter in *John o' London's Weekly*, 17 Dec. 1937, discussing Mr Donald Wolfit's enterprise in producing Shakespeare in the provinces, says, 'His productions certainly do not belong to Mr Prentis's £5 class (than what is more wretched?), nor to his £25,000 class (than what is more vulgar?), but are adequate etc.' There is no grammatical sense in 'than what'; the writer means 'than which, what is more wretched/vulgar?' though the juxtaposition of *which, what* is clumsy, and might be avoided by saying 'and what is more wretched than that?'. Often *than what* is merely tautological for *than*, as in 'It was easier than what he thought.'

that (conj.) misplaced. 'There is just a chance where there is any ornamentation that a stain might creep under it', for 'There is just a chance that, where ..., a stain might ...'. (Vernon Loder, *Choose Your Weapon*).

that (conj.) omitted. The omission of the conjunctive *that* sometimes causes a momentary confusion. In Milton Propper's *The Great Insurance Murders* (an American 'thriller'), we find: 'There were no marks or scratches that indicated the lock had been forced' and 'Rankin ushered her to a chair and learned her name was Mrs Emily Reilly.' 'Indicated the lock' and 'learned her name' might possibly have been independent, self-contained statements: but with something of a jar, one finds that the sentences continue.

that (conj.), redundant. This occurs in such a sentence as 'The sooner that this is altered, the better', where *that* is entirely uncalled for; and by unnecessary repetition, as in 'He said that, as the mistake had been made and was irreparable, that it was useless to discuss the subject again.'

that and **which**; **that** and **who**. See **which and that; who and that.**

that, misused for *so far as* or *for all that*. 'He found that it was unlocked; indeed, that he could see, [it] seemed to have no means of locking' (John G. Brandon, *The Pawnshop Murder*).

that for *thus* or *to that degree* or, loosely, *so very*. 'Oh, it's not that urgent', said the doctor on the telephone – and, in so doing, he used a colloquialism; appropriate in speech but not in formal writing. He might have said 'It is not urgent to that degree', or, less stiffly, 'It's not so urgent as all that.'

that, at. *At that* is a colloquialism, and therefore it should be eschewed in formal, official, and other serious writings. Its most frequent senses are 'moreover', 'even so', and 'in any case'. (British writers often use it without a due regard to its niceties. See my *A Dictionary of Slang*.)

that same day (month, etc.) is not so much incorrect as unnecessarily emphatic for *that day* or the stronger *the same day*; e.g. 'On that same night, he went to London.'

that ... that is clumsy or, at best, cacophonous for *that ... which* or *that ... who(m)*, as in 'That man that you saw yesterday is a swindler' and 'That box that the porter took was valuable.' See also **which and that; who and that.**

the and **The** in titles. See TITLES OF BOOKS AND PERIODICALS.

the said. Inadmissible except in legal documents. 'The said playboy was a millionaire's son' is absurd (Harold Herd).

the which is obsolete and now incorrect for *which*, as in 'The which barn is for sale.'

their, them, they for singular *he* or *she*, *his* or *her*. See **anyone ... they**, and **they, their.**

their's is incorrect for *theirs* – and astonishingly common.

them is constantly used for *they* (as *me* is for 'I'), after *as* and after *is*, *are*, *were*; 'It was not them' is incorrect, but 'It was not them we wanted', quoted by *OED*, has some justification since *them* represents *they whom*.

themselves. See **myself** and **oneself.**

then for *and then* is too abrupt for use in formal or impressive writing or speaking, unless a semi-colon separates the two statements. But 'He slept for a while, then took a walk' is good familiar English.

then for *than* is an error that is much more widespread than highbrows seem to think: it is not merely the illiterate who fall into it. The reason is not that, several centuries ago, *than* and *then* were spellings and pronunciations frequently interchanged, but that, where *than* bears no stress and is spoken very rapidly and lightly, it tends to approximate to *then* in sound.

thence. See **from hence.**

thenceforth. See **thereafter and thenceforth**; also **henceforth and thenceforth.**

theory is occasionally used loosely for *idea* (or *notion*), *view* or *opinion* or *expectation*, as in 'My theory of the war is that the mechanically stronger side will win', where *expectation* or *opinion* would be preferable.

there, introductory, is apt to cause the verb to fail to agree with the subject in number, as in: 'There was at this time, within the horrid confines of that prison, several fellows who were very much respected by the others' (Preface to Anon., *Thieving Detected*, 1777). 'There was my wife and daughter to consider, and my whole career' (W. S. Masterman, *The Perjured Alibi*). Cf. 'There still remains a few wilderness areas on the continent' (Stuart Chase, *The Tyranny of Words*). It is difficult to avoid the impression that these, and other, authors subconsciously regard *there* as a noun (therefore singular), hence as the subject of the sentence. Perhaps there is presumed an analogy in French *il y a*: cf. following entry.

there is many is incorrect for *there are many*, the subject being *many*; contrast French *il y a*. 'There is many a ...' is correct.

thereabout and **thereabouts.** *OED*'s examples (and precept) show that the latter is the more usual form.

thereafter and **thenceforth.** The former = 'after that date or time or place in a sequence': *thenceforth* = 'continually or continuously from that time; indefinitely from that time; from that time *onward*'. *Both are formal words*, not to be used indiscriminately. 'Thenceforth her back upon the world she turned' (Morris); 'This prerogative ... was thereafter ... discontinued' (H. Brooke) (*OED*). See also ARCHAISMS.

therefore and **therefor.** 'The reason *therefor* (i.e. *for it* or *for this*) is *therefore* (i.e. *for that reason*) unsatisfactory' exemplifies the difference between the two words. Many quite good writers do not even know of the existence of *therefor*.

thereof and **theretofore.** See ARCHAISMS.

these kind or **sort of.** George Parker, *A View of Society*, 1781, 'Queer as this *rig*' or underworld dodge 'may appear, there is a larger shop in London where these kind of rings are sold, for the purpose of going on the *Fawney*', i.e. practising the trick of ring-dropping. See also **kind of, all.**

they, their, misused for *he, his* as in 'Anyone thinks twice, when their life is at stake': read 'his life'. See **anyone ... they.** But this locution, technically incorrect, arises from our lack of relative pronouns meaning *he or she, him or her, his or her.* Traditionally, *he* (or *him, his*) has been used for any singular human noun, as in 'A doctor should visit those of his patients whom he knows to be too ill to come to the surgery.' But this may now be taken to imply that doctors are all men. One way to avoid giving offence is to rephrase in the plural: 'Doctors should visit those of their patients …'. Another way is to cut out the pronouns, writing 'A doctor should visit those patients who seem too ill …'.

think as a noun is colloquial, whether for 'an act of thinking; meditation' ('An occasional think does one much good') or for 'an opinion' ('My think is that he's a pretentious fool') (*OED*).

thoroughfare, meaning nothing but *a way through* (for the public), makes ridiculous the following notice, to be seen in Guilford St., WC1, on 18 Dec. 1937, in letters 6 inches high: 'Queen Sq. House. Private. No through Thoroughfare.'

those that; those who. The latter is preferable. See also **which and that.**

though and **although.** *Although* is the more formal; *though* is the usual form in speech and in writings couched in familiar English. But even in dignified writing, *though* is sometimes preferred to *although*; this preference obtains where *though* is more euphonious than *although*, where the metre renders *although* awkward, and in certain combinations such as *even though.* See **although.**

though (or although) is sometimes used to introduce a subordinate clause in a highly irrelevant way; Dean Alford quotes from a Law report in *The Times*, February 1869, 'He, though a gentleman of property, was unhappily paralysed in his lower limbs', and adds, 'What a delightful idea this writer had of the usual exemption of the rich from the ills of humanity!'

thrash, thresh. The latter is retained in reference to corn; in all other references *thrash* is preferred; though one may *thrash*

(or *thresh*) around, and *thrash* (or *thresh*) out a problem.

through for *by means of, by* is allowed by *OED*; nevertheless, the best writers – at their best – avoid it. E.g. 'Through an addition to his salary, he was enabled to purchase the house he wanted' is unsatisfactory.

through for *up to and including,* as in 'Monday through Friday', is a very useful Americanism, but not yet fully accepted in British usage.

tidy. Such expressions as *a tidy step, a tidy few,* are colloquialisms, whereas *pretty good* and *pretty well* are standard speech.

till is inferior to *until* in formal prose or verse. They are otherwise synonymous, and both may create ambiguity in negative sentences; 'he didn't work until midnight' might mean either that he did not start until then, or that he stopped before then. Rephrase.

timid and **timorous; apprehensive.** *Apprehensive* is 'anticipative of something unfavourable; in dread of possible harm or evil', as in *apprehensive of danger* and *apprehensive for one's life. Timid* is 'feeling or evincing want of courage or self-confidence; easily frightened or over-awed', as in 'Poor is the triumph o'er the timid hare' (Thomson of *The Seasons*). *Timorous* is synonymous with *timid,* but with emphasis on 'shrinking (with fear, or from doing something that requires courage)'; but one tends also to use *timid* of temporary fear, and *timorous* of a person habitually lacking in courage (*Webster's*).

titanic. See **gigantic.**

TITLES OF BOOKS AND PERIODICALS. This is a question often neglected: I have already discussed it at the entry *the* in my *A Dictionary of Slang and Unconventional English* (1937; 3rd ed., revised and enlarged, 1948).

Had I chosen the title *Dictionary of Slang,* it would have been incorrect to refer to it either as *A Dictionary of Slang* or as *The Dictionary of Slang* (very pretentious this!, for there are other dictionaries of slang); had the title been *The Dictionary of Slang*, it would have been incorrect (though excusable) to refer to it as either *A Dictionary of Slang* or *Dictionary of Slang*; but as it is *A Dictionary*, why impute telegraphese by calling it *Dictionary*, or conceit by changing it to *The Dictionary*? Hence I write 'My *A Dictionary of Slang*'. If the title had been *The Dictionary* ... I should have referred to the book as 'my *The Dictionary of Slang*'.

And let us italicize the initial 'A' and 'The' or, if the inverted-commas mode is preferred, have inverted commas before them. 'A correspondent on the *Times*' or 'A correspondent on the "*Times*"' is, to put it mildly, a feeble substitute for 'a correspondent on *The Times*' or 'a correspondent on "*The Times*"'. Luckily, few writers fall into the ineptitude of omitting the capital letter in the properly italicized or inverted-comma mode, as in 'a correspondent on *the Times*' or 'a correspondent on "the Times"'.

Admittedly, the general practice is against 'my *A Dictionary of Slang*': but should not exactitude overrule a practice that can hardly be classified as idiom? In familiar speech, 'my *Dictionary of Slang*' is permissible: it is a colloquialism. But I do recommend that scholars and reputable, serious writers (or humorous writers desirous of a reputation for good English as well as for acceptable humour) and cataloguers should retain the *A* and *The* that form the first word in a title. Is it not better to speak of J. M. Barrie's delightful book as 'Barrie's *A Window in Thrums*' than to refer to it as 'Barrie's *Window in Thrums*'? Is not the latter both ambiguous and impertinent – and just a little cheap? After all, we do not speak of 'Michael Sadleir's *Foolish Things*', but of 'Michael Sadleir's *These Foolish Things*'; we speak, not of 'Michael Arlen's *Charming People*' but of 'Michael Arlen's *These Charming People*'. *A* and *The* have their rights no less than *These* and *Those*.

In the titles of periodicals, however, there is an exception, consecrated by usage and justified by convenience: when the title becomes an adjective, *The* is omitted. 'A *Times* correspondent' is more convenient than, and is idiomatic for, 'A correspondent of (generally, on) *The Times*'. I do not suggest that we should either say or write 'a *The Times* correspondent' or 'the *The Times* correspondent'. But, so far as I can see, there is no excuse for 'The editor of the New York Times snorts balefully on discovering this sorry stratagem' (Stuart Chase, *The Tyranny of Words*): either 'The editor of *The New York Times*' or 'The editor of "*The New York Times*"' is required.

There is no doubt concerning what is to be done with 'a' and 'the' *within* titles. They are always written *a* and *the*, as in '*The Lady in the Case* is a good book'; but where a book-title or a periodical-title is involved, the above-enunciated rule is to be observed, as in '*The Ghost at The Times* is an excellent book' or, for the sake of clarity, '*The Ghost at "The Times"* is an excellent book.'

Not only *a* (or *an*) and *the* require small initial letters ('lower case', as printers say). So do prepositions – *at* and *from* and *in* and *of* and the rest of them.

There is no generally accepted rule concerning the other parts of speech. My own practice is to 'capital' every word that is neither an article (*a* or *the*) nor a preposition. I see little reason for writing 'be', 'is', 'are', 'was', 'were', 'will', 'shall', 'would', 'should', 'must', 'ought' in lower case when all other verbs are written in upper case: why *The Lady is Dead* but *The Lady Fell Dead*? Why not *The Lady Is Dead*?

In this matter of titles, I advise authors not to submit to 'the rules of the house' – those rules which printers have formulated in self-protection – when they are *sure* of the rightness of their own titling. (Unless, that is, the printers' rules are those rules which have been proposed in this article.)

[For the citing of titles the most generally available American authority is probably the University of Chicago Press's *A*

Manual of Style. As first words the articles *a* and *the* are part of the titles of books and one would expect them to be so treated – i.e. capitalized and set within the quotation marks or in the italic type that distinguishes the title. However, titles that make for awkwardness or misunderstanding – as in 'his *A Dictionary of Slang*' and 'Dr Vizetelly's *The Standard Dictionary*' – will inevitably be shortened, now and again, when they interfere with the English language. The American rule for capitalization of titles is that the first word and all important words are capitalized. Often, however, on a title page the title is set entirely in caps as is the case with Mr Partridge's dictionary. American librarians have solved the problem in this fashion: Partridge, Eric. Dictionary of slang …, a. They capitalize the first word and no other and treat an initial article as an addendum. Editors, less bold than librarians, muddle along according to publishing house precedents or their own taste. In fact, no one style solves all problems. Authors can help by quoting rather than italicizing special words in titles.

There is no easy way of finding the correct and complete titles – if they exist – of the thousands of American newspapers. The two complete lists are arranged by states, towns, and short titles, as Texas, El Paso, Herald, Post, Times. (Moreover the banner heading on the front page of a paper may not be exactly the same as the masthead above the first column of editorials.) If an editor wishes uniform citations of newspapers, his most practicable course is to italicize or quote only the short title, as in the El Paso *Times*, the New York *Times*, the *Times*. The alternative is to give the masthead titles of newspapers he is acquainted with and to set the others by an arbitrary rule. The *Literary Digest* used to have three ways of citing newspapers (as I remember): one in the text, another in the credit line following a quotation, and still another in the credit line below a cartoon.

Magazines are fonder of their articles than are newspapers. *The Atlantic Monthly* and *The Saturday Review of Literature* wish *The* (and so, by the way, does The Johns Hopkins University – known locally as The Hopkins). It may be difficult to remember whether the *American Mercury* or *The American Mercury* would be most flattering. *The* or *A Life, Time, Fortune* would be ruinous. Should it be *The Reader's Digest*? Some quite literate editors follow what our friend Mr Partridge would call the illiterate practice of ignoring the article in common citations of the periodical press. If we were presenting a Pulitzer prize or a sheepskin suitably inscribed, then we should ask the editor what he liked best. If the reader thinks the problem simple, let him consider — magazine: it is **Harpers** MAGAZINE on the cover, *Harper's Magazine* on the contents page, **Harpers** *Magazine* on the masthead above the first article and HARPER'S MONTHLY MAGAZINE on the running heads. What should an editor do? Call it *Harpers* for short and *Harpers Magazine* for long, and quote it often – that is good practice.]

TITLES OF PERSONS. This is a subject that belongs less properly to a book on English usage than to a book on etiquette. For the curious, however, I list here three books:

'Armiger': *Titles and Forms of Address*: comprehensive and dependable.

R. W. Chapman: *Names, Designations and Appellations*: Tract No. 47 of the SPE.

W. Whitten & F. Whitaker: *Good and Bad English*: a short, popular, and useful account.

to, omitted. 'For years it was disputed as to whom the word referred' (E. R. Suffling, *Epitaphia*). *Whom* is correct, but the *to* of *refer to* has been omitted owing to the influence of *as to*. The sentence should read 'For years it was disputed as to whom the word referred to' or, by substituting *about* for *as to*, 'For years it was disputed about whom the word referred to': the former is preferable because it is more idiomatic.

to for *to* + infinitive is now perfectly Standard English. 'I shall go; he doesn't want *to*.' Here, 'doesn't want to do so' would be too formal. See VERB UNCOMPLETED.

to, in *other to* and *different to*. See **other** and **than**.

to, misused for *as to* (or *in respect of*), is exemplified in 'Since the two of them had been at a loss to what else to do, they had made the journey to St Johns' (Kenneth Roberts, *A Rabble in Arms*). In this example, *to* could have been omitted.

tolerant to. See PREPOSITIONS WRONGLY USED.

to-morrow and **tomorrow.** *Webster's* prefers *tomorrow* and *today*; since *c.* 1940 usage has increasingly tended, even in Britain, to omit the hyphen.

tomorrow is and **tomorrow will be.** The latter is more logical, except, when in a vivid and graphic context, the morrow is pulled back into the present, as in the catch-phrase, 'tomorrow is another day'.

too for *very* is a trivial colloquialism, as in 'Isn't it just too sweet!'

too is occasionally misused for *either* in negative sentences and phrases. 'I don't mean that we should shut our eyes to it; but it shouldn't make us shut our eyes to other things too' (C. Daly King, *Arrogant Alibi*). It is Dr Pons, the psychologist (Daly King himself in fictional shape) who is speaking, not some illiterate moron. A sense construction? Perhaps; but it jars.

toper and **drunkard; drinker.** *Toper* (mainly literary) is synonymous with *drunkard*, 'a hard drinker'; for *drunkard*, see also at **drunk.** The term *drinker* requires a qualifying word or phrase, as in 'a hard drinker', 'a moderate drinker', 'a drinker of nothing but water'. For *dipsomaniac* and *alcoholic* see **drunk.**

topic and **subject** are nowadays virtually synonymous, although a *topic* is often one

subsection or aspect of a more general *subject*.

topography, geography, chorography. Whereas *geography* relates to the entire earth, or a considerable part of it, and treats the subject in general terms, *topography* is the detailed description of, say, a town or a district; *chorography* stands midway between the two – it deals with districts and regions but not with towns, villages, hamlets, valleys, etc. Greek *gē*, 'the earth', *topos* 'a place', *chora*, 'a land'; + Gr. *graphia*, 'descriptive science'.

tornado. See **cyclone.**

tortuous is sometimes misused for *torturous* and for *tortious* (a legal term).

tost for *tossed* is now poetical. Avoid it in prose.

totalitarian is so often misused or loosely used that *OED's* definition may serve to redress the balance. 'Of or pertaining to a policy which permits no rival loyalties or parties', as in 'A reaction ... against parliamentarianism ... in favour of a "totalitarian" or unitary state, whether Fascist or Communist' (*The Times*, 1929).

totally destroyed appears, as a tautology, on the style sheets of many newspaper editors. 'A house is destroyed' is usually sufficient. But suppose that one is describing a row of houses subjected to fire: one house is *half destroyed*, i.e. destroyed as to one-half; the next, however, is wholly destroyed – *totally destroyed* (Frank Whitaker, in the *JIJ*, January 1939). See VOGUE WORDS.

touching. See CONJUNCTIONS, DISGUISED.

tough, 'a street ruffian', is no longer colloquial; but the corresponding adjective ('of criminal or potentially criminal proclivities') and *tough*, 'very unfortunate; unjust' are colloquialisms.

tour. See **trip.**

track record. See VOGUE WORDS.

trade union and **trades union.** The plurals are *trade unions* and *trades unions*. In Britain, the preferred form of the singular is *trade union*, except in the title of the *Trades Union Congress*; in the USA it is *labor union*.

tragedy. See **disaster.**

tragic; tragical. *Tragic* is the correct form (opposed to *comic*) in the sense 'of, pertaining to, belonging to, proper to tragedy (a branch of the drama)'; but 'resembling tragedy in respect of its matter; relating to or expressing fatal or dreadful events, hence sad, gloomy' allows either *tragic* or *tragical*.

transcendent; transcendental. *Transcendent* = 'pre-eminent', as in 'A person of altogether transcendent greatness' (Seeley); as a synonym of '(merely) eminently great or good; excellent', it is loose English. In the sense 'extraordinary', both forms are correct; but for 'superhuman, supernatural' and for 'abstract, metaphysical' (a vague usage to be avoided), *transcendental* is correct. In Theology, the word is *transcendent*; in Mathematics, *transcendental*. In Philosophy, *transcendental* is applied to the system of Emerson and to a tenet of Schilling's system; in Aristotelian philosophy, the word is *transcendent*. Kant distinguishes: for him, *transcendent* = 'outside (or transcending) experience; unrealizable (in human experience)'; whereas *transcendental* = 'not derived from experience; *a priori*', and hence it is applied to any philosophy resembling Kant's 'in being based upon the recognition of an *a priori* element in experience' (*OED*). *Transcendental Meditation* is a method of mental relaxation derived from Hinduism.

transfer is occasionally misused for *convert* and for *transpose*. The former error occurs in '... Some pencilled figures, Ten thousand dollars. Rebecca found him a pen and watched him transfer dollars into pounds' (Warwick Deeping, *Sackcloth and Silk*).

transitory and **transient.** Both are correct in the sense 'temporary; fleeting; momentary'. *Transitory action* is a legal technicality. *Transient* is often preferred for short duration caused by rapid movements, as in 'transient hotel guests', and *transitory* for the inevitable passing of something desirable, as in 'transitory pleasures'.

transmit is officialese for *forward* or merely *send* or *post*.

transpire is loosely used for *happen* or *occur*, its figurative meaning is properly *to become known, to come to light*.

transportation, for *transport* or *pass* or *ticket* or *fare*, is an American word, though it is now coming into British use.

trauma, traumatic, traumatize. See VOGUE WORDS.

travail is 'the labour and pangs of childbirth', also 'to suffer these'; *travel* is '(a) journeying', also 'to journey'.

treachery and **treason.** The former has the wider meaning, being both general (when it is synonymous with *treason*) and particular (= 'an act of treason or perfidy'). In the general sense, 'deceit, cheating, perfidy; violation of faith, betrayal of trust', *treachery* is preferred to *treason*, but in the special application, 'deception or desertion of one's sovereign' or of the government of the state to which one owes allegiance, *treason* is preferred, with the variant *high treason*; and *treason* is, in all references and contexts, the legal term. *Treacherousness* may be used of anything unreliable, such as ice or one's memory.

treasonable and **treasonous.** In the extended sense, 'perfidious', only the former is used. In the nuances, 'of the nature of treason, involving treason, characterized by, hence characteristic of treason', the terms are synonymous: both 'a treasonable conspiracy' and 'a treasonous conspiracy' are correct; 'a treasonous libel', 'a treasonable letter' might also be 'a treasonable libel', 'a treasonous letter': but *treasonable* is gradually superseding *treasonous* (*OED*).

treat; treat of; treat on. *Treat on* is incorrect for *treat of.* To *treat of* is 'to deal with (some matter, whether in speech or in writing); to discourse on', as in 'His book treats of a more abstruse subject.' To *treat* a subject is to discuss it (in speech or writing), now generally 'to deal with [it] in the way of literary art', the former nuance occurring in 'What subjects did he treat?', the latter in 'I wonder how he will treat the subject', 'The life of St Stephen ... has been treated in mural frescoes' (*OED*).

treble and **triple.** In the sense 'three times as much or many; multiplied by three; of three times the measure or amount', *triple* is preferable to *treble*; thus, 'a triple scale' (*not* in music), 'The quantity should not be less than triple the weight of the solids consumed', 'If *A* is the third part of *B*, *B* is the triple (part) of *A.*' In the sense 'consisting of three things (or sets of things) or members; threefold', *treble* and *triple* are synonymous; thus, 'A treble enclosure', 'A kind of shirt of double or treble elk-hide', and 'A triple bank of oars', 'Triple rows of chairs': but *triple* is now the commoner. In the sense 'having three applications or relations; of three kinds', *treble* is preferred, as in 'Every part and episode [of a certain book] has its double and treble meaning.' In music: *triple*, adjective, does not occur – except in the phrases *triple counterpoint*, *triple fugue*, *triple rhythm*, *triple time*; as a noun, *triple* does not occur at all (*OED*).

trek was originally 'a journey performed in an ox-waggon', 'an organized migration or expedition by ox-waggon'; hence, 'any migration or collective journeying' – but it implies a long and arduous journey, and is not properly used of merely a holiday movement to the seaside (etc.). It has, among journalists, become a 'rubber-stamp word' (see **amazing**).

trend. See **tend.**

triad. See **triumvirate.**

trial for *attempt* is incorrect, as in 'Like a fussy old man who' – properly *that* – 'is

afraid of losing his dignity, and in the very trial at keeping it, is seen without it' (Paul Horgan, *A Lamp on the Plains*).

trilogy, trio. See **triumvirate.**

tri-monthly, 'occurring once every three months' or 'lasting for three months'; in the former sense *quarterly* is preferable; in the latter, *of three months*. Yet the sense in which a term is needed is 'occurring three times a month': therefore, why not adopt *tri-monthly* in that sense? See **bimonthly.**

trip is a quick journey there and back, by land, sea, or air, and for business or pleasure; 'a business trip to Tokyo', 'a coach trip round the island'. A *journey* is from one place to another, and takes some time, the word emphasizing the actual process of travelling. A *tour* visits several places, as with 'a city sightseeing tour'.

triple. See **treble.**

triumvirate (etymologically, a set or combination of three men, especially three rulers) is never, *trio* rarely, applied to aught other than persons. (Although *trio* has other senses in music.) To write of 'a triumvirate of test matches' (for three such matches), as I have seen done by one who should know better, is faintly ridiculous. A series of three novels or (long) poems or plays is a *trilogy*; or four, a *tetralogy*. *Triad* may be used of three heroes, three matricides, three film stars, and so on; and is obligatory in certain learned or technical connections (e.g. in music, in Welsh literature).

troop; troops; trooper; troupe; trouper. A *troop* is that sub-division of cavalry which corresponds to a company of infantry and a battery of artillery; *troops* is 'armed forces collectively' without *the*, as in 'to raise troops'; *the troops* is 'soldiers' or 'the soldiers', as in 'The spirit of the troops is excellent'; there is no singular to either *troops* or *the troops*. A *troop* is also three or more patrols of Scouts, or more generally an assemblage of persons or creatures in motion. A *trooper* is a horse soldier, a cavalryman, hence a cavalry horse. A *troupe* is a company of actors, dancers, or performing animals; a member of a troupe is a *trouper*.

troposphere, stratosphere, atmosphere, ionosphere. The third is the gaseous envelope that, sphere-shaped, surrounds the earth; the first, that layer of atmospheric air which extends upwards, for some seven miles, from the surface of the earth and in which the temperature falls, as one moves higher; and *stratosphere* is that layer of air which lies beyond the troposphere and in which the temperature is constant in the lower part and increases as one moves higher. The *ionosphere* begins above the stratosphere, extends to about 600 miles from the earth's surface, and is able to reflect radio waves. In short, the *atmosphere* consists of the *stratosphere*, the *troposphere*, and the *ionosphere*.

troubled; troublesome; troublous. *Troubled* is applied to a sea or other extent of water, or a sky that is stormy; to wine or water that is turbid (coloured with sediment; made muddy or thick). Also to moods, thoughts, attitudes, minds, hearts, sleep, periods of time that are disturbed, disordered, disquieted, agitated, afflicted ('a troubled ghost'; 'these troubled times', 'troubled reign', 'goaded by this troubled thought ...'). *Troublesome* is now used but rarely in any sense other than that of 'giving trouble; causing annoyance; vexatious or distressing', as in 'a troublesome cough', 'troublesome neighbours'. *Troublous* is a literary synonym of *troubled* as applied to a stormy sea; hence it is applied to a violent wind — another literary application; to periods, reigns, lives, state (of an institution); but in its own right, and without the competition of either *troubled* or *troublesome*, it further means '(of persons or their attributes) turbulent, disorderly; restless, unquiet', as in 'Troublous and adventurous spirits, men of broken fortunes ... and boundless desires' (Motley), but even here it is rather literary than general for 'turbulent; restless, unquiet' (*OED*).

trout: pl. **trouts,** except in sporting use: 'He may guddle trouts in a stream', 'Pike

and trout are to be had in the lochs.' When various species (or more than one species) are concerned, the plural is — or should be — *trouts*, as in 'There is a good book on the trouts of the Catskills.' See also SPORTING PLURALS.

truculent is catachrestic in the sense 'base, mercenary'. Nor does it mean 'surly'. It now chiefly = 'aggressively defiant, pugnacious'.

trustworthy; trusty. The former = 'worthy of trust or confidence; reliable'; so does *trusty*, but *trusty* is archaic in this sense, except in the phrase *our trusty and well-beloved* (in letters from sovereign to subject). *Trusty* (n.) means a convict trusted and allowed special privileges, and is not to be confused with *trustee*.

truth. See at **veracity.**

try and do (something) is colloquial for *try to do* (something). It is good English idiom, but it cannot be used in the negative, or with *tries, tried, trying*.

tubercular; tuberculous. The latter is now reserved for pathological and medical contexts ('tuberculous tissue', 'tuberculous meningitis', 'tuberculous pork, tuberculous cows', 'hospitals for the tuberculous sick'), whereas *tubercular* is, in discriminating usage, reserved for natural-history contexts, where it = (*a*) 'of a tubercle, consisting of a tubercle, of the form and/or nature of a tubercle' (a *tubercle* being a small tuber), or (*b*), 'tuberculate', i.e. having tubercles, or covered with tubercles (*OED*). Persons with tuberculosis are *tubercular*.

TURGIDITY is 'inflation of language; grandiloquence, pomposity, bombast' (*OED*); a seeming, but windy, grandeur of language; a grandeur that rings insincere or unsuitable. It is the hall-mark of pretentious and ambitious minor poets — the Montgomerys, Robert Pollok, and their like. (Not a common fault in the 20th century.)

two first. See at **first, two.**

two halves, cut into, is verbose, redundant, absurd for *to cut into halves*. But *two halves make a whole* is, of course, correct.

two twins is tautological for *twins*.

type (of), like *case (of)*, is often used unnecessarily or infelicitously; as in 'He's not that type of person'; 'Events of that type generally arouse suspicion', for 'Such events ...' or 'Events of that kind ...'; 'The rose is not that type of flower.' Keep *type* in its right place. Cf. **typical.**

typhoid (fever) and **typhus.** The former, once supposed to be a mere variety of the latter, is also called *enteric* (*fever*). *Typhus* is a very acute infectious fever. *Typhoid* is derived from *typhus*; *typhus* from Greek *tuphos*, 'smoke' or 'vapour', hence 'stupor'. See esp. *OED*.

typhoon. See **cyclone.**

typical should be modified only after due consideration. Such a sentence as the following strikes one as odd: 'Now there I had Smith's début – a rather typical performance which gave me quite a good idea of his methods' (Cameron McCabe, *The Face on the Cutting-Room Floor*): why *rather*? For living things, *characteristic* is preferable to *typical*.

typist is the person operating a *typewriter* (the machine); 'to *typewrite*' is formal for 'to *type*', and occurs chiefly in the adjectival form *typewritten*.

typographic is perhaps obsolescent; **typographical,** current.

U

uglily sounds ugly in many contexts: not all, for in the following two quotations from *OED* it is not cacophonous (and there are many other instances where it is either tolerable or even euphonious) – 'In those representations man indeed was not more uglily than fearfully made' (Sayce); 'The town is ... uglily picturesque.' And it is much more economical than *in an ugly manner*.

ult., prox., inst. In dates: *last, next, this* (*month*, understood). Commercialese, therefore to be avoided.

ultimate. See COMPARATIVES, FALSE.

ultra (adj.) is both ugly and odd for *excessive* or *immoderate*, as in 'ultra reverence', 'ultra respect'; fortunately it is obsolescent.

umbrage, take, to take offence, is an elegancy, and threatening to become officialese.

umbrella. See **parasol.**

un- with participles may produce curious ambiguities. Something *uncovered* or *unwrapped* may either have been taken out of its covers or wrappings, or never have been *covered* or *wrapped*. The adjective form *unbending* may either mean 'inflexible' or come from the verb *to unbend*, 'to relax', which gives the opposite meaning. There is no problem with such adjectives as *unwashed*, since it is impossible to *unwash* things; but one should look out for these possible dual meanings.

un- and in- in adjectives. See **in-** and **non-.** Here, however, is appended a short list of *im*- or *in*- and *un*- terms. (By the way, *un*- is, like *de*- and *re*-, overworked by officialese and gobbledygook.)

impecunious
impenetrable
impertinent
implacable
inadmissible
incapable
incomparable
inconsequent
inconsolable
incredible
incredulous

indecisive
indelible
indirect
inexact
infamous
infelicitous
inhuman
intransigent
unable (but *incapable*)
unbalanced
unbelievable (but *incredible*)
unblessed
unbounded
uncomparable (see separate entry)
unconsoled (but *inconsolable*)
uncrowned
undecided (but *indecisive*)
unequal
unfaithful
unfavourable
ungrateful
unhappy (but *infelicitous*)
unhorsed
unimaginative
unimportant
unpenetrated (but *impenetrable*)
unpleasant
unpretentious
untenable
untruthful

unable. See **incapable.**

unambiguous should not be used as an exact synonym of *perfectly clear*. Thus Dr L. Susan Stebbing, in *Logical Positivism and Analysis*, writes: 'An *unambiguous expression* is not equivalent to a *perfectly clear expression*, since we may understand more or less clearly' – i.e. more clearly or less clearly. 'It is important not to confuse *ambiguity*, *vagueness*, *unclearness*; these three are quite different, and mutually independent.' This footnote is increased in significance when we see that the passage it glosses is this: 'Moore' – Professor G. E. Moore – 'holds that to *understand an expression* is not equivalent to being able *to give a correct analysis* of its meaning. He has pointed out that the failure to see that these are *not* equivalent has been responsible for a good many mistakes with regard to the nature of philo-

sophical problems and with regard to their possible solution.'

unanimous. See COMPARATIVES, FALSE.

unapt. See **inapt.**

UNATTACHED PARTICIPLES. See CONFUSED PARTICIPLES.

unavoidable, misused for *unchangeable* (or *unchanging*). 'As was his unavoidable custom, he observed the faces of the crowd around him' (Carolyn Wells, *The Clue of the Eyelash*).

unaware is the adjective, **unawares** the chief form of the adverb.

unbeknown is not, as stated by Weseen, dialectal; **unbeknownst** is dialectal and colloquial. As a variant of *unknown*, it is perhaps unusual, but certainly not rare, as in 'the land of the unbeknown'; its commonest role, however, is that which it plays in the phrase *unbeknown to* (= *unknown to*), 'without the knowledge of', as in 'The bottle had been opened, unbeknown to the purchaser'; the elliptical *unbeknown*, 'without anybody's knowledge; unnoticed, undetected', is becoming rare ('My love rose up so early And stole out unbeknown', Housman) (*OED*).

unbelievable and **believable** for *incredible* (or *difficult to believe in*) and *credible*, although theoretically possible and indeed listed in the best dictionaries, are somewhat unusual now and almost catachrestic; certainly they are to be avoided in connection with persons or their representation in books. Obviously 'It is unbelievable' is permissible and even idiomatic when it applies to a fact or a rumour; but *unbelievable* rings oddly in 'The first readers of Mr McCabe's book … rightly refused to believe that there could possibly be a detective as unconventional and unscrupulous as Smith. The critics, therefore, attacked McCabe, the author, for having invented such an unbelievable character' (Cameron McCabe, *The Face on the Cutting-Room Floor*).

unbeliever. See **disbeliever.**

unbend. Under the heading *The 'Unbend' Mystery*, Wilfred Whitten (in *Good and Bad English*) gives an admirable example of the misuse of this word, supplied to him by a correspondent: 'He was a stern and unbending old man, but he could unbend on occasion', and quotes his correspondent's comment: 'This choice specimen of literary English I came across in the work of an author of repute, but he sinned in good company, for they all do it. Only, one would think that the very form of the complete sentence would have shown him, had he taken a moment's thought, that the verb in the second half should be "bend".' See **un-.**

uncomparable is not the same as *incomparable*; it is a hybrid word, but necessary to distinguish its meaning, 'that cannot be compared' from that of *incomparable*, 'above or beyond comparison' (in the sense of likeness). Both words are among the uncomparable adjectives, *q.v.* at **COMPARATIVES, FALSE.**

unconscious and **subconscious.** *Subconscious*, in ordinary language, is 'partly or imperfectly aware', as in 'He was subconscious that he was trying a bold experiment' (Hawthorne, 1864): this sense is now not used of persons, although one might speak of 'a subconscious realization of the danger'. In psychology, it = 'partially or imperfectly conscious; belonging to a class of phenomena resembling those of consciousness, but not clearly perceived or recognized'; hence, 'belonging to that portion of the mental field the processes of which are outside the range of attention'. *Unconscious*, in psychology, means 'performed, employed, etc., without conscious action', as in *unconscious cerebration*. In ordinary language, it = 'unaware, unregarding, or regardless' (as in 'He was unconscious of the danger although it was obvious to everyone else'); 'not characterized by — not endowed with — the faculty or presence of consciousness'; 'temporarily without consciousness' (*knocked unconscious*); 'not known to or thought of as possessed by or existing in oneself' ('The boxer had an unconscious grace'); 'not attended by, or present to, consciousness' ('It is wrong to punish an unconscious act', J. Martineau, 1866). *Subconscious*, then, should be confined to psychological contexts. [With thanks to *OED*.]

uncourteous. See at **discourteous.**

undeceived, as a participial adjective, can be ambiguous, for there is a verb *undeceive*, to tell the truth to, to inform a person of a mistake, with a past participle *undeceived* employable as an adjective. 'But she shook her head, undeceived' (Agatha Christie, *Dumb Witness*), where the meaning is 'not deceived', but where one is delayed by the possibility of the meaning 'informed' (of something). See **un-.**

under and **below** and **beneath.** See **above and over.**

under the circumstances. When in doubt use *in*, which is always correct. See **circumstances** ...

underhand; underhanded(ly). The only sense in which the latter word is necessary (or desirable) is 'short of "hands"; *undermanned*' as in 'The clergy are utterly underhanded' (Samuel Wilberforce, 1874). *Underhand* (with several senses, including *sly[ly]*) is both adjective and adverb (*OED*).

underlay and **underlie.** Apart from the former as a printing technicality and the latter as a geological as well as a mining one, the essential difference is this: *Underlay* is 'to support (something) by placing something else underneath it; to furnish *with* something laid below', as in 'You ought not to stitch any wounded finger, ... but underlay it with little splinters' and 'Their project of underlaying the sea with electric wires' (*The Athenaeum*, 1851).

To *underlie* is 'to form a basis to; to exist beneath the surface-aspect of', as in 'That germ of truth which underlies all falsity and every falsehood': this is the dominant sense. A sense once important but now slightly obsolescent is, 'to be subjected to, to have imposed on one; to submit to, to undergo or suffer', especially in reference to accusation, penalty, punishment, pain, as in 'He underlies also the graver charge of intentional misrepresentation' (Donaldson, 1857), 'Since my last visit to the Russian lines I had underlain a ban' (O'Donovan, 1882) (*OED*).

undersigned, I (or we) **the.** Permissible in Law; affected or tediously jocular elsewhere. In 1868 Dickens could write, 'The undersigned is in his usual brilliant condition'; that was a long time ago.

understand, for *hear* or be *told*, is officialese and sometimes ambiguous.

UNDERSTATEMENT or *Meiosis*; and *Litotes*. *Understatement* is the everyday synonym of the learned *meiosis*; understatement itself is the supreme virtue of the Englishman. If an Englishman says, 'I dislike that woman', that woman should remove herself as expeditiously as possible; if he says that some contretemps is 'rather a nuisance', he means that it is utterly damnable or extremely unfortunate.* But whereas, in speech, understatement is, all in all, a virtue, it may easily, in writing, become very misleading: do not, therefore, overdo British reticence and English *meiosis*.

Litotes is that 'figure of speech, in which an affirmative is expressed by the negative of the contrary; an instance of this' (*OED*), as in 'a citizen of *no mean city*', 'He is no coward.'

undertone and **overtone.** See **overtone and undertone.**

undiscriminating and **indiscriminate.** Usage is tending to confine the former to persons, the latter to aim, purpose, motive, impulse, selection, plan, method, treatment, behaviour; a tendency that, if given effect, makes for clarity and for that distinctiveness which characterizes

*See O. Jespersen, *Growth and Structure of the English Language*, Sec. II.

all sensitive or subtle writing. The senses of *indiscriminate* are: 'not marked by discrimination or discernment; done without making distinctions', hence 'confused or promiscuous'. The person of discrimination or discernment is a *discriminating* (or *discerning*) person.

undue and **unduly** are often – indeed, usually – unnecessary. Examine the need before you employ either of them.

undying. See **deathless.**

unelastic and **inelastic.** Either is permissible, though the latter is preferable. In figurative contexts, *inelastic* is much the commoner.

unendurable. See COMPARATIVES, FALSE.

UN-ENGLISH PLURALS. See PLURALS, UN-ENGLISH.

unfertilized is correct; but rather *infertile* than *unfertile*, rather *infertility* than *unfertility*, etymology demanding *in-* and usage not rejecting it.

unfrequent is inferior to *infrequent*, but *unfrequented* is correct, *infrequented* incorrect; *unfrequency*, however, is rare for *infrequency*.

unharmonious is inferior to *inharmonious*.

unheard of = 'not before heard of, hitherto unknown', hence 'new, strange', hence 'unprecedented'; it is, therefore to be used with care.

unhospitable is inferior to *inhospitable*.

unhuman is much weaker than – not an error for – *inhuman*. *Unhuman* should be reserved for the sense 'not pertaining to mankind'; for the sake of clarity, use it neither for *inhuman* nor for *superhuman*.

unilateral, one-sided, should be left to diplomacy; the more so since some supporters of *unilateral disarmament* appear to have thought that the word means 'unanimous'.

uninhabitable. See **habitable** and COMPARATIVES, FALSE.

unionized = 'formed into a trade union; *un-ionized* = 'not converted into ions'. The hyphen is thus obligatory in the latter.

unique, most or **rather** or **very.** An object that is 'unique' is the only one of its kind in existence; there can be no qualification of the absolute without a contradiction of the quality which it asserts. The frequent use of *unique(ly)* to express mere rarity or excellence is incorrect. See COMPARATIVES, FALSE.

United Kingdom, the. See **Great Britain.**

universal. See COMPARATIVES, FALSE.

unlawful. See **illegal.**

unless, misused for *except*. 'Unless when carried out on a set purpose, it [i.e. alliteration] offends the ear' (Alexander Bain, *English Composition and Rhetoric*, enlarged edition, Part II, 1888).

unloosen is obsolescent for '*to unloose*'. It is not synonymous with *loosen*.

unmeasurable is preferable in the two literal senses 'incapable of being measured, on account of great size, extent, or amount, in reference to material things, to dimensions, to time', as in 'The tower ... was of an unmeasurable height', and 'not admitting of – insusceptible of – measurement', as in 'The Church is unmeasurable by foot-rule' (*OED*). But in the sense of 'too great for measurement, immense', *immeasurable* is preferable, as in 'immeasurable ambition', 'the immeasurable grace of God', 'Religion is immeasurable.'

unmoral, amoral, non-moral, immoral. The last – opposed to *moral* – is positive ('evil; corrupt, depraved'); the first three are negative, and synonymous one with another. Purists prefer *non-moral* to *unmoral*. *Amoral*, however, is the best word for the sense 'not to be judged by a moral criterion; not connected with moral considerations', though Fowler condemns it.

unpracticable is (or should be) obsolete for *impracticable*; **unpractical** is obsolescent as a synonym of *impractical*, but good writers distinguish *unpractical* (merely not practical) from *impractical* (decidedly the opposite of *practical*).

unqualified is not, as some persons assume, exactly synonymous with *unrestricted* or *entire*. This erroneous presumption vitiates the homely force of 'To have unqualified charge of a garden makes a vital difference in a person's outlook on gardening.' Usage confines this sense to assent, approval, success.

unquestionably, for *preferably, surely*, or *certainly*, is often unnecessary or even weak.

unreadable is subjective ('too dull or obscure to be read with patience'); *illegible* is objective ('indecipherable'). Thus, 'Many of the manuscripts of unreadable novels are illegible.'

unreligious is neutral, 'not religious', or pejorative, 'ungodly'; *irreligious* is pejorative, 'ungodly, impious'.

unresenting of is incorrect for *unresentful of* (or *not resenting*), as in 'Unresenting of his old friend's raillery' (Carolyn Wells, *The Clue of the Eyelash*).

unresponsible = 'not in a position of responsibility; not yet at the age at which responsibility sets in'; *irresponsible* may be used in the same sense ('You shouldn't have handed the question-paper to an irresponsible person'), but generally, in current usage, it = 'feckless, shiftless, undependable'.

unsanitary should be reserved for 'not possessing sanitation'; *insanitary* = 'injurious to health; unhealthy'. 'An uninhabited desert is merely unsanitary, but a camp of nomads therein may be offensively insanitary.'

unscathed. See **scatheless.**

unsociable, unsocial. See **antisocial.**

unsuccess means, negatively, 'lack of success'; positively, 'failure'. As one generally opposes *failure* to *success, unsuccess,* if used at all, might well be reserved for the negative sense, 'lack of success'.

until. See **till.**

until such time as. Until.

untouchable. See COMPARATIVES, FALSE.

upon and **on** (prepositions). Of these near synonyms, *upon* is stronger (more emphatic) and more formal and impressive than *on*; but it is slowly falling into disuse in speech (more's the pity!); in writing, *upon* is often preferred to *on* on the score of euphony. In many combinations, however, *on* is the only possibility; 'on Tuesday', 'on foot', 'on the radio', 'on holiday'.

upstair can be only an adverb, and is there obsolescent for *upstairs*; as a noun, only *upstairs* is permissible. The same with *downstair.*

upward and **upwards.** The latter is adverb only; the former is chiefly an adjective, but often functions as an adverb in American English and in older British writing.

upward adjustment. Rise (in price). Economese.

upwards of is incorrect for *rather less than* or *nearly* or *not quite,* as in 'upwards of a hundred' (some number in the 90s). Properly, *upwards of* = 'slightly or rather more than'.

urban is 'of or belonging to or characteristic of or resembling a city', whereas *urbane* is 'having the manners or culture regarded as characteristic of a city', hence 'civil, courteous', hence 'blandly polite', indeed 'suave', and is used in transferred senses ('urbane manners', 'urbane mind'; 'urbane epistle').

urgent is a strong and dignified word. Don't cheapen it.

us both and **us each.** See **we both ...**

USAGE. See IDIOM.

use. See **consume** and **what use.**

USELESS LATIN ADJECTIVES. There are, in English, numerous Latin- and Greek-derived adjectives that are unnecessary, for they duplicate an excellent or, at the least, a satisfactory 'Saxon' adjective (or noun used adjectivally). To speak of the *hodiernal post* (or *mail*) for *today's post, avuncular* for *uncle's* is intolerable; but then, very few of us would! See Jespersen's *Growth and Structure of the English Language,* Sections 131–2.

user-friendly. See VOGUE WORDS.

using. See CONJUNCTIONS, DISGUISED.

utilize, utilization are, 99 times out of 100, much inferior to *use,* verb and noun; the one other time, they are merely inferior.

utmost, utter, uttermost. See COMPARATIVES, FALSE.

Etymologically, *utter* is the comparative, and *utmost* the (double) superlative of Old English *ut,* 'out' ('external'); *uttermost* = *utter + most,* an etymological absurdity.

Utter now = 'extreme, absolute, complete, entire', as in 'utter darkness'; (of denials, refusals, recantations, etc.) 'unmodified' or 'decisive'; (of persons) 'complete', as in 'an utter fool', 'that utter stranger'.

Uttermost is obsolescent in the senses 'outermost' ('He flew to the uttermost island of the Hebridean group'), and 'extreme' or 'utmost', as in Ruskin's 'To speak with the uttermost truth of expression'; its only active sense is the very restricted one, 'last in a series', as in 'I shall pay to the uttermost farthing.' *Uttermost,* in short, is disappearing from general use; it is already rare except in cultured speech and good writing.

Utmost, physically = 'outmost' (most remote; most external), as in 'Knights of utmost North and West' (Tennyson);

hence, it = 'furthest extended', as in 'With my utmost sight I could only just discern it' – a sense now becoming rare; obsolescent, too, is the sense 'latest (in time)' or 'final', as in 'Adding the utmost oil as a lubricant'. The predominant sense is 'of the greatest or highest degree, number, amount; extreme', as in 'The utmost profit of a cow', 'With the utmost cheerfulness'.

V

vacant. See empty.

VAGUENESS. See WOOLLINESS.

valuable is that which has intrinsic value; *valued* is (that which is) regarded as having value. A *valuable* thing is perhaps not properly *valued*; a *valued* one is not necessarily *valuable*.

valueless. See invaluable.

vantage. See advantage.

vapid (pronounced *vappid*) and insipid. *Vapid* (L. *vapidus*, savourless) is (of liquors, beverages) 'flat', (of food) 'flavourless'; hence, fig., 'devoid of animation, zest, or interest' (esp. 'vapid talk', 'vapid amusements'). *Insipid* (L. *insipidus*, tasteless) is, lit., 'Without taste, or with very little taste'; hence, fig., 'lifeless; dull or unexciting', as in 'insipid compliments' and 'kisses, though pleasant in private, are insipid in public' (Lytton). The nouns are *vapidity* and *insipidity*; *vapidness* and *insipidness* are inferior forms (*OED*).

variant, misused. In 'He has heard very variant opinions of his book', 'variant' means 'varying, diverse'. Not strictly incorrect in the adjectival sense, *variant* is met with chiefly in biological and technical connections, as in 'variant spellings'.

varicoloured and variegated are, the former obligatorily, the latter preferably, to be used of or in reference to colour. *Varied* can safely be discarded by those who fear to confound it with *various*, for every sense of *varied* is shared by *various*, which, moreover, has senses lacked by *varied*. As for *various*: the discriminating writer refrains from using it in the weakened senses 'more than one; several; many'. That nuance, 'many', is perhaps inevitable, for the meaning of *various* often merges into that of *many different*. 'We met various times' is, at best, infuriatingly vague: say *several* or *many* as the context demands (*OED*).

varied. See previous entry.

VARIETY. See SYNONYMS, last paragraph.

various. See varicoloured.

venal and venial are often confused, but have opposite meanings; the former being 'purchasable', 'subject to mercenary or corrupt influences', the latter 'pardonable, excusable' (*OED*).

vengeance and revenge (nn.). See avenge.

venom and poison. The former is the poison secreted by snakes and certain animals; also it is used figuratively for 'virulence; bitter spite or malice'.

venture. See adventure.

veracity and truth. *Veracity* = 'truthfulness; accuracy', or even 'a truth', but not 'truth' itself.

VERB + (PRO)NOUN + GOVERNED VERB ('I saw it gain on him'); and VERB + (PRO)NOUN + ing FORM OF VERB ('I saw it gaining on him'). In the former, the second or governed verb expresses a single, definite, time-precise, completed action, whereas in the latter the -ing form ('gaining') expresses a continuous, incomplete action. In the former, the sense is 'I saw that it gained on him', but in the latter the sense is 'I saw that it was gaining on him, but I did not see what eventually happened.' Cf. 'I shall see it gain on him' and 'I shall see it gaining on him', likewise 'I see [the true, not the historic present] it gain on him' and 'I see it gaining on him': the same nuances hold good in those two tenses, except that in the present the limiting of the action in 'I see it gain on him' is less clear-cut than it is in 'I saw it gain on him.' This generalization may seem obvious, as indeed it is; yet the rule therein implicit is often flouted by careless writers.

VERB UNCOMPLETED. 'Political upheavals in Europe influence the Londoner's daily life in strange ways, and they always have' (*The Evening News*). Such short cuts are now commonplace in all but the most formal English, which would here prefer 'and have always done so'. It is not yet, however, fully acceptable to use *do, doing, done* without *so* in such situations, as in 'they always have done' or 'they never should do'.

verbiage and **verbosity** are occasionally confused. Roughly, *verbosity* results in *verbiage*; nowadays, *verbosity* is applied mostly to speaking, *verbiage* mostly to writing; *verbosity* is both tendency and result, whereas *verbiage* is only result. *Verbiage*, by the way, has a further sense, now rare and, indeed, almost obsolete: 'wording, diction, verbal expression'.

VERBOSITY.
> A plethora of words becomes the
> apoplexy of reason.
> (C. A. Ward, *Oracles of
> Nostradamus*, 1891)

OED defines verbosity as 'superfluity of words', with the alternatives 'wordiness; prolixity'.

Verbosity is a general tendency and the resulting practice. (It sometimes overlaps TAUTOLOGY, *q.v.*) Wilson Benington has amplified the *OED* definition in this clarifying way: 'Using more words than are necessary, as though talking for the sake of talking or of hearing the sound of one's own voice; preference of long

words, high-sounding phrases, complicated sentences, to simple language and clear expression: – habits noticeable in speakers afflicted with logorrhoea and equally characteristic of grandiloquent writers.'

A few brief examples of a fault exemplified best by long passages:

'Such are the vicissitudes of this our sublunary existence': for 'Such is life.'

'Lassitude seems to be a word unknown to the vocabulary of the swallows' (Morris, *British Birds*): an amusing instance of ponderous circumlocution, all the heavier because it was intended to lighten the dullness of direct statement.

'Modern Stockholmers, *irrespective of class*, are accustomed to fairly substantial midday meals in restaurants, and typists must have shared the indignation of their managing directors at *being forced this week within the confines of a packet of sandwiches*' (*The Daily Telegraph*, 22 Jan. 1938): the italics are mine.

'Are we quite sure that newly emancipated woman has yet acquired a sound biological status, or secured for herself a harmonious psycho-physiological equilibrium?' (cited by Sir Alan Herbert).

'Your eyes will scarcely believe that cameras could record its roaring climax of catastrophe and desolation' (advertisement of a film).

Verbosity, therefore, is almost the same thing as *pleonasm*, which is 'the use of more words in a sentence than are necessary to express the meaning; redundancy of expression' (generally *redundancy* alone) – except that *verbosity* has certain connotations that are absent from the extended signification of *pleonasm*.

Vergil is usually Anglicized as *Virgil*, but the poet's full name was Publius Vergilius Maro.

vernacular is often used loosely for *low language* and *jargon* (technicalities). Properly, the noun and adjective = '(the language) naturally spoken by the people of a particular country or district', i.e.

'native or indigenous (language)'; hence 'written, spoken, or translated into the native language'; 'belonging to or characteristic of the native language'. In the 16th–17th centuries, English was the vernacular, Latin the learned language, and French the language of diplomacy.

verse and **stanza.** For the sake of the valuable distinction, reserve *verse* (popularly what is here a stanza) for 'one line of verse or poetry' and use *stanza* for 'a small number of metrical lines forming a unit in a longer composition'.

verso and **recto.** The *recto* is the front, the *verso* the back of a manuscript leaf or a printed leaf or sheet. As *OED* remarks, 'The left-hand page of a book is the verso of that leaf, and faces the recto of the next.'

vertebra has pl. *vertebrae.*

very modifies adjective (*very angry*) or adverb (*very foolishly*), but not a past participle (*It is very improved* being wrong, *much improved* being right). Cf. **very interesting.**

very interesting but **much interested** or, less commonly, **very much interested.** Purists object to *very interested, very disappointed, very annoyed,* etc. They prefer *much interested, much* (or *very much*) *pleased, much disappointed.* Some of these participial adjectives with *-ed* have come to be considered as ordinary adjectives, so that *very tired, very pleased, very worried* are as legitimate as *very cold, very hungry.* In marginal cases, however, good writers prefer *much* or *very much.*

Clearly, idiom forbids *much interesting, much pleasing, much disappointing.* See **much and very.**

vest and **waistcoat.** A *waistcoat* is that part of a man's suit of clothes which he wears under his coat and which is of the same material as the coat and trousers, unless it is an *odd* waistcoat or a fancy one, and is usually called a *vest* in the USA. In British usage, *vest* is the more common noncommercial name for a man's or woman's undershirt. In both British and American

usage, *vest* is, with reference to women's apparel, 'part of a woman's dress bodice'. *Singlet* (once a kind of waistcoat) is 'an unlined woollen garment ... worn as a man's undershirt' (adapted from *OED*). Today one should add *T-shirt*, which in Britain is an outer garment only but in American usage is also another word for undershirt.

vestigial, misused for *rudimentary* or *rough-and-ready.* This error occurs several times in John Gunther's *Inside Asia.*

via, 'by way of', refers to the direction of a journey, not to the means of travelling; therefore the following is wrong, very wrong, misleadingly wrong: 'Out at the end of the wharf a man sold tickets to' – 'for' would be better – ' "excursion" trips via a speed boat' (Erle Stanley Gardner, *The Case of the Dangerous Dowager*).

viable. See VOGUE WORDS.

vicar. See **rector and vicar.**

vicinage and **vicinity; neighbourhood.** *Vicinage* is a rarer word than *vicinity* in the sense 'neighbourhood, surrounding district'. Both *vicinage* and *vicinity*, but not *neighbourhood*, also mean 'nearness', as in 'The common white pottery ... will not bear vicinage to a brisk kitchen fire for half-an-hour.' *In the vicinity* (or *vicinage*, or *neighbourhood*) *of* is a verbose way of saying 'about', as in 'in the vicinity of a hundred dollars'.

vicious for '(weather that is) *inclement* or *severe*' is not, as Weseen asserts, incorrect; it is, however, rather unusual and quite unnecessary.

vide = 'see!, consult!'; **viz.** = 'that is to say: namely; to wit'. 'This strange event (*vide* Motley) has never been satisfactorily explained'; 'Three of Plumer's men ..., viz., Troopers Abrahamson, White and Parkin'; *vide* but not viz. (the latter is short for *videlicet*) should be written in italics.

view (v.), misused for *look.* ' "If 'e can git aht o' 'ere", "Big Bill" said, viewing round the place in the light of a candle he had lit, "'e's a dam' sight cleverer'n what 'e looks"' (John G. Brandon). *View* is always transitive except in the sense 'to watch television'.

viewpoint. See **standpoint.**

vigil, properly a prolonged night-watch, is often misused to mean any wait, even if trivial and extremely brief. 'Selecting the most comfortable seat, and placing his beer on the floor beside him, Dick settled down to wait. It was not a long vigil; for in less than a couple of minutes Mr Potter made his appearance' (Victor Bridges, *Blue Silver*).

vigour for *rigour.* Frank Shaw, *Atlantic Murder,* 'Even the crew-quarters underwent a microscopic examination ... [The new hands,] naturally, were the ones to be watched with extra vigour.'

violin. See at **fiddle.**

violincella is an incorrect spelling and pronunciation of *violoncello.*

virility should not be used of sexual power in women.

vis-à-vis. Gobbledygook for *about*; prompted by *regarding.* It needs italics, hyphens, and an accent.

vital. See COMPARATIVES, FALSE.

vitamins.
From *The Observer,* 6 Feb. 1938.
Sir – the uncertainty as to the pronunciation of the word 'vitamins' referred to in the letter from Mr Henry Fields, of Leeds, published in your issue of 30th ult. in 'From the Post Bag', should, I think, be dispelled by bearing in mind that scientific authorities mainly adhere to the old Latin pronunciations.
The derivation of 'vitamin' from *vis, vita* apparently governs the question referred to.
One does not pronounce the word 'vitality' or 'vital' as *vee*-tality or vittality; nor do any of the scientific, medical, advisory, or general staff, nor any of our numerous medical, nursing, or scientific visitors at the laboratories and factory dealing with the treatment of vitamins ever pronounce the word other than as vitamins – with the long 'i'. –
Yours, etc. J. H. Wrentmore,
(Vitamins, Ltd) Hammersmith.
[Since the above was written, the accepted British pronunciations have come to rhyme the first syllable with either *sit* or *fright,* but not with *meet.*]

viz. See **vide.**

vocation. See **avocation.**

VOGUE WORDS. Many words (and a few phrases) have acquired a power and an influence beyond those which they originally possessed; certain pedants say, Beyond what these terms have any right to mean or to imply. But like persons, words cannot always be taken for granted. It just cannot be assumed that they will for ever trudge along in the prescribed rut and for ever do the expected thing! Journalists, authors, and the public whim – sometimes, also, the force of great events, the compulsion of irresistible movements – have raised lowly words to high estate or invested humdrum terms with a picturesque and individual life or brought to the most depressing jargon a not unattractive general currency. Such words gain a momentum of their own, whatever the primary impulse may have been.

Not all 'new' words or new senses that have come into vogue are necessarily to be castigated on that account; we need the new sense of *green* (discussed below) just as we need *fax* and *glasnost,* to name new phenomena; indeed, vogue words are seldom new coinages.

They have a relatively short life. We list here some that are particularly current in the 1990s; but see also those journalistic words dealt with at **amazing** and at OFFICIALESE.

academic in the sense of 'merely theoretical; with no practical bearing'.
acceptable for 'tolerable', as in 'an acceptable rate of casualties'.
aggressive for 'forceful and enterprising', a new appreciative sense.

allergic, 'strongly disliking'. See separate entry.

alternative. For the new sense, see separate entry.

ambience for 'surroundings; atmosphere'.

ambivalence, ambivalent, 'the coexistence of opposed feelings', once a technical term in psychology.

angle for 'approach; technique'. See separate entry.

archetypal, archetype for 'typical example of something', as in 'the archetypal golden-hearted whore'.

astronomical for 'extremely large'.

aware as in 'politically aware'; 'an aware person'.

backlash, 'adverse reaction'.

ball game for 'concern; set of circum-stances', as in 'It's a whole new ball game.' Originally American, so that the 'game' would at first mean baseball.

basically as an almost meaningless 'filler', as in 'This is basically where I disagree.'

blueprint for 'scheme; plan', as in 'The method will serve as a blueprint for our future work.'

born-again for 'converted', and now applied not only to fundamentalist Christianity. One can be a 'born-again conservationist'.

breakthrough for 'a major advance or discovery'.

caring for 'committed; compassionate.' 'The hospice provides a caring environment where people may spend their last days.'

catalyst for anyone or anything that precipitates change. A loose extension of its original sense in chemistry.

charisma, charismatic for the quality in a public figure that inspires devotion, and often now meaning no more than 'great personal charm'.

climate for 'prevailing mood', as in 'the present economic climate', and particularly in 'climate of opinion'.

clone for 'identical copy'. This originally botanical word was popularized in science fiction, and is now used, for instance, of a cheaper computer that simulates the properties of a more expensive one.

committed for 'dedicated', as in 'a committed Christian', 'a committed socialist'.

complex, now often meaning no more than 'a bee in one's bonnet', as in 'She has a complex about tidiness.' In psychology a complex is a whole related group of thoughts and feelings.

constructive for 'positive and helpful', as in 'a constructive approach'.

crash (adj.) for anything intended to give quick results, as in 'crash diet', 'crash course', 'crash programme'.

deliver (both transitive and intransitive) for 'carry out; produce the promised result', as in 'Will the government deliver on tax cuts?'

deploy for 'to use; place'. One deploys forces or arguments.

dialogue for 'discussion between political groups', as in 'East–West dialogue'.

dichotomy for 'discrepancy; conflict'. See separate entry.

dimension for 'aspect; facet', as in 'The rise in house prices added an extra dimension to the problem.'

eco-, from 'ecology', has spawned many popular non-technical compounds concerned with environmental issues, such as *eco-freak* and *eco-friendly*. See the paragraph on *-friendly* below.

environmental(ly), environmentalism, in contexts concerned with the protection of our environment. A product may be 'environmentally friendly', and a geographical area officially designated as 'Environmentally Sensitive'.

escalate (both transitive and intransitive) for 'rise; expand'. Prices can escalate, or a company might escalate its overseas trade.

ethnic for 'foreign; exotic', as used of food, clothes, music.

euphoria for 'happiness', and particularly 'over-optimism'.

Euro- is giving rise to all manner of compounds relating to the European Community, as with *Eurobond, Eurocrat, Eurotunnel,* and *Euro-sceptic.*

extrapolate has escaped from its original sense in mathematics and philosophy to mean 'infer from the known facts'.

face-lift for any procedure to improve the appearance of anything.

feedback is loosely used for 'response', as in 'get some feedback from our advertising campaign'.

flavour of the month (or *week,* or *year*) for 'a temporary fashion'. A cliché.

-free is a fashionable suffix, appearing in such widely different combinations as *nuclear-free, cholesterol-free, meat-free, salmonella-free.*

-friendly is another popular suffix. From the computing term *user-friendly* = 'easy for the non-specialist to use', it has broken away to form such compounds as *ozone-friendly* (of products) and *citizen-friendly* (of comprehensible legal drafting).

gender is a fashionable synonym for 'sex', as in 'prejudices based on the candidate's gender'.

global for 'worldwide', popularized first by Marshall McLuhan's concept of 'the global village', and now occurring constantly in 'global warming'.

grass roots for 'ordinary people; the rank and file'.

green (as adj., n., and v.) for anything to do with environmental issues. We now have green products, green labelling, the Greens or Green party, and of course Greenpeace.

guidelines for 'principles; criteria guiding action'.

hands-on was originally a computer term, but now means 'involving practical participation', as in 'get some hands-on experience of administration'.

image for 'perceived reputation', as in 'his public image', 'image-building'.

implement for 'carry out, fulfil'. One implements plans, promises, policies.

in-depth for 'thorough; detailed', as in 'an in-depth study'.

input originated in electronics and computer technology, but is now used for anything contributed to a system. Ideas, money, or persons might all be input.

integrate (both transitive and intransitive) for 'blend; mix; amalgamate'.

interface for 'point of interaction; frontier' as in 'the interface between technology and design'.

-ism, -ist for 'basis of prejudice'. To the earlier *racism* and *sexism* have now been added *ageism, ableism* (= in favour of the able-bodied), *heterosexism,* and even *fattism* (= against fat people). See separate entry.

knee-jerk for 'automatic; stereotyped', as in 'knee-jerk radicalism'.

lifestyle for 'habits; way of life'. A piece of marketing jargon.

logistics for 'detailed organization for carrying out a plan'; originally a military word.

low profile for 'unobtrusive behaviour'. See also, *profile,* below.

major and *minor* as in 'major surgery', 'of very minor importance'.

marginal for 'insignificant', as in 'a marginal improvement'.

massive for 'substantial; extensive'.

meaningful for 'important'.

mechanism for 'procedure', as in 'the mechanism for claiming a tax rebate'.

mileage for 'advantage; potential'.

minor. See *major, minor,* above.

model as in 'democracy on the Western model'.

motivate, motivation, used particularly in managerial jargon.

objective (adj.) for 'unbiased'.

obscene as a blanket term of disapproval.

ongoing for 'current; in process'.

operative (adj.) as in 'the operative word'.

optimal, optimum for 'best'.

orchestrate for something like 'stage-manage'. 'He orchestrated the whole meeting.'

organic, which has escaped from its
technical senses in medicine and
chemistry to refer to agricultural
production without the use of
chemical fertilizers or pesticides. Such
expressions as 'organic carrots' irritate
those who know that all living things
are technically 'organic'.

osmosis, a term originally from
biochemistry, used figuratively of a
process of gradual influence: 'to pick
up the language by osmosis'.

overall (adj.) for 'total; inclusive', as in
'the overall cost.'

overkill for 'excess', as in 'advertising
overkill'.

palpable for 'obvious', as in 'a palpable
lie'.

paradigm for 'typical example', as in 'This
episode is a paradigm of the problems
that confront us.'

parameter for 'limit; boundary'; ' to work
within the parameters of time and
money'.

paranoid, a technical word from
psychiatry, loosely used for
'suspicious'.

peak (v.); 'Output peaked last March.'

permissive as in 'the permissive society'.

perspective for 'outlook', as in 'get a
different perspective on things'.

prestigious, for 'socially impressive'.

profile for 'description; specification', as in
'job profile'.

quantum leap (or *jump*), which in physics
means an abrupt but minuscule
transition, has come to be used for a
sudden spectacular increase or
advance, as if the *quantum* were
something large.

rat race: a journalistic cliché.

reaction, when used simply for 'opinion;
answer'. See separate entry.

realism, realist, realistic, as in 'charge a
realistic price'.

relate (intransitive) for 'respond; interact'.
This sense originated in psychological
jargon, but is loosely used as in 'I can't
relate to that sort of music.'

repercussions for 'results'.

rewarding for 'worthwhile'.

scenario for 'possible state of affairs'.

significant, as in 'a significant
improvement'.

situation for 'state of affairs'.

sophisticated, as in 'sophisticated
techniques'.

spectrum as in 'a wide spectrum of
opinion'.

spin-off for 'by-product'.

state-of-the-art, as in 'state-of-the-art
engineering'.

subjective for 'biased'.

symbiosis, symbiotic, technical terms in the
life sciences but now applied to
anything mutually beneficial.

syndrome, originally a medical term
but now widely used for 'condition',
as in 'the bored-housewife
syndrome'.

target for 'goal; objective'. It is absurdly
used in such contexts as 'to exceed
one's target', since one might suppose
that the idea of a target is to hit it.

tendentious for 'biased'.

total, totally, as in 'total ignorance' or
'totally unnecessary'.

track record for a person's past
performance.

trauma, traumatic, traumatize, originally
technical terms in medicine and
psychology, but now loosely used of
anything upsetting; 'a traumatic love
affair'.

user-friendly. See *-friendly*, above.

viable, a biological term now loosely used
for 'practicable; sound', as in
'economically viable' or 'a viable
alternative'.

-wise is a suffix meaning 'with regard to'.
Such resultant modish adverbial
compounds as *careerwise, saleswise*, and
taxwise, though concise, are
nevertheless much criticized.

workshop for any meeting for discussion
or practical work, as in 'a theatre
workshop'.

yardstick for 'a standard; criterion'.

yuppie (and even *yuppiedom* and *yuppify*).
It stands for 'young urban
professional', and crops up everywhere
in such contexts as the housing
market, cars, clothes, food and drink.

VULGARISMS AND LOW LAN-
GUAGE. *Vulgarisms and low language (vulgar language)* are often taken to be exactly synonymous. But it is well to differentiate. *Low (or vulgar) language* is of two kinds: (1) words foisted on one social class by a lower class; words brought from trade into drawing-room. And (2) – closely connected and often merging with (1) – those which have originated in and are used mostly by the *proletariat* (a word employed here, as a necessary classification).

With (1) we need not concern ourselves further: (2), however, is important. Examples of (2) are *dotty* and *dippy* for 'mad', *lolly* (a sweet), *codger* and *geezer*, *old woman* (wife), *to cop*, *to bash*, *to do* or *diddle* (the latter being no longer considered low). Of these, some are slangy, others merely lowly and familiar. The connection between the slangy and the lowly words is so intimate that, the moment they cease to be slangy or lowly, they tend to – often do, eventually – become admitted to the class of ordinary colloquialism. Yet the distinction between such lownesses and slang is as desirable as it is legitimate. Low words are those which, used by the poorest and meanest of the poorer classes, are yet neither cant nor 'good' colloquialisms (admitted into Society): some are slang, some are idiom, the idiom being so lowly that often it is ignored. Excellent examples are found in 'deep' Cockney (see the novels and stories of e.g. Pett Ridge, Barry Pain, and Neil Lyons), where we see that some low language is an almost inextricable tangle of slang and idiom; much of it so racy and picturesque and expressive that it may put some Standard English into the shade. Take such a passage as this from *Arthur's*, by Neil Lyons:

' "So it's corfee fur everybody", Jerry the Twister had explained upon his arrival at Arthur's stall. "Give me a quid, 'e did, as a start-off an' then blighted well *fought* me fur it, the blighter. Where am I? ses 'e. Kennington Road, ses I. Lead me to the Strand, ses 'e. It was a lead, I give you *my* word, 'E was a 'ot un. Climb down nigh every airey we passed, stole the milkcans, an' tied 'em up to the knockers. Pinched a rozzer in the leg, give 'im a visitin' card, an' stole his whistle. Put 'is dooks up to a fireman, tossed 'im fur 'is chopper, an' kissed 'is wife. Run fur 'is very life into Covent Garden Market (me after 'im), bought a cabbidge, took it into a resterong where all the nobs was dinin', sends for the boss an' ses: Cully, cook this for my dinner. Boss say: You be damned! Collidge genelman takes off 'is 'at. I call upon you ... to cook this cabbidge. It is the law. I'll be shot if I do, ses the boss. You'll be endorsed if you don't, ses the toff. Give it 'ere, ses the boss; I'll cook it. Cabbidge comes up on a silver dish: charge two thick 'uns. Genelman pays the money, an' breaks a glass: charge ten shillings. Grand lark, ses the toff. I seen cheaper, ses I. Put 'em up, ses the toff. Where's yer money? ses I. 'Ere's a quid, 'e ses; an' afore I can start on 'im up comes a swaddy in a red cap. Give you a bob for that 'at, ses the toff. 'Old 'ard, I tells 'im. That's a policeman, military policeman. Don't you 'ave no larks wiv' 'im. Rats to you, 'e ses. I'll 'ave that to make a wescoat of, ses 'e. An' 'e up an' snatches it. *Then* the trouble began. 'Im an' the swaddy an' two constables an' a cab-tout was mixed up proper fur nigh on ten minutes. Put 'em up grand, 'e did, the toff, I mean. An' they squashed 'is 'at an' tore 'is wescoat, an' the cab-tout bit 'is 'and. An' 'e broke a window, an' lost 'is watch, an' they frog-marched 'im off to Vine Stret. 'Ere's a lark, ses 'e, when they started." '

In such language as that, there are many faults: but it is ruddy with good health, and bursting with life. As G. K. Chesterton said in 'A Defence of Slang' (*The Defendant*, 1901), 'The lower classes live in a state of war, a war of words. Their readiness is the product of the same fiery individualism as the readiness of the old fighting oligarchs. Any cabman has to be ready with his tongue, as any gentleman [had once] to be ready with his sword.' For vividness at a still lower level of language than that of the extract from *Arthur's.* see 'Epsom's Attic Salt' in my *Slang Today and Yesterday* (pp. 241–7).

Now we come to *vulgarisms* in the sense in which I have for some years tried to fix it, to stabilize it, to get it accepted by the pundits and the philologists.

Vulgarisms are words that belong to idiomatic English or denote such objects or processes or functions or tendencies or acts as are not usually mentioned by the polite in company and are never, under *those* names, mentioned in respectable circles. Doctors may speak of them by their medical names, and anyone may refer to them – though not usually before members of the opposite sex – by their technical and generally Latinized or Grecized designations, and persons secretly libidinous or coprological delight to drag such words into their talk in terms of Freud and his followers. *Arse,* an excellent Old English word, is no longer obscene; it occurred in Frederic Manning's great war novel, *The Middle Parts of Fortune,* in 1930, and has, since *c.* 1932, appeared in print with increasing frequency. C. 1850–1920, the usual 'Saxon' word was *backside,* but since the early 1920s – thanks largely to such 'choice spirits' as Sir Alan Herbert – *behind* has taken its place. *Bum,** now decidedly vulgar, has become mainly a schoolboys' word; as used by Shakespeare, Dekker, Jonson, it was much more dignified. And, by the way, it is echoic – not a telescoping of *bottom. Bottom,* in very general use since *c.*1830, has always been con-

sidered more genteel than *backside,* which is mainly a man's word, whereas *bottom* is a woman's word; since *behind* acceded to the throne, *bottom* has taken to itself a moral rectitude even greater than *behind's* and an air of primness happily absent from *behind. Posterior* is politer still, but if we use the plural we connote *buttocks,* which, so much more precise and 'Saxon', is not quite so acceptable to the prudish. Euphemism, here as in all such words, is often employed, sometimes in some such childish form as *sit-me-down.* Chest need not be a euphemism: as a synonym for the breast, it is merely – a synonym. But as equivalent to the female breasts, it is a silly, inexact euphemism. The 'Saxon' words for the male member (*membrum virile* is the technical term) and the female pudend (*pudendum muliebre*) are excellently idiomatic and belong to the aristocracy of the language, but, because they denote these intimate parts, they are – by a mental twist that we may leave to the psychologists – regarded as vulgar and, though they are certainly not slang, even as slangy. (A useful collective noun is *genitals,* usable of either sex.) The 'Saxon' words for 'to urinate' and 'to defecate' are idiomatic and perfect English, but association and prudery put them into quarantine; for the latter function, however, there exists the estimable *stool.*

These are vulgarisms. The slangy synonyms, which are numerous, belong to low language.

*[In American usage *behind* has for a long time been the usual nursery and homely word, much commoner than *backside* and somewhat effeminate as contrasted with the masculine *arse* (always pronounced, and popularly spelled, *ass*). But the present slang is *fanny,* which has had a spectacular career in smart publications and stage-shows; and in the home and nursery, whence it may have come (cf.*doll*), challenges *behind* itself.]

W

wage; wages. In the figurative sense, 'a reward or recompense', use *wage* ('The gods give thee fair wage and dues of death', Swinburne); this sense, however, is obsolescent. *Wages,* construed as a singular ('The wages of sin is death'), is an archaism. In ordinary English, *wages* (construed as plural) = 'the amount paid periodically, especially by the day or week or month, for the labour or service of a workman or servant' (as opposed to a *salary*, which is paid for non-manual or non-mechanical work); but the singular, *wage*, 'has sometimes a special convenience with reference to a particular instance or amount', as in '[Masters] commonly enter into a private bond or agreement, not to give more than a certain wage' and 'a day's wage for a day's work' (though 'a day's wages for a day's work' would also be correct). Note a *wage-slave*, *wage-labour*, and, in Political Economy, *wage-fund* (or *wages-fund*).

wait is the intransitive ('Will you wait, or not?'); **await** (or **wait for**) is the transitive form ('Will you wait for me?'; 'He awaits our arrival'). There is now an awkwardness in 'Wait what she's going to say' (detective novel, 1937); but this transitive use of *wait* is still acceptable in 'wait one's turn' or 'wait (defer) breakfast'. – See also **await**.

waive, 'to relinquish, refrain, forbear', is occasionally confused with *wave*, to make a certain motion with the hands.

wake, waken. See **awake**.

want (wish, desire). *Want* (v.i.) is 'to be lacking'; archaic except as *to be wanting* (to be lacking). To *want for nothing* is 'not to lack the necessaries or comforts of life'. As a transitive verb, *want* = to *desire*, to *wish* for (something); also with infinitive as in 'He wants to do it' (he desires or wishes to do it); also 'to *want* a person to do something'; also it = 'to wish to see, or to speak to, a person', as 'You're wanted at the door' which is familiar, not literary English.

want and **need.** The standard constructions are 'I want my car washed', and 'My car wants (or *needs*) washing.' The alternatives 'I want my car washing' and 'My car wants (or *needs*) washed' are regionalisms, not accepted as standard usage.

-ward is a suffix both adjectival and adverbial, whereas **-wards** is adverbial only.

warn, 'to give timely notice of impending danger or misfortune' (*OED*), with other slightly varying senses all implying danger or penalties, is often misused for *to give preliminary notice or information* without the implication of unpleasant consequences if the *warning* be neglected; *The New Statesman and Nation*, under the heading 'This England', once quoted from a letter in *The Eastern Daily Press*: 'I wonder if it is at all possible to be warned if there is likely to be a return of the aurora borealis at any time?'

warn of is incorrect for *warn against*, in 'Against unwarranted identification Korzybski delivers his major attack. He constantly warns of the *subject-predicate* form' (Stuart Chase, *The Tyranny of Words*). One *warns of* danger in general, but *warns against* specific dangers.

warrant, warranty; guarantee, guaranty. For the last two, see **guarantee.** *Warranty* is noun only; *warrant*, both noun and verb. *Warranty*, in Law, is 'an act of warranting'; in literary use, it = 'substantiating evidence (or witness)', as in 'By what warranty A deed so hateful say you I have wrought?' (Whitelaw's *Sophocles*), and also 'a justifying reason or ground' (*for* an action or a belief), as in 'The Pope was claiming powers … for which there was no warranty in the history of the Church'; for the second literary sense, *warrant* is a synonym ('Have we any warrant for a belief in immortality?'). *Warrant* bears the senses, 'sanction or authorization; an act of authorization; a token or evidence of authorization', as in 'An assembly that is without warrant from the sovereign is unlawful', 'He produced an old rusty sword and cried, "See, my lords, here is my warrant" ' (Stubbs); concretely, *warrant* is 'a document conveying authority or security' (*search warrant*), 'a writ or order issued by some executive body', and there are special senses in stockbroking (*share* *warrant*) and commerce (a form of receipt). The verb *to warrant* has a technical sense in Law. As a general term, it = 'to guarantee as true, to make oneself answerable for (a statement)', especially in *I warrant* or *I will warrant*; 'to attest the truth or authenticity of; to authenticate', as in 'That [his confession] was genuine could not be doubted: for it was warranted by the signatures of some of the most distinguished military men living' (Macaulay); 'to authorize (a person to do something), to authorize or sanction (a course of action)', as in 'Who has warranted this step?' hence (of things), 'to furnish adequate grounds for (a course of action), to justify', as in 'It is impossible to say whether this accusation was warranted by facts' (Washington Irving) and 'We are not warranted in assuming that he has been telling lies'; to 'guarantee (goods, articles) to be of the quality, quantity, make, etc., specified', as in *warranted free from adulteration* or *colours warranted fast* (*OED*).

was or **were** in conditionals. Use *were* for suppositions contrary to fact, as in 'If he were a woman, he would understand'; and in such inverted sentences as 'Were she to resign, it would be a disaster.' Use *was* for real possibilities, as in 'If she *was* here, she must have heard the news'; and with *whether* (or *if* used for *whether*), as in 'We wondered whether it was time to leave.' When there is actual doubt, both *was* and *were* are possible, the latter being preferred in formal contexts, as in 'She spoke as though it *were* (or *was*) already decided.' See also SUBJUNCTIVE.

way (adv.) is short for (*far*) *away* in such phrases as 'sold, way below cost', 'way down South', 'to go way off' (afar), 'way down East', 'from way back' (from a rural, or a remote, district): all are colloquial.

way of being, by. 'I am by way of being an artist' is permissible, except in literary English, when the speaker wishes to make his statement appear more modest; but 'He is by way of being an artist' is a senseless circumlocution when nothing more is meant than 'He is an artist'; as a piece of facetiousness it is bearable – but only just.

ways, in *come* (or *go*) *one's ways*, is now either dialectal or American. So, too, for *a little ways* and *a good* (or *great* or *long*) *ways* – a short or a long distance.

we aren't and **we're not.** [Reversed: only *aren't we* is possible as a shortening of *are not we?*) Weseen says that '*we're not* is preferred'; but let us take *we're not ready* and *we aren't ready.* If the emphasis is on *ready*, at least as many people would say, 'We aren't *ready*, you know', as would say 'We're not *ready*, you know'; if on *not*, 'We're *not* ready' is preferable; if on *we*, '*We* aren't ready' is probably as common as '*We're* not ready.'

we both and **we each; us both** and **us each.** See GENITIVE, VAGARIES OF THE, the last paragraph but one.

weave. See at **wove.**

wed for *marry* is overdone by journalists, especially in headlines, where the short word is *so* convenient. Frank Whitaker has stigmatized it as a 'rubber-stamp word' (see **amazing**). *Wed* is ordinary English inflected thus: *wed – wedded* (*wed* being dialectal) – *wedded* (*wed* being dialectal or poetical). The adjectival form is *wedded*, as in 'wedded bliss'.

wedding for *marriage* is to be used with care. The following example is from an answer in a Scottish Leaving Certificate examination paper: 'Miss Margaret X has much pleasure in accepting Miss Mary Smith's invitation to her wedding to Mr John Brown, in the Marlborough House, on Tuesday, the 22nd March at 2 p.m.' The invitation was presumably sent by Mary Smith's parents *for the wedding of their daughter and John Brown*, and would have been correctly accepted in those terms, but, as Margaret expressed her reply, *marriage* would have been the right word to use. Properly employed, *wedding* = 'the performance of the wedding-rite' or 'the ceremony of a marriage, with its attendant festivities' as in 'weddings, christenings, burials', 'Are you to be at the Milton wedding next week?', 'I am told the wedding went off very well.'

weekend. A *weekend* is Saturday and Sunday, perhaps including Friday evening. A *long weekend* includes Friday, or Monday, or even both.

weigh is incorrect for *way* in *under weigh*, 'in preparation'. 'Getting under weigh' (W. H. G. Kingston, *Lusitanian Sketches*); Louis Bromfield, *It Had to Happen*, ' Now that he had a project under weigh his spirits rose.' (The metaphor is nautical.)

well nigh. See **nigh.**

Welsh Rabbit. See **rabbit, Welsh.**

we're not. See **we aren't ...**

were or **was.** See **was or were.**

westerly and **western.** See **easterly.**

westernly, good English in the 17th century, is in the 20th regarded as a solecism for *westerly* and *western.*

westward; westwards. The latter is an adverb only; the former is chiefly an adjective, but often functions as an adverb in American English and in older British writing.

wet – **wet** or **wetted** – **wet** or **wetted.** With *have*, *wet* is the commoner participle; with *be*, *wetted* is as common as and less ambiguous than *wet*. Usage, I surmise, will finally consecrate *wetted* at the expense of *wet* in both preterite and past participle.

wharfs; wharves. Both are correct; *wharves* is the more euphonious, and the usual American form.

what, as subject, takes the singular verb, whether the complementary noun be singular or plural: thus, 'What I like is sprouts', not 'What I like are sprouts'; 'What the public wants are crime stories' (Anthony Weymouth, *Tempt Me Not*) should be 'What the public wants is crime stories'; for 'It was indeed doubtful if the old man had really been interested in books – what he collected were ideas,

legends, beliefs' (John Gloag, *Sacred Edifice*, 1937), read ' ... what he collected was ...'. But where *what* clearly means 'things that' a plural verb may be correct, as in 'They are eating what seem to be (things that seem to be) sprouts.'

what and **which,** as interrogative adjectives. See **which and what.**

what for *those which* is incorrect. '"The bullets ... known to have been fired by young Mr Moffat ... are the same as what killed this Bennet bloke"' (E. R. Punchon, *The Dusky Hour*).

what, as. 'But that I did see, sir, as plain as what I see you now' (E. C. Bentley and H. Warner Allen in *Trent's Own Case*). The speech of an uneducated person, who should have said '*as plainly as I see you now*'.

what a many for *how many* or *what a number of* is slovenly colloquialism. [Unknown in American usage.]

what ... for?, as an inverted form of *for what*, is sometimes ambiguous, as in the question (overheard), of mother to child: 'What did he change his bright new penny for?', which might mean '*Why* did he change it?'

what ... is when. A not unusual form of grammatical clumsiness, as 'What is really shocking is when an artist comes to a serious subject such as this' (Anthony Blunt in *The Spectator*, 6 May 1938). This sentence might be better expressed in other ways, e.g. 'It is really shocking to see an artist come, etc.', or 'What is shocking is to find that an artist can come, etc.'.

what use is now standard idiom in 'What use is it to learn Greek?' 'Of what use is it ... ?' would be an alternative.

whatever. See **ever.**

when can be used for *in which*, after, e.g., *year*, as 'The year when it happened' (for 'the year in which it happened'); but care must be exercised in extending this usage. Thus *in which* seems to be, and indeed is, preferable to *when* in the following: 'Cases sometimes occur when there is marked disagreement between the cancellation date on the envelope and the date on the sheet it contains' (Nigel Morland).

when, misused for *whereas.* 'When the old Rhetoric treated ambiguity as a fault in language, the new Rhetoric sees it as an inevitable consequence of the powers of language' (I. A. Richards, *The Philosophy of Rhetoric*). Was this particular error the result of a conscientious desire to avoid *while* = *whereas*, and of a too hasty solution of that stylistic crux?

when ... ever is often misused for *whenever.* '"And the next time, Mac, don't tell me that if I'd just buckle down to the job a little sooner I could finish it with time to spare." "When did I ever say that?" I demanded with some heat' (Isabel Briggs Myers, *Give Me Death*). See also **ever.**

whence, from. Though found in the work of good writers, the 'from' is redundant. Swinburne, *Studies in Prose and Poetry.* 'The quarter from whence the following lucubration is addressed': this would be more correctly written 'The quarter whence ...' or 'The quarter from which'. *Whence* and *whither*, with *hence* and *hither*, are now literary, but perfectly admissible in speech. *Whence* is correctly used in the following: Stevenson, *Kidnapped*, 'There was no question put of whence I came or whither I was going', and in these stanzas from Fitzgerald's *Omar.*

> Into this universe, and why not
>   knowing,
> Nor whence, like water willy-nilly
>   flowing:
> And out of, as wind along the
>   waste,
> I know not whither, willy-nilly
>   blowing.

> What, without asking, hither
>   hurried whence?
> And, without asking, whither
>   hurried hence!
> Another and another cup to drown
> The memory of this impertinence!

Whence is clumsily used in 'Here Machiavelli's earth returned to whence it rose' (Byron), where *to whence* = *to that place whence* (WB).

where for *that* is incorrect, as in 'I see where they had a heat wave' – i.e. 'I saw, in the newspaper, that they had a heat wave.'

where for *whither* is now usual, as in 'Where are you going?' ('Where are you going *to*?' is redundant.)

where; wherein; at (or in) which; omitted. Although syntactically and structurally on a par with the omission of the relative pronouns, *that*, *which*, *who*, the omission of *where(in)* and *at* (or *in*) *which* is not the same analytically or verbally, for *where* = *at* (or *in*) *which*, and *wherein* = *in which*; *where* and *wherein* = combinations of preposition + pronoun, whereas *that which*, *who* are simples or singles (pronoun only). The result of omitting *where*, *wherein*, *at* (or *in*) *which*, is subjectively one of momentary ambiguity, objectively one of abruptness, as in 'Neil was for storming Erchany like young Lochinvar and carrying her to some place they could be married in secret' (Michael Innes, *Lament for a Maker*), where one is, for a split second, apt or tempted to think that *in order that* should precede 'they could be married in secret'.

where from and **from where.** *Where* can = to *where* (or *where to*), as in 'Where are you going?' and thus it takes the place of *whither*; but *where* does not take the place of *whence*, for which either *where from* or preferably *from where* must be used. 'I took that passage from Thucydides.' 'From *where*?' 'Where did that man come from?' is more idiomatic than 'From where did that man come?'

whereas; whereat; wherefore; whereof; whereon. See ARCHAISMS.

wherever. See **ever.**

whether, of. 'The whole question of whether we like it is ignored' is redundant for 'the ... question whether' or 'the question of our liking it'.

whether or no; whether or not.
Whether or no, as in 'Whether or no it is possible, I cannot say', is obsolescent for '*Whether or not* it is possible, I cannot say.' But *whether or not* is tautological for *whether*, except where the doubt is to be emphasized.

which and **that; who** and **that.** Of these relative pronouns, *which* refers to things only; *that to* things and persons; *who* to persons only. But *that* is not a syntactical synonym of either *which* or *who*. The discrimination between *which* and *that* and between *who* and *that* is one of the marks of a stylist.

With the caution that 'the tendency to appropriate *who* and *which* to persons and things respectively often outweighs other considerations; thus, "People *who* live in glass houses" is preferred to "people *that*"; this is particularly the case with *those, they,* and other pronouns of common gender. "Those *who* are in favour of this motion", is more usual than "those *that*" [but this may be partly because *they who* and *those who* are *formulas*]', it is to be noted that relative clauses are used for two purposes:

(1) The more sharply to define or to limit the antecedent, which without the ensuing relative clause would either make no sense or convey a sense different from the intended one. 'This is the book that G. K. Chesterton wrote'; 'Uneasy lies the head that wears a crown.' Here, the relative clause is ushered-in by *that*, except after a preposition ('He is a man for whom' – not 'for that' – 'I have the deepest regard') or where *whose* is inevitable ('He is a man whose opinion means much to me'). No comma (or other stop) is to be used to separate this relative clause from its antecedent, a rule applying also when *who* and *which* are used with a preposition or when *whose* is obligatory, as in 'The man whose son is alive is not heirless.' (In 'His recovery was hastened by ... games on the enchanted heath, near which he lived' (*Harrap Book News*), the comma after 'heath' is necessary, for there was only one enchanted heath, whereas 'His recovery

was hastened by games on an enchanted heath near which he lived' would restrict the connotation of 'heath' and imply that there was more than one such heath.) The comma-less form is restrictive; the comma'd form is non-restrictive, i.e. it falls into the next class. The relative may be omitted, as in 'This is the book G. K. Chesterton wrote.' The *that* relative occurs especially where the antecedent is shown to belong to a class, a group, a kind, a species, etc., as in 'All that live must die', 'The greatest dramatist (that) we've ever had', 'Adrian the Fourth is the only Englishman that has been Pope.'

(2) The more fully to give information about something (the antecedent) that is already defined sufficiently to make sense; this class of relative has various names, such as 'non-restrictive', 'parenthetical', 'explicative'. Compare 'His brother is very rich' with 'His brother, who owns a brewery, is very rich'; 'This book is excellent' with 'This book, which was written by Chesterton, is excellent.' Here, the relative clause must be ushered-in by *who* (*whom*) or *which*; a comma separates – or should separate – the relative clause from the antecedent; and the relative pronoun cannot be omitted. Here, too, the relative clause can be supplanted by a conjunction + a noun or a pronoun (and, of course, the rest of a sentence), thus: 'This book is excellent, and Chesterton wrote it.'

A useful rule – at least *I* have found it useful – is this of mine: the restrictive or defining or limitative or necessary relative clause (relatives of Class 1) forms an integral, irremovable part of the sentence and cannot be put within parentheses, whereas the non-restrictive relatives (Class 2) can always be put within parentheses and their omission would not render the sentence senseless.

In speech, the use of *which* for *that* is less reprehensible, for intonation will convey the sense. 'But in the written language the need of discrimination between the two classes described is often felt, and the non-observance of the distinction is liable to lead to misunderstanding. Example: "All the members of the Council, who were also members of the Education Board, were to assemble in the Board-room." This would naturally imply that all members of the Council were members of the Education Board. "That", instead of "who", would clearly express the meaning intended, which is that "those who are members of the Education Board as well as of the Council were to assemble".... Observe the significance of the distinction in the following: "In two of the instances, *which* have come under my notice, the system has worked well"; "In two of the instances *that* have come under my notice, the system has worked well." The first means: "Two of the instances have come under my notice; in [all of] these instances the system has worked well." The second means: "Instances have come under my notice; in two of them the system has worked well." ' (Quoted from Onions, *An Advanced English Syntax*: on which the preceding part of the article has, in the main, been based. For a more leisurely – yet very useful – examination of the *that* and the *who* (and *which*) modes, see Jespersen, *Notes on Relative Clauses*.)

But I wish to add several points that have occurred to me:

A. *Which* can be used for *that* or *who* in such a sentence as 'He's not the man *which* he was', where '*who* he was' would be absurd and ambiguous. But the wise man evades the difficulty: he says, 'He's not the man *that* he was.' By so doing he observes also the distinction between *that* on the one hand and *which* or *who* on the other.

B. (*a*) 'It isn't only homicidal maniacs that are dangerous.'

(*a*¹) 'It isn't only homicidal maniacs who are dangerous.'

(*b*) 'It is not only pictures that are beautiful.'

(*b*¹) 'It is not only pictures which are beautiful.'

In each pair (*a* and *a*¹; *b* and *b*¹), are both forms correct? If not, which?

(Note that in *a* and *a*¹, the answer need not take into account the fact that 'all homicidal maniacs are dangerous', and that in *b* and *b*¹, the answer need not take into account the fact that 'not all pictures are beautiful': the following explanation will show why.)

Of *a* and *a*¹, the second is correct: quite apart from the fact that *a* ('It isn't only homicidal maniacs that are dangerous') implies that some are harmless, its sense is obviously incomplete: *a*¹ conforming to good sense, is complete, for it makes the self-contained statement, 'Homicidal maniacs are dangerous, but they are not the only dangerous persons.' The good writer would say, 'Not only homicidal maniacs are dangerous', and thus avoid both verbosity and ambiguity.

Similarly, of *b* and *b*¹, the second is correct; *b* is obviously incomplete, for nothing has been said about 'pictures that are beautiful' (= 'those pictures which are beautiful'), whereas *b*¹ makes a complete statement, 'Pictures [as a class] are beautiful, but they are not the only beautiful things.'

(The only overriding reason for choosing *a*, *b*, rather than *a*¹, *b*¹ in the above examples might be to suggest that there are dangerous 'things' as well as 'persons', and beautiful 'persons' as well as 'things', since *that* usefully covers both contingencies.)

which and **what**, as interrogative adjectives or pronouns. As, to an unknown visitor – a complete stranger – one says, 'What do you want?' and, to a friend that has indicated the range of his desire, 'Which do you need?', so, if one knows the genus, one says 'Which sort of book?', or, knowing the species, 'Which type of novel – adventure, love, detective?', or, knowing the sub-species, 'Which author?', or, knowing the author, 'Which book of his?' Likewise, with a number of books available, one asks not 'What book do you want?' but 'Which book do you want?': yet one often hears people ask, 'What book do you want?' – 'What book do you choose?' – and so forth. Compare the following questions (where the suitable interrogative is employed): 'What sort of cooking do you get here?' – 'Good, very good!' – 'And which sort of food – English, American, or Continental?' – 'English.' – 'And what drinks are there?' – 'No beers, no ales, no spirits; only wines.' – 'Which wines – the expensive? French or Italian? Or both French and Italian?' – 'The prices range from the absurdly low to the millionairish-high, and as for the country and the growth, why! you choose which(ever) wine you fancy.'

In short, *what* is vague and implies ignorance in the speaker, *which* is precise and therefore implies some degree of specific knowledge. But if you are in doubt (I admit that I'm often doubtful), or wish to widen your knowledge of this debatable land, then consult the Grammars of Curme, Jespersen, Onions – the three greatest grammarians of the 20th century.

which and **who**. *Which* and *who* lead frequently to lapses from good grammar (and good sense); Byron can write (*Childe Harold*, III, 28), 'The thunderclouds close o'er it, which when rent The earth is covered thick with other clay, Which her own clay shall cover.'

Gilbert White commits the error of writing *and which*, where either 'and' or 'which' is unnecessary, 'This is their due, and which ought to be rendered to them by all people' (*OED*). See **and which.**

A more illiterate error is *which he*, as in Dorothy Sayers, *Unnatural Death*: 'Ironsides ... a clerk on the Southern, which he always used to say joking like, "Slow but safe, like the Southern – that's me" '; and 'I believe the gentleman acted with the best intentions, 'avin' now seen 'im, which at first I thought he was a wrong 'un.' (Exact dialogue, of course.)

which for *which fact* is sometimes ambiguous, as in 'That rifle cost me fifteen pounds, which has left me short of cash.' It is legitimate for *which* to refer to a whole preceding clause, as in 'He can cook, which is convenient', but the device should be used with restraint.

which ... were for *which ... was* may, to the sceptical, appear to be an error unlikely to be committed by the educated person. It is an error more frequent than the sceptical realize. For instance, in so good a writer as Wilfranc Hubbard, there occurs this sentence, 'You ask me which of the two lives were least' – better, 'the less' – 'worthy of record' (*Orvieto Dust*).

while and **whilst**. See at **among and amongst.**

while for *although* is now considered to be a legitimate sense of *while*, but it should nevertheless be avoided if there is danger of confusion with the temporal sense, as in 'While she is young, she will learn quickly.'

while, whilst for *whereas* or *and* (or even *but*). Sir Alan Herbert gives a comic example of this: 'The Curate read the First Lesson while the Rector read the Second.' And here is a less amusing but no less instructive example from Stuart Chase, *The Tyranny of Words*: 'The Greeks had no algebra, no graphical methods, while the geometry of Euclid which they did possess dealt only in spaces and made no allowance for times.'

whiskers and **moustache**. *OED* settles the frequent confusion, thus: '[*whiskers.*] The hair that grows on an adult man's face; formerly commonly applied to that on the upper lip, now called *moustache*, and sometimes to (or including) that on the chin (*beard*); now restricted to that on the cheeks or sides of the face.' [*Mustache* is the US spelling.]

whisky; whiskey. 'Scotch' is *whisky*, and this is the usual British spelling. *Whiskey* is distilled in Ireland or in America, and that is the usual US spelling.

who and **that** (relative pronouns). See **which and that.**

who and **whom**. Such phrases as 'the man who I saw there' are very common in speech, for people appear to think that *whom* sounds pedantic. *Whom* for *who*, however, is the more frequent error in literary use. Thus Sir Wm Gell refers to a character 'whom it is possible may be at some future time introduced to my reader'; and *The Daily Mail* has 'Mr Cornelius told a *Daily Mail* reporter that at 2 a.m. yesterday he was aroused by calls for help from a woman, whom he learned later was Lady ...', *he learned later*, a parenthetical phrase, causing all the trouble; and Mrs Beatrice Kean Seymour, in *The Happier Eden*, has ' "We've met several people here, who remember him." She had not said whom they were.' The following example, from a particularly able writer, is instructive: '... To say nothing of two men whom he declared were spies of his rival, but as to whom there was a recurrent little joke about plain-clothes police' (Michael Innes, *The Daffodil Case*). Such a sentence as 'Men say who I am' becomes, as an interrogative, 'Who do men say that I am?', not as in the Authorized Version of the Bible, 'Whom do men say that I am?' (cited by Onions). The rule to remember is that *whom* is not to be used with the verb *to be* (whatever parenthetic material may intervene), except where that verb is in the infinitive; so that 'a man whom we understood to be a policeman' is correct.

who else's. See at **whose else's.**

whoever for *who ... ever*, and vice versa. In 'Whoever saw him do such a thing? I've known him for twenty years and have never known him to do it', *whoever* should obviously be 'Who ever (saw ...)'. But 'Who ever says such a thing is a liar' is incorrect for 'Whoever says such a thing is a liar.' See also **ever.**

whole (adj.). See COMPARATIVES, FALSE, also **complete** ...

whole (adj.) and **the whole** (n.) are sometimes confused, as 'The whole proceedings are in this book' for 'The whole of the proceedings *is* ...' or, better, 'All the proceedings *are*...'. And see following entry.

whole, the. 'The whole three of them' is incorrect for 'all three' or 'all the three'. 'The whole lot', however, is correct. Nesfield quotes *The Daily Telegraph*, February 1900, 'This was the cost for removing snow from the whole of the thoroughfares of the metropolis' ('all the streets of London'). The same error appears in 'The whole three were now grappling on the carpet' (David Haggart (who was hanged in 1821), *Life*, 1821).

whom. See **who and whom.**

whomever, whomsoever; whosoever, whosesoever. These are the correct accusatives and genitives respectively of *whoever* and *whosoever.* But *whosoever* (not *whoseever*) is rare and *whosoever* is archaic, for either of these genitives, modern usage prefers *whatever person's.* *Whomever* and *whomsoever* are subject to the same confusion with *whoever* and *whosoever* as *whom* is with *who*; e.g. 'They shall not be impeded by whomsoever it may be' (Ruskin).

Whoso, whomso: archaic for *whoever, whomever.*

who's for *whose* is an odd yet not infrequent error: cf. *it's* for *its*, *her's* for *hers.*

whose for *which.* Strictly, *whose* refers to persons only. But *whose* for *of which* is permissible when employed to avoid the awkwardness of *the* [noun] *of which*, as in 'A large number of brass discs, *whose* workmanship [= the workmanship of which] shows that they belong to the later period of Celtic art, have been found in Ireland' (Onions).

whose, and, misused for *whose.* 'She who swore away the life of Kidden the porter, and whose (Kidden's) blood still cries aloud for vengeance' (Joseph Cox, *A faithful Narrative of Thief-Takers*, 1756).

whose else's. Agatha Christie, *The Mysterious Affair at Styles*, ' "You are sure it was Mr Inglethorpe's voice you heard?" "Oh, yes, sir, whose else's could it be?" ' The correct form for familiar Standard English is *who else's*; less common but permissible when the noun does not follow is *whose else*. See **else's.**

wide and **broad.** (See **breadth.**) In 'Cliff nodded and clenched and unclenched his wide mobile hands' (Ngaio Marsh, *Died in the Wool*), we feel that *broad* would have been better. Whereas *broad* connotes amplitude (*broad shoulders*), *wide* emphasizes the distance between the limits – underlines the separation (*at wide intervals*). Wherever generosity or freedom from narrowness or pettiness is involved, *broad* is used (*broadminded, in broad outline*). Then take 'a *wide* – a *broad* – range of subjects': in the former, number is chiefly important; in the latter, weight or generosity.

wideness for *width* is unidiomatic. Cf. **breadth; broadness.**

wiggle and **wriggle.** To *wiggle* is now colloquial when it is not dialectal, whether it is an intransitive verb (to waggle; to wriggle) or a transitive verb (to wriggle something about, to cause something to wriggle): so avoid it in good writing or in formal speech.

wildlife (thus). Gobbledygook for all wild creatures – and even for wild plants.

will and **shall.** See **shall and will.**

windward and **windwards.** The latter is obsolescent; it occurs only in *to windwards*, for which *to windward* is much commoner. As an adjective, *windward* = 'moving against the wind', as in 'Windward Great Circle Sailing' (J. Greenwood, *The Sailor's Sea Book, c.* 1850); 'weatherly', as in 'An excellent windward boat'; and 'facing the wind', as in *the Windward Islands* (opposed to *the Leeward Islands*). As a noun, *windward* = 'the side facing the wind' as in 'Tacking about, and so getting to windward of them, they ... gain'd a great advantage' (James Tyrrell, *The General History of England*, IV, 1700) (*OED*).

wing – **winged** – **winged.** *Winged*, as preterite and as true past participle, is pro-

nounced as one syllable. The participial adjective is also pronounced as one syllable when it = 'shot on the wing; disabled in the air', as in 'A winged bird cannot fly far', 'A winged aeroplane must soon descend', or 'having wings'; but in poetry it is often two-syllabled, as in 'winged thunder' (Dryden), 'winged words'.

wireless. See **radio.**

-wise. See VOGUE WORDS.

with. Except where ambiguity would result, I urge that *with* should be used of the instrument and *by* restricted to the agent. 'He was killed with [not by] a spanner.'

with + plural verb. 'Michael, accompanied by his wife, is at the door' is clearly correct; so is 'Michael, with his wife, is at the door.' A singular subject linked by *with* (or by *along with, together with*) to a following noun should take a singular verb.

with a view to (ascertaining) is officialese for (*in order*) to (*find out*); so too *with the object of.* ...

withal is an archaism, except insofar as it has been preserved as an elegancy.

within. See **in for *within*.** NB: this is not an error but an infelicity. When it is so easy to avoid confusion, why not avoid it? A good example occurs in the legend to be seen (in 1937–8, at least) on the vans of a certain London firm: 'Goods delivered in 36 hours.'

without for *unless* is now adjudged illiterate, as 'Without something unexpected happens, the murderer will be hanged tomorrow.'

without doubt should be used as an adjective only with sedulous care. In e.g. 'It is not only McCabe's objectivity – though that is without doubt – but also a natural equality between the two opponents' (C. McCabe, *The Face on the Cutting-Room Floor*), where 'indubitable' or, better still, 'indisputable' would have been preferable.

witness, debased to = 'to *see*'. To *witness* is not merely to *see*, but to *testify*, or by being a spectator to be in a position to testify.

womanish; womanly; womanlike; female; feminine. *Womanish* is now mainly pejorative; *womanly*, generally favourable. *Womanish* = 'resembling a woman in her weakness' (physical disabilities, mental disabilities), as in 'Her spitefulness is, in short, womanish'; but if applied to a (young or youngish) girl, it = 'like a grown woman (in figure or in her ways)'. *Womanish* is often (contrast *mannish, q.v.* at **manlike**) applied to effeminate or effeminate-looking men, as in 'that womanish exquisite!'. *Womanly* = 'of, belonging to, characteristic of a woman' (neutrally or favourably), whether of women or their qualities or their actions, as in 'Her womanly kindness and gentleness redeemed her from insipidity'; also 'having the character of – befitting – a woman as opposed to a girl', as in 'A womanly sort of bonnet'. *Womanlike* is the feminine of *manlike*. *Female* is merely the adjective corresponding to *male* (*q.v.* at **manlike**); *feminine* corresponds to *masculine* (see at **manlike**) (*OED*).

wonder for *wonderful* ('a wonder child') is an example of journalistic 'rubber-stamp words' (*q.v.* at **amazing**).

wonderful – more wonderful – most wonderful. The forms *wonderfuller* and *wonderfullest* are not recommended.

wondrous (adj.) is literary; as adverb, it is archaic for *wondrously* (itself literary).

wooded, wooden, woody. *Wooded* = 'covered with growing trees; abounding in woods and forests', usually with adverb, as in 'The neighbourhood was richly wooded.' *Wooden* = made of wood; consisting of wood ('A waggon with wooden wheels'); hence, 'produced by means of wood; relating to wood; hard or stiff like wood', as in 'The fingers have … become … pale and wooden'; figuratively, 'lifeless, spiritless, dull and inert, unintelligent,

insensitive', as in 'A dry-as-dust antiquary of the most wooden type', 'He has a wooden head', 'a wooden notion'. *Woody* is a synonym of *wooded* (but without adverb), as in 'The rose-hung lanes of woody Kent' (Morris). Its other senses are 'of a wood, situated in a wood' ('a woody nook', 'They left the woody path for a field'); 'of the nature of, or consisting of, wood; ligneous' (as in 'the woody knobs of rosebush roots', 'Fibrous and woody elements … exist … in all vegetable foods'); (of plants) 'having stem and branches of wood'; 'resembling wood; having the consistence and the texture of wood' ('a large, woody apple'); 'characteristic of wood; having some quality (e.g. smell) of wood', as 'clean woody odours'; 'having a dull sound, like that of wood when struck', as in 'A little cottage piano, woody and dull of tone' (*OED*).

WOOLLINESS. '… Many people, either from ignorance or from carelessness, are far from being precise in thought and expression – they mean not, but blunder round about a meaning …' (Jespersen, *Language*, p. 274).

Woolly. Lacking in definiteness or incisiveness; 'muzzy'; (of the mind [style], etc.) confused and hazy (*OED*).

Woolliness is that fault of style which consists in writing around a subject instead of on it; of making approximations serve as exactitudes; of resting content with intention as opposed to performance; of forgetting that whereas a haziness may mean something to the perpetrator, it usually means nothing (or an ambiguity) to the reader or the listener. The ideal at which a writer should aim – admittedly it is impossible of attainment – is that he write so clearly, so precisely, so unambiguously, that his words can bear only one meaning to all averagely intelligent readers that possess an average knowledge of the language used.

But to generalize further on woolliness would serve no useful purpose. I shall particularize by giving, first, a number of brief examples and, in most cases, commenting on them, and, secondly, some longer passages and leaving them to the reader's angry bewilderment.

'Not a ship, nor a gun, nor a man, were on the ground to prevent their landing' (Gladstone, *Gleanings*, 1870). Why *ground*? (If Gladstone means 'at this part of the coast' why does he not write 'at this place'?) Does *gun* mean literally 'a cannon', or does it mean *gun*-crew or, rather, a *gun and its crew*?

'These men would have preferred Halliday [the headmaster elect] to get smaller results by conventional methods than Sam's [the present headmaster's] triumphs by different ones' (R. Philmore, *Short List*). A confusion of past with future, and of two constructions. Perhaps recast in some such form as this: 'These men would have preferred Halliday's minor success, attained by conventional methods, to Sam's major success, attained by unconventional ones.'

'Living in an age of transition, the outlines of the people round us grow insubstantial, are modified, mentally and physically, day by day' (Osbert Sitwell, *Those Were the Days*). This might have been put at AGREEMENT, FALSE.

'After dinner, they drove on to London, and found Mr Pegley's address was on the top floor of a new and very smart block of flats' (E. R. Punshon, *The Dusky Hour*). Better, '... found that Mr Pegley lived on the top floor...'.

'He supposed some information about them might probably be obtained from Norris' (*ibid.*). To begin with, 'He supposed that' would remove an unnecessary ambiguity; 'might probably' arises from a confusion between 'might well' and 'would probably'.

'As essayists, the writings of Addison and of Steele are familiar to all readers of eighteenth-century literature' (John Dennis, *The Age of Pope*). And all he needed to say was 'As essayists, Addison and Steele are familiar...'; the intrusive 'the writings of ... of' has produced a ludicrous example of false agreement and put the reader out of his stride.

'The afternoon gatherings were fewer than the evening ones, and their composition, their man-power, differed considerably. Less definite and of one tint, they included more of compromise with the world' (Osbert Sitwell, *Those Were the Days*). Both of these sentences are so ambiguous, so obscure, as to require an exquisite excogitation.

'It will be for him to decide if we proceed further' (Vernon Loder, *The Button in the Plate*). The author – as the context shows – intends 'whether'; 'if' yields a very different sense.

'His point is, I think, evidently mistaken' (I. A. Richards, *The Philosophy of Rhetoric*). Read, either 'His point is, I think, mistaken' or 'His point is evidently mistaken.' If the error is *evident*, why 'I think'? And if it isn't, why 'evidently'?

'In most prose, and more than we ordinarily suppose, the opening words have to wait for those that follow to settle what they shall mean' (*ibid.*). It is not the opening words which have to wait, but we who read them: *we* must wait for the ensuing words before *we* can settle what the opening words mean in the sentence.

' "Billy the Dip's" job was, as usual, outside man; which most important duty he would perform in the company of another ferrety-eyed person not present, who owned to the name of Abe Snitzler, and in whom was combined the cunning of the rat with the swiftness of the eel. These two would station themselves, the first on the corner of Regent and Maddox Street, the second in the alley at the rear of the premises by which route the loot and getaway would have to be made' (John G. Brandon, *The Regent Street Raid*). Concerning this paragraph, a much longer paragraph might be written.

'They say you can't kill a newspaper man or even one who wants to become one' (Russell Birdwell, *I Ring Doorbells*). The first 'one' is the impersonal 'one' (a person); the second = 'a newspaper man'. Hence, confusion.

'Like many genteel people, their own education was nothing to brag about' (a usually precise, always worth-while author). Read, 'Like that of many other genteel people, their own education was nothing to brag about.'

'Money won at billiards cannot be recovered' (Hay & Son Ltd's *Diary*, 1939). Not *won* but *lost* is the right word.

'It was more as if he lived in the shadow of something that no man could remain quite sane while contemplating' (Michael Innes, *Lament for a Maker*). The sentence has not been worked out; or rather, the thought has not been worked out. Perhaps '... something that no man, while contemplating, could remain quite sane against (*or* in the face of)' or, more elegantly, '... something, in the face of which, no man could remain quite sane while he contemplated it' or '... something that, if he contemplated it, left no man quite sane while he contemplated it'. The original sentence is too condensed and too pregnant with meaning to be either clear or comfortable.

'A man may look over the countryside below him and see it in detail, not too far away to be an indistinguishable blur, sufficiently far to give the sense of breadth and effect' (Robert Eton, *The Journey*), where 'not so far away as to be indistinguishable' is needed.

'Put very simply, a causal law may be taken as saying that, under certain conditions, of two events if one happens the other does' (I. A. Richards, *op. cit.*). Should this not read, 'Put very simply, a causal law may be taken as saying that if, under certain conditions, one of two events happens, the other happens also'?

'These few examples ... show how easy it is to write sentences which are literally nonsensical without seeing that they are nonsensical' (A. J. Ayer, *Language, Truth and Logic*). It is.

'P. Lebrun ... may have owed something to Shakespeare, Pichot ... perhaps drew on Glover's poem ... but external evidence is silent on those two points' (Eric Partridge, *The French Romantics' Knowledge of English Literature*). Read, '... but there is no external evidence on those

two points': *external evidence* has, in the original, been too drastically personified.

'He doesn't go out much, but he gives a man's dinner now and then, which are the best in London' (John Buchan, *The Power-House*). Read, '... now and then, and these are the best dinners in London'.

'The handwriting was like a sick man of ninety' (John Buchan, *The Moon Endureth*); better, 'like a sick man of ninety's' or 'like that of a sick man of ninety'.

'But probably he did, as we still may, find much to interest us in the work of the Lancashire poets' (Eric Partridge, *A Critical Medley*, 1926). For 'us', read 'him'.

'Not only are the frontiers of science traced out, its specialist lines of development where they are most significant, but its social and philosophic meaning are set out in direct form' (a publisher's booklist). Either 'meaning is' or 'meanings are'; the latter is preferable.

'Mr McCabe's is by nature a provocative mind. He does not always want it, but he can never help it' (i.e. avoid it), writes Cameron McCabe. To what do these *its* refer? *It* should refer to a *provocative mind*; but if it did, the second sentence would make less than sense. What the author intends is, I think, this: 'Mr McCabe's is a provocative mind. He does not always want *to be provocative*, but he cannot avoid being so (*or* provocative).'

'Usually he had some clearly defined purpose behind all his actions' (Stephen Maddock, *Doorway to Danger*).

'I am one of these who cannot describe what I do not see' (Russell, *Diary during the Last Great War*). Read, 'I am one of those who cannot describe what they do not see.'

'Another mode of spending the leisure time is that of books' (Cobbett: cited by Nesfield).

'Of this, however, we may be sure, that he has, like every capable general does, put himself in imagination in his enemy's place' (*The Daily Telegraph*: cited by Nesfield).

'The humblest citizen of all the land, when clad in the armour of a righteous cause is stronger than all the hosts of error' (William Jennings Bryan, at the National Democratic Convention, Chicago, 1896).

'You shall not press down upon the brow of labour this crown of thorn. You shall not crucify mankind upon a cross of gold' (*ibid.*).

'I have been a militant Communist and a constitutional Socialist and a Pacifist, and always there have been moments when I see all people ... as frightened children' (article, 'Under Thirty', *The Spectator*, 17 Dec. 1937).

'The fifteenth century has been termed "the golden age" of the English labourer, and up to the middle of the nineteenth century this may have been so' ('Social and Economic History', by W. O. Massingberd, in vol. II of *The Victoria County History* of Lincolnshire).

'A third public school man writes: "If one thinks a little, retailing is a very real, alive and gripping 'profession', and well it may be termed, perhaps never before a profession, it is highly specialized where one brings into play every faculty one has been given. To those men who have been fortunate to have a good education, there is nothing else I know where every subject he has been coached in has been brought into use at one time or another. With his being such he will always be an ever-awake and useful member of the community"' (*The New Statesman*, quoting advertisements by members of the staff of a great London shop). That, I think, is the best example I have had the good fortune to find: it is perfect.

Now for a few examples from Ramsay MacDonald, the Rt Hon. David Lloyd George and Elihu Root. (I might have taken passages from the speeches of other politicians, but I do not think that I should easily have bettered the ensuing infelicities.) They will evoke irreverent chortles from the critical: indeed from all who prefer clear to blurred, and definite to hazy writing.

'Relativity was written plainly across the pages of history long before Einstein applied it to the universe. Relatively, Capitalism has justified itself in relation to the absolute criterion of Capitalist aims; but in relation to the absolute criterion' – as though there were one! – 'of social wealth, harmony and happiness, and individual welfare, Capitalism has not justified itself and has to be transformed into something that is higher' (James Ramsay MacDonald, 'Socialism for Business Men' a speech delivered on 1 Oct. 1925, to the Liverpool Rotarians).

'No employer can appeal straight to the hearts of his people [his employees] to sacrifice themselves in the national interests, because the moment he does that he raises in their minds the problem of the relationship between employer and employed. – He raises in their minds that unfortunate conflict of the economic, industrial, and social interests of the two sides to this economic problem. Until we can abolish the two sides, and unite them in a new form of social service, we shall not be able to appeal to the communal sense of both, in order to do sacrificial work for the benefit of the whole community. There lies the philosophical basis of the class conflict, and you cannot remove it except by reorganization' (*ibid.*).

'Religion, as faith, can be professed under any circumstances' (*ibid.*). For 'any' read 'all'.

'You get a society which is like a pyramid standing on its apex. I would like to turn it round and then I would say, "That is now safe." You cannot do that in a day or a week. There must be a change of faith' (*ibid.*).

'Socialism is an idea. The growth of Socialism is shown by the continued application of sound ideas, modifying the form and structure of the society in which we live, and moulding it so that as time goes on the form becomes more and more like the absolute idea itself. – It is the same in architectural conception and the religious conception. It is the same as the ideas in a man's mind when he starts out to build up a business' (*ibid.*).

'Mr Chairman, I am one of those people who never hide the fact that I am a patriot. You get sometimes queer definitions of patriotism, and in accordance with those definitions I am ruled out. But I am one of those people indifferent to what "they say"' (Ramsay MacDonald, 'Patriotism True and False', a speech delivered in America on 11 Oct. 1929: in his *American Speeches*, 1930).

'I daresay I have not many years now here and certainly I am in the position of a man who feels that the remaining sands in the upper part of the sandglass become more and more golden in their preciousness, and therefore I am not anxious to waste them. I am not interested, therefore, so much in looking back and trying to devise agreements such as might apply under circumstances which I believe, if you and I make up our minds, are now dead' (Ramsay MacDonald, 'Among Old Friends', 11 Oct. 1929: in *American Speeches*). The first sentence is a bewildering abomination, and the second sentence lacks a tail.

'We have been working as well as preaching in Europe and I think we have been working with a considerable amount of success. We have been seeing to this – and this is of fundamental importance – that public opinion is demanding that those responsible for governments should not only take the risk of war, which they take when they begin to build competitively their armaments, but they should take the risks of peace' (Ramsay MacDonald, 'The Risks of Peace', later the same day: *op. cit.*).

'The problem of leisure or how to use leisure is the problem of human life, and there is nothing that a university can do that you will bless it for in your later years more than this – it will give you an opportunity of appreciating things for yourself' (*id.*, 'Education', Toronto, 16 Oct. 1929: *op. cit.*).

(On 21 Oct. 1929, to the assembled staff and students of McGill University, on the occasion of a Doctorate of Laws being conferred on him by that university:) 'As Prime Minister of Great Britain, I take this as an evidence on your part of the abiding and enduring loyalty to the common Empire to which we both belong. As one who has come over in order to try and bring a little closer not in the form of an alliance, but in the form of a closer and more affectionate unity of spirit and understanding these two great nations, I take it in conferring this degree you have also had in mind' (*op. cit.*).

But let us pass to that more celebrated orator, David Lloyd George. His was a different sort of woolliness – the woolliness that results from an excess of metaphor and from a surfeit of words; a woolliness much less woolly than Ramsay MacDonald's, for the general (as opposed to the particular) meaning is nearly always clear, as in 'The Curse of Feudalism' (published in *The People's Will*, 1910) – a speech that begins thus:

'The progressive forces in this country [Great Britain] are bending their energies to the task of uprooting the mischievous power of feudalism. The reactionary elements in the country, on the other hand, are, with the same [i.e. an equal; or, a similar] energy, with the same zeal, but, perhaps, with different weapons, undertaking the task of nourishing and feeding these roots [*which* roots?], and deepening their hold on the soil, and by tariffs and by something they call reform of the House of Lords, real progress in this country is barred in every direction by the feudal power.' Here the luxuriant verbiage rather induces a sense of woolliness than produces sheer woolliness: the passage, indeed, is far from being sheerly woolly: and as it fell, unhalting from the orator's silver tongue, it was, one cannot doubt, eloquent and perhaps even impressive.

'What business could ever be conducted under the conditions in which you conduct agriculture? Would you ever get a businessman risking the whole of his capital on improvements on a year's tenancy?... No businessman would invest and risk his capital without a certain measure of security that he will reap the reward of it' ('Labour the Road to Freedom', in *The People's Will*, 1910).

'I am only concerned with the causes of the shortage in the equipment and material of war in so far as it is necessary to understand them with a view to making that shortage up. That the shortage is serious from the point of view of the standard which has been created by this war is undoubtedly well known' ('The Munitions Bill', 23 June 1915: *Through Terror to Triumph*, 1915). Here the cause of woolliness is verbiage.

'The trenches are not all in Flanders. Every [coal-] pit is a trench in this war, a labyrinth of trenches; every workshop is a rampart, every yard which can turn out the munitions of war is a fortress' ('Coal and the War', 29 July 1915: *op. cit.*). Here it is the inaptitude and the inaccuracy of the metaphor which have caused the haziness and the muzziness.

'We have just emerged from a great peril. We have emerged triumphantly. The greatness of the peril we can hardly conceive at the present moment. It will take time for us fully to appreciate its vastness. The greatness of the triumph we cannot fully estimate now. I met a man the other day who came to me and said, "This victory is so vast that I can only take it in parts." I think that that was one of the truest things said of our triumph. He said, "I see one phase of it today, and tomorrow I see another, and the third day I see another." That is true about the danger we have averted and about the victory we have achieved' ('Reconstruction', 24 Nov. 1918: *Slings and Arrows*, 1929).

'The story of Liberalism has not yet been told. Whether it will have the responsibility, the independent responsibility, for the destiny of this great people and this great Empire as it has in the past, or whether it will act in combination with others as it practically has done since 1886, and what combinations and associations there may be I am not going to predict, but I am quite sure that the central ideas that Liberalism stands for are vital to the life and the continued power and influence of this country and of the world' (20 April 1927, at The 1920 Club: *ibid.*).

But let us take an American statesman, Elihu Root. He is less woolly than the two British statesmen from whom I have quoted; much less woolly, in fact, than Ramsay MacDonald. No one, however, will (I hope) deny that the following passages create a rather blurred impression.

'One accustomed to the administration of municipal law who turns his attention for the first time to the discussion of practical questions arising between nations and dependent upon the rules of international law, must be struck by a difference between the two systems which materially affects the intellectual processes involved in every discussion, and which is apparently fundamental. – The proofs and arguments adduced by the municipal lawyer are addressed to the object of setting in motion certain legal machinery which will result in a judicial judgement to be enforced by the entire power of the state over litigants subject to its jurisdiction and control' ('The Sanction of International Law', 24 April 1908: *Addresses on International Subjects*, 1916).

'The war [1914] began by a denial on the part of a very great power that treaties are obligatory when it is no longer for the interest of either of the parties to observe them. The denial was followed by action supported by approximately one half the military power of Europe and is apparently approved by a great number of learned students and teachers of international law, citizens of the countries supporting the view. This position is not an application of the doctrine *rebus sic stantibus* [affairs being at such a point (or, at such a pass) …] which justifies the termination of a treaty under circumstances not contemplated when the treaty was made so that it is no longer justly applicable to existing conditions. It is that under the very circumstances contemplated by the treaty and under the conditions for which the treaty was intended to provide the treaty is not obligatory as against the interest of the contracting party' ('The Outlook for International Law', 28 Dec. 1915: *ibid.*).

But enough of these.

WORDINESS. See VERBOSITY.

working-man and **working man; workman.** A *working man* is vague, for it = 'a man that is or happens to be engaged in work', whereas a *working-man* is 'a man employed to work for a wage, especially in a manual or industrial occupation'; *working-man* includes *artisan, mechanic, labourer.* (The corresponding female is a *working-woman*.) A *workman* is 'a man engaged, on a wage, to do manual labour', especially if he is 'employed upon some particular piece of work' (an *operative*); often, the context shows that 'a skilled worker' is meant; often too, it is opposed to *employer* or to *capitalist*, though *worker* (especially in the plural) is more usual in this opposition. *Workman* has the further, more general sense, 'one who works – or practises his craft or his art – in some specified manner', e.g. in painting; thus, 'My health makes me a very slow workman.' *Workwoman* is 'a female worker or operative' (*OED*).

workshop. See VOGUE WORDS.

world. See **earth** and **sphere.**

WORLD ENGLISH. See STANDARD ENGLISH, Section IV.

worse is misused in the following, quoted by the *DNB* from Gough the antiquary as his opinion of his contemporary William Maitland (18th century): 'He was self-conceited, knew little, and wrote worse.'

worst, misused for *most*, as 'What I need worst is a haircut.' A thoroughly idiomatic usage of *worst* is that with verbs of liking or loving, allowing, pleasing, as in 'This pleased them worst of all', where *worst* = 'least' (*OED*).

worst two is incorrect for *two worst* in e.g. 'The worst two pupils were sent down to the class below.' Cf. **first two** (for *two first*).

worthless. See COMPARATIVES, FALSE.

worthwhile is an adjective, not an adverb. A trip to Paris may be *worthwhile*, but we must say 'it is *worth* (not *worthwhile*) going to Paris'.

would, misused for *were.* See SUBJUNCTIVE. Here is a particularly glaring example: ' "Would it not be better," Pyke said very slowly, "if you *would* be quite frank with me?" ' (W. S. Masterman, *The Perjured Alibi*). But see final paragraph of **would and should.**

would used for *will.* See PAST MODAL.

would and **should.** *OED* quotes Mrs S. Pennington, 1766, 'I choose rather that you would carry it yourself', as misusing *would* for *should*; cf. 'And as we walked together, I asked Ptah that if I could comfort this woman, she would tell me of her grief' (from a novel published in 1937).

From R. H. Mottram, *The Spanish Farm*, 'He made a gesture, and she accepted the fact that he was rather taken with her. He would be': this use of *would he* is a common colloquialism but verges on slang. It is a short cut; and for its effect, it depends very largely on the peculiar emphasis placed on 'would' by a speaker. It is hardly admissible in literature. But these two paragraphs merely skim the question.

Should and *would* correspond roughly, as past tenses, to *shall* and *will* (*q.v.*). The common contraction *'d*, however, stands only for *would* (unlike the useful *'ll* which subsumes both *shall* and *will*). As with *shall*, *should* is being displaced by *would*, so that such expressions as 'I would be inclined to agree' are now common idiom. This process has probably been hastened for the good reason that the chief use of *should* today is 'ought to', for all persons, as in 'You should really see a doctor about that toe.'

It is therefore clearer to use *would* even in first person situations where ambiguity might arise. 'I thought we should leave early' might mean either 'I expected it would happen' or 'I thought it would be right.' There is probably no ambiguity about 'I should be delighted to go', but even that might be interpreted as 'I ought to be delighted – but I'm not.'

Should, not *would*, is used for all persons in such conditional clauses as 'What would you do if he should die?' (but *if he died* is more usual, and perfectly correct).

Would, not *should*, is used in conditional clauses used as requests; as in 'If you would kindly wait a minute …'. It is also used for all persons, for 'used to', as in 'As children, we would often see him drive past.'

would best is unfortunate for *had best* in 'I think I would best rent a house', 'She would best avoid such a marriage.'

would better is incorrect for *had better* in 'I would better depart now.'

would have, in conditional sentences, is incorrect for *had*, as in 'If he would have wished, he could have spared you a troublesome journey.'

would rather and **had rather.** In the first person, *had rather* is a viable but old-fashioned alternative to *would rather*. ('I had rather die young than live to be a hundred'); in the second and third, *would rather* is the more usual ('He would rather sleep than eat'). It is convenient that *'d* stands for both *would* and *had*. See also **rather, had.**

wove and **woven.** *Wove* is the preterite of *weave*; *woven*, the usual past participle, *wove* being inferior except in such technicalities as *wove mould* and *wove paper*. A second *weave* verb meaning 'move by changing direction' is formed with *weaved*, as in 'He weaved his way through the traffic.'

wrack is misused for *rack* in at least three senses. It should be a *rack* of clouds; *rack*, an instrument of torture, even so good a scholar as Swinburne falling into 'She had no heart's pain, but mere body's wrack'; and it is *rack* of lamb. In the sense 'ruin', both forms are correct, as in go to (*w*)*rack* and *ruin*, but, except in that phrase and its variants (*bring to, put to, run to rack and ruin*), *wrack* – a cognate of *wreck* – is the more general (*OED*).

wrapt and **rapt.** In 'He was absorbed in wrapt meditation', *wrapt* is incorrect for *rapt*. *Wrapt* or, more generally, *wrapped* is the past participle (and participial adjective) of *wrap*, 'to cover or swathe by enfolding in, e.g. a cloth', 'to cover or envelop (an object) by winding or folding something round or about it', etc. *Rapt* is from the Latin *rapere*, 'to take and carry off by force', fig. 'to delight'. *Rapt* = 'taken and carried away', whether lit. or fig.; hence, 'transported with some emotion or thought', as in 'The book held me rapt', 'I stood gazing, rapt in admiration', 'Rapt in adoring contemplation', 'rapt by wonder' (*OED*).

wrath, 'anger', and **wroth,** 'angry' (a literarism), are sometimes confused.

wriggle. See at **wiggle.**

wring – wrung – wrung are the inflections now current. The preterite *wrang* is now dialectal only. The past participle *wringed* is obsolete.

writ. The noun *writ* is obsolete except in the phrase *Holy* (or *Sacred*) *Writ*, the Bible or Holy Scriptures, and in Law (a *writ of certiorari*, *writ of venire facias*, etc.; 'a Parliamentary writ'). The past participle *writ* is archaic, as in 'The moving finger writes, and having writ, moves on.'

writer, the; the present writer. These are not wrong; *OED* admits them without comment. But they are to be used in moderation; in general, the honest *I* is preferable.

wrong (adv.) readily replaces *wrongfully* (unfairly, unjustly) or *wrongly* in the combinations 'to guess wrong', 'to spell it wrong' and 'to go wrong' (in this last it may in any case be interpreted as an adjective). It cannot precede a verb or participle, so that one must write 'a word wrongly pronounced', or 'Wrongly, she refused to sign.'

WRONG TENSE. See TENSE-SEQUENCE.

wroth. See at **wrath.**

X

x and **ct** variants (*connection, connexion; reflection, reflexion*). See **-ection and -exion**.

Xmas as a contraction of *Christmas*, barely allowable in its common use in writing and printing, is intolerable in the pronunciation, *Exmas*.

Y

Yankee, loosely applied (in Britain) to all Americans (i.e. of the USA), means in America only a citizen of the New England states (Massachusetts, Connecticut, etc.), or by extension a citizen of any Northern state, as distinguished from a Southerner.

yardstick. See VOGUE WORDS.

ye in such popular uses as 'Ye olde Englysshe Tea-Shoppe' is founded on a complete misconception of the old symbol Þ, the letter 'thorn', which in Old English and Middle English represented the sound of *th*. In printing, the *y* was substituted for it and has come to be mispronounced.

Yiddish is so often misunderstood and misused that the editor feels it incumbent on him to mention that, although the language is written in Hebrew characters, it is not Hebrew nor yet a dialect of Hebrew. Yiddish is 'the language used by Jews in Europe and America, consisting mainly of German (orig. from the Middle Rhine area) with admixture (according to local or individual usage) of Baltic-Slavic or Hebrew words'. The word is simply the English form of German *jüdisch*, 'Jewish', short for *jüdisch-deutsch*, 'Jewish-German' (*OED*).

Note that the *Yiddisher* is not any Jew, but a Jew that speaks *Yiddish*. And *Yid* is an offensive shortening of *Yiddisher*.

you and **one.** See **one and you.**

you aren't and **you're not.** Cf. the entry at **we aren't.**

you both. See **both of us.**

young and **youthful.** The former is literal with the stress on the mere fact of age; the latter stresses the fact that one has, or is characterized by, youth, or that one is still young; *youthful* also = 'juvenile; characteristic of or suitable for the young'; and especially, 'having the freshness and vigour of youth'. 'Though he is a young man (only 21), one does not think of him as being youthful', 'youthful impatience', 'Here we have ... an unmistakable attack made by the youthful Socrates' (Jowett), 'The world was still at its youthful stage' (*OED*).

Cf. the entries at **juvenile and puerile** and **childish; childlike.**

your's is not to be used for *yours*.

yourself, yourselves. See **oneself.**

yourself; yourselves for *you*. See **myself.**

youth and **youthfulness.** *Youth* corresponds to *young*; *youthfulness* to *youthful*. 'The youthfulness of the old man was astounding'; 'Even in youth, he was like an old man.'

yuppie. See VOGUE WORDS.